HOLLYWOOD
Songsters

HOLLYWOOD
Songsters

SINGERS WHO ACT AND ACTORS WHO SING

A BIOGRAPHICAL DICTIONARY

2ND EDITION

VOLUME 2: GARLAND TO O'CONNOR

JAMES ROBERT PARISH AND MICHAEL R. PITTS

Routledge
New York and London

Published in 2003 by
Routledge
29 West 35th Street
New York, NY 10001
www.routledge-ny.com

Published in Great Britain by
Routledge
11 New Fetter Lane
London EC4P 4EE
www.routledge.uk.co

10 9 8 7 6 5 4 3 2 1

Library of Congress Cataloging-in-Publication Data is available from the Library
of Congress.

Parish, James Robert and Pitts, Michael R.
Hollywood songsters : singers who act and actors who sing.
ISBN: 0-415-93775-2 (set: alk. paper).
ISBN: 0-415-94332-9 (vol. 1: alk. paper)
ISBN: 0-415-94333-7 (vol. 2: alk. paper)
ISBN: 0-415-94334-5 (vol. 3: alk. paper)

for

Kate Smith (1907–1986)

The Songbird of the South

Contents

Volume 1

Volume 2

Volume 3

Authors' Note

As indicated by the title, *Hollywood Songsters* includes performers who have had success both as singers and as film stars of American-made movies. In compiling this volume, we have tried to include a variety of personalities who have been popular since the introduction of sound to movies in the late 1920s. Naturally, some of those included have had more success than others and some are associated more with singing than acting, or vice versa, but all have had an impact in both performance arts.

While we have included 112 performers in this updated and expanded edition of the 1991 original book—and this new edition now includes CD as well as LP discographies for each singer—we realize that not every singer who has worked successfully in United States motion pictures is represented with an individual entry. If you find that a favorite songster is missing, please contact us (in care of the publisher) and tell us so. Also, we welcome additions and corrections for this book. Given the space limitations, we could not offer minute details on all aspects of the lives and careers of the people included. However, we hope we have provided well-rounded coverage of their show business activities, especially in relation to their music and films.

James Robert Parish
Michael R. Pitts

Keys to Abbreviations

LP and CD Album Discography Key

Cap	Capitol Records		Par	Paramount Records
CIF	Classic International Filmusicals Records		SRO	Standing Room Only Records
Col	Columbia Records		ST	Soundtrack (film)
Har	Harmony Records		ST/R	Soundtrack (radio)
Mer	Mercury Records		ST/TV	Soundtrack (television)
MGM	Metro-Goldwyn-Mayer Records		UA	United Artists Records
OC	Original Cast		WB	Warner Bros. Records

Notes

- In the LP section of each discography, the listing 10″ in front of the company name refers to a ten-inch, long-playing record; all others are twelve-inch LPs. The LP section does not include 78s, 45s, EPs, 8-tracks, or audio cassettes. However, CD albums—but *not* CD singles—have their own separate discographic listing following the LP section in each appropriate entry.

- When two code numbers are given for a particular LP listing, the first one is for the monaural release; the second one for the stereo release.

- As for LP reissues, the original LP issue company and code number are listed first, followed by any reissues by other labels. The one exception to this rule is some of the soundtracks from MGM musical films, which have had as many as a half dozen reissues. In that case, we have listed the first issue *only.* When a title first was issued on a ten-inch LP we listed it first, followed by the first twelve-inch LP release (if any). However, an LP album that has the same title but does *not* contain the same tracks as a prior LP release of the performer is listed separately in alphabetical order by title (and subsorted by label name) within the LP section of the songster's discography.

- We had to draw the line on some album listings where one of the *Hollywood Songsters* does not do the entire record. Basically, if a performer is given substantial billing on the disc cover, we listed it, and tried to include any other performers on the release as well.

- In the LP record listings, Amalgamated Records is an umbrella title for a host of small, independent labels. We have used the Amalgamated code numbers for such releases.

- In the CD disc listings for a performer, as in the LP section of each subject's discography, reissues of a particular album by other labels are included as part of the same entry. However, as in the LP section, albums that have the same title but do *not* contain the same tracks as a prior release of the performer are listed separately in alphabetical order by title (and subsorted by label name) within the CD section of the songster's discography.

Filmography Key

AA	Allied Artists	MGM/UA	Metro-Goldwyn-Mayer/United Artists Pictures
ABC	American Broadcasting Corporation	NBC	National Broadcasting Corporation
AIP	American International Pictures	NG	National General Pictures
Aus	Austrian	Par	Paramount Pictures
Avco Emb	Avco Embassy Pictures	PBS	Public Broadcasting System
Br	British	PRC	Producers Releasing Corporation
Braz	Brazilian		
BV	Buena Vista	Rep	Republic Pictures Corporation
CBN	Christian Broadcasting Network [later The Family Channel]	RKO	RKO Radio Pictures
		(s)	Short Subject
CBS	Columbia Broadcasting System	Soundies	Soundies Distributing Corporation of America (SDCA)
Cin	Cinerama Releasing Corporation		
		Sp	Spanish
Col	Columbia Pictures	Tif	Tiffany Film Corporation
Emb	Embassy Pictures Corporation	20th-Fox	Twentieth Century-Fox Film Corporation
Fox	Fox Film Corporation		
FN	First National Pictures (Warner Bros.)	UA	United Artists Pictures
		UI	Universal-International Pictures
Fr	French	Univ	Universal Pictures
Ger	German	Unk	Unknown Distributor
GN	Grand National Pictures	Vita	Vitaphone Corporation (Warner Bros.)
Ir	Iranian		
It	Italian	WB	Warner Bros. Pictures
Lip	Lippert Films	WB-7 Arts	Warner Bros.–Seven Arts Pictures
MGM	Metro-Goldwyn-Mayer Pictures		

Notes

Film titles in brackets following a listing are the alternate release title, reissue title, or British release title for the given film.

Television/Cable Key

ABC   American Broadcasting Corporation

BBC   British Broadcasting Corporation

CBN   Christian Broadcasting Network [later
        The Family Channel]

CBS   Columbia Broadcasting System

Fox   Fox Broadcasting Corporation

NBC   National Broadcasting Corporation

NN   Non Network

PBS   Public Broadcasting System

Synd   Syndicated

TNN   The Nashville Network

Notes

Made-for-television or made-for-cable feature films (telefilms/cable features) are listed with all the other films as part of the appropriate individual filmography.

Acknowledgments

Thanks to: Academy of Motion Picture Arts and Sciences—Margaret Herrick Library, Larry Billman (Academy of Dance on Film), Billy Rose Theater Collection of the New York Public Library at Lincoln Center, Stephen Bourne, John Cocchi (JC Archives), Stephen Cole, Tony Cooper (Frankie Laine International Appreciation Society), Ernest Cunningham, Eleanor Knowles Dugan, Echo Book Shop, Dr. James Fisher, Karin Fowler, Gary Giddins, Laura Gwaltney, Richard K. Hayes (Kate Smith Commemorative Society), Jane Klain (Museum of Television & Radio), Alvin H. Marill, Doug McClelland, Jim Meyer, Donn Moyer, Albert L. Ortega (Albert L. Ortega Photos), Barry Rivadue, Margie Schultz, André Soares, Les Spindle, Allan Taylor (copy editor), George Ulrich, Laura Wagner, Ray White.

Special thanks to literary agent Stuart Bernstein and to our editors, Richard Carlin and Sara Brady.

Judy Garland

(b. Frances Ethel Gumm, Grand Rapids, Minnesota, June 10, 1922; d. London, England, June 22, 1969)

When she died in 1969, *Newsweek* magazine observed, "Judy Garland was the single great musical entertainer who developed within the Hollywood studio system." Her best movie musicals remain classics: *The Wizard of Oz* (1939), *Meet Me in St. Louis* (1944), *The Harvey Girls* (1945), and *A Star Is Born* (1954). In addition, there were her youthful song-and-dance romps with Mickey Rooney, her celluloid teamings with Gene Kelly (including the complex *The Pirate*, 1948), and her pairing with Fred Astaire (*Easter Parade*, 1948). But there was more to "Miss Show Business" (as she was known affectionately) than her activities as an active recording, radio, and TV show artist: There was the "in person—live onstage" Judy Garland. Of twentieth-century American performers who consistently captivated audiences with their own magic—not relying on lighting and sound special effects to do the trick—Judy Garland stands at the pinnacle, with perhaps Al Jolson as her closest rival. Anyone who ever experienced one of her concerts was a witness to and a part of the tremendous emotional control she exuded over audiences as she sang, joked, and toyed with her much-publicized image as Miss Vulnerability. (She said once, "If I'm such a legend, then why am I so lonely?") Like Marilyn Monroe, Garland drew power from audiences' tremendous love of her. It eased the torment of her well-documented insecurities and woes, as well as her harrowing pain that liquor and drugs could not touch.

She was born on June 10, 1922, in Grand Rapids, Minnesota, the third daughter of Frank Avent Gumm and Ethel Marion (Milne) Gumm. He was a struggling Irish tenor, and she was a vaudeville house pianist. When they married they toured the lesser circuits as "Jack and Virginia Lee, the Sweet Southern Singers." Later, they settled in Grand Rapids, where Frank managed the New Grand Theater and Ethel played the piano. Sometimes their two elder daughters, Mary Jane (Suzanne) and Virginia (Jimmie), joined their parents in reviving their act. Their third daughter was named Frances Ethel. She was born with scoliosis, a curvature of the spine, which led to a lifelong insecurity about her figure. (She had long legs but a short, almost dwarflike torso and was not quite five-feet tall.)

When she was two and a half, Frances (known as "Babe" or "Baby" to her family) made an impromptu show-business debut by running onto the stage and joining her parents in singing "Jingle Bells." Immediately she became part of their act. Because Ethel Gumm was so intent on getting her children—especially Frances—into the movies, the family moved to California. They settled in Lancaster, seventy miles north of Los Angeles. Gumm took over management of a silent cinema, and Ethel made the rounds of the studios and booking agents with her three girls. These visits led, eventually, to the young girls signing up with the Meglin Kiddies, a specialty agency that handled child acts in and around Los Angeles. Soon there were scattered bookings and work in at least four film short subjects.

Mickey Rooney and Judy Garland in *Babes on Broadway* (1941).
[Courtesy of JC Archives]

By now the Gumms had moved to Lomita, far closer to Hollywood. While Frank managed another cinema, the unwavering Ethel chaperoned her three daughters whenever they had road engagements. (The girls were never very good as a singing team, and their bookings were always second-rate at best.) The sisters were enrolled at Mrs. Lawler's Professional School, where Joe Yule Jr.—later Mickey Rooney—was a student. In 1934, the trio performed on the midway at the Chicago's World Fair, but were left stranded when they were not paid for their work. They managed a booking at Chicago's Oriental Theater. When they arrived for the play date, they found the theater marquee listed them as "The Glum Sisters." Headliner George Jessel renamed them the Garland Sisters, while Frances chose the new name of Judy for herself (picking it from the popular Hoagy Carmichael song of the same name).

While the Garland Sisters were on a work/vacation at the Cal-Neva Lodge at Lake Tahoe, songwriter Harry Akst and his friends—Columbia Pictures casting agent Lew Brown and talent agent Al Rosen—heard Judy perform. They agreed that Judy was the real talent of the family, and they gave her introductions to the movie studios. Eventually, their contacts led to an audition for Judy at MGM with that studio's musical arranger, Roger Edens (who became a lifelong friend and mentor). He, in turn, had Garland audition for Ida Koverman, executive secretary to studio head Louis B. Mayer. Koverman was so impressed with Judy's singing of "Dinah" that she called in her boss. Two weeks later, Judy Garland was under MGM contract, and Mayer proclaimed, "We have just signed a baby Nora Bayes." Years later, Garland claimed, "I was very thrilled by it, though I actually didn't sign the contract. Nobody asked me. That should be the title of my life: Nobody Asked Me."

Soon after Judy joined MGM in 1935, her father died of meningitis, and the loss deeply affected Garland for the rest of her life. Now the family had to depend on Garland's $150 weekly salary. However, the studio was not sure how to use the plump teenager with the glorious voice. They had her perform at assorted studio functions and then, as a toss away, teamed her with equally young contractee Deanna Durbin in a two-reeler, *Every Sunday* (1936). The gimmick of the short was having Deanna sing "sweet" while Judy sang "hot." MGM still pondered, while Universal Pictures snatched Deanna away and turned her into a major star. Regardless, Mayer still could not decide what to do with Garland. Instead, she guested on radio shows (such as *The Shell Chateau Hour*) and made recordings for Decca Records. Then, to hedge his bets, Mayer loaned Judy to Twentieth Century-Fox for *Pigskin Parade* (1936), where she made her feature film debut singing the swinging "Balboa" number. *Variety* reported, "She's a cute, not too pretty but pleasingly fetching personality, who certainly knows how to sell a pop [tune]."

Roger Edens made a special arrangement of "You Made Me Love You" that he entitled "Dear Mr. Gable." Judy sang the lyrics at Gable's thirty-sixth birthday party (February 1, 1937) at the studio. Mayer was so enthused he ordered the number to be incorporated into *Broadway Melody of 1938* (1937), then in preproduction. In that musical, Judy played Sophie Tucker's daughter and sang the song as she sat writing Gable a fan note. The *New York Times* insisted this solo was "probably the greatest tour de force in recent screen history." Of her next four releases, *Love Finds Andy Hardy* (1938) was the most important. She was teamed with her old pal Mickey Rooney, and it demonstrated that Judy, besides singing, could deliver comedy lines with a delicious tartness.

MGM had hoped to borrow Shirley Temple for their upcoming musical fantasy, *The Wizard of Oz* (1939), but when that proved impossible, they settled on Judy for the lead. With the help of corsets, pigtails, and makeup, the seventeen-year-old Judy looked the innocent young Dorothy from Kansas who discovers in the Land of Oz that there is no place like home. The tremendously expensive color production turned a profit eventually, became a classic through annual TV showings, earned Judy a special Oscar, and provided her with her signature song "Over the Rainbow" (a number the studio almost deleted because of the picture's length).

Judy was number ten at the box office in 1940 as she continued making musicals with and without her peer Mickey Rooney. Already she was engulfed in a regimen of dieting and pill taking (to suppress her appetite and keep her peppy) while continuing her hectic routine of filmmaking, recordings, as well as radio and personal appearances. This unhealthy regimen of dieting and special medications was undertaken with the studio's encouragement because MGM cared only about maximizing its investment in their big moneymaking songstress. In July 1941—much to the annoyance of her mother and the studio—Judy married composer/musician David Rose (twelve years her senior), who had recently been divorced from movie comedian Martha Raye.

In *For Me and My Gal* (1942), Judy first received star billing above the title and sang the memorable "After You're Gone." It was the first of her several musicals with movie newcomer Gene Kelly. It was also in 1942 that Judy, under the encouragement of MGM scriptwriter Joseph

L. Mankiewicz, began seeking psychiatric help. When her mother found out and, in turn, told Louis B. Mayer, a holocaust ensued. Mankiewicz left the studio, Mayer was furious with Garland, and Judy never forgave her mother. (Garland would later refer to Ethel as "the real-life Wicked Witch of the West," and always blamed her for the unhappy/abnormal childhood she endured. They were still feuding when Mrs. Gumm died in 1953.)

Judy sang "The Joint Is Really Jumpin' at Carnegie Hall" in the all-star *Thousands Cheer* (1943), and gave memorable interpretations to "But Not For Me," "Embraceable You," and "Bidin' My Time" in *Girl Crazy* (1943)—teamed yet again with Mickey Rooney. In *Presenting Lily Mars* (1943), originally conceived as a dramatic vehicle for Lana Turner, Judy was the small-town girl who finds love (Van Heflin) and show-business success on Broadway. Also in 1943, Garland played her debut concert engagement on July 1 in Philadelphia, made an extended USO tour, and terminated her marriage to David Rose, much to the relief of Louis B. Mayer, who had never approved of the union. (Mayer the mogul had pressured Judy to have an abortion during her marriage to Rose.) During this period, Judy had brief romances with Artie Shaw and Tyrone Power.

Meet Me in St. Louis (1944) was a joyous excursion into Americana set in 1903 and 1904. It allowed Judy to pine vocally over "The Boy Next Door," whom she fell in love with while "Clang, Clang, Went the Trolley" ("The Trolley Song"). This warmhearted family study was directed by Vincente Minnelli, who understood Judy well. Minnelli also directed her next feature, *The Clock* (1945), a touching dramatic study of her love for a young GI (Robert Walker). It led James Agee (*The Nation* magazine) to assess, "She can handle any emotion in sight, in any shape or size, and the audience along with it." Judy and Minnelli were married on June 15, 1945, and their daughter Liza May was born on May 12, 1946. Judy was back to what the public wanted in the musical, *The Harvey Girls* (1946), as the resourceful restaurant worker in the old West who sang the electric "On the Atchison, Topeka and the Santa Fe." She did a sharp mock send-up of the archetypal lofty movie star in "The Interview" segment of *Ziegfeld Follies of 1946* (1946), and as Broadway's Marilyn Miller in *Till the Clouds Roll By* (1946), she was wistfully effective vocalizing "Who?" and "Look for the Silver Lining."

Judy's escalating insecurities caused production delays on *The Pirate* (1948), a fanciful costume musical with Gene Kelly and directed by Minnelli. The final product proved to be too sophisticated to be a box-office hit. In *Words and Music* (1948), Garland was edgy, drawn, and thin playing herself and singing "Johnny One Note" and dueting with pal Mickey Rooney on "I Wish I Were in Love Again." She was set to reteam with Gene Kelly in Irving Berlin's *Easter Parade* (1948), but he broke his ankle during rehearsals and was replaced by Fred Astaire. The latter proved to be an admirable song-and-dance partner for Garland. Together they performed the indelible "A Couple of Swells," a tramp routine that Judy would use frequently in her stage shows in years to come. MGM set Astaire to be with her in *The Barkleys of Broadway* (1949), but Judy was increasingly unable to deal with career and domestic pressures, and the studio used Ginger Rogers instead.

Judy substituted for a pregnant June Allyson in the period musical *In the Good Old Summertime* (1949), but there was little on-camera chemistry between Garland and Van Johnson. Again there were production delays because Judy was ill and unhappy. MGM had acquired the screen rights to Broadway's *Annie Get Your Gun* as a Garland vehicle. Filming began in May 1949, after Judy had prerecorded the score. Director George Sidney finally had to acknowledge that she was physically and emotionally unable to proceed, and the studio suspended her. Garland was shipped to a Boston sanatorium for a rest "cure," where she underwent shock treatments. The studio replaced her in *Annie Get Your Gun* (1950) with Paramount's Betty Hutton.

When Judy returned to Hollywood, she required an on-the-set psychiatrist during the filming of *Summer Stock* (1950). The tormented star fluctuated between chunky and thin during filming, but still shone in the lustrous "Get Happy" finale number (shot months after the original footage). The increasingly exasperated studio ordered her to replace the pregnant (again) June Allyson in *Royal Wedding* (1951), but Judy was at an emotional breaking point in her life and had an emotional collapse. As a result, Jane Powell was assigned to play in *Royal Wedding* opposite Fred Astaire.

Unable to cope with her array of domestic and professional problems, Garland attempted suicide on June 20, 1950, by slashing her throat with a bit of glass. Metro coworker Katharine Hepburn was among those who gave Garland a pep talk, advising her, "Now listen, you're one of the three greatest talents in the world. And your ass has hit the gutter. There's no place to go but up. Now goddammit. Do it!" But Garland was incapable of changing, and MGM ended her (over $5,000 a week) contract, with planned roles such as Julie in *Show Boat* (1951) going to Ava Gardner. She and Minnelli divorced in 1951, two very artistic types unable to cope with one another any further.

At this crisis, Michael Sidney Luft, former secretary to dancing star Eleanor Powell and ex-husband of screen actress Lynn Bari, entered Judy's life. He was an ambitious promoter who understood how to manage Judy, both onstage and off. He realized she still had value as a stage attraction and encouraged her to perform at the London Palladium in 1951, where she was a sensation. That October, albeit stocky (her weight would fluctuate dramatically over the coming years), Garland was at the Palace Theater in New York, gloriously reviving the two-shows-a-day vaudeville policy. Her engagement was extended for nineteen weeks, grossed $750,000, and won Garland a special Tony Award. Despite the pressures of her schedule, Judy relaxed for the first time in her career. She and Luft wed in June 1952, and that November she gave birth to daughter Lorna. (Their other child, Joseph Wiley, was born in March 1955.)

The manner in which *A Star Is Born* (1954) was conceived and executed has been documented meticulously in Ronald Haver's 1988 book of the same name. The battles of wills between Judy and Luft on the one hand and Warner Bros. studio head Jack L. Warner on the other, while director George Cukor and costar James Mason served as intermediaries, were legendary. Despite the production delays (primarily due to Judy's emotional instability), the wide-screen musical was released in October 1954. And, in spite of the severe editing the picture underwent after road-show engagements, Judy was Oscar-nominated for playing the movie extra who becomes a major screen attraction. The autobiographical "Born in A Trunk" number was one of filmdom's longest production exercises, but "The Man Who Got Away" presented Garland at her chanteuse best. The picture was her career zenith.

Garland's final downhill slide required fifteen years to complete. She debuted on TV on NBC's *Ford Star Jubilee* in a ninety-minute special on September 24, 1955, the first of several such outings where she sang, danced, and joked. She was among the many who enthusiastically supported John F. Kennedy in his presidential bid, and she labeled him "One of the best friends I ever had." In the late 1950s, Judy's weight problem escalated, and at one point when she was hospitalized to deal with the problem, she was informed by the medics that she only had a brief time left to live and that her career was finished. However, she rallied, performed more "comeback" concerts, and on April 23, 1961, she appeared at New York City's Carnegie Hall in a magnificent showstopping performance that drew raves. (The Manhattan event was the culmination of a forty-city tour that had been hugely successful.) The two-disc live recording of the event has sold well over two million copies to date and won two Grammy Awards (Best Album and Best Female Solo Vocal). Despite all these successes, Judy still yearned for a movie return and for $50,000 accepted a small role—as a plump, distraught German hausfrau—in Stanley Kramer's prestigious docudrama, *Judgment at Nuremberg* (1961). It won her an Oscar nomination for Best Supporting Actress.

Garland was at her most hyperactive in 1963, appearing in two additional movies. She played a music teacher at an institution for mentally retarded children in *A Child Is Waiting*, for which director John Cassavetes channeled her nervous energy effectively. For the British-made *I Could Go On Singing*, she was chic in an autobiographical role that required her to vocalize energetically. CBS-TV (who had guided her through popular network specials in 1962 and 1963) thought they could succeed, where MGM and everyone else had failed, in making Judy a disciplined performer. She was the star of a weekly network musical program, *The Judy Garland Show*, which debuted on September 29, 1963. Unfortunately it competed in a time slot against the medium's then most popular show (*Bonanza*), and after twenty-six weeks Judy was off the air. Mel Tormé, Judy's musical writer/advisor on the series, wrote his harsh version of working with such a tormented person in *The Other Side of the Rainbow With Judy Garland on the Dawn Patrol* (1971), although others involved with the series disclaimed his negative portrayal of Garland. Meanwhile, she returned to the concert stage, where frequently her entrances and banter were the most polished parts of the evening.

In 1965, Judy and Luft divorced, and she married (briefly) young actor Mark Herron. She was replaced by Ginger Rogers in a quickie biography film, *Harlow* (1965), and after prerecording two songs for Jacqueline Susann's *Valley of the Dolls* (1967), Garland withdrew from the project. Susan Hayward substituted as the aging Ethel Merman–type Broadway star. In 1968 it was thought that Garland would take over from Angela Lansbury in the Broadway musical *Mame*, but it was Janis Paige who accepted the stage challenge. In 1969, Judy wed discotheque manager Mickey Deams, twelve years her junior. At London's Talk of the Town Club, she made yet another comeback. Typically, there were media accounts of her lateness onstage and fuming audiences. On June 22, 1969, Judy Garland was found dead in the bathroom of her London apartment by her husband. The death was ruled as from an "accidental" overdose of barbiturates. The funeral was held in New York. A hysterical gathering of over twenty thousand crowded the funeral home to mourn and to pay their final respects.

Following Judy Garland's death there were many album reissues of her multimedia performances and several books by ex-husbands and friends analyzing the "real" Judy. Perhaps the most understanding explanation of this enigmatic legend was provided by daughter Liza, herself a show-business phenomenon: "Mama had this great thing. She was different with everyone. . . . She tuned in to individuals on their own wave length. . . . She was all things to all people. . . . I think Mama got everything she ever wanted. . . . Do you know anyone in show business who ever made more comebacks?"

In the 1990s, there was a renewed interest in the artistry and life of Judy Garland. It was sparked by a spate of biographies about the legendary songbird, including David Shipman's *The Secret Life of an American Legend* (1993), Gerald Clarke's *Get Happy: The Life of Judy Garland* (2000), and especially by Lorna Luft's *Me and My Shadow: A Family Memoir* (1998). The later prompted a four-hour TV movie (*Life With Judy Garland: Me and My Shadow*) in 2001 with Tammy

Blanchard as the young Judy and Judy Davis playing the star as an adult. The production—far more graphic than the earlier TV movie about Garland's trouble-prone life (1978's *Rainbow* starring Andrea McArdle as the young Judy)—won several Emmys, including prizes for Davis and Blanchard. In Spring 2002, Scott Schechter's *Judy Garland: The Day-by-Day Chronicle of a Legend* was published.

Filmography

The Meglin Kiddie Revue (Vita, 1929) (s)
Holiday in Storyland (Vita, 1930) (s)
The Wedding of Jack and Jill (Vita, 1930) (s)
The Old Lady in the Shoe (Vita, 1931) (s)
La Fiesta de Santa Barbara (MGM, 1935) (s)
Every Sunday (MGM, 1936) (s)
Pigskin Parade [The Harmony Parade] (20th-Fox, 1936)
Broadway Melody of 1938 (MGM, 1937)
Thoroughbreds Don't Cry (MGM, 1937)
Everybody Sing (MGM, 1938)
Love Finds Andy Hardy (MGM, 1938)
Listen, Darling (MGM, 1938)
The Wizard of Oz (MGM, 1939)
Babes in Arms (MGM, 1939)
Andy Hardy Meets Debutante (MGM, 1940)
Strike Up the Band (MGM, 1940)
Little Nellie Kelly (MGM, 1940)
Life Begins for Andy Hardy (MGM, 1941)
Ziegfeld Girl (MGM, 1941)
Babes on Broadway (MGM, 1941)
Meet the Stars #4 (Rep, 1941) (s)
Cavalcade of the Academy Awards (Vita, 1941) (s)

For Me and My Gal [For Me and My Girl] (MGM, 1942)
We Must Have Music (MGM, 1943) (s)
Presenting Lily Mars (MGM, 1943)
Girl Crazy (MGM, 1943)
Thousands Cheer (MGM, 1943)
Meet Me in St. Louis (MGM, 1944)
The Clock [Under the Clock] (MGM, 1945)
The Harvey Girls (MGM, 1945)
Ziegfeld Follies of 1946 (MGM, 1946)
Till the Clouds Roll By (MGM, 1946)
The Pirate (MGM, 1948)
Words and Music (MGM, 1948)
Easter Parade (MGM, 1948)
In the Good Old Summertime (MGM, 1949)
Summer Stock [If You Feel Like Singing] (MGM, 1950)
A Star Is Born (WB, 1954)
Pepe (Col, 1960) (voice only)
Judgment at Nuremberg (UA, 1961)
Gay Purr-ee (WB, 1962) (voice only)
A Child Is Waiting (UA, 1963)
I Could Go on Singing (UA, 1963)

TV Series

The Judy Garland Show (CBS, 1963–64)

Album Discography

LPs

The ABC Collection (ABC 620)
All of Judy (Telebrity 1228)
Alone (Cap T-835)
Annie Get Your Gun (Sound/Stage 2302, Sandy Hook 2053) [ST]
Babes in Arms/Babes on Broadway (Curtain Calls 100/6-7) [ST]
The Beginning (DRG 5187)
Behind the Scenes at the Making of "The Wizard of Oz"—The Complete "Maxwell House Good News" Radio Broadcast of June 29, 1939 (Jass 17) [ST/R]

The Best of Judy Garland (Decca DX-172/7172, MCA 4003, MCA 1630)
Bing, Bob and Judy (Totem 1009) w. Bing Crosby, Bob Hope
Born in a Trunk (Col CL-762)
Born in a Trunk, Vols. 1-3 (AEI 2108-10)
Broadway Melody of 1938 (Motion Picture Tracks MPT-3) [ST]
By Myself (Sears SP-430)
Christmas With Judy (Minerva MIN LP 6JG-XST) w. Liza Minnelli, Lorna Luft, Jack Jones
Collector's Items (Decca DEA-7-5, MCA 4046)

Dean Martin, Judy Garland & Frank Sinatra (Jocklo International 1007)

Deep In My Heart/Words and Music (MGM 2SES-54ST) [ST]

Deluxe Set (Cap TCL-STCL-2988)

Dick Tracy in B-Flat (Curtain Calls 100/1) [ST/R]

Drive-In (Command Performance 8) [ST/R]

Easter Parade (10″ MGM E-502, MGM E-3227) [ST]

For Collectors Only (Paragon 1002)

For Me and My Gal (Sountrak 107) [ST]

Forever Judy (MGM PX-102)

From MGM Classic Films (MCA 25165) [ST]

From the Decca Vaults (MCA 907)

Garland at the Grove (Cap T/ST-1118)

The Garland Touch (Cap W/SW-1710)

Gay Purr-ee (WB 1479) [ST]

Girl Crazy (10″ Decca DL-5412) w. Mickey Rooney

Girl Crazy/Strike Up the Band (Curtain Calls 100/9-10) [ST]

The Golden Years at MGM (MGM SDP-1-2)

The Great Garland Duets (Paragon 1001)

Greatest Hits (Decca DL-75150)

Greatest Hits (Radiant 711-0104) [ST/TV]

Greatest Performances (Decca DL-8190)

The Harvey Girls (Hollywood Soundstage 5002) [ST]

The Harvey Girls/Meet Me in St. Louis (Decca DL-8498)

I Could Go On Singing (Cap W/SW-1861, EMI 1288) [ST]

I Could Go On Singing Forever (Longines SY-52222)

I Feel a Song Coming On (Pickwick 3053)

If You Feel Like Singing (MGM E-3149)

In the Good Old Summertime (MGM E-3232) [ST]

Judy (Cap T-734)

Judy (Radiant 711-0101) [ST/TV]

Judy All Alone (Take One! TLP 201)

Judy and Bing Together (Legend 1973) w. Bing Crosby

Judy and Her Partners in Rhythm and Rhyme (Star-Tone ST-213)

Judy and Vic (Minerva 6JG-TVD) w. Vic Damone

Judy Garland (Metro M/S-505)

Judy Garland (MGM GAS-113)

Judy Garland and Friends (Minerva MIN-6JG-FNJ) w. June Allyson, Steve Lawrence, Jerry Van Dyke

Judy Garland at Carnegie Hall (Cap WBO/SWBO-1569)

Judy Garland at Home at the Palace (ABC 620)

Judy Garland at the Grove (EMI 26007)

Judy Garland at the Palace (10″ Decca DL-6020)

The Judy Garland Deluxe Set (Cap STCL 2988)

Judy Garland Duets (Broadcast 003)

Judy Garland in Concert (Trophy 2145)

Judy Garland in Concert in San Francisco (Mark 56 632)

Judy Garland in Holland, Vols. 2-3 (Amalgamated 195, 208)

Judy Garland in Hollywood (Radiant 711-0102)

Judy Garland Live (Amalgamated 145)

Judy Garland Live (Cap C2-92343)

Judy Garland Live at the Palace (CIT 2001)

Judy Garland, 1935-51 (Star Tone ST201)

Judy Garland on Radio (Radiola 1040)

Judy Garland Sings (10″ MGM E-82)

The Judy Garland Story (MGM E-4005)

The Judy Garland Story, Vol. 2 (MGM E-4005P)

Judy Garland—The Long Lost Holland Concert (Amalgamated 160)

Judy in Hollywood (Radiant 7112-0102)

Judy in Love (EMI/Pathé 54573)

Judy in Love (T/ST-1036)

Judy! Judy! Judy! (Star-Tone 224)

Judy! That's Entertainment (Cap T/ST-1467)

Judy the Legend (Radiant 711-0103)

Judy's Greatest Hits (Radiant 711-0104)

Judy's Portrait in Song (Radiant 711-0106)

Just for Openers (Cap W/DW-2062)

Lady in the Dark (Command Performance 10) [ST/R]

The Last Concert (Paragon 1003)

The Last Performance—London, 1969 (Juno 1000)

The Legend (Radiant 711-0103)

The Letter (Cap TAO-STAO-1188, EMI 602) w. John Ireland

Little Nellie Kelly/Thousands Cheer (Amalgamated 323) [ST]

Live at the London Palladium (Cap WBO-SWBO-2295, Cap ST-11191) w. Liza Minnelli

Lovely To Look At/Summer Stock (MCA 39084) [ST]

Magic (Decca DL-4199)

The Magic of Judy Garland (DNFR 7632)

Meet Me in St. Louis (Pelican 118) [ST/R]

Meet Me in St. Louis/The Harvey Girls (AEI 3101) [ST]

Merton of the Movies (Pelican 139) [ST/R]

Miss Show Business (Cap W-676)

More Than a Memory (Stanyan 10095)

Musical Scrapbook (Star-Tone 208)

Mutual Admiral Society (Minerva MIN 6JG-FST) w. Mickey Rooney, Jerry Van Dyke

Our Love Letter (Cap T/ST-1941) w. John Ireland

Over the Rainbow (Music for Pleasure 50555)

Over the Rainbow (Pickwick 3078)

Over the Rainbow (Radiant 711-0107)

Over the Rainbow (Springboard 4054)

Pagan Love Song/Hit the Deck/The Pirate (MGM 2SES-43ST) [ST]

Pagan Love Song/The Pirate (MCA 39080) [ST]

Pepe (Colpix 507) [ST]

Pigskin Parade/Everybody Sing (Amalgamated 231) [ST]

The Pirate (10″ MGM E-21, MGM E-3234) [ST]

Presenting Lily Mars (Caliban 6033, Sountrak 117) [ST]

Radio Broadcast Follies of 1936 (Amalgamated 227) [ST/R]

Rare Performance (Windmill 258)

Sixteen Greatest Hits (Trip 16-9)

Sophie (AEI 1130) [OC]

A Star Is Born (Col BL-1201, Col CL-1101/CS-8740, Har HS-11366) [ST]

The Star Years (MGM E-3989)

Summer Stock (10″ E-519, MGM E-3234) [ST]

Terms of Endearment (Cap SV-12329) [ST]

That Old Song and Dance (Minerva MIN 6JG-FSS) w. Donald O'Connor, Jerry Van Dyke

That's Dancing! (EMI America SJ-17149) [ST]

That's Entertainment (Cap SM-11876)

That's Entertainment, Part II (MGM MG-1-5301, MCA 6155) [ST]

Thousands Cheer (Amalgamated 232, Hollywood Soundstage 49) [ST]

Till the Clouds Roll By (10″ MGM E-501, MGM E-3231, Metro M/S-578, Sountrak 115, Vertinge 2000) [ST]

Three Billion Millionaires (UA UXL-4/UXS-54)

Twelve Hits (Oxford 3030)

The Uncollected Judy Garland (Stanyan 10095)

The Unforgettable Judy Garland (Radiant 711-0105)

The Very Best of Judy Garland (MGM E/SE-4204)

The Wit and Wonder (DRG 5179)

The Wizard of Oz (10″ Decca DL-51520)

The Wizard of Oz (Decca DL-8387/78387, MCA 521)

The Wizard of Oz (MGM E-34640 [ST]

The Wizard of Oz (Radiola 1109) [ST/R]

Words and Music (10″ MGM E-505, MGM E-3233, Metro M/S-580) [ST]

The Young Judy Garland (Amalgamated 251)

Ziegfeld Follies of 1946 (Curtain Calls 100/15-16) [ST]

Ziegfeld Girl (CIF 3006) [ST]

CDs

A&E Biography . . . Anthology (Cap/EMI Records 84750)

All the Clouds'll Roll Away (JSP 702) w. Bing Crosby

All-Time Greatest Hits (Curb D21K-77370)

Alone (Cap C21Y-92346)

Always Chasing Rainbows: The Young Judy Garland (ASV CD-AJA-5093)

America's Treasure (DCC Compact Classics DZS-013, Garland GRZ-13)

Annie Get Your Gun (Annie 001, Turner Classic Movies/Rhino R2-76669) [ST]

At Her Best (Dressed to Kill 298)

Back to Back Hits (CEMA Special Markets S21-18250) w. Liza Minnelli

The Best of Judy Garland (BCI Eclipse 64792)

The Best of Judy Garland (EMI 34407)

The Best of Judy Garland (First Choice FCD-4562)

The Best of Judy Garland (Intersound CDC-1027)

The Best of Judy Garland (Polygram HMNCD-15)

The Best of Judy Garland From the MGM Classic Films (MCA MCAD-25165)

The Best of Judy Garland in Hollywood (Turner Clasic Movies/Rhino R2-75292)

The Best of the Capitol Masters—The London Sessions (Cap C21S-99618)

The Best of the Capitol Years (EMI 93438)

The Best of the Decca Years, Vol. 1 (MCA MCAD-31345)

The Best of the Electrifying Judy Garland (Cap 96600)

Bing Crosby With Judy Garland & Al Jolson (Avid 625) w. Bing Crosby, Al Jolson, John Charles Thomas

Changing My Tune: The Best of the Decca Years, Vol. 2 (MCA MCAD-10504)

Chasing Rainbows (Remember RBM-75007)

Child of Hollywood (CDS 321)

Christmas Album (Laserlight 12-467)

Christmas Through the Years (Laserlight 12-534)

Classic Songs from the Stage & Screen (MCI MCCDSE-101)

Cocktail Hour (Columbia River Entertainment Group CRG-21800)

Collector's Gems from the M-G-M Films (Turner Classic Movies/Rhino R2-72543)

Come Rain Or Come Shine (Laserlight 12-480)

The Complete Decca Original Cast Recordings (MCA MCAD-11491)

Dear Mr. Gable (Universal Special Markets 20540)

The Definitive Garland (Pastel 38)

The Definitive Judy Garland (Artists CD-PAST-38)

Dick Tracy in B-Flat (Hollywood Soundstage 4010) [ST/R]

Easter Parade (Sony Music Special Products AK-45392, Turner Classic Movies/Rhino R2-71960) [ST]

50 Hit Songs From the Immortal Judy Garland (Laserlight 15-942)

Fly Me to the Moon (Laserlight 12-484)

For Me and My Gal (Turner Classic Movies/Rhino R2-72204) [ST]

Girl Crazy (Turner Clasic Movies/Rhino R2-72590) [ST]

Golden Memories (Pair PCD-2-1030)

The Great Judy Garland (Redx RXBOX-31048)

The Harvey Girls (Turner Classic Movies/Rhino R2-72151) [ST]

Her 25 Greatest Hits (The Entertainers 271)

The Hits of Judy Garland (Cap C21K-46672)

The Hollywood Years (Blue Moon BMCD-7004)

I Can't Give You Anything But Love (BCI Eclipse 64789)

In Concert: The Beginning of the End (Legend 6011)

In the Good Old Summertime (EMI 794193) [ST]

It Was a Good Time—The Best of Judy Garland & Liza Minnelli (Curb D2-77777)

It's All for You—The Last Yars (Milhy 6265)

Judy (32 Records 32900)

Judy/Judy in Love (EM 533086)

Judy and Liza Together (Curb D2-77587) w. Liza Minnelli

Judy at Carnegie Hall (Cap/EMI 27876)

Judy at Carnegie Hall (DCC Compact Classics DCC-1135)

Judy at the Palace: Palace Two-a-Day (Hollywood Soundstage 4012)

Judy: Complete Decca Masters (MCA MCAD-11059)

Judy Duets: The Platinum Judy Garland (V&R Records 15990)

Judy Garland (Bella Musica BMF-702)

Judy Garland (Laserlight 81-004)

Judy Garland (Sounds of a Century 1880)

Judy Garland (A Touch of Class 85530)

Judy Garland and Mickey Rooney (Turner Classic Movies/Rhino R2-71921)

The Judy Garland Christmas Album (Laserlight 12 467)

The Judy Garland Collection (Delta 85701)

The Judy Garland Collection, Vol. 1 (VALM 1138)

The Judy Garland Collection, Vol. 2 (VALM 1151)

Judy Garland—In Paris (RTE RTE-CD-20012)

Judy Garland—Live (Cap C21S-92343)

Judy Garland on Radio (Vintage Jazz Classics VJC-1043-2)

The Judy Garland Show (Laserlight 15-942)

The Judy Garland Shows (BCD OTA-101911)

Judy: That's Entertainment! (Cap CDP-7-48426-2)

The Ladies of Show Biz (Sony Music Special Products CK-31844) w. Cab Calloway

The Last Years (Artists CD-MICH4-6265)

The Legendary 1960 Amsterdam Concert (Double Gold 53044)

Legends of the 20th Century (EMI 5222282)

Little Girl Blue (Pair PCD-2-1223)

London Sessions (Cap/EMI 99618)

Lovely To Look At/Summer Stock (MCA MCAD-39084) [ST]

The Magic of Judy Garland (EMI 5219842)

The Magic of Judy Garland (Musicrama 747082)

Mail Call (Laserlight 15-413) w. Bing Crosby

The Man That Got Away (Laserlight 12-482)

Meet Me in St. Louis (MGM 305123, Turner Classic Movies/Rhino R2-71959) [ST]

Miss Show Business (Cap C21Y-92344)

Moon Over Miami/Broadway Melody of 1938 (Great Movie Themes 60030) [ST]

A Music Anthology (Cap 94750)

Music Life Legend (Prism PLATCD-120)

The One & Only Judy Garland (Cap C2PO-96600)

The One & Only Judy Garland (The CD Collection OR-0053)

On the Radio (Jazz Classics 5006)

Over the Rainbow (Avid AVC-536)

Over the Rainbow (BCI Eclipse 64791)

Over the Rainbow (Charly 1137)

Over the Rainbow (Disky SI-990402)

Over the Rainbow (The Entertainers 406)

Over the Rainbow (Golden Options 3806)

Over the Rainbow (Laserlight 12-481)

Over the Rainbow (Pilz 449336-2)

Over the Rainbow (ProArte CDD-547)

Over the Rainbow (Promo Sound)

Over the Rainbow (Simply the Best 99040)

Over the Rainbow (Universal Special Markets 20214)

Pagan Love Song/The Pirate (MCA MCAD-39080) [ST]

Pepe (Collectors' Choice Music CCM-113-2, DRG 113) [ST]

The Pirate (Sony Music Special Products AK-48608) [ST]

A Portrait of Judy Garland (MCI Gallerie 407)

Puttin' on the Ritz (ABM ABMMCD-1018)

Puttin' on the Ritz (Musicrama 778802)

The Quintessential Judy Garland (Soundtrack Factory 33520)

The Show That Got Away (32 Records 32220)

Sing-A-Long (Priddis Music 1175)

Sophie (AEI 027) (OC)

The Sound of the Movies (Sound of the Movies 3108) w. Betty Grable

Spotlight on Judy Garland (Cap C21Y-29396)

A Star Is Born (CK-44389) [ST]

A Star Is Born (Radiola 1155) [ST/R]

Stormy Weather (Laserlight 12-483)

Summer Stock (Sony Music Special Products AK-46199) [ST]

Summer Stock/In the Good Old Summertime (Rhino Handmade RHM2 7761)

Sweet Sixteen (All Star ALS-23123)

That's Entertainment! (EMI/Cap Special Markets 57357)

That's Entertainment, Part II (Sony Music Special Products A2K-46872) [ST]

That's Entertainment! III (Angel CDQ-46872) [ST]

Till the Clouds Roll By (MGM/EMI MMG-24) [ST]

Till the Clouds Roll By (Sandy Hook CDSH-2080, Sony Music Special Products AK-47029) [ST]

Together (Curb D21K-77587) w. Liza Minnelli

Touch of Class (EMI TC-885302)

20th Century Masters: The Millennium Collection (MCA MCAD-19952)

25th Anniversary Retrospective (Cap C21Z-29901)

21 Hollywood Hits (Nimbus 2004)

The Unforgettable Judy Garland (MCI ETDCD-073)

Universal Legends Collection (Universal 1122622)

The Very Best of Judy Garland (Prism PLATCD-513)

When You're Smiling (BCI Eclipse 64790) w. Bing Crosby

The Wizard of Oz (Sony Music Special Products AK-45356, Turner Classic Movies/Rhino R2-71964, Turner Classic Movies/Rhino R2-71999) [ST]

Words and Music (MGM/EMI MGM-14, Sony Music Special Products AK-47711) [ST]

You Made Me Love You (Hallmark 304592)

The Young Judy Garland (Pearl Flapper PAST-CD-7014)

Ziegfeld Follies (Turner Classic Movies/Rhino R2-71958) [ST]

Ziegfeld Girl (Great Movie Themes 60026) [ST]

Zing Went the Strings of My Heart (Empress 873)

Mitzi Gaynor in the 1950s.
[Courtesy of JC Archives]

Mitzi Gaynor

(b. Francesca Mitzi Marlene De Charney von Gerber, Chicago, Illinois,
September 4, 1931)

Frequently, being talented, pretty, and ambitious has little to do with the ability of retaining screen stardom. Sometimes it is a case of being in the right place at the wrong time. Such was the situation with gifted, curvaceous, and extremely dedicated Mitzi Gaynor. She made her screen debut in 1950, in a Betty Grable musical at Twentieth Century-Fox just as the musical genre was again peaking. She was touted by the industry as the vivacious successor to Betty Grable and June Haver. However, song-and-dance pictures were waning by the 1950s, and she did her best work after leaving Fox. Her movie career seemed to revive when she was showcased in *South Pacific* (1958), but the momentum did not last for long. Musicals had died again. She was only in her early thirties when she abandoned the "new" Hollywood and turned to TV specials and the club stage. There, she not only displayed musical versatility and glamor, but also exhibited a refreshing comic verve that enhanced her entertainment package value to her public. As such she continued being a highly paid star for decades.

She was born on September 4, 1931 (some sources say 1930; she insisted 1932) in Chicago. Her given name was Francesca Mitzi Marlene De Charney von Gerber. Of Austro-Hungarian descent, her father was a cellist/music director, and her mother was an exhibition ballroom dancer. Her mother recalled, "When there was dance music on the radio, she bounced her bottle up and down in perfect tempo! . . . And before she could walk, she held on to a chair and bounced in time to music." The future star made her first stage appearance at the age of three in one of her mother's recitals, and by the next year was taking dance classes.

When Mitzi was four, the family moved to Detroit. By age nine, Mitzi was determined to be a professional dancer. She studied with her mother and with Mme. Kathryn Etienne (a professional dance instructor). When Mme. Kathryn Etienne moved to Hollywood, Mitzi (along with her mother and her aunt) followed her teacher to the coast. She was enrolled in Los Angeles at Le Conte Junior High School and then at the Powers Professional High School (operated by the mother of actress Mala Powers).

During the World War II years, Mitzi was part of a troupe that entertained at armed services camps; one of her specialties was her imitation of Carmen Miranda. The adolescent made her professional debut in July 1944 as part of the Etienne Ballet in Redlands, California. Later, lying about her age, she was in the 1946 West Coast production of Jerome Kern's *Roberta*—starring Tom Ewell—that played in San Francisco and Los Angeles.

Also with the Los Angeles Civic Light Opera, Mitzi Gerber—as she was then known—appeared in *The Fortune Teller* (1946). Under the title *Gypsy Lady*, the show was transferred to New York City that September, and young Mitzi was part of the cast headed by Melville Cooper and

Helena Bliss. This seventy-nine-performance engagement was followed by a tour of *Song of Norway*, in which Mitzi was cast as Miss Anders. She got to sing and dance to "Bon Vivant Part 2" with Sig Arno. This was followed by roles with the LA Civic Light Opera in *Naughty Marietta* (1948) with Susanna Foster and Wilbur Evans, and *The Great Waltz* (1949) with Walter Slezak and Dorothy Sarnoff, in which Mitzi played the role of Katie. When *The Great Waltz* was playing Los Angeles, producer/actor/raconteur George Jessel saw Mitzi and had her screen-tested at Twentieth Century-Fox. As the would-be movie performer recalled later, "They shot it [the test] in black and white and color. The funniest thing about it was my makeup. They spent the whole morning on it, and I was hoping I'd end up looking like Joan Crawford or Lana Turner or Ava Gardner. When the makeup man stepped aside and let me look in the mirror, I was crushed. I looked just like me." Nevertheless, the applicant was signed by the studio to a one-picture contract for $1,000 a week.

One of Gaynor's escorts in the early 1950s was eccentric billionaire Howard Hughes. In May 2001, she recalled for an A&E cable *Biography* episode devoted to Hughes: "He was generous. Very. With his time and advice. Oh, no, never with money, and I certainly didn't give him any." She mentioned on the same documentary that it was she who broke off with Hughes: "Howard had too many girls, from Terry Moore to Jean Simmons to Janet Leigh."

My Blue Heaven (1950) was the third of four screen teamings of Betty Grable and Dan Dailey. It was all about a husband-and-wife, song-and-dance team who plan to adopt a baby after the Mrs. suffers a miscarriage. What gave this backstage tale some novelty was that it was set in the TV industry, where the leads were stars of a musical variety program. This twist aside, the best surprise of the film was hazel-eyed, brunette Mitzi as Gloria Adams. Not only did she perform several amusing send-ups of TV cosmetic commercials, but she sparkled in the song number "Live Hard, Work Hard, Love Hard." *Variety* lauded this vivacious newcomer: "In addition to a pert and saucy face and the kind of figure boys don't forget, she's long on terping [i.e., dancing] and vocalizing." The studio quickly signed the newcomer—now called Mitzi Gaynor—to a term contract.

Fox was not sure how best further to use Gaynor on-camera. It cast her as Jeanne Crain's no-nonsense campus friend in *Take Care of My Little Girl* (1951), an indictment of the college sorority system. Mitzi's next release, *Golden Girl* (1951), remained her favorite motion picture. Produced by George Jessel, it featured Mitzi in a fictionalized account of stage performer Lotta Crabtree, who rose to renown in the 1860s California gold-rush days. Dale Robertson is her gambler/Confederate spy beau, and Dennis Day (Jack Benny's sidekick) is the shy troupe member who adores her. The film proved to be traditional hokum basically saved by Gaynor's verve. Her best number was "Dixie." The *Golden Girl* lead was the type of part for which Paramount's Betty Hutton would have given her own or anyone's eyeteeth.

Betty Grable and the younger June Haver were still the queens of musical comedy at Twentieth Century-Fox. However, another young blonde starlet named Marilyn Monroe was rising fast at the studio, and she was the one who stood out among the new crowd peppering *We're Not Married* (1952). The comedy deals with separate episodes of five couples who discover they are not really married: the judge (Victor Moore) who wed them had allowed his license to expire. In one of the film's most contrived segments, Gaynor plays a pregnant wife whose G.I. "husband" (Eddie Bracken) is being shipped overseas during the Korean War. If *We're Not Married* was an adequate production at best, *Bloodhounds of Broadway* (1952) was not even of that caliber. It was another George Jessel–produced, poorly conceived musical comedy; this time a Damon Runyon yarn about a New York bookie (Scott Brady) meeting an attractive Georgia yokel (Mitzi Gaynor). She persuades Brady to help her become a name on Broadway. The picture's choreographer, Bob Sydney, would later become Mitzi's dance director on her TV specials. In her off time from the studio, Gaynor appeared in Los Angeles Civic Light Opera's production of *Jollyanna*, which opened in San Francisco in the summer of 1952.

George Jessel not only produced *The "I Don't Care" Girl* (1953), but he played himself in the Technicolor picture. He is the movie producer attempting to find out the facts in the life of vaudeville star Eva Tanguay (Mitzi Gaynor) so he can make a movie about her. The scripting was abysmal, and the direction was inconsistent in its attempt to cover the story's inadequacies. Gaynor was vivacious (one might say frantic) in her title-role performance, but she could not breathe life into this hodgepodge of flashbacks and hackneyed set pieces. She tap-danced with David Wayne, traded quips with acerbic pianist/manic humorist Oscar Levant, and sang such numbers as the title song and "Hello, Frisco, Hello." Jack Cole staged the three production numbers, and Seymour Felix choreographed the tap routines. However, moviegoers were now weary of such sugary, unbelievable musical biopics.

Back in 1951, studio head Darryl F. Zanuck had begun preproduction on a musical *Down Among the Sheltering Palms* (1953), intending it as a June Haver vehicle. She refused to be in it, claiming the storyline was immoral. Those who were corralled into the project, including Jane Greer, Gloria DeHaven, and Mitzi, wished they had *not*. This group included director Edmund Goulding, who did his peevish best to sabotage the production. The film's plot is set at the end of World War II, when an Army captain (William Lundigan) and his troop command are stationed on the South Pacific isle of Midi. The order of the day is nonfraternization with the natives. Mitzi is the luscious Rozouila, daughter of the island king (Billy Gilbert), offered as a goodwill gesture to Lundigan. When the film was finally released, it was considered completely naive foolishness by critics and public alike. Zanuck never forgave any of the cast involved in the mishmash. However, the *New York Times* pointed out, "Miss Gaynor supplements her adroit inquiry, 'What Makes De Diff'rence?' with a couple of electric feats of tribal choreography, stopping the show cold, or hot, as usual."

By 1954, June Haver had left Fox, and Betty Grable was on her way out, as were musicals. The studio was banking heavily on Marilyn Monroe at the box office and would soon have Sheree North and Jayne Mansfield as backups to that sexpot star. Mitzi Gaynor, unfortunately, was caught in midstream. She was considered too talented to be wasted as screen fluff and yet too wholesome (similar to Doris Day) to make a reputation as a sex goddess of musical comedy. She floundered at the studio, finally being cast in an independent "B" Western, *Three Young Texans* (1954), which Fox released in early 1954. It was a pedestrian effort wasting its three young performers, Mitzi, Keefe Brasselle, and Jeffrey Hunter. Although Gaynor was game in her clichéd screen role, it was Vivian Marshall who sang the saloon song "Just Let Me Love You."

Then Fox had second thoughts about Mitzi and cast her in the splashy Irving Berlin musical, *There's No Business Like Show Business* (1954). It was a major production filmed in CinemaScope and boasting Ethel Merman, Dan Dailey, Donald O'Connor, Johnnie Ray, Marilyn Monroe, and Mitzi Gaynor (sixth billed!). It was all about a vaudeville family and their talented offspring. Long-legged Gaynor was the spunky (and sometimes quite sexy) daughter who falls in love with Hugh O'Brian. Everyone had their share of production numbers, but between Merman's belting, O'Connor's soft-shoeing, Ray's wailing, and especially Monroe's sensuous "Heat Wave" number, Gaynor was nearly lost in the shuffle. During production, Fox announced that they were *not* picking up Gaynor's contract option.

In the early 1950s, Mitzi had been dating corporate attorney Richard Coyle, eleven years her senior. However, her constant escort was Jack Bean, an MCA talent agent whom she had met in 1952 when he tried unsuccessfully to sign her for his agency. On November 18, 1954, they were married in San Francisco. He later left the industry and went into real estate, as well as becoming his wife's business manager.

During her Fox period, Richard Rodgers and Oscar Hammerstein II had voiced interest in having Mitzi play the ingénue role in an *Annie Get Your Gun* stage revival. When their *Oklahoma!* (1955) went into production, Gaynor (like Betty Hutton) was considered for the part of Ado Annie, but when Fox would not loan her, Gloria Grahame was signed for the role of the girl who just could not say no. Looking back on her studio contract years, Gaynor admitted in her kidding way, "I went through a very sexy period. Boy, I was full of attitudes. Even my ears were sexy, I thought, and lips—did I have lips! Practically used to put my lipstick up inside my nose, and I'd shave my eyebrows until I looked smolderingly hot. But I knew that the whole thing was kind of ridiculous, too."

More realistically, and with the advice of her husband, Mitzi went about making herself more marketable as a freelance movie personality. She streamlined her figure, sharpened her singing/dancing techniques, adopted a more sensual persona, and became more blonde. She was off the screen all through 1955. However, at a $100,000 salary, she was hired to play opposite Bing Crosby in *Anything Goes* (1956) at Paramount. She is the crooner's shipboard romance who wins a role in his new Broadway musical. In the proceedings, there was quite a contrast between the ballerina dancing of Zizi Jeanmaire and Gaynor's more provocative terpsichorean display. Mitzi had another shipboard romance in RKO's *The Birds and the Bees* (1956), an unsatisfactory remake of the Barbara Stanwyck–Henry Fonda comedy classic *The Lady Eve* (1941). RKO was a dying corporation by this time, and this film, despite the valiant efforts of Gaynor, David Niven, and George Gobel, helped to sink the studio lot.

Twentieth Century-Fox had wanted Mitzi to return to costar in *The Best Things in Life Are Free* (1956), but she declined (the role went to Sheree North). Instead Gaynor joined with Frank Sinatra in *The Joker Is Wild* (1957), again at Paramount. It was a version of the life and times (the Roaring Twenties) of nightclub singer turned comedian Joe E. Lewis (Sinatra), who loves socialite Jeanne Crain but instead marries leggy chorine Mitzi, only to succumb later to booze. Sinatra sang effectively (the title song won an Academy Award), Gaynor was gammy and sexy, and marvelous Sophie Tucker appeared as herself. 1957 proved to be her best year on-screen, because she followed this film with MGM's sophisticated *Les Girls* (1957), directed by George Cukor. It was a stylish Cole Porter original musical that had Gene Kelly doing what he did best: dancing, singing, and playing a heel. Here he is a stage trouper on the Continent who acts fast and loose with his three stage partners: Mitzi, Kay Kendall, and Taina Elg. Gaynor is the one he marries, and with him she dances "Why Am I So Gone (About That Gal)?" With Kendall and Elg, Mitzi performs several routines, including the saucy boudoir spoof "Ladies in Waiting." Unfortunately, the movie was too chic for most moviegoers' tastes.

In the late 1950s, Hollywood had almost abandoned the traditional musical (except for rock 'n' roll efforts). Occasionally, the studios would take a risk if the property was based on a surefire Broadway hit. Such was the case with *South Pacific*, which had begun its run on Broadway in 1949 and nearly a decade later was being translated finally to the screen. It was "the" role of the year. Mary Martin, who had originated the part, was now considered too mature to play frolicking nurse Nellie Forbush on-screen. Thus, talent such as Doris Day, Elizabeth Taylor, Susan Hayward, Ginger Rogers, and Jean Simmons campaigned for the part. Mitzi Gaynor was among those tested by the show's composers, Rodgers and Hammerstein. She auditioned for Hammerstein at the Crystal Ballroom of the Beverly Hills Hotel. As she recalls, "while I was singing, Oscar, who was a little deaf, kept moving farther and farther back. He wanted me to project, as if I were auditioning for the theater! . . . When I was finished, I put my shoes back on and asked, 'How was I?' and he said, 'Thank you, Miss Gaynor, you're a very good sport!' "

Hammerstein was still not sure if Gaynor had the box-office allure required for the heavily budgeted musical. She then did a secret screen test (the other competitors were jumpy about anyone getting the edge) for director Joshua Logan at Twentieth Century-Fox, the distributor of this Magna production. Gaynor won out and was hired at double her past salary. Shot on location in Hawaii in a super-wide-screen process, *South Pacific* should have been a milestone screen musical. But it was not. Logan's direction was heavy-handed and gimmicky (with its multicolored, gassy sky effects); the singing of costars Rosanno Brazzi (as the plantation owner who loves Gaynor) and John Kerr (the second lead male role) was dubbed; and the film was a too-lengthy 171 minutes. Nevertheless, Gaynor cavorted energetically in this $5 million production, acting gaminelike as she admitted to being a "A Cockeyed Optimist," that "I'm in Love With a Wonderful Guy," or "I'm Gonna Wash That Man Right Outa My Hair." She and Brazzi (and his voice double) dueted "Some Enchanted Evening," and with Ray Walston (the brightest personality in the picture) she performed the lively "Honey Bun." Because of the hoopla involved, the picture grossed $17.5 million in domestic film rentals. However, it was generally not liked and damaged Mitzi Gaynor's standing in Hollywood. It was said she had no sex appeal on-screen.

Thereafter, Gaynor turned to another genre, screen comedies. She was vivacious with David Niven in the domestic fluff *Happy Anniversary* (1959), did her best to buoy a leaden *Surprise Package* (1960) opposite Yul Brynner, and was one of the few bright ingredients in *For Love or Money* (1963), paired with Kirk Douglas. However, by now her film career was essentially over. "The movie musical thing was finished, the contract players were flooding the streets, and I was just part of the backwash," she said.

Meanwhile, Mitzi had been testing the waters in other entertainment mediums. Besides appearing on the *Jack Benny Hour* (CBS-TV, March 18, 1959), she was the only female guest on *The Frank Sinatra Show* (ABC-TV, October 9, 1959), shining out in an array of talent that included Bing Crosby, Jimmy Durante, and Dean Martin. More importantly, in 1961 she began performing in Las Vegas. The gambling capital catered to a Southern California crowd, and anyone with a film name was considered potential marquee bait. Morris Landsberg, the owner of the Flamingo Hotel, urged her to star in a cabaret act for him. She claims that she was very dubious about the venture. When Landsberg invited Mitzi and her husband to a Las Vegas middleweight prize fight (Sugar Ray Robinson versus Gene Fullmer) Gaynor said, "If Fullmer wins, I'm going to do the act"; he did and she did. Mitzi pioneered the original (and soon-to-become-standard) Las Vegas production ensemble show: glitzy costumes/sets, high-tech lighting and sound, superb male dancers, and as its focal point, a singing star who could vocalize, dance, and even clown. She was a pre–Carol Burnett type, only a lot prettier. She tested the act in Hot Springs, Arkansas, and then opened in Vegas in July 1961, and it led to a new career for her. In the coming years, she acquired a piece of the Flamingo Hotel, thanks to the business acumen of her agent/manager/husband Jack Bean.

In 1964, Mitzi finally appeared on *The Ed Sullivan Show* (CBS-TV), once he agreed to the proviso that she have at least a fifteen-minute time spot. She shared the spotlight that night with the Beatles, and some viewers thought her act was too suggestive. By 1968, she was earning $45,000 a week in Las Vegas. In her club gambit, she did skits that kidded her sexy screen image and demonstrated her performance versatility. As she could frolic as a leggy dancer, be a stylish chanteuse, and excel as a comedienne with perfect timing, audiences were vastly pleased with her shows. Among her comedy alter egos were Mitzi Goodglove, Nancy Neat, and Betty Bath. She continued demonstrating the independence that had marked (and marred) her Fox contract years. She insisted, "I'd rather work in-person than in a movie I don't like. . . . If I told you the [Broadway] hits I've turned down—but something just has to strike me." She wowed the audience with her showstopping dance number on the April 11, 1967, Academy Award telecast, proving that her reputation as a perfectionist paid dividends.

For her first starring TV special, *Mitzi* (NBC-TV, October 14, 1968), produced by her husband, her guests included George Hamilton and Phil Harris. It had good ratings and led to *Mitzi's Second Special* (NBC-TV, October 20, 1969). She did an hour show with Perry Como on NBC-TV on December 9, 1971. This was followed by such annual entries as *Mitzi . . . The First Time* (CBS-TV, March 28, 1973), *Mitzi and a Hundred Guys* (CBS-TV, March 24, 1975), *Mitzi . . . Roarin' in the 20s* (CBS-TV, March 14, 1976, with guest Linda Hopkins and Ken Berry), *Mitzi . . . Zings Into Spring* (CBS-TV, March 29, 1977, with Roy Clark), and *Mitzi . . . What's Hot, What's Not* (CBS-TV, April 6, 1978). Her most elaborate outing was *Mitzi and a Hundred Guys*, which had an array of guest performers, ranging from Michael Landon to Bill Bixby, Andy Griffith, Monte Hall, and Bob Hope.

Meanwhile, Gaynor pursued her club touring. She annually played three to four months on the road (earning $80,000 weekly) and then devoted the rest of the year to perfecting her next act. When she was at Harrah Club in Lake Tahoe in 1971, *Variety* reported of the typical Gaynor production, "Gaynor herself is an excellent comedienne. In baby pink fluff, she camps 'My Heart Belongs to Daddy' and dressed in hokey hick bloomer outfit worn for 'Doin' What Comes Naturally' she sits on the stage and sings 'Look to the Rainbow,' and comes off superbly." There had been talk in 1972 of her doing a musical picture called *Hollywood! Hollywood!* with Carol Burnett, but it was never realized. "I have no desire to do films any more," Gaynor insisted. "My [annual] television special is my movie. . . . I love television because it's fast. All that waiting around on movie sets while they change the set or the lights isn't for me any more. . . . When people ask me why I work so hard and when am I going to retire, I think they're crazy." When asked about her old films, she said, "I see pictures I've done and I say, 'Ugh, Mitzi, don't act so much.' I'm all eyebrows, teeth and hair. Reaction upon reaction! . . . But Virgo people are hard on themselves."

When Mitzi was at the Westbury Music Fair in October 1979, *Newsday* reminded readers, "She's not just a straight hoofer and singer, but a first-rate musical comedienne, injecting wit and humor into her act that comes out charmingly." By 1982, she was netting $250,000 annually from her club engagements and had done ten network specials. On November 10, 1986, she was honored by the Friars Club as one of the great song-and-dance stars of her generation. Throughout the rest of the 1980s, she continued her cabaret appearances (especially in Las Vegas and Atlantic City venues), wearing Bob Mackie costumes, celebrating and satirizing theme subjects, and dancing up a storm. Her 1987–88 national tour was a celebration to Irving Berlin and was produced at a cost of $350,000. Already in her late fifties, she continued unabated, with an eleven-month, thirty-six-city national tour of the old musical *Anything Goes* for the 1989–90 season. In the updated production, she played the role of Reno Sweeney. Said Gaynor: "I got my Social Security card when I was twelve and I haven't been out of work a single day since then."

During 1992, Gaynor was featured on American Movies Classics, hosting the cable network's *Comedy Classics* for a twenty-six-week period. In February 1996, Mitzi, still vibrant and energetic, was one of the honorees, along with Juliet Prowse, at the Tenth Annual "Gypsy" Awards held at the Century Park Hotel in Los Angeles. During the often-humorous festivities, Gaynor, herself an expert raconteur, acknowledged, "I'm having the best time I've ever had in my whole life. Nothing like this has ever happened to me before." Four years later, at their annual Christmas holiday party at their Beverly Hills home, Mitzi and her husband Jack Bean toasted the publication of Frank DeCaro's book *Unmistakably Mackie: The Fashion and Fantasy of Bob Mackie*. In the publication, Mitzi, who was the designer's first major celebrity client, recalled the key role that Mackie had played in dressing up her later career.

When asked about her career in dancing a few years ago, Mitzi Gaynor said, "You've got to love it. You've got to wake up in the morning and say: 'It hurts so much I can't move and I *love* it.'"

Filmography

My Blue Heaven (20th-Fox, 1950)
Take Care of My Little Girl (20th-Fox, 1951)
Golden Girl (20th-Fox, 1951)
We're Not Married (20th-Fox, 1952)
Bloodhounds of Broadway (20th-Fox, 1952)
The 'I Don't Care' Girl (20th-Fox, 1953)
Down Among the Sheltering Palms (20th-Fox, 1953)
Three Young Texans (20th-Fox, 1954)
There's No Business Like Show Business (20th-Fox, 1954)

Anything Goes (Par, 1956)
The Birds and the Bees (RKO, 1956)
The Joker Is Wild [All the Way] (Par, 1957)
Les Girls (MGM, 1957)
South Pacific (Magna, 1958)
Happy Anniversary (MGM, 1959)
Surprise Package (UA, 1960)
Lykke og krone (Norwegian, 1962) (documentary)
For Love or Money (Univ, 1963)

Broadway

Gypsy Lady (1946)

Album Discography

LPs

Anything Goes (Decca DL-8318) [ST]
Golden Girl (Caliban 6037) [ST]
The Joker Is Wild (Caliban 6024) [ST]
Les Girls (MGM E-3590) [ST]
Mitzi (Verve 2110)
Mitzi Gaynor Sings the Lyrics of Ira Gershwin
     (Verve 2115)

Mitzi Zings Into Spring (ICPR 3-77) [ST/TV]
My Blue Heaven (Titania 503) [ST]
South Pacific (RCA LOC/LSO-1032) [ST]
There's No Business Like Show Business (Decca
     DL-8091, MCA 1723) [ST]

CDs

Les Girls (EMI 794251) [ST]
Mitzi (Verve POCJ-2660)
South Pacific (RCA 3681-2-R) [ST]

There's No Business Like Show Business (Varese
     Sarabande VSD-5912) [ST]

Betty Grable

(b. Elizabeth Ruth Grable, South St. Louis, Missouri, December 18, 1916;
d. Las Vegas, Nevada, July 2, 1973)

An icon in American cultural history, blue-eyed Betty Grable will forever be remembered as the most celebrated of all pin-up girls. The famous World War II poster shot of her in a form-fitting bathing suit looking seductively over her shoulder is embedded in the minds of many Americans. It was just as much a part of the war effort as rationing or helping to retake the beaches at Normandy. Her legs (like those of Marlene Dietrich) were insured for a million dollars, her vital statistics (34-23-35) were legendary, and her spunky personality made her all the more enticing. Although she was one of the top moneymaking stars (in the top ten at the box office for a decade!), she was quite down-to-earth and unaffected by her enormous star status. She quipped, "As a dancer I couldn't outdance Ginger Rogers or Eleanor Powell. As a singer I'm no rival to Doris Day. As an actress I don't take myself seriously." On another occasion she said, "I am what I wanted to be. Just give me the lines that lead into a song-and-dance routine. I'm the girl the truck drivers love."

Grable was the blonde bombshell link between the 1930s' Jean Harlow and the 1950s' Marilyn Monroe. Her peaches-and-cream good looks were highlighted superbly when filmed in splashy color, and her typical film backstage stories were a marvelous excuse for her to parade in abbreviated, revealing costumes. As such, she captivated the moviegoing public during the war years with her ingratiating personality and fluffy screen vehicles. It is somewhat ironic that although she is typed as a movie singer, Betty Grable was a mediocre vocalist at best.

She was born Elizabeth Ruth Grable in South St. Louis, Missouri on December 18, 1916, the daughter of bookkeeper/truck driver Conn Grable and ambitious Lillian Rose Hoffman. She was the second of two girls, preceded in birth by older sister Marjorie. Her mother was insistent that her younger daughter become a show-business success. At an early age, Betty took ballet and acrobatic lessons as well as playing the ukulele, singing, and dancing. By the time she was seven, she was adept enough to appear in local talent shows booked by Jack Haley and Frank Fay. While hardly in her teens, Betty fell in love with Hollywood when the family vacationed there. Against her father's will, Betty and her mother remained in the film capital, where she attended the Hollywood Professional School and did a vaudeville act with Emlyn Pique (Mitzi Mayfair).

At thirteen (but claiming she was two years older), Betty was in the ensemble of *Happy Days* (1929), took part in a blackface chorus bit in Fox's *Let's Go Places* (1930), and was also in the chorus of *The New Movietone Follies of 1930* (1930). When the musical movie craze faded, she auditioned and was signed by producer Samuel Goldwyn to be a "Goldwyn Girl," appearing in a string of features for the producer, including three Eddie Cantor opuses: *Whoopee* (1930), *Palmy Days* (1931; where she met her future lover, actor/dancer George Raft), and *The Kid From Spain* (1933). During this time, her grasping mother put her in a series of educational shorts directed by Fatty Arbuckle (under his real name of William Goodrich), and she used the name Frances

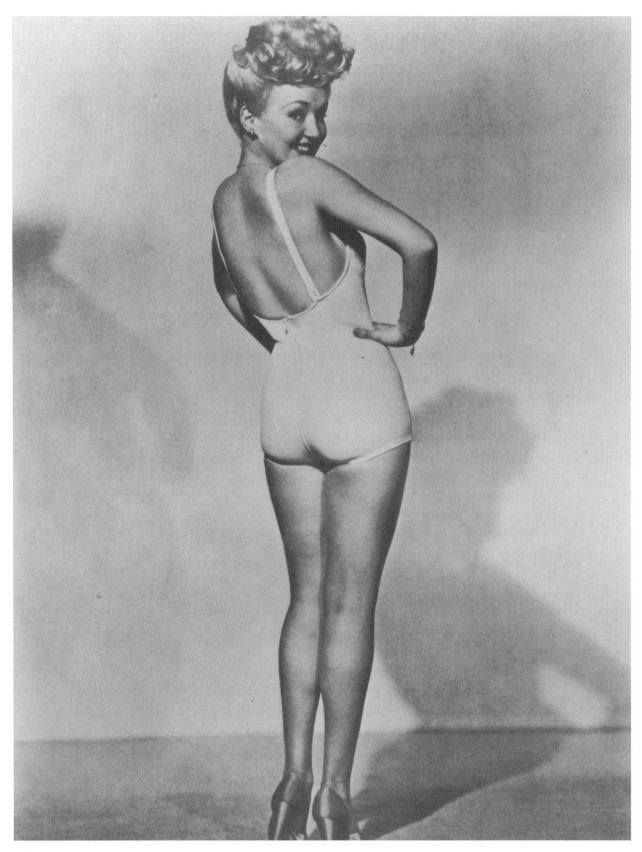

Betty Grable in her famous World War II era pinup pose.
[Courtesy of JC Archives]

Dean. When her Goldwyn contract was terminated ("I had that girl under contract once. I wonder why I never did anything with her," Goldwyn later quipped), she appeared in the revue *Tattle Tales* with Barbara Stanwyck and Frank Fay in 1933, but left the show during its pre-Broadway tryout in San Francisco. Then she did an eight-month tour as the vocalist with Ted Fio Rito and his band. (The candid Grable would admit of her stint as a band singer, "The trouble was, I couldn't sing!") With Fio Rito she appeared in *Sweetheart of Sigma Chi* (1933) and was in a variety of other Hollywood products, several made on poverty row like *Probation* (1932) and *What Price Innocence?* (1933).

Betty had been the ingénue in RKO's Bert Wheeler–Robert Woolsey comedy *Hold 'Em Jail* (1932) and later toured with the comedy team, as well as appearing with them in *The Nitwits* (1935). After she gained some attention singing "Let's K-nock K-neez" in *The Gay Divorcee* (1934) with Edward Everett Horton, RKO signed her to a contract. But as with her Goldwyn tenure, not much happened. When her RKO contract ended, she went to Fox (again) for a colead in *Pigskin Parade* (1936). However, it was Judy Garland (in her first feature picture) and Stuart Erwin (who was Oscar-nominated) who received the most attention. Grable's big number, "It's Love I'm After," was cut from the final release print. She was part of a vaudeville tour with ex–child star Jackie Coogan, and on her birthday (December 19, 1937), they were married. She had already begun her rash of campus cuties roles at Paramount with *Collegiate* (1936), and was soon signed by that studio to a contract. Also in this period, from 1937 to 1938, she coteamed with John Payne in the radio series *Song Time*.

Despite the promise of an expanded career, she continued to play the same type of collegiate roles in a string of "B" features at Paramount, including *College Swing* (1938*), Campus Confessions* (1938) and *Million Dollar Legs* (1939). She was voted "America's Ideal Girl" by the Hollywood Artists and Local Chamber of Commerce. Then she made newspaper headlines by standing by Coogan during his famous court battle to obtain his screen earnings from his mother and stepfather. She was earning $500 weekly when Paramount dropped her option in 1939. It was yet another crisis in her seesawing career, and she later admitted, "Something had to be done or I would be a promising youngster until I was a grandmother."

Grable returned once more to vaudeville, where she earned up to $1,500 weekly. Author Buddy DeSylva caught Grable when she was appearing for two weeks with Jack Haley at the San Francisco Exposition. DeSylva, who cowrote the book for a new Cole Porter vehicle, *DuBarry Was a Lady*, hired her for its 1939 Broadway production. Ethel Merman was the star, but Betty in the second lead got good notices for her dance number "Well, Did You Ever." She appeared on the cover of *Life* magazine. Meanwhile, Twentieth Century-Fox mogul Darryl F. Zanuck noticed the Grable hoopla and signed her to a contract, admitting, "This girl has qualities we missed here."

Grable returned to Hollywood in June 1940. Her marriage to Coogan was over. Her romance with bandleader Artie Shaw had ended when he married Lana Turner in February 1940. She began dating George Raft instead. For her first role under her new Twentieth Century-Fox contract, Betty replaced Alice Faye, the studio's top musical star, in the Technicolor *Down Argentine Way* (1940) when Faye became ill. Betty scored well as the heiress who is mad about horse racing and is romanced by Don Ameche. She and Faye became lifelong friends after they were paired in *Tin Pan Alley* (1940) as dancing sisters. In this delightful period musical, they give a sexy rendition of "The Sheik of Araby," sporting harem-girl outfits. The film also allowed Betty to sing "Honeysuckle

Rose" and "Moonlight and Roses." She and Don Ameche were paired again in another Technicolor musical, *Moon Over Miami* (1941), in which she sang "Kindergarten Conga."

Although Grable always insisted she was not a good actress, her next two features—*A Yank in the R.A.F.* and *I Wake Up Screaming*, both 1941 and filmed in black-and-white—showed that she handled drama well. But exhibitors and moviegoers liked her best in Technicolor fluff such as *Song of the Islands* (1942), in which she was matched with the studio beefcake contractee Victor Mature. She was now receiving more than a thousand fan letters a week, and within a year was to be among the top ten moneymaking Hollywood stars. Her brand of snap and sparkle was definitely in vogue. In 1942, replacing pregnant Alice Faye, she starred in *Springtime in the Rockies*, and this color opus had her appearing with bandleader Harry James. James soon replaced George Raft in Grable's love life, and they were wed on July 5, 1943, in Las Vegas. Meanwhile, Betty churned out more musicals. She was a chorus girl performing "I Heard the Birdies Sing" in *Footlight Serenade* (1942; her final black-and-white starring vehicle), and *Coney Island* (1943) had her singing "Cuddle Up a Little Closer" and "Take It From There." She portrayed a Brooklyn singer who becomes a British music-hall star in *Sweet Rosie O'Grady* (1943), in which she performed "Waitin' at the Church." She had a guest bit as herself in *Four Jills in a Jeep* (1944), and then romanced a sailor (John Harvey) in *Pin-Up Girl* (1944), a lame musical designed by Twentieth Century-Fox to exploit her title as the popular favorite of the GIs. On March 3, 1944, she gave birth to her first child, Victoria. (Her second child, Jessica would be born on May 20, 1947.) Said the ever-candid Grable, "It isn't difficult to be a good mother and a movie star at the same time. It just calls for planning. . . . My family always comes first."

Betty returned to pictures in 1945 in *Billy Rose's Diamond Horseshoe* singing "Welcome to the Diamond Horseshoe" and "Acapulco" in this slight tale of chorine Grable falling for medical student Dick Haymes. Fox had wanted Betty to reteam with Alice Faye in *The Dolly Sisters* (1945), but the latter had retired from the screen, and it was newcomer June Haver who was paired with Grable in this entertaining songfest. Grable sang "I Can't Begin to Tell You." Her only 1946 film appearance was a guest bit at the finale of *Do You Love Me?* which costarred her husband, Harry James. During the 1940s, Grable appeared on radio in such shows as *Gulf Screen Guild Theater, Lux Radio Theater, Philco Radio Time*, and *Suspense*. Despite the fact that she was known as a singer, she cut no records. Twentieth Century-Fox studio chief Darryl F. Zanuck refused to let most of his stars record. Actually she did one commercial record ("I Can't Begin to Tell You") in 1945 for Columbia Records with Harry James. On the record label she was billed as "Ruth Haag" (a pseudonym composed of her and Harry's middle names).

By now Grable was the studio's chief moneymaker and she was earning over $300,000 annually. In 1947, however, her period piece comedy, *The Shocking Miss Pilgrim*, which did not reveal her fabulous legs, lost money. The studio wisely returned her to form in *Mother Wore Tights* (1947), costarring Dan Dailey, where she sang "Kokomo, Indiana," "Burlington Bertie From Bow," and "You Do." She missed again in *That Lady in Ermine* (1948), a musical fantasy production fraught with problems when director Ernst Lubitsch died in the middle of its filming and was replaced by Otto Preminger. She and Dan Dailey were reunited in *When My Baby Smiles At Me* (1948), which had been filmed earlier as *Dance of Life* (1929) and *Swing High, Swing Low* (1937).

The bottom really fell out from under Betty Grable's screen career when she starred in Preston Sturges's *The Beautiful Blonde From Bashful Bend*. Grable never looked lovelier on film, but the movie itself was a vulgar, turgid Western that cast the star as a gun-slinging school marm in the Old West romanced by slick crook Cesar Romero and stuffy millionaire Rudy Vallee. She was back with Dan Dailey for *My Blue Heaven* in 1950. However this marital comedy about radio stars wanting to adopt a baby was mediocre, and young contractee Mitzi Gaynor received the best notices. Much better was a remake of *Coney Island* called *Wabash Avenue* (1950) in which saloon singer Betty (who warbled "I Wish I Could Shimmy Like My Sister Kate") was romanced by her boss (Phil Harris) and a gambler (Victor Mature). She and Mature repeated their roles on *Lux Radio Theater* on CBS on November 13, 1950.

Betty and Dan Dailey were teamed for the final time on the big screen in *Call Me Mister* (1951), about a show-business couple doing a USO tour in Japan. For producer George Jessel, she headlined *Meet Me After the Show* (1951), which was reminiscent of the star's musicals from the '40s. Grable was put on suspension for refusing to do yet another song-and-dance with Dailey (*The Girl Next Door*, 1953; June Haver took the part). Betty also turned down a dramatic role in *Pickup on South Street* (1953), which Jean Peters performed. (Grable's rationale was, "I don't go in for that dramatic stuff; I'm no actress.")

After her suspension, Grable returned to the studio to make *The Farmer Takes a Wife* (1953). However, it was a weak musical and fared poorly. With musicals (and Grable) on the wane, studio plans to star Betty in remakes of *Heaven Can Wait* and *Bad Girl* were dropped. Fox had a new blonde sexpot named Marilyn Monroe who won the lead away from Grable in *Gentlemen Prefer Blondes* (1953). It was Monroe who received top billing in *How to Marry a Millionaire* (1953) over Grable and Lauren Bacall. Nevertheless, always the professional, Grable turned in a deft comedy performance in this picture as the showgirl determined to wed a rich businessman (Fred Clark). Fox loaned Grable to Columbia Pictures for a remake of the 1940 film *Too Many Husbands*, a clumsy musical named *Three for the Show* (1954). Although Grable was good as the show-business star who thinks her husband (Jack Lemmon) has died and marries a dancer (Gower Champion), the picture proved to be a lumbering mess. Her final picture at Twentieth, *How to Be Very, Very Popular*, teamed her with Sheree North. The studio was grooming the latter as a Marilyn Monroe replacement, just as it had groomed Monroe to replace Grable. The two blondes did a fine job in this CinemaScope comedy as burlesque dancers who hide in a men's dormitory after witnessing a murder. But the film was considered old-fashioned and did poor business at the box office. On that note, Grable and Fox ended their contract. Reportedly Grable, typically good-natured, told Marilyn Monroe (who inherited her star dressing room), "Honey, I've had it. Go get yours. It's your turn now."

There were plans for Grable to make films for United Artists, but that didn't happen. Nor did negotiations for her to star in *Guys and Dolls* (1955) for her old boss Samuel Goldwyn come to pass, as she was replaced by another ex-Fox musical star, Vivian Blaine. Following the demise of her film career, Betty worked for a time in television. In 1956, she appeared as "Cleopatra Collins" on NBC-TV's *Stage Door*, and the same year played with Orson Welles, Keenan Wynn, and Ray Collins in *Ford Star Jubilee*'s presentation of "Twentieth Century" on CBS-TV, plus guesting on CBS's *Showers of Stars* TV program with Mario Lanza. On the 1957 Academy Awards telecast, she and Harry James performed "Lullaby of Broadway," and the duo guest-starred the next year on CBS's *The Lucille Ball–Desi Arnaz Comedy Hour*. She and James also appeared together in Las Vegas, and she toured with her revue, *Memories*. However, Grable had no great desire to continue working hard. In fact, she admitted, "I never really had any great drive for my career; it was my mother who wanted it. Even now she's mad at me for not working any more. . . . Once in a while my agents call me, but I couldn't care less."

In the late 1950s Grable and James moved their family to Las Vegas, where his musical activities were headquartered, and they resided in a new $100,000 home located behind the Tropicana Hotel. Never having been happy in Hollywood, Betty found more personal contentment in Las Vegas, although by now her marriage to the heavy-drinking and gambling Harry James was a rocky one.

Late in 1962, Grable and Dan Dailey reteamed for a condensed version of *Guys and Dolls* at the Dunes Hotel in Las Vegas, and they would continue with the show, on and off, both in Vegas and road-show stock productions. In 1965, Betty and Harry James divorced, and Grable sold their home, moving into a smaller house. That same year, Betty took on one of her most successful roles, that of Dolly Levi in one of the many touring editions of *Hello, Dolly!*, this one opening in Las Vegas. A sixteen-month tour followed, culminating in her return to Broadway with the role in the summer of 1967. After the show's successful run, she returned to Las Vegas and did road tours with productions of *Plaza Suite, High Button Shoes*, and *Guys and Dolls*, among other musicals. She needed money badly, because she had loaned Harry James (who had remarried) more than a million dollars to pay off gambling debts.

In 1969, she went to London to star in the expensive musical Western *Belle Starr*, but it flopped badly, closing after sixteen performances. In 1971, she and her old pal Dorothy Lamour costarred in the summer theater revue *That's Show Business*, in Saint Louis. She also made appearances on Carol Burnett's TV variety program and became a TV spokesperson for Geritol. In 1972, Betty worked twice on TV with her movie costar Dick Haymes: first on a TV special and then at the 1972 Academy Awards show. In 1972, it was announced that Grable would take over for Yvonne De Carlo in the Australian company of *No, No Nanette*, but illness intervened as tests showed Betty had cancer. Despite deteriorating health, Grable went to Jacksonville, Florida, early in 1973 to appear in *Born Yesterday*. After the show's run, she returned to Las Vegas and was hospitalized. She died there on July 2, 1973. One of her last visitors was Alice Faye. Grable had earned $5 million from her career, but she died nearly broke. One of the attendees at her funeral on July 5, 1973 was Harry James, who had married her forty years ago to that day. (He died on July 5, 1983.)

In 1986, Betty was the subject of a sensationalized biography *Pin-Up: The Tragedy of Betty Grable* by Spero Pastos. The book revealed that Grable was a woman of many facets, although intellectualism was not one of them. It detailed how she had been victimized by her ambitious mother and had, in turn, been a neglectful mother herself. Betty's main appeal was illustrated by the book's dust jacket; both sides boasted the picture of this glamorous star in her famous World War II pin-up. Subsequent books on the star included the detailed *Betty Grable: A Bio-Bibliography* (1993) by Larry Billman and *The Girl With the Million Dollar Legs* by Tom McGee (1995).

Filmography

Happy Days (Fox, 1929)
Let's Go Places [Mirth and Melody] (Fox, 1930)
Fox Movietone Follies of 1930 [New Movietone
 Follies of 1930] (Fox, 1930)
Whoopee! (UA, 1930)
Kiki (UA, 1931)

Palmy Days (UA, 1931)
Ex-Sweeties (Educational, 1931) (s)
Crashing Hollywood (Educational, 1931) (s)
Once a Hero (Educational, 1931) (s)
Hollywood Luck (Educational, 1932) (s)
Hollywood Lights (Educational, 1932) (s)

Lady! Please! (Educational, 1932) (s)

Over the Counter (MGM, 1932) (s)

The Age of Consent (RKO, 1932)

The Flirty Sleepwalker (Educational, 1932) (s)

The Greeks Had a Word for Them (UA, 1932)

Child of Manhattan (Col, 1932)

Probation [Second Chances] (Chesterfield, 1932)

Hold 'Em Jail (RKO, 1932)

The Kid From Spain (UA, 1932)

Cavalcade (Fox, 1932)

Child of Manhattan (Col, 1933)

Air Tonic (RKO, 1933) (s)

The Sweetheart of Sigma Chi [Girl of My Dreams]
   (Mon, 1933)

Melody Cruise (RKO, 1933)

What Price Innocence? [Shall the Children Pay?]
   (Col, 1933)

Elmer Steps Out (Col, 1934) (s)

Susie's Affairs (Col, 1934) (s)

Love Detectives (Col, 1934) (s)

The Gay Divorcee [The Gay Divorce] (RKO,
   1934)

Student Tour (MGM, 1934)

Hips, Hips, Hooray! (RKO, 1934)

By Your Leave (RKO, 1934)

Love Detectives (Col, 1934) (s)

Business Is a Pleasure (Vita, 1934) (s)

The Nitwits (RKO, 1935)

Old Man Rhythm (RKO, 1935)

A Quiet Fourth (RKO, 1935) (s)

A Night at the Biltmore Bowl (RKO, 1935) (s)

Drawing Rumors (RKO, 1935) (s)

The Spirit of '76 (Astor, 1935) (s)

Sunkist Stars at Palm Springs (MGM, 1936) (s)

Pigskin Parade [The Harmony Parade] (20th-Fox,
   1936)

Follow the Fleet (RKO, 1936)

Don't Turn 'Em Loose (RKO, 1936)

Collegiate [The Charm School] (Par, 1936)

This Way Please (Par, 1937)

Thrill of a Lifetime (Par, 1937)

College Swing [Swing, Teacher, Swing] (Par 1938)

Give Me a Sailor (Par, 1938)

Campus Confessions [Fast Play] (Par, 1938)

Man About Town (Par, 1939)

Million Dollar Legs (Par, 1939)

The Day the Bookies Wept (RKO, 1939)

Down Argentine Way (20th-Fox, 1940)

Tin Pan Alley (20th-Fox, 1940)

A Yank in the RAF (20th-Fox, 1941)

Hedda Hopper's Hollywood (Par, 1941) (s)

I Wake Up Screaming [Hot Spot] (20th-Fox, 1941)

Moon Over Miami (20th-Fox, 1941)

Footlight Serenade (20th-Fox, 1942)

Song of the Islands (20th-Fox, 1942)

Springtime in the Rockies (20th-Fox, 1942)

Coney Island (20th-Fox, 1943)

Sweet Rosie O'Grady (20th-Fox, 1943)

Four Jills in a Jeep (20th-Fox, 1944)

Pin-Up Girl (20th-Fox, 1944)

Billy Rose's Diamond Horseshoe [Diamond Horse-
   shoe] (20th-Fox, 1945)

The Dolly Sister (20th-Fox, 1945)

All Star Bond Rally (20th-Fox, 1945) (s)

Do You Love Me? (20th-Fox, 1946)

Hollywood Park (20th-Fox, 1946) (s)

The Shocking Miss Pilgrim (20th-Fox, 1947)

Mother Wore Tights (20th-Fox, 1947)

Hollywood Bound (Astor, 1947) (s)

That Lady in Ermine (20th-Fox, 1948)

When My Baby Smiles at Me (20th-Fox, 1949)

The Beautiful Blonde From Bashful Bend (20th-
   Fox, 1949)

Wabash Avenue (20th-Fox, 1950)

My Blue Heaven (20th-Fox, 1950)

Call Me Mister (20th-Fox, 1951)

Meet Me After the Show (20th-Fox, 1951)

The Farmer Takes a Wife (20th-Fox, 1953)

How to Marry a Millionaire (20th-Fox, 1953)

Three for the Show (Col, 1955)

Screen Snapshot: Hollywood Shower of Stars (Col,
   1955) (s)

How to Be Very, Very Popular (20th-Fox, 1955)

Broadway Plays

DuBarry Was a Lady (1939)

Hello, Dolly! (1967) (replacement)

Radio Series

Song Time (CBS, 1937–38)

Album Discography

LPs

Betty Grable (Curtain Calls 100/5, Scarce Rarities 5501)

Betty Grable (Sandy Hook 2014)

Betty Grable, 1934-60 (Star-Tone 219)

Billy Rose's Diamond Horseshoe (Caliban 6028) [ST]

Call Me Mister (Titania 510) [ST]

Collegiate (Caliban 6042) [ST]

Coney Island/Moon Over Miami (Caliban 6001) [ST]

The Dolly Sisters (CIF 3010) [ST]

Down Argentine Way/Springtime in the Rockies (Hollywood Soundstage 5013) [ST]

Down Argentine Way/Tin Pan Alley (Caliban 6003) [ST]

Footlight Serenade (Caliban 6002) [ST]

Four Jills in a Jeep (Hollywood Soundstage 407) [ST]

The Gay Divorcee (EMI 101, Sountrak 105) [ST]

Meet Me After the Show (Caliban 6012) [ST]

Mother Wore Tights/The Shocking Miss Pilgrim (CIF 3008) [ST]

My Blue Heaven (Titania 503) [ST]

Pigskin Parade (Pilgrim 4000) [ST]

Pin-Up Girl/Song of the Islands (Caliban 6009) [ST]

Springtime in the Rockies (Pelican 128 [ST/R]

Sweet Rosie O'Grady (Titania 507) [ST]

Three for the Show (10″ Mer MG-25204) [ST]

Wabash Avenue (Caliban 6029) [ST]

CDs

Always the Ladies (Sound of the Movies 3109) w. Alice Faye

The Dream Duo (Vintage Jazz Band VJB-1948) w. Harry James

Lady Be Good/Four Jills in a Jeep (Great Movie Themes 60029) [ST]

Moon Over Miami/Broadway Melody of 1938 (Great Movie Themes 60030) [ST]

The More I See You (Golden Options GO-3834)

The Pin-Up Girl (Jasmine 10314)

Rose of Washington Square/The Dolly Sisters/Gold Diggers of 1933 (Great Movie Themes 6009) [ST]

The Sound of the Movies (Sound of the Movies 3108) w. Judy Garland

Those Bombastic Blonde Bombshells (Wallysnite Records BGM42)*

*Compilation album

Kathryn Grayson

(b. Zelma Kathryn Hedrick, Winston Salem, North Carolina, February 9, 1922)

Kathryn Grayson was groomed by MGM in the 1940s as that studio's answer to Universal's Deanna Durbin. However, despite good looks, acting ability, and a fair coloratura operatic voice, she never really was in competition with Durbin, nor did she ever become a top singing star even at her home studio. She was limited by poor scripts and was often used merely used as window dressing, rather than as an integral part of the story. Her on-camera appeal was limited, too, because she usually came across as overtly coy and mannered. It was not until the 1950s that she blossomed as a star of movie operettas. However, by then this genre was in its twilight, and her film career ended when that type of light screen fare became passé. In the years afterward, Grayson carved for herself a career in nightclubs and onstage, doing her movie songs and operettas, sometimes in tandem with screen costar Howard Keel. The star admitted she was never sufficiently ambitious about her movie career and was content to appear in whatever MGM offered her, preferring financial security to tremendous stardom. Her initial goal had always been to be an opera diva and, when that did not happen, being a movie star was always second best. After she retired from filmmaking she said, "I want to do something intelligent, and movie musicals don't classify."

Kathryn Grayson was born Zelma Kathryn Hedrick on February 9, 1922, in Winston Salem, North Carolina, the daughter of a building contractor–realtor. Most of her childhood was spent with her family in transit, but they lived for some years in Saint Louis. Her interest in music was evident from an early age. At Saint Louis's Municipal Opera, she performed for Chicago Civic Opera star Frances Marshall, who encouraged Kathryn and her family to continue with her music lessons. While she was a teenager, Kathryn's family moved to Hollywood and she went to Manual Arts High School and took vocal training from Minna Letha White. Louis B. Mayer heard Kathryn sing at a city festival and offered her an MGM contract without even a screen test. Much to White's chagrin, the young lady accepted the lucrative studio offer, and in 1940 she began a year's training in drama, elocution, and voice. To provide her with actual show-business experience, the studio negotiated for her a steady job singing on *The Eddie Cantor Show* on NBC radio.

Like many MGM starlets of the period, Kathryn made her screen debut in an "Andy Hardy" feature, *Andy Hardy's Private Secretary* (1941). She played an aspiring singer whom Andy (Mickey Rooney) engages to be his secretary and get his mixed-up affairs at high school in order. In her positive film bow, Kathryn not only emoted well, but also provided pleasing vocals to "Voci de Primavera" and a scene from Gaetano Donizetti's famous opera *Lucia di Lammermoor. Variety* observed of the pretty miss with the heart-shaped face and dimpled cheeks, "Looks like Metro has a name nugget in Miss Grayson." She did even better in *The Vanishing Virginian* (1941) as the daughter of a small Southern town public servant (Frank Morgan); she sang in it "The World Was Made for You." In 1940, Kathryn married another MGM player, John Shelton. Their marriage would be plagued with separations, reconciliations, a miscarriage, and more highly charged partings. They finally divorced in 1946, and he died in May 1972.

Kathryn Grayson and Mario Lanza in *The Toast of New Orleans* (1950).
[Courtesy of JC Archives]

For Grayson's first starring role, MGM cast the singer opposite Bud Abbott and Lou Costello in *Rio Rita* (1942), a remake of the 1929 Radio Picture that had starred John Boles, Bebe Daniels, and the comedy team of Bert Wheeler and Robert Woolsey. Kathryn was seen as the sweetheart of radio star John Carroll, with her ranch being invaded by Abbott and Costello and Nazi spies. A fairly bright effort, it gave Grayson the new Harold Arlen/E. Y. Harburg song "Long Before You Came Along" to perform. In 1942, she also did well in the overly cute comedy *Seven Sweethearts* as the oldest of seven daughters, none of whom can marry until she weds; within the picture, Kathryn sang "You and the Waltz and I."

The young star's operatic training was again evidenced in the all-star *Thousands Cheer* (1943), in which she was romanced by Army private Gene Kelly and sang the aria "Sempra Libre" from Giuseppe Verdi's opera *La Traviata,* and the novelty tune, "I Dug a Ditch in Wichita." In this big-budget affair, she played the daughter of John Boles and Mary Astor. She commented later, "There's so much one can learn from people like them." Kathryn was then off the screen for two years, but in the interim she did war-effort entertaining and appeared on radio programs like Paul Whiteman's *Radio Hall of Fame* on NBC in 1943. In the early 1940s, Grayson wished to return to her operatic studies, leading to recurring battles with studio head Louis B. Mayer (he called her an "ungrateful little bitch"). However, she eventually gave in to the tough-minded executive. (Some insist her studio career was perpetuated by an amorous mentor in the Metro hierarchy.)

Grayson returned to the screen in 1945 in MGM's *Anchors Aweigh*, in which Navy men Gene Kelly and Frank Sinatra romance her. However, in the story line the prim singer is more intent on dropping her film-extra jobs and auditioning for concert pianist José Iturbi. She sang "My Heart Sings." Next she and studio rival June Allyson costarred in the title roles of *Two Sisters From Boston* (1946), a period musical with a mediocre score. Its plot has somewhat uppity Kathryn becoming the singing star at a Bowery saloon run by Jimmy Durante and being romanced by Peter Lawford. Once again, her screen image was too lofty for broad audience acceptance. The singer's last two 1946 films were guest appearances in the all-star musicals, *Ziegfeld Follies of 1946* and *Till the Clouds Roll By.* In the former (shot in 1944), she was stuck with the dud production number "There's Beauty Everywhere," while in the second outing, a biopic of Jerome Kern, she had a well-staged sequence from *Show Boat* in which she and Tony Martin shone in a splendid, if stagy, duet of "Make Believe." Five years later, she took the role of Magnolia in MGM's remake of *Show Boat*, while in 1953 she and Tony Martin reteamed on RCA Victor Records for a very fine rendering of the score to *The Desert Song.*

MGM unwisely teamed Kathryn Grayson and Frank Sinatra for two additional glossy feature films, neither of which helped their careers. *It Happened in Brooklyn* (1947) has them as part of a theatrical group out to stage a musical show. Kathryn performed music from Léo Delibes's opera *Lakme*, but the results were less than satisfying. Next she was the object of outlaw Sinatra's affections in the hokey Western *The Kissing Bandit* (1948), which was so badly received it was almost laughed off the screen. Its only asset for Grayson was allowing her to vocalize on "Love Is Where You Find It."

Far better for the songstress were her two teamings with Mario Lanza in *That Midnight Kiss* (1949) and *The Toast of New Orleans* (1950). Lanza made his screen debut in the former as a singing truck driver, and he and Grayson made an attractive screen pairing. In *The Toast of New Orleans*, he is a singing fisherman who becomes an opera star, and the film gives Kathryn the chance to perform excerpts from Puccini's *Madame Butterfly* as Cho-Cho-San (her favorite operatic part). Following the movie's release, she and Lanza embarked on a successful cross-country tour with the picture, and she became close to the tenor and his family and would remain so even after his tragic death in 1959 and his wife's demise the following year. (When Grayson's daughter, Patricia, married in 1969, the maid of honor was Colleen Lanza, Mario's daughter and Kathryn's best friend.) On-screen, Grayson was cast as an opera star in the comedy *Grounds for Marriage* (1950), but most of its footage was devoted to the efforts of reconciling she and her ex-husband doctor (portrayed by Van Johnson).

In her personal life, Kathryn had wed actor Johnny Johnston in 1947, and on October 7, 1948, she gave birth to her only child, Patricia Kathryn. She and Johnston would divorce in 1951, and she never remarried, although she would be seen frequently on the Los Angeles social scenes with attractive dates. (In the late 1950s, actor Robert Evans was her frequent escort.) Grayson would say of Tinseltown social life, "You can never tell what a man has in mind when he asks you for a date in this town. He may be thinking of romance or he may just want his name in the papers."

After a decade on the screen, Grayson finally came into her own when MGM teamed her with Howard Keel for its color remake of *Show Boat* and top-billed Kathryn in the role of Magnolia. In it, she and baritone Keel did beautiful duets on "Make Believe," "You Are Love," and "Why Do I Love You?" The musical grossed over $5 million at the box office. Its success led to a second teaming of Grayson and Keel in a thin remake of *Roberta* (1935) entitled *Lovely to Look At* (1952). Neither star wanted to do this lavish, but bland, production, and after it was completed Kathryn, earning $4,000 weekly, went on loan to Warner Bros. (That same year, Metro's Jane Powell also went on loanout to that studio.)

Initially, Grayson was set to make a quartet of musicals for Warner Bros., but only two ensued: *The Desert Song* and *So This Is Love*, both in 1953. She was cast as Margot in *The Desert Song*. She and costar Gordon MacRae battled valiantly with the mildewed script about the Riffs in North Africa as they dueted on "One Alone" and Kathryn soloed with "Romance." The color musical only proved that Sigmund Romberg's score was more fit for the stage than the screen, although this was its third movie rendering. While at MGM, Kathryn had wanted to portray opera star Grace Moore on-screen, and she had just that chance at Warner in *So This Is Love*. However, she was defeated by a mundane script and moviegoing audiences who were already tiring of musicals and were hardly interested in operatic arias.

Warner Bros. and Grayson concluded their joint ventures, and the star returned to MGM to star in the delightful *Kiss Me, Kate* (1953), reteamed with Howard Keel. In the dual roles of Lili and Katherine, she made a fine shrew. She soloed on "I Hate Men" and dueted spiritedly with Keel on "So in Love," "We Open in Venice" (with Ann Miller and Tommy Rall), "Wunderbar," and the title song. MGM then announced Kathryn would star in musical versions of *Trilby* and *Camille*, but they never came about, and her planned role in *Brigadoon* (1954) went to Cyd Charisse. Grayson very much wanted the lead of the disabled opera singer in *Interrupted Melody* (1955), but the role was handed to Eleanor Parker (whose voice had to be dubbed for the singing interludes).

In the fall of 1955, Grayson made her dramatic television debut on CBS-TV's *G. E. Theater* on "Shadows of the Heart," for which she was nominated for an Emmy Award. She did another segment of the anthology series the next year. Her final screen role came also in 1956 in *The Vagabond King*, which was supposed to have reunited her with Mario Lanza. However, he lost the role due to health problems, and it was assumed by a little-known opera singer named Oreste, who played Francois Villon to Grayson's Catherine. They both interpreted the film score nicely, especially their duet of "Only a Rose," but the age of the screen operetta was long over. Kathryn then returned to television for roles in two CBS-TV programs: *Playhouse 90* in 1957 and *Lux Playhouse* the following year.

Although regarded primarily as a singer, Kathryn Grayson did very little recording during her career. While at MGM, she did perform some of her movie songs for the company's label, MGM Records, like "My Heart Sings," "Love Is Where You Find It," and "You Are Love." In the mid-'50s she cut an album for them called *Kathryn Grayson Sings*. She had done concert work in the early 1950s, both in Hollywood and London, so it was natural for Kathryn to return to this work following her screen career finale. (She was offered low-budget film properties, which she rejected, as she did a 1958 offer for a $1 million over five years to be the television spokeswoman for Revlon Cosmetics.)

In 1960, Grayson was onstage in productions of the operas *Madame Butterfly, La Bohème,* and *La Traviata*. In 1961, she starred in stage productions of *The Merry Widow, Rosalinda,* and *Naughty Marietta*. She toured in 1963 with an elaborate edition of *Camelot* with Louis Hayward, but plans for her to replace Julie Andrews as Queen Guenevere in the Broadway edition fell through. She continued to be active in cabaret work and onstage, and in 1969, she and Howard Keel reteamed for a club act. During their run at the Fremont Hotel in Las Vegas in 1969 *Variety* commented, "Miss Grayson is earnest in her soprano scalings, which occasionally have a metallic edge at the top. . . . Identified with melodies of limpid nostalgia, Miss Grayson, nevertheless, gives a very good accounting of the strong modern ballad, 'Both Sides Now.'" She and Keel continued their club act together, on and off, through the 1970s, and during that decade they also appeared together to advantage in the stage production of *Man of La Mancha*. A much heavier Kathryn Grayson occasionally appeared on television in the 1980s; late in the decade she and Gloria DeHaven were guests on another ex-MGM star's (Angela Lansbury) teleseries, *Murder, She Wrote*. Grayson played her role of Ideal Molloy on three episodes of the popular whodunit series.

In the 1990s, Kathryn, who still lived in her twenty-room mansion in Santa Monica that she had acquired after World War II, remained mostly out of the limelight. In her personal life, she remained pals with many of her MGM peers, including June Allyson, Esther Williams, Janet Leigh, Betty Garrett, and Cyd Charisse. In July 1997, Kathryn was part of the contingent who appeared behind the footlights in New York City for *Carnegie Hall Celebrates the Glorious MGM Musicals*, joined by such fellow studio alumnae as June Allyson, Leslie Caron, Van Johnson, and Mickey Rooney. Similarly, in January 2000, Grayson was among those at the Pasadena (California) Civic Theater, where she joined June Allyson, Cyd Charisse, Tony Martin, Gloria DeHaven, and Betty Garrett onstage for A *Celebration of the Classic Hollywood Musicals*.

Always a level-headed woman, Kathryn Grayson never took her stardom too seriously. Regarding her screen vehicles she once admitted, "Well, most of them were big budgeted and seemed to take forever to make. I didn't have very good directors on most of them." As to her studio alma mater, she commented, "Everything is gone now. The MGM backlot is leveled. The whole studio system fell apart when Mr. Mayer left MGM. He loved quality. I hear the Sony people who now owner the former MGM studio have beautiful gardens there. . . . I wish they'd make beautiful pictures instead."

Filmography

Andy Hardy's Private Secretary (MGM, 1941)
The Vanishing Virginian (MGM, 1941)
Rio Rita (MGM, 1942)
Seven Sweethearts (MGM, 1942)
Thousands Cheer (MGM, 1943)
Anchors Aweigh (MGM, 1945)
Two Sisters From Boston (MGM, 1946)
Ziegfeld Follies of 1946 (MGM, 1946)
Till the Clouds Roll By (MGM, 1946)
It Happened in Brooklyn (MGM, 1947)
The Kissing Bandit (MGM, 1948)

That Midnight Kiss (MGM, 1949)
The Toast of New Orleans (MGM, 1950)
Grounds for Marriage (MGM, 1950)
Show Boat (MGM, 1951)
Lovely to Look At (MGM, 1952)
The Desert Song (WB, 1953)
So This Is Love [The Grace Moore Story] (WB, 1953)
Kiss Me, Kate (MGM, 1953)
The Vagabond King (Par, 1956)

Radio Series

The Eddie Cantor Show (NBC, 1940)

Album Discography

LPs

Always (Azel AZ 105)

Anchors Aweigh (Curtain Calls 100/17, Sandy Hook 2024) [ST]

Annie Get Your Gun/Show Boat (MGM 2SES-42ST) [ST]

The Desert Song (10″ RCA LPM-3105) w. Tony Martin

Grounds for Marriage (10″ MGM E-536) [ST]

It Happened in Brooklyn (Hollywood Soundstage HS-5006) [ST]

Kathryn Grayson (Lion 70055)

Kathryn Grayson Sings (10″ MGM E-551, MGM E-3257)

Kiss Me, Kate (MGM-3-077, Metro M/S-525, 25003) [ST]

Kiss Me, Kate/The Band Wagon (MGM 2SES-44ST) [ST]

The Kissing Bandit (Motion Picture Tracks MPT-7) [ST]

Lovely to Look At (10″ MGM E-150, MGM E-3230) [ST]

Lovely to Look At/Brigadoon (MGM 2SES-50ST) [ST]

Lovely to Look At/Summer Stock (MCA 39084) [ST]

Let There Be Music (Azel AZ-102)

Make Believe (Azel AZ-101)

Nelson Eddy With Shirley Temple, Jane Powell, Kathryn Grayson, Lois Butler, Norma Nelson (Mac/Eddy JN 128)

Opera and Song (Azel AZ-103)

Show Boat (10″ MGM E-559, MGM E-3230, Metro M/S-527, MCA 1439) [ST]

So This Is Love (10″ RCA LOC-3000) [ST]

That's Entertainment! (MCA MCA2-11002) [ST]

That's Entertainment, Part 2 (MGM MG-1-5301, MCA 6155) [ST]

Thousands Cheer (Hollywood Soundstage 409) [ST]

Till the Clouds Roll By (10 MGM E-501, MGM E-3231, Metro M/S-578, Sountrak 115, Vertinge 2000) [ST]

The Toast of New Orleans (Azel-104) [ST]

20 Golden Favourites of Kathryn Grayson (Bulldog BDL-2043)

Ziegfeld Follies of 1946 (Curtain Calls 100/15-16) [ST]

CDs

Anchors Aweigh (Sandy Hook CDSH-2024) [ST]

Brigadoon/Lovely to Look At (MCA MCAD-5947) [ST]

It Happened in Brooklyn (Great Movie Themes 60034) [ST]

Kiss Me, Kate (Sony Music Special Products AK-46916, EMI 854356, Turner Classic Movies/Rhino R2-72152, CBS UK 70278) [ST]

Lovely to Look At (MCA MCAD-39084, Sony Music Special Products AK-47027) [ST]

Make Believe (Azel AZCD-1021)

My Heart Sings (Flare 1021)

Remember (Azel AZCD-1032)

Show Boat (MCA MCAD-1439, Turner Classic Movies/Rhino R2-71998, EMI 836024, CBS UK 70281) [ST]

Show Boat/Annie Get Your Gun/Pagan Love Song (Great Movie Themes 60005) [ST]

Softly (Azel AZCD-1051)

Stairway to the Stars (First Night Cast 6021) [OC]

Till the Clouds Roll By (MGM/EMI MGM24, Sandy Hook CDSH-2080) [ST]

Time After Time (Broad Music EMD-020)

Ziegfeld Follies (Turner Classic Movies/Rhino R2-71958) [ST]

June Haver

(b. June Stovenour, Rock Island, Illinois, June 10, 1926)

Pretty and talented June Haver starred in a dozen features for Twentieth Century-Fox in the 1940s and early 1950s, with the bulk of them in Technicolor. The studio groomed her as a rival and possible successor to Betty Grable. In turn, Marilyn Monroe, who was in two of Haver's features, was brought on to succeed June. Like most of Darryl F. Zanuck's blonde stars of the period, June Haver was "a film personality," a movie player who had little outside experience on stage, radio, or television. As was true with most Fox stars, she was not permitted to make recordings.

Ironically, June first came to the attention of the film industry through her vocalizing in the big-band era. However, it was as a singer, dancer, and actress that she made her mark on the musicals of post–World War II vintage. Looking a lot like Betty Grable, June rarely earned plum screen assignments at Fox, because they were usually reserved for the reigning Pin-Up Queen. Thus, Haver rarely had occasion to display her full potential on-camera. Always deeply religious, June Haver tired of Hollywood eventually and for a time in the early 1950s, entered a convent. Later, she resumed her acting career briefly and then settled down to raise a family after her marriage to Fred MacMurray.

She was born June Stovenour in Rock Island, Illinois, on June 10, 1926. As a precocious child, guided by a very determined mother, she showed an interest in music as well as singing, dancing, and oratory. At the age of eight, she won the Cincinnati (Ohio) Conservatory of Music's Post Music Contest, and then played piano (as a guest artist) with the Cincinnati Symphony Orchestra. As a teenager, she studied dramatics, dance, and vocalizing, and she landed a job singing with bandleader Dick Jurgens. This led to a brief association with Freddy Martin's band, and then, with her mother chaperoning, she embarked on a tour with Ted Fio Rito's musical group. (Betty Grable had also been a band vocalist with Fio Rito.) June made her screen debut with the bandleader in the Universal musical short *Skyline Serenade* (1941) and did other shorts at the studio, including *Tune Time* (1942) with Jan Garber and His Orchestra, and *Trumpet Serenade* (1942), a short entry with Tommy Dorsey and his band.

Now living in Beverly Hills with her family, June Haver (which had become her new professional name) attended high school there. While appearing in community theater, she came to the attention of Twentieth Century-Fox executives who screen-tested her and soon placed the five-feet two-inches, blue-eyed blonde under contract, starting at $75 weekly. Both June and Jeanne Crain made their feature film debuts in the Alice Faye musical *The Gang's All Here* (1943), with June on-screen briefly at the beginning of the proceedings as hatcheck girl Maybelle. Seeing potential in her looks and screen presence, Darryl F. Zanuck groomed June as a possible replacement for Betty Grable, the studio's top moneymaking star. Haver was cast as little sister Cri-Cri in *Home in Indiana* (1944), the plot of which concerns a farm youth (Lon McCallister) who becomes a successful small-town jockey while finding love with a local girl (Jeanne Crain). At this time, June

June Haver and Betty Grable in *The Dolly Sisters* (1945).
[Courtesy of JC Archives]

became a protégée of studio producer George Jessel, and he personally cast her in the role that was to bring her stardom in *The Dolly Sisters* (1945).

Prior to *The Dolly Sisters*, June was given the female lead in *Irish Eyes Are Smiling* (1945), the biopic of Irish composer Ernest Ball (Dick Haymes). She is a chorus girl whom Ball follows to Manhattan, where both of them achieve stardom. Next she had the supporting role of Lucilla in the fantasy *Where Do We Go From Here?* in which her future real-life husband Fred MacMurray starred. He is a 4-F salvage depot guard who finds an old lamp. Its genie (Gene Shelton) gives him three wishes, which allows him to be a hero at three different crucial periods in American history. Then came *The Dolly Sisters*, which showcased Haver and Betty Grable as show-business siblings whose act brings them stardom at the turn of the century. This colorful production offered lots of the era's peppy tunes, and it really boosted June's career status, although (understandably) she and her costar were personally cool to one another during its filming.

June was top-billed for the first time in *Three Little Girls in Blue* (1946), in which she costarred with Vivian Blaine and Vera-Ellen as one of three sisters hunting for rich husbands in 1902 Atlantic City. The musical, which offered such songs as "Somewhere in the Night" and "This Is Always," grossed over $3 million at the box office. It was a remake of *Three Blind Mice* (1938) and *Moon Over Miami* (1941), and would be reworked yet again as *How to Marry a Millionaire* (1953).

For her next two vehicles, June was guided by veteran director Lloyd Bacon. The dramatic *Wake Up and Dream* (1946) cast her as a young woman seeking her missing brother. She sang the song "Give Me the Simple Life." One critic said of her in this failed patriotic fantasy, "June Haver . . . looks good in Technicolor, but never comes to fair grips with the script." She was back in her forte with the musical *I Wonder Who's Kissing Her Now?* (1947), the fictional biography of 1890s' composer Joseph E. "Joe" Howard (played by Mark Stevens). June portrays an entertainer who performs many of Howard's tunes (the title song, "Honeymoon," and "What's the Use of Dreaming"). The feature was June's sole 1947 release, because she married childhood boyfriend trumpeter Jimmy Zito. They eloped to Las Vegas on March 9 and were wed in a civil ceremony and then were remarried in a Catholic Church service on March 26. The marriage was not a happy one, and it ended in divorce two years later, with the actress then dating dentist Dr. John Duzik (who had been her fiancé *before* her marriage to Zito). Duzik's sudden death in October 1949 was a sobering experience for the once-exuberant and carefree June.

Meanwhile, in 1948 Fox reteamed June Haver with Lon McCallister in another bucolic love story, *Scudda-Hoo! Scudda-Hay!*, in which he plays a Hoosier farm boy who trains a pair of mules who, by accident, help him win the young woman (Haver) he adores. Then she was assigned to another screen biography of a composer, this time that of Fred Fisher (S. Z. Sakall) in *Oh, You Beautiful Doll!* It is set in the colorful 1890s with serious composer Fisher having his works made into popular melodies by a song seller (again, Mark Stevens). June is featured as the singer Doris who performs many of the Tin Pan Alley standards of the day.

Indicating that her home studio felt June was more profitable as a loanout star, Darryl Zanuck made an agreement with Warner Bros. whereby June was borrowed by that studio for four movies. (This was in contrast to Betty Grable, who was never loaned out during her fourteen-year rule at Fox.) At Warner Bros., June had what was probably her best screen assignment, that of musical comedy star Marilyn Miller. *Look for the Silver Lining* (1949) told of Miller's rise to Broadway stardom, and it offered well-staged production numbers built around such songs as "Who," "Time on My Hands," "A Kiss in the Dark," "Sunny," and the title tune. It pleased undemanding filmgoers, but not severe film critic Bosley Crowther (*New York Times*) who sniped, "Her lack of vitality is a volume of blonde inconsequence in a shimmering void."

Also at Warner Bros., June starred in *The Daughter of Rosie O'Grady* (Grable had starred in *Sweet Rosie O'Grady* at Fox in 1943), another turn-of-the-century musical in which her screen father (James Barton) forbids her to have a movie career. In it, she performed the title song and "As We Are Today." There was discussion at Warner Bros. of starring June in *The West Point Story* (1950) and *Lullaby of Broadway* (1951), but it was that studio's rising blonde singing star Doris Day who snared those leads. At this point, June and Warner Bros. came to a professional impasse.

Back at Fox, June showed a disinterest in her career. She turned down a lead in *When Willie Comes Marching Home* (1950; Colleen Townsend was featured). She refused to appear in *Friendly Island* and went on suspension. She said, "I don't think people would like me in the picture because of several objectionable elements in the story." (The film was eventually made as the unsuccessful *Down Among the Sheltering Palms*, 1953, starring Jane Greer, Mitzi Gaynor, and Gloria DeHaven.) She did agree to appear in *I'll Get By* (1950), an updated version of Alice Faye's *Tin Pan Alley* (1940). It was a thin tale of a songwriter (William Lundigan) who finds success and his lady love (Haver). Gloria DeHaven, as June's screen sister, gained the better notices. Offscreen, with 1950 being a Holy Year, June made a pilgrimage to Rome and to the Vatican.

Fox felt June's box-office draw was dwindling, so her next entry, the comedy *Love Nest* (1951), was shot in economical black and white. It was nevertheless an amusing affair in which she is the wife of a former soldier (William Lundigan). Together they purchase an apartment building and must deal with its zany denizens, including an ex-WAC played by Marilyn Monroe (who had had a bit role in Haver's *Scudda-Hoo! Scudday-Hay!*).

In 1952 June, Haver was given a Betty Grable castoff assignment, *The Girl Next Door* (1953), teamed with Dan Dailey, who had become Grable's frequent costar. June was the musical-comedy star who moves next door to a widowed cartoonist (Dailey) and his young son. While shooting one of the picture's athletic dance routines involving gyrating tables, June fell off of one of the tables and suffered a concussion. By the time she had recovered from the injury, her costars (Dailey and Dennis Day) were busy elsewhere, and production was not completed until the next year.

At this point, June began withdrawing farther from the filmmaking world. Although her studio contract would not expire until February 20, 1953—she was earning $3,500 weekly—she continued to refuse offers. (Columbia Pictures wanted to borrow her for the musical remake of *My Sister Eileen*; Janet Leigh was eventually used in this 1955 picture.) In February 1952, June announced that she planned to become a nun. She informed the media, "I know what I want to do. But what I want must also be what God wants. May His will be done." She entered Saint Mary's Academy in Leavenworth, Kansas, as a novice in the Order of the Sisters of Charity. She remained at the convent for several months, but was forced to leave due to health reasons. Her always very vocal mother had her own interpretation of the events: "I think Junie realized almost from the start she had made a mistake. All her life she has been devoted to her family—a real home girl. You can understand this made it difficult to readjust to a religious life."

Meanwhile, June's *The Girl Next Door* had been released to less-than-stellar results, and her studio contract was not renewed. Fox was also ending their association with veteran Betty Grable and was preoccupied with promoting younger Marilyn Monroe as their latest blonde star. (The lot also would soon have Sheree North as their backup blonde singing/dancing starlet.) As her performance comeback, June starred (February 13, 1954) in a *Lux Radio Theater* adaptation of "Trouble Along the Way," with Jack Carson as her colead. June explained, "I decided to go back to acting after I received letters from all over the world—thousands of them. They wanted to know when I was going back. They said they were happy I was contemplating it and wanted to see me, especially in happy stories."

In the spring of 1954, she attended a birthday party for John Wayne, and there she became reacquainted with Fred MacMurray, whose wife Lillian had died eleven months before. June and MacMurray began dating, and a month later, on June 28, 1954, they were married in Ojai, California. She was twenty-eight; he was forty-five. Late in 1956, the couple adopted two baby girls, twins Katie and Laurie. Early in 1958 (January 3), the MacMurrays made their second and last professional acting appearance together in a segment of *The Lucy-Desi Comedy Hour* on CBS-TV called "Lucy Hunts Uranium." (Coincidentally, a month later Betty Grable and her husband Harry James would appear on the Ball-Arnaz series.) After that television outing, June announced, "You can say definitely that I have retired." June opted for the life of a wife and mother in her Brentwood home with Fred MacMurray and their girls, although she did do volunteer work as a nurse's aide at Los Angeles' Saint John's Hospital. Fred went on to great fame and additional fortune with his long-running sitcom series, *My Three Sons* (1960–72).

In 1979, MacMurray successfully beat throat cancer, but in the late 1980s the disease returned and he became a virtual recluse at home. June, then a grandmother, was his contact to the outer world and did her best to keep his spirits up during this trying period. (She took time out in fall 1987 to be the recipient of the Thalians annual award at their Los Angeles gala.) Haver helped in the supervision of their extensive real-estate holdings in Los Angeles as well as their 2,300-acre cattle ranch. When he was able, Fred took walks with June or helped her work in his beloved gardens. On November 3, 1991, the badly ailing MacMurray lapsed into a coma, and two days later, the veteran star died of pneumonia, at age eighty-three. His last words were, "I love you, Junie." After that, June Haver MacMurray remained out of the limelight, except for charity fundraising galas and events close to her heart. In February 2002 she was one of the Gypsy Awardees given by the Professional Dance Society. At the event, held at the Beverly Hilton Hotel, she announced that she was establishing a ten-year scholarship for the society.

Filmography

Skyline Serenade (Univ, 1941) (s)
Swing's the Thing (Univ, 1942) (s)
Tune Time (Univ, 1942) (s)
Trumpet Serenade (Univ, 1942) (s)
The Gang's All Here [The Girls He Left Behind] (20th-Fox, 1943)
Home in Indiana (20th-Fox, 1944)
Irish Eyes Are Smiling (20th-Fox, 1945)
All-Star Bond Rally (20th-Fox, 1945) (s)
Where Do We Go From Here? (20th-Fox, 1945)
The Dolly Sisters (20th-Fox, 1945)

Three Little Girls in Blue (20th-Fox, 1946)
Wake Up and Dream (20th-Fox, 1946)
I Wonder Who's Kissing Her Now? (20th-Fox, 1947)
Scudda-Hoo! Scudda-Hay! [Summer Lightning] (20th-Fox, 1948)
Oh, You Beautiful Doll! (20th-Fox, 1949)
Look for the Silver Lining (WB, 1949)
The Daughter of Rosie O'Grady (WB, 1950)
I'll Get By (20th-Fox, 1950)
Love Nest (20th-Fox, 1951)
The Girl Next Door (20th-Fox, 1953)

Album Discography

LPs

The Dolly Sisters (CIF 3010) [ST]

I'll Get By/Look for the Silver Lining (Titania 604) [ST]

Kurt Weill in Hollywood [Where Do Go From Here?] (Ariel KWH 10) [ST]

Oh, You Beautiful Doll/I Wonder Who's Kissing Her Now? (Titania 502) [ST]

Three Little Girls in Blue (Hollywood Soundstage HS-410) [ST]

CDs

Rose of Washington Square/The Dolly Sisters/Gold Diggers of 1933 (Great Movie Themes 60009) [ST]

Dick Haymes

(b. Richard Benjamin Haymes, Buenos Aires, Argentina, September 13, 1916;
d. Los Angeles, California, March 28, 1980)

Like Frank Sinatra, Dick Haymes was a product of the big-band era. For a time, their career had other parallels, with both starting off as band vocalists to be catapulted to stardom via Gotham clubs and then records, radio, and motion pictures. In fact, of the two, Dick Haymes probably had the better voice. He certainly was more handsome, even if his antiseptic acting style kept him from enduring screen popularity. Somewhere along the way, Haymes's multimedia career fizzled, due mostly to his own personal excesses. He spent the remainder of his life eking out a living while Sinatra became so wealthy he worked only when he wished. Nevertheless, talented Dick Haymes had a varied and, at times, successful career. During the '40s, he was one of the most popular singers of his day, when this baritone was known as "the King of the Juke Boxes."

He was born Richard Benjamin Haymes in Buenos Aires, on September 13, 1916, the son of Argentinean cattleman Benjamin Haymes and his wife Margaret, a musical comedy singer. When Dick was a small boy, the family ranch folded due to a drought. Subsequently, his parents separated, and Dick and younger brother Robert (later known as actor Bob Stanton) went with their mother to Rio de Janeiro. When they were of school age, the boys were educated in Europe, and in 1936, the family settled in Connecticut. Later, Dick enrolled at Montreal's Loyola University.

Because his mother was a fine vocal coach, she taught Haymes how to sing at an early age. (She once admitted that as a child Dick was "a little ham running around the house.") After Haymes quit college, he sang for a time in New Jersey before working as a vocalist for bandsmen Johnnie Johnston and Bunny Berigan at $25 weekly. Engagements then came with Orin Tucker, Freddy Martin, and Carl Hoff, with Haymes eventually forming his own group, the Katzenjammers. He also worked as a radio announcer and had hopes of becoming a pop composer as well.

Wanting to better himself, Haymes hitchhiked to Hollywood, where he wrote songs and did stunt and extra work in the movies, even getting a small role in MGM's *Dramatic School* (1938). A fall from a horse ended his stunt career, and in 1940 he was back East in New York City. He attempted to peddle his songs to bandleader Harry James, who was not impressed with the tunes but thought Haymes such a good singer that he hired him for his band. This was the break the young man needed, and during his stay with James, the singer recorded a number of good-selling records, including the ballads "You've Changed" and "I'll Get By."

Leaving the James organization late in 1941, Haymes went to work for Benny Goodman and again scored with "Idaho" / "Take Me" and "Serenade in Blue" / "I've Got a Gal in Kalamazoo." Also in 1942, Dick hired Bill Burton as his agent and maneuvered a two-week singing engagement at La Martinique, a famous nightclub in New York City. He was such a sensation he stayed for three months. He was signed by Decca Records, and by the end of July 1943 this smooth

Vivian Blaine and Dick Haymes in *State Fair* (1945).
[Courtesy of JC Archives]

vocalist had three singles simultaneously on the Hit Parade: "You'll Never Know" was number one, "It Can't Be Wrong" was number two, and "In My Arms" was in the number ten position. Later, during the course of a nine-week gig with Tommy Dorsey and His Band (after Sinatra had left the group), Haymes traveled with them to California to join the group in appearing at MGM in *Du Barry Was a Lady* (1943). In this costume musical, Haymes was disguised in a powdered wig and barely noticeable. He then replaced Buddy Clark on the CBS radio program *Here's to Romance*.

Dick's most popular recording in the mid-'40s was "Little White Lies," which sold over 2.25 million copies and earned him $75,000. Twentieth Century–Fox studio head Darryl F. Zanuck was so impressed by the personality's impact as a vocalist that he signed him to a seven-year contract. By now Dick Haymes was the father of a son, Dick Jr., from his September 1941 marriage to dancer Joanne Marshall (later known as actress Joanne Dru). It was his second union; he had been wed briefly to singer Edith Harper in 1939.

The singer's first Twentieth Century–Fox film was *Four Jills in a Jeep* (1944), in which he portrayed a lieutenant romantically interested in one of the title characters (Mitzi Mayfair). He sang "How Blue the Night," "You Send Me," and "How Many Times Do I Have to Tell You."

Next, he played Irish composer Ernest R. Ball in *When Irish Eyes Are Smiling* (1944). Thanks to this film plus his records and radio work, Dick Haymes was fast becoming a serious rival to Bing Crosby and Frank Sinatra (and certainly far above Perry Como, who was also making movie musicals at Fox). In 1944, Haymes also costarred with Helen Forrest on the popular NBC radio show *Everything for the Boys*, and he and Forrest cut several successful duets on Decca Records, the best-selling being "I'm Always Chasing Rainbows."

Probably Dick's best-remembered film role was as the farmer's son lead in Richard Rodgers and Oscar Hammerstein II's *State Fair* (1945), lensed in color. He sang "It's a Grand Night for Singing" and also recorded (although he did not sing it in the movie) "It Might as Well Be Spring." His film acting of the hayseed young lover in *State Fair* was earnest but wooden. Nevertheless, he was a distinct improvement over the work of Norman Foster in the initial screen version (in 1933), and better than Pat Boone would be in the tattered remake (of 1962). With his boyish genuineness, Haymes was a proper leading man for Betty Grable in *Billy Rose's Diamond Horseshoe* (1945), one of her lesser musicals. He portrayed a medical intern who thinks he wants to follow in the show-business footsteps of his father (William Gaxton) but has a change of heart after marrying a sensible chorine (Grable). He had a hit recording with "The More I See You," one of his *Diamond Horseshoe* numbers. It was much to his disappointment that the studio would not allow him the role of the downtrodden Irish drunk Johnny Nolan in *A Tree Grows in Brooklyn* (1945), but Fox considered him too young and too inexperienced as a dramatic actor. The role went to eleven-years-older James Dunn, who won an Academy Award as Best Supporting Actor.

The next year, Dick had a reunion with Harry James, playing a big-band vocalist in *Do You Love Me?* (1946). This time he was teamed on-camera with Maureen O'Hara, who was seen as the fiery college dean he romances. The picture provided him with the title tune and "I Didn't Mean a Word I Said." He and Grable were rematched in *The Shocking Miss Pilgrim* (1947), set in turn-of-the-century Boston and boasting a George and Ira Gershwin score. He sang "For You, For Me, For Ever More," which was popular with audiences, while the period picture was not. He was top-billed for the first time in *Carnival in Costa Rica* (1947), in which he crooned "Mi Vida." The picture itself was mundane in its tale of newlyweds (Haymes and Vera-Ellen) coping with bickering in-laws. The authentic Costa Rican color footage received better reviews than Haymes's emoting.

Twentieth Century-Fox sold Dick's contract to Universal Pictures. He made two musicals there. *Up in Central Park* (1948), originally a Broadway play, was trite historical froth, with Deanna Durbin and newsman Haymes uncovering the corruption of Boss Tweed (Vincent Price). His second and last Universal feature, *One Touch of Venus* (1948), also a transplanted Broadway show, was a fantasy in which Robert Walker and Ava Gardner had the leads, and Haymes had a throwaway part as the hero's best friend. He crooned "Speak Low."

Although Dick's movie career had sputtered out by the late 1940s, he was still much in vogue thanks to his radio and Decca recording work, plus his many personal appearances. On radio, he starred in *The Dick Haymes Show* on NBC from 1944 to 1945 and on CBS from 1945 to 1947. In 1947, he joined with Bob Crosby on CBS's *Club 15* offering and also appeared on CBS's *Your Hit Parade*. In addition, he guest-starred on such radio shows as *Command Performance, Guest Star, The Jack Benny Program, Philco Radio Time,* and *Showtime* (in a radio adaptation of 1938's *Alexander's Ragtime Band* with Tyrone Power, Al Jolson, Dinah Shore, and Margaret Whiting).

On December 23, 1946, on CBS's *Lux Radio Theater*, he and Maureen O'Hara recreated their *Do You Love Me?* roles.

In 1949, Haymes and Joanne Dru divorced, and she received $350,000 from him in alimony over the next seven years, as well as support payments for their three children. That year in July, Haymes wed Nora Eddington, the ex-wife of Errol Flynn. Their brief marriage, however, proved to be a stormy one, due mainly to Haymes's excessive drinking. His career, on the other hand, continued. He returned to films as a crook in *St. Benny the Dip* (1951), a low-budget entry that received unexpected good reviews. *Variety* noted that Haymes "as the youngest of the con men, surprises with a smooth performance." He sang "I Believe" in the film. He made his musical comedy stage debut that year in Dallas playing in *Miss Liberty* in the role Eddie Albert had originated on Broadway. Dick also starred in 1951 in the radio series *I Fly Anything* on ABC as aviator Dockery Crane; the show ran for one season. At the time, he also started doing dramatic work on television, appearing in such series as *Ford Theater, Lux Video Theater*, and *Suspense*.

In 1952, Haymes became enamored with Rita Hayworth, and they were soon a much-reported upon item in the national press. It was through her efforts that her home studio, Columbia Pictures, provided Haymes with screen assignments. He supported Mickey Rooney in *All Ashore* and starred in *Cruisin' Down the River*. Both were 1953 "B" movies and proved to be Haymes's last significant big-screen appearances. Trouble developed for Haymes when he visited Hayworth on location in Hawaii on the set of *Miss Sadie Thompson* (1953), where it was revealed/announced that Haymes was not an American citizen. Further, it was rumored that he intentionally avoided military service during World War II by keeping his Argentine citizenship. The singer was declared an alien who had left the country without special government permission. (Hawaii was not yet then a state.) It was not until the U.S. Supreme Court ruled on the matter that it was decreed that Haymes could remain in the United States. Meanwhile, on September 24, 1953, he and Rita Hayworth were married in Las Vegas, where he was singing at the Sands Hotel. Because he had married a citizen, he was assured of legal residence in the United States. Nevertheless, court battles still ensued. While he eventually won the right to remain in the United States, the effort cost Haymes a great deal in legal fees. Plans to costar him with Rita in the biblical film *Joseph and His Brethren* (he was to play Joseph!) fizzled despite a $50,000 personal loan from Columbia boss Harry Cohn. The marriage splintered when Rita claimed that Haymes beat her. They were divorced in 1954, with Hayworth to receive $1 million dollars in alimony.

Dick next wed singer Fran Jeffries in 1955, and they had a winning nightclub act together, while he also appeared on such TV programs as *Screen Directors Playhouse* and *Producers Showcase*. He also cut several well-received albums for Capitol Records. In 1956, however, he lost the lead in a stage production of *The Tender Trap*, because he was still an alien without U.S. citizenship. In 1960, he and Fran Jeffries were divorced; the marriage had produced a daughter, Stephanie. That year, Haymes also declared bankruptcy.

During the 1960s, Haymes worked mostly in Europe. He married British model Wendy Smith early in the decade, and they had two children, Sean and Samantha. He quit drinking in 1965 and made a living by appearing in clubs in England, Australia, Africa, Europe, and Ireland (where he became a citizen in 1965). Dick also made a guest appearance on the British teleseries *The Saint* with Roger Moore; it was aired in the United States in 1965. In 1969, he was hospitalized in England with tuberculosis, but recovered within that year.

Things began to pick up for the singer, despite another bankruptcy in 1971, when in 1972 he made his first U.S. appearance in a decade on the NBC-TV special *The Fabulous Fordies* hosted by Tennessee Ernie Ford. Also on the show were his former Fox screen costars, Betty Grable and Maureen O'Hara. Haymes sang "It Might As Well Be Spring" and "The More I See You," and "showed that the ravages of time had taken very little from what was always conceded as the best voice of his pop era" (*Variety*). This comeback led to successful nightclub engagements in New York City, Los Angeles, and Las Vegas. The *Los Angeles Times* commented, "Dick proved that time hasn't dimmed his smooth voice or ingratiating style of projection. . . . He has returned to headline status."

Daybreak Records issued his Los Angeles Cocoanut Grove performance on the LP album *Dick Haymes Comes Home!* He also acted on such TV series as *McMillan and Wife*, *Hec Ramsey*, *Adam-12*, and *Eddie Capra Mysteries*, as well as costarring in the TV suspense movie *Betrayal* (1974). Mostly, though, he made his living working in nightclubs and by cutting several albums for Audiophile Records. He was among the horde of faded stars paraded forth in *Won Ton Ton, The Dog Who Saved Hollywood* (1976). Haymes admitted, "When I see myself on the late show in an old musical, I think: That person is no longer—he's been reborn."

Despite his professional resurgence throughout the 1970s, Dick did not look well, and, as the 1970s progressed, his health further deteriorated. On March 28, 1980, he died from lung cancer in Los Angeles.

Blessed with a superior singing voice and an ingratiating personality, Haymes might well have become the premier singing star of the twentieth century had he not succumbed so quickly to his own hedonistic ways and had he been able to concentrate more fully on furthering and building his career.

Filmography

Dramatic School (MGM, 1938)
Du Barry Was a Lady (MGM, 1943)
Four Jills in a Jeep (20th-Fox, 1944)
Irish Eyes Are Smiling (20th-Fox, 1944)
State Fair (20th-Fox, 1945)
Billy Rose's Diamond Horseshoe [Diamond Horse-
    shoe] (20th-Fox, 1945)
Do You Love Me? (20th-Fox, 1946)
Carnival in Costa Rica (20th-Fox, 1947)

The Shocking Miss Pilgrim (20th-Fox, 1947)
Up in Central Park (Univ, 1948)
One Touch of Venus (Univ, 1948)
St. Benny the Dip [Escape If You Can] (UA, 1951)
All Ashore (Col, 1953)
Cruisin' Down the River (Col, 1953)
Betrayal (ABC-TV, 12/3/74)
Won Ton Ton, The Dog Who Saved Hollywood
    (Par, 1976)

Radio Series

Here's to Romance (CBS, 1943)
Everything for the Boys (NBC, 1944)
The Dick Haymes Show (NBC, 1944–45; CBS,
    1945–47)

Club Fifteen (CBS, 1947–53)
Your Hit Parade (CBS, c. 1947–48)
I Fly Anything (ABC, 1951)

Album Discography

LPs

As Time Goes By (Audiophile 170, Ballad 6)

The Best of Dick Haymes (MCA 2720, MCA 1651)

Billy Rose's Diamond Horseshoe (Caliban 6028) [ST]

Call Me Madam (10″ Decca DL-5304, Decca DL-8035, Decca DL-9022/79022, MCA 2055) w. Ethel Merman

Christmas Songs (10″ Decca DL-5022)

Club 15 (10″ Decca DL-5155) [OC]

Diner (Elektra E1-60107) [ST]

Dick Haymes (Glendale 9006)

Dick Haymes (Vocalion 3616)

Dick Haymes and the Andrews Sisters—Club 15 (Sounds Rare 5004)

Dick Haymes Comes Home! (Daybreak 2016)

Dick Haymes 1940-41 (Joyce 6006)

Dick Haymes 1941 (Joyce 6009) w. Benny Goodman, Harry James

The Dick Haymes Show (Joyce PIX-3)

The Dick Haymes Show: 1945-47 (Take Two TT-303)

Dick Haymes Sings Irving Berlin (MCA 1773)

Dick Haymes With Harry James (Joyce 6001)

Dick Haymes With Harry James and His Orchestra (Harlequin 2008)

Dick Haymes With Helen Forrest, Vols. 1-2 (10″ Decca DL-5243/4)

Do You Love Me? (Caliban 6011) [ST]

Du Barry Was a Lady (Titania 509) [ST]

Easy (Coral CB-20016)

Featuring Dick Haymes (Viking 1035)

For You, For Me, For Everyone (Audiophile 130)

Four Jills in a Jeep (Hollywood Soundstage 407) [ST]

Haymes in Hollywood 1944-48 (Vedette 8701)

Helen Forrest and Dick Haymes—Long Ago and Far Away (MCA 1546)

Imagination (Audiophile 79)

James and Haymes (Circle 5) w. Harry James

Keep It Simple (Audiophile 200)

Kurt Weill in Hollywood [One Touch of Venus] (Ariel KWH 10) [ST]

The Last Goodbye (Ballad 7)

Little Shamrocks (10″ Decca DL-5038)

Little White Lies (Decca DL-8773)

Look at Me Now! (Hollywood 138)

Love Letters (Memoir 107)

Moondreams (Cap T-787, EMI/Pathé 81989)

The Name's Haymes (Hallmark 301)

Polka Dots and Moonbeams (Memoir 120)

Pop Singers on the Air! (Radiola 1149) w. Perry Como, Vic Damone, Eddie Fisher

Rain or Shine (Cap T-713, Cap 1019)

The Rare Dick Haymes (Ballad 8)

Rare Early Broadcast Performances (Starcast 1002)

The Rarest Cuts (Amalgamated 254)

Richard the Lion-Hearted (Warwick 2023)

Rosemary Clooney and Dick Haymes (Exact 232)

Sentimental Songs (10″ Decca DL-5291)

Serenade (10″ Decca DL-5341)

The Shocking Miss Pilgrim (CIF 3008) [ST]

Songs for Romance (Presto 636)

Souvenir Album (10″ Decca DL-5012)

The Special Magic of Dick Haymes (SRO 1002)

Spotlight on Dick Haymes (Tiara 513/7513) w. Johnny King

State Fair (Box Office Productions 19761, CIF 2009, CIF 3007, Sound/Stage 2310) [ST]

State Fair/I Fly Everything (EOH 99603) [ST/R]

Sweethearts (10″ Decca DL-5335)

The Unreleased Dick Haymes (Amalgamated 255)

The V-Disc Years (SRO 1001)

CDs

The Ballad Singer (Jasmine JASMCD-2525)

The Best of Dick Haymes (Curb/CEMA D21K-77479)

The Best of the Capitol Years (EMI 1364)

Call Me Madam (MCA 10521) w. Ethel Merman

The Classic Years (Pesagus)

The Classic Years (Prestige 214)

Cocktail Hour (Columbia River Entertainment Group CRG-218047)

The Complete Columbia Recordings (Collectors' Choice Music CCM-047-2) w. Harry James, Benny Goodman

Complete Duets (Music Club 208) w. Helen Forrest

Dick Haymes & His Pals—Club 15 (Vocalion CDUS-3013)

Dick Haymes—Legendary Live! At the Cocoanut Grove 1973 (Artistry 524876, Evolution 3203)

Dick Haymes With Harry James (Memoir Classics 510)

Diner (Elektra 60107-2) [ST]

Drifting & Dreaming With Jo Stafford (Jazz Classics 6005)

DuBarry Was a Lady (Great Movie Themes 60010) [ST]

Easy to Listen To (Pair PCD-2-1228)

The 50s Remembered (Varese Sarabande VSD-5782) w. Johnny Desmond, Dick Dale, Don Cherry

For You, More Me, For Evermore (Audiophile ACD-130)

How High the Moon (Memoir CMOIR-510) w. Harry James, Helen Forrest

Imagination (Audiophile ACD-79)

It Had to Be You (Memoir Classics 512)

It Might as Well Be Spring (Hallmark 304612)

It Might as Well Be Spring (Masters 503432)

It's a Grand Night for Singing (President 518787)

James & Haymes (Circle 5) w. Harry James

Keep It Simple (Audiophile ACD-200)

Lady Be Good/Four Jills in a Jeep (Great Movie Themes 60029) [ST]

Legendary Song Stylist (Pulse PLS-CD-307)

Little White Lies (ASV CD-AJA-5387)

My Heart Tells Me (Memoir Classics 521)

On the Air, Vol. 1 (Ballad 1)

On the Air, Vol. 2 (Ballad 2)

On the Air, Vol. 3 (Ballad 3)

On the Air, Vol. 4 (Ballad 4)

On the Air, Vol. 5 (Ballad 5)

Pop Singers on the Air (Radiola 1149) w. Perry Como, Vic Damone, Eddie Fisher

Richard the Lion-Hearted (Fresh Sound FSRCD-119)

Sad Eyes (Jass J-CD-633)

Serenading With the Big Bands (Sony Music Special Products A-26058)

Soft Lights and Sweet Music (Hindsight 265)

Star Eyes (Jazz Classics JCD-6004)

State Fair (Hollywood Soundstage HSCD-4003, Varese Sarabande 302-66075-2) [ST]

State Fair/Centennial Summer (Classic International Film-musicals 3009, Hollywood Soundstage 4003) [ST]

Stella by Starlight (Memoir Classics 547)

Swing Session (Star Line CD-SG-404)

Swingin' Session (Sounds Great 404)

This Is Always (See For Miles 907)

22 Golden Hits (The Good Music Record Company)

Two of a Kind (Mr. Music 7009) w. Helen Forrest

The Ultimate Collection (Prism PLATCD-645)

V-Disc Recordings (Collectors' Choice Music 6671)

The Very Best of Dick Haymes, Vol. 1 (Taragon 1033)

The Very Best of Dick Haymes, Vol. 2 (Taragon 1034)

You'll Never Know (ASV CD-AJA-5232)

You'll Never Know (Planet Music 1021)

You'll Never Know: The Very Best of Dick Haymes (MCA MSD-35197)

Dooley Wilson, Bill "Bojangles" Robinson, and Lena Horne in *Stormy Weather* (1943).
[Courtesy of JC Archives]

Lena Horne

(b. Lena Mary Calhoun Horne, Brooklyn, New York, June 30, 1917)

"I was the first black sex symbol, the first black movie star, and the first black to integrate saloons . . . I had to take a lot of flak from my own people, and everybody else's people." Thus spoke the very forthright, five-feet, five-inches Lena Horne, a musician's singer who overcame a great deal of prejudice to establish herself professionally. No study of her lengthy career can avoid the adversities with which she coped as a black entertainer in a white-dominated show-business environment. Bitterly recalling her tenure as a Metro-Goldwyn-Mayer specialty performer, she said, "I was always told to remember I was the first of my race to be given a chance in the movies, and I had to be careful not to step out of line, not to make a fuss. It was all a lie. The only thing that wasn't a lie was that I did make money; if I didn't; they wouldn't have kept me."

In her several decades as a major singer, the exotic and stunning Lena Horne developed her own rich contralto style, noted for its crisp diction and its perfection of sensual phrasing. Whether performing a sultry romantic ballad or a haunting blues number, she balanced her natural style with professionalism, giving her song interpretations their uniqueness. These special vocal qualities were as basic to Lena Horne the performer as the many career steps that led the star through segregation to integration and to her well-defined black self-identity.

Lena Mary Calhoun Horne was born on June 30, 1917, in Brooklyn, New York. Her grandmother, Cora Calhoun Horne, had graduated from Atlanta University in 1881, in an era when few women attended college. She had been a suffragette and had married a magazine editor and schoolmaster, Edwin Horn (who later added an "e" to his name). They were both active in the newly formed National Association for Advancement of Colored People (NAACP). Her maternal grandfather was the first black member of the Brooklyn Board of Education, and an uncle (Dr. Frank Smith Horne) was an educator and government administrator who would be an occasional unofficial adviser on race relations to President Franklin D. Roosevelt. Her father (Edwin F. "Teddy" Horne) was both a servant and a numbers runner/gambler. Lena was three when he left home. Her mother (Edna Scottron) was stage struck and soon left Brooklyn to tour the East Coast with the black Lafayette Players. Much of Lena's childhood was spent living in foster homes or with her uncle Frank in Fort Valley, Georgia.

At age twelve, Lena returned to Brooklyn to live with her grandmother and later with her mother, who had remarried a Cuban (Michael Rodriguez). She attended a variety of schools in Brooklyn and the South, and sometimes traveled with her mother on her stock-company tours. Because Lena was so light-skinned and considered such a "smarty pants," she was regarded as an outsider by her own race. "I never let myself love anybody, because I knew I couldn't stay around," she recalled. This mixture of independence and hurt shaped her personality and became an integral part of her performing persona.

In the fall of 1933, at the age of sixteen, Lena abandoned schooling to help support her parents. Through family contacts, she got a $25 weekly job at the Cotton Club in Harlem, which was operated by white gangsters. She appeared in the chorus line there, in shows featuring such entertainers as Cab Calloway, Ethel Waters, and Avon Long. Later, she was given her own dance numbers in these revues. Lena remembered, "My mother didn't want me in that atmosphere, and she'd come with me every night—or my stepfather. One night they [the club's owners] pushed his head in the toilet because they didn't want him coming around." Producer Lawrence Schwab saw Lena performing at the Cotton Club and hired her to play a quadroon in *Dance With Your Gods*, which opened at Broadway's Mansfield Theater on October 6, 1934. The play about a skeptic who invokes an ancient voodoo curse lasted a scant nine performances. Horne then joined Noble Sissle's Society Orchestra, hired more for her looks than her talents, where she was a dancer, occasional singer. Under the name "Helena Horne," she even took over as the orchestra's temporary leader when Sissle was injured in an accident.

By 1936, Lena had become reconciled with her father, who had remarried and who owned the Hotel Belmont in Pittsburgh. He introduced her to his friend, Louis J. Jones, a minister's son who was active in politics (as a Democrat) in Pittsburgh. Prompted by her desire to get away from show business and her mother and stepfather, Lena and Jones were married in January 1937. Their daughter Gail was born in December 1937. Because Jones found it difficult to obtain steady work in the Depression, Lena had to continue performing. She made money singing at private parties in the Pittsburgh vicinity.

In 1938, Horne made her film debut in *The Duke Is Tops*, a low-budget effort starring Ralph Cooper, a former emcee at Harlem's Apollo Theater. Filmed in ten days in Hollywood, the independently produced musical cast her as the star of a small-town revue who moves to New York to win show-business success. Looking slightly chubby, she sang "I Know You Remember." *Variety* recorded that Lena "is a rather inept actress, but something to look at and hear . . ." She was in the cast of Lew Leslie's Broadway revue *Blackbirds of 1939*, but the show was short-lived. Her son Edwin (Teddy) was born in 1940, and thereafter Lena and her husband separated (and were divorced in 1944).

Lena returned to New York in the fall of 1940, and after months of rejection because she did not fit the usual racial stereotypes, she joined Charlie Barnet's Orchestra, thus making her one of the first black entertainers to sing with a leading white band. While with the group, she recorded "Good for Nothing Joe," which became a hit single. In March of 1941, she had a seven-month engagement singing at the Café Society Downtown in Greenwich Village, a famous club that attracted a liberal, racially mixed audience and featured singers like Billie Holiday, at $75 weekly. She became noted for her interpretation of blues numbers. During this period, she recorded with Teddy Wilson and his band (who also were working at the Café Society Downtown), Henry Levine's Dixieland Jazz Group, and Artie Shaw (with whom she recorded "Love Me a Little, Little"). Later in 1941, she recorded for the RCA Victor label, including "Moanin' Low" and "I Gotta Right to Sing the Blues." She was also a featured vocalist on several radio shows, and made occasional film appearances.

Along with Katherine Dunham's dancers and other performers, Horne was hired to perform at the Little Troc Club in Los Angeles. Among those attending the well-received show was movie star George Raft, who arranged a screen test for Horne at Universal, but nothing came of it. However, another ringsider was MGM staff arranger/composer Roger Edens. He organized an audition for her with producer Arthur Freed and other MGM executives. When it came time to negotiate terms, her unimpressed father and her agents (who took 40 percent of the singer's earnings, instead of the customary 10 percent) represented her interests with MGM. Lena had reservations about wanting a film career at a major studio, considering the problems facing African-American artists at that time. However, NAACP executive secretary Walter White, bandleader Count Basie, and actor Paul Robeson, among others, encouraged her to accept the deal, insisting it would help make things easier for other black performers. Thus Lena signed a seven-year contract that began at $200 weekly.

Lena made it clear from the start that she did not intend to portray black maids on-screen, and she rejected the suggestion that she play one in Jeanette MacDonald's *Cairo* (1942). (Ethel Waters took the assignment.) Horne also refused to go along with publicity that would suggest she was of Latin-American extraction. However, the studio devised a special "Light Egyptian" pancake makeup to further lighten Lena's skin tones, which she agreed to use. She made her MGM bow in *Panama Hattie* (1942) in what would become a tradition in her Metro years. She sang "Just One of Those Things" and was given a rumba routine to sing called "The Sping." Her segments were so situated in the picture that they could be easily snipped out of release prints distributed in the South. (Lena remembers, "Once I stopped at a train counter for something to eat. The lady behind the counter refused to serve me, but she did want my autograph because I'd just made my first film.") One of Horne's closer friends off-camera was Oscar-winning black actress Hattie McDaniel, who explained to her the political ploys necessary to succeed in a segregated film industry. It was also in this period that she dated married championship boxer Joe Louis who, in 1943, enlisted in the army.

During her periods of free time, Horne returned to café work in New York City. Finally, MGM cast her in the role for which the studio had hired her, as the chanteuse in the all-black *Cabin in the Sky* (1943). She gave a heady performance as the temptress Georgia Brown dispatched by the devil to pull Eddie "Rochester" Anderson away from his wife (Ethel Waters). Lena, who had an off-camera feud with Waters (who felt threatened by the young, slim newcomer) offered a strong, naughty rendering of the song "Honey in the Honeycomb" and dueted with Anderson on "Life's Full of Consequences." One of Horne's scenes, in which she sang "Ain't It the Truth" while luxuriating in a bubble bath, was deleted by the censors.

Under other circumstances, her performance in *Cabin in the Sky* should have led to further dimensional celluloid roles at the studio. But not at MGM, which already had developed a love-hate relationship with their determined contractee. She was loaned to Twentieth Century-Fox for their all-black *Stormy Weather* (1943), a musical ensemble based loosely on the career of Bill "Bojangles" Robinson. She soloed "Stormy Weather" and "Digga Digga Doo," dueted with Robinson on "I Can't Give You Anything But Love, Baby," and was with Robinson and Cab Calloway on "There's No Two Ways About Love." The *New York Times* enthused that the picture was "a joy to the ear, especially when Miss Horne digs deep into the depths of romantic despair to put across the classic blues number . . . in a manner that is distinctive and refreshing." The song "Stormy Weather," which she had sung previously in clubs and on record, would become closely linked with Horne throughout her career.

Despite having excellent notices for two major film roles, Lena's screen career stagnated. MGM could only envision her in stereotypical ethnic roles and was quite concerned that African Americans did not accept her because she was so fair-skinned and fine-featured. ("I just couldn't be my own person . . . The only other black person at MGM was the shoeshine man.") Thus Metro, which had an agreement that only called for Lena's services a few months a year, used her merely as an added attraction for some of its musical features.

Usually Horne was seen on-screen leaning seductively against a pillar and singing a number or two. In *Thousands Cheer* (1943), she performed "Honeysuckle Rose" and was paired with black pianist-singer Hazel Scott in a brief interlude of Red Skelton's *I Dood It* (1943), for a heated rendering of "Jericho." She sang "You're So Indifferent" in *Swing Fever* (1943), and in *Broadway Rhythm* (1944, in which she actually had a character name, Fernway De La Fer) she performed "Somebody Loves Me" and "Brazilian Boogie." For *Two Girls and a Sailor* (1944), she crooned "Paper Doll," and in a West Indies club setting for *Ziegfeld Follies of 1946* (1946) she sang "Love."

When Lena vocalized "Can't Help Lovin' Dat Man" and "Why Was I Born?" as Julie in the *Show Boat* segment of *Till The Clouds Roll By* (1946), it was clear she should be the one to play the troubled mulatto when the studio filmed that musical. However, even in *Till the Clouds Roll By,* the studio had excised her few lines of dialogue with Kathryn Grayson's Magnolia, fearful of enraging racists. By 1951, when the studio finally made its full-blown *Show Boat* remake, Horne and MGM were at loggerheads, and the part of Julie went to Ava Gardner. Meanwhile, Lena was the most sophisticated ingredient of *Words and Music* (1948), singing "The Lady Is a Tramp" and "Where or When." Her last studio assignment was a guest cameo in Esther Williams's *Duchess of Idaho* (1950), performing "Baby, Come Out of the Clouds."

During the war years, Horne became one of the nation's top black entertainers (earning $1,000 weekly at MGM; over $6,500 weekly for nightclubs). She performed regularly at the Hollywood Canteen and frequently toured with the USO to entertain at armed forces bases around the country. She became a favorite pin-up girl for black soldiers. There was much press coverage when she complained publicly while entertaining at Fort Riley, Kansas: She found that several German prisoners of war were seated in the front rows, while American black GIs were seated behind. Meanwhile, Lena continued her cabaret work, becoming the first black entertainer to perform at the Savoy-Plaza Hotel and the Copacabana Club in New York. In 1948, *Life* magazine labeled her "the season's top nightclub attraction." Others noted the icy, aloof style that had become the singer's trademark posture. Years later, Lena reasoned, "The image I chose to give is of a woman the audience can't reach and therefore can't hurt. They were not getting me, just a singer."

In 1947, Lena performed in London and Paris, and on a later return trip to England was presented to the royal family. In December 1947 in Paris, she married a white man, Lennie Hayton, an MGM musical director who later served as her arranger and conductor. The wedding remained a near secret for three years. In the interval, Lena continued feuding with MGM, who kept her on salary only fifteen weeks a year. She asked to be loaned to Twentieth Century-Fox to play the light-skinned black in *Pinky* (1949), but the studio refused. She begged to play Julie in *Show Boat* (1951), but the hierarchy said no. They were still punishing her for refusing in the mid-'40s to appear in a Broadway musical (*St. Louis Woman*) the studio was interested in backing. (Pearl Bailey played the role when *St. Louis Woman* was staged in 1946.) The studio did not renew Horne's contract in 1950. Lena returned to cabarets, where she was soon earning $12,500 weekly. Of her movie years, she would say, "I never considered myself a movie star. Mostly, I just sang songs in other people's movies."

Continuously outspoken and at times bitter, Lena was in the headlines in 1950 when she commented negatively about controversial black entertainer Josephine Baker. (Horne later apologized, and she and the French-based chanteuse became friends.) More damaging was the aftereffects of the Senator Joseph McCarthy anticommunist hearings of the early 1950s. Lena was cited for her friendship with left-winged African-American stage and film star Paul Robeson and for her membership in assorted "leftist" organizations. It caused her to be blacklisted in films, TV, radio, and recordings. She said later of this period, "Sure it hurt me but it educated me to a lot of things. I began to grow as a person . . ." Eventually, by the mid-'50s, she reestablished herself in television and mainstream club work. She made a cameo appearance in MGM's *Meet Me in Las Vegas* (1955) as a favor to her husband, singing "If You Can Dream." She signed a new recording contract with RCA Victor. Her single of "Love Me or Leave Me" was number nineteen on the charts in July 1955. Her live LP *Lena Horne at the Waldorf-Astoria* (1957) became a huge seller (the best-selling LP by a female singer in RCA's history to that date). She appeared frequently as a guest artist on the TV variety shows of Peggy Como, Ed Sullivan, and Steve Allen. Her RCA albums *Give the Lady What She Wants* (1958) and *Porgy & Bess* (1959; with Harry Belafonte) also became best-sellers, with the latter LP winning a Grammy. (She would also win a Grammy for her 1962 album, *Lena—Lovely and Alive.*)

On Broadway, Lena headlined the Harold Arlen–E. Y. Harburg musical *Jamaica* (October 31, 1957). Her costar was another ex-MGM player, Ricardo Montalban. The *New York Post* enthused, "She is one of the incomparable performers of our time." The exotic show ran for 555 performances. She did *Jamaica* largely because she hoped it would set a precedent for more minority-oriented shows on Broadway. To her regret, it did not at that time. Her next stage venture, *Lena Horne in Her Nine O'clock Revue* (1961), never reached Broadway, closing in New Haven after a Toronto tryout.

During much of the 1960s, Lena Horne was a strong civil-rights activist. In 1960 when a patron made a racist remark to her at the Luau Restaurant in Beverly Hills, she threw anything and everything at hand at the harasser. She became a very visible advocate for integration and frequently spoke and sang at rallies and began including message songs in her club act repertoire. In 1966, she participated in the round-table discussions sponsored by the National Council of Negro Women and its affiliated Lamda Kappa Mu sorority. She explained to the press, "Now I have a lot more ease with myself." Meanwhile, in 1965 her autobiography, *Lena*, written with Richard Schickel, was published. Never happy performing in cabaret, she reduced the number of her live appearances in the late 1960s. She insisted that, until 1967, she did not really enjoy performing with live audiences because of the integration chip on her shoulders; but then she realized how prejudiced she had been herself. "I learned to have a ball when I was fifty," she said.

There was considerable press coverage when Lena agreed to costar in Universal's Western *Death of a Gunfighter* (1969). Much was made of the fact that she would play the brothel madam who was the lover-then-wife of the town's marshal (Richard Widmark). The scenario made no reference to the interracial aspect. She sang "Sweet Apple Wine" during the opening/closing credits. In the release print, her role was abbreviated and although (or because) the film was unexploitive, it quickly disappeared from distribution. She continued appearing occasionally in TV specials such as *Harry [Belafonte] and Lena* (ABC-TV, March 22, 1970).

In the troublesome period between 1970 and 1971, her husband Lennie Hayton died (April 24, 1971) of a heart attack; her father passed away; and her son Teddy, age twenty-nine, with whom she had been reconciled after years of misunderstandings, died from a kidney ailment. "I started to change when everybody left me," she said, "When I found out that the worst had happened to me and I was surviving. I began to think about myself, to look back at what I had been given and what I hadn't had. And I slowly grew into my other self." She moved to a New York City apartment and began concertizing around the country, often costarring with Count Basie, Alan King, or Tony Bennett. With Bennett she appeared for three weeks at the Minskoff Theater on Broadway in the fall of 1974. Now at peace with herself and liberated, she confessed, "In my early days I was a sepia Hedy Lamarr. Now I'm black and a woman, singing my own way."

In 1978, she made a movie return in Universal's *The Wiz* based on the Broadway hit show that was an all-black version of the Judy Garland picture, *The Wizard of Oz* (1939). Looking youthful enough to play the lead herself, she was cast as Glinda the Good Witch to Diana Ross's Dorothy and Michael Jackson's Scarecrow. It was directed by Sidney Lumet, then married to Horne's daughter, Gail. Lena sang "Believe in Yourself" with Ross. Made at a cost of $24 million, the overblown musical was not liked and only grossed $13 million domestically.

In 1980, Lena was named one of the world's ten most beautiful women, but after appearing at San Francisco's Fairmont Hotel cabaret in March 1980, she announced her retirement plans. She began a three-month farewell tour that June. However, she had a change of heart and on May 12, 1981, she opened on Broadway in *Lena Horne: The Lady and Her Music*. She performed a host of songs associated with her ("Stormy Weather," "The Lady Is a Tramp," "I Got a Name") and interspersed it with sharp talk and direct reflections on her life. *Newsweek* magazine raved that she was "the most awesome performer to hit Broadway in years." The *New York Times* added, "The lady's range, energy, originality, humor, anger and intelligence are simply not to be believed." For her one-woman production, she received a special Tony Award and a Grammy (for the LP album set), and the show was taped for cable TV (and later released on videocassette). *Lena Horne: The Lady and Her Music* lasted for 333 performances. It closed on June 30, 1982, her sixty-fifth birthday. She went on tour with the production and performed it in London in the summer of 1984. That December 10, she was among the five recipients (including Arthur Miller and Isaac Stern) who received the Kennedy Center Honors Award for Lifetime Achievement. In 1985, there was discussion of her doing a TV series to be spun off from *The Cosby Show*, but that did not materialize. She did a benefit concert at Carnegie Hall on May 20, 1986, for the Yale School of Drama and continued to receive artistic and humanitarian awards. (She previously had been given an honorary L.H.D. degree by Howard University in 1979.) Also in 1986, her daughter, Gail, now wed to journalist Kevin Buckley, wrote *The Hornes: An American Family,* which traced the heritage of her family from 1777 to that date.

With much fanfare, Lena came out with a new LP (*The Men in My Life*) in 1988, singing solos and duets with the likes of Sammy Davis Jr. and Joe Williams. She insisted she made the record because, "My grandchildren and my daughter hate to see me not working. To get them off my back, I went and did it." The *New York Times* noted of her song style, "She brings an emotional generosity to the material that would have been almost inconceivable until recently from someone who for decades maintained a facade of sophisticated reserve." One of the highlights of *Entertaining the Troops* (March 14, 1989), a PBS-TV documentary on World War II, was Lena and Eddie "Rochester" Anderson singing their "Consequences" number from *Cabin in the Sky* on the black radio show *Jubilee.*

In the 1990s, Lena chose to record again. Her first album in six years was 1994's *We'll Be Together Again.* The opening number, "Maybe," was written by her late friend Billy Strayhorn. The album's cuts were tributes to those late musicians who helped to shape her career: orchestra leader Duke Ellington, her husband Lennie Hayton, and pianist/arranger Strayhorn. Reporting on the disc, *Senior Highlights* observed, "Horne is letting her fans know, through her music, even more about her life and her losses and loves . . . Her voice, lower these days than it was a few decades ago, shows some signs of the passing years. But her *Together Again* album is, overall, a rich performance by a remarkable lady who could write the book on how to grow old with style, dignity and amazing grace."

The year 1994 proved to be very productive for Lena. She was one of the cohosts of *That's Entertainment! III,* which showed viewers more clips of the once-great MGM and its flock of stars. In a subdued fashion, Horne referenced the industrywide racial discrimination that stymied her career on the Metro lot in the 1940s. In addition, Horne participated in *A Century of Women,* a three-part documentary aired on TBS Cable that traced the strides and achievements made by twentieth-century women in the arenas of the arts, science, civil rights, and politics. Among the other personalities involved in the insightful production were Maya Angelou, Betty Friedan, Gloria Steinem, Jodie Foster, Sally Field, and Halle Berry. In June 1994, a few days shy of her seventy-sixth birthday, Lena gave a concert at Avery Fisher Hall in New York City, facing her first live audience in several years. The event was a tribute to Billy Strayhorn, who had been Duke Ellington's collaborator and arranger and who had composed the famous "Take the A Train." In September that year, she performed two widely acclaimed concerts, and a few days she held forth at Manhattan's Supper Club. The latter venue was used to tape *An Evening With Lena Horne* (A&E Cable, 12/4/94). Her repertoire for the ninety-minute event included "I'll Always leave the Door a Little Open," "Mood Indigo," "Why Shouldn't?" and "The Lady Is a Tramp." It was also announced that year that United Image Entertainment had acquired the rights to make a Lena Horne screen biography, tentatively entitled *Stormy Weather: The Lena Horne Story.* To date, the project has not come to fruition.

In 1996, when Turner Classic Movies/Rhino released on CD *Lena Horne at MGM: Ain't It the Truth,* the *Los Angeles Times* noted, "Even if you don't know Horne's history, this is an engaging collection of wonderfully stylish movie vocals." On November 25, 1996, PBS-TV's *American Masters* series presented an hour-entry on Lena's life and career. Reflecting on the broadcast, the star said that the show "is like looking in a mirror and everything's left-handed. They have pictures I didn't even know about." Of her past she observed, "I'm the inventor of mood swings. I took refuge in the song 'Stormy Weather' to explain a lot about myself." But nowadays, she added, "my new great-grandson is the most important part of my life."

On June 23, 1997, at Lincoln Center's Avery Fisher Hall, Lena was honored with the Ella Award for Lifetime Achievement by the Society of Singers. She was the recipient for her outstanding musical achievements as well as her devotion to civic causes. The star-studded event was entitled *Lena: An 80th Birthday Celebration. Daily Variety* reported, "Still looking as gorgeous as ever, she [Horne] received her award with her usual combination of grace and self-deprecating humor and then thrilled the crowd by grabbing a microphone and saying, "let's see what happens." She sang—in her inimitable style—"Come Rain or Come Shine" and "As Long As I Live." In mid-1998 her newest album (*Being Myself*) on the Blue Note label was released. *Entertainment Weekly* rated it a "B": "Whether singing a bright 'As Long as I Live' or a darker 'What Am I Here For,' Horne commands attention. Vocalizing naturally poses greater challenges for her at 80, but her highly nuanced sense of drama pulls her through." Remarking on her new album, Lena said, "*Being Myself* represents who I am today. I think that this is one of the better recordings I have made. There is a good feeling in the music." On October 18, 1999, at Lincoln Center's Avery Fisher Hall in New York City, Horne was the subject of *Lena: The Legacy*. The evening featured the likes of Cicely Tyson, Laurence Fishburne, Chita Rivera, Bobby Short, Alan King, and Rosie O'Donnell, and was a benefit for the Lena Horne Youth Leadership Awards. In succeeding years, more compilations and reissues of Lena's past recordings were issued, including 2001's *The Best of the War Years* and *The Classic Lena Horne.*

In the new millennium, Lena Horne continued to be a spokesperson for her race and for older people, and an advocate for the government giving greater support to the arts, education, and health care. Reexamining her past she said, "I was a guinea pig during much of my career, going where blacks had never been allowed before . . . I'm really just a piece of Americana when you come down to it." At her age she insists, "I can do what I damn please and say what I want. Don't you think I've served enough time?"

Filmography

The Duke Is Tops [Bronze Venus] (Million Dollar
    Films, 1938)
Harlem Hot Shot (Metropolitan, 1940)
Boogie Woogie Dream (Soundies, 1942) (s)
Harlem on Parade (Goldberg & Goldberg, 1942)
Panama Hattie (MGM, 1942)
I Dood It [By Hook or By Crook] (MGM, 1943)
Swing Fever (MGM, 1943)
Thousands Cheer (MGM, 1943)
Cabin in the Sky (MGM, 1943)
Stormy Weather (20th-Fox, 1943)
Ziegfeld Follies of 1946 (MGM, 1946)

Till the Clouds Roll By (MGM, 1946)
Studio Visit (MGM, 1946) (s)
Mantan Messes Up (Toddy Pictures, 1946)
Words and Music (MGM, 1948)
Duchess of Idaho (MGM, 1950)
Meet Me in Las Vegas [Viva Las Vegas!] (MGM,
    1956)
Heart of Show Business (Col, 1956) (s)
Death of a Gunfighter (Univ, 1969)
The Wiz (Univ, 1978)
That's Entertainment! III (MGM, 1994) (cohost)

Broadway Plays

Dance With Your Gods (1934)

Jamaica (1957)

Radio Series

Jubilee (Synd, c. 1943–44)

TV Series

A Century of Women (TBS Cable, 6/7-9/94) (documentary) (miniseries)

Album Discography

LPs

Cabin in the Sky (Hollywood Soundstage 5003) [ST]

A Date With Lena (Sunbeam 212)

The Duchess of Idaho (Titania 508) [ST]

The Essential Lena Horne (Buddah 5669-2)

Faberge Presents Harry and Lena (RCA PRS-295) [ST/TV] w. Harry Belafonte

Feelin' Good (UA UAL-3433/UAS-6433)

For Someone in Love (Stanyan 10138)

Give the Lady What She Wants (RCA LPM/LSP-1879, RCA Int'l 89459)

Here's Lena Now! (20th Century-Fox 4115)

I Feel So Smoochie (Lion 70050)

It's Love (RCA LPM-1148)

Jamaica (RCA LOC/LSO-1036) [OC]

The Lady and Her Music (Qwest 2QW3597)

Lena, A New Album (RCA BGL1-1799)

Lena and Gabor (Skye 15) w. Gabor Szabo

Lena and Michel (RCA BGL1-1026) w. Michel Legrand

Lena Goes Latin (DRG 510)

Lena Horne (Tops L-1502)

Lena Horne at the Waldorf Astoria (RCA LOC/SLO-1028)

Lena Horne in Hollywood (UA UAL-3470/UAS-6470)

Lena Horne Live at the Sands (RCA LPM/LSP-2364)

Lena Horne Sings (10″ MGM E-545)

Lena Horne Sings Your Requests (Charter 1010)

Lena Likes Latin (Charter 106)

Lovely and Alive (RCA LPM-2587)

The Men in My Life (Three Cherries TC 44411) w. Sammy Davis Jr., Joe Williams

Merry (UA UAS-6546)

Nature's Baby (Buddah 5084)

On the Blue Side (RCA LPM/LSP-2465)

Once in a Lifetime (Movietone 71005/72005)

Porgy and Bess (RCA LOP/LSO-1507) w. Harry Belafonte

Songs by Burke and Van Heusen (RCA LPM/LSP-1895)

Soul (UA UAL-3496/UAS-6496)

Stormy Weather (Sandy Hook 2037, Sountrak 103) [ST]

Stormy Weather (RCA LPM-1375)

Stormy Weather (Stanyan 10126)

Swing Fever (Caliban 6038) [ST]

Swinging Lena Horne (Coronet CXS-CS-165)

This Is Lena Horne (10″ RCA LPT-3061)

Thousands Cheer (Amalgamated 232, Hollywood Soundstage 409) [ST]

Till the Clouds Roll By (10″ MGM E-501, MGM E-3231, Metro M/S-578, Sountrak 115, Vertinge 2000) [ST]

That's Entertainment! (MCA MCA2-11002) [ST]

That's Entertainment, Part 2 (MGM MG1-5301, MCA 6155) [ST]

20 Golden Pieces (Bulldog 2000)

Two Girls and a Sailor (Sound Stage 2307) [ST]

Watch What Happens (Buddah 185)

The Wiz (MCA 2-14000) [ST]

Words and Music (10″ MGM E-505, MGM E-3233, Metro M/S-580) [ST]

Ziegfeld Follies of 1946 (Curtain Calls 100/15-16) [ST]

CDs

A&E Biography . . . A Musical Heritage (Cap/EMI 94758)

At Long Last Lena (RCA 07863-66021-2)

Being Myself (Blue Note 34286)

The Best of Lena Horne (Pair PDC-2-1055)

The Best of Lena Horne: Love Me or Leave Me (Castle Pulse PLSCD-119)

The Best of Lena Horne: Original Recordings (Curb D21K-77616)

The Best of the RCA Years (Koch 7993)

The Best of the War Years (Stardust 971)

Blood and Sand/Panama Hattie/At War With the Army (Great Movie Themes 60047) [ST]

Cabin in the Sky (Turner Classic Movies/Rhino R2-72745) [ST]

Christmas With Louis Armstrong, Lena Horne & Nat (King) Cole (KRB Music Companies KRB6151-2)

The Classic Lena Horne (RCA 69399)

Cocktail Hour (Columbia River Entertainment Group CRG-218009)

Complete Black & White Recordings (Simitar 5678)

Dinah Washington & Lena Horne (Members' Edition UAE-30722)

The Essential Lena Horne Featuring Gabor Szabo (All That Jazz ATJCD-5950, MMS Classix 9030072)

An Evening With Lena Horne: Live at the Supper Club (Blue Note B212-31877)

The Fabulous Lena Horne: 22 Hits, 1936-46 (ASV CD-AJA-5238)

Forever Gold (St. Clair 5730)

Greatest Hits (CSI 75202)

Greatest Hits (RCA 09026-68041-2)

The Irrepressible Lena Horne (ABM ABMMCD1019)

The Irrepressible Lena Horne, Vol. 2 (ABM ABMMCD1112)

Jamaica (RCA 09026-68041-2) [OC]

Jazz Masters Series (DCC Jazz)

The Lady (DCC Compact Classics)

The Lady & Her Music (Bianco BIA-4187)

The Lady & Her Music (Pearl Flapper 709)

The Lady & Her Music (Recall 305, Snapper SMDCD-305)

The Lady & Her Music: Live on Broadway (Qwest 3597-2)[OC]

The Lady Is a Tramp (Blue Note BN056)

The Lady Is a Tramp (Prestige CDSGP059)

Lena (Prestige CDPC-790)

Lena and Gabor (Audiofidelity) w. Gabor Szabo

Lena Goes Latin/Sings Your Requests (DRG 510)

Lena Horne (GFS GFS-286)

Lena Horne (L'Art 11)

Lena Horne (Pegasus PEG242)

Lena Horne (Pegasus PEG254)

Lena Horne at MGM: Ain't It the Truth (Turner Classic Movies/Rhino R2-72246)

A Lena Horne Christmas (Razor & Tie)

Lena in Hollywood (EMI/Cap Special Markets E21Y-37394)

Lena Sings the Standards (Hallmark)

Lena Sings Your Requests (DaRG 501)

Lena Soul (EMI E21Y-37393)

Love Is the Thing (RCA 07863-66473-2)

Love Songs (RCA 07863-63604-2)

Lovely and Alive (RCA Spain 74321-42125-2)

Lower Basin Street (RCA BVJ-35621) w. Dinah Shore

Mad About the Boy (Quicksilver)

The Master Eagle (EAB CD029)

Men in My Life (Three Cherries Records 7C-44411) w. Sammy Davis Jr., Joe Williams

Merry From Lena (EMI E21K-95145)

More (BCI Music 453)

More of the Best (Laserlight 17-074)

More Than You Know (Pickwick 11622)

Nat & Lena (Forever Music Group 070) w. Nat (King) Cole

Once in a Lifetime (Ronco Silver/Telstar CDSR-9008)

One More For My Baby (Masters 503352)

Quintessential (Soundtrack Factory 33514)

Some of the Best (Laserlight 17-073)

Soul (EMI/Capitol Special Markets 98875, Premier/EMI PRMCD1X)

Stormy Weather (Charly 1084)

Stormy Weather (Hallmark 300322)

Stormy Weather (Pickwick 16006)

Stormy Weather (St. Clair 1371)

Stormy Weather (20th Century-Fox 07822-11007-2) [ST]

Stormy Weather: The Legendary Lena Horne 1941-58 (RCA Bluebird 9985-2-RB)

That's Entertainment, Part 2 (Sony Music Special Products A2K-46872) [ST]

That's Entertainment! III (Angel CDQ-55215) [ST]

Till the Clouds Roll By (MGM/EMI MGM-24) Sandy Hook CDSH-2080, Sony Music Special Products CK-47029) [ST]

Two Girls and a Sailor (Great Movie Themes 60023) [ST]

V-Disc Recordings (Collectors' Choice Music 6657)

The Very Best of Lena Horne (Going for a Song)

Watch What Happens (BCC DJZ-607, Sound Sol 2830.072) w. Gabor Szabo

We'll Be Together Again (Blue Note B21X-28974)

When I Fall in Love (Spotlight On 129)

Whispering (Dove Audio, HIP, 32 Jazz Records, Joker 39052)

With Love From Lena (Parade PAR-2005) w. Gabor Szabo

The Wiz (MCA MCAD-2-11649) [ST]

Words and Music (MGM/EMI MGM-14, Sony Music Special Products AK-47711) [ST]

Ziegfeld Follies (Turner Classic Movies/Rhino R2-271959) [ST]

George Houston

(b. George Fleming Houston, Hampton, New Jersey, January 11, 1896;
d. Hollywood, California, November 13, 1944)

Opera singers are *not* generally associated with low-budget Westerns, but tall, handsome George Houston is better remembered as a cowboy-film hero than as a top-notch operatic baritone. He also starred on Broadway in musicals and revues and had dramatic supporting roles in several big-budget Hollywood productions before embarking on a career as a sagebrush warbler. Like Fred Scott, he did no recording, and today it is the cheap PRC Westerns for which the talented George Houston is recalled.

George Fleming Houston was born in Hampton, New Jersey, on January 11, 1896, the son of the Reverend and Mrs. Charles Houston. He entered Blair Academy in New Jersey in 1910 and was a member of the track team, before leaving the school three years later to attend New York City's Institute of Musical Arts (now Julliard School of Music) from which he received degrees in voice and music teaching. Houston served in World War I from 1917 to 1919; he was with the U.S. Army Ambulance Service attached to the Seventeenth French Division.

Following military service, George Houston studied voice and became a member of the Rochester American Opera Company, which was associated with the Eastman School of Music in Rochester, New York. In 1927, he made his New York City operatic debut in Wolfgang Amadeus Mozart's opera *The Abduction From the Seraglio*. Next, he sang the role of Mephistopheles (from Charles Gounod's *Faust*) and was Escamilio in George Bizet's *Carmen* before appearing in *The New Moon* and other several Broadway productions, including *Chee-Chee* (1928), *Earl Carroll's Fioretta* (1929), *The Venetian Glass Nephew* (1931), *Cyrano de Bergerac* (1932), *Melody* (1933), *Caviar* (1934), and *The O'Flynn* (1934).

George Houston made the first of nearly two-dozen motion picture appearances when he took on the part of Uncle Andy in the Vitaphone two-reel costume musical short *Masks and Memories* in 1934, starring Lillian Roth. Next he had the leading role of opera singer Carlo Salvini in the soap-opera melodrama *The Melody Lingers On* (1935), which at least allowed him to perform selections from the opera *Carmen*. He was also an on-screen opera singer in *Let's Sing Again* (1936), in which he played the father of Bobby Breen, who made his film debut in this Sol Lesser production. Houston had the title role in *Captain Calamity* (1936), a South Seas drama that cast him as a ship captain who romances a beautiful woman (Marian Nixon) while fending off pirates. The picture was issued by Regal, but was soon acquired by Grand National, which also released *Wallaby Jim of the Islands* (1937), in which George had the title role of a singing sailor.

In 1937, George was featured briefly as Grand Marshal George Duroc in MGM's prestige vehicle *Conquest*, starring Greta Garbo. Houston (using the name George Byron) was glimpsed as a singer in Walter Wanger's production of *Blockade* (1938). For MGM, he was featured briefly as

George Houston and Beth Marion in *Frontier Scout* (1938).
[Courtesy of JC Archives]

opera singer Fritz Schiller in *The Great Waltz* in 1938, and the same year he had his first starring role in a Western as Wild Bill Hickok in Grand National's budget entry *Frontier Scout*. The feature, which was George's initial genre pairing with Al St. John, was produced by Fine Arts Pictures. (PDC [later PRC] announced in 1939 that Houston would play Billy the Kid in a series of eight screen adventures. This never happened for George, although Bob Steele did make six Billy the Kid pictures for PRC in 1940 to 1941.)

Thereafter, Houston returned to the stage, where he appeared as the Devil in Max Reinhardt's production of *Faust* in 1938 in Hollywood, with Conrad Nagel, Lenore Ulric, and Margo. The *New York Times* rated him "impressively satanic." Houston came back to movies in 1940 to play a detective in the Frankie Darro–Mantan Moreland Monogram economy mystery *Laughing at Danger*, and the same year he was impressive as George Washington in the historical fiction *The Howards of Virginia*, a major production made at Columbia Pictures.

In 1941, Houston embarked on a series of low-budget Westerns for PRC, which reteamed him with Al St. John, now in the guise of sidekick Fuzzy Q. Jones, a part he originated earlier at Spectrum with Fred Scott. Although cheaply made, the Lone Rider series greatly benefited from Houston's presence as the stalwart hero and St. John's comedy relief. The movies, all produced by Sigmund Newfield and directed by his brother Sam Newfield, also allowed George to sing several songs, most of which were composed by Johnny Lange and Lew Porter. Although Don Miller in *Hollywood Corral* (1976) considered the star "undoubtedly the best singer among the cowboys," Miller noted, "Generally unsmiling and in short supply of humor, Houston often seemed preoccupied, probably musing on better days at the opera with Verdi and Puccini, rather than high noons on the PRC prairies with Charlie King and I. Sanford Jolley." The series opened with *The Lone Rider Rides On* in 1941 and closed with *Outlaws of Boulder Pass* in 1942, for a total of eleven entries. Bob Livingston took over the role of the Lone Rider for six more features for PRC during the 1942–43 season.

It has been claimed that George Houston worked in the Lone Rider series in order to finance his American Music Theater. This Pasadena, California, headquartered group performed opera in English. After leaving the PRC Western series, Houston devoted his time to the group. The star was planning a national tour for the group sponsored by the Theater Guild of New York when he collapsed on a Hollywood street on November 13, 1944. He died from a heart attack on the way to a hospital. He was survived by his wife, light-opera singer and actress Virginia Card.

Filmography

Masks and Memories (Vita, 1934) (s)
The Melody Lingers On (UA, 1935)
Let's Sing Again (RKO, 1936)
Captain Calamity (Regal/GN, 1936)
Conquest (MGM, 1937)
Wallaby Jim of the Islands (GN, 1937)
What Price Safety? (MGM, 1938) (s)
Blockade (UA, 1938)
Marie Antoinette (MGM, 1938)
The Great Waltz (MGM, 1938)
Frontier Scout (GN, 1938)
Laughing at Danger (Monogram, 1940)

The Howards of Virginia (Col, 1940)
The Lone Rider Rides On (PRC, 1941)
The Lone Rider Crosses the Rio (PRC, 1941)
The Lone Rider in Ghost Town (PRC, 1941)
The Lone Rider in Frontier Fury (PRC, 1941)
The Lone Rider Ambushed (PRC, 1941)
The Lone Rider Fights Back (PRC, 1941)
The Lone Rider and the Bandit (PRC, 1942)
The Lone Rider in Cheyenne (PRC, 1942)
The Lone Rider in Texas Justice (PRC, 1942)
Border Roundup (PRC, 1942)
Outlaws of Boulder Pass (PRC, 1942)

Broadway Plays

The New Moon (1927)
Chee-Chee (1928)
Fioretta (1929)
The Venetian Glass Nephew (1931)

Cyrano de Bergerac (1932)
Melody (1933)
Caviar (1933)
The O'Flynn (1934)

Betty Hutton in *Incendiary Blonde* (1945).
[Courtesy of JC Archives]

Betty Hutton

(b. Betty June Thornburg, Battle Creek, Michigan, February 26, 1921)

Exuberant, firecracker, live wire—all of these describe the dynamo that was Betty Hutton, and yet none of them fully do her justice. In addition to her mile-a-minute screen persona (which also exemplified her to some degree in real life), Hutton was a seasoned performer who could act and sing and put over a vehicle by the sheer force of her extremely vibrant personality. In the World War II years, her frenetic energy seemed to be a catalyst for the American people in their struggle against the Axis. While she was never a soldier's sex symbol like Betty Grable, Rita Hayworth, or Dorothy Lamour, she certainly captivated wartime audiences by her looks and talents and, most of all, by her "blonde bombshell" rambunctious screen shenanigans. At one point in the late 1940s, Hutton was ranked second to Judy Garland in her enormous audience appeal. Sadly, Betty Hutton's career began to come apart in the 1950s with a series of bad career moves, followed by several emotional public "retirements" from show business and the inevitable comebacks. She spent most of the subsequent decades a recluse from the limelight, but always managing to be in the news due to one sad event after another.

Betty was born Betty June Thornburg in Battle Creek, Michigan, on February 26, 1921 (a year after her sister). When Betty Hutton was two years old, her father, a railroad brakeman, deserted his family, Betty's mother Mabel Lum Thornburg and an older sister Marion. After Percy Thornburg's desertion, Mabel took her two young girls to Detroit, where she got a job in a car factory but made more money operating a bootleg liquor joint. Mrs. Thornburg could play the guitar, and she taught Marion and Betty to sing and dance. Betty made her first public singing appearance in her mother's cheap speakeasy at age three standing on a kitchen table. Betty recalled later: "[We] were so poor, we never had enough to eat. We lived three families in a flat. It was a nightmare." When she was nine years old, Betty happened upon a church, where she became inspired by religion. It was then she decided to make something of her life. At age thirteen, she got a job as a singer in a Michigan summer resort and then worked with a local band of high-school students.

When she was fifteen, the teenager saved $200 and went to New York City hoping for a break in show business. However, the trip was a brief, unsuccessful one. Back home, she and sister Marion went to a Detroit nightclub, where Betty sang a song. Bandleader Vincent Lopez heard her and soon hired the teenager to be a vocalist with his band for $65 weekly. While touring with Lopez, Betty developed her exuberant singing style as well as using the name "Betty Darling." However, in 1938, when sister Marion became a vocalist with Glenn Miller, the sisters both began using the surname Hutton.

In the autumn of 1938, Betty had her first big professional exposure with Lopez at Billy Rose's Casa Mañana Club in New York City. The next spring, she made her recording debut with the bandleader on Bluebird Records with vocals on "Igloo," "The Jitterbug," and a duet with

Sonny Schuyler on "Concert in the Park." She also made her screen debut in the 1938 Vitaphone short, *Queen of the Air*. The next year she made more Vitaphone short subjects, including *Vincent Lopez and His Orchestra, One for the Book* (with Hal Sherman), and was with Chaz Chase and Hal LeRoy in *Public Jitterbug #1* (1939). Thanks to the success of this short and her Bluebird record, Betty was billed as "America's Number One Jitterbug." (Said Betty about this title, "It was just an unfortunate label that was pasted on. I just was a screwball. I sang crazy songs. I did just whatever came to my mind. They didn't know what to call me, so they called me a jitterbug. I don't dance. A jitterbug has to dance.") Also in 1939, she made her first Paramount picture, the short *Three Kings and a Queen*. Betty continued to tour with Lopez in vaudeville as well as singing on his NBC radio program. Her contract with the bandsman called for him to receive 20 percent of her income in current and all future ventures. It was a clause that was to give her legal headaches in the future.

Early in 1940, Betty Hutton left Vincent Lopez's band and sang and danced to good notice in the Broadway revue *Two for the Show*. During its run, she and Lopez terminated their contract with an out-of-court settlement. Later in the year (October 30, 1940), at $500 weekly, Betty was featured in another Broadway musical, Cole Porter's *Panama Hattie* starring Ethel Merman. (June Allyson was in the chorus and was Betty's understudy.) Again Hutton was a big success, and the show's producer, songwriter B. G. "Buddy" DeSylva, hired her for $1,000 a week to appear in his Paramount film musical *The Fleet's In* (1942). The movie teamed her with light-comic actor Eddie Bracken for the first time. In it, she played the part of Dorothy Lamour's hyperactive roommate, with the plot centering on sailor William Holden trying to get his way with club-singer Dorothy. Betty scored well in the film with the songs "Arthur Murray Taught Me Dancing in a Hurry" and "How to Build a Better Mousetrap." *PM* reported, "[her] facial grimaces, body twists and man-pummeling gymnastics take wonderfully to the screen."

Next, Betty was rematched with Eddie Bracken in *Star Spangled Rhythm* (1942) as a Paramount Pictures telephone switchboard worker who loves sailor Bracken. The sailor's father (Victor Moore) is, in actuality, a studio gateman, but has told his son he is a movie executive, which causes a series of screwball situations—all of which provide comedy relief between the star-filled specialty numbers. By the end of 1942, Betty Hutton was named a Star of Tomorrow by the *Motion Picture Herald*, and she negotiated a comedy and singing job on radio's *The Bob Hope Show*.

Now under contract exclusively with Paramount, the "blitzkrieg bombshell" again appeared with Eddie Bracken in the comedy *Happy Go Lucky* (1943). In it, she was the hoydenish pal of a gold digger (Mary Martin). The latter is pursuing a rich man (Rudy Vallee) at a Caribbean resort, with the aid of her beachcomber boyfriend (Dick Powell). This picture gave Betty the energetic production number "Murder, He Says," which was so popular it became a national catchphrase. Betty then teamed with Bob Hope on celluloid for the screen version of Cole Porter's Broadway musical comedy *Let's Face It* (1943), with Hutton running a fat farm and in love with crafty GI Hope. She sang "Let's Not Talk About Love." The performance solidified her position as one of Paramount's top female box-office attractions.

In 1943, Betty also became one of the first performers to be signed by Johnny Mercer for the newly formed Capitol Records. She sang not only energetic novelty tunes like "His Rocking Horse Ran Away" (from her film *And the Angels Sing*) and "Doin' It the Hard Way," but also ballads such as "Blue Skies" and "It Had to Be You." For her first nonsinging movie role, Hutton scored well in *The Miracle of Morgan's Creek* (1944), a comedy now regarded as a classic. She is the fickle girl who convinces her none-too-bright 4-F boyfriend (Eddie Bracken) to marry her so her pregnancy (from a brief one-night marriage when she was intoxicated) will be blessed with respectability. It proved to be one of screwball comedy writer/director Preston Sturges's most satisfying zany screen works.

Concerning *And the Angels Sing* (1944), in which Betty was part of a sister quartet (along with Dorothy Lamour, Diana Lynn, and Mimi Chandler) at odds with a crooked bandleader, James Agee (*The Nation* magazine) praised, "Betty Hutton is almost beyond good and evil, so far as I am concerned." Hutton negotiated a new Paramount contract, which paid her $5,000 weekly. She went on a vaudeville tour and appeared on several radio shows, including *The Chase and Sanborn Hour, Command Performance,* and *Mail Call.* She closed out 1944 with dual roles as patriotic Wave sisters in *Here Come the Waves* with Bing Crosby. Then, at year's end, she embarked on a two-month South Pacific USO tour.

When Hutton returned to the sound stages, she was granted the dramatic role she long wanted, that of Roaring Twenties speakeasy star Texas Guinan in *Incendiary Blonde* (1945), a title that described the star even better than its subject. The film—thanks to lavish production values and the star's verve—did well. Betty then sang "The Hard Way" in Paramount's all-star *Duffy's Tavern* (1945), based on Ed Gardner's popular radio program. *The Stork Club* (1945) followed, with Betty as a hatcheck girl who comes under the benevolent wing of millionaire Barry Fitzgerald after she saves his life, which complicates matters with her bandleader boyfriend (Don DeFore). She performed "I'm a Square in a Social Circle," and dueted with popular crooner Andy Russell on "If I Had a Dozen Hearts."

By now Betty's studio mentor, B. G. DeSylva, was no longer in charge, and Betty's vehicles became more variable in quality and usually were unworthy of her. *Cross My Heart* (1946) was a mild remake of a Carole Lombard 1930s' comedy, with zany Betty confessing to a murder so her lawyer boyfriend (Sonny Tufts) will gain publicity by proving her innocent. Much better was another biopic, *The Perils of Pauline* (1947), in which Betty played silent-screen serial star Pearl White. Among her songs in this film were "Poppa Don't Preach to Me," "I Wish I Didn't Love You So," and "Rumble, Rumble, Rumble," all of which she recorded for Capitol Records.

By this point, Betty was enjoying a happy domestic life, having wed Ted Briskin, a camera manufacturer. They had two daughters Candy (born November 23, 1946) and Lindsay (born April 14, 1948). Betty's return to motion pictures in 1948 was in the disastrous fantasy *Dream Girl,* which cast her as a self-centered rich girl who daydreams about happiness. In contrast to this career setback, she had a most successful stand at the London Palladium, earning $17,500 per week.

Back on the screen in 1949, Betty costarred with Victor Mature in the pleasant farce *Red, Hot and Blue,* which cast her as a stage actress whom a director (Mature) attempts to make a star, while the two become implicated in murder. She also repeated her role in *Red, Hot and Blue* with John Lund on NBC's *Lux Radio Theater.* However, plans to star her in a biography of Theda Bara fell through, as did subsequent projects in which she was to play Sophie Tucker, Clara Bow, and Mabel Normand. Having lost the lead in a loanout to Warner Bros. for *Romance on the High Seas* (1948) due to her second pregnancy, Betty was even more upset to lose the coveted role of Annie Oakley in MGM's screen version of Irving Berlin's *Annie Get Your Gun* (1950). The choice part went to Judy Garland, who, however, was forced to withdraw after recording the soundtrack. Betty was rushed in to play opposite Howard Keel, who portrayed Frank Butler, the sharpshooter Annie loves. Hutton was sensational as Annie, and the resultant film made a mint at the box office. Betty was featured on the cover of *Time* magazine and named the year's most popular actress by *Photoplay* magazine.

The year 1950 proved to be a good one for the star. She then teamed with Fred Astaire for *Let's Dance* at Paramount, in which she is a singer whose husband dies in the war. She makes a show-business comeback and, meanwhile, is attracted to a dancer (Astaire). On radio's *Theater Guild on the Air* on ABC, Betty starred in "Daisy Mayne" and "Page Miss Glory," the latter with Ronald Reagan. She also signed with RCA Victor Records, recording the *Let's Dance* song "I Can't Stop Thinking About You" and having a top-ten single duet with Perry Como on "A Bushel and a Peck."

In 1951, Hutton and Ted Briskin divorced, and for a time she dated actor Robert Sterling, the ex-husband of MGM's Ann Sothern. Betty returned to the screen in 1952 in Cecil B. DeMille's circus epic *The Greatest Show on Earth* as a high-wire artist, and the movie made $14 million at the box-office. Her next success came with a solid vaudeville engagement, following Judy Garland into the Palace Theater in New York City. After this engagement, she underwent throat surgery (which also required her to retrain her voice). Thereafter, she starred in her third biopic, as vaudevillian Blossom Seeley, in *Somebody Love Me* (1952). It was a Technicolor story about the trials and tribulations of Seeley and her husband Benny Fields (Ralph Meeker). RCA Victor released the movie's soundtrack, and Betty and Gene Barry played the leads on *Lux Radio Theater*.

On March 18, 1952, in Las Vegas, Betty married choreographer Charles O'Curran (her dance director on *Somebody Loves Me*). When Paramount balked at her insistence that O'Curran direct her next vehicle (*Topsy and Eva*), she walked out on her studio contract, which was not scheduled to expire until the end of the year. (Paramount announced it would star Rosemary Clooney in all their planned Hutton vehicles, but that never happened, either.) As suddenly as it had begun, Betty's meteoric film career had been aborted.

Betty returned to the London Palladium for a three-week stint in 1952, and the next year she was performing on the lucrative nightclub circuit. She was back at New York's Palace Theater in late 1953 and began making plans for her television debut in the NBC-TV musical special *Satins and Spurs*. She returned to Capitol Records, doing an album called *A Square in a Social Circle* and the *Satins and Spurs* soundtrack, which was issued prior to the show's debut on September 12, 1954. The much-touted Max Liebman production cast Betty as a rodeo queen in the Annie Oakley tradition. Despite all the hullabaloo, the program was a disaster and was the beginning of the end of Betty's career. She was so distraught over its failure that, after a good run at Las Vegas' Desert Inn, she tearfully announced to the media and public her retirement.

Early in 1955, Betty and Charles O'Curran were divorced, and the next month she wed Capitol Records executive Alan W. Livingston. That summer, she had a miscarriage. At year's end, she made a poorly received special for NBC-TV (the *New York Times* reported, "She worked much too hard and it showed"). After several false starts, Betty returned to films in United Artists' *Spring Reunion* (1957), a project once planned for Judy Garland. It was a low-key, low-budgeted entry with lonely spinster Betty falling for Dana Andrews at a high school reunion, while a classmate is murdered. She sang "That Old Feeling," but audiences passed the movie by. Betty Hutton was no longer a marketable screen name.

Before and after the *Spring Reunion* failure, Betty guested on NBC-TV's *The Dinah Shore Chevy Show* and did a musical revue in Las Vegas. In mid-1958 Hutton retired again from show business stating, "I had never given myself the chance to be a housewife." However, a few months later she was reactivating her career, reasoning, "I still had pride enough in myself as a performer not to simply drop out of the business, leaving people asking 'Say whatever became of Betty Hutton anyhow?'"

In 1959, Hutton starred on CBS-TV in the comedy series *Goldie*, which lasted barely one season, and she recorded an album called *Betty Hutton at the Saints and Sinners Ball* for Warner Bros. Then came more club work, more publicized backstage hassles, a divorce (1960) from Alan Livingston, and her fourth marriage (on December 24, 1960) to trumpeter Peter Candoli. In 1962, her mother died in a tragic fire, Betty did a summer tour in *Gypsy*, and at year's end, she gave birth to her third daughter, Carolyn. Later in the 1960s, she toured in *Annie Get Your Gun* and *Gentlemen Prefer Blondes*, and was a temporary replacement for Carol Burnett on Broadway in *Fade Out, Fade In* during the summer of 1964. She also did guest spots on TV series, such as (ironically) *The Greatest Show on Earth*, *Burke's Law*, and *Gunsmoke*. She and husband Candoli had much publicized martial problems, but were not divorced until 1971. In 1967, the star filed bankruptcy. She bemoaned, "I've been crucified in this racket, crucified, when I only gave out love. I bought houses, Cadillacs, furs, you name it, for people—even churches for my maids. But when the money went, everybody split." Her unbridled demeanor—considered unbecoming in the medium at the time—forced Betty off a daytime quiz show. In the same period, she was dropped from two low-budget Westerns filled with once-major names being shot at Paramount because she could not handle the quick shooting schedules. She was replaced in *Red Tomahawk* (1967) and *Buckskin* (1968) by Joan Caulfield, another ex-Paramount star from the 1940s.

After that, Betty became a recluse who did not reappear before the public until late in 1971, when she rode in the Hollywood Santa Claus Lane Parade. That occasion brought work offers, but nothing worked out for the former star, who admitted she had made and spent over $9 million and was now broke. She mused, "I don't know the 'in' crowd in Hollywood anymore . . . I don't even have many friends anymore because I backed away from them; when things went wrong for me I didn't want them to have any part of my troubles." She became alienated from her two oldest daughters and had a long, bitter feud with her sister Marion (who died in January 1987), and could only obtain work in small-time summer stock. While on tour in Rhode Island, in the early 1970s, she attempted suicide but was helped by a Portsmouth priest, Reverend Peter Maguire. On and off for the next several years, she worked at his rectory as a cook and housekeeper. In the later 1970s Betty moved back to California and was reconciled with her daughters and began making sporadic appearances on TV talk shows.

In the fall of 1980, Betty Hutton returned to Broadway in the role of Miss Hannigan in *Annie*. Rex Reed enthused in the *New York Daily News*, "She is a seemingly endless fountain of comic exuberance, a one-woman fireworks display that lights up the stage at the Alvin and leaves the audience cheering." She also made a guest appearance on the PBS-TV special *Jukebox Saturday Night* singing her old movie hits like "Murder, He Says," "You Can't Get a Man With a Gun," and "His Rocking Horse Ran Away." But once again, her show-business career drifted away. She returned to Portsmouth, Rhode Island, and eventually enrolled at Salve Regina College in Newport, where she earned a Master of Arts degree in liberal studies. In 1986, she was made a member of the college's faculty teaching motion picture and television classes. She was supposed to attend the April 1989 Academy Awards, but again illness and insecurities kept her away from the festivities.

After teaching theater arts at Emerson College in Boston in the 1990s, Betty relocated to the West Coast in 1996. Her good friend/benefactor, Reverend Peter Maguire, had recently died, and, said Hutton: "I figured there's no reason for me to be here [in the East] anymore, now that Father's gone. I can be a good Catholic anywhere." She hoped to get her life story turned into a film, but the project did not materialize. In mid-1999, the ex-Paramount star was in the news again. By then, she'd retired to Palm Springs, where she was living on her Screen Actors Guild pension and Social Security. She had been diagnosed with Epstein-Barr syndrome and was living in seclusion. Earlier that summer, she had fallen and broken her shoulder, and in June she fell at home and broke several ribs. Betty lay on the floor for hours—unable to call for help—until a friend came by and found her.

In July 2000, Betty, candid to a fault, turned up on cable TV on Turner Classic Movies' *Private Screenings* interview program in which the former "Bounding Betty" conversed with host Robert Osborne. During the hour-long chat, the garrulous former star discussed—among other matters—her alcoholic mother and her four "disastrous" marriages. That fall, the restored *Annie Get Your Gun* movie musical was reissued on home video and DVD. Betty did not attend the special screening in Beverly Hills to launch the film's reemergence after fifty years. In July 2001, Hutton was admitted to Desert Regional Medical Center in Palm Springs, this time suffering from a suspected stroke. A born survivor, she rebounded from the episode.

Filmography

Queen of the Air (Vita, 1938) (s)
Vincent Lopez and His Orchestra (Vita, 1939) (s)
One for the Book (Vita, 1939) (s)
Headline Bands (Vita, 1939) (s)
Public Jitterbug #1 (Vita, 1939) (s)
Three Kings and a Queen (Par, 1939) (s)
The Fleet's In (Par, 1942)
A Letter From Bataan (Par, 1942 (s)
Star Spangled Rhythm (Par, 1942)
Happy Go Lucky (Par, 1943)
Let's Face It (Par, 1943)
Skirmish on the Home Front (Par, 1943) (s)
The Miracle of Morgan's Creek (Par, 1944)
Here Come the Waves (Par, 1944)
And the Angels Sing (Par, 1944)

Incendiary Blonde (Par, 1945)
Duffy's Tavern (Par, 1945)
Hollywood Victory Caravan (Par, 1945) (s)
The Stork Club (Par, 1945)
Cross My Heart (Par, 1946)
The Perils of Pauline (Par, 1947)
Dream Girl (Par, 1948)
Red, Hot and Blue (Par, 1949)
Annie Get Your Gun (MGM, 1950)
Let's Dance (Par, 1950)
Sailor Beware (Par, 1952)
The Greatest Show on Earth (Par, 1952)
Somebody Loves Me (Par, 1952)
Spring Reunion (UA, 1957)
Jazz Ball (NTA, 1958)

Broadway Plays

Two for the Show (1940)
Panama Hattie (1940)

Fade Out, Fade in (1964) (replacement)
Annie (1980) (replacement)

Radio Series

Vincent Lopez and His Orchestra (NBC Blue, 1939)

The Bob Hope Show (NBC, c. 1942–43)

TV Series

The Betty Hutton Show [Goldie] (CBS 1959–60)

Album Discography

LPs

And the Angels Sing/Let's Dance (Caliban 6017) [ST]

Annie Get Your Gun (10″ MGM E-509, MGM E-3227, Metro M/S-548) [ST]

Annie Get Your Gun/Show Boat (MGM 2SES-42ST) [(ST]

Annie Get Your Gun/Three Little Words (MGM E-3768) [ST]

Betty Hutton at the Saints and Sinners Ball (WB 1267)

A Blonde Bombshell (AEI 2120)

The Fleet's In (Hollywood Soundstage 405) [ST]

Hutton in Hollywood (Vedette 8702)

Incendiary Blonde (Amalgamated 238) [ST]

Satins and Spurs (10″ Cap L-547, MPT 4) [ST/TV]

Somebody Loves Me (10″ RCA LPM-3097) [ST]

A Square in a Social Circle (10″ Cap H-256, EMI/Pathé 65521)

Star Spangled Rhythm (Curtain Calls 100/20, Sandy Hook 2045) [ST]

Stork Club (Caliban 6020) [ST]

That's Entertainment, Part 2 (MGM MG-1-5301, MCA 6155) [ST]

CDs

Annie Get Your Gun (Annie 001, Turner Classic Movies/Rhino R2-76669) [ST]

The Best of the RCA Years (One Way 34490)

Blonde Bombshell (AEI 005)

Footlight Parade/Star Spangled Rhythm (Great Movie Themes 60013) [ST]

Great Ladies of Song—Spotlight on Betty Hutton (Cap CDP 07777 89942)

Here Come the Waves (Great Movie Themes 60001) [ST]

Show Boat/Annie Get Your Gun/Pagan Love Song (Great Movie Themes 60005) [ST]

Spotlight on Betty Hutton (Cap C21Y-89972)

Star Spangled Rhythm (Sandy Hook CDSH-2045) [ST]

That's Entertainment! III (Angel CDQ-55215) [ST]

Fred MacMurray and Burl Ives in *Smoky* (1946).
[Courtesy of JC Archives]

Burl Ives

(b. Burle Icle Ivanhoe Ives, Hunt, Illinois, June 14, 1909; d. Anacortes, Washington, April 14, 1995)

One of the most versatile performers of the twentieth century, Burl Ives was considered a leading folk singer, but his appeal also extended to the popular and country-music fields. In addition to his singing, he created for himself a fine career in acting, one that earned him an Academy Award along with roles in more than two dozen feature films. He starred on Broadway and television, and gave many popular concerts. In addition, he wrote several books and arranged and popularized many American folk songs. A big man, standing six-feet two-inches and weighing 270 pounds, imposing Burl Ives loomed large over the American entertainment scene for half a century.

Burle Icle Ivanhoe Ives was born in Jasper County in Southern Illinois on June 14, 1909, the son of a tenant farmer who moved with his family frequently. Burl's mother loved to sing, and he and his three sisters and three brothers were all fond of music. At age four, Ives performed for the first time in public at a reunion for veterans. He attended school in Hunt City, Illinois, where he learned to play the banjo. When he was twelve, he performed with great success at a local camp meeting, and during high school he played football. After graduation in 1928, he attended Eastern Illinois State Teachers College, where he continued his avid interest in American folk music.

Predicting no future for himself in school, Ives dropped out. "I grabbed my guitar and hit the road," he commented later. He wandered around the country, working on riverboats and obtaining money as a performer when possible or taking any job available to sustain himself. For a time, he played semiprofessional football, and along the way, he continued collecting folk songs. His interest ranged from not only old English and Scottish ballads but also work songs, children's and nursery songs, cowboy ballads, railroad tunes, and other types of melodies of historical importance. He studied voice with Madame Clara Lyon in Terra Haute, Indiana, and upon arriving in New York City, he continued his voice training with Ella Toedt. At the same time, he also studied acting with Benno Schneider. In the big city, he sang in Greenwich Village cafés and acted in stock companies, all the while continuing his studies at the New York University School of Music.

In 1938, Burl Ives made his Broadway bow in *I Married An Angel* with Vivienne Segal, Vera Zorina, and Walter Slezak, followed the same year by playing the tailor in *The Boys From Syracuse* with Eddie Albert and Jimmy Savo. In 1940, he was on Broadway again in *Heavenly Express* and on the CBS radio series *Forecast*. This led to a successful stand at the Village Vanguard club, well known for presenting folksingers and leading jazz musicians. In 1941 and 1942, he starred in the fifteen-minute CBS radio show *The Wayfaring Stranger* (the show's name came from a traditional African-American spiritual), until Ives was forced to leave it for military service. As a part of his army duties, he was one of the servicemen cast in the Broadway production *This Is the Army*, with music by Irving Berlin. For a time, he had a radio program (*G. I. Jive*) aired on overseas military outposts.

In 1943 and 1944, Burl returned to CBS radio in another fifteen-minute offering. Discharged from the service, he appeared with Alfred Drake in the Broadway production of *Sing Out, Sweet Land!* (1944), a tribute to American folk and popular music written by drama critic Walter Kerr. From 1946 to 1948, Ives again headlined the fifteen-minute *The Wayfaring Stranger* radio program, now broadcast on the Mutual network. That year also saw the publication of his autobiography, also titled *Wayfaring Stranger*, and the following year he joined in the Broadway revival of the Restoration comedy *She Stoops to Conquer*.

In 1946, Burl Ives had made his film debut in the outdoor drama *Smoky*, and in 1948 he had roles in two Westerns, *Station West* and *Green Grass of Wyoming*, as well as appearing in the Walt Disney film *So Dear to My Heart*. In it, he was top-billed as benevolent Uncle Hiram, singing "Lavender Blue" and dueting with Beulah Bondi on "Billy Boy." Said *Variety*, "Ives adds immeasurably as village blacksmith, to the Brown County, Ind. doings." Meanwhile, Burl, known for his very liberal political beliefs, was part of Hollywood Fights Back, a late 1940s' effort to counter the effects of the House Un-American Activities witch-hunt against alleged Communists in the entertainment industry and elsewhere. (Later, Burl had a change of political heart and testified in front of Senator Joseph McCarthy's congressional hearing, giving into and siding with the anti-Communist investigation. His about-face seemed geared to save his career.) In 1950, he returned to the screen in another Western, *Sierra*, starring World War II hero-turned-actor Audie Murphy.

During World War II, Burl Ives made recordings for the Office of War Information. After his medical discharge from the service, he continued to record for minor commercial labels, introducing the songs "Mule Train" and "Ghost Riders in the Sky" before they became gold records for Frankie Laine and Vaughn Monroe, respectively. When the popularity of folk music increased greatly after the war, Ives was much in demand for personal appearances. In 1950, he filmed ten Snader Telescriptions (short subjects) for television, performing such folk songs as "John Henry," "On Top of Old Smokey," "Sweet Betsy From Pike," "Hush Little Baby," "The Cowboy's Lament," and "Noah Found Grace in the Eyes of the Lord." In 1953, Ballantine Books published two best-selling paperbacks by the folk singer, *The Burl Ives Songbook* (which contained 115 American folk songs) and *Burl Ives' Sea Songs of Sailing, Whaling and Fishing* (with a total of 68 songs). Commercially, he recorded with both Columbia and Decca Records, and he recorded over 120 songs for Encyclopedia Britannica Films in its six-album set, *Historical America in Song*.

In 1954, Ives was featured as Captain Andy in the Broadway revival of *Show Boat*, and the next year he won critical acclaim for his stage performance as domineering Big Daddy in Tennessee Williams's dark drama *Cat on a Hot Tin Roof*. Burl was now very much in demand for dramatic acting roles, and he returned to motion pictures as Sam in John Steinbeck's *East of Eden* (1955) and in the minor tale of corporate manipulations *The Power and the Prize* (1956).

Continually active professionally, Burl Ives began his dramatic work on network television in 1957, appearing on the CBS-TV shows *U.S. Steel Hour* and *Playhouse 90*, the latter in "The Miracle Worker." (He also made a brief, unbilled appeared in the 1957 theatrical release *A Face in the Crowd*.) The following year, 1958, was an important one for Ives's film career. He repeated his role of the patriarchal Big Daddy in the film version of *Cat on a Hot Tin Roof*. Then, he won an Academy Award as Best Supporting Actor for his performance in *The Big Country*, playing the grasping Rufus Hannasy in this sprawling, William Wyler–directed Western. He was impressive as the older man whose young wife (Sophia Loren) is attracted to his son (Anthony Perkins) in Eugene O'Neill's *Desire Under the Elms*. He then trekked to Florida to film *Wind Across the Everglades*. In 1959, he was the brutal outlaw gang leader who takes over a small town in *Day of the Outlaw*, and he had substantial roles in the comedy *Our Man in Havana* and in the melodrama *Let No Man Write My Epitaph*, both filmed in 1960.

After a thankless role in *The Spiral Road* (1962)—Rock Hudson's attempt to go "dramatic"—Ives returned to work for Disney in the box-office success *Summer Magic* (1963) with Hayley Mills, based on the old stage favorite, *Mother Carey's Chickens*. He was also the jovial genie in *The Brass Bottle* (1964), struggled with the other actors to enliven the disappointing follow-up to *Mister Roberts* (1955) called *Ensign Pulver* (1964), and provided the songs for *Mediterranean Holiday* (1964). In 1966, he was one of the voices in the animated feature *The Daydreamer*. Reaching in a different genre direction, he next starred in a slapped-together science-fiction period piece, *Those Fantastic Flying Fools*, (1967) based on a Jules Verne novel. Thereafter, he was again on Broadway briefly, playing the euthanasia-minded, small-town physician in *Dr. Cook's Garden* (1967). (In the 1971 telefeature version, Bing Crosby inherited Ives's role.) Burl was seen as a slave-owning rancher in the violent Western *The McMasters* (1970), and was in such later contrasting types of features as *Baker's Hawk* (1976; a wholesome family story), *Just You and Me, Kid* (1979; with George Burns and Brooke Shields), *Earthbound* (1981; a science-fiction tale), and the little-seen racial study *White Dog* (1982).

Since coming to television in the late 1950s, Burl Ives was quite active, appearing in such diverse series as *Zane Grey Theater, The Name of the Game, Daniel Boone, Alias Smith and Jones, Night Gallery, Little House on the Prairie*, and *Hallmark Hall of Fame* (in "Pinocchio"). He also starred in three TV series: *High-Low* (NBC, 1957; a quiz show), *O.K. Crackerby* (ABC, 1965; a comedy), and *The Lawyers* (NBC, 1969–72; one of the rotating series on *The Bold Ones*). He made several telefeatures, as well being the narrator of *The Ewok Adventure* (1984). He appeared in the miniseries *Captain and the Kings* (1976) and *Roots* (1977; as Justin), as well as having his own TV special, *The Burl Ives Thanksgiving Special* (1968; syndicated), and taking part in the animated offerings *Rudolph the Red-Nosed Reindeer* and *The First Easter Rabbit*.

As a recording artist, Burl was most prolific in his work for Decca from the early 1950s until the late 1960s. In the early-to-mid-1960s, he had a number of best-selling singles for Decca, including "A Little Bitty Tear" in 1961, "Funny Way of Laughin'" (which won him a Grammy Award as Best Country and Western Song), "Mr. In-Between" and "Mary Ann Regrets" in 1962, "This Is All I Ask" in 1963, and "True Love Goes On and On" and "Pearly Shells" in 1964. He also scored with most of these songs on the country charts, along with "Evil Off My Mind" in 1966 and "Lonesome 7-7203" in 1967. His Decca albums proved to be steady sellers, and he had charted LPs for the label with *The Versatile Burl Ives* and *Funny Way of Laughin'* in 1962 and *Pearly Shells* in 1965. After leaving Decca, Ives recorded for a number of labels, including Bell, Caedmon, United Artists, and Word (for the latter he cut several religious LPs).

In addition to television and recordings—and his role as a very active conservationist—Ives continued to make concert-hall appearances throughout the 1970s and into the 1980s. In the fall of 1988, he debuted his one-man show, *The Mystic Trumpeter: Walt Whitman* (which he wrote with his wife Dorothy, whom he wed in 1970), with Ives enacting the title role. "Seldom are an actor and the subject of a one-man show so perfectly matched as are Burl Ives and Walt Whitman," observed *Daily Variety*. The reviewer added that the show "looks to be a permanent addition to

America's stage literature." Thus at nearly age eighty, Burl Ives set out on still a new show-business career.

In private life, Burl married twice: His 1945 union to Helen Peck Ehrlich produced a son, Alexander, and ended in divorce; he and his second wife, Dorothy—twenty years his junior—had three children. For years Ives maintained both a New York apartment and a California ranch. His hobbies included flying and boating. As he grew older, the entertainer suffered from circulatory problems and congestive heart failure, but he continued to perform, his last work being *Imagination Celebrations*, in which he sang for children not only in the United States but also in Central and South America. His final recording, "The Magic Balladeer," was issued in 1993. Ives died April 14, 1995—at his rustic Anacortes, Washington, home—of complications from mouth cancer. (The malady had first been discovered when he had back surgery in the summer of 1994.) Just before he fell into a coma he told his family: "It's time to say farewell. I'm going to sing in heaven now."

Burl Ives's versatile show-business persona was best summarized in his *Burl Ives Songbook*: "His whole large person and personality radiate with the vigor and warmth that international audiences have come to love. . . ." Carl Sandburg said he was "the mightiest ballad singer of this or any other century."

Filmography

Smoky (20th-Fox, 1946)
Green Grass of Wyoming (20th-Fox, 1948)
Station West (RKO, 1948)
So Dear to My Heart (RKO, 1948)
Sierra (Univ, 1950)
East of Eden (WB, 1955)
The Power and the Prize (MGM, 1956)
A Face in the Crowd (WB, 1957)
Desire Under the Elms (Par, 1958)
The Big Country (UA, 1958)
Cat on a Hot Tin Roof (MGM, 1958)
Wind Across the Everglades (UA, 1958)
Day of the Outlaw (UA, 1959)
Let No Man Write My Epitaph (Col, 1960)
Our Man in Havana (Col, 1960)
The Spiral Road (Univ, 1962)
Summer Magic (BV, 1962)
The Brass Bottle (Univ, 1964)
Ensign Pulver (WB, 1964)

Mediterranean Holiday [The Flying Clipper] (Continental, 1964) (songs only)
The Daydreamer (Emb, 1966) (voice only)
Those Fantastic Flying Fools [Rocket to the Moon] (AIP, 1967)
The Sound of Anger (NBC-TV, 12/10/68)
The Whole World Is Watching (NBC-TV, 3/11/69)
The Man Who Wanted to Live Forever [The Only Way Out Is Dead] (ABC-TV, 12/15/70)
The McMasters (Chevron, 1970)
Baker's Hawk (Doty-Dayton, 1976)
The Bermuda Depths (ABC-TV, 1/27/78)
The New Adventures of Heidi (NBC-TV, 12/13/78)
Just You and Me, Kid (Col, 1979)
Earthbound (Taft International, 1981)
White Dog (Par, 1982)
Uphill All the Way (New World, 1985)

Broadway Plays

I Married an Angel (1938)
The Boys From Syracuse (1938)
Heavenly Express (1940)
This Is the Army (1942)
Sing Out, Sweet Land! (1944)

She Stoops to Conquer (1949) (revival)
Show Boat (1954) (revival)
Cat on a Hot Tin Roof (1955)
Dr. Cook's Garden (1967)

Radio Series

Forecast (CBS, 1940)
Burl Ives (NBC, 1940–41; CBS, 1941)
The Burl Ives Coffee Club (CBS, 1941–42)
The Wayfaring Stranger (CBS, 1941–42)

God's Country (CBS, 1942)
The Burl Ives Show (CBS, 1942, 1944; Mutual, 1946–48; ABC, 1949)

TV Series

High-Low (NBC, 1957)
O.K. Crackerby (ABC, 1965–66)

The Lawyers (NBC, 1969–72)

Album Discography

LPs

All-Time Gospel Favorites (Suffolk Marketing)
American Folk Songs (10″ Decca DL-5490)
Americana (Album Globe AC-820)
America's Musical Heritage (Longines LW-199)
Animal Folk (Disneyland 3920)
Australian Folk Songs (Decca DL-8749)
Ballads (UA UAL-3060/UAS-6060)
Ballads and Folk Songs, Vols. 1-3 (10″ Decca DL-5013, 5080, 5093)
The Best of Burl Ives (Decca DX-167/DXS-7167, MCA 4034)
The Best of Burl Ives, Vol. 2 (MCA 4089)
The Best of Burl Ives for Boys and Girls (Decca DL-4390)
Best of Burl's for Boys and Girls (MCA 98)
Big Country Hits (Decca DL-4972/74972)
Big Rock Candy Mountain (Pickwick 3393)
Blue Tail Fly and Other Favorites (Stinson 1)
Burl (Decca DL-4361)
Burl Ives (Camay 3005)
Burl Ives (Coronet CX/CXS-271) w. Chad Willis and the Beachstones
Burl Ives' Coronation Concert (Decca DL-8080)
Burl Ives' Korean Orphan Choir (Word 8140)
Burl Ives Live (Everest FS-340)
Burl Ives Sings (Col CL-980)
Burl Ives Sings for Fun (Decca DL-8248)
Burl Ives Sings Irving Berlin (UA UAL-3117/UAS-6117)
Burl's Broadway (Decca DL-4876/74876)
Burl's Choice (Decca DL-4734/74734)
Captain Burl Ives' Ark (Decca DL-8587)
Cheers (Decca DL-8886/78886)
Children's Favorites (10″ Col CL-2570)
Christmas Album (Col CS-9728)
Christmas at the White House (Caedmon TC-1415)
Christmas Day in the Morning (10″ Decca Dl-5428)

Christmas Eve (Decca DL-8391/78391)
A Day at the Zoo (Disneyland 1347)
The Day Dream (Col OL-6540/OS-2940) [ST]
Down to the Sea in Ships (Decca DL-8245)
The Environment (U. S. Department of the Interior—no number)
Faith and Joy (Word 3259/8140)
Favorites (Sunset 5280)
Folk Lullabies (Disneyland 3924)
Folk Songs (10″ Decca DL-5467)
Got the World by the Tail (Har/his-11275)
Greatest Hits (Decca DL-4850/74850, MCA 114)
Have a Holly Jolly Christmas (Decca DL-4089/74089, MCA 237)
Historical America in Song (Encyclopedia Britannica Films)
How Great Thou Art (Word 8537)
Hugo the Hippo (UA LA-637-G) [ST]
Hymns (10″ Col CL-6115)
I Do Believe (World 3391/8391)
In the Quiet of the Night (Decca DL-82470)
It's Cool in the Furnace (Word 8580)
It's Just My Funny Way of Laughin' (Decca DL-4279/74279)
Joy Unspeakable (Word 8391)
Little Red Caboose (Disneyland 1859)
The Little White Duck (Har HL-9507/his-14507, Col C-33183)
The Lollipop Tree (Har HL-9551/His-14551)
Lonesome Train (10″ Decca DL-5054) w. Earl Robinson, Richard Huey, Lon Clark
Lonesome Train (Decca DL-9065)
Manhattan Troubador (UA UAL-3145/UAS-6145)
More Folk Songs (10″ Col Cl-6144)
My Gal Sal (Decca DL-4606/74606)
Old Time Varieties (Decca DL-8637)
On the Beach at Waikiki (Decca DL-4668/74668)
Paying My Dues Again (MCA 318)
Pearly Shells (Decca DL-4578/74578, MCA 102)

Return of the Wayfaring Stranger (10″ Col CL-6058, Col CL-1459)

Rudolph, the Red-Nosed Reindeer (Decca DL-4815/74815, MCA 247) [ST/TV]

Scouting Along With Burl Ives (Columbia Special Products 3471)

Shall We Gather at the River (Word 3339/8339)

Sing Out, Sweet Land! (Decca DL-8023) [OC]

Singin' Easy (Decca DL-4433/74433)

Softly and Tenderly (Col CS-9925)

Something Special (Decca DL-4789/74789)

Song Book (Coral CB-20029)

Songs for Men (Decca DL-8125)

Songs for Women (Decca Dl-8246)

Songs I Sang in Sunday School (Word 8130)

Songs of Ireland (Decca Dl-8444)

Songs of the West (Decca DL-4179/74179, MCA 196)

The Special Magic of Burl Ives (Suffolk Marketing)

Summer Magic (Buena Vista 4025) [ST]

Sweet, Sad and Salty (Decca DL-5028/75028)

Sweeter as the Years Go By (Word 8583)

Time (Bell 6055)

The Times They Are A-Changin' (Col CS-9675)

True Love (Decca DL-4533/74533)

The Versatile Burl Ives (Decca DL-4152/74152)

The Wayfaring Stranger (10″ Col Cl-6109, Col CL-628/CS-9041)

The Wayfaring Stranger (10″ Stinson 1)

We Americans (National Geographics 07806)

The Wild Side of Life (Decca DL-8107)

CDs

All My Best (MCA MSD-38733)

America's Favorite Balladeer (Heartland Music 5983-2)

America's Folk Singer: 38 All-Time Greatest Hits (Gemini Gems Music)

Another Day Another Year (Hallmark 311142)

The Best of Burl Ives (Sony 47108)

Big Rock Candy Mountain (Half Moon HMNCDX102) w. Bing Crosby, Danny Kaye

Burl Ives (Sounds of a Century 1780)

Burl Ives (World of Music CD-12533)

Burl Ives & The Weavers Sing the Biggest Christmas Hits (Sony Music Special Products 13349)

Burl Ives Sings Country (Broadway BRCD-115)

Burl Ives Sings His Favorites (Collectors' Blues CBCD007)

Chim Chim Cheree and Other Children's Choices (Walt Disney Records 60410)

Christmas Album (Legacy Records 64771)

Christmas Eve With Burl Ives (MCA, Universal Special Markets 1071)

Gospel Music Treasury (The Beautiful Music Company)

Greatest Hits (MCA 11439)

Have a Holly Jolly Christmas (MCA MCAD-25992, Universal Special Markets 25992)

How Great Thou Art (BIV 0003D)

How Great Thou Art (Echo 003)

I'm Goin' Away (Col River Entertainment Group CRG-140000)

In Memoriam (Legacy International 418)

Inspirational Favorites (Universal Special Markets 112-108)

Lavender Blue—Songs of Charm, Humour and Sincerity (Jasmine JASMCD-3524)

The Legendary Burl Ives (Reader's Digest)

A Little Bitty Tear (Half Moon HMNCD006)

A Little Bitty Tear (MCA MACD-20280, Universal Special Markets 20280)

Little Bitty Tear—The Concert Collection (Prism PLATCD-124)

A Little Bitty Tear: The Nashville Years (Bear Family BCD-15667)

Little White Duck & Other Children's Favorites (Col CK-33183)

Member's Edition (United Entertainment UAE-30862)

Misty Music (United Audio UAE-30862)

More of the Best (Laserlight 12-650)

On Top of Old Smoky (Sony Music Special Products A28451)

Poor Wayfaring Stranger (Flapper 7090)

Return of the Wayfaring Stranger (Collectables COL-CD-6662)

The Riddle Song (ZZM 9071)

Rudolph the Red-Nosed Reindeer (Universal Special Markets 22177)

Some of the Best (Laserlight 12-649)

Songs I Sang in Sunday School (Echo 002)

20 Gospel Favorites (Madacy/Cedar HCP2-0741)

Twinkle in Your Eye (Legacy CK-63421)

The Very Best of Burl Ives Christmas (Uni/MCA 12018)

The Wayfaring Stranger (Collectables COL-CD-6474)

We'll Meet Again (Word INCLD-002)

A Well Respected Man (Javelin CWNCD-2021)

Gloria Jean

(b. Gloria Jean Schoonover, Buffalo, New York, April 14 1927)

Gloria Jean was brought to Hollywood by producer Joe Pasternak to be groomed as a future Deanna Durbin by Universal Pictures. An immediate success at the studio, she remained there for seven years. Unfortunately, as she grew older, her vehicles became more pedestrian. With her combination of fresh looks, a fine singing voice, and sweet personality, Gloria Jean successfully exhibited a picture of American youth so popular during the World War II era. Eventually, however, her career faded, and she spent many years thereafter attempting to regain a small foothold in the entertainment industry.

Gloria Jean was born in Buffalo, New York, on April 14 1927, the daughter of Ferman Schoonover, a music-store owner, and his wife, Eleanor. She was raised in Scranton, Pennsylvania, along with her three older sisters. As a youngster, she exhibited a strong interest in music, and her uncle taught her songs and gave her voice lessons. (Her mother hoped she might become an opera singer one day.) She made her stage debut at age three, billed as Baby Schoonover. At the age of five, she had her own radio program in Scranton. The next year she was offered an opportunity to sing with Paul Whiteman's orchestra, but the deal was rejected by her parents because of the amount of travel it would entail. When she was ten, Gloria went to New York to study opera. Universal producer Joe Pasternak heard her singing there, and she was signed to a seven-year contract with Universal. Her entire family eventually moved to Hollywood, where her father later worked in real estate.

Because of her natural abilities and outgoing personality, Gloria Jean was not required to take acting lessons. In 1939, she made her film bow in *The Under-Pup* in the starring role of a young girl from a poor family who wins a vacation to a summer camp with a group of rich girls. *Variety* bubbled, "youngster has warm poise, winsome personality and a screen presence that is remarkable. . . . She also has vocal ability which is demonstrated briefly in several sequences. . . . Gloria Jean is well qualified for starring responsibilities in the future. . . ." Next came the actress's most successful picture, *If I Had My Way* (1940) with Bing Crosby. In it, she is an orphan who is brought to Gotham by a steel worker–crooner (Crosby), and they become enmeshed in the opening of a nightclub. This movie contained several pleasant songs, including the title number by James V. Monaco and Johnny Burke, and it allowed Gloria full opportunity to both emote and sing in a top-flight production.

Jean's third picture, *A Little Bit of Heaven* (1940), was equally good. She plays a young singing star who supports her family. When they become snobbish due to her success, she pretends to lose her voice. An interesting plot twist cast several once-famous movie stars (Maurice Costello, Monte Blue, William Desmond, Noah Beery, Charles Ray, and Kenneth Harlan) as her "uncles." Gloria recorded the movie's title tune for Decca Records, the company for which she also provided a trio of songs from *The Under-Pup*.

Gloria Jean, El Brendel, Bing Crosby, and center right: Claire Dodd, Brooks Benedict, Allyn Joslyn, and far right: Ed Mortimer in *If I Had My Way* (1940).
[Courtesy of JC Archives]

Fourteen-year-old Gloria was next matched with W. C. Fields in *Never Give a Sucker an Even Break* (1941), an uneven comedy in which she is adopted by con artist Fields after her trapeze artist mother is killed making a circus movie. Although not one of Fields's best outings, he (not Gloria) had the lion's share of screen time. During this period, Gloria appeared as guest artist on a number of radio shows, including *The Chase and Sanborn Hour, Screen Actors Guild Theater*, and the programs of Bob Hope and Bing Crosby. In addition, she sang at President Franklin D. Roosevelt's birthday party in 1940.

In 1942, Universal, which was cranking out lots of low-budget musicals, began teaming Gloria Jean with Donald O'Connor in a string of features. Despite the quantity, these pictures were *not* quality, and they marked the beginning of her decline as a screen star. The first in this series was *What's Cookin'?* (1942), and she was fourth-billed behind the Andrews Sisters, Jane Frazee, and Robert Paige. Gloria portrayed a young vocalist hoping to get on a big radio show. The picture's emphasis was definitely on the musical numbers featuring the sisters Andrews, Woody Herman and His Orchestra, and the Jivin' Jacks and Jill. A better showcase for Gloria came with

Get Hep to Love (1942), which cast her as a young songster who runs away from her parasitic aunt. She sang "Villanelle," "Siboney," "Drink to Me Only With Thine Eyes," and "Sempre Libre" from Giuseppe Verdi's opera *La Traviata*. Her third 1942 release was *When Johnny Comes Marching Home*, which had Jane Frazee as the love interest to soldier Allan Jones. Gloria was left to romance Donald O'Connor.

Gloria and Donald carried on their romantic involvement in *It Comes Up Love* (1942), with Jean singing "Love's Old Sweet Song," "Say Si Si," and "What the Rose Said." The peripatetic teenagers were again paired in *Mister Big* (1943), which had them changing a dramatic school's play into a lively musical. (All of these budget productions made by the duo were poor cousins to the far more lavish musicals Judy Garland and Mickey Rooney were featured in together at MGM.) The final screen pairing of Gloria and O'Connor occurred in *Moonlight in Vermont* (1943), which found Gloria as the Granite State native who heads to Gotham to enroll in a drama school. Her songs were: "Something Tells Me," "Be a Good, Good Girl," "Dobbin and a Wagon of Hay," and "Pickin' the Beets." She was outstanding in presenting these tunes, but the melodies, unfortunately, were mediocre. By now Universal was ignoring Gloria in order to focus on its latest contracted young musical talents: Susanna Foster and Ann Blyth.

Following a guest bit in Universal's all-star *Follow the Boys* (1944), Gloria had a thankless role in the Olsen and Johnson wacky comedy *The Ghost Catchers* (1944). Somewhat better was *Pardon My Rhythm* (1944), in which she was a high school singer who helps her bandleader (Bob Crosby) enter a musical contest. She sang "Do You Believe in Dreams?" As 1944 ended, Gloria Jean found herself top-billed in another programmer musical, *The Reckless Age*. For a change, she played a more mature young woman who leaves the big city for a job in a small-town store owned by her grandfather (Henry Stephenson). She closed out the year with a straight dramatic role in *Destiny*, a finely directed (by Reginald LeBorg) but minor production about a man (Alan Curtis) wrongly sent to prison. She was seen as the young woman who loves him. The film had been conceived originally as an episode of *Flesh and Fantasy* (1943), but when that prestige Universal production—a multipart drama—was considered overlong, *Destiny* was deleted and expanded for a solo outing.

The year 1945 found Gloria closing out her Universal tenure in a trio of "B" features, beginning with *I'll Remember April*, in which she portrayed the daughter of a wealthy man accused of murder. She sang the film's lovely title song. Kirby Grant was her leading man in this feature as he was again in *Easy to Look At*, in which she is a fashion designer accused of selling her firm's designer to a competitor. The picture's best number, "Is You Is, or Is You Ain't My Baby?" was sung by the Delta Rhythm Boys. Gloria's final Universal project was the murder mystery *River Gang*, about a young woman and her uncle (John Qualen) mixed up in a killing.

Following the expiration of her Universal contract, eighteen-year-old Gloria went on a lengthy personal appearance tour, and at her agent's suggestion, did *not* accept several lucrative studio offers. She was offscreen for nearly two years, finally returning in *Copacabana* (1947) where she was almost lost amidst the mugging of Groucho Marx and Carmen Miranda, Andy Russell's singing, and Steve Cochran's romancing. She had a better opportunity in a lesser movie, *I Surrender Dear* (1948), as a band singer in love with her boss (David Street), while in the period piece *An Old-Fashioned Girl* (1949) she was a music instructor in Boston during the 1870s. Next she played an advertising agency worker who saves a youth center from being razed by a greedy businessman in *Manhattan Angel* (1949). *There's a Girl in My Heart* (1949) gave her the second feminine lead, but a chance to sing as the denizen of a theater that is about to be taken over by a crooked politician (Lee Bowman). It was her last screen work for six years.

During the early 1950s, Gloria again toured the United States, but her appearance at the London Casino was so poorly received (she broke down onstage) that a planned vaudeville tour was cancelled. In Hollywood, she got minor work on television, including recording several songs for TV's Snader Telescriptions: "Conchita Lopez" (1950), "Deep in the Heart of Texas" (1950), "Fools Rush In"(1951), "Moon's Song" (1951), "Shrimp Boats" (1952), and "Soon" (1952).

In 1955, Jean obtained the female lead in a "B" movie called *Air Strike* for Lippert. However, her assignment was a background one in the plot of a navy commander (Richard Denning) working to develop an efficient jet fighter plane. After that, Gloria Jean disappeared from show business, working as a hostess in an Encino, California, restaurant, because her movie money had long since gone to pay back taxes. In the early 1960s, Jerry Lewis promised to launch her comeback in his film *The Ladies' Man* (1961), but all she got was a bit assignment. In 1962, she did obtain a starring role in the little-seen comedy *The Mad Cappers* [*Laffin' Time*]. In 1965, she took a job as a receptionist at Redken Laboratories, a cosmetics firm in Van Nuys, California. She needed the job to support her son Angelo; she had married in 1962 and was divorced in 1966.

In the 1980s, Gloria attempted to obtain a Nashville recording contract. ("I can still sing," she said to an interviewer in this period.) She also made occasional appearances on shows like Merv Griffin's TV program and Richard Lamparski's *Whatever Became Of . . . ?* radio series. "I had a wonderful career, but I want people to know how happy I am today," she said. More recently, Gloria Jean told the *Los Angeles Times*: "I'm not saying that I'd mind if I got a call from [TV producer] Aaron Spelling or someone like that. I'd be delighted. They use everybody else in town. But it's not the top priority for me." Gloria Jean retired in 1995 after thirty years of employment at Redken Laboratories. Today she enjoys being with her two grandchildren, and although she lives in the present she has no qualms about discussing her acting career.

Filmography

The Under-Pup (Univ, 1939)
If I Had My Way (Par, 1940)
A Little Bit of Heaven (Univ, 1940)
Winter Serenade (Univ, 1941) (s)
Never Give a Sucker an Even Break (Univ, 1941)
What's Cookin'? [Wake Up and Dream] (Univ, 1942)
Get Hep to Love [She's My Lovely] (Univ, 1942)
It Comes Up Love [A Date With an Angel] (Univ, 1942)
When Johnny Comes Marching Home (Univ, 1942)
Mister Big (Univ, 1943)
Moonlight in Vermont (Univ, 1943)
Follow the Boys (Univ, 1944)
Ghost Catchers (Univ, 1944)

Pardon My Rhythm (Univ, 1944)
The Reckless Age (Univ, 1944)
Destiny (Univ, 1944)
Easy to Look At (Univ, 1945)
I'll Remember April (Univ, 1945)
River Gang [Fairy Tale Murder] (Univ, 1945)
Copacabana (UA, 1947)
I Surrender Dear (Col, 1948)
An Old-Fashioned Girl (Eagle-Lion, 1948)
Manhattan Angel (Col, 1949)
There's a Girl in My Heart (AA, 1949)
Air Strike (Lip, 1955)
The Ladies' Man (Par, 1961)
The Madcaps [Laffin' Time] (Boots and Saddles, 1962)

Herb Jeffries

(b. Herbert Jeffrey, Detroit, Michigan, September 24, 1911)

One of the ironies of motion picture history is that Herb Jeffries, "The Bronze Buckaroo," the only black cowboy star in 1930s' movies, was not Afro-American. His ancestry was Irish-Italian with a great-grandmother who was Ethiopian. Still the talented Jeffries was always identified as black and worked his way from band singer to film star to bandleader. Along the way, he was also a composer, nightclub entrepreneur, record producer, and movie director. Herb Jeffries remained active as an entertainer for many decades, attributing his longevity to Eastern religious study and practice.

Herbert Jeffrey was born September 24, 1911, in Detroit, Michigan, to a theatrical family. As a youth he learned to ride on his grandfather's farm, and he also began singing with a piano-playing friend, the duo appearing on local radio. By the early 1930s, he was singing in New York City and Chicago with Erskine Tate and other bandleaders. In Chicago, Earl "Fatha" Hines hired him as the vocalist for his revue at the Grand Terrace, and Herb also briefly sang with Blanche Calloway's band. He then began to tour with Hines, and the trek took them through the South, where he saw black children flocking to small segregated theaters to see cowboy movies. Having grown up in Detroit idolizing Tom Mix and Buck Jones, Jeffrey decided black youngsters needed their own cowboy hero, and he set out to make such film fare.

In the mid-1930s, Jeffrey tried to enlist support from the black community, including the underworld leaders in the urban numbers rackets, to finance "B" Westerns with him as their singing hero star, an effort to emulate the success of Gene Autry. He was not successful until he met white independent producer Jed Buell, who agreed to produce *Harlem on the Prairie* (1937). In order to fit the bill as a cowboy hero, Jeffrey spent three months on a ranch in Santa Ynez, where he learned to work with cattle, do horse tricks, and spin a rope. (In the early 1920s, champion bulldogger Bill Pickett had become the first black to star in cowboy movies, but he made only two features, *The Bull-Dogger* and *The Crimson Skull*.) Billed as Herbert Jeffries, the actor starred as Jeff Kincaid, a cowboy who with his sidekick (Mantan Moreland) comes to the aid of a robber (Spencer Williams), who, in turn, is being threatened by a vicious gang. Filmed at N. B. Murray's Dude Ranch in Southern California, the film proved successful. When it played in New York City, it was called *Bad Man of Harlem*.

Three more "All-Colored Cast" Westerns followed for the star, and in them he was billed as Herbert Jeffrey. This trio were produced and directed by Richard C. Kahn. As in the initial feature, the star wrote the songs used in the picture, including "I'm a Happy Cowboy," which was his theme song. In all three features, he played cowpoke hero Bob Blake, and Spencer Williams, later of TV's *Amos 'n' Andy* fame, appeared in each of them. The films were *Two-Gun Man From Harlem* (1937), *The Bronze Buckaroo* (1938), and *Harlem Rides the Range* (1938), the latter being

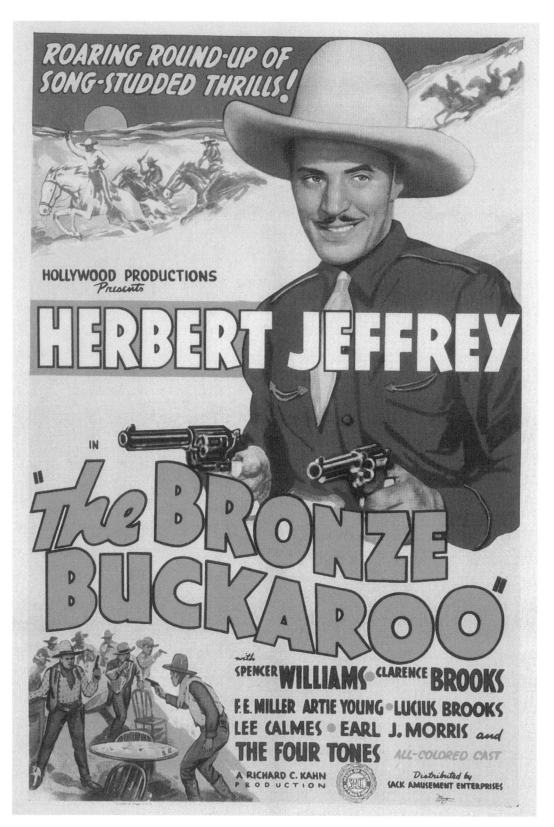

Herb Jeffries aka: Herbert Jeffrey in *The Bronze Buckaroo* (1939).
[Courtesy of JC Archives]

coscripted by Williams. In the features, the star rode a white horse called Stardusk. A fourth feature, *Ten Notches to Tombstone*, was begun but not completed. In a 1995 interview, Jeffries recalled his days as a black cowboy movie hero: "I had a Cadillac with steer horns up front and my name in gold rope on the side and after the picture I'd do rope tricks, spin my gun and sing songs from the movie. Wherever I went kids would follow me through the street, not only black kids but white kids too, which was unusual to see down South. They'd seen cowboys before but not movie cowboys."

While the Herb Jeffries's black Westerns were financially successful, the number of all-black theaters was beginning to dwindle, thus narrowing the market for such features. In 1939, now billed as Herb Jeffries, the star joined Duke Ellington's band as a vocalist and in the next three years recorded a number of songs for Victor Records, including the 1940 million-seller "Flamingo." Jeffries enlisted in the army in 1942, and when World War II ended he opened a jazz club called The Flamingo in Paris, catering to such clientele as Ali Khan, King Farouk of Egypt, and Orson Welles. In the late 1940s, he was back in the United States fronting a band and recording for such labels as Exclusive (on which he had the best-selling "Basin Street Blues"), Trend, Coral, Mercury, and Columbia. He cut several more versions of "Flamingo," which sold over 14 million copies. He was also the composer or lyricist of such songs as "The Singing Prophet," "Which Way Does the Wind Blow?" "Deep Down in the Middle of Your Heart," and "Don't Weep Little Children."

In 1949, Herb's composition "Candy Store Blues" was heard in the picture *Manhattan Angel* starring Gloria Jean. In 1951, Jeffries was back on the screen in *Disc Jockey*, for which he wrote and performed the title song and "In My Heart." In the early 1950s, the talent starred in eleven three-minute musicals made for television by Snader Telescriptions. They included: "After Hours," "Basin Street Blues," and "A Woman Is a Worrisome Thing." He performed the title song in the 1954 melodrama *Wicked Woman*, and then appeared as himself in three all-black musicals, *Rhythm and Blues Revue* and *Jazz Festival*, both 1955 releases that were filmed at Harlem's Apollo Theater, and *Basin Street Revue* (1956). In 1957 Jeffries starred in the Allied Artists feature *Calypso Joe*, playing the title character, as well as composing the feature's half dozen songs. It was around this time that he recorded an album of calypso music for the RKO-Unique label called *Jamaica*.

In the late 1950s, Herb opened another Flamingo Club, this time in Los Angeles. He also found employment as a writer of special material for theaters and nightclub acts. He wrote and directed the 1967 feature film *Mundo Depravado*, which Box-office International released in the United States as *World of the Depraved*. It spotlighted stripper Tempest Storm in the story of two silly detectives (Johnnie Decker and Larry Redd) who are on the trail of a serial killer who murders young women at a health spa. Jeffries provided the voice of Freight Train in the 1970 animated TV series *Where's Huddles* for Hanna-Barbera Productions, and the next year, he returned to features in the violent motorcycle yarn, *Chrome and Hot Leather*. After acting in a few TV movies, *Jarrett* (1973) and *Twice in a Lifetime* (1974), Jeffries played gangster Charlie Blue in the Jack Palance theatrical release *Portrait Of A Hitman* in 1977. Herb also made appearances on such TV series as *I Dream of Jeannie, Hawaii Five-O*, and *The Virginian*.

During the early 1990s, Jeffries toured with Barbara McNair and the Mills Brothers in the Duke Ellington tribute show *Mostly Duke*, and he also worked with his own band. In addition, he did concerts with classical orchestras. In 1992, Herb appeared at the Gene Autry Western Heritage Museum with Autry, Rex Allen, and Patsy Montana in a tribute concert to the singing cowboys, and he was featured in the 1993 PBS-TV series *California's Gold* in a segment on warbling cinema cowpokes. In part two of a three-part TV documentary, *The Untold West*, in 1994, Herb researched and narrated the segment "The Black West," which also used footage from his Western features. The next year he recorded a compact disc for the Warner Western label called *The Bronze Buckaroo*. On it, he was joined by guests like Rex Allen Jr., Michael Martin Murphy, the Mills Brothers, Hal Linden, and the Sons of the San Joaquin. For this new CD, in addition to performing his Western theme song, "I'm a Happy Cowboy," Jeffries did traditional genre tunes and also wrote two compositions ("Down Home Cowboy" and "Lonesome River Blues") especially for the project.

The veteran entertainer was interviewed in the TV documentary movie *Midnight Ramble* (1994), which dealt with the career of pioneer African-American filmmaker Oscar Micheaux. In 1996, Jeffries played himself in the comedy Western telefeature *The Cherokee Kid*, starring Sinbad. Sinbad also presented Herb with the Golden Boot Award that year at its fourteenth annual ceremony, honoring his contributions to Western movies. Herb also was on-screen in the full-length *Keepers of the Frame* (1999), a documentary about film preservation. With the dawning of the twenty-first century, Jeffries continued to make personal appearances, and he also recorded a CD, *The Duke and I*, commemorating the one hundredth birthday of Duke Ellington. Married five times (one of his wives was Tempest Storm), Jeffries is the father of a son and four daughters.

Filmography

Harlem on the Prairie [Bad Man of Harlem] (Associated Features, 1937) (also songs)
Two-Gun Man From Harlem (Merit Pictures, 1937) (also songs)
The Bronze Buckaroo (Sack Amusement, 1938) (also songs)
Harlem Rides the Range (Sack Amusement, 1939) (also songs)
Manhattan Angel (Col, 1949) (song only)
Disc Jockey (AA, 1951) (also songs)
Wicked Woman (UA, 1954) (also song)
Rhythm and Blues Revue (Studio Films, 1955)
Jazz Festival (Studio Films, 1955)
Basin Street Revue (Studio Films, 1956)

Calypso Joe (Allied Artists, 1957)
Mundo Depravado [Depraved World] (Monique Productions, 1967) (U.S. title: World of the Depraved) (director, script only)
Chrome and Hot Leather (American International, 1971)
Jarrett (NBC-TV, 3/17/73)
Twice in a Lifetime (NBC-TV, 3/16/74)
Portrait of a Hitman (ANE, 1977)
Midnight Ramble (Northern Lights Productions, 1994) (documentary)
The Cherokee Kid (HBO Cable, 12/14/96)
Keepers of the Frame (1999) (documentary)

Television Series

Where's Huddles (CBS-TV, 1970) (voice only)

Album Discography

LPs

Devil Is a Woman (Golden Tone C4066)
Herb Jeffries (Har HL-7048)
Herb Jeffries Sings (10″ Mer MG-25090)
Jamaica (RKO/Unique SLP-1280)

Just Jeffries (10″ Mer MG-25091)
Magenta Moods (10″ Mer MG-25089)
Say It Isn't So (Bethlehem 72, Rep 215)
Time on My Hands (10″ Coral CRL-56044)

CDs

The Bronze Buckaroo (Warner Western 45639)
The Duke and I (no further information available)
Four Winds and the Seven Seas (Sony Music Special Products 28452)

Jamaica (RKO/Unique 1001)
Say It Isn't So (Rhino 76680)

Al Jolson in *The Singing Kid* (1936).
[Courtesy of JC Archives]

Al Jolson

(b. Asa Yoelson, St. Petersburg, Russia, May 26, 1886; d. San Francisco, California, October 23, 1950)

"The World's Greatest Entertainer," as Al Jolson was often called, sang for over half a century and endeared himself to millions. Jolson's success encompassed vaudeville, minstrel shows, revues, Broadway, movies, records, radio, and concerts. He probably introduced more popular songs than any other entertainer, and he was one of the highest-paid performers of his day. His electric personality and emotional delivery of songs made him a household name. Despite the fact he was a Russian Jew, he will be forever remembered as the black-faced minstrel man singing con brio about the old South. Beneath his show-business facade, however, was an extremely complex, egotistical man who could be generous, kind, and considerate and yet also cruel, sadistic, and violent. Although many of his contemporaries disliked him personally, he was one of the few performers to be almost universally lionized by his peers. George Jessel summed it best by saying, "What a great artist he was!" It was Jolson, though, who had the final word, as usual, when he declared, "I've got so much dough that fourteen guys couldn't spend it in their lifetime. But I'd rather die than quit this business." And that is just what happened.

Al Jolson always claimed he was born May 26, 1886, in St. Petersburg, Russia. His father was a cantor, and Al's given name was Asa Yoelson. Because of the anti-Jewish pogroms that persistently swept Russia, the Yoelsons came to America when Al was a small boy. They lived in Washington, DC, where his father planned for him to follow in his footsteps and enter the synagogue as a cantor. Young Al, however, proved to be a problem child, especially with his newfound taste for the popular music of the day. To discipline him, he was placed, for a time, in a Catholic school in Baltimore. However, after being inspired by witnessing Fay Templeton perform on the stage and meeting minstrel man Eddie Leonard, Al joined a traveling burlesque company as a comic stooge. He soon graduated to becoming a singer; his voice had been impressive even as a boy before he left Russia.

Al made his stage debut in 1899 in Washington, DC, as one of the young mob in the pre-Broadway production of *The Children of the Ghetto*. The next year he teamed with his older brother Harry for a routine called "The Hebrew and the Cadet." In 1901, Al and Harry worked with Joe Palmer in a vaudeville act called Joelson, Palmer, and Joelson. However, since the billing was too long for the theater marquee, the "e" was dropped from the brothers' surname, thus becoming Jolson. By 1906, Al was working solo in San Francisco, which had just suffered the devastating earthquake. It was there he enjoyed his first real success as a dynamic singer of popular songs. At the time he was still performing without heavy makeup. But on the advice of his dresser, a black man, he begun using burnt-cork makeup. He found his act was even more enthusiastically received when he worked in blackface with white gloves. (Several of Jolson's peers, including Eddie Cantor, had a similar affinity to performing in minstrel blackface, a practice common among many vaudeville era entertainers, and a carryover from the days of minstrel shows.)

In 1909, Al Jolson became a member of Lew Dockstader's Minstrels, the most popular touring minstrel group of the day, and this even furthered his success as a singer of "dialect songs." In the spring of 1911, he made his Broadway debut playing Erastus Sparkler in *La Belle Paree*. After a good run, he headlined *Vera Violetta* in the fall. It too was a success, and in the show he sang "That Haunting Melody," which he recorded for Victor Recordings late in 1911. (It was his recording debut.) The show also featured a young Mae West. Both his Broadway shows had been at New York City's Winter Garden Theater, and there he would remain for the rest of the decade. In 1912 he starred in *The Whirl of Society* followed by *The Honeymoon Express* in 1913, both with Gaby Deslys. In *Dancing Around* (1914), he sang "It's a Long Way to Tipperary." *Robinson Crusoe, Jr.* debuted early in 1916 with Jolson as its focal point. The show provided him with two big numbers: "Where the Black-Eyed Susans Grow" and "Where Did Robinson Crusoe Go With Friday on Saturday Night?" It was during these shows that Jolson would cause a sensation by interrupting the planned proceedings and then devoting fifteen to twenty minutes singing popular songs of the day and telling the enthusiastic audience, "You ain't heard nothin' yet!"

In 1918, Jolson did his final Winter Garden show, *Sinbad*, which had a score by Sigmund Romberg, but also additional numbers, some cowritten by Jolie (as Al was called by friends) including "I'll Say She Does." However, his biggest hits in the long-running *Sinbad* were "Swanee," "Rock-a-Bye Your Baby With a Dixie Melody" (which he recorded that year along with another *Sinbad* song, "Hello Central, Give Me No Man's Land"), and "My Mammy." Jolson had begun recording with Columbia in 1913 and stayed with the label for a decade, lining up a number of best-selling records like "You Made Me Love You," "Sister Susie's Sewing Shirts for Soldiers," "Yaaka Hula Hickey Doola," "Who Played Poker with Pocahontas (When John Smith Went Away)," "Toot Toot Tootsie," and "Avalon."

The Roaring Twenties opened with Al starring in *Bombo* (1921) at his own Jolson's 59th Street Theater. This New York show lasted for over two hundred performances and featured such songs as "Who Cares?" "April Showers," and "California, Here I Come." After its Broadway run, Jolson toured with the production through 1924. In 1925 he was back on Broadway in *Big Boy*, and although it ran for only forty-eight performances, it included several noted Jolson tunes, such as "If You Knew Susie," "Hello, 'Tucky, Hello," and "Miami." The previous year, Jolson had signed with Brunswick Records. To sweeten the deal, the company had made him a member of their board of directors as well as allotting him a hefty advance on each song he recorded. The advances were so sizeable that none of his Brunswick records showed a profit for the company until he recorded "Sonny Boy" in 1928. Although Al had a number of best-sellers for Brunswick, his record sales were easily eclipsed by Nick Lucas, who was the label's top artist from 1926 to 1930.

In 1927, Al made show-business history when he starred in Warner Bros.' part-talkie feature film *The Jazz Singer*, doing songs like "My Mammy," "Blue Skies," and "Toot Toot Tootsie." Actually he had made his sound film debut earlier in the year in the short subject *Al Jolson in a Plantation Act*, which Vitaphone filmed in New York City in the fall of 1926. The short, in which he sang "April Showers," had been more or less a screen test for Jolson, who replaced George Jessel as the lead in *The Jazz Singer*. The film was based on Jolson's real life in that its story of a young Jewish boy who goes against his cantor father's will and becomes a pop singer obviously paralleled Jolson's experiences. (Jessel had balked at the studio's offer of "only" $30,000 to re-create his stage role. Eddie Cantor was the next choice, but he declined the assignment, thinking it was too identified with Jessel. Jolson accepted the part for $75,000.) *Variety* reported, "Jolson, when singing, is Jolson.

There are six instances of this, each running from two to three minutes. . . . As soon as he gets under cork the lens picks up that spark of individual personality solely identified with him."

The trendsetting *The Jazz Singer* was such a commercial sensation (earning over $3.5 million) that Jolson followed it with the even more popular ($5.5 million) *The Singing Fool* for Warner Bros. in 1928. It was another part-talkie in which he sang such ditties as "It All Depends on You," "There's a Rainbow 'Round My Shoulder," and "Sonny Boy." The latter tearjerker (sung to little Davey Lee in the movie) sold over three million copies when Al recorded it for Brunswick. In fact, Jolson's movie work revitalized his record sales, as he had several good sellers from his pictures during this period.

Jolson's first all-talkie was *Say It With Songs* (1929), and among his tunes in this overly sentimental drama (with little Davey Lee on hand again to milk audience tears) were "Little Pal," "One Sweet Kiss," and "I'm in Seventh Heaven." In the summer of 1929 Jolson had an interesting stage "return" when his second wife Ruby Keeler (he was married to Henrietta Keller from 1906 to 1911), whom he had married the previous year, starred in the Florenz Ziegfeld musical production of *Show Girl* with Nick Lucas, Clayton-Jackson-Durante, and Eddie Foy Jr. During *Show Girl*, Jolson, seated in the audience, would rise when Keeler came onstage and sing the production's chief tune, "Liza," which he also recorded for Brunswick.

In 1930, Jolie starred in two additional features for Warner Bros.: *Mammy* (he made separate trailers for both *The Singing Fool* and *Mammy* to promote the features) and *Big Boy*. By now, however, the public was used to the novelty of sound and were tiring of Jolson's sugary tearjerkers overladen with popular songs. The studio determined that the nearly $1 million dollars they paid Jolson per picture was no longer worth it. Meanwhile, the Depression was making inroads into the record industry, and after a 1930 recording session with Brunswick in which he did songs from *Mammy*, Jolson did not record again for nearly three years. His popularity, however, was still so great that in the fall of 1930 he was offered $12,000 per week to headline a vaudeville show at the Palace Theater in New York City; he declined the lavish bid.

Nevertheless, Al returned to Broadway in 1931 in *The Wonder Bar*, but it lasted for only eighty-six performances. Meanwhile, he had begun broadcasting on radio in 1929, and after guest appearances on several programs, he starred in his own half-hour series on NBC radio, from November 1932 to February 1933. In the summer of that year, he and Paul Whiteman cohosted *The Kraft Music Hall*, a one-hour musical program for NBC that ran for a year. Jolson was earning $5,000 weekly for his radio work. Also in 1933 Jolson returned to films in *Hallelujah, I'm a Bum* for United Artists (as part of an abortive long-term contract), but the innovative musical comedy was unsuccessful, mainly because all of its dialogue was in rhyme. He did record the film's title song and "You Are Too Beautiful," also from the picture, in his last session with Brunswick late in 1932. Jolson would not make another commercial recording for thirteen years.

Plans to star Jolson in a Broadway version of Dubose Hayward's novel *Porgy* did not materialize, but he did return to Warner Bros. where his wife, Ruby Keeler, was now a star thanks to her success in *42nd Street* (1932). His initial vehicle back at the studio was a picture version of *Wonder Bar* (1934). It was loaded with diverse studio talent (Kay Francis, Dick Powell, Dolores Del Rio, and Ricardo Cortez). As the owner of a chic Paris nightclub, Jolson joked, emoted, and had a big production number (in blackface), "Goin' to Heaven on a Mule." The entry was popular, and Jolson signed a film-a-year-contract with the studio, which chose to team him on-camera with Keeler in *Go Into Your Dance* (1935). The film provided Al with two more standards: "About a

Quarter to Nine" and "She's a Latin From Manhattan." However, it was too evident on-screen that Ruby's career was on the rise while his was ebbing. Ironically, the duo starred in a radio adaptation of "Burlesque" on CBS's *Lux Radio Theater* on June 15, 1936, which had a story line about a one-time headliner seeing his career fall apart while his young wife becomes a big success! Warner Bros. wanted to rematch Jolson and Keeler, but he refused, instead choosing to do *The Singing Kid* (1936). It was a rehash of all that he had done before, seemed antiquated, and even worse, was a relatively low-budget entry. The picture offered him only one good song, "Here's Looking at You." From December 1936 to December 1939, the singer starred in *The Al Jolson Show* on NBC radio with Martha Raye and Victor Young and His Orchestra. Also in 1939, Jolson and Keeler were divorced; they had one adopted child, Al Jolson Jr.

Jolson was back on-screen in 1939 with three films for Twentieth Century-Fox, but now he was no longer the top-billed star. In *Rose of Washington Square,* he was featured third behind Alice Faye and Tyrone Power, but had a good role (a variation of himself) as a vaudevillian with the opportunity to reprise "Toot Toot Tootsie," "My Mammy," and "Rock-a-Bye Your Baby With a Dixie Melody." In *Hollywood Cavalcade,* he appeared briefly as himself singing "Kol Nidre" in a recreation of the synagogue sequence from *The Jazz Singer*. Finally, he costarred with Don Ameche in a biopic of Stephen Foster called *Swanee River*, and the film may well have provided Jolson with his finest movie showcase. He played legendary minstrel man E. P. Christy and had occasion to sing a quartet of Foster favorites, "Oh! Susanna," "De Camptown Races," "My Old Kentucky Home," and "Old Folks at Home." (On April 2, 1945, Jolson repeated the Christy role on *Lux Radio Theater* with Dennis Morgan now as Stephen Foster.)

The fifty-four-year-old Jolson relaunched his Broadway career in 1940 with a good run of *Hold On to Your Hats* with Martha Raye. During the 1942–43 radio season, the star headlined *The Al Jolson Program* on CBS. During World War II, he was a tireless entertainer of Allied troops, both at home and abroad. He continued to work on radio, guesting in such series as *Soldiers in Greasepaint*, and *Philco Radio Hall of Fame*. Late in 1943, Jolson sang "Swanee" as a part of an appearance as himself in Warner Bros.' *Rhapsody in Blue*, which was finally issued in 1945. In the summer of 1945, he resumed recording when he cut old favorites "April Showers" and "Swanee" for Decca Records.

During his overseas trips to entertain troops, Jolson contracted malaria. Eventually the condition forced an operation that required the removal of most of one lung. While recuperating, he romanced a young woman named Erle Galbraith, and they were married in March 1945. (In 1948 they adopted a son, Asa Jr.) After recovering, Jolson guested on Milton Berle's radio program and then was hired to sing the songs for the soundtrack of a movie about his life called *The Jolson Story* (1946). It was made by Columbia Pictures, with Larry Parks playing Al. Jolson actually appeared in one scene of the film, a musical number ("Swanee") done in blackface with the star on bended knee on the theater's ramp way. The picture's huge success (which netted Jolson several million dollars) revitalized Al's career, and he began recording again for Decca. Several of his old standards becoming best-sellers again, in addition to new tunes like "The Anniversary Song," which he cowrote. (By 1948, the "new" Jolson was ranked the number-one singer in the United States, ahead of Frank Sinatra, Bing Crosby, Perry Como, and Frankie Laine.)

Al guest-starred on many radio programs of the time, especially the *Kraft Music Hall* with Bing Crosby. When Crosby left the NBC show in 1947, Jolson was hired to take his place. He remained with the variety show as its star until the spring of 1949. In 1949, he also did the soundtrack recording of the songs to *Jolson Sings Again* (1949), a biographical sequel to *The Jolson Story*; Larry Parks again played Al. In addition, Jolson reprised *The Jazz Singer* on *Lux Radio Theater*, and also portrayed himself when the series adapted *The Jolson Story* and *Jolson Sings Again* to radio.

Jolson's health deteriorated in the late 1940s, but in 1950 he insisted on a hectic schedule of entertaining troops in Korea and Japan in the Far East command. The tour proved too much for him and, a month after he returned home, he died of a heart attack in San Francisco on October 23, 1950. After private arrangements were made monetarily for his widow and adopted sons, the bulk of his $3 million estate was divided between Catholic, Jewish, and Protestant institutions. At the time RKO had planned to team him with Dinah Shore in a project entitled *Stars and Stripes Forever*. Said Eddie Cantor of the late star, "This great personality never learnt to live. The moment the curtain came down he died."

The star's memory has been kept alive by the International Al Jolson Society, which was formed following his death and continued to thrive in the new century. Younger generations were introduced anew to Jolson in the late 1990s when Mike Burstyn did a national tour in the title role of *Jolson*, a one-man show that drew rave reviews. In these politically correct times, however, the character of Al Jolson was not shown much in blackface.

Filmography

Al Jolson in a Plantation Act (Vita, 1926) (s)
The Jazz Singer (WB, 1927)
The Singing Fool (WB, 1928)
Sonny Boy (WB, 1929)
New York Nights (WB, 1929)
Say It With Songs (WB, 1929)
Screen Snapshots #1 (Col, 1929) (s)
Mammy (WB, 1930)
Big Boy (WB, 1930)
Screen Snapshots #20 (Col, 1930) (s)
Showgirl in Hollywood (FN, 1930)
 Hallelujah, I'm a Bum [Hallelujah, I'm a Tramp]
   (UA, 1933)
Wonder Bar (FN, 1934)
Go Into Your Dance [Casino de Paree] (FN, 1935)
Kings of the Turf (Vita, 1935) (s)

Broadway Highlights (Par, 1935) (s)
The Singing Kid (WB, 1936)
A Day at Santa Anita (Vita, 1937) (s)
Hollywood Handicap (MGM, 1938) (s)
Rose of Washington Square (20th-Fox, 1939)
Hollywood Cavalcade (20th-Fox, 1939)
Swanee River (20th-Fox, 1939)
Cavalcade of the Academy Awards (Vita, 1941) (s)
The Voice That Thrilled the World (WB, 1943) (s)
Show Business at War (20th, 1943) (s)
Rhapsody in Blue (WB, 1945)
The Jolson Story (Col, 1946)
Screen Snapshots #166 (Col, 1948) (s)
Jolson Sings Again (Col, 1949) (voice only)
Memorial to Al Jolson (Col, 1951) (s) (documen-
   tary)
The Great Al Jolson (Col, 1955) (s) (documentary)

Broadway Plays

The Children of the Ghetto (1899)*
La Belle Paree (1911)
Vera Violetta (1911)
The Whirl of Society (1912)
The Honeymoon Express (1913)
Dancing Around (1914)
Big Boy (1915)
Robinson Crusoe, Jr. (1916)

Sinbad (1918)
Bombo (1921)
The Wonder Bar (1931)
Hold On to Your Hats (1940)

*It is disputed if Jolson was actually an extra in the
   Broadway production of this show.

Radio Series

Presenting Al Jolson (NBC, 1932–33)
The Kraft Music Hall (NBC, 1933–34)
Shell Chateau (NBC, 1935–36)

The Al Jolson Show [The Lifeboy Program/Rinso
    Program/Tuesday Night Party] (CBS, 1936–39)
The Al Jolson Show (CBS, 1942–43)
The Kraft Music Hall (NBC, 1947–49)

Album Discography

LPs

Al Jolson (10″ Decca DL-5316)
Al Jolson and Steve Allen Together (Mark 56 759)
The Al Jolson Collection (Ronco 5A/5B)
Al Jolson 1885-1950 (Epitaph E-4008)
Al Jolson Onstage (Memory 2575)
Al Jolson on the Air (Sandy Hook 2003)
Al Jolson on the Air, Vols. 1-5 (Totem 1006, 1012,
    1019, 1030, 1040)
Al Jolson Overseas (Decca DL-9070)
Al Jolson With Oscar Levant (Decca Dl-9095)
Al Jolson's Scrapbook of Memories (Gemini 1001)
Among My Souvenirs (Decca DL-9050, MCA
    2064)
The Best of Al Jolson (Decca DX-169/DXS-7169,
    MCA 1000)
The Big Broadcast of 1935 (Kasha King 1935)
    [St/R]
Bing and Al, Vols. 1-6 (Totem 1003, 1007, 1013,
    1015, 1016, 1017) w. Bing Crosby
Bing Crosby and Al Jolson Duets (Amalgamated
    0003)
Broadway Al (Totem 1010)
Brunswick Rarities (MCA 1560)
Burlesque (Star-Tone 505) [ST/R]
California, Here I Come (Sunbeam 505)
The Early Years (Olympic 7114, Kaola 14126)
An Evening With Al Jolson (ASA 1)
The Famous Al Jolson Show (Memorabilia 701)
The Films of Al Jolson (Golden Legends 2) [SDT]
Go Into Your Dance/Wonder Bar (Golden Legend
    200012, Hollywood Soundstage 402, Sandy
    Hook 2030) [ST]
The Greatest of Al Jolson (Columbia Special Prod-
    ucts PD-12668, Telehouse 12070)
The Immortal Al Jolson (Decca DL-9063, MCA
    2066)
Immortals—Jolson and Cantor (10″ Epic LN-
    1128) w. Eddie Cantor
In the Heart of New York/Say It With Songs
    (Subon 1234) [ST]
The Jazz Singer (Sountrak 102) [ST]
The Jazz Singer (Pelican 125, Radiola 1070) [ST/R]
Jolie (Decca DL-9099)
Jolie and Ginger Live (Elgog 887) w. Ginger
    Rogers

Jolie Live in '35 (Amalgamated 124, Sandy Hook
    2079)
Jolson Rehearses, Reminisces and Rambulates
    (Quango 126)
Jolson Sings (Silver Eagle 1014)
Jolson Sings Again (10″ Decca DL-5006)
Jolson Sings Again (Pelican 145) [ST/R]
The Jolson Story (Pelican 129) [ST/R]
The Jolson Story—Outtakes and Alternate Takes
    (Take Two TT-103) [ST]
A Legend Named Jolson (Show Biz 1011)
The Legendary Al Jolson (Col P15530, Murray Hill
    15528)
The Legends of Al Jolson, Jimmy Durante & Eddie
    Cantor (Ambassador Artists 1003-3)
Let Me Sing and I'm Happy (Ace of Hearts 33)
Mammy (Amalgamated 223) [ST]
The Magnificent Al Jolson (Windmill 273)
The Man and the Legend, Vols. 1-4 (Rhapsody
    1-4)
Memories (Decca DL-9038, MCA 2061)
Old Favorites (10″ Decca DL-5080)
Radio Broadcast Follies of 1935 (Amalgamated
    252) [ST/R]
Radio Rarities—You Ain't Heard Nothin' Yet (Ra-
    diola 3MR1-2)
Rainbow 'Round My Shoulder (Decca DL-9036,
    MCA 2059)
Rock-a-Bye Your Baby (Decca DL-9035, MCA
    2058)
Rose of Washington Square (Caliban 60023) [ST]
Say It With Songs (Ace of Hearts 87)
The Singing Fool (Take Two TT-106, Sandy Hook
    2107) [ST]
The Singing Kid (Caliban 6013) [ST]
Sitting on Top of the World (Vocalion 3)
Songs He Made Famous (10″ Decca DL-5026)
Souvenir Album, Vols. 1-6 (10″ Decca DL-5028/
    31, 5314/15)
Stephen Foster Songs (10″ Decca DL-5308)
Steppin' Out (Sunbeam 503)
Swanee River (Totem 1028) [ST/R]
A Tribute to Al Jolson (Audio Rarities 2285)
The Vintage Jolson (Pelican 111)

The Vitaphone Years (A-Jay 3749)

The World's Great Entertainer (Music for Pleasure 5813)

The World's Greatest Entertainer (Decca DL-9074, MCA 1734, MCA 2067)

The World's Greatest Entertainer—The Jazz Singer (Halycon 102)

You Ain't Heard Nothin' Yet (ASV 5038)

You Ain't Heard Nothin' Yet (Decca DL-9037, MCA 1808, MCA 2060)

You Made Me Love You (Decca DL-9034, MCA 2057)

CDs

Al Jolson (CBS 300)

Al Jolson (Intersound 3554)

Al Jolson—Live! (Onstage 6001)

Al Jolson 1911-48 (Sounds of a Century 1828)

Al Jolson on Broadway (Intersound 3592)

Al Jolson on the Silver Screen (Sandy Hook SH-2030)

April Showers (Golden Options 3813)

April Showers (Memories of Yesteryears SAM-BACD-5060)

The Best of Al Jolson (Going for a Song—no number)

The Best of Al Jolson (Half Moon HMNCD-004)

The Best of Al Jolson (Polygram HMNCD-4)

The Best of the Decca Years (MCA CRP-10505)

Best of the War Years (Stardust 759)

Black & White (Magnum Collectors 28)

Bullets Over Broadway (Sony Classical SK-66822) [ST]

California, Here I Come (Movie Stars 008)

Cantor Meets Jolson (Original Cast 9753) w. Eddie Cantor

Coast to Coast (Crystal Stream Audio IDCD-SPEC13)

Cocktail Hour (Columbia River Entertainment CRG-218034)

Complete Recordings, Vol. 1 (Naxos Nostalgia NX-8.120514)

Duets (Original Cast 8722)

First Choice: Best of Al Jolson (Intersound 4625)

For Me & My Gal (Classic World Productions 9995)

From Broadway to Hollywood (Pearl Flapper PAST-CD-7045)

The Great Al Jolson (BCD GLD-3103)

The Greatest Entertainer of All Time (FMCG FMC018)

Greatest Hits (Tring International GRF081)

Guest Starring Al Jolson (Crystal Stream Audio ID-CDSPEC12)

Hits (Public Music 9013)

The Jazz Singer 1924-32 (Halcyon 102)

The Jazz Singer (Radiola CDMR-1080) [ST/Radio]

The Jolson Story (Great Movie Themes 60021) [ST]

The Jolson Story (MCA MCAD-27052, Universal Special Markets 27052)

King of the Airwaves (Memories of Yesteryears MTLCD-5061)

Let Me Sing and I'm Happy (Golden Stars 5108)

Let Me Sing and I'm Happy (Parrot 004) w. Bing Crosby

Let Me Sing and I'm Happy (Turner Classic Movies/Rhino R2-72544)

Mammy (ProArte CDD-436)

Memories of a Legend (Legacy Entertainment 043)

My Greatest Hits (Universal 1183502)

Original Records of Al Jolson (Intersound 3554)

A Portrait of Al Jolson (Gallerie 542)

Rainbow 'Round My Shoulder (MCA MCAD-27053, Universal Special Markets 27053)

Rhapsody in Blue (Great Movie Themes 60028) [ST]

Rose of Washington Square (Varese Sarabande 302-066-009-2) [ST]

Rose of Washington Square/The Dolly Sisters/Gold Diggers of 1933 (Great Movie Themes 60009) [ST]

The Salesman of Song 1911-23 (Pearl PAST-CD-9796)

The Singing Fool (Promo Sound)

Snap Your Fingers (Columbia River Entertainment Group CRG-120015)

Sonny Boy (BCD GSS-5162)

Sonny Boy (Pilz Entertainment 449338-2)

Stage Highlights (Pearl Flapper PAST-CD-9748)

30 Great Hits (The Entertainers 276)

The Twenties: Broadway to Hollywood (Flapper PAST-CD-7045)

22 Greatest Hits (Masters 502532)

The Very Best of Al Jolson (Prism PLATCD-30)

Wonder Bar/Go Into Your Dance (Hollywood Soundstage HS-402) [ST]

The World's Greatest Entertainer: Al Jolson—The Jazz Singer (Halcyon 102)

The World's Greatest Entertainer (Nimbus 2009)

You Ain't Heard Nothin' Yet (ASV CD-AJA-5038)

You Ain't Heard Nothin' Yet: Jolie's Finest Columbia Recordings (Legacy CK-53419)

You Can't Have Everything/Go Into Your Dance/You'll Never Get Rich (Great Movie Themes 60014) [ST]

You Made Me Love You: His First Recordings (Stash ST-CD-564)

Allan Jones, Walter Connolly, and Mary Martin in *The Great Victor Herbert* (1939).
[Courtesy of JC Archives]

Allan Jones

(b. near Scranton, Pennsylvania, October 14, 1907; d. New York City, June 27, 1992)

A handsome tenor, Allan Jones carved for himself a well-etched career onstage, in films, and in the recording field, as well as on radio. While many knew him in later years as the father of popular singer Jack Jones, Allan Jones was a multitalented performer whom the great composer Rudolf Friml considered to be his favorite singer. (Frank Sinatra labeled Jones "a singer's singer.") Of course, it was Jones's rendering of Friml's "The Donkey Serenade" that provided Allan with his biggest record success, and for many years, it was the third best-selling record in RCA Victor's catalog. Longevity was the key in keeping Jones before the public in assorted media during his six decades of professional career.

Of Welsh ancestry, Allan Jones was born near Scranton, Pennsylvania, on October 14, 1907, the son of a coal mine foreman. The boy learned to sing at an early age and did his first public singing in church. When he was sixteen, he joined Philadelphia's National Welsh Eisteddfod at the Academy of Music. During high school, Jones worked at odd jobs to earn money, and when he graduated from high school he worked as a coal miner to save enough money to study music. In 1926, he obtained a scholarship from Syracuse University, but soon left and enrolled at New York University to study voice with Claude Warford. There Jones was soloist with the University Glee Club, and he also performed solos at the University Heights Presbyterian Church (which helped to keep him going financially). Going to Paris with Warford for further study, Jones took up the study of opera with Felix Leroux of the French National Opera, and then he moved to London to study oratorio singing with noted British conductor Sir Henry Wood. Returning to the United States in 1927, Allan worked as a professional singer. During this time he became acquainted with famous opera singer Dame Nellie Melba, who became something of a mentor to the young talent.

Allan continued to study and perform, and in 1929 he wed Marjorie Buel, his teenage sweetheart. They had a son, Theodore, but the marriage was short-lived, and when they went their separate ways she took their son with her. Late in the year, Jones returned to Paris and, the next year, sang with the Cannes Opera Company. The year 1931 found him back in the United States performing at Carnegie Hall with the New York Symphony and Philharmonic Orchestras directed by Walter Damrosch. Later in the year, Jones debuted on Broadway in *Boccaccio*, and the next summer he performed in operettas with the St. Louis Municipal Opera Company. In 1933, the handsome performer toured for the Shuberts in *Blossom Time*, *The Only Girl*, and *The Student Prince*. For the same theatrical producers, he did a tour of *Bitter Sweet*, and in the spring of 1934 he starred in the production on Broadway. The Shuberts, who had him firmly under contract, put Jones in as star in the Friml operetta *Annina* on the road, and this was followed by an aborted presentation of *America Sings*, which played in Boston but never opened on Broadway due to a stagehand strike.

By now, MGM talent scouts from Hollywood had spotted Allan Jones. It required a great deal of negotiation with the Shuberts to get him out of his long-term stage commitment. Metro-Goldwyn-Mayer had planned originally to star Jones with Jeanette MacDonald in *Naughty Marietta*, but by the time he could sever his relationship with the Shuberts, the studio had opted to match her with Nelson Eddy. Thus Jones made his delayed movie debut in *Reckless* (1935), a Jean Harlow vehicle in which he sang "Everything's Been Done Before." He was the hero in the Marx Brothers *A Night at the Opera* (1935), and in it he sang "Alone" and "Cosi Cosa," two songs associated closely with his career. In 1936, Jones supported Jeanette MacDonald and Nelson Eddy in the expansive *Rose-Marie*, in which he played opera singer Jeanette's stage costar. Together they performed the death scene from Charles Gounod's opera *Romeo and Juliet*. Much of Jones's footage, however, ended up on the cutting room floor. Rumor had it that this dumping was due to the insistence of the firmly entrenched Nelson Eddy, who did not relish competition from his fine-looking rival. Jones also dubbed Dennis Morgan singing "A Pretty Girl Is Like a Melody" in *The Great Ziegfeld* (1936), and he can be spotted doing a brief song in a crowd sequence in Twentieth Century-Fox's *Ramona* (1936).

Allan's greatest movie success came in 1936, when he was loaned to Universal to costar with Irene Dunne in the expensively produced remake of *Show Boat*. In it, he and Dunne dueted on "Make Believe" and "You Are Love," plus a new song for the production, "I Have the Room Above." (On June 24, 1940, Jones and Dunne re-created their role for CBS's *Lux Radio Theater of the Air* production of the Jerome Kern–Oscar Hammerstein II musical.) On June 26, 1936, Allan wed actress Irene Hervey, and two years later, they had a son, John Allan Jones, who grew up to be pop singer Jack Jones.

Now at the height of his screen popularity, Allan returned to MGM as costar with the Marx Brothers in *A Day at the Races* (1937), and then Metro, wanting to test Jeanette MacDonald's appeal away from Nelson Eddy, paired Jones with her in *The Firefly* (1937). This well-mounted operetta produced his most popular song, Friml's "The Donkey Serenade." On January 13, 1938 (the day before the birth of his son), Jones recorded "The Donkey Serenade" and "Giannina Mia" from *The Firefly* for Victor Records, and the disc sold over three million copies. The same day he also did "The One I Love" and "Cosi Cosa" for the company, two songs he sang in his final MGM starrer, *Everybody Sing* (1938), which also featured Judy Garland and Fanny Brice.

By now strong-willed Allan Jones, who refused to be a docile contract player waiting for his screen break to happen at the studio, was feuding with MGM's chieftain Louis B. Mayer, who favored the already-established Nelson Eddy in assigning lead roles in music. As a result, Jones was forced to sit out the rest of his studio contract. However, he was allowed to host *The Metro–Maxwell House Radio Hour* on NBC, and he continued to make lucrative personal appearances. When his MGM contract expired, Jones went to Paramount to headline *The Great Victor Herbert* (1939), a plodding musical biography that costarred Mary Martin. At least the picture provided him an opportunity to sing "Sweethearts," "Someday," "Thine Alone," and "I'm Falling in Love With Someone" (all of which he recorded for Victor), but he was overshadowed on-screen by Walter Connolly in the title role. For the same studio, Jones appeared in support of Madeleine Carroll and Fred MacMurray in *Honeymoon in Bali* (1939), a vapid comedy that afforded him the occasion to sing the famed tenor aria "O Paradiso" from the opera *L'Africaine* by Giacomo Meyerbeer.

In 1940, being professionally at loose ends, Allan Jones signed a contract with lesser Universal Pictures. During the next half-dozen years, he starred in ten features for this production-line studio, along with two loanouts to Paramount. (Ironically, during this period Nelson Eddy starred at MGM in *Bittersweet* [1940], *The New Moon* [1940], and *The Chocolate Soldier* [1941]—*all* of which Jones had starred in onstage.) Jones's Universal tenure began with *The Boys From Syracuse* (1940), which costarred his wife Irene Hervey. In the picture, Jones sang "Falling in Love With Love" and "Who Are You?" both of which he recorded for the Victor label. Next, he again supported a comedy team, this time Bud Abbott and Lou Costello, who were making their screen debut in *One Night in the Tropics* (1940). The low-budget picture gave Jones the opportunity to sing "Remind Me," but little else of distinction. Allan returned to Paramount to costar with Susanna Foster (who had made her screen debut in *The Great Victor Herbert*) in *The Hard Boiled Canary* [aka: *There's Magic in Music*], a comedy about a burlesque performer becoming an opera star. He stayed at that studio for *True to the Army* (1942), where he played second fiddle to Judy Canova (as a backwoods girl on the run from gangsters) and Ann Miller's hoofing.

By now World War II was in progress, and Allan Jones became the first Hollywood entertainer to volunteer to perform for service personnel, and he also cut a number of V-Discs, which were designed for military entertainment use. Back at Universal, he starred with Jane Frazee in the quickie *Moonlight in Havana* (1942) as a baseball player who tries for a singing career. He and Jane Frazee were matched with Gloria Jean and Donald O'Connor for *When Johnny Comes Marching Home* (1942), a drama that featured Phil Spitalny and His All-Girl Orchestra and the Four Step Brothers. The programmer *Rhythm of the Islands* (1943) found Jones and rotund Andy Devine attempting to start a resort on a tropical isle, but the picture's sole tune, "I've Set My Mind Up to It," went to Jane Frazee. Meanwhile, with MGM's comedic songstress, Virginia O'Brien, Jones performed in a war-bond drive at New York City's Capitol Theater in 1943. (Allan was also an active volunteer at the Hollywood Canteen during the war.).

Jones did get to sing a trio of songs in *Larceny With Music* (1943) as a singer masquerading as the heir to an estate. The low-budget entry featured Kitty Carlisle (who had costarred with Allan in *A Night at the Opera*), as well as Alvino Rey and His Orchestra and the King Sisters. This was followed by *You're a Nice Fellow, Mr. Smith* (1943) with Jones as a GI who marries a young woman (Evelyn Ankers) so she can gain an inheritance. He rounded out the year with a guest cameo in *Crazy House*, featuring the studio's zany comedy team of Olsen and Johnson.

Jones's solo 1944 feature was *Sing a Jingle*, in which he was a vocalist who goes to work in a manufacturing plant as his contribution to the war effort. Meanwhile, that year he returned to network radio starring in *The Allan Jones Show* on CBS, and for the same network he and Woody Herman alternated as stars of *The Old Gold Show*. Allan also guest-starred on such series as *The Radio Hall of Fame* and *Music America Loves Best*. Back at Universal, the star headlined *Honeymoon Ahead* (1945) in which he was a paroled convict singing "Time Will Tell and "Now and Always." He closed out his studio contract with *The Senorita From the West* (1945) about a girl (Bonita Granville) who wants to be a singer and who becomes involved with Jones, who dubs the radio voice of a noted crooner.

When not making motion pictures, Allan Jones joined with Benny Baker, Nanette Fabray, Betty Garrett, and Mary Wickes in the 1944 musical comedy *Jackpot*, which did better business on the road than on Broadway. After the war, Jones had a successful two-year tour of Great Britain, even giving command performances for King George VI and Queen Elizabeth II (who succeeded King George in 1952). Back in the States in 1947, he and Irene Hervey toured in the drama *State of the Union*. When its run was over, Jones worked in vaudeville and then joined Ed Wynn's *Laugh*

Carnival, a pre-Broadway show that never made it to the Great White Way. (Jones sang "The Donkey Serenade," "This Is the Moment," "Begin the Beguine," and the famed tenor aria, "Vesti la Giubba," from Ruggero Leoncavallo's opera *Pagliaci*.)

In the early 1950s, Allan Jones filmed eleven three-minute songfests for television, produced by Snader Telescriptions. Included was his signature tune, "The Donkey Serenade," along with such items as "Questa o Quella" from Giuseppe Verdi's *Rigoletto*. He also did popular numbers like "All My Love," "The World Is Mine Tonight," and "Over and Over and Over." Thereafter, to keep busy professionally, he toured in such road shows as *Guys and Dolls* (in which he played Sky Masterson). His reviews were glowing, but Hollywood was no longer interested in the middle-aged performer. In 1957, Jones and Irene Hervey divorced, and he soon wed Mary Florsheim Picking; but they parted in 1964. In the meantime, by the end of the 1950s, Allan's son Jack was beginning his own singing career, and father and son did some nightclub work together. They would, on occasion, reteam well into the 1980s. (In April 1989, Jack Jones got a star on the Hollywood Walk of Fame right next to his dad's.)

During the early 1960s, Allan Jones relaxed his show-business activities, but as the decade progressed he was still making personal appearances. In 1962 he recorded his first long-playing album (Victor had reissued his earlier recordings on LPs) called *Allan Jones Sings Only the Greatest* for the Star label. He also resumed his screen career with character roles. He was the corrupt mayor in Paramount's quickie Western *Stage to Thunder Rock* (1964) and a businessman on a holiday in *A Swingin' Summer* (1965). He began doing summer theater work in plays like *How to Succeed in Business Without Really Trying* in 1966, and that year found him in heavy demand for nightclub appearances. In the fall of 1967, the *New York Post* reported the singer had "only 12 days free in the next 12 months."

Regarding his performance at Manhattan's The Living Room at the time, *Variety* noted, "Jones still suggests the robustness and vigor of his voice. There is sufficient power to go the whole route and he does a full turn, asks no quarter and gives out in the best tradition. . . . He does not work as a period piece, but as an entertainer recalling a treasured era, who also gives out with tunes for moderns as well." In 1967, the singer cut another album, the best-selling *Allan Jones Sings for a Man and a Woman* on Scepter Records, and he continued to appear in such varied stage productions as *Silk Stockings*, *The Happy Time*, *The Fantasticks*, and *Paint Your Wagon*. When Merv Griffin presented a TV tribute to Rudolf Friml in 1968, Jones appeared and sang several Friml melodies, and on the show the composer reaffirmed that Jones was his favorite singer.

In 1971, Jones undertook the role in which he gave his best work, that of the aged Don Quixote in the musical *Man of La Mancha*, a show he would do on and off for the next decade. He also did other productions like *The Big Show of 1936* (a pre-Broadway nostalgia revue that closed in Philadelphia) and *110 in the Shade*. He guest-starred on such TV programs as *The Steve Allen Show*, *Over Easy*, *The Mike Douglas Show*, and *The Love Boat*, the latter in an episode with son Jack (who sang the program's title song). Allan also worked the lecture-tour circuit successfully, as noted by the *Indianapolis Star* review of his October 1972 performance at Clowes Hall: "With a voice strong and steady enough to belie his age by many years, he sang well-remembered melodies from both his pre- and post-retirement days, enchanting audiences with sidelight stories between numbers." In 1976, Jones starred at New York City's Town Hall as well as continuing his tours of *Man of La Mancha*.

During the 1970s, Jones also found domestic happiness in his marriage to dancer Maria Villavincie, who was many years his junior. In 1971, Jones narrated the Sherpix documentary *Sub Rosa Rising*, and in 1978 (with soprano Patti Stevens) he recorded the album *Allan Jones Sings Friml Favorites*, which was issued by Glendale Records in 1982. "That Allan Jones recorded the Friml 'gems' on disk well into the fifth decade of his career speaks volumes, not only for the lyric beauty and purity of his tenor voice, but as well for the remarkable soundness of his vocal technique," wrote Fred Tyatt on the album's liner notes. Allan Jones remained active into the early 1990s, completing a successful concert tour of Australia just a few weeks prior to his death from lung cancer on June 27, 1992, at Lenox Hill Hospital in New York City.

Filmography

Reckless (MGM, 1935)
A Night at the Opera (MGM, 1935)
The Great Ziegfeld (MGM, 1936) (voice only)
Rose-Marie (MGM, 1936)
Ramona (20th-Fox, 1936)
Show Boat (Univ, 1936)
Lest We Forget (WB, 1936) (s)
A Day at the Races (MGM, 1937)
Cinema Circus (MGM, 1937) (s)
The Firefly (MGM, 1937)
Everybody Sing (MGM, 1938)
Honeymoon in Bali [Husbands or Lovers] (Par, 1939)
The Great Victor Herbert (Par, 1939)
Hollywood Hobbies (MGM, 1939) (s)
The Boys From Syracuse (Univ, 1940)

One Night in the Tropics (Univ, 1940)
The Hard-Boiled Canary [There's Magic in Music] (Par, 1941)
Moonlight in Havana (Univ, 1942)
True to the Army (Par, 1942)
When Johnny Comes Marching Home (Univ, 1942)
You're a Lucky Fellow, Mr. Smith (Univ, 1943)
Rhythm of the Islands (Univ, 1943)
Larceny With Music (Univ, 1943)
Crazy House (Univ, 1943)
Sing a Jingle [Lucky Days] (Univ, 1944)
Honeymoon Ahead (Univ, 1945)
The Senorita From the West (Univ, 1945)
Stage to Thunder Rock (Par, 1964)
A Swingin' Summer (United Screen Arts, 1965)
Sub Rosa Rising (Sherpix, 1971) (narrator)

Broadway Plays

Boccaccio (1932)
Bitter Sweet (1934)

The Chocolate Soldier (1942) (revival)
Jackpot (1944)

Radio Series

The Metro-Maxwell House Hour (NBC, 1937)

The Allan Jones Show (The Old Gold Show) CBS, 1944)

Album Discography

LPs

Allan Jones Sings for a Man and a Woman (Scepter 566)
Allan Jones Sings Friml Favorites (Glendale GL-9004) w. Patti Stevens
Allan Jones Sings Only the Greatest (Star 1253)
Allan Jones Sings Show Tunes (Camden (CAL-268)

The Best of Allan Jones (RCA International 90065)
The Donkey Serenade (Camden CAL/CAS-2256)
Everybody Sings (Amalgamated 231) [ST]
Falling in Love (10″ RCA LM-95)
The Firefly (Caliban 6027) [ST]
The Firefly (10″ RCA LM-121)

The Great Ziegfeld (CIF 3005) [ST]
It's a Grand Night for Singing (Westwood 505)
Night and Day (RCA LM-1140)
One Night Stand With Woody Herman—Allan
    Jones (Joyce 1037)
Rose-Marie (Hollywood Soundstage 414) [ST]
Showboat (Sunbeam 501) [ST/R]

Showboat (Vertinge 2004) [ST]
Showboat (Xeno 251) [ST]
That's Entertainment! (MCA MCA2-11002) [ST]
    (uncredited)
Victor Herbert—Beyond the Blue Horizon (Cali-
    ban 6033) [ST]

CDs

Allan Jones (Music & Memories MMD-1142)
The Donkey Serenade (ASV CD-AJA-5348)
A Night at the Opera (PCI 33502) [ST]
A Night at the Opera/Animal Crackers/At the Cir-
    cus/Room Service (Sound Track Factory
    SFCD33502) [ST]

On the Air (Collectors' Choice Music CCM-1025)
There's a Song in the Air (Jasmine JASCD-110)
The Ultimate Show Boat (Pavilion GEMS-0060)
    [ST]
The Wonderful Voice of Allan Jones (Broadway
    BRCD-133)

Shirley Jones

(Shirley Mae Jones, b. Smithton, Pennsylvania, March 31, 1934)

When Shirley Jones made her screen debut in *Oklahoma!* in 1955, Bosley Crowther in the *New York Times* enthused that she was "so full of beauty, sweetness and spirit that a better Laurey cannot be dreamed." Thus, at twenty-one, Jones found movie stardom. Although her ingénue period in films was brief, the lovely actress not only developed into a seasoned dramatic performer, but she also found success on the musical stage and television. In addition, she had a successful club act with her first husband, Jack Cassidy, and later carved out a new career for herself when she and her stepson, David Cassidy, starred in the popular early 1970s TV sitcom *The Partridge Family*. Throughout her movie career, both on film and TV, Shirley Jones managed to score well in a variety of parts that demonstrated her acting range. In the 1970s, she branched out into assorted show-business activities with her second husband, Marty Ingels, although in middle age religion played an increasingly important role in her life.

The future star was named for Shirley Temple. She was born on March 31, 1934, in Smithton, Pennsylvania, the only child of brewery owner Paul Jones and his wife Marjorie. Shirley had a natural knack for singing that she developed while still very young. By the age of five, she was performing solos at her local Methodist Church. Later she studied voice with Pittsburgh vocal coach Ken Welch. After graduating from South Huntingdon High School in 1952 (as a student she had acted in school plays and had won a stage singing contest), the buxom Shirley won the Miss Pittsburgh contest and placed second for Miss Pennsylvania. She then studied drama at the Pittsburgh Playhouse and made her professional stage debut in *Lady in the Dark* at the Pittsburgh Civic Opera Company, followed by *Call Me Madam*.

In the summer of 1953, Shirley vacationed in New York City, and while there, Ken Welch arranged for her to audition for theatrical agent Gus Schirmer. He was so impressed with her that he, in turn, arranged for her to audition with one of Richard Rodgers–Oscar Hammerstein II's casting directors. That director took her directly to the composers, who signed her to a seven-year contract, thus canceling Shirley's plans to attend Centenary Junior College in Hackettstown, New Jersey. Given vocal and acting lessons, she was placed in the naval nurse chorus of the long-running *South Pacific* on Broadway and then was given a small role in *Me and Juliet*. When that Rodgers–Hammerstein II show went on tour, Shirley assumed the starring role.

In 1954, Shirley went to Hollywood to screen test for Laurey in Rodgers and Hammerstein II's film version of *Oklahoma!* (1955). She made her film debut in the coveted part of the pretty farm girl romanced by a handsome rancher (Gordon MacRae). In it she sang "Many a New Day" and "Out of My Dreams" and dueted with MacRae on "The Surrey With the Fringe on Top" and "People Will Say We're in Love." *Variety* endorsed, "This is Miss Jones's first picture, and it is sure to make her a much sought-after star almost overnight."

Shirley Jones in *The Music Man* (1962).
[Courtesy of JC Archives]

It was logical that this wholesome beauty would be cast in the screen adaptation of Rodgers and Hammerstein II's *Carousel* (1956). When Frank Sinatra walked off the production, Gordon MacRae was brought in to portray the self-centered carnival barker, Billy Bigelow, with whom innocent factory worker Julie Jordan (Jones) falls in love. Shirley sang "What's the Use of Wonderin'," "You'll Never Walk Alone," and dueted with MacRae on "If I Loved You." Following the making of *Carousel*, Shirley performed *Oklahoma!* in Paris and Rome on a goodwill tour for the U.S. Department of State. Back home she was a guest on CBS-TV's *Person to Person* and then went to Cambridge, Massachusetts, to appear in *The Beggar's Opera*. There she met actor-singer Jack Cassidy, whom she married on August 5, 1956. That November, she appeared as an alcoholic in "The Big Slide" episode of CBS-TV's *Playhouse 90* opposite Red Skelton and on February 19, 1957, was on that network's *U.S. Steel Hour*.

For her third film, shapely Shirley portrayed a farm girl who helps a juvenile delinquent (Pat Boone) reform as he becomes a silky driver on the racetrack in *April Love* (1957) for Twentieth Century-Fox. In the feature, Shirley soloed on "Give Me a Gentle Girl," and sang the title song, "Do It Yourself" and "The Bentonville Fair" with Boone. By now Shirley was becoming bored with her pristine screen image, and following the birth (September 27, 1958) of her son, Shaun (who later became a TV and singing star in the 1970s), Shirley and her husband undertook a successful nightclub tour. They had worked together the previous spring in stock, while Shirley alone had appeared in the CBS-TV production of *The Red Mill* in 1958. Shirley and Cassidy also cut two LP albums for Columbia, *Speaking of Love* and *With Love From Hollywood*, performing show tunes. In 1958, also for Columbia Records, the couple made a studio cast version of *Brigadoon*. After appearing with James Cagney in the labor union exposé *Never Steal Anything Small* (1959), an oddball musical comedy/drama, she went to England to costar with Max Bygraves as the parents of a talking baby in *Bobbikins* (1960).

In post–studio system Hollywood, it was up to performers and their agents to shape careers. Shirley chose to do a complete about-face when she played the young woman who turns to prostitution after being violated by an evangelist (Burt Lancaster) in *Elmer Gantry* (1960). For her turnabout performance, she won the Best Supporting Actress Academy Award. After that, however, she did a summer stock tour of *Oklahoma!* and then provided a guest cameo as a far-out actress in *Pepe* (1960). Following her work in the John Ford Western *Two Rode Together* (1961), Shirley returned to the musical for the last time when she was seen as Marian, the small-town librarian who finds love with a charming con man (Robert Preston) in *The Music Man* (1962). In it she did full justice to the haunting "Till There Was You," along with "Goodnight My Someone," "Being in Love," and in her reprise duet with Preston on "Goodnight My Someone."

After the highly profitable *The Music Man*, Shirley Jones continued to work in a variety of mediums, but the success she had enjoyed in her earlier movies would not be repeated. In 1962 her TV pilot, *For the Love of Mike*, failed to sell as a CBS-TV series. She continued to make pictures, but none of them were outstanding. By the middle of the 1960s, she was no longer considered a major film name. In 1968, Shirley and Jack Cassidy appeared on Broadway in a period musical *Maggie Flynn*, which had a modest run, and in 1969 she starred in the first of her several made-for-television movies, *Silent Night, Lonely Night*. For this drama about two lonely souls (Shirley, Lloyd Bridges) who find love at a remote resort, she was nominated for an Emmy Award.

In the fall of 1970, Shirley starred in the ABC-TV series *The Partridge Family* as Connie Partridge, a spunky widowed mother who forms a singing act with her children (David Cassidy, Susan Dey, Danny Bonaduce, Jeremy Gelbwaks [later replaced by Brian Foster], and Suzanne

Crough), and they become a hot act. The comedy, based on the real-life group the Cowsills, became a huge success that ran for four seasons. In addition, *The Partridge Family* group had several successful single records and albums on the Bell label. Their 1970 single of "I Think I Love You" sold over four million copies and was followed by best-sellers like "Doesn't Somebody Want to Be Wanted" and "Looking Through the Eyes of Love." The act also had nine charted albums for Bell between 1970 and 1973 with their first LP, *The Partridge Family Album*, having impressive sales for over seventy weeks. Moreover, *The Partridge Family* series was the subject of a massive merchandising campaign, which extended from books to toys. The show, which briefly made a teenage idol of Shirley's stepson, David Cassidy, ran its course and left the network in the summer of 1974. For the public, Shirley was again "Miss Wholesomeness."

In the mid-1970s, Shirley and Jack Cassidy were divorced. (He died in a fire on December 12, 1976.) In 1977, she married comic-actor-agent Marty Ingels, and they became involved in an assortment of business projects including a lucrative talent bureau. During the mid-to-late 1970s, Shirley appeared in more TV movies. In 1979, she returned to the big screen for the first time since playing a madam in the Western *The Cheyenne Social Club* (1970). The new project, *Beyond the Poseidon Adventure* (1979), was a tepid disaster genre picture.

Jones attempted a new teleseries with *Shirley* (NBC-TV), but the comedy lasted only three months in the 1979–80 season. Two years later, she appeared on the CBS-TV pilot *The Adventures of Pollyanna*, but that failed to sell, and the following year she was in the pilot for the ABC-TV series *Hotel* (which did sell, but she was not on the program again until she made a guest appearance early in 1987). She returned to feature films in *Tanks* (1984) opposite James Garner, and the next year starred in the poignant PBS-TV special on Alzheimer's disease, *There Were Times, Dear*. In the early-to-mid-1980s, Shirley was a TV and print media spokesperson for the West Coast chain of Ralph's Supermarkets. In 1988 she had the running role of love-starved grandmother Kitty Noland in the ABC-TV comedy series *The "Slap" Maxwell Story*.

The year 1988 was extremely productive for Jones as she and Marty Ingels guest-starred on Oprah Winfrey's TV talk show and Shirley was named Woman of the Year by Childhelp USA. She and Marty were also awarded the National Leukemia Council's first Gift of Life Award for their fifteen years of volunteer work in fighting the disease. In August, she closed the thirty-fourth Republican National Convention in New Orleans by singing "America the Beautiful," and she also took part in the PBS-TV special *In Performance at the White House* by singing "If I Loved You" and "You'll Never Walk Alone" from *Carousel*. She closed the auspicious year by cohosting a TV special, *Christmas in DC,* with opera singer Kathleen Battle. She opened 1989 by singing at the Inaugural Ball at the request of President George Bush. That year, she coauthored with her husband Marty Ingels and Mickey Herskowitz the book *Shirley & Marty: An Unlikely Love Story*. She also signed a pact with Diadem Records to record gospel music and undertook a sixteen-week tour of *The King and I* with David Carradine. In addition, in this period, Jones had two how-to home videos in the marketplace. Moreover, energetic Shirley also made a pilot (*Sister Kate*) for a new TV situation comedy series, in which she would have starred as the owner of a bail-bond business; the project did not sell. Meanwhile, she continued to make guest appearances on others' TV shows, including the revived *Burke's Law* (1994–95).

By the mid-1990s Shirley's marriage to Ingels was an off-and-on situation and became fodder for the supermarket tabloids. (Ironically in fall 1995 the couple took over the leads in a Los Angeles production of the play *Love Letters*.) The next year Jones hosted a TV special entitled *Rodgers and Hammerstein: The Sound of Movies*. Sporadically she appeared in TV movies (1997's *Dog's Best

Friend) and made occasional independent features that often verged on the ridiculous (2000's *Shriek If You Know What I Did Last Friday the 13th*). In April 1998, the Oscar winner received the Harvey Award, presented by Jimmy Stewart's hometown of Indiana, Pennsylvania; she had costarred twice with the late star on the big screen. Later that year, Shirley made one of several amusing appearances on the sitcom *The Drew Carey Show*, cast as his mature girlfriend. (In real life, Jones was twenty-seven-years older than the stand-up comic.)

Also in fall 1998, Shirley had a guest role on the television nighttime drama *Melrose Place*. Her appearance on that series raised eyebrows because Jones was then the honorary chairperson of the Parents Television Council Media watchdog group, which had just listed *Melrose Place* on its "Dirty Dozen" roster. When ABC-TV presented its two-hour feature (*Come On, Get Happy: The Partridge Family Story*) on November 13, 1999, this behind-the-scenes fiction cast Eve Gordon as Shirley during the period she starred as the head of the singing Partridge clan. That same fall Shirley appeared as Melissa Joan Hart's grandmother on an episode of *Sabrina, The Teenage Witch* (ABC-TV), which was reported to become a recurring role, but did not. In July 2000, A&E Cable presented a two-hour biography of the singing star entitled *Shirley Jones: Hollywood's Musical Mom*. In reviewing the program, *Hollywood Reporter*'s Marilyn Moss noted, "This extremely satisfying bio paints Shirley Jones as down-to-earth and forthright, not to mention multitalented."

In spring 2001, Shirley, who had recently reconciled with husband Marty Ingels after a six-month separation, put her 7,000-square-foot Beverly Hills mansion up for sale. Bought for $165,000 in 1965, Jones sold the property for $2.5 million. Thereafter, she and Ingels purchased a gated $1.2 million home in nearby Encino. (They also were longtime owners of property at Fawnskin, a small town on Big Bear Lake in San Bernardino County, California, where they bought additional land in December 2001 to be turned into a public park.) While making such movies as *Ping!* (2000, in which she was cast as a saxophone-playing grandmother who rides a motorcycle) and *Manna From Heaven* (2001), Jones continued to concertize throughout the United States. She acknowledged that for the first time in several years, she was again taking vocal lessons. "As we age," she explained, "the voice changes, it drops and the support system weakens. . . . The lessons reiterate things we've known all our lives—but we get lazy." In March 2002, Shirley ended her long, seesawing relationship with Ingels by filing for divorce. She cited "irreconcilable differences" as the grounds for the split-up.

When asked once what she'd like to do if for some reason she could not perform, she admitted, "I'd like to be a personal shopper for the movie stars. I like shopping, and I'm good at it. I also love animals and would like to raise them or work with a veterinarian."

Filmography

Oklahoma! (Magna, 1955)
Carousel (20th-Fox, 1956)
April Love (20th-Fox, 1957)
Never Steal Anything Small (Univ, 1959)
Bobbikins (20th-Fox, 1960)
Elmer Gantry (UA, 1960)
Pepe (Col, 1960)
Two Rode Together (Col, 1961)
The Music Man (WB, 1962)
The Courtship of Eddie's Father (MGM, 1963)

A Ticklish Affair (MGM, 1963)
Dark Purpose [L'Intrigo] (Univ, 1964)
Bedtime Story (Univ, 1964)
Fluffy (Univ, 1965)
The Secret of My Success (MGM, 1965)
Silent Night, Lonely Night (NBC-TV, 12/16/69)
The Happy Ending (UA, 1969)
El Golfo (Mercurio Films, 1969)
The Cheyenne Social Club (WB, 1970)
But I Don't Want to Get Married (ABC-TV, 10/6/70)

The Girls of Huntington House (ABC-TV, 2/14/73)

The Lives of Jenny Dolan (NBC-TV, 10/27/75)

The Family Nobody Wanted (ABC-TV, 2/19/75)

Winner Take All (NBC-TV, 3/3/75)

Yesterday's Child (NBC-TV, 2/3/77)

Who'll Save Our Children? (CBS-TV, 12/16/78)

Evening in Byzantium (Synd-TV, 8/14–15/79)

A Last Cry for Help (ABC-TV, 1/19/79)

Beyond the Poseidon Adventure (20th-Fox, 1979)

The Children of An Lac (CBS-TV, 10/9/80)

Inmates: A Love Story (ABC-TV, 2/13/81)

Tank (Univ, 1984)

There Were Times, Dear (PBS-TV, 6/3/87) [made in 1985]

Charlie (MGM-TV, 1989)

Cops 'n' Roberts (Unk, 1995)

Dog's Best Friend (Family Channel-cable, 3/23/97)

This Is My Father (Cinema Guild, 1998) (documentary)

Gideon (Baldwin/Cohen, 1999)

Shriek If You Know What I Did Last Friday the 13th (Lions Gate Films, 2000)

Ping! (Initial Entertainment, 2000)

The Adventures of Cinderella's Daughter (Creative Light Entertainment, 2000)

Manna From Heaven (Five Sisters Productions, 2001)

Broadway Plays

South Pacific (1953) (replacement)

Me and Juliet (1953)

Maggie Flynn (1968)

TV Series

The Partridge Family (ABC, 1970–74)

Shirley (NBC, 1979–80)

The "Slap" Maxwell Story (ABC, 1988)

Album Discography

LPs

Always in the Mood (Manhattan ST-53031)

April Love (Dot 9000) [ST]

Brigadoon (Col CL-1132; Col OL-7040/OS-2540)

Carousel (Cap W/SW-694) [ST]

An Evening With Diana Ross (Motown M7-877R2) [OC]

Free To Be . . . You & Me (Arista 4003) [ST/TV]

Maggie Flynn (RCA LOCD/LSOD-2009) [OC]

The Music Man (WB 1499) [ST]

Oklahoma! (Cap WAO/SWAO-595) [ST]

The Partridge Family Album (Bell 6050)

The Partridge Family at Home With Their Greatest Hits (Bell 1107)

The Partridge Family Bulletin Board (Bell 1137)

The Partridge Family Christmas Carol (Bell 6066)

The Partridge Family Shopping Bag (Bell 6072)

The Partridge Family Sound Magazine (Bell 6064)

The Partridge Family—Up to Date (Bell 6059)

Pepe (Colpix 507) [ST]

Speaking of Love (Col CL-991) w. Jack Cassidy

With Love From Hollywood (Col CL-1255) w. Jack Cassidy

The World of the Partridge Family (Bell 1319)

CDs

Always in the Mood (Manhattan CDP-46423)

Carousel (Angel ZDM-077-7-64692-2-5) [ST]

Free To Be . . . You & Me (Arista 18325) (ST/TV)

The Music Man (WB 1459-2) [ST]

Oklahoma! (Angel ZDM-077-764691-2-6) [ST]

Oklahoma!/Carousel (Capitol 7-466312; Capitol 7-46635-2) [ST]

The Partridge Family Album (Razor & Tie RE-2012)

The Partridge Family Christmas Card (Razor & Tie RE-2006)

The Partridge Family—Greatest Hits (Razor & Tie RE-8604)

The Partridge Family Shopping Bag (Razor & Tie RE-2022)

The Partridge Family Sound Magazine (Razor & Tie RE-2021)

The Partridge Family Up to Date (Razor & Tie RE-2013)

Pepe (Collectors' Choice Music CCM-113-2; DRG 113) [ST]

Shirley (A&M—no number)

Show Tunes (Sony Music Special Products A-26113) w. Jack Cassidy

Silent Strength (Diadem—no number)

Howard Keel

(b. Harry Clifford Leek, Gillespie, Illinois, April 13, 1919)

It is not uncommon for performers to have ups and downs in their careers. However, it is rare for an entertainer to attain his greatest success after the age of sixty, especially if stardom was initially his during his early career. This is just what happened to Howard Keel, who had the biggest boost to his show-business standing thanks to the television soap opera *Dallas*. From that sprung successful concert tours both here and abroad and, for the first time for the booming baritone of so many MGM musicals of the 1950s, a successful recording career. Furthermore, it is ironic that his TV success was based on his acting ability, whereas previously he had mainly been thought of as the star of glossy screen operettas, a later-day Nelson Eddy.

Born Harry Clifford Leek on April 13, 1919, in Gillespie, Illinois, he and his young brother moved with their mother to a suburb of San Diego, California, in 1930, following the death of his coal miner father. After graduating from high school, he worked at a variety of jobs, including that of an aviation mechanic. Young Harry had always enjoyed singing, but never took it seriously until his landlady encouraged him and gave him voice lessons. He found a job as a singing busboy at the Paris Inn Café in Los Angeles, but for higher wages accepted a factory job at Douglas Aircraft, studying voice at night. At Douglas he took part in various in-plant shows, and there he met singer George Houston, who took him on as a pupil at his American Music Theater in Pasadena. As tall as the budding songster, Houston was a baritone who had appeared in movies and at the time was headlining Producers Releasing Corporation's (PRC) "Lone Rider" Western series before his sudden death in 1943. Keel worked in some of the operas staged by Houston but was soon on the road representing Douglas Aircraft across the country and also taking part in talent shows and giving occasional concerts.

Keel auditioned for celebrated lyricist Oscar Hammerstein II hoping for a part in the movie *State Fair* (1945) but, instead, was placed in the Broadway company of Hammerstein II and his songwriting partner Richard Rodgers's *Carousel*. This was followed by a year's run in the London production of Rodgers and Hammerstein II's *Oklahoma!* While in England, Keel made his screen debut in *The Small Voice* (1948) and was impressive as the oafish criminal who takes refuge in the country home of a married couple (Valerie Hobson and James Donald). By a mistake, he was billed as "Harold Keel"; the film was issued in the United States as *Hideout*.

Upon his return to the United State, the actor, now calling himself Howard Keel, was hired by MGM for the lead of the macho cowboy Frank Butler in the film version of *Annie Get Your Gun* (1950). He got the role based on a screen test he had made earlier for Warner Bros. and his work in *The Small Voice*. Despite long delays, including Keel breaking his leg when a horse fell on him, and Judy Garland being fired and replaced by Betty Hutton, the musical saga proved to be a big success and was the beginning of the actor's tenure in posh screen musicals. Howard was

Howard Keel and Betty Hutton in *Annie Get Your Gun* (1950).
[Courtesy of JC Archives]

especially impressive in singing "My Defenses Are Down." *Variety* assessed, "Keel's baritone is particularly adaptable to the show tunes and he sounds them out with resonance."

Despite the resounding success of *Annie Get Your Gun*, the studio was then passing from the control of Louis B. Mayer to Dore Schary, and in the transition little thought was given to the focus of Keel's career. He was shoved into the Technicolor musical *Pagan Love Song* (1950)—starring Esther Williams—that was set in Tahiti and offered lovely scenery, empty plot threads, and lackluster songs. The next year he was teamed with Kathryn Grayson for the first time as swaggering Gaylord Ravenal in the third movie rendition of *Show Boat*. They made a pleasing screen couple. Howard was the narrator of the Clark Gable frontier epic *Across the Wide Missouri* and then starred in one of his finest comedies, *Callaway Went Thataway*, a sharp satire of the "Hopalong Cassidy" craze. Keel was the has-been Western film star whose movies are resurrected by TV, making him much in demand again. After being rematched with Kathryn Grayson in a pallid remake of *Roberta* (1935) called *Lovely to Look At* (1952), Keel and Grayson went on a concert tour of South America to promote it and other MGM movie products.

Upon his return from South America, the singing star was shunted to an action programmer, *Desperate Search* (1952). Far better was his appearance in *Ride, Vaquero!* (1953), in which he was a rancher whose wife (Ava Gardner) is attracted to a handsome cowboy (Robert Taylor).

To earn much-needed revenue, the financially troubled MGM loaned several of its musical stars to other studios in 1953. Keel was sent to Warner Bros. where he costarred opposite Doris Day in *Calamity Jane*. It was totally her movie, and her solo "Secret Love" won an Academy Award as Best Song. Howard's final 1953 outing was the lavish MGM production of *Kiss Me, Kate*, again with Kathryn Grayson. He was virulent, effective, and on the mark in the role of egocentric Petruchio in this 3-D production of Cole Porter's Broadway smash hit.

Keel may have insisted the role of the Mountie was "a blithering idiot" but he finally agreed to star in the remake of *Rose Marie* (1954) with Ann Blyth. It was a colorful, wide-screen entry, but unsatisfying. His manly interpretation of Captain Mike the Mountie—earlier played by Nelson Eddy—gave the picture its only anchor. A happier project was *Seven Brides for Seven Brothers* (1954), in which he is the oafish frontiersman who weds Jane Powell. Although the movie's songs were mediocre, the production was lavish and the plot entertaining. Following this success, his MGM salary rose to $3,000 weekly. Ironically, he was to do only three more features for the studio.

In the purported screen biography of Sigmund Romberg, *Deep in My Heart* (1954), Howard Keel made a guest appearance singing "Your Land and My Land," and then he suffered through his third disastrous picture with Esther Williams, *Jupiter's Darling* (1955), which derived from Robert Sherwood's sophisticated Broadway comedy. In this unlavish musical (leftover sets, stock shots from 1951's *Quo Vadis*, etc.), Williams had the title role of the patrician beauty who delays an attack on Rome by romancing Hannibal (Keel). The finale parade of elephants (dyed pastel colors) was the entry's sole highlight. Also in 1955 Keel reteamed with Ann Blyth for the fourth screen rendition of *Kismet*. Despite the usual MGM pomp and gloss, and their duet of "Stranger in Paradise," the transplanted Broadway musical was a weak one, and it concluded Keel's studio contract.

By now industry executives realized the public was cold toward screen operettas, and Howard was too typecast in the genre to succeed as a dramatic actor. Thus he was off the screen for four years performing in stage productions, concerts, and nightclubs, and working in Europe, where he remained popular. He served a term as president of the Screen Actors Guild and came to TV in 1957 on *Zane Grey Theater*. He then appeared in such small-screen shows as *Tales of Wells Fargo, Death Valley Days*, and *Run for Your Life*. A case of pneumonia prevented him from starring on Broadway as Franklin D. Roosevelt in *Sunrise at Campobello* (Ralph Bellamy took the part). However, on September 19, 1958, Howard headlined the NBC-TV musical special *Roberta*, and that year he also returned to Broadway in a revival of *Carousel*. A 1959 musical *Saratoga* (based on Edna Ferber's novel *Saratoga Trunk*), which costarred him with Carol Lawrence, was a flop.

Searching for venues to pursue his craft, Keel returned to pictures in the British-made *Floods of Fear* (1959) as an escaped prisoner who becomes a hero during a flood. Back in Hollywood, he was commanding as Simon-Peter in Walt Disney's failed biblical opus, *The Big Fisherman* (1959). In 1961, he traveled to West Germany for the combat tale *Armored Command* as an army colonel who foresees the German resistance that became the Battle of the Bulge. Continuing his string of low-budget films, he was in England for the science-fiction feature *The Day of the Triffids* (1963) as a temporarily blinded man. He is the one who regains his sight as the world is invaded by plantlike aliens. Keel wrote much of his own dialogue for the picture, which later became a popular TV and videocassette/DVD item. While in England he starred in a BBC-TV special of *Kiss Me, Kate* with Patricia Morison (from the original Broadway cast).

Back home again, Howard led the road company of the musical *No Strings*, and in 1965 sang the title song for the animated feature film *The Man From Button Willow*. Keel was hired by producer A. C. Lyles for a trio of low-budget Paramount Westerns. The gimmick was to pepper the pictures with former film stars. *Waco* (1966) matched him with Jane Russell and for *Red Tomahawk* (1967) he was to be reunited with Betty Hutton (not one of his favorite performers). However, she withdrew and was replaced by Joan Caulfield, while Yvonne De Carlo was his vis-à-vis in *Arizona Bushwackers*. Sandwiched between the Lyles minifeatures was the John Wayne–Kirk Douglas Western, *The War Wagon* (1967), in which Keel enjoyed his best film assignment in years, that of comical Native American Levi Walking Bear. In 1969 he also made a guest appearance on the CBS-TV sitcom *Here's Lucy*.

From the late 1960s until the early 1980s, Howard Keel kept active in a variety of show-business activities. He and Kathryn Grayson formed a successful club act that debuted in Las Vegas in 1968 and then ran throughout the country along with TV appearances and a six-week engagement in Australia. In 1969, he began a ten-month tour in the play *Plaza Suite* and then toured on and off in the musical *Man of La Mancha* for several years. He also did tours of *I Do! I Do!* and *The Unsinkable Molly Brown*. In 1972, Howard starred in London in Henry James's *The Ambassador*, which he reprised on Broadway later in the year. Keel was frequently reunited with MGM alumnus Jane Powell in road shows, including *Seven Brides for Seven Brothers* and *South Pacific*. In 1975, Howard did a concert tour singing Cole Porter tunes and also appeared at the London Palladium. While in England, he and Ethel Merman recorded the score for *Annie Get Your Gun*. In the early 1980s, he was on such TV nostalgia-cast programs as *The Love Boat* and *Fantasy Island*, but real stardom returned in 1981 when he began appearing on the popular CBS-TV prime-time soap opera *Dallas*.

Jim Davis, the actor who played Jock Ewing, the patriarch on *Dallas*, had died in 1981, and the producers were seeking a strong, handsome older actor to take his place on the nighttime drama. Keel began appearing as rancher Clayton Farlow and soon was a show regular. During the

1984–85 season, he and Donna Reed (who had temporarily replaced Barbara Bel Geddes) made a particularly attractive TV couple. The success Keel attained from *Dallas* resulted in several SRO tours of England, and in 1984 his record album *And I Love You So* became one of the top five LPs in that country, selling over 100,000 copies within a week. When it was issued in the United States as *With Love, Howard Keel*, the album sold so well it resulted in a follow-up, *Reminiscing With Howard Keel*. In 1985, he also recorded the song "J. R.! Who Do You Think You Are?" for Warner Bros./Lorimar Records' album *Dallas, the Music Story*. Heart surgery in the mid-1980s did not slow Keel down. He continued to make successful appearances as well as performing his *Dallas* duties as J. R.'s father-in-law. On July 15, 1989, Keel made his Los Angeles concert debut when he appeared at the Greek Theater for a one-night performance. The *Los Angeles Times* reported, "Keel's rich bass-baritone cruised easily through [Broadway/film musicals] medleys . . . But his finest moments came during his interpretations of smaller tunes—notably 'Wind Beneath My Wings' . . . and Jacques Brel's 'We Never Learn.' His empathy for the more interior emotions of songs like these suggested that maturity may have endowed Keel with a creative sensitivity to match the sunny glow of his voice."

Toward the end of 1989, Howard Keel again did a successful concert tour of England. He opened the 1990s with a PBS-TV special, *Howard Keel at the Royal Albert Hall*, but the next year his tenure in *Dallas* came to an end when the part of Clayton Farlow was written out of the series due to the withdrawal of costar Barbara Bel Geddes from the program. He kept busy in 1991, however, with guest roles on the TV series *Good Sports* and *Murder, She Wrote*, plus headlining another PBS-TV special, *Howard Keel: Close to My Heart*. In 1992, he appeared in *South Pacific* in St. Louis, Missouri, and the next year he guest-starred on the series *Walker, Texas Ranger* as well as doing a United Kingdom farewell tour. He was back on the big screen in 1994 as one of the hosts of *That's Entertainment! III*, and the same year he played the villainous role of Captain Jack in the telefilm *Hart to Hart: Home Is Where the Hart Is*. After another British tour in 1995, Keel drastically slowed the pace of his career, giving only an occasional concert and appearing in celebrity golf tournaments, including the annual Shell/Howard Keel Golf Classic. Over the years, his main hobbies were golf and flying. In 1997, he hosted the television documentary *The Making of "Seven Brides for Seven Brothers."*

Howard Keel married three times, first to actress Rosemary Cooper (1943–1948). In 1950, he wed dancer Helen Anderson, and they had three children: Kaija (who was married to actor Edward James Olmos from 1971 to 1992), Kristine, and Gunnar. Howard and Helen divorced in 1970. In 1971, he married former airline stewardess Judy Magamoll, and they had a daughter, Leslie. For many years the Keels owned a ranch in Sherman Oaks, California, but in the mid-1990s they moved to a spread near Palm Springs, and they also have a home in Telluride, Colorado.

Looking back on his film career, Keel assessed that the short duration and unevenness of his Hollywood career was due to his independence and his naive refusal to embrace the industry's favorite pastime: studio politics. He also said of his career options, "I'd rather sing [than act]. There's nothing like being in good voice, feeling good, and having good numbers to do and having a fine orchestra."

Filmography

The Small Voice [Hideout] (Br, 1948)
Annie Get Your Gun (MGM, 1950)
Pagan Love Song (MGM, 1950)
Three Guys Named Mike (MGM, 1951)
Texas Carnival (MGM, 1951)
Show Boat (MGM, 1951)
Across the Wide Missouri (MGM, 1951) (narrator)
Callaway Went Thataway [The Star Said No!] (MGM, 1951)
Lovely to Look At (MGM, 1952)
Desperate Search (MGM, 1952)
Fast Company (MGM, 1953)
I Love Melvin (MGM, 1953) (scene deleted from release print)
Ride, Vaquero! (MGM, 1953)
Calamity Jane (WB, 1953)
Kiss Me, Kate (MGM, 1953)

Rose Marie (MGM, 1954)
Seven Brides for Seven Brothers (MGM, 1954)
Deep in My Heart (MGM, 1954)
Jupiter's Darling (MGM, 1955)
Kismet (MGM, 1955)
Floods of Fear (Univ, 1959)
The Big Fisherman (BV, 1959)
Armored Command (AA, 1962)
The Day of the Triffids (AA, 1963)
The Man From Button Willow (United Screen Arts, 1965) (voice only)
Waco (Par, 1966)
Red Tomahawk (Par, 1967)
The War Wagon (Univ, 1967)
Arizona Bushwackers (Par, 1968)
That's Entertainment! III (MGM, 1994) (cohost)
Hart to Hart: Home Is Where the Hart Is (ABC-TV, 2/18/94)

Broadway Plays

Carousel (1945) (replacement)
Carousel (1958) (revival)

Saratoga (1959)
The Ambassador (1972)

TV Series

Dallas (CBS, 1981–91)

Album Discography

LPs

Ambassador (RCA SER-5618) [OC]
Ambassador of Song (Polydor 2353-042)
And I Love You So (Warwick WW-45137)
Annie Get Your Gun (Amalgamated 145, Sandy Hook 2053) [ST] w. Judy Garland
Annie Get Your Gun (10″ MGM E-509, MGM E-3227, Metro M/S-548, Sound/Stage 2302) [ST]
Annie Get Your Gun/Easter Parade (MGM E-3227) [ST]
Annie Get Your Gun/Show Boat (MGM 2SES-42ST) [ST]
Annie Get Your Gun/Three Little Words (MGM E-3768) [ST]
Calamity Jane (10″ Col CL-6273, Columbia Special Products 19611) [ST]
Deep in My Heart (MGM E-3153) [ST]
Deep in My Heart/Words and Music (MGM 2SES-54ST, MCA 5949) [ST]
General Motors 50th Anniversary Show (RCA LOC-1037) [ST/TV]

Kismet (MGM E-3281, Metro M/S-5260 [ST]
Kismet (MCA 1424) [ST]
Kiss Me, Kate (MCA 25003) [ST]
Kiss Me, Kate (MGM E-3077, Metro M/S-525) [ST]
Kiss Me, Kate (RCA LOP/LSP-1505) w. Gogi Grant, Anne Jeffreys
Kiss Me, Kate/The Band Wagon (MGM 2SES-44ST) [ST]
Lovely to Look At (10″ MGM E-150, MGM E-3230) [ST]
Lovely to Look At/Brigadoon (MGM 2SES-50ST) [ST]
Lovely to Look At/Show Boat (MGM E-3230) [ST]
Lovely to Look At/Summer Stock (MGM 39084) [ST]
Oklahoma!/Annie Get Your Gun (Stanyan SR-10069)

Oklahoma!/Annie Get Your Gun/Carousel (World Records SH-393) [OC]

Pagan Love Song (10″ MGM E-534, MGM SES-43ST) [ST]

Pagan Love Song/Hit the Deck/The Pirate (MGM 2SES-43ST) [ST]

Pagan Love Song/The Pirate (MCA 39080) [ST]

Reminiscing With Howard Keel—His Stage and Screen Favorites (Silver Eagle TLS-2259)

Rose Marie (MCA 25009) [ST]

Rose Marie (10″ MGM E-229, MGM E-3228, Metro M/S-616) [ST]

Rose Marie/Seven Brides for Seven Brothers (MGM E-3769, MGM 2SES-42ST) [ST]

Saratoga (RCA LOC/LSO-1051) [OC]

A Selection of His Screen Successes (10″ MGM D-146)

Seven Brides for Seven Brothers (MCA 20021, MCA 25021) [ST]

Seven Brides for Seven Brothers (10″ MGM E-244, MGM E-3235) [ST]

Show Boat (MCA 1439) [ST]

Show Boat (10″ MGM E-559, MGM E-3230, Metro M/S-527) [ST]

Show Boat (RCA LOP/LSO-1515) w. Gogi Grant, Anne Jeffreys

That's Entertainment! (2-MCA MCA2-11022) [ST]

That's Entertainment, Part 2 (MGM MG-1-5301, MCA 6155) [ST]

With Love—Yesterday, Today and Tomorrow (Silver Eagle SE-1026, CAL-268)

CDs

All Time Favorites (Disky 96)

Americans in London 1947-51: Oklahoma!/Annie Get Your Gun/Carousel/Zip Goes a Million (Encore's Box Office ENBO-CD-5/92) [OC]

And I Love You So (Spectrum U4034)

Annie Get Your Gun (Annie 01, Rhino 76669) [ST]

The Best of Howard Keel (Emporio 559)

The Best of Howard Keel (Pearl 5305441)

The Best of Howard Keel (Success 16176)

The Best of Howard Keel (Tring International JHD014)

Calamity Jane/I'll See You in My Dreams (Columbia Special Products M/P-19611) [ST]

Calamity Jane/Pajama Game (Columbia 467610, Sony Music Special Products 5018712) [ST]

Close to My Heart (Music for Pleasure 795846-2)

Collection (Castle—no number)

Deep in My Heart (Sony Music Special Products AK-47703) [ST]

Deep in My Heart/Words and Music (MCA MCAD-5949) [ST]

An Enchanted Evening With Howard Keel (MCI MCCD-006)

Film and Musical Favorites (Laserlight 15-093)

Great Songs (Entertainment UK—no number)

Great Songs (Musketeer MU-5024)

Howard Keel (Disky HR-877092)

Howard Keel Live in Concert—UK Tour (Pickwick PWKS-860)

I'll See You in My Dreams/Calamity Jane (Columbia 6689) [ST]

The Incomparable Howard Keel (MCI ETDCD-060)

Just For You (Telstar TCD-2318)

Kismet (EMI 854536, MCA MCAD-1424, Sony Music Special Products AK-45393) [ST]

Kiss Me, Kate (EMI 854538, MCA MCAD-25003, Sony Music Special Products AK-46196, CBS UK 70728) [ST]

Lovely to Look At (MCA MCAD-39084, Sony Music Special Products AK-47207) [ST]

Musical Highlights (Remember H489366)

Oklahoma! (Angel 52657) [OC]

Pagan Love Song (MCA MCAD-5950) [ST]

Pagan Love Song/The Pirate (MCA MCAD-39080) [ST]

Reminiscing: The Howard Keel Collection (Telstar TCB-2259)

Reminiscing With Howard Keel—His Stage & Screen Favorites (Silver Eagle SED-10612)

Rose Marie (MCA MCAD-25009) [ST]

Saratoga (RCA 63690-2) [OC]

Seven Brides for Seven Brothers (EMI 853047, Sony Music Special Products AK-52422, MCA MCAD-6176, MCA MCAD-20021) [ST]

Show Boat (EMI 836024, Sony Music Special Products AK-45436, MCA MCAD-1439, Turner Classic Movies/Rhino R2-71988, CBS UK 70281) [ST]

Show Boat/Annie Get Your Gun/Pagan Love Song (Great Movie Themes 60005) [ST]

That's Entertainment, Part 2 (Sony Music Special Products A2K-46872) [ST]

That's Entertainment! III (Angel CDQ-55215) [ST]

This Is Howard Keel (Sovereign)

The Very Best of Howard Keel (Summit 114)

The Very Best of Howard Keel—And I Love You So (Prism PLATCD-112)

With Love (Laserlight 15-105)

Cyd Charisse and Gene Kelly in *The Band Wagon* (1952).
[Courtesy of Michael R. Pitts]

Gene Kelly

(b. Eugene Curran Kelly, Pittsburgh, Pennsylvania, August 23, 1912; d. Beverly Hills, California, February 2, 1996)

Two male dancers are associated indelibly with twentieth-century American screen musicals: dapper Fred Astaire and ingratiating Gene Kelly. Elegant Astaire would be forever associated with sophistication and romance, a polished performer who could charm and woo his partner in the ballroom, park, or skating rink. Convivial Kelly, far more athletic in his approach, used his masculine Irish good looks to make hoofing more appealing to the average viewer. Exuberant Gene propelled dancing into a fresh dimension where soft shoe, ballet, or other Terpsichorean activity replaced dialogue and became an integrated part of the scenario's structure. Like Astaire, Kelly could sing (in a raspy, decent voice), and he choreographed much of his own screen dancing. But Kelly went several steps farther than Astaire, with whom he costarred occasionally. Gene became a film producer and director, doing a better job in those projects (such as 1952's *Singin' in the Rain*) where he was in front of the camera as well. It was always Kelly's ambition "to get rid of the idea that dancing was not manly and get it across that it is just as manly as any other form of athletics. Being a dancer is closely allied to being an athlete, and that is the premise on which my whole style is based. I was always a pretty good athlete." (In fact, Gene said once, "I never wanted to be a dancer. . . . I wanted to be a shortstop for the Pittsburgh Pirates.")

Eugene Curran Kelly was born in Pittsburgh, Pennsylvania, on August 23, 1912, the third of five children of James Patrick and Harriet (Curran) Kelly. His father was a traveling gramophone salesman; his strong-willed, stage-struck mother encouraged her children to take lessons in music, dance, and French. Gene and his younger brother Fred excelled at dance, but Gene far preferred playing sports. He admitted, "I hated dancing. . . . I thought it was sissy. I bless her now for making me go. . . ." Kelly studied journalism at Pennsylvania State College, but when the Depression hit, he quit school and taught gymnastics at a YMCA camp near Pittsburgh. He and Fred developed a hoofing act—tap-dancing on roller skates—that they displayed at local amateur nights.

When Gene had the money he returned to his schooling, this time at the University of Pittsburgh, where he graduated in 1933 as an economics major. He began law school in the fall of 1933, but realized dancing was his true career and dropped out of classes. During this period, he and Fred continued their dance teaming, and Gene began teaching in the Pittsburgh dance school where he had studied as a child. Each year he would take two weeks of classes from the Chicago Association of Dancing Masters, where he was later accepted as a member. He developed his teaching into the Gene Kelly Studio of the Dance, which soon had a branch location in Johnstown, Pennsylvania. It was at this time that Kelly realized, "As much as I loved classical ballet, I had to face the fact that my style of dancing was more modern." As such, he rejected an opportunity to join the Ballet Russe de Monte Carlo, which passed through Pittsburgh on their way to Chicago.

The Kelly brothers performed their dance routines at local clubs, and during the Chicago World's Fair of 1933 to 1934 they were part of a children's theater unit and also did nightclub work. Meanwhile, the reputation and fortunes of the Kelly dance studios grew. In the summer of 1935, the Kellys visited California relatives, and while in Los Angeles, Gene was screen-tested (unsuccessfully) at RKO, where Fred Astaire was a dancing star. In the summer of 1937 Gene was offered the chance—so he thought—to choreograph an upcoming Broadway show. When he arrived in New York, he found he was wanted only to appear in one dance number. Disappointed, he chose to return to Pittsburgh. But in August 1938, he returned to New York, encouraged by his mother not to be so prideful this time around.

He joined the chorus of Cole Porter's *Leave It to Me*, which opened on November 9, 1938. The show's overnight sensation was Mary Martin, who sang "My Heart Belongs to Daddy." (Gene was one of the chorus boys in this number.) Kelly quit this production to join the revue *One for the Money* (1939), for which he was paid $115 weekly as one of the six performers who sang, danced, and performed in the skits. When the show went on the road, Gene not only continued to costar, but coached the replacements in their routines. In the summer of 1939, he choreographed three shows for the Theater Guild's strawhat season in Westport, Connecticut. He was hired for the comedic role of Harry the Hoofer in William Saroyan's *The Time of Your Life* (October 25, 1939) and played the role for twenty weeks, after which he choreographed *Billy Rose's Diamond Horseshoe Revue* at the New York's World Fair. (Brother Fred took over Kelly's role in *The Time of Your Life* when the show went on the road.) Meanwhile, Gene met a sixteen-year-old dancer named Betsy Blair while directing dance for Billy Rose's *Revue*. They were married on September 22, 1941; their only child, daughter Kerry, was born in October 1942.

Richard Rodgers had seen Kelly in *The Time of Your Life* and had him audition for his new Broadway show, *Pal Joey*, which led to Gene being hired for the lead role. The show opened at the Ethel Barrymore Theater on December 25, 1940, and ran for 270 performances. Gene Kelly was now a star. John Martin (*New York Times*) lauded, "A tap-dancer who can characterize his routines and turn them into an integral element of an imaginative theatrical whole would seem to be pretty close, indeed, to unique. . . ." MGM displayed interest in signing him, but when studio head Louis B. Mayer demanded that he screen-test (after Kelly had been promised he would not have to), he refused to proceed. A few months later, movie producer David O. Selznick (Mayer's son-in-law) offered Gene a screen contract with no audition required; this time he accepted. Selznick thought Kelly would be ideal for a nonmusical, *Keys of the Kingdom*, in which he would play a missionary priest. Selznick abandoned this concept finally (the part was played eventually by Gregory Peck in 1944) and, instead, the movie newcomer was loaned to MGM to costar with Judy Garland in *For Me and My Gal* (1942).

Kelly had played a charismatic heel in *Pal Joey*, and his role as an opportunistic 1910s' vaudevillian in *For Me and My Gal*—originally planned for the film's other star, George Murphy—was quite similar. Kelly acknowledged later, "I knew nothing about playing to the camera. . . . It was Judy who pulled me through." He also analyzed, "In my first picture, I made a startling discovery—things danced on the screen do not look the way they do on the stage. On the stage dancing is three dimensional, but a motion picture is two dimensional."

Selznick then negotiated a deal with MGM for it to take over Gene Kelly's seven-year contract, with Kelly receiving initially $1,000 weekly. Not sure what to do with their new song-and-dance man, Metro ordered Kelly into *Pilot No. 5* (1943), a World War II drama. He was a gloomy Italian-American lieutenant in support of star Franchot Tone. Next came two nondescript musical roles at MGM, and then a role as a belligerent French soldier in *The Cross of Lorraine* (1943).

Gene was among the many who tested to play the Oriental lead opposite Katharine Hepburn in MGM's *Dragon Seed* (1944), but he did not get the part. Instead, it was another studio that provided his career rescue. Columbia Pictures was shooting a major Rita Hayworth musical, *Cover Girl* (1944), and desperately needed a leading man. Initially, studio head Harry Cohn insisted Kelly was wrong for the part, "That tough Irishman with his tough Irish mug! You couldn't put him in the same frame as Rita!" But he relented, and that picture made Kelly a movie star. As the proprietor of a small Brooklyn club, he not only got to sing serviceably and dance brilliantly to the Jerome Kern–Ira Gershwin score (including the memorable "Long Ago and Far Away"), but also for the unique "Alter Ego" number (in which he danced around and with his own conscience), he and Stanley Donen (whom Kelly met when Donen was a chorus boy on Broadway in *Pal Joey*) took over for choreographer Seymour Felix. Said Kelly of the intricate number, "It was the most difficult thing I've ever done, a technical torture, and I wouldn't want to have to do it again."

After going stridently dramatic in Universal's *Christmas Holiday* (1944), a nonmusical vehicle for that studio's Deanna Durbin in which he played a charming killer, Kelly returned to MGM, where he was allowed to choreograph his next starring vehicle, *Anchors Aweigh* (1945). His costars were Frank Sinatra and Kathryn Grayson. As a sailor on shore leave in Hollywood, Kelly performed "The Mexican Hat Dance," shared a soft-shoe routine with Sinatra in "I Begged Her," and in the unique "The King Who Couldn't Dance" mingled with cartoon characters such as Tom and Jerry in a fantasy sequence that cost $100,000 to make. He was nominated for an Academy Award, but the Oscar went to Ray Milland for *The Lost Weekend*. In 1944, after filming "The Babbitt and the Bromide"—a disappointingly ordinary dance number with Fred Astaire—for *The Ziegfeld Follies of 1946*, Kelly joined the navy. He spent most of his time directing propaganda films, which, because the war was nearly over, were irrelevant.

Kelly was discharged from the navy in May 1946, and Metro used him to add box-office appeal to a stalled vehicle for Marie "The Body" McDonald. *Living in a Big Way* (1947) was not salvaged by Kelly's presence, nor by the dance routines he and Stanley Donen devised. Cole Porter's *The Pirate* (1948) paired him again with Judy Garland, and it was directed by her then-husband, Vincente Minnelli. It was flamboyant and colorful, but production was hindered by Garland's emotional instability. Gene starred as the flirtatious entertainer Serafin and with Robert Alton cochoreographed the athletic "The Pirate Ballet" and the tuneful "Be a Clown." The picture was too sophisticated to succeed with the general public, and Kelly was too coy as the clown hero. Like many other MGM contractees tossed into the swashbuckling *The Three Musketeers* (1948), Kelly seemed more foolish as D'Artagnan than heroic, although he considered the lavish film one of his favorite nonmusical projects. He wanted to do next a musical version of *Cyrano de Bergerac*, but instead he choreographed "Slaughter on Tenth Avenue" (by Richard Rodgers) for *Words and Music* (1948) in which he danced with Vera-Ellen.

Kelly and Sinatra reunited for two additional musicals. Kelly cowrote and choreographed with Stanley Donen, *Take Me Out to the Ball Game* (1949), a period piece in which Esther Williams was the love object and Busby Berkeley was the director. (Kelly and Donen actually directed most of the musical scenes.) Much more potent was *On the Town* (1949), made as part of the Arthur Freed–MGM musical film unit, with music by Leonard Bernstein. Kelly and Sinatra were again sailors, this time on the loose in New York City. According to Gene, the movie's cochoreographer and codirector along with Donen, "Everything we did in the picture was innovative. . . . The fact that make-believe sailors got off a real ship in a real dockyard, and danced through a real New

York was a turning-point in itself." *On the Town* was Kelly's favorite picture. Now the film may seem dated, but then it was innovative and trendsetting.

After two unremarkable films released in 1950 (including *Summer Stock,* his last with Judy Garland) came *An American in Paris* (1951) directed by Vincente Minnelli. The most cited segment of this Technicolor musical was its seventeen-minute ballet sequence set to George Gershwin's music. The segment cost $450,000 to shoot, with Kelly choreographing it and dancing with Leslie Caron (a Kelly discovery from the Paris ballet). *An American in Paris* won an Oscar as Best Picture of 1951, and Kelly received a special Oscar: "In Appreciation of his versatility as an actor, singer, director and dancer, and especially for his brilliant achievement in the art of choreography on film." *An American in Paris* was a big money earner. The last Kelly musical of MGM's golden era was *Singin' in the Rain* (1952), which he codirected and cochoreographed with Donen. It is a classic, with its satirical story about Hollywood at the time talkies arrived. Robust, snappy, and fun, it provided Kelly with his landmark screen moment of dancing jubilantly in the rain. (The iconic musical later spawned a Broadway musical adaptation.)

To take advantage of the new U.S. income tax law that benefited Americans who worked abroad for eighteen months or more (and to escape the House Un-American Activities Committee, which was making life unpleasant for liberal-minded entertainers such as Kelly and his wife), Gene and his family moved to Europe. Unfortunately, everything soured. *The Devil Makes Three* (1952) was shot in Germany and was a box-office dud. In England he filmed the arty, all-ballet *Invitation to the Dance* (which an unhappy MGM did not distribute until 1955) and continued with *Crest of the Wave* (1954), a very parochial British military comedy that did not appeal to Americans. He was back in Hollywood for a guest stint with brother Fred in *Deep in My Heart* (1954) and, then, for *Brigadoon* (1954). The latter was a wide-screen musical that suffered from being too studio-bound. (This was an economy device demanded by new MGM studio boss, Dore Schary.) Neither Kelly's performance nor his dance staging was inspired.

MGM refused to loan Kelly to Samuel Goldwyn for the role of Sky Masterson in *Guys and Dolls* (1955); Marlon Brando got the part. Kelly's final picture for the Arthur Freed–MGM unit was *It's Always Fair Weather* (1955). It was also the end of Gene's professional association with Stanley Donen, with whom he codirected this film. Unlike their earlier collaborations, the two often feuded during the filming. Moreover, sharing the choreography chores with Michael Kidd was a bad decision. Far more satisfying was the witty and top-drawer *Les Girls* (1957), directed by George Cukor, in which Kelly romanced three leading ladies: Mitzi Gaynor, Kay Kendall, and Taina Elg. It provided him with the type of role he knew so well: the Pal Joey–type heel. However, it did not satisfy moviegoers who wanted more basic fare. A screen musical was planned as his next project, to be shot in England, called *Gentleman's Gentleman* but it never materialized. To end his MGM contract, he directed *The Tunnel of Love* (1958), starring Doris Day and Richard Widmark. There was little that was original about Kelly's direction of this Broadway sex comedy hit.

The late 1950s proved to be a time of transitions in Kelly's life. He and his actress wife, Betsy Blair, were divorced in April 1957, and on August 6, 1960, he wed Jeanne Coyne, a dancer whom he had known since their days at Gene Kelly's Dance Studio. (They had a son, Timothy, born in 1962 and a daughter, Bridget, born in 1964.) Gene stretched unsuccessfully to play the failed Jewish showman in *Marjorie Morningstar* (1958) opposite Natalie Wood and then returned to Broadway to direct the musical *Flower Drum Song* (1959) for Rodgers and Hammerstein II. Kelly went dramatic again as the idealistic newspaperman in Stanley Kramer's *Inherit the Wind* (1960), failing to match up to the dramatic intensity of costars Spencer Tracy and Fredric March. Also in 1960, he wrote and choreographed the ballet *Pas de Duex*, set to George Gershwin's Piano Concerto in F Major, which was presented by the Paris National Opera Ballet. Kelly returned to France to direct the Paris-lensed *Gigot* (1962), geared to present Jackie Gleason in a Charlie Chaplin–type movie role as a lovable bum. Kelly and Gleason quarreled over artistic matters, and the resulting sentimental comedy was unpopular.

Kelly had made his TV bow on the *Schlitz Playhouse of Stars* (CBS-TV, March 1, 1957) in "The Life You Save," and two years later he had two television specials: one for *Omnibus* called *Dancing Is a Man's Game* and the other in which he performed dancing to a poem written/read by Carl Sandburg. Unlike Fred Astaire, Kelly did not like the small screen medium—he found it too limiting—but he returned in the fall of 1962 to star in the short-lived series *Going My Way* (ABC-TV), taking over Bing Crosby's 1940s' film role as the happy-go-lucky priest.

Plans for Kelly to work in tandem as producer/director/star for Frank Sinatra's production company in 1963 fell through. Although he was now over fifty, Kelly danced in (and choreographed) a segment of Shirley MacLaine's fitfully entertaining *What a Way to Go!* (1964), and he starred in the well-received *Jack and the Beanstalk* (NBC-TV, 1967), which won an Emmy as Outstanding Children's Program. If anything marked Gene Kelly's screen decline, it was the French-made *The Young Girls of Rochefort* (1968), in which he played a dancing American concert pianist. Directed by Jacques Demy, this fiasco emphasized just how much Gene Kelly's success *and* image belonged to the 1940s and 1950s.

Kelly was adequate shepherding guest stars through the big-screen sex comedy *A Guide for the Married Man* (1967), but he was overwhelmed by the star (Barbra Streisand) and the public expectations for the screen translation of *Hello, Dolly!* (1969). He turned in a very old-fashioned piece of workmanship. Thereafter, the producing studio, Twentieth Century-Fox, cancelled plans for Kelly to direct an adventure musical based on the Tom Swift novels.

After helming the pedestrian Western *The Cheyenne Social Club* (1970), Gene next ventured into mounting a traveling children's show by directing *Clown Around* in April 1972, starring Ruth Buzzi and Dennis Allen of TV's *Laugh-In* popularity. The arena show folded in May of that year in San Francisco. He was asked to direct the movie version of *Cabaret* (1972) abroad, but had to turn it down because his wife Jeanne was dying of leukemia. He did accept a few days' work acting in the romantic comedy *Forty Carats* (1973) because he could go to the studio (Columbia) and be home in twenty minutes. His spouse died on May 10, 1973, the same year in which Gene's mother passed away.

In 1974, Gene did a summer-stock engagement of the musical *Take Me Along* in Dallas, Texas, playing the role of the ne'er-do-well Sid. Thereafter, because Kelly had sparkled as one of the cohosts of *That's Entertainment!* (1974), he was asked to costar, direct, and choreograph the new bridging sequences with Fred Astaire for *That's Entertainment, Part 2* (1976). A few years later, he was drawn out of retirement to costar as a soured clarinetist in a musical fantasy, *Xanadu* (1980). He and colead Olivia Newton-John did a brief dance together. The expensive movie was a big flop. Wanting to keep active in the industry in whatever capacity he could, he allied with

Francis Ford Coppola, intending to create an Arthur Freed–type unit for Coppola's Zoetrope Studios. He worked a bit on *One From the Heart* (1982), but soon ended the relationship with the studio and Coppola.

Kelly continued to make forays into television. He had hosted the brief-running comedy anthology series *The Funny Side* in 1971 for NBC-TV and starred/hosted in a variety of telespecials, including *Gene Kelly; An American In Pasadena* (1978). In 1980 the University of Southern California hosted a tribute to his career, and he looked back, saying, "Now that there isn't any studio system, I can see the advantages of it." When his Beverly Hills house burned in the early 1980s, he lost a lifetime of memorabilia, including his Oscar.

Turning seventy in 1982, Kelly announced he had retired from dancing, stating, "When you get to that age, you can dance, but it's not very exciting. I can't swing from lamp posts anymore." He made occasional acting appearances on TV—such as in *The Love Boat* (1984)—and dealt with the devastating blaze (causing by a Christmas tree catching fire) that destroyed his home and memorabilia. (Thereafter, Kelly supervised the rebuilding of the home.) Now with too much time on his hands, the star was often on hand to talk about his past career (he toured with his stage presentation *An Evening With Gene Kelly*) and to be the focal guest of more retrospectives. Already a recipient of the Kennedy Center Honors, he was the thirteenth recipient of the annual Life Achievement Awards of the American Film Institute on March 7, 1985. At the gala he discussed his career and admitted, "It was a lot of work, but we had fun. We had the best of times. It was because we all thought we were trying to create some sort of magic and joy. If I can make you smile . . . then I'm very proud to be a song-and-dance man." In the TV miniseries *North and South* (1985)—about the Civil War—Kelly played Senator Charles Edwards, while in another miniseries, *Sins* (1986)—set in World War II times—Gene played Eric Hovland.

For yet another compilation of musical filmmaking, *That's Dancing!* (1985), he served as executive producer, director, and cohost. It led Hugh Downs on TV's *20/20* to interview Gene Kelly, of whom he said, "He could sing a few bars and dance a little and when he did, time stood still." In December 1988, he was the twenty-fifth recipient of the Screen Actors Guild's Achievement Award "for fostering the finest ideals of the acting profession," and in April 1989 he received the Pied Pier Award from the American Society of Composers, Authors and Publishers for his contributions to the music industry.

In July 1990, in Santa Barbara, California, Gene married Patricia Ward, his girlfriend of five years. She was forty-four years his junior. The union caused a rift between Kelly and his three grown children by his previous wives. The long-lasting dissention between the dance star and his offspring was mended during 1994 and 1995, when the actor suffered two life-threatening strokes. Meanwhile, in 1994, Gene was one of the cohosts of the long-delayed release of the compilation feature *That's Entertainment! III*. When interviewed at this time about his old studio boss, Louis B. Mayer, Kelly was forthright: "I hated the man. I thought he was bizarre and he never liked me. Fortunately, I never dealt directly with him, and, of course, I made the studio money."

A recluse for his last few years due to illness, Gene died at his Beverly Hills home in his sleep on February 2, 1996, succumbing to a stroke. In 1999 Kelly was the biographical subject of Alvin Yudkoff's *Gene Kelly: A Life of Dance and Dreams*, which focused largely on his years and his efforts to achieve professional success. On March 15, 2000, Gene's younger brother Fred died of cancer in Tucson, Arizona. He was eighty-three. On March 4, 2002, PBS-TV aired *Gene Kelly: Anatomy of a Dancer*. In reviewing this ninety-minute documentary, Lewis Segal (*Los Angeles Times*) observed, "It'll take more than complaints about Gene Kelly's perfectionism and deep competitive streak to make audiences dislike one of the most devastatingly appealing men ever to dance across movie and television screens."

A few years before Gene passed away, the star told a reporter: "Kids talk to me and say they want to do musicals again because they've studied the tapes of the old films. We didn't have that. We thought once we had made it, even on film, it was gone except for the archives. Now, when I look at TV, I see a lot of my old steps being used and I'm delighted."

Filmography

For Me and My Gal [For Me and My Girl] (MGM, 1942)

Pilot No. 5 (MGM, 1943)

DuBarry Was a Lady (MGM, 1943)

Thousands Cheer (MGM, 1943)

The Cross of Lorraine (MGM, 1943)

Cover Girl (Col, 1944) (also choreography)

Christmas Holiday (Univ, 1944)

Anchors Aweigh (MGM, 1945) (also choreography)

Ziegfeld Follies of 1946 (MGM, 1946)

Living in a Big Way (MGM, 1947) (also choreography)

The Pirate (MGM, 1948) (also choreography)

Words and Music (MGM, 1948) (also choreography)

The Three Musketeers (MGM, 1948)

Take Me Out to the Ball Game [Everybody's Cheering] (MGM, 1949) (also story, choreography)

On the Town (MGM, 1949) (also director, choreography)

The Black Hand (MGM, 1950)

Summer Stock [If You Feel Like Singing] (MGM, 1950)

An American in Paris (MGM, 1951) (also choreography)

It's a Big Country (MGM, 1951)

Singin' in the Rain (MGM, 1952) (also director, choreography)

The Devil Makes Three (MGM, 1952)

Crest of the Wave [Seagulls Over Sorrento] (MGM, 1954)

Brigadoon (MGM, 1954) (also choreography)

Deep in My Heart (MGM, 1954)

It's Always Fair Weather (MGM, 1955) (also director, choreography)

Invitation to the Dance (MGM, 1955) (also director, screenplay, choreography)

The Happy Road (MGM, 1956) (also producer, director)

Les Girls (MGM, 1957)

Marjorie Morningstar (WB, 1958)

The Tunnel of Love (MGM, 1958) (director only)

Inherit the Wind (UA, 1960)

Let's Make Love (20th-Fox, 1960)

Gigot (20th-Fox, 1962) (director only)

What a Way to Go! (20th-Fox, 1964) (also choreography)

The Young Girls of Rochefort (WB-7 Arts, 1967)

A Guide for the Married Man (20th-Fox, 1967) (director only)

Hello, Dolly! (20th-Fox, 1969) (director only)

The Cheyenne Social Club (NG, 1970) (producer, director only)

40 Carats (Col, 1973)

That's Entertainment! (MGM, 1974) (cohost)

That's Entertainment, Part 2 (MGM, 1976) (cohost; director of new sequences)

Viva Knievel! (WB, 1977)

Xanadu (Univ, 1980)

Reporters (Fr, 1982)

That's Dancing! (MGM, 1985) (cohost, executive producer, director)

That's Entertainment! III (1994) (cohost)

Broadway Plays

Leave It to Me (1938)

One for the Money (1939)

The Time of Your Life (1939)

Pal Joey (1940)

Flower Drum Song (1959) (director only)

TV Series

Going My Way (ABC, 1962–63)
The Funny Side (NBC, 1971)

North and South (ABC, 11/3–10/85) (miniseries)
Sins (CBS, 2/2–4/86) (miniseries)

Album Discography

LPs

An American in Paris (10″ MGM E-93, MGM E-3232, Metro M/S-552) [ST]
Anchors Aweigh (Curtain Calls 100/17) [ST]
The Best of Gene Kelly From MGM Classic Films (MCA 25166)
Brigadoon (MGM E-3135) [ST]
A Clockwork Orange (WB BS-2573) [ST]
Cover Girl (Curtain Calls 100/24) [ST]
Deep in My Heart (MGM E-3153) [ST]
Deep in My Heart/Words and Music (MGM 2SES-54ST, MCA 5949) [ST]
DuBarry Was a Lady (Titania 509) [ST]
For Me and My Gal (Sountrak 107) [ST]
Gene Kelly on the Air (Totem 1034)
It's Always Fair Weather (MGM E-3241) [ST]
Jack and the Beanstalk (Hanna Barbara HLP-8522) [ST/TV]
The King Couldn't Dance (Col J-25)
Les Girls (MGM E-3590) [ST]
Lovely To Look At/Brigadoon (MGM 2SES-50ST) [ST]
The Man Who Came to Dinner (Star-Tone 226) [ST/R]
Marjorie Morningstar (RCA LOC-1044) [ST]
Nursery Songs and Stories (Col CL-1063, Har HL-9521)
On the Town (Show Biz 5603, Caliban 6023) [ST]
Pagan Love Song/Hit The Deck/The Pirate (MGM 2SES-43ST) [ST]
Pagan Love Song/The Pirate (MCA 39080) [ST]

Peter Rabbit/The Pied Piper of Hamlin (Har HL-9527)
Peter Rabbit/When We Were Very Young (10″ Col JL-8008)
The Pied Piper of Hamlin/The Shoemaker and the Elves (10″ Col JL-8007)
The Pirate (10″ MGM E-21, MGM E-3234) [ST]
Les Poupees de Paris (RCA LOC/LSO-1090) [OC]
Singin' in the Rain (10″ MGM E-113, MGM E-3236, Metro M/S-599) [ST]
Song and Dance Man (10″ MGM E-30)
Song and Dance Man (Stet 15010)
Song and Story Time (Har HL-9529)
The Special Magic of Gene Kelly (MGM 2353-120)
Summer Stock (10″ MGM E-519, MGM E-3234) [ST]
Take Me Out to the Ball Game (Curtain Calls 100/18) [ST]
That's Dancing! (EMI America SJ-17149) [ST]
That's Entertainment! (MCA MCA2-11002) [ST]
That's Entertainment, Part 2 (MGM MG-1-5301, MCA 6155) [ST]
Thousands Cheer (Amalgamated 232, Hollywood Soundstage 409) [ST]
What a Way to Go! (20th Century-Fox 3143) [ST]
Words and Music (JJA 19822) [ST]
Xanadu (MCA 6100) [ST]
Ziegfeld Follies of 1946 (Curtain Calls 100/15-16) [ST]

CDs

An American in Paris (Turner Classic Movies/Rhino R2-71961) [ST]
Anchors Aweigh (Sandy Hook CDSH-2024) [ST]
The Best of Gene Kelly From MGM Classic Films (MCA MCAD-31177)
Brigadoon (Sony Music Special Products AK-45440, EMI 852765) [ST]
A Clockwork Orange (WB 2573-2) [ST]
Cover Girl/You Were Never Lovelier (Great Movie Themes 60035) [ST]
Deep in My Heart (Sony Music Special Products AK-47703) [ST]
Deep in My Heart/Words and Music (MCA MCAD-5949) [ST]

DuBarry Was a Lady (Great Movie Themes 60010) [ST]
For Me and My Gal (Turner Classic Movies/Rhino R2-72204) [ST]
Gotta Dance: The Best of Gene Kelly (Columbia CK-47713)
It's Always Fair Weather (Sony Music Special Products AK-47026) [ST]
Les Girls (EMI 794251) [ST]
Marjorie Morningstar (RCA 74321720542) [ST]
Pagan Love Song/The Pirate (MCA MCAD-39080) [ST]

Singin' in the Rain (Sony Music Special Products AK-45394, Turner Classic Movies/Rhino R2-71963, Great Movie Themes 60006) [ST]

Summer Stock (Sony Music Special Products AK-46199) [ST]

Summer Stock/In the Good Old Summertime (Rhino Handmade RHM2 7761)

That's Entertainment, Part 2 (Sony Music Special Products A2K-46872) [ST]

That's Entertainment! III (Angel CDQ-55215) [ST]

Words and Music (Words and Music (MGM/EMI MGM-14, Sony Music Special Products AK-47711) [ST]

Charlotte Henry and Felix Knight in *Babes in Toyland* (1934).
[Courtesy of Echo Book Shop]

Felix Knight

(b. William Felix Knight II, Macon, Georgia, November 1, 1908; d. New York City, June 18, 1998)

Although he appeared in only a handful of feature films, Felix Knight was one of the most versatile of Hollywood songsters, having been in opera and operettas as well as popular music. In addition, he carved out a successful and lengthy career in radio, Broadway, television, the concert stage, nightclubs, and recordings. While he will always be best remembered by film fans as Tom-Tom, the Piper's Son, in the classic movie version of *Babes in Toyland* (1934), Knight proved to be one of the best tenors ever to grace the screen.

William Felix Knight II was born November 1, 1908, in Macon, Georgia, the son of a cotton farmer who was killed in a hunting accident when the boy was five. Seven years later, the youngster moved with his family to Pensacola, Florida, where an older brother was in the Naval Air Service. There the adolescent began playing the guitar, and by his mid-teens he was already singing at nightspots and dances. By 1925, Knight was featured on a local radio station, and a movie company manager on location in Florida to make a feature urged the young man to try his luck in California.

Taking the manager's advice, Knight went West and found a voice teacher, but was unable to engineer a movie contract. In the meantime, he did local singing jobs as well as church work and gained financial support from the Harkness Scholarship Foundation to help pay for his voice lessons. By 1929, he was singing on a Columbia network (later CBS) station in Santa Barbara, and he also had a national show, *WCC Presents Felix Knight*. He entered the Atwater Kent Foundation Scholarship Auditions of the Air and made it to New York City before placing second in the judging.

Returning to California, Knight sang at the Hollywood Bowl in Giuseppe Verdi's opera *La Traviata* with Lily Pons and then went to San Francisco, where he did Hector Berlioz's *Damnation of Faust* with that city's opera company. Once again back in Hollywood, he continued to study voice and work on radio, including the CBS program *Shell Mountain House* with Raymond Paige and his Orchestra. In 1934, Felix finally made his screen debut in RKO Radio's *Down to Their Last Yacht* as a South Seas native who sings "Malakamokolu." This was followed by the role of a gypsy in the Charles Boyer–Loretta Young picture *Caravan* (1934) at Fox; in it, Knight had two numbers: "Ha Cha Cha" and "The Wine Song." He also did the same part in the French-language version of the feature, *Caravane* (1934), which starred Boyer.

Late in 1934, Felix's most famous picture, *Babes in Toyland*, was issued by MGM. In this Stan Laurel–Oliver Hardy delight, based on Victor Herbert's famed 1903 operetta, Felix was Tom-Tom, the young piper who tries to save his pretty sweetheart (Charlotte Henry) from the evil Barnaby (Henry [Brandon] Kleinbach) and his giant wooden soldiers. Not only did the actor have the romantic lead, but he also performed several numbers, including "A Castle in Spain." Both

Ramon Novarro and Donald Novis were considered for the role of Tom-Tom before it went to Knight in this movie, later also known as *Revenge Is Sweet* and *March of the Wooden Soldiers.*

Although Knight was placed under MGM contract, he did no films directly for the studio but was, instead, loaned out for other assignments. For example, Felix went to Warner Bros. for two musical shorts: *Springtime in Holland* (1935) and *Carnival Day* (1936). The former cast him as a Dutch milk seller, and he sang "The Girl on the Little Blue Plate" and "By the Zuyder Zee," while in *Carnival Day* he was a jockey who romances a flower girl (Geraine Grear [Joan Barclay]) and vocalizes "The Rose in Her Hair" and "Steppin' Along."

MGM did release his next feature, *The Bohemian Girl* (1936), but like *Babes in Toyland,* it was made independently by producer Hal Roach. It reteamed Knight with Stan Laurel and Oliver Hardy, but this time Felix had only a small role as a gypsy singer who does a selection from the Michael William Balfe–Alfred Bunn opera of 1843. A test Felix had done for filmmaker Hal Roach ended up in *Pick a Star* (1937), a comedy that also had Laurel and Hardy in a nonspeaking guest bit; Felix was seen briefly as a nightclub singer in this MGM release. Although he studied acting with Irving Pichel, no more movie opportunities came to Knight, other than a potential movie series in Australia that eventually failed to materialize.

In 1937, Felix Knight moved to New York City, where he made radio recordings for Thesaurus Transcriptions with Nathaniel Shilkret and his Orchestra, and the next year he waxed nine songs with Leo Reisman's orchestra for Victor Records. He also began performing again on network radio, first with the *Schaefer All-Star Parade* on NBC, which ran from 1938 to 1940. Knight was on the NBC Blue Network's *Music Appreciation Hour* in 1938 and the *RCA Magic Key* [*The Magic Key*] during the 1938–39 season. He also had a weekly program on radio station WEAF each Thursday. In 1938, he was one of the finalists on NBC's *Metropolitan Opera Auditions of the Air,* losing to John Carter by only one vote. In 1939, he made his concert recital debut at Town Hall, singing selections from Johannes Brahms, Pier Francesco Cavalli, Alessandro Stradella, and Richard Strauss. Felix made his Broadway bow in October 1940, as the featured singer in *It Happens on Ice,* and two years later, he sang the role of Camile de Jolidon in Franz Lehar's *The Merry Widow* at Carnegie Hall. In his final Broadway outing, Knight played Almaviva in *Once Over Lightly* in 1942 with Igor Gorin and Grace Panvini; it was based on Rossini's opera *The Barber of Seville.*

In 1940, Felix Knight married radio actress Ethel Blume, who appeared in such audio series as *The Adventures of Helen, The Aldrich Family, Easy Aces, John's Other Wife,* and *Joyce Jordan, M.D.* He recorded for Victor Records and continued to be heard on radio in such musical programs as *The Ford Sunday Evening Hour* and *Music Hall of the Air* [*Radio City Music Hall*], as well as the game program *So You Think You Know Music.*

The year 1946 proved to be a good one for Felix in that he not only continued to be very active in radio, but he also signed with Decca Records and became a member of the Metropolitan Opera. At Decca, he recorded popular songs and operettas and was a vocalist with the Guy Lombardo and Russ Morgan orchestras. For his debut at the Met, he sang the role of Count Almaviva in *The Barber of Seville,* the same part he did in the English-language version of the opera, *Once Over Lightly,* four years before. He remained at the Met for nearly a decade, but he also continued to appear on radio in such series as *The Pet Milk Show* and *American Album of Familiar Music.*

Knight had his own television series, *Felix Knight Sings,* in the early 1950s, which aired each Tuesday and Thursday afternoon. (His other TV work included appearances on *NBC Television*

Concert Hall in 1948, singing Rudolfo's aria from *La Bohème* on *Your Show of Shows* in April 1950 and performing Christmas hymns on a holiday edition of *Juvenile Jury* in December 1951.) During this period, Felix also made more records for RCA Victor.

After leaving the Metropolitan Opera, Felix appeared for two months at the Capitol Theater in New York City, and then spent the next several years giving concerts (he appeared with the Philadelphia Orchestra and the Detroit Symphony, among others) and performing in summer stock, as well as working supper- and nightclubs. In 1960 he and Mimi Benzell did an album from the musical shows *Can-Can* and *Kiss Me, Kate* for Design Records. On TV, Knight could be seen as an occasional guest on late-night talk programs such as *The Jack Paar Show* in September 1961.

Toward the end of the 1960s, Knight grew weary of constant traveling and launched still another musical career, this time as a teacher of vocal technique. His students included both Broadway and opera singers, and he continued to teach for the rest of his life. He was a member of the Founding Tent of the Sons of the Desert, the Laurel and Hardy international society, and he attended several of their conventions. Felix Knight died in New York City on June 18, 1998, and was survived by his wife and son, William Felix Knight III. Not long before his passing, he told writer Laura Wagner (*Classic Images*, June 1998): "I did my best, I tried to be a nice guy. I helped people whenever I could, and I never complained. . . . For a country boy from a cotton patch in Macon, Georgia—I think I did pretty good."

Filmography

Down to Their Last Yacht (RKO, 1934)
Caravan (Fox, 1934)*
Babes in Toyland [March of the Wooden Soldiers/ Revenge Is Sweet] (MGM, 1934)
Springtime in Holland (WB, 1935) (s)

Carnival Day (WB, 1936) (s)
The Bohemian Girl (MGM, 1936)
Pick a Star [Movie Struck] (MGM, 1937)

*Also appeared in the French-language version

Broadway Plays

It Happens on Ice (1940)

The Merry Widow (1942)
Once Over Lightly (1942)

Radio Series

WCC Presents Felix Knight (CBS, 1930)
Shell Mountain House (NBC, 1934)
Schaefer All-Star Parade (NBC, 1938–40)
RCA Magic Key [The Magic Key] (NBC Blue, 1938–39)
Music Appreciation Hour (NBC Blue, 1938)
The WEAF Revue (WEAF, 1938–39)
The Ford Sunday Evening Hour (CBS, 1939–41)
The Treasury Hour (NBC Blue, 1941)
Lavender and New Lace (NBC, 1941–42)
Music Hall of the Air [Radio City Music Hall] (NBC, 1943)

Pabst Blue Ribbon Show (NBC, 1945)
Coke Time (Mutual, 1945)
So You Think You Know Music (Mutual, 1945)
The Electric Summer Hour (CBS, 1945)
Harrington Root Beer Show (NBC, 1946)
Your Song and Mine (CBS, 1948)
The Pet Milk Show (NBC, 1948–49)
American Album of Familiar Music (NBC, 1949–50)
Al Goodman's Musical Album (NBC, 1951–53)

TV Series

Felix Knight Sings (c. 1950s)

Album Discography

LPs

Babes in Toyland (Mark56 577) [ST]
Can-Can/Kiss Me Kate (Design DLP-111/DCF-1001, Spectrum SDLP-111/SS-54)
The Desert Song (10″ Decca DL-7000, 10″ Brunswick LA-8501)
Gems From Gershwin (10″ RCA LPT-3055)
Mademoiselle Modiste (10″ RCA LPM-3153)
The Merry Widow (Decca DL-8004, Decca DL-8819)

Musical Comedy & Operetta Favorites, Vol. 1 (Hollywood LPH-114)
Musical Comedy & Operetta Favorites, Vol. 2 (Hollywood LPH-115)
The Red Mill (Decca DL-8016, Decca DL-8458)
Showboat: Hit Selections From the MGM Production (10″ Mercury MG-25104)

CDs

Babes in Toyland/Way Out West (Soundtrack Factory 33546) [ST]
Gems From Gershwin (RCA Victor 63275)
Historic Gershwin Recordings (RCA Victor 63276)

Lucia de Lammermoor (Melodram CDM-27513)
The Merry Widow/The Desert Song (Box Office 1195)

Kris Kristofferson

(b. Kristoffer Kristofferson, Brownsville, Texas, June 22, 1936)

Kristofferson was one of the few entertainers who etched for himself almost separate careers in music and dramatics. This onetime Rhodes scholar not only became a top-notch songwriter and performer, but he also proved to be a very fine actor who became one of the screen's most popular players in the late 1970s. It is ironic, however, that despite the fact he had best-selling single and record album releases, he rarely sang on film. Most of his motion-picture appearances were in solidly dramatic roles. Although Kris was plagued with personal problems several times over the years, he survived to make new inroads in his show-business career. It was Kristofferson, through his songs and personal appearances, who almost single-handedly ended Nashville's monotonous country sounds of the early 1970s. Yet he was also the same actor whom the Foreign Press Association named as Best Actor for his performance in the otherwise flat musical *A Star Is Born* (1976). In addition, the talent, who became a very prolific screen actor, had the dubious honor of starring in one of the biggest box-office fiascoes of all time, the $40 million Western dud *Heaven's Gate* (1980).

Kristoffer Kristofferson was born in Brownsville, Texas, on June 22, 1936, the son of a two-star U.S. Air Force major general who retired to become air operations manager for the oil conglomerate Armco in Saudi Arabia. As a boy Kris moved often, but the family finally rooted down in California, where he developed a liking for country music, particularly that of Hank Williams. While in high school, he learned to play the guitar, and at Pomona College in Claremont he excelled in both athletics (football, soccer, boxing) and academics. As a writer he won a quartet of *Atlantic Monthly* magazine short-story writing contests, and he was awarded a Rhodes scholarship to Oxford University in England, where he wrote a study of the works of William Blake.

When several of his books failed to be published, Kristofferson became disillusioned with academic life and began writing songs. In turn he started performing in England under the name of Kris Carson and was managed by entertainer Tommy Steele's organization, which handled pop-rock acts. However, Kris failed to make much of an impression. As a result, he enlisted in the army, where he served five years, first in West Germany and later going through hangar school, pilot, and parachute jump training, eventually becoming a helicopter pilot. In 1960, he married Fran Beir, and they had two children, Tracy and Kris. Leaving the service in 1965, he got a position teaching English at West Point. However, with his marriage dissolving, he went to Nashville, where he met songwriter Marijohn Wilkin and he decided to remain in Music City.

The mid- and late 1960s proved to be rough years for Kristofferson. He worked as a janitor by night at Columbia Records and as a bartender by day at the Tally-Ho Tavern, all the time trying to promote his songs. His pro–Vietnam War ballad, "Vietnam Blues," was recorded by Dave Dudley, while Roy Drusky waxed "Jody and the Kid," but for the most part, Kristofferson made little headway. He was forced to hire out as a laborer and as a pilot flying workers and

Kris Kristofferson in 1980.
[Courtesy of Echo Book Shop]

equipment for Gulf of Mexico oil rigs. Kristofferson was persistent, however, in pushing his material. In the summer of 1969, Roger Miller had a hit record for Smash with Kris's "Me and Bobby McGee," which also became a pop hit for Janis Joplin. Kristofferson made a successful appearance at the Newport Folk Festival in 1969, and Johnny Cash featured him several times on his ABC-TV variety program. In 1970, Cash had a best-selling record for Columbia with Kris's song "Sunday Morning Comin' Down."

By now Kristofferson's career was gaining momentum. He was signed to a record contract by Monument, and his songs became popular items for other performers: Ray Price's "For the Good Times" and "I Won't Mention It Again," Sammi Smith's "Help Me Make It Through the Night," Jerry Lee Lewis's "Once More With Feeling," Ronnie Milsap's "Please Don't Tell Me How the Story Ends," and Christy Lane's "One Day at a Time." Kris had a successful engagement at the Troubadour in Los Angeles in the summer of 1970, thus establishing himself as a nightclub draw. In 1971 he sang (with Rita Coolidge) on the soundtrack of the motion picture *The Last Movie,* as well as making his film debut in a small role in this Dennis Hopper film. The same year, he received critical acclaim for his portrayal of a drug dealer in Columbia's *Cisco Pike,* and his songs "Me and Bobby McGee" and "Help Me Make It Through the Night" earned him Grammy nominations, as did "For the Good Times" for Best Country Song.

In the summer of 1973, Kristofferson married Rita Coolidge, and that year he had his first really big-selling single for Monument of his own song, "Why Me," although his earlier recordings of "Loving Her Was Easier" and "Watch Closely" had done well. His albums *The Silver Tongued Devil and I* and *Jesus Was a Capricorn* went on to become gold-record award winners. Although he continued to tour, during this period Kristofferson focused primarily on his movie career. Nevertheless, he netted a Grammy nomination in 1973 for "Why Me," while he and Rita Coolidge won a Grammy for Best Vocal Performance by a Duo for "From the Bottom of the Bottle," and they repeated that distinction in 1975 for "Lover Please." On the big screen, he won favorable comments as Susan Anspach's boyfriend in the otherwise deficient comedy *Blume in Love* (1973). In that same year, he was straightforward as outlaw William Bonney in *Pat Garrett and Billy the Kid,* made by esteemed filmmaker Sam Peckinpah for MGM. Ironically, it was not Kris but Bob Dylan, in a guest role in the film, who provided the movie soundtrack singing. Next Kristofferson made a guest appearance as a violent biker in the embarrassing adventure *Bring Me the Head of Alfredo Garcia* (1974). He was paid $150,000 for his brief role. His sole 1975 film was Martin Scorsese's *Alice Doesn't Live Here Anymore.* In it, he offered, perhaps, his best performance to date, as the man who falls in love with a waitress (Ellen Burstyn) who is trying to put the pieces of her life back together following her husband's death. (*Variety* noted, "Kris Kristofferson brings the film to attention as the man who makes life meaningful for mother and son.")

In 1976 he made a trio of pictures, beginning with the violent potboiler *Vigilante Force,* as a Vietnam vet who is hired to bring order to a small California town and ends up as its murderous dictator. While the film was exploitive, he gave a shaded performance as the complex central figure. For the British-made *The Sailor Who Fell From Grace With the Sea,* he was cast as a fun-loving sailor who has an affair with a beautiful widow (Sarah Miles). The arty film's production resulted in offscreen publicity involving the two lead players, and explicit photos from the movie were published in *Playboy* magazine. Next Kristofferson took over for Elvis Presley in the third screen version of *A Star Is Born,* playing an alcoholic rock star who sees his career fade while his wife (Barbra Streisand) rises to stardom. In the indulgent proceedings, Kristofferson performed "Watch Closely Now," "Hellacious Acres," and "Crippled Crow," while he and Streisand (with whom he often feuded during the production) dueted on the project's theme song, "Evergreen," and "Lost Inside of You." With a box-office gross of $37 million, it gave Kristofferson the commercial impetus his screen career required.

Thereafter his screen career was a mixed bag, heading in no particular direction. In 1977 he teamed with Burt Reynolds as two football players who share the same girlfriend (Jill Clayburgh) in the all-too-tepid comedy *Semi-Tough* (with a soundtrack drawn from Gene Autry records). Again for director Sam Peckinpah, Kris starred as a trucker leading a protest in *Convoy* (1978), based on the popular C. W. McCall recording. He played the role of Abner Lait in the production of *Freedom Road* (1979), also starring Muhammad Ali, which was shown in the United States on television while it was screened theatrically in Europe. The year 1980 found Kristofferson toplining the much-maligned *Heaven's Gate*, a sprawling Western about an educated man (Kris) siding with homesteaders against corrupt railroad bosses. The cinematography was beautiful, but the scenario meandered so persistently and for so long (originally 219 minutes; later cut to 149 minutes) that audiences avoided the picture with a passion. Almost as nullifying to his career was his role as a slick banker involved with an oil heiress (Jane Fonda) in the vapid big-business exposé *Rollover* (1981).

Although the 1970s found Kris Kristofferson a highly paid movie performer, singer, and songwriter, his personal life was in turmoil. He and Rita Coolidge had a son, Casey, in 1977, but they were divorced in 1979. By then the star had kicked his dependence on alcohol, which had plagued him for two decades, and in the early 1980s, he ceased to use marijuana. He also began touring with Willie Nelson, and in 1981 appeared in another medium when he made the music video "A Celebration." In the dwindling record market he had minor success with "Prove It to You One More Time Again" for Columbia in 1980 and with a couple of other tunes; "Here Comes That Rainbow Again" (for Monument) and "Nobody Loves Anybody Anymore" (for Columbia) in 1981. After a three-year hiatus, Kris returned to movies in 1984 in the CBS-TV telefeature *The Lost Honor of Kathryn Beck* about a woman (Marlo Thomas) persecuted because she spends the night with a suspected terrorist (Kristofferson). Kris was among the many artists (including Johnny Cash, Hank Williams Jr., Willie Nelson, Carl Perkins) interviewed for MGM/UA videocassette *The Other Side of Nashville* (1984). Theatrically, in 1984 he also starred in two TriStar features: *Flashpoint* and *Songwriter*. The former was a fairly intriguing mystery in which Texas Rangers Kristofferson and Treat Williams stumble onto money taken in a robbery several years before, while in *Songwriter* Kris teamed with Willie Nelson as two popular singers out to have revenge on a dishonest backer (Richard C. Sarafin). (Kristofferson's title song for *Songwriter* was nominated for an Academy Award.) By now, his personal life had become more tranquil with his marriage to attorney Lisa Meyers in 1983. They had five children: Jesse, Jody, John Robert, Kelly, and Blake.

In 1985, this multitalented personality won critical acclaim for his role of an ex-cop just out of prison who finds love and adventure with a group of youths in the futuristic *Trouble in Mind*. Then on TV he played a police captain investigating an alleged brutal rape in 1930s' Hawaii by four men of mixed Asian heritage in *Blood and Orchids* (1986). That year he also starred in two made-for-television features, *The Last Days of Frank and Jesse James* (NBC-TV) and *Stagecoach* (CBS-TV). In the first he was cast as the renowned outlaw, with Johnny Cash playing his brother Frank; while the third version of *Stagecoach*—which featured a host of country singers in dramatic roles—had Kristofferson playing the Ringo Kid, the role that had brought film stardom to John Wayne in 1939. Neither telefilm was much liked. Also in 1986 he was among those starring in the ABC-TV miniseries *Amerika*, as a man leading a rebellion against the Soviet seizure of the United States. In 1987 Kristofferson starred in his own cable TV special *Welcome Home*, for Home Box Office, which was shot at his Washington, DC, stage appearance that year. He turned up as the circus owner in *Big Top Pee-wee* (1988), a foolish exploitation of the bizarre Pee-wee Herman. Many noted that Kristofferson, with his snowy white beard, closely resembled the late character actor George "Gabby" Hayes.

While Kristofferson remained an active actor in the late 1980s, he did not neglect his music, having a successful album, *Repossessed*, as well as being professionally reunited with Rita Coolidge onstage in Las Vegas; both events occurred in 1987. Onstage Kris not only performed his famous songs of the past but used his act as a handy forum for compositions about subjects dear to his very liberal political viewpoint. His left-of-center politics influenced Kris in becoming involved in documentaries such as *Armageddon Express* (1988), in which he appeared with Joan Baez in two stories about activists protesting U.S. weaponry. He was also a supporter of the 1992 project *The Panama Deception*, which claimed to tell the true story of the ouster of Manuel Noriega in Panama.

The decade of the 1990s found the singer-actor-composer appearing in over thirty movies, many of them done for television. In 1990, he and Willie Nelson starred in the CBS-TV film *A Pair of Aces*, with Kris as a Texas Ranger out to protect his daughters from a serial killer while entrusted with bringing a benign outlaw (Nelson) to justice, with the two forming a bond.

The next year they did a sequel, *Another Pair of Aces: Three of a Kind*, in which the same characters team to help a Texas Ranger falsely accused of murder. During the decade Kris appeared in a number of TV Westerns, such as *Miracle in the Wilderness* (1992), and as narrator of *Dead Man's Gun* (1997). He and Willie Nelson reteamed in 1998 for *Outlaw Justice*.

Among the actor's better films of the period were *No Place to Hide* (1992), which cast him as a detective trying to solve the case of a ballerina murdered onstage during a rehearsal, the modern-day Western *Lone Star* (1996), in which he played crooked lawman Charlie Wade, and *Blue Rodeo* (1996), in which he helps a woman (Ann-Margret) whose son has learning disabilities. Also memorable were *Fire Down Below* (1997), which cast Kris as a greedy businessman who orders toxic waste dumped in the Kentucky hills; Showtime's *Girls' Night* (1998) where he played an adventurer, Cody, and *A Soldier's Daughter Never Cries* (1998) in which he played one of his best parts as a hard-drinking expatriate American author. In the sci-fi thriller *Knights* (1993) he was Gabriel, a robot designed to kill vampire cyborgs, while the horror film *Blade* (1998) showcased him as Abraham Whistler, a part he did in a follow-up, *Blade 2: Bloodlust* (2001). He was impressive as Abraham Lincoln in the telefilm *Tad* (1995), in which Jane Curtin played his wife, Mary Todd Lincoln. In 1990 Kris, Johnny Cash, Waylon Jennings, and Willie Nelson appeared in the video documentary *Highwaymen Live*, and three years later the group's European tour was documented in *The Highwaymen: On the Road Again*. The year 1993 also saw the performer being the subject of the White Star Video documentary *Kris Kristofferson*, and in 1998 Kris was a Kennedy Center Honors recipient, along with Bill Cosby, John Kander, Willie Nelson, Andre Previn, and Shirley Temple. Although the star rarely appeared on TV outside of telefilms or musical programs, he did do an episode of the HBO sitcom *The Larry Sanders Show* in 1992 (in 1976 he had guested on *The Muppet Show*). He also narrated the Showtime TV series *Dead Man's Gun* in 1997, and in 1999 he did the same chore for the show *VH1 Legends*. That year he played the role of Steve Day, head of the U.S. government's elite crime division in the ABC-TV four-hour sci-fi movie *Tom Clancy's Netforce*.

The new century saw Kris Kristofferson as active as ever, making personal appearances, recording for the One Way label and starring in a number of theatrical and TV movies. In 2000, he was Lou Smit in the CBS-TV miniseries *Perfect Murder, Perfect Town*, and his theatrical appearances included the remake of *Planet of the Apes* (2001), the comedy *Wooly Boys* (2001), and *Last Word in Paradise* (2001), a drama about the lives of people in a New York City hotel during a twenty-four-hour period. The prolific actor was also featured in *D-Tox* (2002—made in 1999), a cop thriller starring Sylvester Stallone. Meanwhile, in November 2001, Kris received the Lifetime Achievement Award at the Ninth Annual Diversity Awards.

Filmography

Ned Kelly (United Artists, 1970) (song only)

Clay Pigeon (MGM, 1971) (song only)

The Last Movie (Univ, 1971)

Cisco Pike (Col, 1971)

Fat City (Columbia, 1972) (songs only)

Blume in Love (WB, 1973)

The Gospel Road (20th-Fox, 1973) (also song)

Pat Garrett and Billy the Kid (MGM, 1973)

Free to Be . . . You & Me (Artisan Entertainment, 1974) (s)

Janis: A Film (Crawley Films, 1974) (documentary)

Bring Me the Head of Alfredo Garcia (UA, 1974)

Alice Doesn't Live Here Anymore (WB, 1975)

Vigilante Force (UA, 1976)

The Sailor Who Fell From Grace With the Sea (Avco Emb, 1976)

A Star Is Born (WB, 1976)

Semi-Tough (Par, 1977)

Convoy (UA, 1978)

Freedom Road (NBC-TV, 10/29–30/79)

One Trick Pony (WB, 1980) (song)

Heaven's Gate (UA, 1980)

Rollover (Orion/WB, 1981) (also song)

Traveller (Irish, 1981) (song only)

Maeve (British Film Institute, 1982) (song only)

Beyond Reasonable Doubt (Satori, 1983) (song only)

The Lost Honor of Kathryn Beck [Acts of Passion] (CBS-TV, 1/24/84)

Flashpoint (TriStar, 1984)

Songwriter (TriStar, 1984) (also co-songs)

Trouble in Mind (Alive Films, 1985) (also song)

The Last Days of Frank and Jesse James (NBC-TV, 2/16/86)

Something Wild (Orion, 1986) (song only)

Blood & Orchids (CBS-TV, 2/23–24/86)

Stagecoach (CBS-TV, 5/18/86)

Mascara [Makeup for Murder] (Praxino Pictures, 1987) (song only)

The Tracker (Home Box Office-TV, 3/26/88)

Armageddon Express (Documentary Films, 1988) (documentary)

Big Top Pee-wee (Par, 1988)

Charles Haughey's Ireland (Rego, 1988) (documentary)

Walking After Midnight (Kay Film, 1988)

Millennium (20th-Fox, 1989)

Tennessee Nights (Condor, 1989) (song only)

Welcome Home (Col, 1989)

Night of the Cyclone [Perfume of the Cyclone] (Video One Canada, 1990)

Pair of Aces (CBS-TV, 1/14/90)

Sandino (Umanzor Beta Films, 1990)

Another Pair of Aces: Three of a Kind (CBS-TV, 4/9/91)

No Place to Hide (Cannon, 1992)

Original Intent (Skouras Pictures, 1992)

Miracle in the Wilderness (TNT Cable, 12/9/91)

Christmas in Connecticut (TNT Cable, 4/13/92)

Trouble Shooters: Trapped Beneath the Earth (NBC-TV, 10/3/93)

Paper Hearts [Cheatin' Hearts] (Trimark, 1993)

Knights (Kings Road Entertainment, 1993)

Sodbusters (Showtime Cable, 7/17/94)

Big Dreams & Broken Hearts: The Dottie West Story (TNN Cable, 1/22/95)

Adventures of the Old West (Disney Channel Cable, 1995) (host) (documentary)

Brothers' Destiny [Long Road Home/The Road Home] (Concorde/New Horizons, 1995)

Inflammable (CBS-TV, 11/28/95)

Pharoah's Army (Orion, 1995)

Tad (Family Channel Cable, 2/12/95)

Lone Star (Col/TriStar, 1996)

Blue Rodeo (CBS-TV, 10/20/96)

Fire Down Below (WB, 1997)

Big Guns: The Story of the Western (TNT Cable, 7/22/97) (documentary)

Dead Man's Gun (Showtime Cable, 3/20/97) (narrator)

Message to Love: The Isle of Wight Festival (Strand Releasing, 1997) (documentary)

Two for Texas (TNT Cable, 1/18/98)

Girls' Night (Showtime Cable, 12/6/98)

Blade (New Line Cinema, 1998)

Dance With Me (Col, 1998)

A Soldier's Daughter Never Cries (October Film, 1998)

The Land Before Time VI: The Secret of Saurus Rock (Univ, 1998) (voice only) (direct to video)

Outlaw Justice (CBS-TV, 1/24/99)

Tom Clancy's Netforce (ABC-TV, 2/1/99, 2/4/99)

Payback (Par, 1999)

Molokai: The Story of Father Damien (Unapix/Vine International, 1999)

Limbo (Col/TriStar, 1999)

The Joyriders (Trident Releasing, 1999)

The Ballad of Ramblin' Jack (Lot 47 Films, 2000) (documentary)

Planet of the Apes (20th-Fox, 2001)

Wooly Boys (PFG Entertainment, 2001)

Last Word on Paradise (IFC/Killer Films, 2001)

D-Tox [Eye See You] (Univ 2002) (made in 1999)

Disappearances (Kingdom County Productions, 2002)

Blade 2: Bloodlust (New Line Cinema, 2002)

TV Series

Amerika (ABC, 2/15/87–2/22/87) (miniseries)

Dead Man's Gun (Showtime, 1997) (narrator)

VH1 Legends (VH1, 1999) (narrator)

Perfect Murder, Perfect Town (CBS, 2/27/2000, 3/1/2000) (miniseries)

Album Discography

LPs

Border Lord (Monument/Col P-31302)

Breakaway (Monument/Col PZ-033278)

Easter Island (Col/Monument JZ-35310)

Full Moon (A&M 4403) w. Rita Coolidge

Highwayman (Col 40056) w. Willie Nelson, Waylon Jennings, Johnny Cash

Jesus Was a Capricorn (Monument/Col PZ-31909)

Kristofferson (Monument SLP-18139)

Me and Bobby McGee (Monument/Col PZ-30817)

My Songs (Pair PDL-2-1078)

Ned Kelly (UA UAS-5213) [ST]

Repossessed (Mer 830406-1)

Sideshow (Col PZ-32914)

Songs of Kris Kristofferson (Monument/Col PZ-34687)

Songwriter (Col FC-39531) [ST]

Spooky Lady's Sideshow (Monument KZ-32914)

A Star Is Born (Col JS-34403) [ST]

Surreal Thing (Col PZ-34254)

That Silver Tongued Devil and I (Monument/Col PS-30679)

To the Bone (Col JZ-36885)

Who's to Bless and Who's to Blame (Monument PZ-33379)

Winning Hand (Monument 38389-1) w. Willie Nelson, Dolly Parton, Brenda Lee

CDs

All-Time Greatest Hits (Varese Sarabande 0662744)

The Austin Sessions (Atlantic 83208)

The Best of Kris Kristofferson (CBS Select 1026)

The Best of Kris Kristofferson (Sony Music Special Products AK-17915)

The Best of Kris Kristofferson, Vol. 2 (CBS Select BUK-50122)

Border Lord (One Way A-26172)

Breakaway (Monument AK-47065) w. Rita Coolidge

Country Collection (Polygram 5540092)

Easter Island (One Way A-26176)

Highwayman (BCD GLD-25380) w. Johnny Cash, Waylon Jennings, Willie Nelson

Highwayman (Col CK-40056) w. Johnny Cash, Waylon Jennings, Willie Nelson

Highwayman 2 (Col CK-45240) w. Johnny Cash, Waylon Jennings, Willie Nelson

His Life & Work (White Star 1696)

Jesus Was a Capricorn (Monument AK-47064)

Live at the Philharmonic (Monument AK52415) w. Willie Nelson, Rita Coolidge, Larry Gatlin

Me & Bobby McGee (Monument AK-44351)

Millennium (Artisan Entertainment 60491)

A Moment of Forever (Buddha 99720)

My Songs (Pair PDC2-1078)

Natural Act (Polygram 550770) w. Rita Coolidge

The Road Goes on Forever (Liberty C21Z-28091) w. Johnny Cash, Waylon Jennings, Willie Nelson

Shake Hands With the Devil (One Way A-26177) w. Rita Coolidge

The Silver Tongued Devil and I (Monument AK-44352)

Singer/Songwriter (GSC Music 15062)

Singer/Songwriter (Sony Music Special Products A2K-48621)

The Songs of Kris Kristofferson (Monument AK-44350)

Spooky Lady's Sideshow (One Way A-26173)

A Star Is Born (Columbia CK-57375) [ST]

Super Hits (Monument AK-69788)

Surreal Thing (One Way A-26175)

Third World Warrior (Mercury 824629-2) w. Willie Nelson, Sam Waterston, T-Bone Barnett

To the Bone (One Way A-26178)

The Very Best of Kris Kristofferson (Sony 645872)

Who's to Bless & Who's to Blame (One Way A-26174)

Frankie Laine

(b. Francesco Paolo LoVecchio, Chicago, Illinois, March 30, 1913)

A true legend in the entertainment world, Frankie Laine's diverse show-business career began in the early 1930s and continued into the twenty-first century. While his initial years in the profession were rough and offered little success, the star hit it big in 1947 with the song "That's My Desire." After that his career skyrocketed, expanding to include not only records and personal appearances but also radio, television, movies, and composing. As popular abroad (especially in Great Britain) as in his homeland, Frankie earned twenty-one gold singles with records sales over the 200 million mark. Known as "Mr. Rhythm," the singer was equally at home with jazz, popular songs, ballads, religious music, and country tunes.

The oldest of eight children of Sicilian immigrants, Frankie Laine was born Francesco Paolo LoVecchio on March 30, 1913, in Chicago's Little Italy. His father was a barber (one of his private clients was mobster kingpin Al Capone), and his maternal grandfather was murdered by gangsters. That aside, Francesco had a happy family life. His lifelong love of music and singing developed when he was part of the choir at the Church of the Immaculate Conception. He later attended Lane Technical School, from which he was to derive his stage name. As a teenager he sang with the house band at the Merry Garden Ballroom, and at seventeen he became a marathon dancer. He and partner Ruth Smith set the all-time marathon dance record in the early 1920s in Atlantic City, dancing 3,501 hours for 145 consecutive days and splitting a $1,000 prize.

In 1935 Frankie left the marathon circuit and went east to make a living as a singer. For a time he worked with jazz pianist Art Hodes and was a vocalist with Freddy Carlone's band in Cleveland. In New York City, he sang on radio station WINS and then returned to Chicago and then Cleveland, again with no success. For a period, he managed a female singing trio in Hollywood. While on the West Coast, Laine did chorus vocal work at MGM and briefly dubbed an actor's singing in *The Kid From Brooklyn* (1946).

During the war years, Frank worked in a Los Angeles–area defense plant, but lost the job when the conflict ended. Fortunately, he began singing on *Make Believe Ballroom* on KFWB in Hollywood as well as collaborating as a songwriter with pianist Carl Fisher. While performing at Billy Berg's club, he did a jazz version of "That's My Desire" (which had been a best-selling record for Nick Lucas back in 1931), and he waxed it for Mercury Records in 1947. Laine had already recorded for the Beltone and Atlas labels, and his initial Mercury disc, "I May Be Wrong," had done well. "That's My Desire" eventually sold over 3.5 million copies and launched Frankie's stardom after seventeen years of professional struggle.

Following the success of "That's My Desire," the singer signed with Mercury Records, and a steady stream of successful numbers followed, including "A Sunday Kind of Love," "September in the Rain," "Georgia on My Mind," and such gold records as "Two Loves Have I," "Mule Train," and "Cry of the Wild Goose." Laine and his conductor Carl Fisher toured constantly, and they

Frankie Laine in *He Laughed Last* (1956).
[Courtesy of JC Archives]

also collaborated on a number of songs, the best known being "We'll Be Together Again," which was not only a best-seller for Frankie but, thereafter, was recorded by over one hundred other singers. In addition Laine guest-starred on such radio shows as *The Chesterfield Supper Club, The Big Show*, and *The Spike Jones Show*. Early in 1950, Frankie made his television debut on Ed Sullivan's *Toast of the Town*, and during the next two decades, Laine would make many appearances on that variety program. In April 1950, he hosted his first TV special, *The Frankie Laine Hour*.

The singer made his official screen debut in Columbia's 1949 musical *Make Believe Ballroom*, singing "On the Sunny Side of the Street," and he signed with the studio. During the next half dozen years he starred in a series of musicals that emphasized songs over plot. In *When You're Smiling* (1950) he performed the title song and "Georgia on My Mind," and *Sunny Side of the Street* (1951) again had him performing the title tune along with such ditties as "I'm Gonna Live Till I Die." The delightful *Rainbow 'Round My Shoulder* (1952) costarred talented and pretty Charlotte Austin (the daughter of crooner Gene Austin). Frankie sang such numbers as "Wonderful, Wasn't It?" *Bring Your Smile Along* (1956), the directorial debut of Blake Edwards, gave Frankie the title theme plus had him performing such other numbers as "When a Girl Is Beautiful."

On June 15, 1950, Frankie Laine married actress Nan Grey, who had two daughters from a previous marriage. The next year the entertainer signed a lucrative long-term contract with Columbia Records, and more hit records followed, beginning with the two-sided gold disc "Jezebel" / "Rose, Rose I Love You." Among his other popular Columbia platters were "Rainbow 'Round My Shoulder," "Tell Me a Story" with Jimmy Boyd, "Hummingbird," and "The 3:10 to Yuma." The recording sessions led to more gold records, such as "High Noon," "I Believe" (his biggest hit, with over 7.5 million copies sold), and "Moonlight Gambler." Frankie had best-selling duets with Jo Stafford on such singles as "In the Cool, Cool, Cool of the Evening" and "Way Down Yonder in New Orleans." He and Doris Day also did well in 1952 with "Sugarbush."

In 1953 Frankie's recording of "I Believe" stayed at number one on the British charts for eighteen weeks (a record yet to be broken), and he appeared at the London Palladium, where he was mobbed by adoring fans. His popularity in England was so great he continued to make successful tours there well into the 1980s. In addition to being a top nightclub attraction in the United States, the singer also had success in venues in Europe, South America, Australia, and the Orient. In England, he filmed a series of fifteen-minute television programs that were syndicated in the United States during the 1954–55 season as *The Frankie Laine Show*. During 1955 and 1956, his one-hour program *Frankie Laine Time* was a summer series on CBS-TV.

Another aspect of the singer's career was launched in 1953 when he sang the title song over the credits of the Warner Bros. melodrama *Blowing Wild*. He would do the same chore in a series of Westerns: *Man Without a Star* (1955), *Strange Lady in Town* (1955), *Gunfight at the O.K. Corral* (1957), *The 3:10 to Yuma* (1957), and *Bullwhip!* (1958). In 1956 he sang "Hell Hath No Fury" in MGM's *Meet Me in Las Vegas*, and that same year he headlined his last Columbia feature, *He Laughed Last*. This time he performed only "Danny Boy" and "Save Your Sorrow for Tomorrow" in this serio-comedy directed by Blake Edwards. The movie gave the singer an opportunity to do dramatics, although it was on such TV series as *Perry Mason*, *Rawhide* (in a 1960 episode with his wife, Nan Grey), and *Burke's Law* that the performer revealed his fine acting ability. Just as he sang theme songs in big-screen Westerns, he also achieved one of his greatest successes with the title song to the CBS-TV series *Rawhide*, which aired from 1959 to 1966. The singing star also performed the themes for three other TV series: *Gunslinger* (1961), *Rango* (1967), and the first season of *The Misadventures of Sheriff Lobo* (1979–80).

During the early 1960s, things began to slow for Frankie Laine in the record field, although he remained an international audience favorite as well as a much-in-demand TV guest star. Following a chart success with "Don't Make My Baby Blue" in 1963, he left Columbia and signed with Capitol Records. However, his two-year stay with that label proved unfruitful, except for a good-selling LP, *I Believe*. In 1967, Frank joined ABC-Paramount Records, and his career had a resurgence with several top-selling singles: "I'll Take Care of Your Cares," "You Wanted Someone to Play With," and such gold singles as "Making Memories" and "You Gave Me a Mountain." In 1972, Frankie, who had such a long association with sagebrush tales, sang the title theme for the satirical western *Blazing Saddles*. Thereafter, he was later heard singing "Maxwell's Silver Hammer" in *All This and World War II* (1977) and "On the Sunny Side of the Street" in *House Calls* (1978). During the 1970s, he recorded for labels like Amos, Warner Bros., Mainstream, and his own company, Score Records. During the late 1970s, Laine made two albums for the Polydor label in England.

Frankie began the 1980s with a one-man special on BBC-TV in Great Britain, and in 1982 he had a gold album, *The World of Frankie Laine*, in Holland and England, for Arcade Records. He continued to make club and concert appearances here and abroad as well as doing TV, like the small-screen special *Moments to Remember* in 1980 and the subsequent *Over Easy*, both for PBS-TV. In 1985, the singer was briefly sidelined by quadruple heart bypass surgery but he was soon working again, and in 1987 he was back on the record charts, this time the classical list, with the compact disc *Roundup*, which he made with Eric Kunzel and the Cincinnati Pops Orchestra. A second heart bypass surgery in 1990 caused the singer to slow his career somewhat as he and his wife moved into a new home in San Diego, California, a city where they'd lived for some forty years. Laine's autobiography, *That Lucky Old Son*, was published in 1993; on July 25 of that year, his wife Nan died on her seventy-second birthday.

In 1996, Frankie Laine received a Lifetime Achievement Award from the Twenty-Seventh Annual Songwriters Hall of Fame, and in 1998 his compact disc, *Wheels of a Dream* for After 9 Records, earned solid reviews and substantial sales in the United States and abroad. One of its cuts, "Song of India," was issued as a single in England, where it made the charts, giving Frankie another hit record at age eighty-five. That year he also received the Golden Boots Award for this contribution to Western cinema. In 1999, Laine set an attendance record at the Orleans Hotel in Las Vegas, and he remarried, to Marcia Ann Kline. With the new century the veteran songster continued to make personal appearances, record, and do charity work. He received the "Living Legend Award 2000" from the San Diego–based Women's International Center. His eighty-eighth birthday party in 2001, feted by the National Association of Music Merchants (NAMM), drew over seven hundred people, with greetings from dozens of personalities, including Mitch Miller, Tony Martin, Pat Boone, and astronaut Wally Schirra. For the occasion the San Diego Padres baseball team designated a special jersey reading "Laine 88." In June 2001, Laine was inducted into the Western Music Association Hall of Fame.

Filmography

The Harvey Girls (MGM, 1946) (voice only)
The Kid From Brooklyn (RKO, 1946) (voice only)
Make Believe Ballroom (Col, 1949)
When You're Smiling (Col, 1950)
Sunny Side of the Street (Col, 1951)
Rainbow 'Round My Shoulder (Col, 1952)
Blowing Wild (WB., 1953) (voice only)
Bring Your Smile Along (Col, 1955)
Man Without a Star (UI, 1955) (voice only)
He Laughed Last (Col, 1956)
Rock 'Em Cowboy (Col, 1957) (short)
Strange Lady in Town (WB, 1955) (voice only)
Meet Me in Las Vegas [Viva Las Vegas!] (MGM, 1956)

Gunfight at the O.K. Corral (Par, 1957) (voice only)
The 3:10 to Yuma (Col, 1957) (voice only)
Bullwhip! (AA, 1958) (voice only)
The Last Picture Show (Col, 1971) (voice only)
Blazing Saddles (WB, 1973) (voice only)
All This and World War II (Deluxe, 1977) (voice only)
House Calls (Universal, 1978) (voice only)
Eskimo Limon [Lemon Popsicle] (Noah Films, 1978) (voice only)
Yotzim Kavua [Going Steady] (Noah Films, 1978) (voice only)
Raging Bull (UA, 1980) (voice only)
Whore (Vidmark, 1991) (voice only)

Radio Series

Make Believe Ballroom (KFWB, 1945) (local)

TV Series

Frankie Laine Time (Synd, 1954–55)
The Frankie Laine Show (CBS, 1955, 1956)
Rawhide (CBS, 1959–66) (voice only)
Gunslinger (CBS, 1961) (voice only)

Rango (ABC, 1967) (voice only)
The Misadventures of Sheriff Lobo (NBC, 1979–80) (voice only)

Album Discography

LPs

The ABC Collection (ABC AC-30001)
All of Me (Bulldog BDL-1035)
All of These . . . And More (FLIAS FL-3)
All This and World War II (20th-Fox 522) [ST]
All Time Favorites (Wing MGW-12110/SRW-16110)
American Legend—16 Greatest Hits (Embassy 31599)
Back to Back (ERA BU-5710) (w. Johnnie Ray)
Balladeer (Col CL-1393/CS-8188)
The Best of Frankie Laine (Hallmark SHM-515)
Blazing Saddles (WB BS-2781) [ST]
A Brand New Day (Amos AAS-7013)
Call of the Wild (Col CL-1829/CS-8629)
Command Performance (Col CL-625)
Concert Date (Mer MG-20085)
A Country Laine (Playback PP1-12004)
The Country Sounds of Frankie Laine (Music for Pleasure MFO-50256)
Deuces Wild (Col CL-1696/CS-8496)
Favorites (10″ Mer MG-25007)
Foreign Affair (Col CL-1160) w. Michel Legrand
Foreign Exchange (FLSOA OVL-98-1)
Frankie Laine (Everest 4105)
Frankie Laine (Hit Parade International HP-31)
Frankie Laine (10″ Mer MG-25024)
Frankie Laine (10″ Mer MG-25025)
Frankie Laine (10″ Mer MG-25026)
Frankie Laine (10″ Mer MG-25027)
Frankie Laine and Billy Daniels (10″ Mer MG-25100)
Frankie Laine and His Guests (Wyncote W-9161)
Frankie Laine and the Four Lads (Col CL-861)
The Frankie Laine Collection (Hallmark PDA-016)
Frankie Laine Sings (Allegro 4132)
Frankie Laine Sings (Galaxy 4821)
Frankie Laine Sings (Kaola AW-14133)
Frankie Laine Sings/Andre Previn Plays (Rondo R/RS-2015)
Frankie Laine Sings His Very Best (Springboard SPX-6011)
Frankie Laine Sings "That's My Desire" (Rondo-lette A21)
The Frankie Laine Songbook (World Record Club SM-531-6)

Frankie Laine's Best (Exact EX-242)
Frankie Laine's Best (Hallmark SHM-538)
Frankie's Gold (Jubilate J1506)
Golden Hits (Mer MG-20587/SR-60587)
The Golden Years (Wing PKW-2-111)
Greatest Hits (Amos AAS-7009)
Greatest Hits (Col CL-1231/CS-8636)
Greatest Hits (QMO 126/SPX-6011)
Greatest Hits (Spot SPR-8538)
Greatest Hits (Springboard SP-4009)
Gunslinger (FLSOA OVL-99-1)
Heartaches Can Be Fun (Pickwick SPC-3151)
Hell Bent for Leather (CBS 62-062)
Hell Bent for Leather (Col CL-1615/CS-8415)
Hell Bent for Leather (Phillips BL.7468)
High Noon (Harmony H-30406)
I Believe (Cap T/ST-2277)
I Wanted Someone to Love (ABC AB/BCS-608)
I'll Take Care of Your Cares (ABC AB/BCS-604)
I'm Gonna Live Till I Die (Contour 6870-616)
I'm Gonna Live Till I Die (Hallmark SHM-650)
I'm Gonna Live Till I Die (Har HS-11345)
In South Africa—A Souvenir Album (CBS ALD-8112)
It Only Happens Once (FLIAS FL-4) (British)
Jazz Spectacular (Col CL-808, Col JCL-808) w. Buck Clayton
The Last Picture Show (Col D-31143) [ST]
Life Is Beautiful (Polydor 2382-488)
Lover's Laine (10″ Col CL-2504)
Memories (Harmony HL-7425/HS-11225)
Memories of His Greatest Hits (Wing SRW-16349)
Memory Laine (Tower T/ST-5092)
Milestones (FLSOA 103)
Mr. Rhythm (10″ Col CL-6278)
Mr. Rhythm (10″ Phillips BBR-8068)
Mr. Rhythm Sings (10″ Mer MG-25097)
Music, Maestro, Please (10″ Mer MG-25124)
A Musical Portrait of New Orleans (10″ Col CL-6268) w. Jo Stafford
A Musical Portrait of New Orleans (Col CL-578) w. Jo Stafford
Now and Then (CBS P15166)
One for My Baby (10″ Col CL-2548)
One for My Baby (10″ Col CL-6200)

The Pick of Frankie Laine (51 West QR-16047)

Place in Time (Score FLP-102)

Reflective Years (FLP 501)

Reunion in Rhythm (Col CL-1277/CS-8087, Col ACS-8087) w. Michel Legrand

Rockin' (Col CL-975)

The Roving Gambler (Har HL-7329/HS-11129)

Showcase of Hits (Phillips BBL-7263-1958)

Singing the Blues (Mer MG-22069)

Singing the Blues (Wing MGW-12158/SRW-16158)

Sixteen Greatest Hits (Trip TOP-16-3)

So Ultra Rare (Score FLP-101)

Songs by Frankie Laine (10″ Mer MG-25098)

Songs by Laine (Mer MG-20069)

Songs for Losers (FLIAS 79/CUS/415)

Songs for People Together (Mer MG-20083)

Songs That Made Him Famous (10″ Mer MG-25007)

Sunny Side of the Street (10″ Mer MG-25100) [ST]

Take Me Back to Laine Country (ABC ABCS-657)

That Lucky Old Sun (Pickwick SPC-3526)

That's My Desire (Har HL-7382/HS-11182)

That's My Desire (Mer MG-20080)

That's My Desire (Wing MGW-12202/SRW-16202)

3:10 to Yuma (Citadel GD-2) [ST]

To Each His Own (ABC ABC/ABCS-628)

Too Marvelous for Words (Encore P-14392)

Torchin' (Col CL-1176/CS-8024)

Twenty Incredible Performances (ABC X-790)

20 Incredible Performances (Probe GTSP-205)

20 Memories in Gold (Polydor 2382-457)

The Uncollected Frankie Laine (Hindsight HSR-198)

The Uncollected Frankie Laine, Vol. 2 (Hindsight HSR-216)

The Very Best of Frankie Laine & Johnnie Ray (Realm 2V8078)

The Very Best of Frankie Laine—20 Greatest Hits (Warwick PR-5032)

Wanderlust (Col CL-1962/CS-8762)

With All My Heart (Mer MG-20105)

The World of Frankie Laine (Arcade ADEH-19)

You Are My Love (Col CL-1317/CS-8119)

You Gave Me a Mountain (ABC ABCS-682)

You Gave Me a Mountain (Pickwick SPC-3601)

CDs

All of Me (Memories of Yesteryear MTLCD-5053)

All Time Greats (AZ CDSOV-7)

All Time Greats (EMI 59085M)

All Time Hits (KK CDMFP5907)

Balladeer/Wanderlust (Col 487191-2, Globetrotter 753062)

Best From the West (Music Net GFS-384)

The Best of Frankie Laine (BMG TRTCD-166)

The Best of Frankie Laine (Curb DZ-77596)

The Best of Frankie Laine (Fat Boy FATCD-252)

The Best of Frankie Laine (Hindsight FCD-4419)

The Best of Frankie Laine (Musketeer MU-3011)

The Best of Frankie Laine (Spectrum 5444282)

The Best of Frankie Laine (Start 3011)

The Best of Frankie Laine (Sunflower SUN-2023)

The Best of Frankie Laine—Jezebel (Pulse PLS-CD-118)

The Best of Frankie Laine—Songs of Fortune (Newsound—no number)

Christmas Wishin' (Score—no number)

Classic Country (Direct Source 7530)

Cocktail Hour (Columbia River Entertainment Group GRG-218024)

The Collection (Col 039)

Collection (Emporio EMPRCD-845)

The Collection (Polygram 241596)

Country and Western (Hallmark 309442)

A Country Laine (Laurie BCD-1009)

A Country Laine (Prestige PRSCD-250)

The Country Store Collection (Castle CST-43)

Deuces Wild/Call of the Wild (Col 48107-2, Globetrotter 753102)

The Diamond Star Collection (Arcade RH-16973)

Dueling Country (Direct Source 90211) w. Kenny Rogers

The Dynamic Frankie Laine (Masters MACD-61106-2)

Early Classics (Spectrum 5444282)

18 All Time Hits (Music for Pleasure CDMFP-5907)

The Essence of Frankie Laine (Legacy CK-53573)

The European Concert, Vol. 1 (Score—no number)

The European Concert, Vol. 2 (Score—no number)

The Fabulous Frankie Laine (Reader's Digest A3-28442/0838)

Favourites (Pegasus PEGCD-263)

14 Great Country Songs (TH-CO TC-004)

Frankie Laine (Arcade 5300214)

Frankie Laine (Beautiful Music Company LND-1)

Frankie Laine (Cameo CD-3643)

Frankie Laine (The Entertainers 296)

Frankie Laine (The Entertainers 433)

Frankie Laine (Pegasus 372338)

Frankie Laine (Time TM-1236)

Frankie Laine (Timeless Treasures 108)

Frankie Laine (Trumpets of Jericho 20.4808-2051)

Frankie Laine and Friends (Castle PIESD-061)

Frankie Laine and Friends (Classic 7571)

Frankie Laine and Friends (Hallmark 31122)

Frankie Laine and Friends (KRB Music Companies 5016-2)

Frankie Laine and Friends (Pegasus PEG3263)

Frankie Laine and Friends (Prestige PRCDSP-301)

Frankie Laine and Friends (Score FLCD-0691)

Frankie Laine and Jo Stafford—The Duets (Bear Family BCD-15620)

Frankie Laine and Lynn Anderson (United Audio UAE-30782)

The Frankie Laine Collection (Mer 510-435)

Frankie Laine/Johnnie Ray (Dominion 863-2)

Golden Greats (Goldies 25421)

Golden Moments, Vol. 1 (Yankee Marketing—no number)

Golden Moments, Vol. 2 (Yankee Marketing—no number)

Gospel Revival (Sony Music Special Products 30732)

The Great Frankie Laine (Goldies GLD-63240)

The Great Frankie Laine (RedX RXBOX031068)

Greatest Hits (CeDe International CD-66094)

Greatest Hits (Cleopatra 667999)

Greatest Hits (Col CK-8636)

Greatest Hits (Good Music Record Company A21173)

Greatest Hits (MV CDGRF-44)

Greatest Hits (ONN ONN-1)

Greatest Hits (Pegasus PEG-CD-055)

Greatest Hits (Pegasus Flight Productions 493)

Greatest Hits (Prime Cut 2121)

Greatest Hits (Solo PEGCD-055)

Greatest Hits (Spectrum U4022)

Greatest Hits, Vol. 1 (Laurie BCD-1010)

Greatest Hits, Vol. 2 (Laurie BCD-1011)

Gunfight at O.K. Corral (Starlite CDS-5111)

Gunfight at O.K. Corral (Theen CD-0296)

High Noon (Charly 309238)

High Noon (Classic Hits CDCD-1023)

High Noon (ARC TOP-941023)

High Noon (Mu-Op MO-3017)

High Noon: 20 Greatest Hits (Remember RMB-75088)

Hitmaker (Hallmark 300272)

The Hitmaker (Pink RH-648935)

I Believe (Bear Family BCD-16367)

I Believe (Prism PLATCD-177)

I Believe—20 Great Songs (Delta Music CD-6055)

I Hear Music (Sony Music Special Products A-26056)

The Incomparable Frankie Laine (Start 29503)

It Ain't Over Till It's Over (In-Sight)

Jazz Spectacular (Legacy KC-65507) w. Buck Clayton

Jezebel (Castle Communications PCD-10217)

Jezebel (MSI 52147)

The Last Picture Show (Col CK-31143) [ST]

The Legend at His Best (Collectables 0045)

Life Is Beautiful (Prestige CDSG-0227)

The Lost Singles (Hebeto International HBT-04371)

Love Is a Golden Ring (International IMC-3204808)

Lyrics by Laine (Score—no number)

Making Memories (Satril SATCD-5001)

Memories (Samba—no number)

Memories in Gold (Prestige PRCDSP-5004)

Memories in Gold (Score FLCD-0592)

Memories in Gold (Sony 0438433)

Moonlight Gambler (CD Sounds CDFX-6747)

New Directions (Prestige CDSG-251)

On the Trail (Bear Family BCD-15480)

On the Trail Again (Bear Family BCD-15632)

One for My Baby/Mr. Rhythm (Collectables COL-CD-6058)

The Original Recordings (Col 4851249)

Original Recordings (Sony 4851242)

The Platinum Collection (Solo PC-634)

Portrait in Rhythm (Hebeto International HBT-0195)

Portrait of a Legend (Touchwood TWCD-2009)

Portrait of a Song Stylist (Har HARCD-102)

Portrait of Frankie Laine (Penny PYCD-147)

Rare & Rockin' (Hebeto International HBT-03287)

Rawhide and More Big Hits (Javelin HADCD-206)

Rawhide—The Best of Frankie Laine (Woodm WMCD-5665)

Rawhide: 20 Golden Greats (Platinum Collection CDPLAT-072)

Rawhide: 20 Greatest Hits (Tring International GRF044)

Rawhide: 20 of His Best (Hollywood Nites HNC00081)

Return of Mr. Rhythm (Hindsight HCD-256)

The Return of Mr. Rhythm—I Believe (Bianco BIA-4013)

Reunion in Jazz (Score SRCD-5194)

Rewind (CRN Music 5300214)

Riders in the Sky (Prestige CDSGPO-248)

Rockin'/Hell Bent for Leather (Collectables COL-CD-6077)

Round-Up (Telarc CD-80141) w. Erich Kunzel and Cincinnati Pops Orchestra

Sacred Jazz (Hebeto International HBT-03287)

Setting the Standard: The Complete Transcriptions Recordings (Jasmine JASCD-385)

The '70s Country Collection (SMS 4723082)

16 Great Hits (Weton RH-28087)

16 Greatest Hits (Deluxe DLX-07897)

16 Greatest Hits (Hollywood 7897)

16 Most Requested Songs (Legacy CK-45029)

So Ultra Rare (Prestige CDSGPO-249)

Someday Sweetheart (ABM ABMMCD-1022)

Somethin' Old, Somethin' New (Prestige PRCDSP-300)

Songs of Fortune (New Sound NST-042)

Teach Me to Pray (Score—no number)

That Lucky Old Sun (Bear Family BCD-16361)

That Lucky Old Sun (Prism PLATCD-556)

That's My Desire (Pho PUCE-10050)

That's My Desire (Pickwick 11602)

That's My Desire (Pilz Entertainment 449343-2)

That's My Desire (Polygram 4493432)

That's My Desire: 36 All-Time Greatest Hits (GSC Music 15441)

Torchin'/You Are My Love (Sony 4946232)

Le Trilogie D'Amour (Hebeto International HBT-03896/1-2)

20 All-Time Hits (Music for Pleasure—no number)

20 Great Hits (Durec RH-618069)

20 Great Tracks (Prestige PRCDSP-301)

20 Greatest Hits (MR PLATCD-11)

20 Greatest Hits (Prestige PRCDSP-5004)

20 Greatest Hits (Prism PLATCD-1128)

20 of His Best (Obj.E.—no number)

20 Top Hits (Masters 502572)

22 Greatest Hits (King 2804)

The Uncollected Frankie Laine (Hindsight HCD-198)

The Very Best of (ABC Years) (Taragon TARCD-1017)

The Voice of Our Choice, Vol. 1 (Hebeto International HBT-04236)

The Voice of Our Choice, Vol. 2 (Hebeto International HBT-04247)

Wanted Man (Sony France 4723812)

The Weton Collection (Weton RH-91475)

Wheels of a Dream (After 9 TWCD-2020)

You Gave Me a Mountain/To Each His Own (GOT 3703)

The Young Master (Flapper PAST-CD-7826)

Your Cheatin' Heart (Pegasus PEG-CD-273)

Dorothy Lamour

(b. Mary Leta Dorothy Kaumeyer, New Orleans, Louisiana, December 10, 1914;
d. Los Angeles, California, September 22, 1996)

Forever associated with exotic South Seas sarong girls, Dorothy Lamour was the queen of jungle movies during the 1930s and 1940s. She grew to hate this stereotype, which limited her growth as an actress (she was a fine comedienne, a competent actress, and a pleasant vocalist). Sadly though, playing an alluring native in exotic garb remained her screen niche. In the famous "Road" comedy series she made with Bing Crosby and Bob Hope she definitely was in a supporting role to their antic mayhem, deserving a medal for surviving these lunatic celluloid excursions. As for being a pin-up favorite, Dorothy—she of the sloe eyes and penciled eyebrows—ranked behind Betty Grable and Rita Hayworth. Still the always underrated actress enjoyed a long show-business career and was quite popular with the public for many years.

She was born Mary Leta Dorothy Kaumeyer on December 10, 1914, in the charity ward of a New Orleans hospital. Her father was a waiter and her mother a waitress. After her parents were divorced, her mother married a man named Lambour and Dorothy also took that name. (When she went into show business, she dropped the "b" from her last name.) She started performing as a child during the First World War, selling war stamps and singing patriotic tunes. While she planned to be a teacher, finances forced her to quit school at fourteen and take a business course. She became a secretary. After winning several beauty contests (inspired by her childhood friend Dorothy Dell who became a movie actress), she became Miss New Orleans. Five-feet Five-inches Dorothy used her prize money in order to support herself while working with a stock company. Then, accompanied by her mother, she moved to Chicago, where she found employment as a sales clerk at Marshall Field Department Store. (She earned a weekly salary of $17.) Through a talent night competition at the Hotel Morrison she came to the attention of orchestra leader Herbie Kaye and after several auditions for him became a vocalist with his group, quickly displaying a fine sense of rhythm in her delivery of songs. She went on tour with Kaye, and the two fell in love. They were married in Waukegan, Illinois, on May 10, 1935.

When they arrived in New York City, Kaye got his pal and former Yale classmate Rudy Vallee to promote Dorothy. As a result she was hired as a singer at the Stork Club at $150 weekly. She teamed briefly with pianists Julius Monk and Joe Lilly for a vaudeville act and then won a spot on NBC radio's *The Dreamer of Songs* program. Dorothy made her film debut in Vitaphone shorts, including *The Stars Can't Be Wrong* (1936) and then went with the NBC radio show to the West Coast. She was among those who auditioned for, but lost, the role of mulatto Julie to Helen Morgan (from the original Broadway cast) in Universal's *Show Boat* (1936). However, Dorothy tested at Paramount and was awarded a contract at that studio lot, winning out over MGM who also expressed interest in signing the personality.

She made her feature debut in a bit in 1936's *College Holiday* (as a coed). That same year, she enjoyed the title role of *The Jungle Princess*, as a sultry native girl who saves a British hunter

Dorothy Lamour in the early 1940s.
[Courtesy of JC Archives]

(Ray Milland) after he is injured. The two of them battle a crook (Akim Tamiroff) and fall in love. Dorothy's dark beauty, coupled with a tight-fitting sarong and her waist-length hair, did the unreasonable story justice, and she immediately found a place with filmgoers. *Variety* reported "she lands powerfully in spite of the highly improbable story." During the picture, she sang "Moonlight and Shadows," and early in 1937 she recorded the song with Cy Feuer and His Orchestra for Brunswick Records, along with a trio of songs from her second film. *Swing High, Swing Low* (1937) was a remake of the play *Burlesque* and cast Dorothy as a vamp dancer attempting to break up singer Carole Lombard and bandsman Fred MacMurray in sultry Panama.

Along with other studio contractees, Dorothy refined their acting techniques by performing in front of the camera. In the slick programmer *Last Train From Madrid* (1937), which dealt with the Spanish Civil War, she was Gilbert Roland's mysterious girlfriend. One of the benefits of the studio system was that a performer could jump from such a "B" picture to an "A" picture like *High, Wide and Handsome* (1937), an elaborate musical about Pennsylvania oil-well pioneering in the 1850s. Irene Dunne was the star, with Dorothy subordinate as the immoral honky-tonk torch singer (she warbled "The Things I Want"). Independent filmmaker Sam Goldwyn traded the services of his company's Joel McCrea in order to borrow Paramount's Dorothy Lamour for his $2 million South Seas idyll *The Hurricane*. This lushly lensed romance tale boasted a spectacular storm sequence, and Lamour performed her most famous screen song, "The Moon of Manakoora." She closed out 1937 with the "B" picture *Thrill of a Lifetime* as a guest performer singing the title song.

The year 1937 also found Dorothy becoming a regular on NBC radio's *The Chase and Sanborn Hour*, where she would remain for two years. During the summer of 1937 she and Don Ameche costarred in the coffee maker's summer program. Meanwhile, her husband and his band were touring, primarily in the Midwest, where they had a big following.

There were plans to include Dorothy in Jack Benny's *Artists and Models* (1937) and Cecil B. DeMille's *The Buccaneer* (1938). Instead, she began 1938 with *The Big Broadcast of 1938* as the romantic interest singing "You Took the Words Right Out of My Heart." She recorded this song for Brunswick, along with "Thanks for the Memory," which Bob Hope (in his feature film debut) and Shirley Ross dueted in the feature. With the success of *The Jungle Princess* and *The Hurricane*, it was only a matter of time before Dorothy returned to the tropics and the sarong. She was reteamed with Ray Milland for the Technicolor *Her Jungle Love* (1938) as the uninhibited native girl Tura who rescues a British pilot (Milland) after a plane crash. She looked alluring and sang a trio of tunes, including "Lovelight in the Starlight," which she recorded for Brunswick with husband Herbie Kaye and His Orchestra. With Kaye she also recorded "Tonight We Live" and "On a Tropic Night," which she sang in *Tropic Holiday* (1938), yet another teaming with Ray Milland, this one set in Mexico. She had a solid dramatic role ("at least she is trying" judged the *New York Times*) in the fishing saga *Spawn of the North* (1938) as a local gal in love with a fisherman (George Raft). She repeated her role as Nicky Duval on *Lux Radio Theater*.

In 1939, Lamour, who was tired of being categorized so narrowly in the cinema, kidded her screen image in *St. Louis Blues*. She was a stage star who plays saronged characters and who runs away and becomes enamored of a showboat captain (Lloyd Nolan). She sang a quartet of songs, which she recorded for Brunswick Records with Jerry Joyce and His Orchestra since she and Herbie Kaye were separated and would divorce that year. Next Dorothy vocalized on "Strange Enchantment" in the Jack Benny comedy *Man About Town* (1939) and then returned to drama—portraying an Eurasian—for *Disputed Passage* (1939). That year also saw her appearing for a time on Rudy Vallee's radio show.

Dorothy was loaned to Twentieth Century-Fox to be a gun moll in *Johnny Apollo* (1940), a part she re-created the next year on *Lux Radio Theater*. Regardless of her preference, it was back to the South Seas and a sarong for Dorothy in *Typhoon* (1940), another Technicolor jungle opus where she sang (and recorded for Bluebird) "Palms of Paradise." She then began the "Road" pictures with Bing Crosby and Bob Hope. In *Road to Singapore* (1940), she performed "The Moon and the Willow Tree" and "Too Romantic" (again recording them for Bluebird). She demonstrated that she could match "wits" with the frantic shenanigans of Hope and Crosby on any level. She sang (and recorded) the title song in *Moon Over Burma* (1940) where she was a stranded singer saved by lumber men Preston Foster and Robert Preston. (She had an offscreen romance with Preston in this period.) Her final 1940 feature was again at Twentieth Century-Fox for *Chad Hanna*, a period circus drama that cast her as a bareback rider. In that busy year, three of her features were in the top twenty at the box office.

By now Paramount was paying Dorothy $5,000 weekly. During the World War II years, she would become one of the studio's most valuable properties in a series of top-notch pictures, although she ceased to record until the war's end due to the various union strikes by musicians. In this period she starred in a variety of properties, ranging from the popular "Road" series, to a teaming with Bob Hope (her best screen foil) in *Caught in the Draft* (1943) and *They Got Me Covered* (1943; on loanout to Samuel Goldwyn). There were more sarong efforts, such as *Aloma of the South Seas* (1941), *Beyond the Blue Horizon* (1942), and *Rainbow Island* (1944; a genre spoof), plus high-budgeted musical comedies like *The Fleet's In* (1942), *Dixie* (1943; with Bing Crosby), and *Riding High* (1943; with Dick Powell). She benefited from good songs in several of her offerings: "Pagan Lullaby" and "Full Moon and Empty Arms" in *Beyond the Blue Horizon*, and "Constantly" in *Road to Morocco* (1942). In *Star Spangled Rhythm* (1942), she, Paulette Goddard, and Veronica Lake teased their screen trademarks with "A Sweater, A Sarong and a Peekaboo Bang." During the war years, Lamour appeared frequently on radio shows like "Lux Radio Theater" (doing an adaptation of "Dixie"), *Mail Call*, and *Palmolive Party* (a Saturday night NBC show she hostessed). During one of the many war-bond drives in which she participated, Lamour auctioned off two of her sarong outfits for $2 million. (One of her original sarongs was later given to the Smithsonian Institute for display.)

The World War II years were the apex of Dorothy Lamour's career. Also during that period (April 7, 1943) she married Captain William Ross Howard II of Baltimore, Maryland. The star admitted, "I got serious about my acting for the first time, I can't explain it. I wanted to start all over again on a different basis. Maybe to prove something to somebody." At the end of the war, when her husband returned to Los Angeles and entered the field of advertising, the couple adopted a son, Ridgley, late in 1945.

By the mid-1940s, Lamour was wearying of her South Seas roles: "Ten years is a long time to be in pictures. But ten years in a sarong is too long. Personally I've had enough." Paramount heeded her feelings: In *Road to Utopia* (1945; completed in May 1944), the setting was the northern Klondike. In *My Favorite Brunette* (1947), with Bob Hope as a private eye, she was an heiress in distress. The stars re-created both roles on radio's *Showtime*. She was steamy on the prairie with Robert Preston and Alan Ladd in *Wild Harvest* (1947) and returned to an exotic role in *Road to Rio* (1947) where she sang "Experience." In the summer of 1947, she was hostess of the NBC radio show *Front and Center*. In late 1947, like several other Paramount stars (Paulette Goddard and Veronica Lake), Lamour left the studio. Being so typecast in the public's mind and also in her mid-thirties, she found it difficult to obtain suitable screen roles. The vehicles selected for her were creaky melodramas (*Lulu Belle*, 1948), insipid comedies (*The Girl From Manhattan*, 1948), or lumbering murder mysteries (*The Lucky Stiff*, 1949).

On October 20, 1949, Dorothy gave birth to a son, Richard, and the family moved to her husband's hometown of Baltimore. In 1950, Lamour had a successful engagement at the London Palladium and in Glasgow, Scotland. She also recorded an LP album for Decca entitled *Favorite Hawaiian Songs*. The next year she appeared in a guest cameo in Bing Crosby's *Here Comes the Groom* at Paramount and was a substitute hostess on ABC radio's *The Louella Parsons Show*. She played Las Vegas in 1951, but no Hollywood offers were forthcoming until Cecil B. DeMille cast her as the aerialist in his circus epic, *The Greatest Show on Earth* (1952) at Paramount. However, she was subordinate to the three-ring acts and the romancing of Charlton Heston and Betty Hutton. Hope and Crosby were still at Paramount, and they had Lamour as a teammate yet again for *Road to Bali* (1952), which was more labored than funny, but was in color. Although this was her last picture for a decade, she made her TV debut with Eddie Cantor on NBC-TV's *The Colgate Comedy Hour* in 1952 and the same year starred in a segment of *Hollywood Opening Night* (NBC-TV). Three years later she appeared on *Damon Runyon Theater* (CBS-TV) and in 1956 was the subject of a *This Is Your Life* segment. Mostly she concentrated on being a housewife.

In 1956 and 1957, Lamour worked the nightclub circuit and then toured in the comedy *Roger the Sixth*. She was on Broadway for only a week as Abbe Lane's replacement in *Oh! Captain* before returning to the London Palladium in 1958. She recorded an LP called *Road to Romance* for the budget Design label. In 1960 she participated on *The Arthur Murray House Party* (NBC-TV) and guested with Bob Hope on one of his NBC network TV specials. In 1961 Dorothy was back doing cabaret work, marketing a line of beauty products, and authoring the volume *Road to Beauty*.

There was much publicity when Hope and Crosby announced a new "Road" project—*The Road to Hong Kong* (1962) for United Artists—and even more media coverage when it was revealed that Joan Collins and *not* Dorothy Lamour (who was to have a guest cameo) would be the distaff distraction. (It was Crosby who insisted that the far younger Collins have the lead.) After this entry, Dorothy did another Bob Hope NBC-TV special, but Bing Crosby only used pictures of Lamour in his concurrent small-screen special. A better film assignment occurred in the John Wayne vehicle *Donovan's Reef* (1963), which cast Dorothy as a salty Hawaiian Island saloon singer. The same year she toured in *DuBarry Was A Lady*, and in 1964 she made two guest shots on ABC-TV's *Burke's Law*. She sang as the head saleslady in the teenage science-fiction comedy *Pajama Party* (1965; looking plump and tired), and in 1966 she entertained troops in Vietnam, where her son Ridgley was stationed. Late in the year, she appeared with Bing Crosby on *The Hollywood Palace* (ABC-TV). Dorothy embarked on a grueling tour in *Hello, Dolly!* and later starred in the show at the Riviera Hotel in Las Vegas doing one of the two nightly shows, while Ginger Rogers did the other.

Late in 1967, Lamour guest starred on *I Spy* (NBC-TV), and the next spring she and her husband bought a Hollywood home. She was reunited with Bing Crosby and Bob Hope on a TV special. In 1971, she and long-time pal Betty Grable dueted in the Saint Louis summer theater revue *That's Show Business*. That year she also toured in *Anything Goes* but rejected several screen bids. One script offered her $120,000 for a few scenes as a madam, but she told the press, "I'm not happy with a lot of dirty movies."

She continued making personal appearances throughout the 1970s, and in 1980 her autobiography *The Other Side of the Road* was published. She lamented the fact that neither Crosby nor Hope included her in their lucrative percentage deal with Paramount on the "Road" treks. In the 1980s, the now-widowed (her husband died in 1978) Dorothy Lamour remained active by touring with a cabaret act plus working on episodes of such TV shows as *The Love Boat*, *Hart to Hart*, *Remington Steele*, *Crazy Like a Fox*, and *Murder, She Wrote*. In 1987 she made her final feature film, *Creepshow 2*. In this horror anthology entry, she was paired with George Kennedy in the segment "Old Chief Wood'nhead." Among her last TV appearances were two specials: *Stars and Stripes; Hollywood and World War II* (American Movie Classic Cable, 1991), and *Bob Hope and Friends: Making New Memories* (NBC-TV, 1991).

The sultry Lamour, who never visited the South Sea Islands (where so many of her movies took place) until she was almost seventy, died at Saint Vincent's Hospital of cardiac arrest on September 22, 1996, at age eighty-one. She was survived by two sons from her second marriage, a stepson, a grandson, and a granddaughter.

Bob Hope once quipped of Dorothy Lamour, "She did more for a piece of cloth than any American woman since Betsy Ross." However, Dorothy admitted the profitable sarong image hurt her badly in the long run: "Nobody has ever wanted to take me seriously or admit I can act." Also she did not push herself to her own advantage when she was at Paramount: "I just took what they gave me, didn't argue because I didn't want to be put on suspension." She also had a sense of humor about her talents. Once, when asked by a reporter if she'd ever studied acting or vocalizing, she quipped, "No. Can't you tell?"

Filmography

The Stars Are Singing (Vita, 1936) (s)
The Stars Can't Be Wrong (Vita, 1936) (s)
Star Reporter in Hollywood No. 1 (Vita, 1936) (s)
College Holiday (Par, 1936)
The Jungle Princess (Par, 1936)
Swing High, Swing Low (Par, 1937)
High, Wide and Handsome (Par, 1937)
Last Train From Madrid (Par, 1937)
The Hurricane (UA, 1937)
Thrill of a Lifetime (Par, 1937)
Her Jungle Love (Par, 1938)
Hollywood Handicap (MGM, 1938) (s)
The Big Broadcast of 1938 (Par, 1938)
Tropic Holiday (Par, 1938)
Spawn of the North (Par, 1938)
St. Louis Blues (Par, 1939)
Man About Town (Par, 1939)
Disputed Passage (Par, 1939)
Typhoon (Par, 1940)
Johnny Apollo (20th-Fox, 1940)
Moon Over Burma (Par, 1940)
Road to Singapore (Par, 1940)

Chad Hanna (20th-Fox, 1940)
Aloma of the South Seas (Par, 1941)
Road to Zanzibar (Par, 1941)
Caught in the Draft (Par, 1941)
Beyond the Blue Horizon (Par, 1942)
Road to Morocco (Par, 1942)
The Fleet's In (Par, 1942)
Star Spangled Rhythm (Par, 1942)
They Got Me Covered (RKO, 1942)
Dixie (Par, 1943)
Riding High [Melody Inn] (Par, 1943)
Show Business at War (20th-Fox, 1943) (s)
Rainbow Island (Par, 1944)
And the Angels Sing (Par, 1944)
Road to Utopia (Par, 1945)
Duffy's Tavern (Par, 1945)
A Medal for Benny (Par, 1945)
Masquerade in Mexico (Par, 1945)
My Favorite Brunette (Par, 1947)
Variety Girl (Par, 1947)
Road to Rio (Par, 1947)
Wild Harvest (Par, 1947)

A Miracle Can Happen [On Our Merry Way]
(UA, 1948)
Lulu Belle (Col, 1948)
The Girl From Manhattan (UA, 1948)
Slightly French (Col, 1948)
Manhandled (Par, 1948)
The Lucky Stiff (UA, 1949)
Here Comes the Groom (Par, 1951)
The Greatest Show on Earth (Par, 1952)
Road to Bali (Par, 1952)

Screen Snapshots #205 (Col, 1952) (s)
The Road to Hong Kong (UA, 1962)
Donovan's Reef (Par, 1963)
Pajama Party (AIP, 1964)
The Phynx (WB, 1970)
Won Ton Ton, The Dog Who Saved Hollywood
(Par, 1976)
Death at Love House (ABC-TV, 9/3/76)
Creepshow 2 (New World, 1987)

Broadway Plays

Oh! Captain (1958) (replacement)

Radio Series

The Dreamer of Songs (NBC Blue, 1935–36)
The Chase and Sanborn Hour (NBC, 1937–38)
The Rudy Vallee Show (NBC, 1939)

Palmolive Party (NBC, c. 1944–45)
Front and Center (NBC, 1947)
The Dorothy Lamour Show (NBC, 1948–49)

Album Discography

LPs

And the Angels Sing (Caliban 6017) [ST]
Bing Crosby and Bob Hope With Dorothy Lamour
(Radiola 1044)
Bing Crosby and Dorothy Lamour—Live (Amal-
gamated 237)
Dorothy Lamour (Interfusion L-25232)
Dorothy Lamour (Legends 4)
Favorite Hawaiian Songs (10″ Decca DL-5115)
The Fleet's In (Hollywood Soundstage 405) [ST]
Moon of Manakoora/Thanks for the Memory
(West Coast LP-14002)

Pajama Party (Buena Vista 3325) [ST]
Riding High (Caliban 6034) [ST]
The Road to Hong Kong (Liberty 16002) [ST]
The Road to Romance (Design 45)
St. Louis Blues (Caliban 6014) [ST]
Star Spangled Rhythm (Curtain Calls 100/20) [ST]
Thrill of a Lifetime (Caliban 6046) [ST]
Variety Girl (Caliban 6007) [ST]
Victor Herbert—Beyond the Blue Horizon (Cali-
ban 6033) [ST]

CDs

Cocktail Hour (Columbia River Entertainment
Group CRG 218053)
Dorothy Lamour (Allego/CRG 218053)
Footlight Parade/Star Spangled Rhythm (Great
Movie Themes 60013) [ST]
Lovelight in the Starlight (Jasmine JASCD-117)
The Moon of Manakoora (ASV CD-AJA-5231)

On a Tropic Night (Movie Stars 009)
On the Road (Vintage Jazz Band VJB-1949) w.
Bing Crosby, Bob Hope
Stairway to the Stars (First Night Cast 6021) [OC]
Star Spangled Rhythm (Sandy Hook CDSH-2045)
[ST]
Variety Girl (Great Movie Themes 60034) [ST]

Frances Langford and Smith Ballew in *Palm Springs* (1936).
[Courtesy of JC Archives]

Frances Langford

(b. Frances Newbern Langford, Lakeland, Florida, April 4, 1913)

In the pre–rock music era, Frances Langford was one of the best-known and -appreciated pop vocalists. With her smoky and sultry contralto voice, she became America's favorite female vocalist in 1938. But there was much more show-business depth to this feisty five-feet two-inches songstress. During World War II she became known as the "Sweetheart to the GIs" for her years of touring the battlefronts to entertain the troops. She gained a whole new audience after the war when she revealed her sharp comic flair in the course of teaming with Don Ameche in *The Bickersons*. This domestic comedy about spatting spouses was a big hit on radio, TV, and recordings. Although she made over two dozen feature films and was a frequent television variety performer, Frances was at her best as a radio and recording artist, shading her lyrical interpretations with honesty and an easygoing but authoritative sell of the lyrics.

Frances Newbern Langford was born in Lakeland, Florida, on April 4, 1913. (Her mother was well-known concert pianist Annie Newbern.) She attended Southern College in Florida, majoring in music and planning a career in opera. All this changed when she had a tonsillectomy in 1930, which altered her soprano voice to contralto. She adjusted her ambitions, and now focused on popular music. Tampa millionaire and cigar manufacturer Eli Witt heard Frances perform at an American Legion party and hired her for thirteen weeks to be on his local radio show at $5 (later $10) per session. Vacationing crooner Rudy Vallee, always on the lookout for fresh talent, heard Frances singing on the radio and quickly offered her a guest spot on his network radio program, which was broadcasting some of his shows from New Orleans. Thereafter, Vallee continued to take an interest in Frances's career, and when she moved to New York City he helped to foster show-business opportunities for her. She was hired by Victor Records in 1931, but the singles she did for them were not released. By August 1932 she was recording for Columbia Phonograph Company with such tunes as "I Can't Believe It's True" and "Having a Good Time, Wish You Were Here." She was heard on WOR radio (NYC) in the 1932 to 1933 period, made two musical short subjects for a Warner Bros.' Vitaphone release, and had a minor role in the Peter Arno musical *Here Goes the Bride* (November 7, 1933), which lasted only seven performances on Broadway. More importantly, all through this period—on radio (singing and doing commercials), on Broadway, in vaudeville, and in cabaret—she was perfecting her already superior performing skills.

During her singing engagement at New York's celebrated Waldorf-Astoria, Frances was asked to perform at a private party in honor of ace songwriter Cole Porter. Among the guests attending was Paramount producer Walter Wanger, who hired her to sing in motion pictures—without a screen test. Her feature film debut was Paramount's *Every Night at Eight*, a trite but exceedingly engaging rehash. It concerned three songsters (Alice Faye, Frances, and Patsy Kelly) determined to be the singing sensations of the airwaves, with George Raft tossed in as a suave bandleader who romances Langford. *Variety* reported that Langford "gives promise of going places. . . ." In this musical, Frances joined in the harmony on several numbers, including the title tune. She also did a torchy rendition of "Then You've Never Had the Blues" (which she coauthored), and made her mark with "I'm in the Mood for Love," which she reprised several times in the picture. Langford recorded four songs from *Every Night at Eight* for Brunswick Records in late July 1935, with Mahlon Merrick's orchestra providing backup.

Now a growing screen personality, Frances was borrowed by MGM for its *Broadway Melody of 1936* (1935), in which she played herself and provided vocals to "You Are My Lucky Star" and "Broadway Rhythm," while Eleanor Powell exhibited spectacular tap-dancing. Back at Paramount, Frances was part of a campus romp, *Collegiate* (1936), and sang "You Hit the Spot." For *Palm Springs* (1936), she sang "I Don't Want to Make History," one of the tunes she recorded under her Decca Records' contract that began in late 1935. In MGM's *Born to Dance* (1936), a Cole Porter musical designed to showcase Eleanor Powell, Frances was cast as Peppy Turner, who vocalizes "Swinging the Jinx Away" and "Easy to Love" to support Miss Powell's dancing. While Virginia Bruce sang "I've Got You Under My Skin" in this film, Frances recorded it for Decca, and it became a big hit for her. As a matter of fact, this song, along with "I'm in the Mood for Love," was most associated with her.

While some performers have an affinity for moviemaking and audiences are drawn to them, Frances continued to be a "film personality," an individual appreciated when on-camera, but not missed when she was offscreen. Walter Wanger cast her for his *Vogues of 1938* (1937), but her scenes were deleted from the release print of this United Artists release. She was demoted to Republic Pictures for *The Hit Parade* (1937), a congenial low-budget musical costarring Phil Regan and featuring the orchestras of Duke Ellington and Eddie Duchin. *Variety* endorsed, "as the warbling ingénue, [Frances Langford] looks good as photographed and plows into her numbers with authority." Her final entry in this period was Warner Bros.' elaborate *Hollywood Hotel* (1937). It was based on the popular CBS network radio variety program (1934–38) originated by columnist Louella Parson and hosted by Dick Powell. By this time Frances was a regular on this variety radio show. Thus, she was spotlighted in the Busby Berkeley–directed film version singing "Let That Be a Lesson to You" (backed by Benny Goodman's Orchestra) and "Silhouetted in the Moonlight" (dueting with Jerry Cooper).

After *Hollywood Hotel,* there was a three-year gap before Frances returned to picture making. On June 4, 1938, in Arizona, she married movie actor Jon Hall, who, although on-screen since 1935, made his first substantial impression in Samuel Goldwyn's *The Hurricane* (1937), in which his abbreviated native togs vied for attention with Dorothy Lamour's scanty sarong. (Publicity billed handsome Hall as "Goldwyn's Gift to Women.") Frances continued to record for Decca until 1942, often backed with such popular musical figures as Victor Young, Jimmy Dorsey, Harry Sosnick, and organist Eddie Dunstedter. Having performed regularly on radio with Dick Powell on the show *Hollywood Hotel,* from 1939 to 1940 she was heard on CBS's *The Texaco Show,* costarring Ken Murray and Kenny Baker. Already, in 1938, she had been voted the country's most popular female vocalist and soon became known as the "All American Girl" of the airwaves.

With America being drawn into World War II, Hollywood increased its output of mind-diverting musicals, and Frances found herself in demand again, but still as a featured "film personality." RKO utilized her in support of the radio team of Lum and Abner (in their movie debut) for *Dreaming Out Loud* (1940). In the campus musical *Too Many Girls* (1940), she supported Lucille Ball (whose songs were dubbed), Desi Arnaz, and Ann Miller. In Republic's *The Hit Parade of*

1941 (1940), yet another musical about radio-station antics, when the focus was not on the comic shenanigans of Phil Silvers, Patsy Kelly, Hugh Herbert, and Mary Boland, the spotlight was on Frances and Kenny Baker as they dueted "Who Am I?" and on her solo "Swing Low, Sweet Rhythm."

Because blondes Alice Faye and Betty Grable were the reigning queens of screen musicals, brunette Frances changed hair colors for *All-American Co-Ed* (1941), a forty-eight-minute stream-lined musical comedy produced by Hal Roach for United Artists. It remained her hair shade throughout the rest of her career. In *Swing It Soldier* (1941), a "B" musical from Universal featuring Ken Murray and Skinney Ennis and His Orchestra, Langford's big-screen moment was singing "I'm Gonna Swing My Way to Heaven."

In 1941, Frances was reunited with Dick Powell on the radio series *American Cruise* and then joined Bob Hope's popular NBC comedy/variety radio program. After America entered World War II, she volunteered to join Hope on his many USO tours entertaining the troops in the European and African theaters of war. (Hope would remark, "She knows just how much sex to pour and still be dignified.") It is estimated Langford logged over 250,000 miles during this period, becoming the most traveled female of World War II. With her engaging singing voice, pert figure, and knack for relating with GIs (as she visited hospital wards everywhere) she was quickly labeled the "No. 1 Girl of World War II." (She was also known as "The GI's Nightingale," "The Armed Forces Sweetheart," and "The Sweetheart of the Fighting Fronts.")

Sometimes, Frances's wartime treks were dangerous excursions onto the frontlines to perform; other times the peril lay in the flights, with long hops from one Allied base to another. ("I've had my share of close calls on these trips," Frances admitted, "but the rewards are worth every nervous twinge.") Once, over Alaska, Langford's plane began to have serious engine problems, and it seemed the passengers would have to bail out. According to Frances, her concern at the moment was not fear, but how exhilarating it would feel to make a parachute landing! Another time, Langford and Bob Hope's plane was reported missing when they were island-hopping in the Pacific and it was feared they had been lost. Although General Dwight D. Eisenhower had been opposed to women entertaining in the danger zones, he was won over by Frances's spunk and would later present her with a cherished citation: "To Miss Frances Langford, with appreciation for a grand job in North Africa." Later in the war, Frances wrote a syndicated column for the Hearst newspapers entitled "Purple Heart Diary," in which she retold her experiences meeting wounded GIs.

Universal may have tossed Frances into such small-budgeted musicals as *Mississippi Gambler* (1942) and *Cowboy in Manhattan* (1943), but Warner Bros. was more gracious to her in *Yankee Doodle Dandy* (1942), in which James Cagney won an Oscar as the zealously patriotic George M. Cohan. Langford was seen to advantage as entertainer Nora Bayes, who sings, among other tunes, the flag-raising "Over There" at a bond rally with Cagney. The same studio also used her for *This Is the Army* (1943), based on Irving Berlin's morale-boosting stage musical. For the film—starring Ronald Reagan, Berlin, Joan Leslie, and Kate Smith—Berlin wrote one new song "What Does He Look Like?" which was performed by Frances in a café sequence. Then it was back to supporting-bill fodder at Universal. She was a guest performer, singing "My Melancholy Baby" in *Follow the Band* (1943) and the same year played with the zany Ritz Brothers in *Never a Dull Moment* (1943), managing to sing "Sleepy Time Gal" and "My Blue Heaven" amidst the brothers' comic mayhem.

In between USO tours, Frances turned out two weak films in 1944. *Career Girl*, at poverty-row Producers Releasing Corporation (PRC), was a variation on 1937's *Stage Door* and had four undistinguished songs for Kansas City hopeful Langford to sing as she nurtures her Broadway dream. At RKO, in *Girl Rush*, she was the distaff distraction in a period tale featuring the comedy duo of Wally Brown and Alan Carney. Her romantic interest was newcomer Robert Mitchum. In the last of the war years, 1945, she was back at PRC on a showboat in *Dixie Jamboree* and at RKO for another Brown-Carney musical comedy, *Radio Stars on Parade*. In the latter she offered fine versions of "Don't Believe Everything You Dream" and "Couldn't Sleep a Wink Last Night." Paramount's *People Are Funny* (1946) emerged a double-bill item revolving around the then-popular radio show. She played herself, and her onetime mentor Rudy Vallee was on hand as a stuffy radio show sponsor.

Although the war and her USO foxhole circuit chores were now over, blue-eyed Frances continued to be a spokesperson for the GIs, often contributing articles to national magazines on concerns of returning war veterans and what awaited them at home. Her movie assignments remained pedestrian: RKO's *The Bamboo Blonde* (1946) was a cheap song-and-dance outing vaguely taking advantage of Frances's World War II fame with the GIs. She sang to advantage "Dreaming Out Loud." In RKO's economy musical *Beat the Band* (1947), the highlights were Gene Krupa and his jiving band, with Frances cast as a small-town girl wanting to break into show-business big time. Even after a dozen years on-screen, her dramatics here were weak, but she excelled in her stylish renditions of "I've Got My Fingers Crossed," "I'm in Love," and "Kissin' Well."

If Langford's screen career was stagnating, Frances was excelling on the radio airwaves. On September 8, 1946, she (as Blanche Bickerson) and Don Ameche (as John Bickerson) began a long run on NBC (and later CBS) network radio as the battling love mates in the comedy hit *The Bickersons*. The routine had begun as a sketch on an episode of the Charlie McCarthy–Edgar Bergen radio show. Meanwhile, Langford was in the headlines in 1948 when she helped authorities corner a salesman attempting to extort money from her. For Walt Disney's musical potpourri *Melody Time* (1948), part live action, part animation, Frances was in the "Once Upon a Wintertime" animated segment dealing with lovers bickering while ice skating, and she was heard singing the Bobby Worth–Ray Gilbert tune.

Meanwhile, just as her film career had passed its peak, so had her husband's. Jon Hall had been at his most popular during World War II teaming with exotic Maria Montez in a series of colorful fantasies at Universal Pictures. Now, more portly, he was making action quickies at Columbia Pictures and elsewhere. In 1949 Langford and Hall teamed for their only time on-camera in *Deputy Marshal*, an overly talky Western from independent Lippert Pictures. Frances sang "Hideout in Hidden Valley" and "Levis, Plaid Shirt and Spurs."

Still a champion of service veterans, Frances was much in the nation's headlines in May 1950. President Harry S. Truman had announced his decision to relocate a military hospital (for paraplegics) from its Van Nuys, California, base to Long Beach. Frances was the unofficial spokesperson for the GIs and met Truman when his train stopped in Coulee City, Washington. When the iconoclastic politician dismissed her abruptly after a ten-second meeting, there was a huge national outcry.

Later in 1950, Frances was among the many radio/film/recording personalities who turned to television. She and her congenial *Bickersons* costar, Don Ameche, hosted *Startime*, a variety series featuring music, comedy (including *The Bickersons*), and songs. The show lasted four months, until February 1951. By mid-1951 Frances was making a new film for low-budget picture maker Sam Katzman, for whom her husband Jon Hall also made movies. *Purple Heart Diary* (1951) was supposed to be the first of a ten-picture pact with the producer, but proved to be the only project. The melodrama exploited her World War II efforts as an entertainer/humanitarian in a contrived celluloid biography that blended action, comedy, romance, and of course music. Her best numbers were "Hi, Fellow Tourists" and "Bread and Butter Woman." On television, Frances and Don Ameche hosted a variety hour (September 10, 1951, to March 14, 1952) on the ABC network, which featured Jack Lemmon in a recurring domestic comedy sketch. Later in 1952, Frances flew to Korea to entertain the troops. Late the next year (December 19, 1953), she guest-starred as herself on an episode ("Honeymooners' Christmas Party") of Jackie Gleason's CBS-TV show *The Honeymooners*, a segment that is still frequently shown in syndication. What proved to be her final motion-picture appearance was a guest-starring spot in *The Glenn Miller Story* (1954) in which she appeared with the Modernaires and the Glenn Miller Orchestra entertaining troops overseas during World War II. As always, she was vivacious and stylish in her full-throated song renditions.

For years, Langford and Jon Hall had been publicized as Hollywood's Happy Couple. In the early 1950s, they purchased property in Florida near Lakeland, and she began spending more time there. As their career paths and life's interests further diverged, their marriage faltered. In April 1954, she and Hall separated, and in late August 1955 they were divorced in Titusville, Florida. In the interim, while on a nightclub tour that played Milwaukee, Wisconsin, she met forty-eight-year-old Ralph Evinrude, a marine motor company magnate. On October 6, 1955, they were married aboard his 110-foot yacht (*The Chanticleer*) anchored in Long Island Sound. This was multimillionaire Evinrude's third wedding; he had two children from his first marriage.

When Frances wed Evinrude, she had agreed to subordinate her career to their marriage, but in August 1956 she signed with the RKO Unique label to record "When You Speak With Your Eyes" and "Rocking in the Rocket Room." In late 1956, Charles Wick, president of Splendex Enterprises, announced that he would star Frances in a teleseries as one of the revolving stars of filmed musical short subjects. Neither that nor a planned Broadway musical Wick was going to produce for Frances materialized. Throughout the decade, Frances, still a languid beauty, continued to appear sporadically on television, often as a guest on one of Bob Hope's network specials. On March 15, 1959, she was the hostess on *Frances Langford Presents* on NBC-TV. It comprised two half-hour unsold pilots, and featured songs, dance, and comedy from the likes of Bob Hope, Julie London, Edgar Bergen, and the Four Freshmen. Then she was back on television with a variety special, *The Frances Langford Show* (NBC, May 1, 1960), with Don Ameche, Johnny Mathis, Bob Cummings, and the Three Stooges as her disparate guests.

By the mid-1960s, Frances was semiretired from show business and living on her three-hundred acre estate in Florida with her husband. She operated The Outrigger, a club in Stuart, Florida, where she would perform occasionally for her audiences. She told the press, "Vaughn Monroe lives down the road, and Perry Como has a house nearby, and they often drop in for a songfest. So I've been able to keep my voice in trim." When the Vietnam War hostilities broke out, she volunteered to entertain, going overseas in 1966 both with and without Bob Hope to sing for the servicemen. She said kiddingly, "Oh, I suppose there might be a few of the older officers who will remember me." On May 13, 1967, she and long-standing friend Don Ameche appeared on ABC-TV's *The Hollywood Palace* performing one of their classic skits from *The Bickersons*, which through several record albums had remained audience pleasers.

In the 1970s, Frances Langford was out of the limelight until March 1978, when the sixty-four year old entertainer underwent successful open-heart surgery at Miami Heart Institute. She and her husband Evinrude continued their home life in Florida, residing in Jensen Beach, Florida, with a summer retreat at Georgian Bay, and taking frequent trips aboard their yacht, as well as occasionally flying to the Philippines, where they owned an engineering plant. He died in May 1986, and she then sold their Fox Point, Wisconsin, place, preferring to remain full-time in Florida.

In the early 1989 PBS-TV documentary *Entertaining the Troops,* Frances opened the ninety-minute program by singing "It's Been a Long, Long Time." She was interviewed about her war efforts and termed her entertaining at the battle fronts as "fun." Later in the show she took part in the "Bob Hope Troop Reunion," sitting around a table reminiscing with her World War II coperformers Hope (comedian), Patty Thomas (cheesecake), and Tony Romano (guitarist). Hope remembered the time when he and Langford got fungus—he in his feet and she in her ear. Toward the end of these positive and nostalgic tidbits, Frances sang "I'm in the Mood for Love." As always, she was professional and relaxed.

On November 18, 1994, Frances wed Tulsa, Oklahoma, attorney Harold Stuart at her Jensen Beach, Florida, home. Patty Thomas, who had toured with Langford overseas during World War II, was the matron of honor. In June 2001, the veteran entertainer was back in the news when neighbors rallied to support her against local authorities who demanded she control the one hundred peacocks that roamed free on her fifty-seven-acre ranch near Rio, Florida. The county had wanted her to build a fence around her ranch and clip the birds' wings—or move them off the property.

Although Langford no longer performed, several CDs were issued in the 1990s and thereafter featuring her warm contralto. It revealed anew her high-caliber musicianship filled with intelligent phrasing and a distinctive, beautiful voice.

Filmography

The Subway Symphony (Vita, 1932) (s)
Rambling 'Round Radio Row #5 (Vita, 1933) (s)
Every Night at Eight (Par, 1935)
Broadway Melody of 1936 (MGM, 1935)
Collegiate (Par, 1936)
Palm Springs (Par, 1936)
Born to Dance (MGM, 1936)
Vogues of 1938 (UA, 1937) (scenes deleted)
The Hit Parade (Rep, 1937)
Hollywood Hotel (WB, 1937)
Dreaming Out Loud (RKO, 1940)
The Hit Parade of 1941 (Rep, 1940)
Too Many Girls (RKO, 1940)
All-American Co-Ed (UA, 1941)
Picture People #4 (RKO, 1941) (s)
Swing It Soldier (Univ, 1941)
Mississippi Gambler (Univ, 1942)
Yankee Doodle Dandy (WB, 1942)
Hedda Hopper's Hollywood #4 (Par, 1942) (s)
Cowboy in Manhattan (Univ, 1943)
Follow the Band (Univ, 1943)

This Is the Army (WB, 1943)
Never a Dull Moment (Univ, 1943)
Combat America (U.S. Army Air Force, 1943) (documentary)
Career Girl (PRC, 1944)
Memo for Joe (RKO, 1944) (s)
Girl Rush (RKO, 1944)
Dixie Jamboree (PRC, 1945)
Radio Stars on Parade (RKO, 1945)
Tropical Moon (Soundies, 1945) (s)
A Dream Came True (Soundies, 1945) (s)
Some Day When the Clouds Roll By (Soundies, 1945) (s)
People Are Funny (Par, 1945)
The Bamboo Blonde (RKO, 1946)
Beat the Band (RKO, 1947)
Melody Time (RKO, 1948) (voice only)
Deputy Marshal (Lip, 1949)
Purple Heart Diary [No Time for Tears] (Col, 1951) (also story idea)
The Glenn Miller Story (Univ, 1954)

Broadway Plays

Here Goes the Bride (1933)

Radio Series

The Spartan Hour (NBC, 1933–34)
Hollywood Hotel (CBS, 1935–40)
The Texaco Star Theater (CBS, 1939–40)
Summer Cruise (American Cruise) (NBC, 1941)
The Bob Hope Pepsodent Show (NBC, 1941–46)

The Spike Jones Show (NBC, 1945)
The Bickersons (NBC, 1946–47; CBS, 1947–48, 1951)
Musical Americana (NBC, 1947)

TV Series

Star Time (Dumont, 1950–51)

The Frances Langford–Don Ameche Show (ABC, 1951–52)

Album Discography

LPs

The Bickersons (Col CL-1692/CS-8492) w. Don Ameche
The Bickersons (Radiola 1151) w. Don Ameche
The Bickersons Fight Back (Col Cl-1883/CS-8683) w. Don Ameche
The Bickersons Rematch (Col G-30523) w. Don Ameche
Born to Dance (CIF 3001) [ST]
Collegiate (Caliban 6042) [ST]
Every Night at Eight (Caliban 6043) [ST]

Hollywood Hotel (EOH 99601, Hollywood Soundstage 5004) [ST]
I Feel A Song Coming On: 1935-37 (Take Two TT 214)
Old Songs for Old Friends (Cap T/ST-1865)
Rainbow Rhapsody (10″ Mer MG-25005)
The Return of the Bickersons! (Radiola 3MR-4) w. Don Ameche
This Is the Army (Hollywood Soundstage 408, Sandy Hook 2035) [ST]
Yankee Doodle Dandy (Curtain Calls 100/13) [ST]

CDs

Best of Radio Comedy: Ozzie & Harriett & the Bickersons (Laserlight 12-689)
The Bickersons (Radiola CDMR-1115)
Born to Dance (Great Movie Themes 60031) [ST]
Flying Down to Rio/Hollywood Hotel (Great Movie Themes 6008) [ST/R]
Hollywood Hotel (Facet FCD-8110, Hollywood Soundstage HSCD-4008) [ST/R]
I'm in the Mood for Love (ASV CD-AJA-5219)
Serenade (Flare ROYCD-220)

So Many Memories (Jasmine ASMCD-2583)
Someone to Watch Over Me (Happy Days 204)
Sweet Heartache (Flare ROYCD-203)
Sweetheart of Song (Collectors' Choice Music CCM-1006)
This Is the Army (Hollywood Soundstage HSCD-4009) [ST]
Yankee Doodle Dandy (Hollywood Soundstage HSCD-4002) [ST]

Mario Lanza and Sarita Montiel in *Serenade* (1956).
[Courtesy of JC Archives]

Mario Lanza

(b. Alfred Arnold Cocozza, Philadelphia, Pennsylvania, January 31, 1921; d. Rome, Italy, October 7, 1959)

Although Mario Lanza has been dead for several decades, he continues to retain a degree of popularity, due mainly to his many RCA recordings that are constantly being re-released. In the decade from 1949 to 1959, he was featured in eight feature films that were successful because of his vocalizing. Yet for all his screen success as a powerful, if undisciplined, tenor, Lanza had a self-destructive streak that eventually cost him his life. Dogged by weight problems (similar to many operatic stars both before and after him) and possessing a temperament to match his poundage, Lanza essentially destroyed himself on a never-ending merry-go-round of drinking, eating, diets, and barbiturates. Despite having earned well over $5 million from his performing, he had little money on hand at the time of his death in 1959.

Mario Lanza's biography would make a good motion-picture scenario. He was born in South Philadelphia on January 31, 1921, the son of Antonio and Maria Cocozza. He was christened Alfred Arnold Cocozza, and he grew up poor. His father was a disabled World War I veteran, and his mother scratched out a living as a seamstress at a local army quartermasters' depot. As a boy, young Alfred first heard the recordings of Enrico Caruso on a neighbor's phonograph, and the famous tenor became the youngster's idol. His sole goal in life was to become a great opera singer like Caruso. While he did poorly in academics and well in sports in school, Alfred (known as Freddie) was able to take voice lessons, drawing from his mother's meager income.

Two months before he was to graduate from high school, Alfred was expelled and he took a job in his grandfather's grocery business. He worked there for three years until Irene Williams, his music instructor, maneuvered him into an audition with the concert manager (William Huff) of the Philadelphia Academy of Music. Huff was impressed with the young man's vocal abilities and arranged an audition with Serge Koussevitzky, conductor of the Boston Symphony Orchestra and head of the Berkshire Music Center in Tanglewood, located in Lenox, Massachusetts. Alfred got a scholarship there and began using the name Mario Lanza, the surname taken from his mother's maiden name.

In the summer of 1942, Lanza made an impressive debut at Tanglewood in Otto Nicolai's *The Merry Wives of Windsor*. Columbia Concerts signed him for a tour, but it never materialized because he was drafted into World War II service the next January. Because of his vocal talents, Mario was assigned to the army's Special Services and appeared in the service shows *On the Beam* and *Winged Victory*. With the latter production, he was on Broadway and went on the West Coast tour, appearing in Los Angeles with the show (but not in the 1944 film version of the play). He did get a break, however, when he sang at a party hostessed by actress Irene Manning. He so impressed her with his singing that she gained him an audition with Jack Warner. However, the

Warner Bros. studio chief, while liking Mario's voice, did not feel the soldier (now weighing over 250 pounds) had a screen future.

When Lanza sang at a party at Frank Sinatra's home, Mario met agent Art Rush (who managed Roy Rogers and Dale Evans until his death in 1989). Rush thought his singing was so good he negotiated a recording contract for the young tenor with RCA Victor. A serious inflammation of the nose resulted in Lanza being discharged from the army in early 1945, and he kept active with his concert bookings and recordings. On April 13, 1945, he married Betty Hicks, the sister of an army friend. His big break came two years later when he sang at the Hollywood Bowl; after seeing him perform, Louis B. Mayer signed the singer to a seven-year screen contract. Lanza began at $750 a week, and his salary eventually rose to $100,000 a picture.

For his movie debut, Mario was featured in Joe Pasternak's production of *That Midnight Kiss* (1949). Kathryn Grayson was the heiress who wants to become an opera singer and who falls in love with a singing truck driver (Lanza). During the proceedings, he performed operatic arias from Giuseppe Verdi's *Aida*, Pietro Mascagni's *Cavalleria Rusticana*, and Gaetano Donizetti's *L'Elisir d'Amore*, as well as the contemporary songs "They Won't Believe Me" and "I Know, I Know, I Know." *Variety* assessed his voice as "excellent" and added, "far from resembling the caricatured opera tenor, he's a nice-looking youngster of the 'average American boy' school who will have the femme customers on his side from the start." The movie was a solid box-office success, and Lanza caused a sensation in his screen debut.

Louis B. Mayer was so pleased with his new discovery that he gave Lanza a bonus of $10,000 and cast him again with Kathryn Grayson in *The Toast of New Orleans* (1950), this time as her costar. Here he was a singing fisherman who becomes an operatic star. Again, he sang opera, performing arias from Georges Bizet's *Carmen*, Amilcare Ponchielli's *La Gioconda*, Verdi's *La Traviata*, and Frederich von Flotow's *Martha*. However, his best number was his booming rendition of the song "Be My Love," which Nicholas Brodsky had written expressly for Lanza. The song was the highlight of the picture, and his RCA Victor recording of it in 1951 remained on the charts for nearly six months. It sold over two millions copies, becoming Lanza's best-selling single record.

After making *The Toast of New Orleans*, Lanza and Grayson went on a tour around the country to promote the feature. Because Lanza idolized Enrico Caruso, he had long wanted to portray him on film. But there were many delays, some caused by the fact that mogul Louis B. Mayer was being dethroned at the studio. Mario fumed, "Who the hell do they think can play Caruso! Nelson Eddy? There is nobody but me who can play that role. I am Caruso!" Finally the studio assigned him to the picture, a largely fictional account of the legendary Italian tenor. However, it provided Lanza with a fine showcase for singing traditional Caruso opera favorites. He and costar Ann Blyth performed the new song "The Loveliest Night of the Year." (This number was also popular as a Lanza single record for RCA. In fact it almost duplicated his sales of "Be My Love.") While the elaborate *The Great Caruso* was another personal triumph for Mario, grossing $4.5 million at the box office, it was also the beginning of his movie career downfall. During its production, Lanza became excessively temperamental. After the movie's success, his ego swelled and he became increasingly difficult to work with.

From June 1951 to September 1952, the tenor starred on the weekly CBS radio series *The Mario Lanza Show* sponsored by Coca-Cola. In 1952, he balked at starring in the MGM production of *Because You're Mine*, thinking the vehicle too shabby and that producer Joe Pasternak was betraying him. (He said of the producer, "I make the pictures—I sing—and that bastard thinks it's him.") Lanza was also fuming at the studio for allowing a national magazine to profile him in an unfavorable light. Finally, he was upset that Kathryn Grayson had declined to do the new picture and that Broadway's Doretta Morrow had been substituted. Because of his studio contract, Mario begrudgingly went through with the filming. However, during the shooting, he was uncooperative, often showing up on the set intoxicated and being extremely rude and crude toward his costar. The resultant picture was a slim production. It offered Lanza as a drafted opera star falling in love with the sister (Morrow) of his sergeant (James Whitmore). He sang the title tune, "The Song Angels Sing," plus "The Lord's Prayer." Once again, because of his personal popularity, the movie made money.

For his next showcase, MGM assigned Lanza the lead in Sigmund Romberg's classic *The Student Prince* (1954), to be lensed in the wide-screen process. However, after recording the soundtrack prior to filming, Lanza walked off the project, and MGM sued him for $5 million. An agreement was arranged with the new studio regime headed by Dore Schary. Some filming actually began, but there were more clashes and Mario walked out yet again. A final settlement permitted Metro to use his singing voice in the movie with a hastily substituted Edmund Purdom mouthing the words. After this, however, Lanza's studio contract was nullified. The star huffed to the press, "My biggest beef with Metro was that the studio wanted to be commercial and I wanted artistic betterment. Put them together—they don't mix. I rebelled because of sincerity to the public and my career."

On October 28, 1954, Lanza made his dramatic television debut in "Lend an Ear," a revue seen on CBS-TV *Shower of Stars*. However, his vocals were dubbed from his own recordings. As a result, he lost the lead in Paramount's film of Rudolf Friml's evergreen *The Vagabond King* (1956) opposite Kathryn Grayson because it was rumored his voice was gone. (Paramount instead chose a relative unknown, Oreste, as a budget-saving replacement.) In reality, excessive dieting had made Lanza too weak to vocalize on that TV program. There was more unfavorable publicity when Mario was booked into the New Frontier Hotel in Las Vegas in 1955 for a week's engagement. He was unable to appear on opening night because a combination of tranquilizers and champagne had felled him. The engagement was cancelled.

Anxious for ways to support his expensive lifestyle, Lanza negotiated a two-picture deal with Warner Bros. at $150,000 per film. The initial vehicle was *Serenade* (1956), a project that had sat around for years due to the steamy nature of the James Cain book original. The distilled new version had Lanza being used by an older woman (Joan Fontaine) and his manager (Vincent Price), but loved by a younger girl (Sarita Montiel). Lanza sang the title song and "My Destiny," but *Serenade* had fewer opera sequences than usual for a Lanza picture. Although it was modestly successful, Warner Bros. decided to pay off troublesome Lanza rather than make the second picture.

By now Mario Lanza's career was in as deep trouble as his personal life. With a wife and four children (Colleen, Elisa, Damon, and Mark) to support, he had little income outside his earnings from records. In Hollywood, he was now persona non grata. Also he was coping with eating binges, plus excessive drinking, ballooning his weight to three hundred pounds. All this would be followed by rounds of mammoth crash dieting and excessive use of barbiturates. While his RCA soundtrack albums of *The Student Prince* and *Serenade* had sold quite decently, he had no new movie work for further soundtrack albums.

After a film layoff of nearly a year in which he did concerts, Lanza signed a two-picture contract with Italy's Titanus Films. He moved his family to his ancestor's homeland, renting the luxurious Rome villa that Benito Mussolini had once given to Marshal Badoglio. ("I'm a movie star and I think I should live like one," he reasoned.) His first Italian production, *Seven Hills of*

Rome (1958), benefited from beautiful locations and a decent plot about a TV star (Lanza) who comes to Rome to find peace and quiet and falls in love with a beautiful young woman (Peggie Castle). He sang the title song, "Lolita," "Come Dance With Me," "Come Prima," and "Arrivederci Roma." (The latter song brought him back to the single record charts for a six-week run, the first time one of his RCA singles had charted since his 1952 recording of "Because.") Ironically, *Seven Hills of Rome* was released in the United States by MGM, which had a distribution arrangement with Titanus. Metro also released *For the First Time* (1959), which typecast Mario as a temperamental opera singer who retreats to Capri, where he finds love with a pretty deaf girl (Johanna von Koszian). Here he performed "Neapolitan Dance," "Mazurka," "The Pineapple Pickers," and "Tarantella." The picture did only average business.

Following the making of *For the First Time*, the self-indulgent Lanza's health worsened due to his ever-increasing dieting, plus bouts of pneumonia and phlebitis. He died on October 7, 1959, when a blood clot in the leg went to his heart and killed him. Following his sudden demise, the RCA soundtrack album of *For the First Time* became a best-seller, as did several of his other albums. On March 11, 1960, Betty Lanza, who had been in deep depression since her husband's death, died of asphyxiation, and the Lanza's four children (whom family friend Kathryn Grayson had tended for a spell) became wards of Mario's parents. Most of the star's earnings had vanished, but the children had an income from his record royalties of some $100,000 yearly. Only Lanza's daughter Colleen followed in his footsteps by becoming a singer.

In the years since his death, the memory of Mario Lanza has been kept alive not only by his films, but by RCA's constant reissuing of his recordings, which to date have sold in excess of well over 50 million copies. In June 1998, there was a tribute to Mario given in Grant Park in Chicago, where fifty years earlier—shortly before Hollywood discovered him—he'd given an open-air concert. In the late 1990s, Charles GaVoian performed the *Mario Lanza Story*, a one-man tribute to the late artist. In 1999, *Be My Love: A Celebration of Mari Lanza,* was published. It was written by Damon Lanza (the star's surviving son), Bob Dolfi, and Mark Muller.

Filmography

That Midnight Kiss (MGM, 1949)
The Toast of New Orleans (MGM, 1950)
The Great Caruso (MGM, 1951)
Because You're Mine (MGM, 1952)
The Student Prince (MGM, 1954) (voice only)

Serenade (WB, 1956)
Seven Hills of Rome (MGM, 1958) (also Italian-
    language version: Arrivederci Roma)
For the First Time (MGM, 1959)

Broadway Plays

Winged Victory (1943) (replacement)

Radio Series

The Mario Lanza Show (CBS, 1951–52)

Album Discography

LPs

Be My Love (RCA LSC-3289)

Because You're Mine (10″ RCA LM-7015) [ST]

The Best of Mario Lanza (RCA LM/LSC-2748)

The Best of Mario Lanza, Vol. 2 (RCA LM/LSC-2998)

Carols (RCA LM-2029)

Caruso Favorites (RCA LM/LSC-2393)

Cavalcade of Show Tunes (RCA LM-2090)

Christmas Carols (RCA LM/LSC-2333)

Christmas Hymns and Carols (Camden CAL/CAS-777)

Christmas Songs (10″ RCA LM-155)

The Desert Song (RCA LM/LSC-2440)

Double Feature: That Midnight Kiss & The Toast of New Orleans (RCA LM-2422) [ST]

Favorite Arias (RCA LM/LSC-2932)

For the First Time (RCA LM/LSC-2338) [ST]

The Great Caruso (LM/LSC-1127) [ST]

Greatest Hits From Operettas and Musicals (RCA VCS-6192)

If You Are but a Dream (RCA LM/LSC-2790)

I'll See You in My Dreams (RCA LM/LSC-2720, RCA International 89060)

I'll Walk With God (RCA LM/LSC-2607)

A Kiss and Other Love Songs (RCA LM-1860)

Lanza on Broadway (RCA LM-2070)

A Legendary Performer (RCA CRL1-1750)

Love Songs (RCA LM-1860)

Love Songs and a Neapolitan Serenade (RCA LM/LSC-1188)

Magic Mario (RCA LM-1943)

The Magic of Mario Lanza (Heartland Music)

Mario! (RCA LM/LSC-2331)

Mario Lanza (Golden Age of Opera 457)

Mario Lanza (Unique Opera 127)

The Mario Lanza Collection (RCA CRM5-4158)

Mario Lanza in Opera (RCA LSC-3101)

Mario Lanza Live (A Touch of Magic 2)

Mario Lanza Memories (RCA LSC-3102)

Mario Lanza on Radio (Radiola 1121)

A Mario Lanza Program (RCA LM/LSC-2454)

Mario Lanza Sings Caruso (RCA ARL1-0314)

Opera's Greatest Hits (RCA VCS-7073)

Pure Gold (RCA ANL1-2874, RCA International 5005)

Serenade (RCA LM-1996) [ST]

The Seven Hills of Rome (RCA LM-2211) [ST]

Speak to Me of Love (RCA LSC-3103)

The Student Prince (RCA LM-1837, RCA LSC-3216) [ST]

The Student Prince (RCA LM/LSC-2339)

That Midnight Kiss (10″ RCA LM-86) [ST]

The Toast of New Orleans (10″ RCA LM-75, Azel 104) [ST]

The Touch of Your Hand (RCA LM-1927)

The Vagabond King (RCA LM/LSC-2509)

You Do Something to Me (Camden CAL/CAS-450)

Younger Than Springtime (RCA LSC-3049)

CDs

At His Best—Granada (BMG PLSCD-205)

Ave Maria (CLS 4370)

Because You're Mine (Fat Boy FATCD-173)

Be My Love (Prism PLATCD-148)

Be My Love (RCA 09026-60720-2-RG)

Be My Love (Ronco Silver CER-002)

Be My Love—Classic Live Performances (Hallmark 302432)

Be My Love: Mario Lanza's Greatest Performances at MGM (Turner Classic Movies/Rhino R2-72950)

Best Recordings (Musicrama 0641)

Christmas Hymns & Carols (Laserlight 21-724)

Christmas With Mario Lanza (RCA 09026-61420-2)

Classic Performances (Castle PIESD-064)

Cocktail Hour (Columbia River Entertainment CRG-218006)

The Collection (Castle Communications LC-6369)

The Concert Collection (Prism PLATCD-3946)

La Donna e Mobile (GP 2012)

Don't Forget Me (RCA 09026-61420-2)

The Entertainers (Sarabands CD-341)

For the First Time/That Midnight Kiss (RCA 09026-60516-2-RC) [ST]

42 Great Performances (Prism PLATBX-2209)

Gold (San Juan Music Group GOLD-078)

Golden Age (Fremus FR0320)

The Great Caruso/Mario Lanza Sings Caruso Favorites (RCA 09026-60049-2-RG)

The Great Mario Lanza (Goldies 63201)

The Great Mario Lanza, Vols. 1 & 2 (Vienna Dream Classic World LC-6369)

Great Moments in Music (ML 941007)

Greatest Hits (RCA 09206-68134-2)

The Greatest Hits of Mario Lanza (RCA/BMG/Avon Cosmetics 59104)

The Greatest Hits of Mario Lanza, Vol. 2 (RCA/BMG/Avon Cosmetics 88525)

Historic Radio Broadcast (QED 139)

Historical Recordings 1949-1959 (Gala GL-306)

Hollywood Bowl (Melodram MEL-16512)

Lanza Sings Christmas Carols (RCA 9026-63178-2)

A Legendary Tenor (RCA 09026-6218-2-RC)

Ein Liederabend (Notablu 920709)

Live From London (RCA 09026-61884-2)

The Loveliest Night of the Year (Fat Boy FATCD-248)

Love Songs by Mario Lanza (BMG DRC-11655)

Love Songs by Mario Lanza (Ranwood 8268)

The Magic of Mario Lanza (Heartland Music 1919-2)

Mario Lanza (Collection COL-061)

Mario Lanza (DVM CDSC-0205)

Mario Lanza (The Entertainers 245)

Mario Lanza (Naxos Nostalgia NX8.120547)

Mario Lanza (Penny PNCD-0103)

Mario Lanza (Penny PYCD-257)

Mario Lanza (Superstars SUPER024)

Mario Lanza at His Best (PLS 205)

Mario Lanza at His Best (RCA 09026-68130-2)

The Mario Lanza Collection (RCA 09026-60889-2)

The Mario Lanza Collection (Ronco DSR-123)

Mario Lanza in Concert (Castle Communications MACCD-105)

Mario Lanza in Concert (Castle Communications MATCD-287)

Mario Lanza in Concert (Delta)

Mario Lanza in Concert (Music Digital CD-6017)

Mario Lanza in Concert—The Essential Collection (Pickwick PWKS-4230)

Mario Lanza in Hollywood (DRG 4104)

Mario Lanza Live (Submarine DATOM2)

Mario Lanza Live (A Touch of Magic 2)

Mario Lanza Live at the Hollywood Bowl—Historical Recordings 1947 & 1951 (Gala GL-311)

Mario Lanza on Radio (Radiola CDMR-1121)

The Mario Lanza Shows (On the Air OTA-101910)

The Mario Lanza Story (DVREC 62)

Mario Lanza, Vol. 1 (The Entertainers 341)

Mario Lanza, Vol. 2 (The Entertainers 345)

Il Meglio di Mario Lanza (Fremus CDFR041)

Memories: Where It All Began (Gems of the Past GEMS-101650)

My Romance (RCA 09026-63751)

My Song of Love (Tring International FMC020, Tring International JHD111)

O Sole Mio (Madacy 2-2348)

O Sole Mio (Sarabands 290)

O Sole Mio—Greatest Hits Live (Success PK-510)

O Sole Mio—22 Love Songs (Prism PLATCD-147)

Opera Arias & Duets (RCA 09026-63491-2)

Original Soundtracks (Hollywood 16)

The Platinum Collection (Platinum PC-603)

A Portrait of Mario Lanza (Stylus SMD-741)

RCA Diamond Series—16 Top Tracks (RCA/BMG CD-90125)

Serenade (Summit SUMCD-4029)

Silent Night (NL 25201)

The Student Prince/The Desert Song (RCA 09026-60048-2-RG)

That Midnight Kiss/The Toast of New Orleans (Soundies 4104) [ST]

20 Classic Opera Highlights (KB Imports & Exports KBCD-034)

The Ultimate Collection (RCA/BMG 7432-118574-2)

The Very Best of Mario Lanza (Reader's Digest K92015-KK3)

Virtuoso Collection (Newsound PNCD-0103)

When Day Is Done (RCA 09026-63254-2)

With a Song in My Heart (Camden 74321-40058-2)

Without a Song (Musketeer MU-9019)

The Wonderful World of Mario Lanza (SPA Distributors RMB-75620)

You Do Something to Me (Camden CAD1-450)

You'll Never Walk Alone (RCA 09026-68073-2)

Your Startime (RUS 010153)

Nick Lucas

(b. Dominic Antonio Nicholas Lucanese, Newark, New Jersey, August 22, 1897;
d. Colorado Springs, Colorado, July 28, 1982)

"I've been the luckiest guy in the world. If you disc jockeys had been on hand when Nick Lucas first hit his stride he'd be the biggest name in show business." This statement was made by Bing Crosby at a disc jockey convention in the 1950s, and it exemplified the fact that Nick Lucas, the five-feet eight-inches tenor who could sing in three ranges, was one of the music world's biggest stars in the era before radio dictated record-buying tastes. In fact, Nick Lucas was one of the biggest record sellers of the late 1920s and early 1930s (with over 84 million records sold), and he was one of vaudeville's top names, at one time earning $3,000 per week with two years' advanced bookings. In addition, he scored successes on Broadway, films, radio, nightclubs, and later on television. Also a songwriter, Nick Lucas did a great deal to cement the guitar in the world of popular music. He not only had one of the first custom-made guitars that was merchandised, but he also composed well-received guitar instruction books and had his own line of popular guitar picks. While his motion-picture career spanned more than four decades, Nick Lucas was more focused on the lucrative field of personal appearances. Nevertheless, to his credit is the fact he introduced and popularized one of filmdom's most memorable songs, "Tip Toe Through the Tulips."

Born Dominic Antonio Nicholas Lucanese in Newark, New Jersey, on August 22, 1897, the son of Italian immigrants, he was one of nine children. Because his entire family loved music, Nick started playing the mandolin at age five and then graduated to the guitar. By the time he was nine years old, he and his older brother Frank were making extra money for the family by performing at parties, christenings, weddings, and even in saloons or streetcars.

By 1912, brother Frank went into vaudeville, while Nick made his recording debut that year making test cylinder pressings for the Edison Company. The next year he graduated from school and took a job in a leather tannery. However, music was his primary interest, and he was now adept at not only the mandolin and guitar, but also the banjo. Not long afterward he got a job with a band at a Newark cabaret, and in 1917 he married Catherine Cifrodella. They remained together until her death in 1971; they had one daughter, Emily (born in 1918). While appearing at the Iroquois Club in Newark, Nick was approached about forming a vaudeville act. With friend Ted Fio Rito and three other musicians he formed the Kentucky Five, which toured successfully for six months.

After that run, Nick joined Vincent Lopez's orchestra in New York City as a banjo player and in 1919 became a part of the Vernon Country Club Orchestra. By now he was using the professional surname of Lucas. He recorded with that group for Columbia, and in addition he and brother Frank recorded for Pathé as the Lucas Ukulele Trio and the Lucas Novelty Quartet.

Nick Lucas in the 1930s.
[Courtesy of Michael R. Pitts]

For the same label, he recorded with the Don Parker Trio. In 1922, Nick recorded the first pop-jazz guitar solos ever waxed, his own compositions of "Pickin' the Guitar" and "Teasin' the Frets," for Pathé, and the recording would become a milestone in the history of American guitar music.

Late in 1921, Nick joined Sam Lanin's orchestra, and he also recorded with Lanin on Gennett Records as a part of Bailey's Lucky Seven. During this period, Lucas replaced the banjo with the guitar as his recording instrument of choice, thus beginning the guitar's popularity as an accompaniment instrument on recordings. He remained with Lanin in New York City for three years and in 1924 relocated to Chicago, where he joined the Oriole Terrace Orchestra led by Ted Fio Rito and Danny Russo. Not only was he an instrumentalist with the group, but he also began singing with the band, which led to solo appearances with his guitar on radio station WEBH. That Windy City station had exposure across the nation, and tremendous amounts of fan mail for Lucas poured in, leading him to be signed as a solo performer by Brunswick Records.

Nick Lucas's initial Brunswick disc was "My Best Girl," and it was an immediate hit. He then went on his own in vaudeville. In the next few years, Lucas became one of the nation's favorite entertainers, both in vaudeville and on records, where he was dubbed "The Crooning Troubadour," thus making him the first official crooner. Among his hit Brunswick records were "Because They All Love You," "In a Little Spanish Town," and several of his own compositions, such as, "I've Named My Pillow After You" and "I'm Tired of Everything But You."

Early in 1926, Lucas made his Broadway debut in *Sweetheart Time*, popularizing the song "Sleepy Time Gal." In the fall of that year, Nick enjoyed his greatest career success with a three-month stint in London, England, headlining at the Café de Paris. *Variety* noted he was "Acclaimed one of the biggest receptions ever given any artist in that establishment." While in London he also appeared at the Palladium and other venues, along with giving private recitals for the prince of Wales and the queen of Spain.

Following his acclaim abroad, Nick Lucas was even in greater demand in his homeland. For the next several years, he toured the Keith-Orpheum vaudeville circuit, commanding up to $3,000 weekly, making him one of the medium's highest-paid star attractions. Because of his record and vaudeville popularity, the demand for six-string guitars increased greatly. The Gibson Guitar Company produced the Nick Lucas Special, from Lucas's own design, which became a perennial favorite well into the late 1930s. (Several decades later, Gibson revived a Nick Lucas limited-edition guitar.) At the same time, he created guitar instruction books for Mills Music, eventually authoring a score of guitar method volumes and song folios, making the *Nick Lucas Guitar Method* one of the best-selling guitar instruction books. In addition he also lent his name to a brand of guitar picks, which, along with his books, remained good sellers well into the 1980s.

In the summer of 1929, Nick Lucas returned to Broadway in Florenz Ziegfeld's *Show Girl*, which starred Jimmy Durante. In it, Lucas introduced George Gershwin's "Liza" as well as performing "Singin' in the Rain," which was a big-selling record for him on Brunswick. Earlier in the year, Lucas had completed the Technicolor motion picture *Gold Diggers of Broadway* (1929) for Warner Bros. in which he played entertainer Nick and performed his two most famous songs, "Tip Toe Through the Tulips" and "Painting the Clouds With Sunshine." His Brunswick record of the two tunes sold in excess of two million copies, and the sheet music for the songs topped the best-seller list for over four months. That spring vaudeville audiences voted Nick Lucas the eighth most popular performer in the country, and that fall *Gold Diggers of Broadway* was issued to critical acclaim. *Variety* reported of this entertainer with his striking, dark Italian look, "there's no voice on the discs like Lucas' for the type of number sung by him."

Warner Bros. signed Lucas to appear in its all-star production *The Show of Shows* (1929), in which he sang "Lady Luck" and "The Only Song I Know," as well as headlining "The Chinese Fantasy" production number with Myrna Loy in which he sang "Li-Po-Li." Again his notices were so good that the studio quickly offered him a seven-year contract, but he turned it down (he was not interested in acting) in favor of the more immediately profitable vaudeville arena. His Brunswick records also continued to be top sellers, with such songs as: "My Tonia," "Coquette," and "Running Between the Raindrops."

The Depression hit hard at the two main areas of Nick Lucas's success: vaudeville and recordings. However, despite the difficult times, he remained a highly paid headliner in both fields and in the fall of 1931 came to network radio on NBC with his own program for Campbell Soups at $2,000 per week. Early the next year, Lucas began recording for Hit of the Week Records before returning to Brunswick, where he would remain through 1934. Lucas was also the last act to headline the legendary Palace Theater late in 1932 before it was converted into a movie house. During the mid-1930s, Nick Lucas starred on his CBS radio program, and he fronted a band, Nick Lucas and His Troubadours.

It was also in the mid-1930s that thirty-seven year old Lucas returned to films, where Bing Crosby, Russ Columbo (until his untimely death in 1934), and Dick Powell held sway as the crooning stars of musical feature films. Lucas starred in short subjects for both Universal and Vitaphone (Warner Bros.). In *What This Country Needs* (1934), he performed "Tip Toe Through the Tulips," "How Can You Lose?" and "It Happened in Spain." In *Nick Lucas and His Troubadours* he sang "Tip Toe Through the Tulips," "Goody Goody," and "Sing an Old Fashioned Song," while in *Vitaphone Headliners* (1936) he crooned "Broken Hearted Troubadour." From 1936 to 1938, Lucas was the main vocalist with Al Pearce on CBS radio and in 1938 Nick began working the nightclub circuit before embarking on a world tour. Due to the growing worldwide war fever, his tour ended with a six-month engagement in Australia, where he not only headlined on the Tivoli circuit, but also had his own weekday radio program in Melbourne and recorded for Regal Zonophone Records.

Once back in the United States, Lucas made the short films *Yankee Doodle Home* (1939) and *Congamania* (1940) and remained active in club appearances and in the diminished world of vaudeville. In 1944, he was featured in a quartet of shorts for Soundies Corporation of America, and in 1947 he began a two-year run in *Ken Murray's Blackouts* in Hollywood, which also featured Marie Wilson. When the revue went to Broadway for fifty-nine performances as *Blackouts of 1949*, he was among the star players.

Early in 1950, Nick made his network TV debut on *The Ken Murray Show*. During this time, he also recorded for Diamond and Capitol Records. In 1951, he made seven musical shorts geared directly for television by Snader Telescriptions, including *Looking at the World Thru Rose Colored Glasses* and *Marie Ah Marie*. That same year also found him back on network radio as the headliner of ABC's *Saturday Night at the Shamrock*. Lucas also returned to movies, appearing as himself in Allied Artists' low-budget musical *Disc Jockey* (1951), which also showcased the likes of Sarah Vaughan, Foy Willing and the Riders of the Purple Sage, and twenty-eight radio disc jockeys from across the country; Nick sang "Let's Meander Thru the Meadow."

Throughout the 1950s, Nick Lucas appeared in clubs across the United States, with lengthy annual stays in Las Vegas, Reno, and Lake Tahoe. He also recorded for Cavalier, Accent, and Crown Records; his 1957 Decca album *Painting the Clouds With Sunshine* sold so well it remained in the company's active catalog for fifteen years. In 1962, he was a semiregular on Lawrence Welk's TV variety program, and he also appeared on many other network shows, including those of Ed Sullivan, Art Linkletter, Liberace, Kate Smith, and Patti Page's *The Big Record*. During the mid-1960s, Lucas began appearing at fairs and fraternal organization shows, and in 1966 he starred in the Lake Tahoe production of *Blackouts of 1966*. In the late 1960s, when Tiny Tim popularized once again "Tip Toe Through the Tulips," Lucas found himself overwhelmed with job offers. When Tiny Tim was married on Johnny Carson's' *The Tonight Show* late in 1969, Nick Lucas sang on this program, the most watched outing in the show's history.

Lucas returned to feature films again in 1974 singing "When You and I Were Seventeen" on the soundtrack of Paramount's elaborate period piece *The Great Gatsby*. During the same year he crooned "I Wished on the Moon" for the soundtrack of the studio's *Day of the Locust*, set in

1930s Hollywood. The next year he performed "I'll See You in My Dreams," "Happy Days Are Here Again," "Ja Dá," "Let's Make Hay While the Sun Shines," "Wang Wang Blues," and "My Blue Heaven" on the soundtrack of MGM's *Hearts of the West*, starring Jeff Bridges and Andy Griffith. Besides personal appearances, Nick continued to appear on TV (he was especially popular on Sam Yorty's West Coast program) as well as making commercials. He opened the 1980s by appearing on worldwide television in the Tournament of Roses Parade atop a float aptly entitled "Tip Toe Through the Tulips." He remained active on the personal-appearance circuit and on TV shows such as those of Merv Griffin and Wally George before succumbing to pneumonia on July 28, 1982 at the age of eighty-four. In 1983, Nick's 1930 recording of "I'll Get By" was used (uncredited) on the soundtrack of the Woody Allen comedy *Zelig*, a movie presented in a pseudodocumentary format.

One of the best summaries of the singer's productive career was given in the December 4, 1981, issue of Newark, New Jersey's *Italian Tribune* newspaper: "For sheer musical expertise, and durability, the likes of Nick Lucas, the kid from the streets of Newark, has never been equaled."

Filmography

Gold Diggers of Broadway (WB, 1929)
The Show of Shows (WB, 1929)
Nick Lucas Song (Vita, 1929) (s)
Organloguing the Hits With Nick Lucas (Master Art Products, 1931) (s)
Home Again (Master Art Products, 1933) (s)
On the Air and Off (Univ, 1933) (s)
What This Country Needs (Vita, 1934) (s)
Nick Lucas and His Troubadours (Vita, 1936) (s)
Vitaphone Headliners (Vita, 1936) (s)
Yankee Doodle Home (Col, 1939) (s)
Congamania (Univ, 1940) (s)

Goodnight, Wherever You Are (Soundies, 1944) (s)
An Hour Never Passes (Soundies, 1944) (s)
Tip Toe Through the Tulips With Me (Soundies, 1944) (s)
Side by Side (Soundies, 1944) (s)
Big Time Revue (WB, 1947) (s)
Disc Jockey (AA, 1951)
The Great Gatsby (Par, 1974) (voice only)
Day of the Locust (Par, 1974) (voice only)
Hearts of the West (MGM, 1975) (voice only)
Zelig (WB/Orion, 1983) (voice only)

Broadway Plays

Sweetheart Time (1926)
Show Girl (1929)

Blackouts of 1949 (1949)

Radio Series

The Nick Lucas Show (NBC, 1931–32; CBS, 1934–35)

Al Pearce and His Gang (NBC, 1936–38)
Saturday Night at the Shamrock (ABC, 1951)

Television Series

The Lawrence Welk Show (ABC, 1962)

Discography

LPs

Day of the Locust (London PS-912) [ST]
An Evening With Nick Lucas (Take Two 1001)
The Great Gatsby (Paramount PAS-2–3001) [ST]
The Nick Lucas Souvenir Album (Accent 5027, Beacon SBEAB-4)
Painting the Clouds With Sunshine (Decca DL-8653)

Rose Colored Glasses (Accent 5043)
The Singing Troubadour (ASV 5022)
Tip Toe Through the Tulips With Nick Lucas (10″ Tip Toe Through the Tulips with Nick Lucas (Cavalier CVLP-6007) Cavalier 5033

CDs

The Crooning Troubadour (Cool Forever CD081)
The Crooning Troubadour (Crystal Stream Audio 1DCD81)
Nick Lucas, Vol. 1 (Sounds of a Century 1875-A)
Nick Lucas, Vol. 2 (Sounds of a Century 1875-B)
Nick Lucas, Vol. 3 (Sounds of a Century 1875-C)

Nick Lucas, Vol. 4 (Sounds of a Century 1875-D)
Nick Lucas, Vol. 5 (Sounds of a Century 1875-E)
Painting the Clouds (Soundies 4134)
The Singing Troubadour (ASV CD-AJA-5022)
Tip-Toe Thru the Tulips (ASV CD-AJA-5329)

Jeanette MacDonald

(b. Jeannette Anna McDonald, Philadelphia, Pennsylvania, June 18, 1903;
d. Houston, Texas, July 14, 1965)

A beautiful, cultured, redheaded singing star of films, stage, and radio, Jeanette MacDonald is mainly remembered today for her eight movie operettas with Nelson Eddy and for resolutely singing "San Francisco" in the 1936 earthquake film epic of the same title. One of the most successful of movie singers and certainly a woman of sturdy determination (she was known as "The Iron Butterfly"), Jeanette MacDonald failed to realize her true goal, that of operatic stardom. Her forte, at least with her adoring and very faithful public, was filmed operettas, notably the glossy, luxurious MGM musicals of the 1930s.

She was born Jeannette Anna McDonald on June 18, 1903 (her grave marker insists 1907), in Philadelphia, Pennsylvania, the youngest of Daniel and Anne McDonald's three daughters. (Before the future star was four, her family had dropped an "n" from her first name; and later she would change the spelling of her surname to "MacDonald" to emphasize her father's Scottish roots. Because all three sisters were musically inclined, they were educated in private schools where they learned singing, dancing, and dramatics. At an early age Jeanette made her stage debut in a children's revue. As a teenager she came to New York City to visit her older sister Blossom (later billed as Marie Blake and then as Blossom Rock), who was working in the chorus of *The Demi-Tasse Revue,* which was the prologue show for the movie program at the Capitol Theater. Producer Ned Wayburn hired Jeanette to join the chorine lineup. Next she appeared in the chorus of *The Night Boat* (1920) and supplemented her income with modeling jobs. In 1921, she had roles in two Broadway productions *Irene* and *Tangerine*, and in 1922 she appeared in *A Fantastic Fricasse*. Her success in that Greenwich Village revue led to a big part in *The Magic Ring* (1923) in which she sang, and in 1925 she was the ingénue in George Gershwin's *Tip-Toes*. Her first starring Broadway musical was the Shubert Brothers' *Bubbling Over* in March 1926. As a Shubert contract star, she appeared in *Yes, Yes, Yvette* (1927; in which she received top billing for the first time), *Sunny Days* (1928), *Angela* (1928), and *Boom-Boom* (1929). Richard Dix saw her onstage and had Paramount Pictures test her for one of his vehicles at the company's Long Island facility. However, her current stage contract would not permit her to make films.

In 1929 filmmaker Ernst Lubitsch screened the test footage of Jeanette, and after coming to Chicago to hear her in the touring company of *Boom! Boom!* (to see if she could really sing), he hired her for the leading role in the Paramount musical *The Love Parade* opposite Maurice Chevalier. This sophisticated froufrou cast her as Queen Louise of Sylvania who marries a prince (Chevalier) with a scandalous past. In the film, she sang "March of the Grenadier" and "Dream Lover," both of which she recorded for Victor Records late in 1929 in her recording debut. *Variety* enthused of MacDonald, "Her personality, looks and voice make *Love Parade* all the more a charming, intriguing picture. . . ." The *New York Herald Tribune* agreed: "Blessed with a fine voice, a sense

Nelson Eddy and Jeanette MacDonald in *Rose-Marie* (1936).
[Courtesy of Michael R. Pitts]

of comedy and a definite screen personality, she registers an individual success that makes her future in the new medium an enviable one."

Ensconced in Hollywood with her mother (and keeping in touch with her New York–based stockbroker beau Robert Ritchie, who soon arrived on the scene to become her full-time business manager) Jeanette next costarred with Dennis King in the color production of Rudolf Friml's *The Vagabond King* (1930). It was just another of the many ponderous screen operettas in distribution that year, and it gave her no opportunity to display her wit, although she had a big production number ("Only a Rose"). Thereafter, eager to maximize MacDonald's availability, Paramount tossed her into the all-star *Paramount on Parade* (1930), but her rendition of "Sweeping the Clouds Away" was removed from the release print. (However, it was used in the Spanish-language edition, *Galas de la Paramount.*) She worked for Lubitsch again, this time opposite Britisher Jack Buchanan, in the polished *Monte Carlo* (1930), singing "Beyond the Blue Horizon," which she recorded for

Victor. The studio stuck her with a singing part in the scatterbrained comedy *Let's Go Native* (1930). Paramount then ended her contract feeling that as movie musicals (especially operettas) were becoming moribund, so was Jeanette's usefulness to the studio lot.

She was at United Artists for *The Lottery Bride* (1930), which despite Rudolf Friml's original score, was embarrassing to all concerned, including Jeanette, who was cast as a Norwegian contestant in a marriage lottery that lands her in Nome, Alaska. At least the pretentious project offered her top-starring billing on the screen for the first time. Meanwhile, she made her radio debut over NBC. Next she made a trio of pictures for Fox that are both her least-revered and least-known screen work today. Because the musical film cycle had passed, the Fox entries de-emphasized her singing talents and highlighted her ability for ladylike risqué comedy in a drawing-room atmosphere. In fact, in *Oh, for a Man!* (1930) most of her singing numbers were deleted; only her aria from Richard Wagner's opera *Tristan and Isolde* remained.

In the fall of 1931, MacDonald went to London, where she recorded four songs for Victor's British label, HMV (His Master's Voice). The trip to England was part of a concert tour on which she embarked to disprove a French newspaper account insisting she had been killed there in a car crash. The singing engagement took her to several European cities, in addition to Paris and London (where she performed at the Dominion Theater).

Back in Hollywood, Ernst Lubitsch convinced Paramount to reteam Jeanette with Chevalier for *One Hour With You* (1932), which George Cukor began as director and Lubitsch completed. In this superior fare, MacDonald and Chevalier were a married couple whose harmony is interrupted by another woman (Genevieve Tobin). Jeanette sang the title song and "We Will Always Be Sweethearts." She and Chevalier (who were not fond of one another) also starred in the French-language version of this entry with Lily Damita in the Tobin part. Their next vehicle, *Love Me Tonight* (1932), was directed stylishly by Rouben Mamoulian and utilized a Rodgers and Hart score, including the popular "Isn't It Romantic?" It presented Chevalier as a French tailor who becomes infatuated with the guest (Jeanette) of a nobleman who cannot pay his bills. However, with the musical picture definitely out of vogue, Paramount again bid good-bye to MacDonald.

Jeanette went to Europe, ostensibly on a concert tour, but actually to cement film offers. She was in London to star in *The Queen's Affair* (1933) with Herbert Marshall, but both performers left the project, and Anna Neagle took MacDonald's role in that and the next announced project, *Bitter Sweet* (1933). Meanwhile, on the coast of France, MacDonald had become friendly with MGM star Norma Shearer and her studio executive husband Irving Thalberg. He was starting his own production unit at the studio and needed a roster of stars. Thalberg acknowledged that screen musicals had come back into fashion (buoyed by Warner Bros.' 1933 hit *42nd Street)*, and he persuaded an already willing Jeanette to sign a contract with that studio.

After Jeanette returned to Hollywood, both Thalberg and his MGM rival/boss Louis B. Mayer debated and delayed about what should be the first project to showcase their new talent. With her friend Ritchie, MacDonald began negotiations at United Artists for a project that fell through. Then MGM agreed she was to be showcased in *I Married an Angel* based on a Rodgers and Hart original, but the musical was too risqué to be endorsed by the industry's newly restructured Production Code. (The show was transformed into a Broadway musical in 1938 and in 1942 would finally become a MacDonald vehicle, made with her constant costar, Nelson Eddy.) Instead MacDonald starred in *The Cat and the Fiddle* (1934) opposite ex–silent film star Ramon Novarro. Jeanette sang "Tonight Will Teach Me to Forget" and "Try to Forget." The entry, however, lacked a needed light touch and was only mildly successful.

When Grace Moore could not come to terms with MGM, Jeanette replaced her opposite Maurice Chevalier (much to his chagrin) in a remake of *The Merry Widow* (1934) staged elaborately by Ernst Lubitsch. MacDonald sang "I Love You So" and "Vilia." The expensive, bubbly film was more popular with critics than the public.

Jeanette had rejected doing *Naughty Marietta* (1935) several times, but now under a five-year studio pact, she was persuaded to star with a newcomer, Nelson Eddy, in this old-fashioned operetta. MGM reasoned it would be a change from her cosmopolitan outings with Lubitsch and, hopefully, would make her more popular with grassroots America. On-camera she did "The Italian Street Song" and dueted with Eddy on "Ah, Sweet Mystery of Life." The elaborate outing proved to be a substantial hit and made her a top industry personality again. The new screen team was reunited (after Grace Moore dropped out) in the even better *Rose-Marie* (1936). It provided them with their most famous duet, "Indian Love Call," which sold over one million records when they recorded it for Victor. Jeanette also sang arias from Charles Gounod's opera *Romeo et Juliette* and Giacomo Puccini's *Tosca* in this account of an opera singer who falls in love with a persistent Canadian Mountie (Eddy). Despite playing the role of a demanding opera diva, MacDonald displayed a winning tongue-in-cheek rapport that made her seem far less lofty to appreciative moviegoers. The picture was a top money earner of the year, and Jeanette and Nelson Eddy were again hailed as the best screen team since Fred Astaire and Ginger Rogers.

Always a shrewd businesswoman, Jeanette had sold MGM the story of *San Francisco* (1936) on condition that Clark Gable be her costar. He was disinterested in pairing with MacDonald (who had a reputation for being overly demanding on the set). But she was determined, and Louis B. Mayer supported her decision. In the course of this classic exercise, she belted out the title tune, did excerpts from Gounod's *Faust* and Giuseppe Verdi's *Il Trovatore*, and sang "Nearer My God, to Thee." When added to the magnetic presence of Gable, reliable Spencer Tracy (as a priest), and a re-creation of the Bay City quake, the resultant film was destined for huge box-office results.

By this time MacDonald was at the peak of her screen career. The studio dug into the vaults for future MacDonald-Eddy screen matchings. In the schmaltzy *Maytime* (1937)—the production of which had to start all over again due to Irving Thalberg's death in 1936—John Barrymore was her jealous impresario/husband who kills the handsome opera star (Eddy) she loves. She and Eddy provided excerpts from Giacomo Meyerbeer's grand opera *Les Huguenots* and Herbert Stothart's *Czaritza*, plus giving memorable duets on "Farewell to Dreams," "Will You Remember?" and "Song of Love." It was a sugary success. But there were some roles that even the studio agreed were not right for the MacDonald-Eddy on-camera combination. Thus Allan Jones costarred with Jeanette in *The Firefly* (1937). In the opinion of many people (including MacDonald), Jones was a more spirited movie leading man than Eddy. In *The Firefly* he sang "The Donkey Serenade" (which became his trademark song), and Jeanette did Friml's "Giannina Mia," as she essayed her role as a spy in Napoleonic times. However, the box-office grosses on the costly *The Firefly* did not match the screen teamings of MacDonald and Eddy.

On June 17, 1937, Jeanette married actor Gene Raymond in a lavish wedding at the Wilshire Methodist Church in Beverly Hills. (Nelson Eddy sang at the ceremony.) After her marriage, she was encouraged in her operatic pursuits by her husband. For a time she studied with the great opera star Lotte Lehmann, and when she recorded "Let Me Always Sing" and "From the Land of the Sky Blue Water" for Victor Records in 1939, Raymond accompanied her on the piano. In 1938, she starred on radio in the CBS program *Vick's Open House*, and that year she and Nelson Eddy made *Girl of the Golden West* (1938). In this labored screen fare, she sang "Liebestraum" and "Ave Marie," trying to bolster the lumbering production that did not display Eddy to any advantage. Much more popular was the studio's Technicolor production of *Sweethearts* (1938), a contemporary story of a married (and feuding) couple who star in Broadway operettas. The joyful picture was a big moneymaker.

MacDonald and Eddy both sought new screen partners in 1939 to test their individual marquee power and, hopefully, to find other movie teammates. It was also an excellent opportunity for Louis B. Mayer to merchandise his screen team individually to great profit. But Jeanette's *Broadway Serenade* (1939) was absurd and had a miscast, nonsinging Lew Ayres as her show-business, piano-playing husband. By this point Jeanette had fought once too often with studio head Mayer, and it harmed her future at the studio. Her career began going downhill.

She and Nelson Eddy were back in tandem with *New Moon*, the first of two 1940 releases for the duo. A revamping of the 1930 film with Lawrence Tibbett and Grace Moore, this *New Moon* was set in 1790s' New Orleans, with newly rich Jeanette attracted to rakish bondsman Eddy. They offered "Wanting You," perhaps their most effective duet. Their next outing, *Bitter Sweet*, was not as good in its contrived account of a music teacher (Eddy) who marries his pupil (Jeanette) and writes an opera for her only to die in a duel. They harmonized on "I'll See You Again." *Bitter Sweet* was abhorred by its author (Noël Coward) and, to a great extent, ignored by the public; it lost money. Exploiting her offscreen marriage to Gene Raymond, Metro matched her on-camera with him in the remake of *Smilin' Through* (1941), a lachrymose Technicolor opus. By now MacDonald was too mature to play a young ingénue, and Raymond was even more one-dimensional than critics had accused Nelson Eddy of being on-screen.

In 1942 MacDonald and Eddy were teamed for the final time on-screen in the much-delayed *I Married an Angel*. As watered down for the movies, it was a failed fantasy about a wealthy banker (Eddy) dreaming he has wed an angel (Jeanette). It went through retakes and reediting, and the final results were not well received by World War II–weary moviegoers. The same year, MacDonald had a tongue-in-cheek dramatic role (at which she excelled) in the low-budgeted spy spoof *Cairo*, in which she was a film star involved in espionage and romance (with Robert Young).

Nelson Eddy engineered his MGM release in 1942, the same year Metro terminated Jeanette's studio agreement. She chose to appear in grand opera, making her debut in Gounod's *Romeo et Juliette* in Montreal with tenor Armand Tokatyan as Romeo and a cast that included Ezio Pinza. It was followed by a run of the opera in Chicago and elsewhere in the States, but the rumored debut of Jeanette MacDonald at New York's Metropolitan Opera never transpired. She then appeared in Gounod's *Faust* with the Chicago Civil Opera Company. Her reviews were again mixed, with some critics insisting her voice was not sufficiently strong enough to excel in grand opera.

During the World War II years, Jeanette was a tireless civilian entertainer at USO shows for troops. In 1944, she returned briefly to the screen as herself in Universal's *Follow the Boys*, singing "I'll See You in My Dreams" and "Beyond the Blue Horizon." While recurring news stories insisted that MacDonald and Eddy would be reteamed on-screen, nothing materialized, although she was a frequent guest on radio's *The Electric Hour* and *Kraft Music Hall*, both starring Nelson Eddy.

On *Lux Radio Theater* they did radio versions of *Naughty Marietta, Maytime*, and *Rose-Marie*, and on December 23, 1948, on NBC's *Camel Screen Guild Theater*, they reprised "Sweethearts." Jeanette had been recording with Victor Records, and she would remain with the label until the early 1950s, recording a variety of songs, ranging from her movie tunes to opera to inspirational numbers.

Producer Joe Pasternak convinced Jeanette to return to MGM for her two final feature films: *Three Daring Daughters* (1948) and *The Sun Comes Up* (1949). The former had her sing "You Made Me Love You" as she played the mother of three teenage girls, while the latter teamed her as a widowed concert singer with Lassie the dog. She sang excerpts from Puccini's evergreen lyric opera *Madame Butterfly* as well as a few folk songs in her final film. She looked gorgeous in both features, but chose to make no more pictures.

In 1948, MacDonald starred in a very popular Hollywood Bowl concert. In 1951, she and Gene Raymond revived *The Guardsman* on Broadway. Both of them did occasional tours in tandem. She had the title role of "The Prima Donna" on *Directors Playhouse* (NBC-TV) in 1956, and the next year she was in "Charley's Aunt" on *Playhouse 90* (CBS-TV). The year 1957 also found her doing a nightclub act at the Sahara Hotel in Las Vegas and at Los Angeles' Cocoanut Grove; the previous year she and Nelson Eddy had been reunited on Gordon MacRae's TV show. (Her voice had shown signs of age, while Eddy's had not.) In 1958, the duo recorded the LP album *Jeanette MacDonald and Nelson Eddy Favorites* for RCA Victor, and it proved a good seller, attaining a gold record in 1967. When Louis B. Mayer died in 1957, she sang "Ah, Sweet Mystery of Life" at his funeral.

In her last years, MacDonald and Gene Raymond, who had had their periods of marital difficulties, lived a quiet and comfortable life in their Bel-Air home. There were occasional career "almosts" in this period. In late 1960, producer Harold Prince wanted to star Jeanette in a stage musical of the movie *Sunset Boulevard* (1950), even suggesting that Eddy be cast as her once-costar turned her chauffeur. It was to be called *The Iron Butterfly*. But that show idea took too many years to write, and by then MacDonald had passed away. There was also talk of Jeanette and young Liza Minnelli costarring in a Broadway show by composer Hugh Martin and librettist Marshall Barer; that did not come to be. Film producer Ross Hunter wanted MacDonald for a role in his Doris Day screen comedy *The Thrill of It All*, and there were rumors (which proved to be only talk) of Jeanette being considered to play the Mother Abbess in the movie version of *The Sound of Music* (1965). While none of these projects came to pass for MacDonald, she spent her time traveling abroad, accepting awards, and planning her memoirs. Later the Raymonds sold their house and moved into a large apartment in Los Angeles. Heart problems plagued Jeanette in her final years, and the condition became serious in 1963. She died on July 14, 1965, following open-heart surgery in Houston, Texas. Her husband was at her bedside. At her funeral, Nelson Eddy sang "Ah, Sweet Mystery of Life."

Over the decades since Jeanette MacDonald starred on-screen with and without Nelson Eddy, her movie operettas have been in and out of vogue. To some she became a camp figure, while to others (especially her remarkably devoted fan club) she could do no wrong. Today there is a vast canon of her work available on recordings and film. They demonstrate her sharp ability with a comic line, her flair for popularizing highbrow music, and an attractive, vivacious presence that overcame her arch coyness in her later films.

The singing star was the subject of two recent biographies: Sharon Rich's *Sweethearts: The Timeless Love Affair—On-Screen and Off—Between Jeanette MacDonald and Nelson Eddy* (1994) and Edward Baron Turk's *Hollywood Diva: A Biography of Jeanette MacDonald* (1998). In addition there was the publication of Tom Tierney's *Jeanette MacDonald and Nelson Eddy: Paper Dolls in Full Color* (1992). In spring 2002, a $1 million grant from Gene Raymond's trust established the Jeanette MacDonald Operetta Scholarship and Performing Fund at the USC Thornton School of Music.

Filmography

The Love Parade (Par, 1929)*
The Vagabond King (Par, 1930)
Paramount on Parade (Par, 1930)**
Let's Go Native (Par, 1930)
Monte Carlo (Par, 1930)
The Lottery Bride (UA, 1930)
Oh, For a Man! (Fox, 1930)
Annabelle's Affairs (Fox, 1931)
Don't Bet on Women (Fox, 1931)
One Hour With You (Par, 1932)*
Love Me Tonight (Par, 1932)*
Hollywood on Parade #7 (Par, 1933) (s)
The Cat and the Fiddle (MGM, 1934)
The Merry Widow (MGM, 1934)*
Naughty Marietta (MGM, 1935)
Rose-Marie (MGM, 1936)

San Francisco (MGM, 1936)
The Firefly (MGM, 1937)
Maytime (MGM, 1937)
Girl of the Golden West (MGM, 1938)
Sweethearts (MGM, 1938)
Broadway Serenade (MGM, 1939)
New Moon (MGM, 1940)
Bitter Sweet (MGM, 1940)
Smilin' Through (MGM, 1941)
I Married an Angel (MGM, 1942)
Cairo (MGM, 1942)
Follow the Boys (Univ, 1944)
Three Daring Daughters [The Birds and the Bees] (MGM, 1948)
The Sun Comes Up (MGM, 1949)
*Also starred in the French-language version
**Spanish-language version only

Broadway Plays

The Night Boat (1920)
Irene (1921)
Tangerine (1921)
A Fantastic Fricassee (1922)
The Magic Ring (1923)
Tip-Toes (1925)

Bubbling Over (1926)
Yes, Yes, Yvette (1927)
Sunny Days (1928)
Angela (1928)
Boom-Boom (1929)
The Guardsman (1951) (revival)

Album Discography

LPs

Apple Blossom (Mac/Eddy JN 122) [ST/R] w. Gordon MacRae
Bitter Sweet (Amalgamated 200) [ST/R]
Bitter Sweet (Mac/Eddy JN 117) [ST/R] w. Gordon MacRae
Broadway Serenade (Caliban 6020) [ST]
The Cat and the Fiddle (Caliban 6049) [ST]
Dream Lover (Conifer 133)
Favorites (RCA International 89059)
The Firefly (Caliban 60270) [ST]

Follow the Boys (Hollywood Soundstage 5012) [ST]
Hollywood Bowl Concert (Mac/Eddy JN 104)
I Married an Angel (Caliban 6004) [ST]
Irene (Mac/Eddy JN 109) [ST/R]
Jeanette MacDonald (Empire 809)
Jeanette MacDonald and Nelson Eddy (Mac/Eddy JN 111)
Jeanette MacDonald and Nelson Eddy (Murray Hill X14078)

Jeanette MacDonald and Nelson Eddy (RCA LPV-526)

Jeanette MacDonald and Nelson Eddy: Christmas Album (Mac/Eddy JN 119)

Jeanette MacDonald and Nelson Eddy Favorites (RCA LPM/LSP-1738, RCA ANL1-1075)

Jeanette MacDonald and Nelson Eddy: Legendary Performers (RCA CPL1-2468)

Jeanette MacDonald and Nelson Eddy: Patriotic Songs (Mac/Eddy JN 118)

Jeanette MacDonald and Nelson Eddy: Religious Songs (Mac/Eddy JN 127)

Jeanette MacDonald and Nelson Eddy: The Early Years (Mac/Eddy JN 110)

Jeanette MacDonald and Nelson Eddy—Together Again (Sandy Hook 2101)

Jeanette MacDonald Favorites (10″ RCA LM-73)

Jeanette MacDonald Sings! (Sunbeam 514)

Jeanette MacDonald Sings San Francisco and Other Silver Screen Favorites (RCA International 89059)

Love Me Tonight (Caliban 6047) [ST]

Love Parade/One Hour With You/Love Me Tonight (Ariel CMF 23) [ST]

Mail Call (Mac/Eddy JN-129) w. Nelson Eddy, Ronald Colman, George Burns and Gracie Allen

Maytime (Pelican 121, Sandy Hook 2008) [ST/R]

The Merry Widow (Mac/Eddy JN 120) [ST/R] w. Gordon MacRae

The Merry Widow/The Cat and the Fiddle (Hollywood Soundstage 5015) [ST]

Monte Carlo (Caliban 6037) [ST]

Naughty Marietta (Hollywood Soundstage 413) [ST]

Naughty Marietta (Mac/Eddy JN 115) [ST/R] w. Gordon MacRae

Naughty Marietta (Pelican 117) [ST/R] w. Nelson Eddy

Nelson and the Ladies (Sounds Rare 5002) w. Nelson Eddy

Nelson Eddy and Jeanette MacDonald—America's Singing Sweethearts (RCA/Suffolk Marketing DVM1-0301)

Nelson Eddy on the Air (Totem 1035) w. Nelson Eddy

The Nelson Eddy Show (Mac/Eddy JN 101, JN 102, JN 103, JN 106, JN 107)

New Moon/I Married an Angel (Pelican 103) [ST]

New Moon/Rose-Marie (Columbia Special Products P-13878)

One Hour With You (Caliban 6011) [ST]

Opera and Operetta Favorites (RCA LM-2908)

Operatic Recitals III (Mac/Eddy JN 123) w. Nelson Eddy

Operetta Favorites by Jeanette MacDonald and Nelson Eddy (10″ RCA LCT-16)

Romantic Moments (10″ RCA LM-62)

Rose-Marie (Hollywood Soundstage 414) [ST]

Rose-Marie/Naughty Marietta/I Married a Angel/ Bitter Sweet (Sandy Hook 3-SH-1) [ST]

Rose-Marie/New Moon/Naughty Marietta (Col GB-3)

San Francisco (Caliban 6026) [ST]

San Francisco (Victrola VIC-1515)

Silver Screen Favorites (RCA International 89059)

Smilin' Through (Camden CAL-325)

Smilin' Thru (Mac/Eddy JN 125) [ST/R] w. Brian Aherne

Songs of Faith and Inspiration (Camden CAL-750)

Sweethearts (The Good Music Record Company/ RCA Special Products DMM2-0876) w. Nelson Eddy

Sweethearts (Pelican 143, Sandy Hook 2025) [ST/R]

Tonight Or Never (Mac/Eddy 112) [ST/R] w. Melvyn Douglas, Mary Garden

A Tribute to Jeanette MacDonald (O.A.S.I. 594)

CDs

Ah, Sweet Mystery of Life (Flapper PAST-CD-7026) w. Nelson Eddy

Always Together (Hallmark 301672) w. Nelson Eddy

America's Singing Sweethearts (The Beautiful Music Company/RCA Special Products DMC1-1001) w. Nelson Eddy

The Best of Jeanette MacDonald and Nelson Eddy (Sound Waves—no number)

Change Partners (Box Office Records 2793) w. Nelson Eddy

Cocktail Hour (Columbia River Entertainment Group 218065) w. Nelson Eddy

Dames/San Francisco/Suzy (Great Movie Themes 60022) [ST]

Dream Lover (Flapper PAST-CD-7824, Jasmine JASCD-2558) w. Nelson Eddy

Follow the Boys/To Have and Have Not/Star Dust/ Waterloo Bridge (Great Movie Themes 60032) [ST]

Indian Love Call (Golden Options GO-3822) w. Nelson Eddy

Interviews #1 (Mac/Eddy JN-136) w. Nelson Eddy

Interviews #2 (Mac/Eddy JN-137) w. Nelson Eddy

Jeanette MacDonald & Nelson Eddy (Again LBACD-004)

Jeanette MacDonald & Nelson Eddy (Sounds of a Century 1835)

Legendary Performers (Great Movie Themes 60012) w. Nelson Eddy

Love's Old Song (Master Song 503132) w. Nelson Eddy

Nelson Eddy & Jeanette MacDonald (The Good Music Record Company—no number)

One Hour With You (Encore's Box Office ENBO-CD-18/97)

Radio Promos (Mac/Eddy JN-135)

Rose-Marie (Delta—no number) w. Nelson Eddy

Rose-Marie (Music CD-6226) w. Nelson Eddy

San Francisco and Other Jeanette MacDonald Favorites (RCA 09026-60877-2)

16 Most Requested Songs (Javelin CWN-CD-2042) w. Nelson Eddy

Sweethearts (RCA Special Products DMC1-0876) w. Nelson Eddy

Sweethearts—20 Favorites (Prism PLATCD-140) w. Nelson Eddy

Together Again (Sandy Hook CDSH-2101) w. Nelson Eddy

A Tribute to Jeanette MacDonald, Vol. 1 (OASI 7007)

A Tribute to Jeanette MacDonald, Vol. 2 (OASI 7011)

The Very Best of Jeanette MacDonald & Nelson Eddy (Soundwaves SWNCD005)

Vick's Open House, Vol. 1 (Mac/Eddy JN-130)

Vick's Open House, Vol. 2 (Mac/Eddy JN-132)

When I'm Calling You (ASV CD-AJA-5124) w. Nelson Eddy

Shirley Jones and Gordon MacRae in *Oklahoma!* (1955).
[Courtesy of Michael R. Pitts]

Gordon MacRae

(b. Albert Gordon MacRae, East Orange, New Jersey, March 12, 1921; d. Lincoln, Nebraska, January 24, 1986)

Possessing an outstanding tenor voice, virile good looks, and an easygoing, pleasing personality, Gordon MacRae became one of the more popular of semiclassical singers in the 1950s. He inherited the mantle of King of the Operetta that had once belonged to Nelson Eddy, although he was more active in that genre on records, radio, and TV than on celluloid. MacRae was a well-rounded entertainer and was quite successful in all media. However, the heights he might have achieved will never be known due to a long, and for years unknown, battle with alcohol. After finally overcoming his addiction in the mid-1960s, MacRae set about to reestablish his career. He was able to do so, but without attaining the many successes he had known in the 1940s and 1950s. Like entertainer Lillian Roth, MacRae spent his last years as a national spokesman against alcohol abuse, becoming the honorary chairman of the National Council on Alcoholism. Sadly, having overcome one enormous problem, he was struck with cancer of the jaw that eventually killed him. Those close to MacRae noted that his battle with the disease was just as valiant as had been his earlier conflict.

Albert Gordon MacRae was born on March 12, 1921, in East Orange, New Jersey. He came from a theatrical family; his father William was a pioneer radio performer, and his mother was a concert pianist. (After his father died, his mother married Philip Osborne, and they had a son, Jasper.) Gordon became interested in music at an early age. As a child actor on radio he developed a character called Wee Willie MacRae and later was a juvenile soloist in the touring *The Ray Bolger Revue*. When not performing, MacRae worked as a pageboy at NBC Studios in New York City. At the 1939 to 1940 World's Fair, he won a singing contest that resulted in his performing for two weeks with Harry James and his band. He continued his NBC job, but in 1940 he was hired by orchestra leader Horace Heidt (who had spotted him singing in the NBC lounge) to be a band vocalist. He remained with Heidt for two years, although in 1941 he took a respite to make his stage debut at the Long Island Millpond Playhouse in Roslyn, New York, followed by a Broadway run as a replacement in the comedy *Junior Miss* (1941).

In the spring of 1942, MacRae was in Hollywood with Heidt's group, and with the orchestra, he made his recording debut for Columbia Records, providing the vocals on "Heavenly Highway" and "When Your Lips Met Mine." The previous year (May 21, 1941) he had married actress Sheila Stevens, and he served in the military during World War II from 1943 to 1945.

Returning home from the service, the singer landed his own fifteen-minute radio show each Sunday night on CBS called *The Gordon MacRae Show* that lasted for one season. In March 1946, he costarred with Ray Bolger, Arthur Godfrey, and Brenda Forbes in the Broadway musical revue *Three to Make Ready*, which had a 327-performance run, with MacRae singing "If It's Love." During this period, he also cut a number of records for the Musicraft label with Walter Gross and

His Orchestra, including "Prisoner of Love," "They Say It's Wonderful," "Slowly," and "Anybody's Spring." Following his Broadway appearance, Gordon returned to network radio during the 1947–48 season with *The Gordon MacRae Show*, broadcast by CBS each Monday evening for a half hour.

The year 1948 proved to be a high-water mark in MacRae's career. Moving to Los Angeles, he began his six-year association with the popular radio program *The Railroad Hour*, which he hosted on ABC during the 1948–49 season, and then the show switched to NBC from 1949 to 1954. Sponsored by American railroads, this popular production presented capsule operettas and dramas hosted by MacRae, who also starred in them with various guest stars such as Jane Powell, Betty Garrett, Dorothy Kirsten, Margaret Truman, and Mimi Benzell. He also made guest appearances on other radio series, like *The Johnson Wax Program, Navy Star Time, Showtime*, and Perry Como's *The Chesterfield Supper Club*. In the latter he appeared in *Lady Be Good* with Groucho Marx and *The Red Mill* with Gene Kelly and Lucille Norman.

MacRae also signed a five-year contract with Warner Bros., as they were seeking a successor to their aging Dennis Morgan. Like future screen rival Howard Keel (who would be based at MGM), MacRae made his film debut in a dramatic role. In Warners' "B" melodrama *The Big Punch* (1948), Gordon was the boxer falsely accused of murder who is aided by a former pugilist (Wayne Morris) turned minister. *Variety* said of MacRae, "He should get along in films, presenting an easy personality and an ability to read lines credibly. He doesn't need vocalizing to sell himself." In 1948 MacRae signed with Capitol Records, and he would have a profitable association with the label that would last until well into the 1960s. For Capitol he had a string of moderately good-selling singles plus a host of best-selling record albums that included a range of music. During this period, he and his wife had a growing family, with children Meredith, Heather, Gordon, and Bruce.

MacRae's image as the handsome, manly film singer was promoted in his second Warner Bros. production, *Look for the Silver Lining* (1949). This bouncy, colorful biopic of entertainer Marilyn Miller (portrayed by June Haver, on loan from Twentieth Century-Fox) gave Gordon a chance to sing several vintage pop songs. Since *The Big Punch* demonstrated that he could easily handle dramatics, he was assigned to *Backfire* (1949), a taut melodrama with Virginia Mayo, in which he portrayed a man who becomes involved in murder while searching for a missing pal. MacRae's actress wife was also in the cast.

Gordon was reteamed with June Haver in another period musical, *The Daughter of Rosie O'Grady* (1950), in which he played top restaurateur Tony Pastor. This was followed by an updated remake of *No, No, Nanette* called *Tea for Two* (1950). It was the first of several features he made with the studio's top musical star, Doris Day; the wholesomeness of Day nicely complemented that of MacRae. A more rugged role came MacRae's way when he played a young man falsely accused of murder and jailed by his lawman father (Jack Holt) in the spirited Western *Return of the Frontiersman* (1950). Gordon's fifth and final 1950 release was another musical, *The West Point Story* (1950), in which he was a cadet coping with a martinet Broadway director (James Cagney). The latter, in his first dancing role in years, garnered more attention than did costars MacRae, Virginia Mayo, or Doris Day.

Following a guest appearance as himself entertaining troops in *Starlift* (1951), Gordon was reunited again with Doris Day for *On Moonlight Bay* (1951), in which MacRae, as a small-town lad, falls for the tomboy (Doris Day) next door. Filmed in color and boasting a host of nostalgic period (1915–1918) songs, the picture is an adroit piece of Americana. Gordon wanted to do the role of tune composer Gus Kahn in *I'll See You in My Dreams* (1951), but Danny Thomas was given the lead opposite Doris Day. Instead, MacRae was a military cadet secretly wed to Phyllis Kirk in *About Face* (1952), a song-and-dance remake of *Brother Rat* (1938). *On Moonlight Bay* had proved to be so popular that the studio reunited MacRae and Day for a sequel, *By the Light of the Silvery Moon* (1953), with soldier MacRae returning home to face life with bride Day.

This sequel also did good box-office business, but MacRae was to make only two more features for the studio, which had become cavalier about their contractee. In *The Desert Song* (1953), he was the secret leader of the North African "The Riffs" who battles a wicked Arab (Steve Cochran) while winning the love of Kathryn Grayson (on loan from MGM). He nicely handled the title song and dueted with Grayson on "One Alone." While this third remake of the Sigmund Romberg operetta was pictorially and musically colorful, it was stiff in plot and little pleased 1950s' filmgoers. Ironically Nelson Eddy, who was MacRae's elder by a decade, would handle the production much better two years later in an NBC-TV special. MacRae's final Warner Bros. feature, *Three Sailors and a Girl* (1953), was taken from George S. Kaufman's play *The Butter and Egg Man*. It was about a trio of sailors (MacRae, Gene Nelson, Sam Levene) who use their ship's money to back a musical starring Jane Powell (on loan from MGM), who dueted with MacRae on the number "Face to Face." The comedy antics of Levene and Jack E. Leonard were the picture's highlights.

Because Warner Bros. and MacRae had lost interest in one another, he negotiated his studio release, which prevented his doing *Lucky Me* (1954) with Doris Day. He turned to TV because his radio show (part of a fading medium) also ended in 1954, so he hosted NBC-TV's *The Colgate Comedy Hour*. On that program on April 10, 1955, he starred in a production of *Roberta*. More importantly, in 1955 he achieved his goal of being cast as Curly in the screen version of the Richard Rodgers–Oscar Hammerstein II musical *Oklahoma!* (1955). Filmed in an expansive wide-screen process with stereophonic sound, MacRae was the Midwestern rancher who romanced pretty Laurey (Shirley Jones) but had a rival in nasty Jud (Rod Steiger). MacRae sang "Oh, What a Beautiful Morning" and the title song, as well as dueting with Jones on "The Surrey With the Fringe on Top" and "People Will Say We're in Love." The screen adaptation was hardly innovative, but it was sufficiently popular to boost MacRae's industry standing. The Capitol soundtrack album remained on the national record charts for over one hundred weeks.

From March to August 1956, the singer starred in the fifteen-minute NBC-TV series *The Gordon MacRae Show*, a live production that took place on a set modeled after the star's own living room. That year, thanks to Frank Sinatra, MacRae had what is perhaps his best-remembered screen part. Sinatra had been hired to star as Billy Bigelow in the musical fantasy *Carousel* (1956) for Twentieth Century-Fox. However, he refused to film each scene twice (once for CinemaScope, and then again for normal ratio) and walked off the project. Fox quickly substituted MacRae. With total commitment, Gordon became the swaggering carnival barker who carries out a robbery with unsavory Jigger (Cameron Mitchell) to gain money for his wife (Shirley Jones) and baby. Billy is killed, but fifteen years later he returns from Heaven to help his wife and teenage daughter. MacRae and Jones dueted "If I Love You," and he performed the famous "Soliloquy," measuring up favorably to John Raitt, who had created the role so indelibly on Broadway. MacRae made *Carousel* his starring vehicle.

Also for Twentieth Century-Fox, MacRae had his final starring role in a feature film in the entertaining musical *The Best Things in Life Are Free* (1956). He provided a good-natured portrayal of songwriter Buddy DeSylva. During the 1956–57 TV season, he hosted the NBC network series *Lux Video Theater*, and on this program in 1957 he starred in presentations of *One Sunday Afternoon* and *Eileen*. Gordon was to have done *Bells Are Ringing* (1956) on Broadway but could not come to terms with the producers, so Sydney Chaplin was cast opposite Judy Holliday in the hit musical.

In the late 1950s, MacRae—who admitted he was "lazy" and only worked to support his hobby (gambling)—continued to be active, appearing in top nightspots as well as guesting on TV variety shows. (He made an unsold TV pilot called *No Place Like Home*.) In 1958 he had a hit single for Capitol called "The Secret." The next year he appeared on several *Voice of Firestone* shows on NBC-TV, and late in 1959 he starred in the CBS-TV special *Gift of the Magi*. The next year, he and wife Sheila (now billed as Sheila MacRae) hosted several segments of CBS-TV's *The Revlon Revue* before embarking on their successful cabaret club act in the early 1960s. By now, MacRae was having cumulative personal problems due to his longtime drinking problem, and in the middle of the decade his marriage ended (just as he began pulling himself together). Following his divorce in April 1967, he wed candy heiress Elizabeth Lambert Schrafft on September 25, 1967, and they later had a daughter, Amanda. He returned to Broadway in 1967, replacing Robert Preston in the hit musical *I Do! I Do!* and in 1968 he was named Star of the Season by the March of Dimes.

During all this time MacRae's daughters were also involved in show business, with Meredith MacRae having a hit record ("Image of a Boy") in 1964. In addition, she was a regular on the teleseries *My Three Sons* (1963–65) and *Petticoat Junction* (1966–70), as well as being featured in the movie *Norwood* (1970). Heather MacRae appeared in such pictures as *Everything You Always Wanted to Know About Sex But Were Afraid to Ask* (1972) and *Bang the Drum Slowly* (1973).

In the late 1960s, Gordon resumed his club appearances with great success. When he appeared at the Saint Regis Hotel's Maisonette Room in New York, Gotham columnist Earl Wilson commented on his "good, rich voice," while Dennis Sheahan (*Women's Wear Daily*) observed, "He is an untiring entertainer who is completely at ease with the audience. He laughs, tells jokes, mingles with guests and he is not beyond poking a little fun at himself." Gordon continued to appear in clubs throughout the country, with long stands in Las Vegas and New York City. When he appeared at New York's Plaza Hotel in 1970, *Variety* noted, "With consummate authority spawned in the niteries, legit and major filmusicals, MacRae has the Persian Room customers with him from the start. . . ." In the fall of 1974, MacRae resumed his dramatic efforts with a guest appearance on *McCloud* (NBC-TV). In 1979, he returned to films in the costarring role of North American Airlines executive Mike Barnes in *The Pilot* about the alcoholic title character (Cliff Robertson); Robertson also directed the feature, which received little theatrical release.

Into the 1980s, Gordon continued to be active in clubs and in various stage productions as he settled with his family in Lincoln, Nebraska. Then, however, in 1982 he suffered a crippling stroke. Following a long and painful battle with cancer of the jaw, he died there on January 24, 1986, at the age of sixty-four. In 1992, Sheila MacRae's autobiography, *Hollywood Mother of the Year: Sheila MacRae's Own Story*, was published. In it she told of her years with the alcoholic/gambler Gordon and her eventual decision to separate from him and renew her own career. In 1999, the MacRaes' daughter Heather performed at the Manhattan Eighty Eight club, with her act being a tribute to her late father by including many songs associated with Gordon. (Her show was recorded and released by Harbinger Records.) The MacRaes' other daughter, actress Meredith, died on July 14, 2000.

Filmography

The Big Punch (WB, 1948)
Look for the Silver Lining (WB, 1949)
Backfire (WB, 1950)
The Daughter of Rosie O'Grady (WB, 1950)
Tea for Two (WB, 1950)
Return of the Frontiersman (WB, 1950)
The West Point Story [Fine and Dandy] (WB, 1950)
The Screen Director (Vita, 1951) (s)
Starlift (WB, 1951)
On Moonlight Bay (WB, 1951)

About Face (WB, 1952)
Screen Snapshots #205 (Col, 1952) (s)
By the Light of the Silvery Moon (WB, 1953)
So You Want a Television Set (Vita, 1953) (s)
The Desert Song (WB, 1953)
Three Sailors and a Girl (WB, 1953)
Oklahoma! (Magna, 1955)
The Last Command (Rep, 1955) (voice only)
Carousel (20th-Fox, 1956)
The Best Things in Life Are Free (20th-Fox, 1956)
The Pilot (New Line International, 1979)

Broadway Plays

Junior Miss (1941) (replacement)
Three to Make Ready (1946)

I Do! I Do! (1967) (replacement)

Radio Series

The Gordon MacRae Show (CBS, 1945–46)
Skyline Roof (CBS, 1946)
Teentimers Club (NBC, 1947)

The Gordon MacRae Show [Texaco Star Theater] (CBS, 1947–48)
The Railroad Hour (ABC, 1948–49; NBC, 1949–54)

TV Series

The Colgate Comedy Hour (NBC, 1954–55)
The Gordon MacRae Show (NBC, 1956)

Lux Video Theater (NBC, 1956–57)

Album Discography

LPs

Apple Blossom (Mac/Eddy JN 122) [St/R] w. Jeanette MacDonald
The Best Things in Life Are Free (Cap T-765) [ST]
Bitter Sweet (Mac/Eddy JN 117) [ST/R] w. Jeanette MacDonald
By the Light of the Silvery Moon (10″ Cap H-422, Caliban 6019) [ST]
Carousel (Cap W/SW-694) [ST]
Christmas at Boys' Town (Sandcastle SCR-1043) w. The Boys' Town Choir
Cowboy's Lament (Cap T-834, Stetson HAT-3054)
The Desert Song (10″ Cap L-351, Cap W/SW-1842, Angel S-37319) w. Dorothy Kirsten, Lucille Norman
The Desert Song (Titania 505) [ST]
The Desert Song/Roberta (Cap T-384)
Gordon MacRae (Galaxy 4805, Rono-lette A5)

Gordon MacRae (10″ Royale 18106)
Gordon MacRae and Orchestra (Royale 18155)
Gordon MacRae in Concert (Cap T/ST-980)
Gordon MacRae Sings (10″ Cap H-231)
Gordon MacRae Sings (Evon 320)
Gordon MacRae Sings Broadway's Best (Sutton SSU-292)
Gordon MacRae Sings Songs for Lovers (Ember 2007)
Gordon MacRae Sings With Walter Gross' Orchestra (Allegro/Royale 1606)
Hallowed Be Thy Name (Cap T/ST-1466)
Highlights From the World's Greatest Operettas (Cap T-1510)
If She Walked Into My Life (Cap T/ST-2578)
Kismet (Cap W/SW-2022, Angel S-37321) w. Dorothy Kirsten

Kiss Me, Kate! (10″ Cap H-157) w. Jo Stafford

The Last Command (Citadel CT 7019) [ST]

Look for the Silver Lining (Titania 504) [ST]

Memory Songs (Cap T-428) w. Jo Stafford

The Merry Widow (10″ Cap L-335) w. Lucille Norman

The Merry, Widow (Mac/Eddy JN 120) [ST/R] w. Jeanette MacDonald

Motion Picture Soundstage (Cap T-875, EMI/Cap 1183)

Naughty Marietta (10″ Cap L-468) w. Marguerite Piazza

Naughty Marietta (Mac/Eddy JN 115) [ST/R] w. Jeanette MacDonald

Naughty Marietta/The Red Mill (Cap T-551)

New Moon (10″ Cap H-217) w. Lucille Norman

New Moon (Cap W/SW-1966, Angel S-37320) w. Dorothy Kirsten

Oklahoma! (Cap W/SW-595) [ST]

The Old Rugged Cross (EMI 5798) w. Jo Stafford

On Moonlight Bay (Caliban 6006, Titania 501) [ST]

Only Love (Cap ST-125)

Operetta Favorites (Cap T-681)

Our Love Story (Cap T/ST-1353) w. Sheila MacRae

Prisoner of Love (10″ MGM E-104)

The Red Mill (10″ Cap L-530) w. Lucille Norman

Roberta (10″ Cap L-334) w. Lucille Norman

Romantic Ballads (Cap T-537)

Seasons of Love (Cap T/St-1146)

Songs for an Evening at Home (Cap T/ST-1251)

South Pacific (10″ Cap H-163) w. Margaret Whiting, Peggy Lee

Spotlight on Gordon MacRae (Tiara 7250/520) w. Johnny King

Starlift (Titania 510) [ST]

The Student Prince (10″ Cap H-407) w. Dorothy Warenskjold

The Student Prince (Cap W/SW-1841, Angel S-37318) w. Dorothy Kirsten

The Student Prince/The Merry Widow (Cap T-437)

Sunday Evening Songs (10″ Cap H-247) w. Jo Stafford

Tea for Two (Caliban 6031) [ST]

There's Peace in the Valley (Cap T/ST-1916) w. Jo Stafford

This Is Gordon MacRae (Cap T-1050)

Three Sailors and a Girl (10″ Cap L-485) [ST]

The Two of Us (Empress 917) w. Jo Stafford.

The Vagabond King (10″ Cap H-218)

The Vagabond King/New Moon (Cap T-219)

The West Point Story (Titania 501) [ST]

Whispering Hope (Cap T/ST-1696) w. Jo Stafford

Young Man From Boston (label unk-MXWR-4546) [ST/TV] w. the Kingston Trio

CDs

All the Music America Loves Best (The Beautiful Music Company GVC)

The Best of Gordon MacRae (10 Best Series S23-18933)

The Best of Gordon MacRae: The Early Years (Collectors' Choice Music CCM-066)

The Best of the Capitol Years (EMI 93749)

The Best Things in Life Are Free/Motion Picture Soundstage (EMI 4930662)

The Broadway Album (Pair PDC-2-1348)

Carousel (Broadway Angel ZDM-64692, RCA 09026-68071-2) [ST]

The Desert Song (Sony BT-831) [ST]

Down Memory Lane (Memoir 402) w. Jo Stafford

Gordon MacRae Sings (Vocalion CDUS-3014) w. Jo Stafford

I Married an Angel (AEI 002)

It's Magic (ASV CD-AJA-5384) w. Jo Stafford

Music of Sigmund Romberg (EMI/Angel Studio 69062-2) w. Dorothy Kirstin

Oklahoma! (Angel 7243-5-27350-2-0, Broadway Angel ZDM-64691) [ST]

The Old Rugged Cross (Music for Pleasure MFP-99140) w. Jo Stafford

Songs of Praise (Original Cast 2002)

Madonna

(b. Madonna Louise Veronica Ciccone, Bay City, Michigan, August 16, 1958)

The top mega pop star to emerge in the late 1980s was Madonna. In her initial incarnation as the gum-chewing, sex kitten of the rock world, she produced a slew of recording hits that ranged from "Like a Virgin" (1984) to "Like a Prayer" (1989). The determined, five-feet four-and-a-half-inches blonde, strutting wantonly on the concert stage, became an icon of rebellion for her young fans. Her choreographed cavorting made her the distaff counterpart to Michael Jackson and Prince. In performance she typically wore black toreador pants and black T-shirt, topped by a black leather jacket; or sometimes her outfit might be a variation of a corset ensemble complete with boots. The public Madonna delighted in creating for a new generation the blonde bombshell image, as successor to past sexpots such as Jean Harlow, Kim Novak, and Marilyn Monroe (her favorite).

As a sign that she was a terrific attraction, Madonna was a constant headline creator. Her courtship, marriage, spats, and divorce from actor Sean Penn were constant news-making events, as was her later romance with producer/director/actor Warren Beatty. When she starred on Broadway in 1988 in a new work by playwright David Mamet, the critics and her public gave the event dramatic coverage. When Madonna signed a multimillion-dollar spokesperson contract with Pepsi-Cola that same year, it was the cause of extensive speculation in a variety of diverse arenas: stock market circles, the show-business industry, and the tabloids. These events were only equaled by the airing of her controversial "Like a Prayer" video on television in 1989—as part of her Pepsi ad campaign. That sensationalized event and the huge aftermath of controversy over its appropriateness were major news makers. Madonna had become the latest queen of the media. Even after she was no longer the young newcomer on the show-business scene, the mature Madonna continued to surprise, upset, and baffle the public: her single motherhood, her later marriage to filmmaker Guy Ritchie, her new millennium tour with its ultra-high-priced tickets, her British "matron" period as the mother of two. Clearly, Madonna was a unique personality with many layers beneath her ever-changing show-business alter ego.

Like Elvis Presley thirty years before her, Madonna delighted her youthful audiences and irked the older generations. The latter hardly related to her loud rhythmic messages of independence, assertiveness, and nonestablishment behavior. Also like Presley, Madonna expanded her activities beyond concertizing and recording. She made a vivid impression in her debut feature film, *Desperately Seeking Susan* (1985), displaying a freshness of personality and sensitivity that captivated even the more mainstream viewers. Since then, as one industry wit phrased it, she was an actress "desperately seeking a role." With the exception of *A League of Their Own* (1992; in which she was part of an ensemble cast) and *Evita* (1996; the years-in-the-making screen adaptation of the stage hit from years earlier), Madonna has not fared well on the big screen.

She was born Madonna Louise Veronica Ciccone on August 16, 1958, in Bay City, Michigan, to Sylvio (Tony) Ciccone and Madonna Ciccone. She was the third child of three girls (she was

Madonna on the Tinseltown scene in the 1990s.
[photo by Albert L. Ortega]

the eldest) and three boys. Her father, a first-generation Italian-American, was a design engineer for General Motors. Madonna recalled, "I was always precocious as a child. I was just one of those little girls who crawled on everybody's lap. I flirted with everyone. . . . I was aware of my female charm." When Madonna was six, her mother died of breast cancer. Mr. Ciccone moved with his children to Pontiac, Michigan. Some three years later he remarried, to the family's housekeeper. Madonna rebelled at the change in the household; she recalled, "From that time on I felt like Cinderella with a wicked stepmother. I couldn't wait to escape."

As a youngster with a devout Catholic father, Madonna decided she would like to become a nun. "I just thought they were so superior." Later, she became "incredibly disenchanted." Looking back on her childhood, she reflected, "I had a very middle-lower-middle-class sort of upbringing, but I identify with people who have had, at some point in their lives, to struggle to survive. It adds another color to your character." As for her persuasive manner, she says, "From the time that I was very young I just knew that being a girl and being charming in a feminine sort of way could get me a lot of things, and I milked it for everything I could."

In junior high school, Madonna found escape by participating in class plays, but her delight was dance, and it became her addiction throughout her teenage years. When she was in the eighth grade, she made a home movie (which she would use years later in her "Like a Prayer" video). In 1972, when she was fourteen, she met Christopher Flynn—some twenty years her senior—who became her dance instructor, mentor, and best friend. It was he who took the adolescent Madonna to Detroit's racy downtown discos, where she developed her skill on the dance room floor. Despite her distractions, Madonna excelled in academics at Adams High School in Rochester, Michigan, and graduated early, in January 1976. She won a dance scholarship to the University of Michigan, where Flynn joined her by becoming a dance instructor there. After more than a year of college where she studied jazz dancing, Madonna dropped out. She had decided, with Flynn's encouragement, to go to New York to make a career for herself in dance.

Madonna arrived in New York in the summer of 1978 with very few dollars and no clothing besides what she wore. She lived in a run-down tenement in the East Village. She worked in a Times Square donut shop for a time, did figure modeling, and in 1979 she made her first movie. The underground opus was called *A Certain Sacrifice*, created by director/cinematographer Stephen Jon Lewicki and coproducer/cowriter/star Jeremy Pattnosh. The sixty-minute color foray was a crude expedition into softcore pornography. It featured a few scenes of Madonna topless as well as participating in a mild "orgy" while being pursued and molested by a young dropout (Pattnosh) in New York City. The movie would resurface as a video and midnight film in the mid-1980s when Madonna became a celebrity. When the much-discussed (thought lost) film was shown finally, it was regarded by most as a "so what" item.

In New York, Madonna auditioned for the Alvin Ailey Dance Troupe and won a position with the Theater's third company. "Everybody was Hispanic or black, and everyone wanted to be a star," she recalled. She left the troupe after a few months and began taking dance classes with Pearl Lang, formerly a Martha Graham choreographer. It was not a happy teacher-student relationship. When Madonna met rock musician Dan Gilroy (with whom she had a romance), she became interested in rock 'n' roll music, and he taught her to play the guitar, keyboards, and drums. After auditioning for French disco singer Patrick Hernandez, Madonna took off for Paris, where she was to be part of his concert show. She did backup singing for him on a few recording sessions. However, her overly independent nature irked Hernandez and his associates, and she was soon jobless.

Back in New York, Madonna became the vocalist/drummer for the rock group Breakfast Club, fronted by Dan Gilroy and his brother. She composed some of their songs while living with her peers in an abandoned synagogue in Queens. When that relationship dissolved (she wanted to be their lead singer), she returned to Manhattan and formed her own group with Steve Bray, a songwriter/drummer she had known in her brief college days. Together they started the group known as the Millionaires (aka: Modern Dance, Emmy), with their new-wave rock music heavily influenced by such rock leaders as the Police and the Pretenders. Meanwhile, intent on promoting her solo career, Madonna became a frequent attendee at such trendy rock discos as the Roxy and Danceteria, where she developed a strong liking for rap-dance music rather than the hard metal rock her group preferred. From her arresting disco forays, Madonna became friendly with Danceteria deejay Mark Kamins. She provided him with a copy of a demo tape she had made, and her song "Everybody" quickly became a favorite with the disco customers. Kamins introduced Madonna to executives at Sire Records, who signed her to a contract. The label's president, Seymour Stein, remembered his first meeting with the exuberant Madonna: "It hit me right away. I could tell she had the drive to match her talent." It was at this time that Madonna ended her business relationship with her manager, Camille Barbone.

Her first album, *Madonna*, was released in mid-1983, but it took a while for the potpourri of pop disco tunes to catch on. But thanks to her increasingly popular appearances at the Manhattan disco clubs, plus exposure over the airwaves, two selections ("Borderline" and "Lucky Star") from the LP reached the top ten of the charts, while "Holiday" topped at the number-sixteen spot. The video to "Lucky Star" played on cable television's MTV, which helped to establish Madonna's national image as the pouting, strutting sex kitten whose outfit boasted a provocative bare midriff. (The music video medium would play a tremendous role in boosting Madonna's career.) It was, however, her "Like a Virgin" single, with its racy connotations, that made Madonna an acclaimed figure. Released as part of the same-titled album, the song rose to number one in late 1984, and its album, which remained on the charts for fifty-one weeks, also moved into top position. Other cuts ("Material Girl," "Angel," "Dress You Up") from the album scored big and made Madonna an international attraction.

The film *Vision Quest* (1985) was a Rocky-like story of a Spokane, Washington, high-school wrestler (Matthew Modine) who wants to win the state championship and the love of a twenty-year-old drifter (Linda Fiorentino). Produced by Jon Peters and Peter Guber and directed by Harold Becker, it featured a sequence where the two lead performers dance together at a club. For that scene, Madonna was hired to sing on-camera the song "Crazy for You." When released, the picture was considered derivative of plot line but nicely executed as to characterizations. More importantly, the song "Crazy for You" rose to number one on the charts in May 1985, displacing "We Are the World," sung by the all-star charity ensemble. With her offbeat costumes, her unbridled enthusiasm, and her wild dancing, Madonna became a national craze. Her expressions like "boy toy" (referring to males) became a necessary idiom to her followers. Her posture as the New Wave 1980s' gold digger, bent on outmaneuvering the opposite sex, caused an outcry from feminists worldwide. As had become habitual, everything Madonna did, said, or wore caused controversy.

To the surprise of many who followed show business, Madonna gained critical respect for her first starring role in a feature film. According to the movie's coproducer, Sarah Pillsbury, one of the compelling reasons Madonna was hired for the project was because she represented "a punk Mae West." Said the filmmaker, Madonna was "a total fantasy for both men and women." *Desperately Seeking Susan* (1985) was made on a $5 million budget by director Susan Seidelman. It was a wacky screwball comedy told from a feminist's point of view. The picture was set in New York City, where two disparate types—a bored housewife (Rosanna Arquette) and a trampy, punk drifter (Madonna)—find their lives intertwining in a case of escalating mistaken identities that involve a mobster's murder, a leather jacket (the trademark of Madonna's character), and Arquette becoming a temporary amnesiac. *Variety* noted that Madonna "turns in a rounded, interesting performance." The picture grossed $10.937 million in domestic film rentals and established the fact that Madonna not only possessed a unique screen charisma, but she could act. Her single "Into the Groove" was from this picture.

In 1985 Madonna embarked on her cross-country *Like a Virgin* concert tour, an event that gained tremendous momentum as it went with its several truckloads of equipment, scenery, and costumes. Media observers noted quickly that many of Madonna's audience (known as "Madonna wannabes") came to the concerts dressed as Madonna look-alikes, complete with scanty outfits, heavy moussed wild hairdos, and piles of face makeup. When sporting her mod bridal outfit for her "Like a Virgin" number, Madonna was the queen to her screaming fans.

Madonna had first met actor Sean Penn (the bad-boy thespian of the Brat Pack era) on the set while filming her "Material Girl" video. Their first public date was at the New York club Private Eyes in February 1985. They became a much-tracked media couple and in July 1985 Madonna, rumored to be pregnant, wore black to her bridal shower. On August 16, 1985, Madonna and combative Sean Penn were married on a Malibu, California, cliff where the eager press buzzed the ceremony in a fleet of helicopters. The couple honeymooned up the coast in Carmel. That September, both *Penthouse* and *Playboy* magazine published artistic nude photo layouts of Madonna taken in 1979, none of which met the approval of the hot-tempered Penn. That November, while hostessing TV's *Saturday Night Live*, Madonna insisted again that she was not pregnant.

In 1986 her third album, *True Blue*, became an international success. It was dedicated to Sean Penn, "the coolest guy in the universe." One of the LP's most controversial cuts was "Papa Don't Preach," about a pregnant teenager who optimistically intends to keep her baby. Another cut was "Live to Tell" coauthored by Madonna and Patrick Leonard (who was music director on her *Like a Virgin* tour), which was drawn from the heavy movie drama *At Close Range* (1986), starring Christopher Walken, Sean Penn, and the latter's brother, Christopher. "Live to Tell," like "Papa Don't Preach," rose to number one on the charts. Yet another single from *True Blue*, "Open Your Heart," became a number-one tune. It had been conceived originally for Madonna's closest songstress rival of the period, Cyndi Lauper.

Madonna returned to filmmaking with husband Sean Penn in MGM's *Shanghai Surprise* (1986) in which she portrayed a quiet Massachusetts missionary in 1937 China. Penn was cast as a sleazy American salesman. In the slight story, both were looking for a missing opium shipment. The growing media backlash against hot-tempered Penn (who was extremely pugnacious with reporters) and Madonna (having been for such a long time fodder for the press) did not help the film when it opened. The expensively mounted feature, with songs by (and sung by) ex-Beatle George Harrison, fizzled. Audiences would not accept the sexy Madonna in the role of a missionary.

In early 1986, Madonna and Penn purchased a $850,000 Manhattan apartment, and later in the year, between much-publicized public altercations and reconciliations, they appeared at New York's Lincoln Center in the play *Goose and Tomtom*. They received the most attention when, one night after a performance while walking home, Sean got into a fight with a roving photographer.

Madonna had been scheduled to star in *Blind Date* (1987). However, when Blake Edwards joined the lineup as director and Bruce Willis as costar, she dropped out. Instead, she appeared in the unfunny screwball comedy *Who's That Girl?* (1987). She portrayed a New York City bimbo who, after four years in jail, is released and is bent on finding out who framed her for her boyfriend's murder. She is joined on her merry chase by a stuffy yuppie lawyer (Griffin Dunne). He falls in love with the free-spirited waif and eventually becomes liberated from his conservatism. Like *Shanghai Surprise, Who's That Girl?* failed to draw in Madonna's fans to movie theaters. However, the title song (cowritten and coproduced by Madonna and Patrick Leonard), rose to number one on the charts in August 1987. Despite her poor track record, moviemakers were still interested in having Madonna work in the medium. Diane Keaton wanted her to star in a remake of 1930's *The Blue Angel* (which had starred Marlene Dietrich), but that intriguing project did not come to be.

Meanwhile, Madonna continued to be enormously successful in her recordings and music videos. As such, she embarked on her *Who's That Girl?* worldwide concert tour. Her trademark funky dancing was choreographed by Jeffrey Hornaday (of *Flashdance* fame), and her shows were extravaganzas of mixed media: multiple videos, flashing lights, high-tech accoutrements, and precision dancing. In such settings, Madonna sang her hits in a variety of costumes that highlighted her fame as a punk sex goddess. The *Chicago Tribune* reported when she played Soldier Field in July 1987, "There are few performers who would be able to carry off many (or any) of Madonna's campy turns with her graceful élan, which is, we marvel, a strange combination of self-effacement and grand ego." Madonna's tour took her to Japan (where her popularity outshone that of Bruce Springsteen and Michael Jackson) and to England. In the latter country, her four British dates were estimated to have netted her about $6.4 million.

In June 1987, Sean Penn was sentenced to jail for sixty days for violating his probation. His latest offenses included the beating up of a movie extra and reckless driving. In mid-September 1987, he was released from jail on a reduced sentence, but by that November the couple (Madonna in particular) were planning to divorce. By December, they had reconciled—temporarily.

When production of Pulitzer Prize–winning David Mamet play *Speed-the-Plow* was first announced, it was to be an off-Broadway production. But because Madonna was later set to costar, the vehicle was rescheduled for an on-Broadway showing, where it opened on May 3, 1988, at the Royale Theater. It was a satirical study of contemporary Hollywood with Madonna cast as a temporary, supposedly naive studio secretary who becomes the object of lust for sycophant Ron Silver. The play quickly became a hotly contested debate of not how good the work was, but whether Madonna could act. Most encouraging was the *New York Times*, which decided, "She delivers the shocking transitions essential to the action and needs only more confidence to relax a bit and fully command her speaking voice." Dissenting were such sources as the *New York Daily News*, which observed, "What's interesting about Madonna is that she misses the musicality of Mamet's writing."

Speed-the-Plow had amassed a near $1 million advance sale, but did not last the year. Sean Penn, who had not attended her play's opening (he was in Thailand shooting a war film), and Madonna continued their domestic battles when they returned to the West Coast. In November 1988, Penn was onstage in Los Angeles in *Hurlyburly*. In a turnabout, Madonna showed up for his opening late, accompanied by her frequent companion Sandra Bernhard. In this period, Madonna also had a new videocassette in distribution. *People* magazine noted of *Ciao: Italia: Live*

From Italy, "Madonna shows plenty of warmth—heat, actually—but unhappily slobbers it all over a teen-age dancer in this concert tape."

In January 1989, Madonna filed for divorce from Penn and days later dropped an assault charge against her spouse. No sooner had these headlines died down than Madonna instigated another media frenzy. She had signed a $5 million contract with Pepsi-Cola to star in several commercials for them. Part of the tie-in was her new album *Like a Prayer* (1989) and its title single, for which she made a highly stylized music video. In mid-March 1989, it was debuted on national television (and satellite TV throughout the globe and on MTV the next day) and caused an incredible furor among conservative elements who felt the video mocked the Catholic church. The American Family Association asked the soft-drink company to cancel its contract with Madonna, claiming Madonna was not a proper role model for youth. Quietly the ad was dropped from circulation. However, the song as well as the related LP (probably the first to be introduced as a TV commercial) became a number-one hit. One of the singles, "Love Song," featured her in duet with Prince. Another single (also made into a music video) from the big-selling album was "Express Yourself," which rose high on the charts. (The song was written by her and Stephen Bray.)

It was touted in the press that Madonna was set to play a concentration camp internee in the film *Triumph*. However, because she signed a pact with Columbia Pictures (that had first right of refusal on her projects), she chose instead to be Breathless Mahoney in Warren Beatty's long-planned feature film, *Dick Tracy* (1990). The $30 million production began filming in February 1989. By then, Madonna, who was scheduled to sing two songs in the picture, had become Beatty's latest liaison. Meanwhile the songster had wanted to be in 1989's *The Fabulous Baker Boys*, but the part went to Michelle Pfeiffer.

In late May 1989, *Bloodhounds of Broadway*, originally filmed in 1988 for the *American Playhouse* series on PBS-TV and long sitting on the shelf, was screened at the Seattle Film Festival. The movie was based on classic Damon Runyon stories and featured Madonna, Matt Dillon, Esai Morales, Jennifer Grey, and Rutger Hauer. The multipart story was set on New Year's Eve on Broadway in 1928. Madonna was cast as Hortense Hathaway, the comely showgirl eager for the limelight and for financial success. *Variety* thought she "adeptly played" her role but judged the production a "fluffy little piece," and that her commercial prospects appeared "dim."

Despite the fanfare given *Dick Tracy* (1990), the most engaging facet of this stylized version of the enduring comic strip was the clever makeup used to disguise such name actors as Al Pacino and Dustin Hoffman in their on-screen gangster caricatures. As Breathless Mahoney—caught in a nasty relationship with a hoodlum and wanting to alter her bad reputation—Madonna's song numbers as the club chanteuse proved an interesting distraction to the film's slow pacing. Nevertheless, with its star cast, the movie generated $60.611 million in domestic distribution and renewed filmmakers' faith in casting her in new pictures. By the time the movie was in release, Madonna and filmmaker/star Beatty's oddball romance had fizzled. Meanwhile, in April 1990, she had embarked on her *Blonde Ambition* tour, which lasted for several months. Her end-of-the-year greatest hits album (*The Immaculate Collection*) contained two new songs: "Justify My Love" (which became a number-one single and also led to a sexy, controversial music video that MTV and VH1 banned from airing) and "Rescue Me," which popped onto the record charts at the number fifteen position.

During her enormously successful *Blonde Ambition* tour, Madonna was the subject of a feature-length documentary that was released successfully in spring 1991 as *Truth or Dare*. It was a revealing study of a major celebrity both on- and offstage. It reflected a woman in control of her art, but one who could sometimes reveal her childish inner person.

Wanting very much to promote her filmmaking career, Madonna accepted a subordinate role in Woody Allen's moody and ambiguous movie *Shadows and Fog* (1992). That same year, the singer had much better luck with a supporting role in the baseball comedy *A League of Their Own*. This popular entry starred Tom Hanks and Geena Davis and was nearly stolen by comedian/actress Rosie O'Donnell (who became good friends with Madonna). In this sports lark, besides appearing as one of teammates on a woman's baseball team during World War II, Madonna's sang "This Used to Be My Playground" on the picture's soundtrack. As a disc single, the song became a smash.

Intent on capturing attention in all the media, the star published *Sex* (1992), an expensively produced book of softcore erotic photography (including shots of herself and in tandem with such celebrities as Isabella Rossellini, Naomi Campbell, and Vanilla Ice). The highly controversial volume pushed the boundaries of "good taste," won many scathing reviews, and—like most projects involving Madonna—sold very well. The accompanying album, *Erotica*, sold over two million copies, which compared to the megasuccess of her past albums, was considered disappointing.

In 1993, neither the courtroom "thriller" *Body of Evidence* nor *Dangerous Game*, about a filmmaker playing out his private life on-screen, received much theatrical release, and these flops greatly damaged Madonna's chance to become a real movie star. Her 1994 album, *Bedtime Stories*, confounded some critics who thought its more low-keyed qualities and its slower-than-usual success with music buyers meant the star was fading in appeal. However, the album provided her greatest hit single ("Take a Bow") and went multiplatinum. On the film scene, Madonna lost out to Sharon Stone for the colead in 1995's *Casino*, which portrayed Las Vegas movers and shakers and was directed by Martin Scorsese. On the other hand, the Material Girl turned down a role in *Showgirls*, another film release of 1995 dealing with the gaming capital.

Madonna took on a more subdued tone for her compilation album *Something to Remember* (1995), a disc focusing on ballads. It reflected her desire to soften her persona—all part of her campaign to get the coveted lead role in the long-discussed screen adaptation of *Evita* (1996). She won the part in the Alan Parker–directed feature. When released, the critical response to Madonna was not consistently positive. For example, the *San Francisco Chronicle* complained, "Unfortunately, this movie needed an attractive, irresistibly charismatic performer to give us some reason for watching. Madonna is made up to look like Eva, but this is hardly enough to carry the movie. The singer's appeal has always had to do with chutzpah rather than charisma, crudeness and aggression rather than grace. Through most of the movie she resembles Valerie Harper in [the TV sitcom] *Rhoda* more than Eva Peron. Madonna is an MTV phenomenon and *Evita* is one interminable music video." Made on a $55 million budget, *Evita* grossed $49.994 million in domestic distribution.

While *Evita* had been in production, Madonna announced that she was pregnant and that she did not intend to wed the father (who was Carlos Leon, her personal fitness trainer). Her daughter Lourdes (named in memory of Madonna's mother, who had always wanted to visit the religious shrine at Lourdes, France) was born on October 16, 1996, just in time to give Madonna and the newly released *Evita* a promotional push. The star received a Golden Globe for Best Actress in a Musical or Comedy, but no Oscar nomination was forthcoming. When the soundtrack album to the movie was released, both the newly composed "You Must Love Me" and a dance version of "Don't Cry for Me Argentina" became hits for the actress.

Again reinventing herself for the changing time, Madonna went in a new direction for her 1998 album *Ray of Light*. Her first album of new songs in four years, it was distinguished by the use of electronic (synthesized) sounds in a style known as "electronica." It was extremely well reviewed and did exceedingly well with album buyers. Having worked so well with record producer William Orbit on *Ray of Light*, two years later Madonna reteamed with him for *Music*. (One of the innovative album's cuts, "What It Feels Like for a Girl," inspired a 2001 music video that was banned by MTV.)

As the 1990s ended, the single mother had not settled down in her domestic life. While she no longer dated the likes of musician Vanilla Ice, unorthodox basketball star Dennis Rodman, or fitness trainer Carlos Leon, she still had not chosen a mate for life—that is until she met British filmmaker Guy Ritchie, who had gained currency by directing *Lock, Stock and Two Smoking Barrels* (1998) and *Snatch* (2000). Ten years Madonna's junior, he was the father of her child Rocco, born prematurely by emergency C-section on August 11, 2000. Four months later, on December 22, 2000, Madonna and Ritchie wed in a medieval castle in Skibo, Scotland.

Professionally, Madonna had not yet succeeded in turning the life of singer Anita O'Day into a film biography and had dropped out of *Music of the Heart* (1999) at the last minute and been replaced by Meryl Streep. Instead she made the fitful comedy *The Next Best Thing* (2000). As the heroine's gay friend who fathers her child and wants custody of his offspring, Rupert Everett received the entry's best notices. Made on a $25 million budget, *The Next Best Thing* earned a relatively mild $14.98 million in domestic distribution. Madonna's next movie was *Swept Away* (2002), written and directed by her husband Ritchie and featuring Jennifer Aniston and Bruce Greenwood. It was a remake of the 1975 Italian feature directed by Lina Wertmuller.

On the music front, she embarked on a highly promoted world tour (her first in eight years), proving that her fans were still more than willing to pay high ticket prices for the privilege of seeing their diva sing and dance to hip electronic music accompaniment, model through a wide array of costumes, and ride a mechanical bull. Her *Drowned World* tour ended in September 2001 in Los Angeles. Also that year she was the subject of two revealing biographies: Andrew Morton's *Madonna* and Barbara Victor's *Goddess: Inside Madonna*. She also had the distinction of an original tartan pattern being designed in her honor and registered with the Scottish Tartan Society Registry.

In the new millennium, Madonna was based in England with her family. She was very well to do—thanks to her savvy and shrewd self-promotion over the decades—and still embarked on new creative frontiers including her British stage debut. No longer a young newcomer, the megapop icon still lived by this creed: "When I'm hungry, I eat. When I'm thirsty, I drink. When I feel like saying something, I say it." As to her wild road to success, she reflected, "I sometimes think I was born to live up to my name. How could I be anything else but what I am having been named Madonna? I would either have ended up a nun or this."

Filmography

A Certain Sacrifice (Virgin Video, 1979)
Vision Quest (WB, 1985) (also song)
Desperately Seeking Susan (Orion 1985) (also song)
At Close Range (Orion, 1986) (voice, song only)
Shanghai Surprise (MGM, 1986)
Who's That Girl? (WB, 1987) (also song)

Bloodhounds of Broadway (Col, 1989)
Dick Tracy (BV, 1990)
Truth or Dare [Madonna: Truth or Dare (Miramax, 1991) (also executive producer) (documentary)
Shadows and Fog (Orion, 1992)

A League of Their Own (Col, 1992) (also song)
Body of Evidence (MGM, 1993)
Dangerous Game (MGM, 1993)
With Honors (WB, 1994) (song only)
Blue in the Face (Miramax, 1995)
Four Rooms (Miramax, 1995)
Girl 6 (Fox Searchlight, 1996)

Evita (Hollywood Pictures, 1996)
Austin Powers: The Spy Who Shagged Me (New Line Cinema, 1999) (song only)
The Next Best Thing (Par, 2000) (also song)
Snatch (Sony, 2000) (song only)
Star (BMW of North American, 2001) (s)
Swept Away (SKA Films, 2002)

Broadway Plays

Speed-the-Plow (1988)

TV Series

Wonderland (ABC, 2000) (song only)

Album Discography

LPs

Like a Prayer (Sire 1-25844)
Like a Virgin (Sire 1-25157)
Madonna (Sire 1-23867)
True Blue (Sire 1-25442)

Vision Quest (Geffen 240063) [ST]
Who's That Girl? (Sire 1-25611) [ST]
You Can Dance (Sire 1-25535)

CDs

Absolute Madonna (Griffen Music 2468, CHROM CTCD-7015)
American Pie (Polydor 9362448372)
American Pie, Part 1 (Warner 936244839-2)
American Pie, Part 2 (Warner 936244040-2)
American Pie, Part 3 (Warner W519CD)
Angel/Into the Groove (WB WEA-759920335)
Austin Powers: The Spy Who Shagged Me (Maverick 47348, Maverick 243386) [ST]
Austin Powers: The Spy Who Shagged Me, Vol. 2 (Maverick 47358) [ST]
Bad Girl (Maverick 40793-2)
Baktabak Interview (Baktabak CBAK-4019)
Beautiful Stranger (Warner 9362446992, PHAM 532672, WEA 2446992)
Bedtime Stories (Maverick 45767-2)
Bedtime Story (Maverick 41895-2)
Bedtime Story, Part 2 (Warner WO-285CD)
Causing a Commotion (WB WE-759920762)
Cherish (Warner K-7599213262)
Complete Audio Bio (Chrome Dreams 6002)
Crazy for You (Warner W0-88CD)
Dear Jessie/Til Death (WB WEA-759921421)
Deeper & Deeper (WB 2452882, Maverick 40722-2, Warner 9362452882, Warner WO-146CD)
Don't Cry for Me Argentina (WB 9362438, MSI/WEA 43830)
Don't Tell Me (Maverick 9362449692)

Don't Tell Me, Part 1 (WEA 9362449462)
Don't Tell Me, Part 2 (WEA W547CD2)
Don't Tell Me, Part 3 (WEA 9362449492)
Dress You Up (Warner K-0759920)
Drowned World (WEA WPCR-36921983)
Drowned World/Substitute for Love (WEA WO453CD1)
Drowned World/Substitute for Love, Part 1 (WUK 4452)
Drowned World/Substitute for Love, Part 2 (WUK 4456)
The Early Years (Receiver CDRR-118)
Early Years: Give It To Me (Receiver CDRR-144)
Erotica (Warner 9362405852)
Evita (WB 946346) [ST]
Express Yourself (WB WEA-759921249)
Fever (Warner WO168CD)
Frozen (Warner WO433CD, MSI/Sound Product 434722)
Greatest Hits, Vol. 2 (Maverick/WB 9-48000-2)
Hanky Panky/Something (WB WEA-759921557, Sire 21577-2)
Holiday/Lucky Star (Warner K-7599201762)
I'm Breathless (Music From Dick Tracy) (Sire 26209-2)
In the Beginning (Gravity 20012)
In the Beginning (Receiver CDKNOB1)
In the Spotlight With Madonna (Matrix Music Marketing 3045)

Interview (Sonot CD-1134)

Interviews, Vol. 2 (Arabe CBAK-4078)

Into the Groove (Warner K-7599203522)

Justify My Love (Warner 9218200)

La Isla Bonita (WB WEA-759920633)

Like a Prayer (WB WEA-759971190, Sire 25844-2)

Like a Virgin (WB 47901, Sire 25157-2)

Like a Virgin/Stay (WB K-7599202392)

Live to Tell (WB K-7599204612)

Love Don't Live Here Anymore (WB WEA-936243692)

Lucky Star (WB K-7599201492)

Madonna (WB 236867, WB 38101, WB 47907, Sire 23867-2)

Material Girl (WB K-7599203042)

Maximum Madonna (CRHOM ADCD03)

Miss American Pie: The Madonna Interviews, Vol. 3 (Baktabak 4132)

Music (WB 47598)

Music + 1 (WEA WPCR-10900, WEA 947865.2)

Music + 2 (Warner 9367478662)

Music—Limited Edition (WEA 9362478832)

Music—Remix (WEA WPCR-10900)

One More Chance, Part 1 (WB WO-337CD)

Open Your Heart (WB WEA-84920597)

Papa Don't Preach (WB K-7599205032)

Power of Goodbye (WB 936244502)

Ray of Light (WB 46847, Warner WPCR-1860, Warner WPCR-1055617, Maverick WPCR-2000)

Ray of Light/Has to Be (Wave 9362445352)

Remixed Prayer (Warner 7599260222)

Rock on Rom (STP-STPROM5)

Secret (CP WB41772, WB WEA-093624180, Edoya WPCR-1513)

Secret/Let Down Your (WB WEA-936241785)

Sing-a-Long (Priddis Music 1127)

Sing-a-Long, Vol. 2 (Priddis Music 1234)

Something to Remember (Maverick 46100-2)

Take a Bow Remixer (PID 379352)

True Blue (WB 47902, WB 25442-2, Sire 25442-2)

Vogue/Keep It Together (WB 9215252)

Volume 2—The Best & Rest of Madonna (Baktabak 4078)

What It Feels Like for a Girl (Maverick 9362437426)

Who's That Girl (WB K-7599206022)

Wild Dancing (TRO)

Wow (DGMDE)

You Can Dance (Sire 25535)

You Must Love Me (WB WEA-962343791)

You'll See/Rain (WB WEA-936243623)

Jerry Lewis and Dean Martin in *My Friend Irma* (1949).
[Courtesy of JC Archives]

Dean Martin

(b. Dino Paul Crocetti, Steubenville, Ohio, June 17, 1917; d. Beverly Hills, California, December 25, 1995)

Being the straight man/stooge to a professional prankster is never easy, even under the best of circumstances. Sooner or later there is bound to be an effect on the ego of the quieter teammate. Moreover, such a position can hamper a career for years after such a successful partnership breaks up.

During Dean Martin's working relationship (1946–1956) with Jerry Lewis, the lion's share of attention always went to funny man Lewis. Sleepy-eyed, congenial Martin was dismissed generally as the better looking of the duo who sang and handled romancing with the team's leading ladies on-camera. Martin could indeed sing very pleasantly (in the Perry Como crooner tradition), and he had several singles in the top-forty charts, including his signature tune, "Everybody Loves Somebody." As a solo performer, he astounded Hollywood continuously with his "hidden" range of talent. He performed in screen drama with a surprising agility. He starred in his own very successful series of James Bond–like movie spy spoofs (the Matt Helm series). In clubs and on television, he was a congenial bon vivant who sang effortlessly, kidded with his coworkers and the audience, and traded heavily on his image as the world's greatest lush ("ole red eyes"). However, despite all his years of tremendous success as a single act, most people still thought of him mainly in connection with frantic Jerry Lewis. Decades after their well-publicized breakup, he still remained the ex-partner of the crazy one.

He was born Dino Paul Crocetti in Steubenville, Ohio, on June 17, 1917, son of immigrant barber Guy Crocetti and his wife Angela. There was an older boy named Bill who later would be Dean's business manager until Bill's death in 1963. Dino attended Grant Junior High School and completed the tenth grade at Wells High School. At this point the sixteen-year-old Dino dropped out of the educational system. Martin quipped, "I had a bicycle and I never missed a meal. But I was just too smart for those teachers in school." His father gave him five dollars to attend barber school, but that didn't hold his interest either. He tried a succession of jobs, including drugstore clerk, gas jockey, milkman, coal miner, steel puddler, and wire bundler. For a time he was a boxer. As Kid Crochet, he was a welterweight fighter and had three knockouts to his credit. However, when he was floored in a match, he quit the ring.

Meanwhile, Steubenville was not known as "Little Chicago" for nothing. There were many distractions in town for the young man, including the Rex Smoke Shop, which was a front for one of the town's more popular gambling centers. Dino was soon working in the back room as a chips-and-dice man, earning up to $8 per day plus tips and his occasional pilfering. (He recalled, "During the course of a day, I could steal maybe as many as five silver dollars.")

Besides his gaming activities at the shop, Dino liked to sing and occasionally entertained his friends there with a song. Bandleader Ernie McKay heard him and offered the young man a job with his group at $50 weekly. Because he was earning $125 a week as a croupier and blackjack dealer, he initially refused. He continued working at the Rex Smoke Shop, with his employers sometimes loaning him out to other gambling establishments in Ohio, Florida, West Virginia, and Washington, DC. Finally, encouraged by his employers, he accepted the job with McKay and became the band's lead singer.

By the late 1930s, Dino Crocetti had changed his name to Dino Martini. However, when people told him he would be confused with the Italian-American singer (and occasional film actor) Nino Martini, he switched his name to Dino Martin, and then to Dean Martin. He was now singing with the Sammy Watkins Band, a group based in Cleveland. In that city on October 2, 1940, at Saint Anne's Church, he married Elizabeth MacDonald. (They would have four children: Craig, 1942; Claudia, 1944; Gail, 1945; Deana, 1948.) Hoping to improve his image as a 1940s' crooner, Martin had his oversized nose reshaped by plastic surgery. He worked with a succession of bands, and then as a single act in clubs, where he was earning $300 weekly. By 1943 he was performing at the Riobamba Club in New York City, but had yet to make a distinctive impression with the public.

In 1945 Martin came to the attention of MGM, who considered him for a role in a forthcoming movie musical (*Till the Clouds Roll By*, 1946). After his screen test, studio executives wired Martin's agent, "We already have Tony Martin under contract. Why do we want another Italian singer?" (Actually, Tony Martin was Jewish.) It was about this time that Dean was living with his family at Manhattan's Belmont Plaza Hotel and performing at the Glass Hat Club. Also staying at the Hotel and performing at the Glass Hat was nineteen-year-old Jerry Lewis and his wife Patti. It became a habit for "big brother" Martin to help out younger Jerry when audiences grew restless with the latter's fledgling comedy act; while Lewis developed the knack for interrupting Martin's onstage singing sessions with improvised mayhem. After their "joint" appearance at the Glass Hat, each performer went his separate way, but they stayed in touch. Meanwhile, Martin was recording for Diamond Records.

It was during the week of July 20, 1946, that Martin and Lewis became a joint act officially. Lewis was doing his lip-synching record routine at the Club 500 in Atlantic City and faring badly. He phoned Martin's agent (because his own agent was persona non grata at the club) for advice. (Lewis later insisted he had phoned Martin telling him of an opening on the club's bill.) In any event, Martin came to Atlantic City and on July 25, 1946, began performing in tandem with Jerry. Soon the impromptu mayhem developed into inspired pandemonium as Lewis would interrupt Martin's singing with braying and screaming. Martin would chase Lewis through and around the audience, and customers would frequently be soaked with streams of seltzer or drinks tossed into their face. So successful was their improvised routine that the club held them over for six weeks at $750 weekly.

After months of touring the country's cabaret circuit to increased success, the duo appeared at New York's Copacabana Club in April 1948 as a backup act to singer/movie actress Vivian Blaine. So popular were Martin and Lewis that Blaine quickly disappeared from the bill and the wacky twosome remained at the Copa for eighteen weeks. Meanwhile, the team appeared at the Roxy Theater for three weeks of personal appearances and were now earning a total of $15,000 weekly. When the pair played Slapsie Maxie's Club in Hollywood in the summer of 1948, it proved to be an audition for the film studios, who were already eager to sign this sensational comedy team—the new successors to slapstick kings Bud Abbott and Lou Costello. Producer Hal B. Wallis, operating at Paramount Pictures, signed the team to a five-year, seven-picture contract. The terms called for them to be paid $50,000 per picture (later raised to $75,000 per movie), and the stars could produce their own pictures through their York Productions.

Hedging his bets, Wallis first introduced Martin and Lewis to filmgoers in *My Friend Irma* (1949), a black-and-white screen translation of a popular radio series starring that program's wacky blonde lead, Marie Wilson. But for critics and moviegoers alike, it was Martin and Lewis who were the picture's hits. The comedy established the format that would hold sway throughout their sixteen features together: Lewis did his juvenile antics, Martin sang (here "Just for Fun," "My Own, My Only, My All," and "Here's to Love"), and together they created mayhem. Said *Variety*, "Martin is a handsome straight man singer. . . . His voice is pleasant and easy, but his nightclub posturing needs toning down for films."

On April 3, 1949, Martin and Lewis debuted as a weekly radio series on NBC, a variety hour that would last through 1953. The next year they were guests on Milton Berle's NBC-TV comedy program and were such audience pleasers that later that year they joined with Abbott and Costello, Eddie Cantor, and Donald O'Connor as rotating hosts (each once monthly) of *The Colgate Comedy Hour* (NBC-TV). For their television appearances, Martin and Lewis were paid initially $25,000 per show, but because of their popularity, it quickly escalated to $75,000 per program. They would remain with the *Comedy Hour* through 1954. Additionally, they continued to star on the nightclub circuit to hefty audience response. Meanwhile, Martin, who was in and out of financial problems (he had to declare bankruptcy in January 1949), had met Florida beauty queen Jeanne Beiggers. It led to his divorcing Elizabeth in August 1949 and on September 1 in Beverly Hills, marrying the second Mrs. Martin. Jerry Lewis was his best man. (The new Mr. and Mrs. Martin would parent: Dean "Dino" Jr., 1951; Ricci, 1953; and Gina, 1956.)

The extremely profitable Martin and Lewis features ran the gamut of Hollywood genres. They were entangled in the military service in *At War With the Army* (1951), *Sailor Beware* (1951), and *Jumping Jacks* (1952). They were involved in show business in *The Stooge* (1952), toyed with the golfing game in *The Caddy* (1953; in which Dean sang his hit song "That's Amore"), teased the haunted-house motif in *Scared Stiff* (1953), went wild under the big top (*Three Ring Circus*, 1954), created lunacy at a Damon Runyonesque racetrack in *Money From Home* (1954; filmed in the 3-D process), were the worst of the West in *Pardners* (1956), and tore up Tinseltown in *Hollywood or Bust* (1956). By the time of the latter picture, it was no secret to the public that the mutual admiration society between suave Martin and spastic goofball Lewis had run its course.

When Dean learned that for the duo's next joint offering, *The Delicate Delinquent* (1957), he was to be the friendly local policeman—another stooge—he refused the assignment (which went to Darren McGavin). In short order, he ended their joint moviemaking, which had been netting the team $4 million annually. "I hated being a dumb stooge," Martin explained. "I was happier making $100 a week." The two performers fulfilled a contract at the Copacabana Club in New York, with their final show on July 25, 1956, ten years to the date of their first professional teaming.

When Martin and Lewis broke up, the industry concluded that Martin was washed up in the business, reasoning that Lewis had been carrying him. After Martin's first disastrous solo picture—MGM's flat romantic comedy *Ten Thousand Bedrooms* (1957)—the dire predictions seemed to be true. Martin took a job in a Pittsburgh nightclub, and after that engagement, he sat in his hotel room with his wife and said, "This is it, baby. I've got nothing else lined up now."

The next day Dean received a call from his agent that he had a screen role for him (as the result of a talent agency package deal) in Twentieth Century-Fox's *The Young Lions* (1958). It was the third-lead part of the draft dodger in a World War II drama. Because Martin's track record as a dramatic actor was zero, the assignment paid only $20,000, $230,000 less than he had received for his role as the prowling playboy in *Ten Thousand Bedrooms*. Dean took the gamble and amazed everyone by his resilient performance, which compared favorably to his two costars, Marlon Brando and Montgomery Clift. Later in the year, Martin, who had been a Capitol Records recording artist since 1948, had hit singles with "Angel Baby" and "Volare." (His single "Memories Are Made of This" had been number one on the charts in early 1956.)

Martin and Lewis as a team had been members of Frank Sinatra's Rat Pack in the 1950s, and as a single, Dean became more closely associated with the Crooner both on and offscreen. Together they made *Some Came Running* (1958) in which Martin was cast as the good-hearted gambling pal of ex-GI Sinatra. Again Martin received plaudits for his credible, relaxed acting. He went Western in John Wayne's *Rio Bravo* (1959), and comedic in *Who Was That Lady?* (1960) with the husband-and-wife team of Tony Curtis and Janet Leigh. He made an effective leading man in the movie musical *Bells Are Ringing* (1960), paired with the star of the Broadway original, Judy Holliday. As a charter member of the Rat Pack, Dean frolicked in the group's on-camera clowning in *Ocean's 11* (1960), *Sergeants Three* (1962), *4 for Texas* (1963), and *Robin and the 7 Hoods* (1964). Martin was paired with Sinatra (without the Pack) in *Marriage on the Rocks* (1965) and earlier had a cameo role in Frank's comedy *Come Blow Your Horn* (1963). To outsiders it seemed that in these Rat Pack excursions Dean was portraying the happy stooge again, but this time to kingpin Sinatra. Before Marilyn Monroe was fired from her last feature, *Something's Got to Give* in 1962, Dean Martin, who had become an adept screen farceur, was her leading man. By the time the project was recast with Doris Day (as *Move Over, Darling*, 1963), Martin had quit the production and was replaced by James Garner.

Along the way in the 1960s, Dean starred in several average Westerns that included *Texas Across the River* (1966), *Five Card Stud* (1968; with Robert Mitchum), and the much superior sagebrush offering *The Sons of Katie Elder* (1965; with John Wayne) But in this decade Martin proved most effective as the freewheeling, girl-chasing, gun-toting, wisecracking Matt Helm, the star of four colorful Columbia pictures: *The Silencers* (1966), *Murderers' Row* (1966), *The Ambushers* (1967), and *The Wrecking Crew* (1968). The popular movie series featured extremely shapely leading ladies (e.g., Stella Stevens, Ann-Margret, and Nancy Kwan), a flow of gadgets and gimmicks, and most importantly, hip Martin as the girlie photographer turned American spy agent for ICE (a U.S. government organization devoted to intelligence and counterespionage). At a time when there was a slew of 007-like spy spoofs, Dean's Matt Helm series was among the top contenders. A fifth entry, *The Ravagers*, had been planned to start in the fall of 1969 but when its projected leading lady (Sharon Tate) was murdered that August, production was postponed indefinitely and Martin went on to other film projects. Thereafter, the Matt Helm series was shelved, and plans to team him with Sinatra in *Matt Helm Meets Tony Rome* never materialized.

When Frank Sinatra began his Reprise Records in the early 1960s, Sammy Davis Jr. was the first artist signed, and Dean Martin soon followed in 1962. During the 1960s, Martin had a variety of top forty hits, including "Everybody Loves Somebody" (1964), which rose to number-one position; "You're Nobody Till Somebody Loves You" (1965); and "Little Ole Wine Drinker, Me" (1967). Between 1964 and 1969, he had eleven albums in the top forty, including *Dream With Dean* (1964), *Houston* (1965), *Welcome to My World* (1967), and *Gentle on My Mind* (1969).

As a solo act, Dean was an occasional TV performer. He had his own specials in 1958, 1959, and two in 1960. He also guested as an aging gunslinger on the "Canliss" episode of the Western series *Rawhide* (CBS-TV, October 30, 1964). Then, on September 16, 1965, *The Dean Martin Show* debuted on the NBC-TV network. Using "Somewhere There's a Someone" as his theme song, he employed a group of curvaceous showgirls (a group labeled the Golddiggers), and traded heavily on his created image of being America's favorite drunk (he would sing "Every time it rains, it rains bourbon from heaven . . ."). As such, he held forth for nine successful seasons. It was an industry wonder that Martin, who abhorred rehearsal, could be so successful in his impromptu hosting of the weekly program. His summer replacement shows fostered the careers of many talents, including Bobby Darin, Charles Nelson Reilly, Lou Rawls, and such country-music talents as Loretta Lynn, Lynn Anderson, and Jerry Reed. In the last season (1973–74) of Dean's variety series, he began a celebrity roast segment that became so popular that, later (1974–79), the format (with Martin hosting) became recurring NBC-TV specials.

In 1970, Martin was the romantic leading man of the extremely commercial disaster epic *Airport* (1970). Then, he made two additional Westerns: *Something Big* (1971) and *Showdown* (1973; with Rock Hudson). However, he looked bored and tired in both entries, and they were not successful. He continued to perform in clubs, having become a major staple of Las Vegas, especially at the MGM Grand Hotel. As part of his pact with that entertainment combine, he appeared in MGM's *Mr. Ricco* (1975), a tattered melodrama in which he was a San Francisco attorney caught up in a murder case. It was his last leading role in movies. In the late 1970s, he guested on TV's *Charlie's Angels* (1978), *The Misadventures of Sheriff Lobo* (1979), and *Vega$* (1979) as well as doing occasional specials.

Meanwhile, in 1972 he and Jeanne were divorced, and at the time of the costly settlement, his worth was estimated at $26 million. On April 24, 1973, at his Bel Air, California, home, he married young Hollywood beautician Catherine Mae Hawn. He adopted her daughter (Sasha) by a prior marriage. They were soon involved in separations and reconciliations, and in February 1977 their split was finalized. It is estimated that Martin's three marriages and divorces cost him an approximate $10 million, but it never stopped his much-touted womanizing. Meanwhile, in 1976, on Jerry Lewis's annual Labor Day charity telethon, a relaxed Dean Martin came by the television studio in Las Vegas for a surprise appearance. It was the public ending of a two-decades-long feud.

In the early 1980s, Dean Martin had occasional television specials (e.g. *Dean Martin in London;* NBC-TV, November 8, 1983), and he returned to filmmaking with a cameo in the stupid cross-country car chase picture *Cannonball Run* (1981). That Burt Reynolds "comedy" also had a guest appearance by Sammy Davis Jr., and for the unnecessary sequel, *Cannonball II* (1984), Rat Pack chairman Frank Sinatra made an appearance in tandem with Martin and Davis. On March 24, 1985, NBC-TV premiered a new teleseries, *Half Nelson*, in a two-hour premiere episode. It featured Joe Pesci as a pint-sized former New York City undercover cop who is hired by a private security service in Beverly Hills. One of his clients (and later confidant) was series' regular Dean Martin. The show, which never garnered good ratings, went off the air on May 10, 1985. On March 21, 1987, Martin's actor son, Dean Paul Martin, died at age thirty-five in the crash of his Air National Guard jet plane.

In the late 1980s, Martin, still very much a Las Vegas headliner, agreed to join with Sinatra and Davis in an extensive club tour both in the United States and abroad. After a few initial joint engagements, Dean dropped out (with assorted causes, including health reasons, being cited), and

Liza Minnelli replaced him. Martin returned for occasional performances at Bally's in Las Vegas, but towards the end he worked onstage seated in a chair. Still quite depressed over the death of his son Dean Paul in 1987, Dean's health continued to deteriorate, and he died on Christmas Day, 1995, of acute respiratory failure, in his Beverly Hills home.

Besides the extensive reissuance of Dean's many recordings in recent years, Martin's memory has been kept alive in other media. In the book field, besides the several biographies dealing with the Rat Pack, Frank Sinatra, and Jerry Lewis, there have appeared such books as Nick Tosches's *Dino: Living High in the Dirty Business of Dreams* (1992), William Schoell's *Martini Man: The Life of Dean Martin* (1999), and Ricci Martin's *That's Amore: A Son Remembers Dean Martin* (2002). When the TV movie *The Rat Pack* aired in 1998, Joe Mantegna was cast as Dino to Ray Liotta's Ol' Blue Eyes. Also, Dean Martin's popular celebrity TV roasts that aired decades ago have often been revived on television and have sold extremely well in home video/DVD format versions. In 2002 a cable TV movie was in the works detailing the tumultuous working relationship between Martin and his once-partner Jerry Lewis. The latter was to be an executive producer of the project.

Filmography

With Jerry Lewis

My Friend Irma (Par, 1949)
My Friend Irma Goes West (Par, 1951)
At War With the Army (Par, 1951)
That's My Boy (Par, 1951)
Screen Snapshots #197 (Col, 1951) (s)
Sailor Beware (Par, 1951)
Screen Snapshots #207 (Col, 1952) (s)
The Stooge (Par, 1952)
Jumping Jacks (Par, 1952)
Road to Bali (Par, 1952)
Hollywood Fun Festival (Col, 1952) (s)

Scared Stiff (Par, 1953)
The Caddy (Par, 1953)
Money From Home (Par, 1954)
Living It Up (Par, 1954)
Three Ring Circus (Par, 1954)
You're Never Too Young (Par, 1955)
Artists and Models (Par, 1955)
Hollywood Premiere (Col, 1955) (s)
Pardners (Par, 1956)
Hollywood or Bust (Par, 1956)

Dean Martin Alone

Ten Thousand Bedrooms (MGM, 1957)
The Young Lions (20th-Fox, 1958)
Some Came Running (MGM, 1958)
Career (Par, 1959)
Rio Bravo (WB, 1959)
Who Was That Lady? (Col, 1960)
Bells Are Ringing (MGM, 1960)
Pepe (Col, 1960)
Ocean's 11 (WB, 1960)
All in a Night's Work (Par, 1961)
Ada (MGM, 1961)
Sergeants Three (UA, 1962)
The Road to Hong Kong (UA, 1962)
Who's Got the Action? (Par, 1962)
Canzoni Mondo [38/24/36] (It, 1962)
Come Blow Your Horn (Par, 1963)
Toys in the Attic (UA, 1963)
Who's Been Sleeping in My Bed? (Par, 1963)
4 for Texas (WB, 1963)
What a Way to Go! (20th-Fox, 1964)

Robin and the 7 Hoods (WB, 1964)
Kiss Me, Stupid (Lopert, 1964)
The Sons of Katie Elder (Par, 1965)
Marriage on the Rocks (WB, 1965)
The Silencers (Col, 1966)
Texas Across the River (Univ, 1966)
Murderers' Row (Col, 1966)
Rough Night in Jericho (Univ, 1967)
The Ambushers (Col, 1967)
Bandolero! (20th-Fox, 1968)
How to Save a Marriage—And Ruin Your Life
    (Col, 1968)
The Wrecking Crew (Col, 1968)
Five Card Stud (Par, 1968)
Airport (Univ, 1970)
Something Big (NG, 1971)
Showdown (Univ, 1973)
Mr. Ricco (MGM, 1975)
Cannonball Run (20th-Fox, 1981)
Cannonball Run II (WB, 1984)

Radio Series

With Jerry Lewis

The Martin and Lewis Show (NBC, 1949–53)

TV Series

With Jerry Lewis

The Colgate Comedy Hour (NBC, 1950–55)

Dean Martin Alone

The Dean Martin Show (NBC, 1965–74)
The Dean Martin Celebrity Roasts (NBC, 1974–79)

Half Nelson (NBC, 1985)

Album Discography

LPs

Bells Are Ringing (Cap W/SW-14350) [ST]
The Best of Dean Martin (Cap T-2604, CAP SM-2601)
The Best of Dean Martin (Silver Eagle)
The Best of Dean Martin, Vol. 2 (Cap SKAO-140)
Cha Cha de Amor (Cap T/ST-1702)
Cha Cha de Amor (Starline SRS-5095)
Christmas Album (Reprise 6222)
The Country Side of Dean Martin (Reprise 32432)
The Country Style of Dean Martin (Reprise 6061)
Dean Martin (Pickwick 2051)
Dean Martin and Frank Sinatra (Jocklo International 89315)
The Dean Martin and Jerry Lewis Show (Memorabilia 714)
Dean Martin Favorites (Cap DT-2941)
Dean Martin, Judy Garland & Frank Sinatra (Jocklo International 1007)
Dean Martin Sings (Audition Supertone AUD-33-5936) w. Nicolini Lucchesi
Dean Martin Sings (Cap T-401)
Dean Martin Sings, Frank Sinatra Conducts (Cap T/ST-2297), (Pickwick 3465)
The Dean Martin TV Show (Reprise 6233)
The Deluxe Set (Cap DTCL-2815)
Dino (Cap T/ST-1659)
Dino (Reprise 2053)
Dino Latino (Reprise 6054)
The Door Is Still Open to My Heart (Reprise 6140)
Dream With Dean (Reprise 6123)
Everybody Loves Somebody (Reprise 6130)
For the Good Times (Reprise 6428)

French Style (Reprise 6021)
Gentle on My Mind (Reprise 6330)
Greatest (Cap DKAO-378)
Greatest Hits, Vols. 1-2 (Reprise 6301, 6320)
Happiness Is Dean Martin (Reprise 6242)
Happy in Love (Tower T/ST-5036)
Heart-Touching Treasury/Famous Love Songs (Suffolk Marketing)
Hey Brother, Pour the Wine (Cap T/ST-2212)
The Hit Sounds of Dean Martin (Reprise 6213)
Hits Again (Reprise 6146)
Holiday Cheer (Cap T/ST-2343)
Houston (Reprise 6181)
I Can't Give You Anything But Love (Pickwick 3089)
I Have But One Heart (Pickwick 3307)
I Take a Lot of Pride in What I Am (Reprise 6338)
The Lush Years (Tower T/ST-5006)
Moonstruck (Cap C1-90231) [ST]
Movin' With Nancy (Reprise R/RS-6277, Reprise ST-91349) (ST/TV)
My Woman, My Woman, My Wife (Reprise 6403)
One More Time (World Record Club ST-1001)
Pretty Baby (Cap T-849)
Relaxin' (Tower T/DT-5018)
Remember Me, I'm the One Who Loves You (Reprise 6170)
Robin and the 7 Hoods (Reprise 2021) [ST]
The Silencers (Reprise 6211) [ST]
Sleep Warm (Cap T/ST-1150)
Somewhere There's Someone (Reprise 6201)
Southern Style (Cap T/DT-2333)
The Stooge (10″ Cap H-401) [ST]

Summit Meeting at the 500 (Souvenir 247-17) w. Frank Sinatra, Sammy Davis Jr.
Swingin' (Pickwick 2001)
Swingin' Down Yonder (Cap T-1047)
That's Amore (Longines SYS-5235)
This Is Dean Martin (Cap T-1047)
This Is Dean Martin (World Record Club ST-1087)
This Time I'm Swingin' (Cap T/ST-1442)
This Time I'm Swingin' (Starline SRS-5138)

The Very Best of Dean Martin (Cap EST-23166)
Welcome to My World (Reprise 6250)
Winter Romance (Cap T/ST-1285)
You Can't Win 'Em All (Pickwick 3057)
You Were Made for Love (Pickwick 3175)
Young and Foolish (Pickwick 3136)
You're Nobody 'Til Somebody Loves You/Return to Me (Cap STBB-523)
You're the Best Thing (Reprise 2174)

CDs:

All of Me (Castle Pulse PLSCD-372)
All the Hits 1948-63 (BCD PRS-23015)
All the Hits 1948-69 (BCD DBP-102005)
All the Hits 1964-69 (BCD PRS-23016)
All-Time Greatest Hits (Curb D21K-77383)
All-Time Hits (Double Platinum DBP-102005)
Baby, It's Cold Outside (PIE PIESD-211)
Back to Back Hits (Music for Pleasure MFPCD-496843) w. Nat (King) Cole
The Bells Are Ringing (Cap CDP-7-92060-2) [ST]
The Best of Dean Martin (Applause 80024)
The Best of Dean Martin (Cap C21K-46627, EMI-Cap Special Markets 57261)
The Best of Dean Martin (Cap CDP 7 90718 2)
The Best of Dean Martin 1962-68 (Charly CD6R-106)
Blood and Sand/Panama Hattie/At War With the Army (Great Movie Themes 60047) [ST]
A Bronx Tale (Tribeca EK-57560) [ST]
Bye Bye Love (Giant 24609-2) [ST]
Capitol Collectors Series (Cap C21Y-19633, Cap-EMI CDP-7-91633-2)
The Capitol Years (Cap-EMI 98409, EMI CDP-790718 2)
Christmas With Bing Crosby, Nat (King) Cole & Dean Martin (EMI-Cap Special Markets 17742)
Christmas With Nat & Dean (EMI DC-863082) w. Nat (King) Cole
The Clan in Chicago (The Entertainers 389) w. Frank Sinatra, Sammy Davis Jr.
Cocktail Hour With Dean Martin (Golden Stars 5281)
The Complete Dean Martin (Dressed to Kill 427)
Country Dino (The Entertainers 426)
The Country Side of Dean Martin (Heartland Music 6452-2)
Country Style/Dean "Tex" Martin Rides Again (Collectors' Choice Music CCM-512-2)
A Couple of Swells (New Sound—no number) w. Frank Sinatra
A Date With Dean (Pulse PBXCD-347)
Dean Martin (BCD GLD-63325)
Dean Martin (The Entertainers 388)
Dean Martin (Pegasus PEG199)
Dean Martin Hits Again/Houston (Collectors' Choice Music CCM-552-2)

Dean Martin Sings Country Favorites (Goldies—no number)
The Dean Martin Television Show/Songs from "The Silencers" (Collectors' Choice Music CCM-562-2)
Dino: Italian Love Songs/Cha Cha De Amor (Cap-EMI 7243-8-55393-2-9, EMI CTMCD-108)
Dino/You're the Best Thing That Ever Happened to Me (Collectors' Choice Music CCM-262)
The Door Is Still Open to My Heart/I'm the One Who Loves You (Collectors' Choice Music CCM 532-2)
Dream With Dean/Everybody Loves Somebody (Collectors' Choice Music CCM-542-2)
Dreams and Memories (Pair PCD2-1029)
The Essential Dean Martin (Redx RX-1031)
Everybody Loves Somebody (BCD GLD-25325)
Everybody Loves Somebody (Golden Stars 5203)
Everybody Loves Somebody (Goldies—no number)
Everybody Loves Somebody (Prism PLATBX-167)
Everybody Loves Somebody (Prism PLATCD-574)
Everybody Loves Somebody—The Reprise Years: 1962-1966 (Bear Family BCD-343)
Everybody Loves Somebody: 25 Hits (Masters 502972)
40 Easy Listening Classics (Master Song 550342)
Frank Sinatra & Friends (Artanis 8104) w. Bing Crosby, Sammy Davis Jr.
Frank Sinatra at Villa Venice, Chicago, Live 1962, Vol. 1 (Jazz Hour 1033) w. Frank Sinatra, Sammy Davis Jr.
Frank Sinatra at Villa Venice, Chicago, Live 1962, Vol. 2 (Jazz Hour 1034) w. Frank Sinatra, Sammy Davis Jr.
French Style/Dino Latino (Collectors' Choice Music CCM-522-2)
Gentle on My Mind/Take a Lot of Pride in What I Am (Collectors' Choice Music CCM-260)
Gold Collection (Retro R2CD40-52)
Golden Memories (Time-Life Music 18130)
Golden Voices (Madacy 416) w. Frank Sinatra
Great (BCD GLD-63147)
Great, Vol. 2 (BCD GLD-63183)
Greatest Hits (EMI-Cap Entertainment 94961, EMI 49528.2)

Greatest Hits (MPBV)

Happiness Is Dean Martin/Welcome to My World (Collectors' Choice Music CCM-259)

Happy Hour (Pair PCD-2-1177)

Hurtin' Country Songs (Cap-EMI 21509)

I'll Always Love You (Ce De International CD-66153)

I've Got My Love to Keep Me Warm (Goldies GLD-25389)

I Wish You Love (EMI DC-863752)

Italian Love Songs (Cap/EMI 33751)

Just for Fun (Delta CD-6210)

Just for Fun (Music CD-6210)

Just in Time (Ce De International CD-66065)

Ladies & Gentlemen (ABM ABMMCD1025)

Late at Night With Dean Martin (Cap-EMI 521508)

Lay Some Happiness on Me—The Reprise Years and More: 1966-1985 (Bear Family BCD-586)

The Legends Collection (Dressed to Kill 512)

Live at the Sands (Bianco 4020)

Live at the Sands Hotel (Prism PLATCD-575)

The Long-Lost Reprise Hits of Dean Martin (Collectors' Choice Music CCM-053)

Love Songs (Masters 501172)

Love Songs (Ranwood 8259)

The Magic Memories (Prism PLATCD-432)

Making Spirits Bright (Cap-EMI 4957352)

Making Spirits Bright (Hearland Music 7322-2)

Memories Are Made of This (Bear Family BCD-15781)

Memories Are Made of This (EMI DC-86043.2, EMI HR-883302)

Memories of Dean Martin (New Sound NST-117)

A Million and One (Goldies GLD-25368)

Moonstruck (Cap C21Y-90231) [ST]

My Woman, My Woman, My Wife/For the Good Times (Collectors' Choice Music CCM-261)

On the Sunny Side of the Street (Music CD-6213) w. Frank Sinatra

The Rat Pack (Armoury ARMCD-050) w. Frank Sinatra, Sammy Davis Jr.

The Rat Pack (TKO Magnum CECD038) w. Frank Sinatra, Sammy Davis Jr.

The Rat Pack (TKO/United Audio Entertainment UAE-30492) w. Frank Sinatra, Sammy Davis Jr.

The Rat Pack Collection (Madacy 5315) w. Frank Sinatra, Sammy Davis Jr.

Relax, It's Dean Martin (Recall 301, Snapper SMDCD-301)

Return to Me (Bear Family BCD-15959)

Robin and the 7 Hoods (Artanis ARZ-104-2) [ST]

Season's Greetings (CEMA Special Markets 521-57688, EMI-Cap Special Markets 57688)

Singles (EMI G-CDMFP-6129)

Sitting on Top of the World/Once in Awhile (Collectors' Choice Music CCM-257)

61 Great Performances (Prism PLATBX-2202)

Sleep Warm (Cap 37500)

Smooth 'n' Swingin' (Castle Pie PIED1-122)

Solid Gold (Madacy 57958)

Some Enchanted Evening (Hallmark 31232)

Someone Like You (Joker 39040)

Somewhere There's Someone/The Hit Sound of Dean Martin (Collectors' Choice Music CCM-258)

Spotlight on Dean Martin (Cap C21Y-29389, Cap-EMI CDP-7243-8-29389-2-7)

The Summit—In Concert (Artanis 102) w. Frank Sinatra, Sammy Davis Jr.

Sunny Side of the Street (Delta 6213) w. Frank Sinatra, Sammy Davis Jr.

Super Collection (Jasdac EVC-306)

Swingin' Down Yonder (Cap 21Y-94306)

That's Amore (The Entertainers 224)

That's Amore: The Best of Dean Martin (Cap C21Z-37571)

Things to Do in Denver When You're Dead (A&M 31454-0424-2) [ST]

This Time I'm Swingin'!/Pretty Baby (Cap-EMI 7243-8-54546-2-2, EMI CTMCD-104)

Touch of Class (EMI TC-886292)

20 Great Love Songs (EMI LS-886332)

31 Favorites (Heartland Music 12348-2

32 Songs for Lovers (Going for a Song/Cedar GFS335)

The Very Best of Dean Martin (EMI 4932842, EMI 4967212)

The Very Best of Dean Martin (Heartland Music 6449-2)

The Very Best of Dean Martin (Music for Pleasure MFPCD-493284)

The Very Best of Dean Martin: Capitol & Reprise Years (EMI 5277712)

Volare (Delta 15140)

A Winter Romance (Cap CDP-7-93115-2, EMI G-4968282)

Wonderful Music of Dean Martin (BCD WMO-90317)

Mary Martin in 1941.
[Courtesy of JC Archives]

Mary Martin

(b. Mary Virginia Martin, Weatherford, Texas, December 1, 1913; d. Rancho Mirage, California, November 3, 1990)

Somehow the winning combination of Mary Martin's rich singing voice, her pleasing looks, and a warm personality never translated properly to the motion-picture screen. It became one of the mysteries of Hollywood history. In her dozen Hollywood features (mostly for Paramount Pictures in the early 1940s), the vivacious redhead sang engagingly, acted unself-consciously, and looked attractive. Perhaps audiences sensed that she never enjoyed the slow pace of filmmaking and much preferred to perform for live audiences.

From the late 1930s onwards, Mary Martin appeared on Broadway in an assortment of star roles that quickly made her a rival with Ethel Merman for the title of the First Lady of Musical Comedy. She was more dainty than the brassy Merman, but she could be equally feisty (as when she did her own version of *Annie Get Your Gun*). In an array of long-running Broadway hits (including *South Pacific, Peter Pan, The Sound of Music*, and *I Do! I Do!*), she displayed a versatility of performance and a clearness of voice that sustained her as a major figure on the New York stage.

She was born Mary Virginia Martin on December 1, 1913, in Weatherford, Texas, the daughter of Preston Martin (an attorney) and Juanita (Presley) Martin (a former violin teacher at the local college). An older child (Geraldine) was eleven at the time of Mary's birth. At the age of five, Mary made her performing debut at an Elks' carnival singing "When Apples Grow on Lilac Trees." At her mother's insistence, Mary took violin lessons, but much preferred singing and acting. One of her mother's friends was concert singer Helen Cahoon, and she made quite an impression on Mary in choosing a future career. Mary finished high school at age sixteen and was sent to the Ward Belmont Female Academy, a fashionable finishing school in Nashville, Tennessee. However, she dropped out to marry (November 3, 1930) her high school sweetheart, Benjamin J. Hagman, an accountant. Their child Lawrence Martin Hagman (who would become the star of TV's *Dallas* in the late 1970s) was born on September 21, 1931, in Fort Worth, Texas. When Ben Hagman decided to become an attorney, the family moved back to Weatherford, and Juanita Martin took over raising Mary's child. Mary recalled, "I was only seventeen when he was born, so my mother was the mother to both of us."

To help bring income into the household (it was the Depression) and to keep busy (her marriage with Ben Hagman was already foundering), Mary and her friend Mildred Woods opened a dance school in Weatherford, first using her uncle's grain storage loft as a rehearsal studio. The teachers expanded their circuit, and by the time she was nineteen, Mary had three hundred pupils. Meanwhile, she had already made annual treks to Hollywood (financed by her parents) to study dance technique at an academy run by the famous dance team of Fanchon and Marco. On her second stay in Hollywood, she was contracted to perform for a week in a stage revue in San Francisco.

By 1936 Mary realized that she wanted to return to Hollywood to try her luck, and her marriage to Ben Hagman was a mistake. By the next year, she and Hagman were divorced, and she was already in Hollywood, where she won a few jobs singing on radio (but with no pay). Her assorted agents kept getting her auditions. On one occasion, she was taken to perform for Oscar Hammerstein II, where she sang "Oh, Rock It for Me" and then did "Indian Love Call," not realizing (she always claimed) he had written the latter song. Hammerstein was impressed with her presence and promised that some day they would work together. He introduced her to Jerome Kern, who advised her to stop trying to be a prima donna (a la Lily Pons) and just be herself. She auditioned for the film studios, where many saw promise in her, but no one offered her a job. Martin remembers she was known as "Audition Mary" in those days.

Although she could not get screen work, Mary had a few assignments dubbing the singing voices of movie stars in films, including Margaret Sullavan and Gypsy Rose Lee. She finally made her screen debut at RKO playing the dance teacher of Danielle Darrieux in *The Rage of Paris* (1938). One Sunday night at the Trocadero Club she was part of the "amateur showcase" and sang "Il Bacio" first in a classical mode then in a swing tempo. In the audience that evening was Broadway producer Laurence Schwab, who was so impressed with her lively soprano voice that he contracted her for a new Broadway show (*Ring Out the News*) he was planning. She was to receive $150 weekly for a year; $300 if she had a starring part in the show.

By the time she reached New York, Schwab had abandoned that project. Not wanting to pay her salary for nothing, he took her to meet the collaborators (Bella and Sam Spewack and Cole Porter) of a pending Broadway musical *Leave It to Me* at the Waldorf-Astoria Hotel. She sang four songs for the assemblage, which included the show's stars, Sophie Tucker, Victor Moore, Tamara, and William Gaxton. It was Martin's singing of the naughty "A Weekend in the Life of a Private Secretary" that won her the part of the sultry femme fatale. The show tried out in Boston (where she lost one of her two song numbers because one of the show's stars, Tamara, objected) and New Haven. *Leave It to Me* bowed on Broadway on November 9, 1938. Mary stopped the show with the song "My Heart Belongs to Daddy," which was full of Cole Porter's typical spicy rhymes. Sung innocently by Martin, it made the lyrics all the more enticing. (The number was performed in a Siberian setting with Mary in ermine, fur hat, and gloves—most of which she removed to a more basic outfit. She was lifted by and danced with six Eskimos. One of those chorus boys was Gene Kelly.)

Not only was *Leave It to Me* a big hit, but Mary became the latest toast of Broadway with her risqué number. She was on the cover of *Life* magazine and was the columnists' new darling. During the run of *Leave It to Me,* Mary's father died and the papers were full of "Daddy Girl Sings About Daddy as Daddy Dies." Now the Hollywood studios were interested in her, and she signed a contract with Paramount Pictures. She admitted later, "What on earth possessed me to accept it, I don't know. . . . Having been tested and rejected so many times by so many studios, I couldn't wait to get back out there and show them all."

Martin's official screen debut came with *The Great Victor Herbert* (1939), an elaborate biography of the famous operetta composer filled with twenty-eight of his songs. In typical Hollywood fashion, Paramount had hired Mary because of her Broadway fame in the revealing "Daddy" strip number. In this movie, however, she was buried beneath period costumes and her individuality disguised by makeup and hair styles that mimicked the fashion of Claudette Colbert, then the studio's reigning queen. Mary's costars were Allan Jones and Walter Connolly (as the turn-of-the-century composer), and the child coloratura Susanna Foster. *Variety* reported, "Although Miss Martin's voice is limited in its range. . . . Her trouping stamps her immediately as a capable film artist." Much better was her role in *Rhythm on the River* (1940), in which she and Bing Crosby were ghost songwriters for Broadway tunesmith Basil Rathbone. The duo finally get their just recognition and find love with one another. In *Love Thy Neighbor* (1940), she played Fred Allen's niece brightly and tried to intercede in his long-standing feud with fellow radio star Jack Benny. Within the picture she reprised "My Heart Belongs to Daddy."

Discouraged by her Hollywood experience, Mary left after her first three pictures to work for producer Laurence Schwab in *Nice Goin'*. It was a musical based on the hit play *Sailor Beware!*, costarring Bert Wheeler, and with songs by Ralph Rainger and Leo Robin. The show opened on October 21, 1939, in New Haven, but closed in Boston on November 4. *Variety* noted of Mary's contributions in her first musical lead: "It is in the dramatic rather than the vocal department that she showed best at the preem. . . ." (Ironically, Paramount Pictures, which had already filmed *Sailor Beware!* as *Lady Be Careful* in 1936, refilmed it as a musical in 1941—*The Fleet's In*—headlining the studio's sarong queen Dorothy Lamour and its newest singing discovery, Betty Hutton.)

Martin returned to Paramount, where she costarred with Don Ameche (borrowed from Twentieth Century-Fox) and tart-mouthed Oscar Levant in *Kiss the Boys Goodbye* (1941). It was a not-so-bright satire on Hollywood's perennial search for fresh talent à la Scarlett O'Hara in *Gone With the Wind*. Mary was the Southern chorus girl (here her slight Texas twang was properly fitting) with whom a film director (Ameche) falls in love. The movie's highlight was Mary's singing "That's How I Got My Start" and Connee Boswell's interpretation of "Sand in My Shoes."

Even better was *Birth of the Blues* (1941), which reunited her with one of her favorite performers, Bing Crosby. (She would guest on his radio variety show several times over the years.) The picture was a simplistic rendition of the history of jazz with Crosby as a clarinetist who opens a New Orleans club on Bourbon Street with Mary as his prime singer. Her solo highlight was a rousing "Wait Till the Sun Shines Nellie," and with Crosby and Jack Teagarden she did "The Waiter and the Porter and the Upstairs Maid." Her third 1941 film was *New York Town* in which she courted wealthy Robert Preston but really loved down-and-out Fred MacMurray. Her single song was "Yip I Adde I Ay."

In 1942 Mary's only film release (although she was busy making other pictures) was the studio's all-star salute *Star Spangled Rhythm*, in which she teamed with Dick Powell and the Golden Gate Quartet in singing "Hit the Road to Dreamland." The next year she was rematched with Powell in a Technicolor wartime comedy called *Happy Go Lucky*. She was the ex-cigarette girl from New York who arrives in the Caribbean to make her fortune. Despite the opportunity of marrying a wealthy snob (Rudy Vallee), she falls in love with a beachcomber (Powell). While she was bright and chipper, it was Betty Hutton, the studio's "blonde bombshell," who stole the limelight with her snappy rendition of "Murder He Says."

On the other hand, Mary showed a delicious sense of screwball comedy in *True to Life* (1943). In this farce, Franchot Tone and Dick Powell are radio scriptwriters who visit waitress Martin's home to gain fresh material for their radio soap opera. Martin presented "Mr. Bluebird." Thus ended Mary Martin's movie years, except for guest cameos (as herself) in *Night and Day* (1946), singing "My Heart Belongs to Daddy," and in *Main Street to Broadway* (1953). She would insist later, "My Hollywood period is almost nonexistent in my memory."

Two benefits from her Hollywood years were her friendship with screen star Janet Gaynor and her marriage to Richard Halliday. He had been the East Coast story editor for Paramount when she opened on Broadway in *Leave It to Me* but had slept through her "My Heart Belongs to Daddy" number. (He had the flu.) When Paramount had considered signing her to a contract, Halliday had been against it. About the time she went to California to make *The Great Victor Herbert*, he was transferred (against his will) to being Paramount's West Coast story editor. The two of them met during a party while she was making *The Great Victor Herbert*, but there was no chemistry. Later, they met again and fell in love, and were married in May 1940. Their daughter Heller was born in 1941. In 1942, when she was deciding to quit the movies and return to Broadway, Halliday opted to leave filmmaking and become her manager.

For her stage return, Martin selected *Dancing in the Streets*, which had music by Vernon Duke and lyrics by Howard Dietz. The show opened on March 23, 1943, in Boston and closed there on April 10; it never reached New York City. To accept this musical comedy, Mary had turned down the lead in *Oklahoma!* Fortunately, at just about this time, Marlene Dietrich decided not to make her Broadway bow in the Kurt Weill musical *One Touch of Venus*. Producer Cheryl Crawford offered the role to Mary, who became the heavenly muse who comes down to Earth. Her costar was Kenny Baker, and the hit show lasted for 567 performances. When the successful play closed in New York, it was launched on a national tour. It was during this trek that Mary concluded that, for the sake of her marriage, Halliday would be the decision maker of the family and that, thereafter, their daughter would always tour with them to keep the family together. (Her son Larry had been brought up largely by Mary's mother; when the latter died and Martin took over the upbringing, there were years of friction.) By now the Hallidays had settled into a home in Norwalk, Connecticut.

Lute Song (1946) was based on a Chinese play *Pi-Pa-Ki*, with music by Raymond Scott and lyrics by Bernard Hanighen. Mary was the young Chinese wife who goes in search of her straying husband (Yul Brynner). Her best number was "Mountain High, Valley Low." The show lasted for 142 performances, but this time she did not go on the road with it after the Broadway stint. Instead she sailed for England to star in *Pacific 1860*, more because she adored the musical's author (Noël Coward) than because the period vehicle was correct for her. Realizing her error, but already contracted for the show, she continued on with the project. The play ran for nine (unhappy for Martin) months on the West End.

While Mary had been doing *Lute Song*, another hit show had opened on Broadway, Irving Berlin's *Annie Get Your Gun*. She had not been considered for the part of the rough-and-tumble lead because of her refined stage image. However, during Martin's *Pacific 1860* engagement, she was asked to headline the London company of *Annie Get Your Gun*. Being homesick, she declined. However she agreed to star in the U.S. national road company of the musical western. Mary's daughter Heller played her little sister onstage. The popular tour lasted for eleven months, into late 1948. Martin acknowledges that her happiest moment on the tour was during the dress rehearsal run-through in New York before they left for their opening engagement in Dallas. Broadway's original musical Annie Oakley, Ethel Merman, was in the second row of the orchestra and gave her replacement an enthusiastic response.

According to Martin she almost rejected the chance to star in *South Pacific*, thinking the idea that Richard Rodgers and Oscar Hammerstein II put forth of a love-struck nurse on a tropical isle during World War II was an unexceptional concept. Fortunately she (or someone) changed her mind. When the show opened on Broadway on April 7, 1949, Martin was the lead, portraying Nurse Nellie Forbush. Her leading man was Metropolitan Opera star Ezio Pinza. For hundreds of Broadway performances, she shampooed her close-cropped tresses onstage as she sang "I'm Gonna Wash That Man Right Outa My Hair," dueted with bass Pinza on "Some Enchanted Evening," and cavorted as she performed "A Cockeyed Optimist," "I'm in Love With a Wonderful Guy," and "Honey Bun." She went to London (November 1, 1951) to star in the West End Production, remaining with it for a year. (As with *Lute Song*—played on the screen in 1948 by Ava Gardner—when *South Pacific* finally became a film in 1958, Martin was not seriously considered for the lead role. She was thought too old at forty-five to play the lead.)

Once again back in New York, Martin chose to rest her throat. Thereafter, for her next vehicle, she rejected a musical (Cole Porter's *Kiss Me, Kate*) and instead selected to do the drawing room comedy *Kind Sir* (1953). The show received no raves. ("What a waste of talent!" insisted the *New York Times*.) Thanks, however, to its luminous two stars (Martin and Charles Boyer) it lasted for 166 performances. (When it was filmed as *Indiscreet*, 1958, it costarred Ingrid Bergman and Cary Grant.)

Mary had already made an illustrious television bow on *The Ford 50th Anniversary Show* (CBS-TV, June 15, 1953). The program's highlight was the show-tune medleys sung in tandem by Martin and Ethel Merman. It was a video milestone that remains legendary to this day. Then, under her husband's auspices, Mary created another industry stir when, on Easter Sunday, March 29, 1954, she appeared in two NBC-TV specials telecast live from New York. The first, *Magic With Mary Martin*, was geared for a children's audience and featured music by Mary Rodgers (Richard's daughter); the second was *Music With Mary Martin* for adults.

The perennial favorite *Peter Pan* by Sir James M. Barrie had last been revived on Broadway in 1950 with Jean Arthur and Boris Karloff. For the new, musical version (October 20, 1954), Mary—in her early forties—was showcased as the perpetual youthful male lead with Cyril Ritchard as the dastardly Captain Hook. For 152 performances, she flew (thanks to special wiring) and sang "I've Gotta Crow." Her daughter Heller was in the cast and joined with her when the show was transferred into a hugely popular TV special (NBC-TV, March 7, 1955), which earned Martin an Emmy Award. The small-screen *Peter Pan* received such high ratings that it was restaged for a new TV airing in 1956, and then yet another new edition was mounted with Martin on December 8, 1960 in color. (The latter, taped while she was doing *The Sound of Music*, was the version that was restored and retelecast to much fanfare by NBC-TV on March 24, 1989.) By now, it had become customary for the Hallidays, after each stage venture, to take a long relaxing cruise on a freighter. After *Peter Pan*, they booked passage on such a ship bound for South America. They were berthed in Brazil when their good friends (former movie star) Janet Gaynor and her clothes designer husband Adrian invited them to their farm retreat in Anápolis (in the state of Golanz). The Hallidays were so intrigued by the landscape that they bought a farm on a neighboring mountain, eventually acquiring several thousands acres and turning it into a working farm.

After *Peter Pan*, Mary agreed to go abroad on a State Department goodwill tour of Thornton Wilder's comedy, *The Skin of Our Teeth*, playing the role of the maid Sabina (originated on Broadway in 1942 by Tallulah Bankhead). The tour opened in Paris, and later Mary re-created the role in a TV special (NBC-TV, September 11, 1955). A month after that special, she was reunited with Noël Coward for another television variety outing, *Together With Music* (CBS-TV, October 22, 1955). While these mainstream offerings appealed to Martin's fans, there was an outcry when she appeared as the dicey mistress of a junkyard magnate (Paul Douglas) in the TV adaptation of *Born Yesterday* (NBC-TV, October 28, 1956). Although she was splendid in the role, she learned from this experience not to step so far away from her good-girl image in the future.

In 1957, Mary did a ten-week West Coast tour of *South Pacific* and *Annie Get Your Gun* and brought the latter to television in a two-hour special on November 27, 1958. Perhaps her greatest triumph was starring as Maria Von Trapp, the Austrian novitiate who, during World War II, falls in love with a widowed baron and his brood of children in *The Sound of Music* (November 16, 1959). The Richard Rodgers–Oscar Hammerstein II musical, of which she and her husband had a 25 percent investment, ran for 1,443 performances on Broadway. During its New York stay, her husband was hospitalized for alcoholism. For her performance in *The Sound of Music*, Mary was given her fourth Tony (having won the Award previously for her general contributions in 1948, *South Pacific* in 1950, and *Peter Pan* in 1955), and her best-selling original cast album won a Grammy in 1961. When *The Sound of Music* was brought to the screen in 1965, it was Julie Andrews who inherited the coveted lead role.

In December 1962, the songstress was a guest on *The Bing Crosby Christmas Show*, (ABC-TV) and the following October she was back on Broadway in a new musical *Jennie*, based on the life of stage star Laurette Taylor. The show was a failure, closing after only 82 performances. In 1965, Martin agreed to star in a State Department tour of *Hello, Dolly!*, which played in Vietnam, Japan, and also in parts of the United States. She had another special on NBC-TV (April 3, 1966), *Mary Martin at Eastertime With the Radio City Music Hall*. She returned to the Broadway stage—her voice now very throaty and deeper-timbered—in the musical *I Do! I Do!* (May 16, 1968), a two-person show with Robert Preston (her coleading man from their long-ago movie *New York Town*). The show had a lengthy run (561 performances) and she then went on tour with it.

After *I Do! I Do!*, Mary planned a short hiatus that stretched into several years. In March 1973, her husband died as a result of abdominal surgery, and thereafter she took a long European holiday. As therapy, she wrote her sentimental autobiography *My Heart Belongs to Daddy* (1976), which the *New York Times* thought was gracious but warned "she maintains her distance." She returned to the stage in *Do You Turn Somersaults?* (1977), playing a sixty-year-old woman in an autumnal comedy about a former actress turned circus cashier. Her costar was Anthony Quayle, and the show had her dancing a Charleston, doing somersaults, and singing songs from an upside-down position. The show was successful and on the road for seven months.

In 1979, Mary did a cross-country tour as a designer of linen/performer for the Fieldcrest Company (the revenue went to charity). She made her telefeature debut in *Valentine* (ABC-TV, December 7, 1979) as a seventy-one-year-old woman having an affair with a man (Jack Albertson) from the same retirement home.

Martin had already begun her cohosting duty on the *Over Easy* (PBS-TV) talk show series aimed at senior citizens when in September 1982 (in San Francisco where the show was taped), the taxi she was in was hit by a drunken driver. Her fellow passengers included her agent (who was killed), Janet Gaynor (who was severely injured and who died two years later), and Gaynor's husband. Martin suffered a fractured pelvic bone and punctured leg. Doctors thought Mary would never walk again, but she did. She returned for a time to *Over Easy*, and she did a benefit at San Francisco's Davies Symphony Hall for the trauma center (where she had been brought after the accident). For the latter occasion she even flew again briefly as Peter Pan. She guested on *The Love Boat* (1983) and *Hardcastle and McCormick* (1985), and later in 1985, she was the focus of a tribute at the Shubert Theater in New York City, a benefit for the Theater Collection of the Museum of the City of New York.

In 1986, Mary Martin and Carol Channing—two former Dolly Levis of the stage musical *Hello, Dolly!*—contracted to costar in *Legends*, a play by James Kirkwood of *A Chorus Line* fame. It was a tale of two theatrical greats who agree to do a stage play together to revive their careers, but who hate one another. In the course of the macabre comedy, they perform one song together. The show played over 350 performances in a thirty-two-city tour during 1986–87, but never reached Broadway. (James Kirkwood authored a tell-all *Diary of a Mad Playwright: How I Toured With Mary Martin and Carol Channing and Lived to Tell About It*, published in 1989 after his death. The book reveled the myriad controversies, jealousies, and frustrations that beset the much-troubled production.)

In August 1988, Mary Martin was part of *Broadway at the Bowl*, a multistar salute at the Hollywood Bowl. She sang "My Heart Belongs to Daddy," "A Cockeyed Optimist," as well as teaming with the famed opera tenor Placido Domingo for "Some Enchanted Evening." In early 1989, it was announced that Mary would tour in a musical version of *Our Town* called *Grover's Corner* created by Tom Jones and Harvey Schmidt (*I Do! I Do!*), but in May of that year, she was diagnosed as suffering from cancer of the liver and colon. Said the feisty star, "I'm fighting this illness. But none of us live forever."

After withdrawing from the stage project, Martin underwent surgery at Cedars-Sinai Medical Center in Los Angeles. By early 1990, Martin was recuperating at her Martha's Vineyard home. She was to make an appearance at the Schubert Theater in New Haven that May, but she was too ill to attend. Instead, she sent a taped message. She made a trip to Great Britain that summer intent on visiting friends there. That September the home video/laser disc version of Mary's TV production of *Peter Pan* was released. (Within three months, over four million copies were sold.) By late October 1990, she was at the Eisenhower Medical Center at Rancho Mirage, California. By November 1, the dying Martin returned to her home nearby, where she passed away on November 3. One of her last visitors was former costar Carol Channing.

After Mary's passing, London's Hospital of Sick Children, to whom playwright J. M. Barrie had bequeathed his copyright to *Peter Pan*, published a memorial tribute to Martin in *Variety* newspaper. Calling her the "greatest portrayer" of *Peter Pan*, the text read, "Wherever she has flown, her bright light will be forever visible to millions of children who, because of her, will never grow old."

Filmography

The Rage of Paris (RKO, 1938)
The Great Victor Herbert (Par, 1939)
Rhythm on the River (Par, 1940)
Love Thy Neighbor (Par, 1940)
Chinese Garden Festival (Unk, 1940) (s)
Kiss the Boys Goodbye (Par, 1941)

Los Angeles Examiner Benefit (Unk, 1941) (s)
Birth of the Blues (Par, 1941)
New York Town (Par, 1941)
Star Spangled Rhythm (Par, 1942)
Happy Go Lucky (Par, 1943)
True to Life (Par, 1943)

Night and Day (WB, 1946)
Main Street to Broadway (MGM, 1953)

Valentine (ABC-TV, 12/7/79)

Broadway Plays

Leave It to Me (1938)
One Touch of Venus (1943)
South Pacific (1949)
Kind Sir (1953)

Peter Pan (1954)
The Sound of Music (1959)
Jennie (1963)
I Do! I Do! (1966)

TV Series

Over Easy (PBS, 1980–83)

Album Discography

LPs

Annie Get Your Gun (Cap W-913) [ST/TV]
Anything Goes (10″ Col ML-2159, 10″ Col CL-2582)
Anything Goes/The Bandwagon (Col ML-4751, Columbia Special Products 4751)
Babes in Arms (Col ML-4488, Col CL-823, Col OL-7070/OS-2570, Columbia Special Products 2570)
The Bandwagon (10″ Col ML-2160)
Bing and Mary—Rhythm on the Radio (Star-Tone 225) w. Bing Crosby
Cinderella/Three to Make Music (RCA LPM/LSP-2012)
The Ford Fiftieth Anniversary Television Show (10″ Decca DL-7027) [ST/TV] w. Ethel Merman
Girl Crazy (Col ML-4475, Col CL-822, Col OL-7060/OS-2560, Columbia Special Products 2560)
The Great Victor Herbert (Caliban 6033) [ST]
Guideposts for Living (Guideposts GP-100) w. Norman Vincent Peale
Happy Go Lucky (Caliban 6021) [ST]
Hello, Dolly! (RCA LOCD/LSOD-2007) [OC]
Hi-Ho (Disneyland 4016)
I Do! I Do! (RCA LOC/LSO-1128) [OC]
Jennie (RCA LOC/LSO-1083) [OC]
Leave It to Me (Smithsonian P-14944) [OC]
Let's Face It/Leave It to Me/Red, Hot and Blue (Smithsonian RO-16) [OC]

Lute Song/On the Town (Decca DL-8030) [OC]
Mary Martin on Broadway (Columbia Special Products 14282)
Mary Martin Sings for Children (YPR 731)
Mary Martin Sings for You (10″ Col ML-2061)
Mary Martin Sings, Richard Rodgers Plays (RCA LPM-1539)
Musical Love Story (Disneyland 3031)
Night and Day (Motion Picture Tracks MPT-6) [ST]
One Touch of Venus (Decca DL-9122/79122) [OC]
Pacific 1860 (Show Biz 5602) [OC]
Peter Pan (RCA LOC/LSO-1019) [OC]
The Sleeping Beauty (Disneyland 3911)
Snow White (Disneyland 4016)
Songs From "The Sound of Music" (Disneyland 1296)
The Sound of Music (Col KOL-5450-KOS-2020, Col S-32601) [OC]
South Pacific (Col OL-4180/OS-2040, Col S-32604) [OC]
Star Spangled Rhythm (Curtain Calls 100/20) [ST]
Three to Make Music (RCA LPM/LSP-2012) [OC]
Together With Music (DRG-21103, Radiola 10136) w. Noël Coward
Twenty-Five Years of Life (10″—no label nor code number) [ST/TV]
Victor Herbert—Beyond the Blue Horizon (Caliban 6033) [ST]

CDs

Annie Get Your Gun (Broadway Angel ZDM-64765)

Blue Skies/Rhythm on the River (Great Movie Themes 60025) [ST]

The Decca Years (Koch 7906)

Footlight Parade/Star Spangled Rhythm (Great Movie Themes 60013) [ST]

Girl Crazy (Col SK-60704) [OC]

Hello, Dolly! (RCA 7768-2-RG) [OC]

I Do! I Do! (RCA 1128-2-RC) [OC]

Jennie (RCA 09026-60819-2) [OC]

Marty Martin Sings, Richard Rodgers Plays (RCA 07863-6058-2)

My Heart Belongs to Daddy (Flapper 7838)

On the Town (MCA MCAD-10280) [OC]

One Touch of Venus (MCA MCAD-11354) [OC]

Pacific 1860 (Encore Box Office ENBO-8193) [OC]

Peter Pan (RCA 3762-2-RG) [OC]

16 Most Requested Songs (Col CK-53777)

The Sound of Music (Col CK-32601) [OC]

South Pacific (Col CK-32604) [OC]

Together With Music (DRG 1103) w. Noël Coward

Tony Martin and Arlene Dahl in *Here Come the Girls* (1953).
[Courtesy of JC Archives]

Tony Martin

(b. Alvin Morris, Oakland, California, December 25, 1913)

For more than sixty years, Tony Martin proved to be one of the most accomplished and polished of show-business singers. His strong, yet subtle, singing style and beautiful baritone voice guaranteed him successful careers on records, radio, television, films, and as a much-in-demand singer worldwide. For all his success, however, Martin never truly registered as a movie star, although he appeared, sometimes to advantage, in more than two dozen feature films. His reputation as a show-business legend, however, remained solid, and on Hollywood's Walk of Fame his name was embedded four times, for records, radio, television, and motion pictures.

The son of Russian Jewish immigrant parents (Edward Morris and Hattie Smith), the future star was born Alvin Morris in Oakland, California, on Christmas Day in 1913. When Al, as the boy was called, was small his parents were divorced; his mother, Hattie, remarried a man named Mike Myers, whom the youngster always considered as his father. (His real dad committed suicide when Al was a young boy.) Financially, Al's family was poor, but they were strong-knit. He developed a love of music and took up the saxophone and clarinet. (The father of future crooner Russ Columbo gave young Al clarinet lessons.) At age twelve, Al and three other boys formed a group called the Clarion Four, and a couple of years later, he was in a small jazz band, the Five Red Peppers.

After graduating from high school, Al continued to appear with various bands in the Bay area while he attended a Catholic school, Saint Mary's College, studying pre-law. Music was dominant in his life, however, and he joined Tom Coakley's band, recording the song "Here Is My Heart" for Brunswick Records, and then joining Tom Gerun's Orchestra. He sang with this band at the World's Fair in Chicago in 1933, and upon returning to the West Coast, he formed Al Morris and His Orchestra. The group was hired for short broadcasts on NBC's Blue Network. Next there was a screen test at MGM that was not successful, but at that time Nat Goldstone became Al's agent, and they remained together for more than three decades.

While MGM executives were not impressed with twenty-two-year-old singer Al Morris, the powers that be at RKO Radio were, and he won a contract with that lesser studio, making his film debut in two of the studio's two-reel *Headliner* abbreviated musicals. Believing he was now ready for bigger assignments, the studio cast him in a featured role in their upcoming Fred Astaire musical *Follow the Fleet* (1936), and he was chosen to sing a new song, "You and the Night and the Music." Wanting no competition, Astaire took the song for himself, leaving Al with merely a one-line bit. The screen newcomer fared even worse in his next RKO outing, *Muss 'Em Up* (1936), because his part was cut out of the script even before filming started. He wound up on-screen only as John Carroll's deceased brother.

With two cinema strikeouts, Al returned to nightclub work, and while singing at Hollywood's Trocadero Club, he was spotted by Twentieth Century-Fox chief Darryl F. Zanuck, who signed him for his studio. However, bad luck continued to dog Al's film career. The young man (now called Tony Martin because he liked both the name Tony and bandleader Freddy Martin) was assigned to the Shirley Temple feature *Poor Little Rich Girl* (1936) and sang "When I'm With You." But when the movie was issued, Martin discovered that his voice had been dubbed by another singer. His big break, nonetheless, came in his next project, *Sing, Baby, Sing* (1936), in which he had a featured part singing "When Did You Leave Heaven?" a song he recorded successfully for Decca Records. The star of that picture was popular Alice Faye, and after its completion she and Martin began dating. On September 4, 1937, they were married in Yuma, Arizona.

Success came quickly for Tony Martin at Twentieth Century-Fox in 1936. After playing the boyfriend in the Jones Family series entry *Back to Nature* (1936), the studio cast him in a number of well-received musicals and comedies, although for a time he was billed as Anthony Martin. Following a decent supporting role in *Pigskin Parade* (1936), in which he sang "It's Love I'm After," he was given his first starring role in the minor musical comedy *The Holy Terror*. Next he and Alice Faye dueted on "Afraid to Dream" in *You Can't Have Everything* (1937), and he was the leading man in the Ritz Brothers knockabout comedy, *Kentucky Moonshine* (1938), after having done the same for Eddie Cantor's *Ali Baba Goes to Town* (1937). Martin then costarred again with his wife in the remake of *Sally, Irene and Mary* (1938).

By now, Fox had begun to give Tony dramatic screen roles, such as the football hero in the prison drama *Up the River* (1938) and a boxer in *Winner Take All* (1939). His favorite film assignment in this period was in the 1936 musical drama *Banjo on My Knee* (1938), which showcased him beautifully as cabaret entertainer Chick Bean, singing "There's Something in the Air," and dueting with star Barbara Stanwyck on "Where the Lazy River Goes By."

In addition to movies, Martin continued to branch out into other show-business areas. Along with personal appearances, he was briefly heard on radio's *The Jack Benny Program* before joining *The George Burns and Gracie Allen Show*. On radio he also costarred with Andre Kostelanetz on CBS's *Tune-Up Time* during the 1939–40 season, and in 1940 and 1941 he headlined *The Tony Martin Show* on the NBC network. Tony also maintained his recording career, working for Decca and Brunswick in 1936. He was the vocalist on a number of 1938 records for Brunswick with Ray Noble and His Orchestra, and the same year he cut eight songs for the Vocalion label with Manny Kelin and His Swing-a-Hulas. In 1939 Martin signed a recording contract with Decca, and his first offering, "Begin the Beguine"/ "September Song" sold over a million copies, quite a feat because the record industry was still in the post-Depression doldrums.

When his Twentieth Century-Fox contract expired in 1940—the same year he and Alice Faye were divorced—the songster freelanced as an actor and starred in the delightful Columbia Pictures musical *Music in My Heart* (1940). The film highlighted not only Rita Hayworth in her first major role (Martin chose her specifically for the part), but also showcased Tony's singing of several songs, including "It's a Blue World," which was a best-seller for him on Decca Records. In 1941, Tony was featured in the posh MGM musical *Ziegfeld Girl* singing "You Stepped Out of a Dream" to Lana Turner, Hedy Lamarr, and Judy Garland; again the song was a hit for him on Decca. Among his other successful platters for the label were "Does Your Heart Beat for Me?" "Don't Take Your Love From Me," and a duet with Frances Langford on "Our Love Affair"/"Two Dreams Met."

In 1942, Tony Martin was enjoying substantial success as a multimedia star earning $12,000 per week. It all ended when he joined the navy that year and the darkest part of his life began.

He was accused falsely of trying to bribe an officer for a commission and was drummed out of the service. Next he joined the army, where for a time his peers made his life a living hell. Finally he was sent to the Far East front and participated in a number of bombing missions and acquitted himself with honor, receiving the Bronze Star and the Presidential Unit Citation before being honorably discharged as a sergeant in 1946.

Returning to Hollywood in 1946, Martin not only found himself broke, but also the recipient of protests due to the 1942 navy scandal. He was signed to host NBC's *Carnation Contented Hour* but was soon fired due to listener complaints. He also lost out on a major role in a Twentieth Century-Fox musical. Fortunately, he remained active in personal appearances, and he signed a recording contract with Mercury Records that resulted in the million-selling single "To Each His Own." In 1947, Tony contracted with more powerful RCA Victor Records, and in 1948 he was a big success performing at the London Palladium, the highlight being his singing the song "Tenement Symphony" that he had introduced originally in the Marx Brothers feature *The Big Store* in 1941. Martin remained with RCA until 1960. During that time, he recorded many of his best popular records, including eighteen tunes on the *Billboard* charts (such as "I Get Ideas" in 1951 and "It's Better in the Dark" in 1956). His popularity was just as strong abroad, particularly in England and South Africa.

Martin returned in films in 1946 in the MGM musical potpourri *Till the Clouds Roll By*, singing "All the Things You Are" in the *Show Boat* sequence. In 1948, he starred in Universal's *Casbah*, in which he played amorous thief Pepe Le Moko (a role done previously on the screen by Jean Gabin and Charles Boyer). In this picture, he sang a quartet of Harold Arlen songs: "For Every Man There's a Woman," "What's Good About Goodbye," "Hooray for Love," and "It Was Written in the Stars." Following offscreen love affairs with Rita Hayworth and Lana Turner, Martin married MGM dancer-actress Cyd Charisse in 1948, and their union proved to be one of Hollywood's most durable. Their only child (Cyd had a son, Nicky, from her first marriage), Tony Jr., was born in 1950.

From the late 1940s well into the early 1960s, Tony Martin was one of the most in-demand singers in the world. He was the first big-name singer to headline in Las Vegas, and he was equally in style throughout the country, as well as in London, Paris, Cuba, Buenos Aires, and South Africa. On television he was extremely successful in guest appearances on NBC's *The Colgate Comedy Hour*, and for two seasons he headlined his own program, *The Tony Martin Show* (1954–56), on the same network.

Meanwhile, on the big screen Martin starred with Janet Leigh in the entertaining RKO release *Two Tickets to Broadway* (1951), in which he reprised his hit record of "There's No Tomorrow," as well as singing "Manhattan" and the prologue to Ruggero Leoncavallo's opera *Pagliacci*. (Martin gave serious thought at the time to the study of opera.) Two years later, he played a semivillainous role when he costarred with Bob Hope and Rosemary Clooney in the comedy *Here Come the Girls*. Also in 1953, he appeared as the other man with Esther Williams and Van Johnson in the vapid musical *Easy to Love*, the highlight of which was Martin's singing "That's What a Rainy Day Is For."

For MGM's musical biography of Sigmund Romberg, *Deep in My Heart* (1954), Martin had a guest appearance singing "Lover Come Back to Me." In 1955 veteran Martin was among those trying to buoy up *Hit the Deck*, in which he sang the Vincent Youmans's tunes, "More Than You Know" and "Keepin' Myself for You." With musical films on the wane and Tony now over forty years old, he had to stretch for screen assignments. He did a responsible job in the title role of the Western *Quincannon, Frontier Scout* (1956), and in 1957 he starred in his last major film, the British-made musical *Let's Be Happy*.

Besides his numerous appearances on TV on musical, variety programs, and specials, Martin also acted occasionally on TV, such as on *Showers of Stars* (1955), *The George Burns Show* (1958), *The Donna Reed Show* (1961), *Death Valley Days* (1963), and *The Name of the Game* (1970). In 1960 Martin left RCA and joined Dot Records and had several good-selling singles like "Fly Me to the Moon" and "Convicted." During the rest of decade, he recorded for such labels as Park Avenue, Charter, Twentieth Century-Fox, Motown, NAN, Dunhill, and Chart. For the latter label, he even cut a country-music album, *Tony in Nashville*, in 1970. His main source of income, however, still came from personal appearances. Throughout the 1960s and 1970s, he was much in demand, both as a single and sometimes in tandem with his strikingly attractive and talented wife, Cyd Charisse.

Regarding his solo appearance at New York City's Copacabana in 1967, *Variety* reported, "Tony Martin has been major boxoffice for many years. He remains a superior entertainer. . . ." In the early 1960s, the singer was active in the national People-to-People Sports Program, and in 1969 baseball commissioner William Eckert authorized him to head the Centennial Baseball Committee to celebrate the sport's one hundredth anniversary. In 1969, Martin headlined the syndicated TV special *Spotlight on Tony Martin*, as well as touring in *Guys and Dolls*, and in 1972 he starred in another syndicated special, *The Tony Martin Show*.

In 1975, it was announced that Martin would star as Harry Richman in a musical film of Richman's autobiography *A Hell of a Life* for which Martin owned the rights, but American-International Pictures, who touted the project, was sold before it could become a reality. In 1976, Martin and Charisse published their memoirs, *The Two of Us* (also the title of a song he had recorded for Motown in 1966) as told to Dick Kleiner. Each performer told their own stories in separate chapters. The duo also did a lengthy tour promoting the volume.

During the early 1980s, Tony returned to feature films, appearing as himself in two international productions. The 1980 Spanish-made *Todos Los Dias un Dia* starred Julio Iglesias as a famous singer who finds romance, and in the feature he and Tony dueted on "As Time Goes By." *Dear Mr. Wonderful* (1982), a West German production, was about a mediocre singer (Joe Pesci) who dreams of stardom. Tony's appearance in the feature was its highlight, but unfortunately all the singing was left to star Pesci.

During much of the 1980s, Tony Martin and Cyd Charisse continued to work in tandem, but as the decade progressed Mrs. Martin pretty much gave up dancing, leaving her husband to work solo. He made successful tours of Great Britain in the 1980s and early 1990s and continued his international club and concert appearances into the new century. Regarding an appearance in Los Angeles in 1996, Archie Rothman noted in the (Los Angeles) *Village Vantage* that Martin hit "high notes much younger singers would find difficult to reach." In the summer of 1997, Tony was one of several guest stars at a MGM musical tribute at Carnegie Hall. Stephen Holden reported in the *New York Times*: "Mr. Martin, now 84, came out and sang a beautifully nuanced, pitch-perfect 'All the Things You Are.' The voice, with its virile overtones, seemed only to have grown richer over the years, and the audience response was rhapsodic." Skitch Henderson did the piano accompaniment for him at the show, and the next year Tony was back in Carnegie Hall, singing at Henderson's eightieth birthday tribute, which was telecast on PBS-TV. Regarding Martin's appearance Gary Stevens wrote, "As an octogenarian, who is still singing, Tony is nothing short of amazing. . . . He sang the rangy 'Tenement Symphony,' a cantata of sorts, just about the way he belted it out in the Marx Bros. movie *The Big Store* back in '41. Hard to believe, but true."

In 1993, the Martins moved into a condominium on Wilshire Boulevard's Golden Mile in Los Angeles, and in 1997 they were the recipients of the "Mrs. and Mrs. Hollywood" award. (The couple were renowned for being available to glamorize openings of new clubs and restaurants in the Los Angeles area.) The next year they celebrated their fiftieth wedding anniversary.

Although well into his late eighties, Martin remained a superb entertainer with a voice singers decades younger envy. While all of his contemporaries (except Frankie Laine) had either retired or died, the indefatigable baritone continued to make international concert appearances. (He joined with his wife Cyd, June Allyson, Gloria DeHaven, and Betty Garrett in February 2000 for a week of *A Celebration of the Classic Hollywood Musicals* at the Pasadena Civic Center.) Perhaps the title of one of Tony's British reissue CDs best summed up his amazing show-business longevity: *Tony Martin: The Greatest Singer of Them All!*

Filmography

As Al Morris

Educating Father (RKO, 1935) (s)
Murder on the Bridle Path (RKO, 1936)

Follow the Fleet (RKO, 1936)

As Tony Martin

Poor Little Rich Girl (20th-Fox, 1936)
Sing, Baby Sing (20th-Fox, 1936)
Back to Nature (20th-Fox, 1936)
Pigskin Parade (20th-Fox, 1936)
Banjo on My Knee (20th-Fox, 1936)
The Holy Terror (20th-Fox, 1937)
You Can't Have Everything (20th-Fox, 1937)
Life Begins at College (20th-Fox, 1937)
Ali Baba Goes to Town (20th-Fox, 1937)
Kentucky Moonshine (20th-Fox, 1938)
Sally, Irene and Mary (20th-Fox, 1938)
Up the River (20th-Fox, 1938)
Thanks for Everything (20th-Fox, 1938)
Winner Take All (20th-Fox, 1939)
Music in My Heart (Col, 1940)
Ziegfeld Girl (MGM, 1941)
The Big Store (MGM, 1941)

Meet the Stars—Stars at Play (Rep, 1941) (s)
Till the Clouds Roll By (MGM, 1946)
Casbah (UI, 1948)
Two Tickets to Broadway (RKO, 1951)
Here Come the Girls (Par, 1953)
Easy to Love (MGM, 1953)
Deep in My Heart (MGM, 1954)
Hit the Deck (MGM, 1955)
Meet Me in Las Vegas [Viva Las Vegas!] (MGM, 1956)
Quincannon, Frontier Scout (UA, 1956)
Let's Be Happy (AA, 1957)
Party Girl (MGM, 1958) (voice only)
Todas Los Dias un Dia [All Days in One Day] (Coral Films/Promafilm Internacional/Alfred Fraile II, 1980)
Dear Mr. Wonderful (Pierpont Films, 1982) (video title: Ruby's Dream)

Radio Series

The Jack Benny Program (NBC, 1937)
The George Burns and Gracie Allen Show (NBC, 1937–38)
Tune-Up Time With Tony Martin (CBS, 1939–40)

The Tony Martin Show (NBC, 1940–41)
The Carnation Contented Hour (NBC, 1946)
The Tony Martin Show (ABC, 1947–48)

TV Series

The Tony Martin Show (NBC, 1954–56)

Album Discography

LPs

Casbah (Radiola 1099) [ST/R]
The Days of Wine and Roses (Charter 100)
Deep in My Heart (MGM 3153) [ST]
The Desert Song (10″ RCA LPM-3105) w. Kathryn Grayson
Dream Music (Mer MG-20079)
Dreamland Rendezvous (10″ Mer MG-25122)
Fly Me to the Moon (Dot 3466/25466)
Go South, Young Man (RCA LPM/LSP-1778)
Golden Hits (Mer 20644/60644)
His Greatest Hits (Contour 2870-318)
His Greatest Hits (Dot 3360/25360)
Hit the Deck (MGM 3163) [ST]
Hit the Deck/Pagan Love Song/The Pirate (MGM 2SES-43ST) [ST]
Hotel Hollywood (Medallion 301) [ST/R]
I Get Ideas (Camden CAL-412)
I'll See You in My Dreams (Applause APLP-1003, Diamond 3-82005)
I'm Always Chasing Rainbows (Kaola 14140)
In the Spotlight (Decca DL-8366)
It's Just Love (Wing MGW-12115)
Live at Carnegie Hall (Movietone 71007/72007)
Live at Carnegie Hall (20th-Fox 3138)
Live at the Americana (Motown MS-645)
A Melody by Tony Martin (Coral CB-20019)
Mr. Song Man (Mer MG-20075)
Mr. Song Man (Wing MGW-11203)
A Night at the Copacabana (RCA LPM-01357)
The Night Was Made for Love (RCA LPM-1218)
One for My Baby—Harold Arlen Songs (10″ RCA LPM-3136)
Our Love Affair (Decca DL-8287)
Pigskin Parade (Amalgamated 2312) [ST]

Pigskin Parade (Pilgrim 4000) [ST]
Les Poupees de Paris (RCA LOC/LS)-1090) [OC]
The Romantic Sound of Tony Martin (Time-Life TL-7021-24)
Sally, Irene & Mary (Caliban 56031) [ST]
Sing, Baby Sing (Caliban 6029) [ST]
Something in the Air (Conifer CMS-004)
Songs From the Motion Picture "Gigi" (RCA LPM/LSP-1716) w. Gogi Grant
Speak to Me of Love (RCA LPM-1263)
A Stroll Through Melody Lane (Decca DL-8286)
Tenement Symphony (RCA International 90069)
Till the Clouds Roll By (MGM 3231, Metro 578, Sountrak 115) [ST]
Todas Los Dias Un Dia (Discos CBS International DML-50316) [ST]
Tonight (Camden CAL-576)
Tony in Nashville (Chart 1029)
Tony Martin (Audio Fidelity 6200)
Tony Martin (MCA 1515)
Tony Martin (10″ Mer MG-25004)
Tony Martin (10″ Mer MG-25036)
Tony Martin (Vocalion 3610)
Tony Martin at the Desert Inn (RCA LPM/LSP-2146)
Tony Martin at the Plaza (Audio Fidelity 6223)
Tony Martin Sings (10″ Decca DL-5189)
Tony Martin Sings of Love (Camden CLA-484)
20 Golden Pieces (Bulldog BDL-2047)
Two Tickets to Broadway (RCA LPM-39) [ST]
World Wide Favorites (10″ RCA LPM-3126)
You and the Night and the Music (10″ RCA LPM-3038)
You Can't Have Everything (Titania 508) [ST]
Ziegfeld Girl (CIF 3006) [ST]

CDs

As Time Goes By (Prism PLATCD-450)
The Best of Tony Martin on Mercury (Mer 314-532-875-2)
The Best of Tony Martin on RCA (Collectors' Choice Music CCM-046-2)
Blue Lights of Yokohama (Saturn SVCD-001)
Cocktail Hour (Columbia River Entertainment Group CRG-218057)
Deep in My Heart (Sony Music Special Products AK-47703) [ST]
Flying Down To Rio/Hollywood Hotel (Great Movie Themes 60008) [ST/R]

Go West/The Big Store (Soundtrack Factory 33503) [ST]
Greatest Hits (RCA 565626)
Greatest Hits (RCA 69327)
Greatest Love Songs (Classic World 9928)
The Greatest Singer of Them All! (BMG/RCA TYR)
Hear My Song (Flare ROYCD-216)
Hit the Deck (Turner Classic Movies/Rhino R2-76668-2, EMI 794193) [ST]
Hit the Deck/Royal Wedding (MGM/EMI MGM-15) [ST]

Hollywood Hotel (Facet FCD-8110, Hollywood Soundstage HSCD-4008) [ST/R]

Hooray for Love (Flare ROYCD-228) w. Dinah Shore

I'll See You in My Dreams (Allegiance D2-72910)

I'll See You in My Dreams (DRG 5248)

The King and I (Flare 227) w. Dinah Shore, Patrice Munsel, Robert Merrill

Legendary Song Stylist (Castle MAC-CD-359)

Something in the Air (Conifer CMSCD-004)

Stairway to the Stars (First Night Cast 6021) [OC]

Tenement Symphony (Memoir CDMOIR-545)

That's Entertainment! III (Angel CDQ-55215) [ST]

This Could Be the Night (ASV CD-AJA-5099)

Till the Clouds Roll By (Sandy Hook CDSH-2080, Sony Music Special Products AK-47029) [ST]

Tonight With Tony Martin (Vocalion CDUS-3016)

Tony Martin (Music & Memories MMD-1033)

Two Family House (RCA 07863-63733-2) [ST]

Very Warm for May (AEI 008) [OC]

You Can't Have Everything/Go Into Your Dance/You'll Never Get Rich (Great Movie Themes 60014) [ST]

Yours (Fat Boy FTB-191)

Ziegfeld Girl (Great Movie Themes 60026) [ST]

Lauritz Melchior, Kathryn Grayson, Jimmy Durante, and June Allyson in *Two Sisters From Boston* (1946). [Courtesy of JC Archives]

Lauritz Melchior

(b. Lauritz Lebrecht Hommel Melchior, Copenhagen, Denmark, March 20, 1890;
d. Santa Monica, California, March 18, 1973)

In the early 1930s, Hollywood delighted in the novelty of "presenting" Metropolitan opera stars such as Grace Moore and Lawrence Tibbett in screen vehicles, usually in heavy-handed operettas. The studios enjoyed the prestige of having such vocal luminaries under contract, and it was believed that the public deserved the cultural uplift these renowned stage figures could provide. In the mid-1940s, Joe Pasternak, who had made Deanna Durbin a star at Universal Pictures in the late 1930s, was thriving at MGM, producing a string of colorful, lucrative musical confections. He decided it would be fun for moviegoers (and profitable for he and Metro) if he mixed the likes of classical pianist José Iturbi (or, on occasion, pop organist Ethel Smith) with such contrasting studio regulars as Esther Williams, Jimmy Durante, Kathryn Grayson, Jane Powell, or Xavier Cugat. One of his more inspired coups was coaxing the Metropolitan Opera's leading Wagnerian tenor, Lauritz Melchior, to appear in four of the studio's Technicolor musical comedies.

Fifty-five-year-old Melchior brought to the screen his massive tenor voice, as well as his massive girth (240 pounds), which caused one film critic to describe him as Sophie Tucker in a suit. More importantly, jovial Melchior possessed a delightful sense of theatrics that Pasternak allowed to flourish on-camera. For some more conservative music lovers, Melchior hamming it up on-screen was an insult to his lofty stage reputation. But for most film viewers, including Melchior himself, it was a grand lark and another profitable forum in which to share his love of music. Moviegoers responded immediately to his zestful personality and the richness of his deep voice. If this famous singer's acting lacked the finer shadings of true actors, that was all right; he obviously was having such a good time in front of the cameras.

Lauritz Lebrecht Hommel Melchior was born in Copenhagen, Denmark, on March 20, 1890, the son of Jorgen Conradt and Julie (Moller) Melchior. From 1896 to 1905, he attended the voice school conducted by his father and grandfather. As a boy soprano at the English church in Copenhagen, he came to the attention of Queen Alexandra. During these early years, two individuals greatly influenced Melchior in pursuing his singing career. His blind sister Agnes (who later taught at the Royal School for the Blind) frequently was given free (because of her handicap) box seats under the stage for the Royal Opera. She took her brother along, and he would sneak up into the wings to report on the visual goings-on. He soon became the "eyes" for Agnes and the other blind children attending the opera. The other person was Froeken Kristine Jensen, the housekeeper who brought up the Melchior children after their mother died (when Lauritz was one month old). She not only encouraged her young charge to become a singer, but later she would publish cookbooks to help pay for his singing lessons.

At the age of eighteen, Melchior began seriously to take singing lessons. In 1912, he was accepted by the Royal School of the Opera in Copenhagen, where his voice now registered as a baritone. On April 2, 1913, he made his debut—as a baritone—at the Royal Opera in Copenhagen as Silvio in Ruggero Leoncavallo's *Pagliacci* and five years later made his bow as a tenor. It had been Mme. Charles Cahier, a member of a traveling opera company with Melchior, who had convinced him that he was actually a "tenor with the lid on." In 1919, Melchior was performing in concert at Queen's Hall in London, where British novelist Hugh Walpole happened to be in the audience. Walpole was impressed with the intrepid singer, and thereafter the famed writer took a great interest in Lauritz's career, giving him advice, funds, and encouragement. The two artists became good friends, and Walpole dedicated several novels to his friend, often sending him copies of his manuscripts for criticism. Thanks to his growing fame, on July 30, 1920, Melchior was invited by the inventor Guglielmo Marconi to be heard on the debut worldwide radio broadcast from the Marconi Experimental Station in Chelmsford, England. His singer partner was Dame Nellie Melba.

Walpole suggested that Lauritz go to Germany to study Wagnerian roles. Following his friend's advice, Melchior, in 1924, made his debut there as Parsifal and the same year was heard performing Siegmund in Wagner's *Die Walkure*. He made his U.S. debut at the Metropolitan Opera in February 1926 singing the title role in *Tannhauser*. By now, his first wife Inger Nathansen had died. (He had two children by her, a daughter and a son. The latter, Ib, became a film and television writer/director in the United States.)

In 1925, Lauritz had married Maria Hacker, a German film actress who specialized in daring screen acrobatics. Their first meeting had been most unusual. For one of her movie stunts, she had to jump out of an airplane with a parachute. While practicing this routine, she landed in Melchior's garden at his hunting estate at Chossenwitz. Because he was six-feet, three-inches and she was barely five-feet tall, he called his wife *Kleinchen* (little one). She became his business manager, leading Melchior to say, "I make the noise, she make the business."

The seemingly inexhaustible singer performed a wealth of roles (including both Siegmund and Siegfried in the entire Ring cycles of Richard Wagner and the title role of Tristan in Wagner's *Tristan und Isolde* at the Metropolitan Opera), quickly becoming the Metropolitan's most famous Wagnerian Heldertenor (heroic tenor). By the start of the 1940–41 Met season, he had accumulated a staggering record of Wagnerian performances: 215 Siegfrieds, 171 Tristans, 146 Siegmunds, 109 Tannhausers, 73 Lohengrins, and 57 Parsifals.

But Melchior was not content with just being on the opera stage (both at the Metropolitan and around the world). He performed in concert throughout the continental United States and in Hawaii. He was heard frequently on radio, and throughout his career he made many recordings both in America and abroad. When questioned how he maintained such a grueling momentum, he responded, "I never strain. I always sing with the interest, never use my principal." Other outlets for his boundless energy were cooking (he was famous for his oxtail soup and smorgasbord), hunting, antique collecting, teaching the therapeutic value of music to the handicapped (at Columbia University's Teachers College), and endless practical jokes. He was given the title "Singer to the Royal Court of Denmark" by the Danish King, and his birth land gave him the Knighthood and Silver Cross of Dannebrog as well as the gold medal of "Ingenio et Arti." France bestowed on him the rosette of the Legion of Honor, Bulgaria the Cross for Service to Art, and Germany-Sachen-Coburg-Gotha the Carl Eduard Medal, First Class (for his participation at the Bayreuth Festivals). He had also a Saxonian knighthood and a gold medal from Vassar College for his many services to the arts in the United States.

In 1943, Melchoir performed a joking singing commercial (for an imaginary "Pasternak's Pretzels") on Fred Allen's Sunday-night CBS network radio show. Producer Joe Pasternak heard Melchior in this antic stunt. Appreciating the tenor's sense of fun, he began negotiations to bring Lauritz to the screen, courtesy of Metro-Goldwyn-Mayer.

Melchior made his motion picture debut in *Thrill of a Romance* (1945), an Esther Williams vehicle set at a Sierra Nevada mountain lodge where she is about to start her honeymoon. Her stuffy husband is called off to Washington, DC, before their marriage begins, and a romance develops between her and a freckled-faced army major (Van Johnson). Serving as chaperone for this courtship is a sizeable cupid named Nils Knudsen (Melchior) who has a penchant for eating and singing. In between Williams's swimming, Johnson's smiling, and the swinging of Tommy Dorsey and His Band, the film newcomer sang "Please Don't Say No" and a "Serenade'" by Franz Schubert. *Variety* endorsed Melchior for "flitting in and out with his bombastic vocal gymnastics dressed up to please the masses."

On February 17, 1946, Melchior celebrated his twentieth year at the Metropolitan, appearing in several sequences from various Wagner operas. Four months later, he was seen on-screen in *Two Sisters From Boston*, playing Olaf Olstrom, a temperamental Metropolitan opera tenor. The airy plot contrivance concerned Kathryn Grayson as a chanteuse (at Jimmy Durante's Bowery saloon) who must pretend to be an opera singer when her stuffy relatives come to New York City. As such, during one of Melchior's arias, Grayson jumps forth from the chorus to join him in song. In more controlled moments, Melchior sang "The Prize Song" from Wagner's *Die Meistersinger*, as well as snatches of a created opera contrived from music by Franz Liszt and Felix Mendelssohn.

For *This Time for Keeps* (1947), Melchior was reunited with shapely Esther Williams. He received second billing as Hans Herald, a portly opera star. The setting was Michigan's Mackinaw Island, where Lauritz's rebellious son (Johnnie Johnson), a GI who wants a career in swing not opera, is romancing the star (Williams) of the Aquacaper. For variety there was Xavier Cugat and His Orchestra, razzmatazz Jimmy Durante (delightful in his murderous renditions of "Inka Dinka Do" and "The Man Who Found the Lost Chord"), Stanley Donen's choreography, and the spectacular Technicolor scenery. Jovial Melchior, who continued to kid his stage image, sang "La Donna e Mobile" from Giuseppe Verdi's *Rigoletto*, "M'Appari" from Flotow's *Martha*, an excerpt from Verdi's *Otello*, and to further demonstrate his versatility, Cole Porter's "You'd Be So Easy to Love."

For his final MGM foray, Melchior was Olaf Eriksen in *Luxury Liner* (1948). He was the opera tenor sailing for a South American tour aboard a vessel skippered by George Brent and bedeviled by Brent's stowaway teenager (Jane Powell), who insists upon playing matchmaker for her widowed dad. Aboard this "love boat" were Xavier Cugat and His Orchestra (performing "Cugat's Nougat"), the Pied Piers (harmonizing "Yes We Have No Bananas"), and classical soprano singer Marina Koshetz, who did a surprisingly effective comic rendition of Cole Porter's "I've Got You Under My Skin." Melchior was front and center to do a rendering—with Powell—of the Act II duet from Verdi's *Aida* and to solo "Come Back to Sorrento." He also managed a hearty Danish drinking song as a teasing acknowledgment of his beer-drinking fame.

Melchior, MGM, and filmgoers were all delighted with his movie forays. However, Rudolf Bing, the new manager of the Metropolitan Opera, was not. He had decided upon a new regime of discipline and decorum for all the stars of the Metropolitan. One of the prime offenders, in Bing's eyes, was Melchior, who was too accustomed to setting his own time schedule for rehearsals, and selecting his own repertoire. Bing also thought it improper for a Met luminary to be appearing in Hollywood trifles. After singing *Lohenrgrin* on February 2, 1950, the peevish Lauritz resigned from the opera company, charging Bing with a lack of "natural courtesy." (Some insist that his contract was not renewed by Bing.) It was his 513th performance of his twenty-year association with the Met.

Undaunted, Melchior continued to perform in concerts, radio, television, clubs, and recordings. He did a personal appearance turn at the Palace Theater in February 1952, and in 1953 he returned to motion pictures. The project was Paramount's *The Stars Are Singing*. It was Rosemary Clooney's film debut, and she performed her big 1951 hit "Come On-a My House," among other numbers. Melchior was mirthful Poldi, her Greenwich Village neighbor, who helps to shelter refugee Anna Maria Alberghetti in his digs. Melchior sang "Vesti la Giubba" from Leoncavallo's *Pagliacci*, the pop tune "Because," and dueted on "My Heart Is Home" with Clooney. The film was not popular, and Melchior turned back to television guesting (including an appearance on *Arthur Murray's Dance Party*). He also joined with tenor James McCracken in June 1954 for a run of Guy Lombardo's *Arabian Nights*, which played at the Jones Beach Marine Theater on Long Island.

In the late 1950s, Lauritz made a singing beer commercial that became popular. In March 1960, he sang the role of Siegmund in Wagner's *Die Walkure* with the Danish Radio Orchestra to honor his seventieth birthday. In 1963, he starred in a Carnegie Hall concert to commemorate the fiftieth anniversary of his operatic debut. That same year his wife Maria died, and in 1964 he wed his secretary Mary Markan, who was thirty-four years his junior. They divorced two years later.

It was in 1972, that the still tall, imposing (and now white-bearded) Melchior received Germany's top recording award (Deutschen Schallplattenpreises) in recognition of EMI's two-LP album *Melchior: The Wagner Tenor of the Century* (1971), composed of recordings made between 1926 and 1935. He lived in California on a five-and-one-half acre mountaintop retreat (which he named the Viking) and devoted much energy to his foundation, which nurtured new generations of heldentenors to handle the great heroic opera roles. He died on March 18, 1973, in Santa Monica, following an emergency gallbladder operation. Interment was in Copenhagen.

Filmography

Thrill of a Romance (MGM, 1945)
Two Sisters From Boston (MGM, 1946)
This Time for Keeps (MGM, 1947)
Luxury Liner (MGM, 1948)
The Stars Are Singing (Par, 1953)
Glamorous Hollywood (Col, 1958) (s)

Album Discography

LPs

Arabian Nights (Decca DL-9013) [OC]
Five Duets (RCA LM-2763)
Great Scenes From Wagner: Gotterdammerung
    (Victorla VIC-1369)
Heldentenor of the Century (RCA CRM3-0308)
The Lauritz Melchior Album (Seraphim 6086)
The Lauritz Melchior Anthology, Vol. 1 (First Recordings) (Danacord DACO-115/116)

The Lauritz Melchior Anthology, Vol. 2 (1923-26)
    (Danacord DACO-117/118)
The Lauritz Melchior Anthology, Vol. 3 (1928-
    1931) (Danacord DACO-119/120)
The Lauritz Melchior Anthology, Vol. 4 (Part 1)
    (Danacord DACO-171, 172, 173)
The Lauritz Melchior Anthology, Vol. 4 (Part 2)
    (Danacord DACO-174, 175, 176)

Lauritz Melchior: 50th Anniversary—1911-61
(Asco-121)

The Legendary Lauritz Melchior (Odyssey Y-31740)

Lohengrin/Tristan and Isolde (RCA LM-2618)

Melchior in Copenhagen (Danacord DACO-168)

Melchior: The Wagner Tenor of the Century (EMI)

Thrill of a Romance (Camden CAL-424)

Wagner: Arias (1923-36) (Pearl 228/9)

Wagner: Die Walkure (Act I) (RCA LM-2452, Seriphim 60190)

Wagner/Melchior (Victrola VIC-1500)

Wagner: Siegfried (Abridged) (Electrola/Odeon E-80744/80745)

Walkure (RCA LM-2452)

CDs

The German & Italian Repertoire (Grammofono GRM2-78504)

Lauritz Melchoir (EMI 7697892)

Lauritz Melchoir (Nimbus Prima Voce 7816)

Lauritz Melchoir (Preiser 89032)

Lauritz Melchoir II (Preiser 89068)

The Lauritz Melchoir Anthology, Vol. 1 (Danacord 2-311)

The Lauritz Melchoir Anthology, Vol. 2 (Danacord 2-313)

The Lauritz Melchoir Anthology, Vol. 3 (Danacord 2-315)

The Lauritz Melchoir Anthology, Vol. 4 (Danacord 2-317)

The Lauritz Melchoir Anthology, Vol. 5 (Danacord 3-319)

The Lauritz Melchoir Anthology, Vol. 6 (Danacord 3-322)

Lauritz Melchoir, Vol. 2 (Preiser 89086)

Legendary Repertoire (Grammofono GRM-78526) w. Kirsten Flagstad

Opera Arias (Lavial PH-5094)

Vocal Archives—Greatest Hits on Record (Enterprise VA-1113)

Wagner: Gotterdammerung (Naxos Historical 8.110041-43)

Wagner: Tristan und Isolde (Naxos Historical 8.11088-10)

Wagner: Tristan und Isolde (Video Arts 8994810042)

Wagner/Verdi/Leoncavallo (Pearl PEA-500)

Ethel Merman and Donald O'Connor in *Call Me Madam* (1953).
[Courtesy of JC Archives]

Ethel Merman

(b. Ethel Agnes Zimmermann, Astoria, Long Island, New York, January 16, 1909;
d. New York City, February 15, 1984)

When Ethel Merman sang, there was never any question who it was. She had a unique brassy voice that may have lacked subtlety but had verve, personality, and volume. She claimed her range extended from "G below to C above." As to her singing technique, this direct, meat-and-potatoes lady once remarked candidly, "I just stand up and holler and hope that my voice holds out." However, this naturalness was fine with America's great songwriters. George Gershwin told her, "Ethel, don't ever take a music lesson."

Regarding her legendary title as the Belter, composer Irving Berlin warned his confreres, "You better not write a bad lyric for Merman, because people will hear it in the second balcony." Cole Porter insisted (affectionately) that Ethel Merman sounded like a band going by. One Broadway reviewer described the vivacious five-feet six-inches songstress as "a doll from Astoria [Long Island] with a trumpet in her throat." Another said, "Even before the atomic bomb, there was Ethel Merman. She may never have flattened a playhouse but she has always shaken the rafters and laid an audience low." The Merm herself admitted of her lusty vocalizing, "If you hear me, you know who it is. I guess I'm blessed with good lungs."

She was an oversized star onstage and a high-octane gal away from the lights (she loved flea markets, thick steaks, raunchy jokes, and was a stickler for details). It was this oversized quality that confounded Hollywood. Although she made several feature films, she never became a big movie name. It was not that she was unattractive (she had a pleasing kewpie-doll look) or too mature when she first came to pictures (she was in her early twenties). It was her exultant presentation. No matter how Merman toned down her performance in front of the cameras, it was always too much for close-ups. Onstage, she had two rules about performing: "Why should I get scared, I know my lines," and "I've been told that I'm round-eyed and look surprised. What's wrong with that? Who wants a girl who knows everything." If motion pictures kept rejecting her as leading lady material, she was still the First Lady of the American Musical Theater, where she always felt more at home. She quipped, "Broadway has been very good to me, but I've been very good to Broadway too."

She was born Ethel Agnes Zimmermann on January 16, 1909, in Astoria, Long Island, New York, the daughter of Edward and Agnes Zimmermann. Her father was a bookkeeper. As a child, she exhibited vocal talents, sang in amateur talents contests, and appeared in singing entertainments at nearby army camp shows during World War I. She completed a commercial course at William Cullen Bryant High School (Long Island City) and after graduation, began working as a stenographer. It was at the B. K. Vacuum Booster Brake Company in Long Island that she persuaded her millionaire boss, Caleb Bragg, who had many acquaintances in the entertainment industry, to provide her with a letter of introduction to his friend, producer George White. This noted theatrical producer offered Ethel a job in the chorus line of his current *Scandals*. However, she wanted to sing, so she returned to her secretarial job. Nevertheless, she continued to sing at every available evening or weekend social function.

During a singing engagement at the Little Russia Club on Manhattan's West Fifty-seventh Street, Ethel came to the attention of theatrical agent Lou Irwin. He signed her to a nine-year pact and soon arranged for an audition with Warner Bros. at their Brooklyn studio on Avenue J. She was contracted for six months at $125. Merman quit her secretarial job, hoping for great things. Instead, her only acting assignment was to wear jungle garb in a studio short subject, *The Cave Club* (1930). Anxious to get her singing career moving, she negotiated her release from the contract, and she was soon appearing with the team of Lou Clayton, Eddie Jackson, and Jimmy Durante at Les Ambassadeurs Club. She performed her numbers, and they did their routines. Later, in early 1930, Merman teamed with piano player Al Siegel and appeared in vaudeville. By this time she was singing in Long Island clubs under her new shortened professional name of Ethel Merman.

While she was billed at the Brooklyn Paramount Theater Broadway producer Vinton Freedley heard Ethel sing. He had George Gershwin listen to the self-assured miss, and Ethel was hired as a rhythm singer for the upcoming *Girl Crazy*. Meanwhile, during play rehearsals, she appeared at the Palace Theater in Times Square. With songs by George and Ira Gershwin and Ginger Rogers as star, *Girl Crazy* opened at the Alvin Theater on October 14, 1930. Rogers was paid $1,500 a week, Ethel was salaried at $350 weekly. (Ethel always claimed she never said, in a jealous peak about Rogers, "She's okay, if you like talent.") With her dynamic singing of "I Got Rhythm," Ethel quickly established herself as a major Broadway force. She recalled, "I held a high C note for sixteen bars" and did several encores. Ethel said, "I was nobody before the show opened, and the next day everybody on Broadway knew about me."

Girl Crazy ran for 272 performances. During the engagement, Merman sang at the Central Park Casino (after the show) and began making movies again (during the days). This time she was under contract to Paramount Pictures and worked at their Astoria, Long Island, studio. Her first feature—as a last-minute replacement for Ruth Etting—was *Follow the Leader* (1930), a vehicle for stage comedian Ed Wynn that featured Ginger Rogers as the ingénue. Farther down in the cast was Merman, who had one song, "Mary." *Variety* noted, "Faulty make-up marked down her true appearance and the recording didn't carry her voice naturally." This lackluster feature film debut was an omen of her screen future. The studio used her thereafter in a series of musical short subjects (such as *Roaming*, 1931) and several cartoons (like *Time on My Hands*, 1932) in which Merman provided the singing voice.

On Broadway, Ethel was in *George White Scandals of 1931* (1931), in which she sang "Life Is Just a Bowl of Cherries." She teamed with Rudy Vallee for an appearance at the New York Paramount in June 1931 and the next month was doing a vaudeville stand at the Palace Theater. In the Broadway show *Take a Chance* (1932, which began as *Humpty Dumpty*), she did "You're an Old Smoothie" and turned the ballad "Eadie Was a Lady" into a boisterous number. The successful show lasted for 243 performances.

After *Take a Chance*, Ethel, accompanied by her mother, went to Hollywood for the first time. Paramount had cast her in *We're Not Dressing* (1934) starring Bing Crosby, Carole Lombard, and the team of George Burns and Gracie Allen. It was all about a cruise yacht whose passengers are shipwrecked on a desert isle. Merman was the girlfriend of eccentric Leon Errol, and together they dueted "It's Just a New Spanish Custom." The rest of the songs, however, belonged to star Crosby.

When Ethel was between Paramount pictures, Samuel Goldwyn borrowed her for *Kid Millions* (1934), his latest Eddie Cantor musical. She portrayed the practical-minded girlfriend of Warren Hymer, both out to grab the $77 million that Cantor's nebbish character has inherited. She sang "An Earful of Music," and with her energetic, comedic performance, she almost stole the picture away from Cantor and newcomers Ann Sothern and George Murphy. One of Ethel's leftover numbers ("It's the Animal in Me"), excised from *We're Not Dressing*, was pulled from the cutting-room floor and used for *The Big Broadcast of 1936* (1935). However, Paramount clearly did not know what to do with high-voltage Ethel Merman.

With William Gaxton and Victor Moore, Merman next costarred on Broadway in Cole Porter's *Anything Goes* (1934), in which she had an abundance of hit songs that became fully associated with her: "I Get a Kick Out of You," "Blow, Gabriel, Blow," and "You're the Top." The *New York Times* applauded her for "the swinging gusto of her platform style." On radio, she starred in the variety program *The Ethel Merman Show* over New York City's WABC. Before *Anything Goes* closed its 261-performance run, Merman returned to Hollywood to costar again with Eddie Cantor in *Strike Me Pink* (1936).

When that Samuel Goldwyn picture was delayed, Paramount used Merman to re-create her stage role in its movie version of *Anything Goes* (1936). Bing Crosby was the star, and while Ethel repeated some of her stage song numbers, it was his picture all the way. On the other hand, *Strike Me Pink*, which proved to be Cantor's final movie for Goldwyn and that had Sally Eilers as the comedian's leading lady, was really a Merman showcase; she sang three of the four numbers ("First You Have Me High, Then You Have Me Low," "Calabash Pipe," and "Shake It Off With Rhythm"). She was definitely the lively highlight of this meandering production, which boasted a Technicolor finale in an ice-cream factory.

On Broadway, Cole Porter's *Red, Hot and Blue!* (1936) provided Merman with such hit songs as "De-Lovely," "Ridin' High," and "Down in the Depths on the Ninetieth Floor." The production caused strategical problems of how to bill equally costars Merman and Jimmy Durante (Bob Hope was "only" featured in the musical) without offending the other. The final compromise was to have Ethel and Jimmy's names intersect on the ads, so neither party would be offended by the other having "top" billing. Not in the same leagues with her earlier vehicles, *Red, Hot and Blue!* ran a more modest 183 performances.

Socially Merman was linked with Philadelphia's burgeoning publishing tycoon Walter Annenberg, but this connection ended when she returned to Hollywood. She was now under a one-picture deal (with options) with Twentieth Century-Fox. There were then three reigning blonde musical stars at that studio: moppet Shirley Temple, songster Alice Faye, and ice-skating champion Sonja Henie. Realistically there was no way a dark-haired singing "broad" from Broadway could compete with that dynamic trio. However, the lure of a healthy salary (in comparison to her already-healthy Broadway income) bewitched Merman. She was convinced the new studio would showcase (and film) her better than had either Goldwyn or Paramount. She was quite wrong.

Happy Landing (1938) starred Sonja Henie and Don Ameche with Ethel as a distaff second banana. There were ice-skating routines by Henie, tap-dancing by the Condos brothers, and Ethel sang "Hot and Happy" and "You Appeal to Me." (Her other number, "You Are the Music to the

Words in My Heart," was cut from the release print.) Her on-screen vis-à-vis was Cesar Romero (whom publicity releases imaginatively insisted she was dating off-camera). *Variety* alerted readers about Merman's latest screen appearance that she was "only effective when she's being a tough, acquisitive, etc., or when she's singing rhythm tunes as only she can sing them."

The love triangle of *Alexander's Ragtime Band* (1938) spotlighted Don Ameche (the composer) and Tyrone Power (the bandleader) both in love with a sultry songstress (Alice Faye). Merman was on hand briefly, but nevertheless effectively, as Jerry Allen, the powerful vocalist later hired by Power's group. She sang a lilting medley of Irving Berlin tunes, including "Blue Skies," "Pack Up Your Sins," "Go to the Devil," "We're on Our Way to France," "My Walking Stick," "Everybody Step," and "Heat Wave." For her third 1938 release she was billed beneath the zany Ritz Brothers in *Straight, Place and Show*, a threadbare racetrack story that lacked class or imagination. Ethel's vocal contributions were "With You on My Mind" and "Why Not String Along With Me?" The *New York Times* branded this insipid comedy as "one of those pictures produced by the trial and error method—a trial to its audience and an error on the part of the producer." Regarding the end of this phase of her moviemaking career, Merman assessed, "I liked to be in control. You couldn't be in films. And I'd already learned that it was cold down there as the face on the cutting-room floor."

Merman was much more comfortable back on Broadway where she could perform at clubs and be the toast of the town. She dated Stork Club proprietor Sherman Billingsley and starred onstage in *Stars in Your Eyes* (1939), again teamed with Jimmy Durante. It was a near flop and closed after 127 performances. Much better was *DuBarry Was a Lady* (1939), Cole Porter's follow-up success to *Leave It to Me* (1938) that had made a Broadway star of Mary Martin. In this new musical comedy, Ethel was teamed with Bert Lahr and sang "Friendship," "Do I Love You?," and "Did You Evah?" The show featured Benny Baker and Betty Grable and went on for 178 performances. When it was made into a 1943 movie musical by MGM, Lucille Ball inherited Merman's boisterous role.

Even more successful for Merman was Cole Porter's *Panama Hattie* (1940), which gave her a rousing characterization as Hattie Maloney and such infectious numbers as "Let's Be Buddies" and "Make It Another Old-Fashioned, Please." Betty Hutton was the play's ingénue, and further down in the cast was June Allyson, who was Hutton's understudy. When *Panama Hattie* became an MGM film in 1942, Ann Sothern played Hattie Maloney. Meanwhile, in 1940 Ethel met and married actor's agent William Smith. They were divorced the next year when he returned to the West Coast to continue working in the film industry. She next wed (in 1941) Robert D. Levitt, a newspaper reporter turned publisher for Hearst Publications. Their daughter Ethel (Jr.) was born in July 1942 and their son Robert in August 1945.

Again for Cole Porter, Ethel starred in the splashy wartime musical *Something for the Boys* (1943) in which she sang "Hey, Good Lookin' " and "He's a Right Guy." By the time that musical concluded after 422 performances (Vivian Blaine starred in the 1944 movie version) Ethel was enmeshed in her bad-luck year of 1944. During that unhappy time, she had a miscarriage, separated and reconciled with her husband, and signed for and dropped out of the stage musical of *Sadie Thompson*. (June Havoc took her place, but the show closed after 32 showings on Broadway.)

Much more felicitous was Merman's association with Irving Berlin's *Annie Get Your Gun*, which registered 1,147 performances after its May 16, 1946, opening. Ethel was exuberant and rambunctious as Annie Oakley, who learns about romance ("They Say It's Wonderful"), courtship

("You Can't Get a Man With a Gun"), and career choices ("There's No Business Like Show Business"). When the hit musical went on the road with a national company, Mary Martin took over the title part; when MGM translated it to the screen in 1950, Betty Hutton was the lead. Meanwhile, in 1949 Ethel Merman had a continuing series over NBC network radio.

Merman made her television bow in a comedy pilot *Thru the Crystal Ball* (June 20, 1949), and the next year was the hostess with the mostest when she top-billed Irving Berlin's Broadway show *Call Me Madam* (1950) as an international darling of the political set, à la Perle Mesta. It was an immense hit, running for 644 performances, and she won a Tony Award for her lively performance. (She would frequently resurrect the show for stock tour appearances.) For many fans, it was a toss-up whether Ethel Merman or Mary Martin was now the First Lady of the American Musical Theater, but the two settled for a draw when they teamed to harmonize medleys of their hit show tunes on *The Ford 50th Anniversary Show* (CBS-TV, June 15, 1953). Their sensational pairing was recorded by Decca Records, and they would reteam on several occasions in future years for charity events.

In 1952, Merman divorced Levitt, and in March 1953 she married Robert F. Six, president of Continental Airlines, a love match that fell apart in the late 1950s and led to a 1960 Mexican divorce. In 1954 Ethel re-created two of her most famous roles when she starred in TV condensed versions of *Anything Goes* (NBC-TV, February 28, 1954) and *Panama Hattie* (CBS-TV, November 10, 1954).

For a change, Hollywood used Ethel (at $150,000) to re-create her starring role in *Call Me Madam* (1953), aided on-camera by George Sanders, Donald O'Connor, and Vera-Ellen. Because the picture was such a close rendition of the Broadway original, Merman shone as she never had on-screen before, delivering one of her zestiest characterizations. The same studio, Twentieth Century-Fox, also employed Ethel to costar with Dan Dailey, Donald O'Connor, Mitzi Gaynor, Johnnie Ray, and Marilyn Monroe in the vaudeville saga *There's No Business Like Show Business* (1954). The movie was gaudy, in color and in wide-screen CinemaScope. Ethel belted forth a host of Irving Berlin melodies. In this picture, she succeeded in showing the movie colony that they had been wrong to pass her off as a Broadway oddity in the 1930s. Unfortunately, however, the great age of screen musicals had passed.

The mid-1950s marriage of movie star Grace Kelly to Prince Rainier of Monaco generated a great deal of global publicity. In 1956, Howard Lindsay and Russel Crouse took advantage of that international social event to spawn *Happy Hunting*, a musical comedy starring Merman and Fernando Lamas. During the show's 412-performance run, there was a great deal of publicity about the continuing feud between the two temperamental costars. At the same time on television, Ethel went dramatic in the "Honest in the Rain" episode (CBS-TV, May 9, 1956) of *U.S. Steel Hour*.

If any show is identified completely with Ethel Merman it is the Jule Styne–Stephen Sondheim musical *Gypsy* (1959). As the stage mother (of stripper Gypsy Rose Lee) to end all stage mothers, she cavorted through the demanding role for over two years during its 702-performance engagement. She mesmerized audiences with her vitality, emotional depth, and vocal renditions of such tunes as "Some People," "You'll Never Get Away From Me," her show stopping "Everything's Coming Up Roses," and her soliloquy "Rose's Turn." The original cast album became a classic, and it won a Grammy Award. When this show went on tour, Ethel went with it. When the Broadway success became a movie, however, it was Rosalind Russell, not Ethel Merman, who starred (inadequately) with Natalie Wood as Mama Rose in *Gypsy* (1962). Losing the movie part in *Gypsy* was one of Merman's saddest professional defeats.

After Mae West and other choices bowed out of James Garner's fluffy screen comedy *The Art of Love* (1963), Ethel Merman substituted. When Stanley Kramer assembled an all-star comic entourage for his cynical *It's a Mad, Mad, Mad, Mad World* (1963), Ethel gamely accepted the role of the archetypical shrewish mother-in-law, standing out strongly in a cast of major comedians. It was during this Hollywood period that she met Oscar-winning actor Ernest Borgnine, and much to the amazement of some (and the amusement of others), they were wed on June 26, 1964, only to separate after thirty-days of marriage. They divorced in 1965.

In 1966, Irving Berlin persuaded Ethel to revive *Annie Get Your Gun* for the New York stage, and he wrote a new song especially for her, "An Old-Fashioned Wedding." The following year (March 19, 1967) on NBC-TV, she appeared in a small-screen version of the classic show. However, in 1968, her daughter Ethel (Jr.) died of an overdose of barbiturates and liquor; some insisted it was suicide.

Producer David Merrick had long wanted Ethel Merman to star in his *Hello, Dolly!* (she had been the original choice for the lead). However, it was not until March 1970 that Merman agreed to go into the long-running Broadway hit for a limited run. For her version, the songs "World Take Me Back" and "Love Look in My Window" (both cut from the original production) were added back into the proceedings. It was Merman who closed the Broadway engagement after its historic 2,844 performance run. The April 21, 1972, Tony Awards gave her a special award for her continuing contributions to the musical theater.

In the 1960s, Ethel had appeared on television in such campy assignments as *Batman* (1967) and later as a guest star on Marlo Thomas's *That Girl* (1968). In the 1970s, Merman was a frequent guest on talk shows and in such specials as *Jack Lemmon in 'S Wonderful, 'S Marvelous, 'S Gershwin* (1972), *Ed Sullivan's Broadway* (1973), and *The Ted Knight Musical Comedy Variety Special* (1976). She made an unsold comedy series pilot *You're Gonna Love It Here* in 1977 and was a guest on *The Love Boat* series in 1979 and 1980. In this series' two-hour musical special in 1982, she teamed with Ann Miller, Van Johnson, and Della Reese. When the disco craze was at its peak in the mid-1970s, Merman turned out *The Ethel Merman Disco Album*, showing she had lost little or none of her vibrato. In 1955 her first autobiography, *Who Could Ask for Anything More?* (written with Pete Martin), was published. Her second life story version, *Merman* (written with George Eels), appeared in 1978. She later made a cameo appearance in *Won Ton Ton, The Dog Who Saved Hollywood* (1976) and had a hilarious moment as herself (in pajamas!) in the zany *Airplane!* (1980).

Unfortunately, Ethel's final years were tragic. She suffered recurrently from ailments and "existed" in her midtown Manhattan hotel suite. She was later diagnosed as having a brain tumor and spent her last days incoherent and speechless. She died in her sleep on February 15, 1984, at her apartment, survived by her son. On the evening of that day, theaters on Broadway dimmed their lights at 9 P.M. in tribute to one of its greatest stars. One newspaper obituary stated, "She had a quality that can never again spring spontaneously into being—call it classicism, call it Olympian simplicity, call it God's unattainable socko, but call it Merman."

Just as the equally unique Judy Garland spawned several mimics and impersonators, so did Ethel Merman. Her greatest impressionist was Rita McKenzie, who in the late 1980s, mounted a one-woman show entitled *Call Me Ethel!* It played cabaret and summer-stock engagements around the country off and on for several years. Said the *Los Angeles Times*, "McKenzie's nuances, her assertive ruby lips, and that scrunched-up hair style is 'De-Lovely' Merman right down to 'The Animal in Me.' "

Filmography

The Cave Club (Vita, 1930) (s)
Her Future (Unk, 1930) (s)
Follow the Leader (Par, 1930)
Devil Sea (Par, 1931) (s)
Old Man Blues (Par, 1931 (s)
Roaming (Par, 1931) (s)
Let Me Call You Sweetheart (Par, 1932) (s) (voice only)
Time on My Hands (Par, 1932) (s) (voice only)
You Try Somebody Else (Par, 1932) (s) (voice only)
Ireno (Par, 1932) (s)
Be Like Me (Par, 1933) (s)
Song Shopping (Par, 1933) (s) (voice only)
We're Not Dressing (Par, 1934)
Kid Millions (UA, 1934)
The Big Broadcast of 1936 (Par, 1935)

Anything Goes (Par, 1936)
Strike Me Pink (UA, 1936)
Happy Landing (20th-Fox, 1938)
Alexander's Ragtime Band (20th-Fox, 1938)
Straight, Place and Show [They're Off] (20th-Fox, 1938)
Stage Door Canteen (UA, 1943)
Call Me Madam (20th-Fox, 1953)
There's No Business Like Show Business (20th-Fox, 1954)
The Art of Love (Univ, 1963)
It's a Mad Mad Mad Mad World (UA, 1963)
Journey Back to Oz (Filmation, 1974) (voice only)
Won Ton Ton, The Dog Who Saved Hollywood (Par, 1976)
Airplane! (Par, 1980)

Broadway Plays

Girl Crazy (1930)
George White's Scandals of 1931 (1931)
Take a Chance (1932)
Anything Goes (1934)
Red, Hot and Blue! (1936)
Stars in Your Eyes (1939)
DuBarry Was a Lady (1939)
Panama Hattie (1940)

Something for the Boys (1943)
Annie Get Your Gun (1946)
Call Me Madam (1950)
Happy Hunting (1956)
Gypsy (1959)
Annie Get Your Gun (1966) (revival)
Hello, Dolly! (1970) (replacement)

Radio Series

The Ethel Merman Program (WABC, 1935) (local)
Rhythm At Eight (CBS, 1935)

The Ethel Merman Show (NBC, 1949)

Album Discography

LPs

Alexander's Ragtime Band (Hollywood Soundstage 406) [ST]
Annie Get Your Gun (Decca DL-8001, Decca DL-9018/79018, MCA 2031) [OC]
Annie Get Your Gun (London XPS-905)
Annie Get Your Gun (RCA LOC/LSO-1123)
Anything Goes (Caliban 6043) [ST]
Anything Goes/Panama Hattie (Larynx 567, Amalgamated 144, Sandy Hooks 2043) [ST/TV]

Call Me Madam (10″ Decca DL-5465) [ST]
Call Me Madam (10″ Decca DL-5304, Decca DL-8035, Decca DL-9022/89022, MCA 1226, MCA 2055)
The Ethel Merman Disco Album (A&M 4775)
Ethel Merman/Lyda Roberti/Mae West (Col CL-2751, Columbia Special Products 2751)
Ethel Merman Onstage (X LVA-1004) w. Gertrude Niessen

Ethel Merman Sings the New Hits From "Hello, Dolly!" (Bar-Mike—no number) [OC]

Ethel Was a Lady (MCA 1804)

Ethel's Ridin' High (London XPS-909)

The Ford Fiftieth Anniversary Television Show (10″ Decca DL-7027) [ST/TV]

Greatest Hits (Reprise R/R9-6032)

Gypsy (Col OL-5420/OS-2077, Col S-32607) [OC]

Happy Hunting (RCA LOC-1026) [OC]

Her Greatest Hits (Stanyan 10070)

Kid Millions (CIF 3007) [ST]

Lee Wiley and Ethel Merman Sing Cole Porter (JC 2003)

Memories (Decca DL-9028)

Merman in Las Vegas (Reprise 6062)

Merman in the Movies, 1930-38 (Encore 101)

Merman Sings Merman (London XPS-901)

The Moon Is Your Balloon (MCA MCL-1839)

Musical Autobiography (Decca DX-153)

Panama Hattie/Anything Goes (Larynx 567, Amalgamated 144) [ST/TV]

Les Poupees de Paris (RCA LOC/LSO-1090) [OC]

Red, Hot and Blue/Stars in Your Eyes (AEI 1147) [OC]

The Return to Oz [Journey Back to Oz] (Filmation—no number) [ST/TV]

Something for the Boys (Sound/Stage 2305) [OC]

Songs She Made Famous (10″ Decca DL-5053)

Stage Door Canteen/Hollywood Canteen (Curtain Call 100/11-12) [ST]

Straight, Place and Show (Vertinge 2000) [ST]

Terms of Endearment (Cap SV-12329) [ST]

There's No Business Like Show Business (Decca DL-8091, MCA 1727) [ST]

Twelve Songs From "Call Me Madam" (MCA 1726) [ST]

The World Is Your Balloon (MCA 1839) w. Jimmy Durante, Ray Bolger

The Young Ethel Merman (JJC 3004)

CDs

Alexander's Ragtime Band (Hollywood Soundstage 4011) [ST]

American Legends (Laserlight 12-741)

Annie Get Your Gun (MCA Classics MCAD-10047, RCA 1124-2-RC) [OC]

Call Me Madam/Panama Hattie (MCA Classics MCAD-10521) [OC]

Cocktail Hour (Columbia River Entertainment Group CRG-218017)

Doin' What Comes Naturally (Jasmine JASMCD-2548)

An Earful of Merman (Movie Stars 015)

The Ethel Merman Collection—There's No Business Like Show Business (Razor & Tie RE-82144)

Ethel Merman/Lyda Roberti/Mae West (Collectors Series 75017, Columbia Special Products 2751, K-tel 75017-2)

Gypsy (Col CK-32607, Sony SK-60848) [OC]

Happy Hunting (RCA 09026-68091-2) [OC]

I Get a Kick Out of You (Pearl Flapper PEACD-7056)

I Get a Kick Out of You (Pegasus PGNCD-823)

Legendary Song Stylist (Castle MACCD-361)

Merman Sings Merman . . . and More (Spectrum 5443882)

Mermania, Vol. 1 (Harbinger 1711)

Mermania, Vol. 2 (Harbinger 1806)

Mighty Merman—22 Show Stopping Standards (Pearl 3036100032)

Red, Hot and Blue/Stars in Your Eyes (AEI 001) [OC]

Something for the Boys (AEI 004) [OC]

Stage Door Canteen (Sandy Hook CDSH-2093) [ST]

There's No Business Like Show Business (Varese Sarabande VSD-5912) [ST]

12 Songs From "Call Me Madam" (Decca 10521)

24 Classic Songs (Prism PLATCD-292)

You're the Top (ProArte/Fanfare CDD-473)

Bette Midler

(b. Bette Midler, Honolulu, Hawaii, December 1, 1945)

More than any entertainment superstar who has emerged in the last half of the twentieth century, Bette Midler's life and career has been filled with the most intriguing contradictions. She began singing professionally in the chorus of Broadway's *Fiddler on the Roof* and graduated to showcasing her vocal and comedic talents as a cabaret performer in a bathhouse catering to homosexuals. Her unconventional stage act soon was acclaimed for its bizarre mixture of versatile vocals, high camp, and zealous comedy (which often was characterized as being just plain raunchy). Bubbly Bette quickly gained fame as "The Divine Miss M." She was renowned as the racy five-feet one-inch redhead known as "The Mouth that Launched Sleaze With Ease" and "The Trash-With-Flash Lady."

However, beneath Midler's surface glitz and kitsch was an instinctive and intense dramatic songstress who provided wonderful interpretations of golden oldie songs as well as new rock numbers. She illustrated the depth of her resourcefulness in her starring movie *The Rose* (1979). Then her career fell apart suddenly. Yet in the mid-1980s everything again changed for her. She married, had a child, and starred in a string of screen comedies that did *Big Business* (1988) and made her an *Outrageous Fortune* (1987). She became one of new Hollywood's most bankable stars, solidified by *Beaches* (1988), a dramatic female buddy picture that she coproduced as well as starred in. The latter movie provided her with her first number-one hit song, "Wind Beneath My Wings," and a huge-selling sleeper LP album from the film's soundtrack. It seemed a typical abrupt career turn for the always unpredictable Ms. Midler. She soon turned into a Hollywood establishment figure herself, surprising the entertainment industry yet again.

She was born in Hawaii on December 1, 1945, the third daughter of Fred and Ruth (Schindel) Midler, who had moved to the islands from New Jersey not long before. Like her older sisters (Judy and Susan), Bette was named by the starstruck Mrs. Midler for a movie celebrity, in her case Bette Davis. (Because it was assumed that Davis pronounced her first name as "Bet," that was how the child was always called.) When Bette was a youngster, the Midlers moved back to Passaic, New Jersey (Mrs. Midler's hometown). However, after a disillusioning six months they returned to Waikiki permanently. Fred Midler was a housepainter employed frequently by the navy. As such, the Midlers had military housing (inexpensive but adequate). Later, when the government required additional space for military personnel, the Midlers were among those sent to a low-level housing development. There the Midlers were the only white people in the community's ethnic mix. The overweight, plain Bette soon convinced the neighborhood children she was Portuguese. She recalled, "It was easier than anything else. Portuguese people were accepted. Jews were not. I was an alien, a foreigner, even though I was born there." When Bette was six, the Midlers had their first son, Danny, who became mentally retarded due to an ailment during infancy.

Always the outsider at school, Bette found a degree of acceptance by becoming the class comedienne. She won a school talent show singing "Lullaby of Broadway," and that became her

Bette Midler in *The Rose* (1979).
[Courtesy of JC Archives]

standard performance number. When she was twelve, she attended her first theater show, reinforcing her love of show business and her determination to follow it as a career and as an escape from her stifling home life. In her senior year at Radford High in Honolulu, she had the lead in the class production of *When Our Hearts Were Young and Gay*. After graduating in 1963, she spent another summer working in a pineapple factory. That fall she enrolled at the University of Hawaii as a drama major, but soon left. In 1965, Julie Andrews and company were filming *Hawaii* on location, and Bette got an extra's job playing a seasick missionary's wife. When an additional extra's role opened up in the picture, she went to Hollywood for the shoot. It provided her with sufficient funds ($1,000) to try stage work in New York. She had decided she was not conventionally pretty enough to be in the movies. Nonetheless, she told her family, "I'm gonna be a star!"

To support herself in Manhattan, Bette held a variety of jobs, as a typist, a hatcheck girl, a department store sales clerk, and a go-go dancer in Union City, New Jersey. She won roles in children's theater (usually as a witch) and then was cast in the Tom Eyen play *Miss Nevertiti Regrets* at the Cafe la Mama. She worked in the Catskill Mountains in *An Evening of Tradition* (based on stories by Paddy Chayefsky and Sholom Aleichem) and sang in showcases. Off-Broadway she was *Sinderella Revisited*, a Tom Eyen play that also was modified into a laundered matinee version for children called *Cinderella Revisited*. After many months of auditioning, in 1966 Bette was given a chorus part in the hit Broadway musical *Fiddler on the Roof*. She also understudied the role of Tevye's eldest daughter. Later she got to play the role, with Adrienne Barbeau and Tanya Everett as her sisters. Altogether she was in *Fiddler* for three years. (It was during this period that her oldest sister Judy came to New York to see the show and was killed in a freak car accident.)

After this long run in a small part on Broadway at frustratingly small pay, Midler left the musical. She had already begun performing on talent nights at Manhattan clubs. At one of the cabarets, the Improv, the club pianist was Barry Manilow. He and Bette became friendly, and he soon become her accompanist. She developed an act that featured nostalgic songs and an eccentric wardrobe, which ranged from toreador pants to sequined gowns from past eras. Meanwhile, she joined the cast of the off-Broadway rock musical *Salvation*.

In July 1970, at $50 a weekend, Bette was hired to sing at the Continental Baths, a gay bathhouse on Manhattan's upper westside. With Barry Manilow as her accompanist, she began a long-run engagement there, developing her act to include audacious, bawdy comedy and altering her costuming to 1950s' flashy trash. When she was a guest on Johnny Carson's *Tonight Show* that summer she told the TV host, "I'm probably the only female singer in America who sings in a Turkish Bath. It's a health club." On a later appearance on his show, Carson and his entourage (Ed McMahon, Doc Severinsen, and guest Orson Bean) became her backup singers, the Bang Bangs. By the fall of 1970, Bette was appearing as Jackie Vernon's opening act at Mr. Kelly's Club in Chicago. She sang "Sh-Boom," wore a purple dress, and had a mass of flaming orange hair. The audience was bewildered by her stream-of-consciousness comedy patter and her outrageousness.

Midler continued to perform at the Continental Baths, dressing up in crazy outfits and sporting thick platform shoes. (In the process, she did a wonderful imitation of Carmen Miranda.) In the spring of 1971, she played the Acid Queen and Mrs. Walker for the Seattle Opera Company's production of *Tommy*. She was again at Mr. Kelly's in Chicago, this time as the opening act for comedian Mort Sahl. By now her theme song had become "Friends." She then was hired to appear at the Downstairs at the Upstairs in New York City. Her two-week engagement turned into a ten-week stand, often filled with celebrity audiences. She made one of her final appearances at the Continental Baths in February 1972 and then went on the road. As part of her troupe, she had Barry Manilow as pianist in the small band and backup singers. The singing trio of backup singers was called the Harlettes (originally Melissa Manchester, Merle Miller, and Gail Kantor). Bette continued to perfect her routines, which one critic called "madcap, manic and melodious." She would skitter across the stage in high heels, stop, and say, "I think it's time for a little vulgarity. What do ya say, folks?" Next she would recite with relish one of her outrageous Sophie Tucker jokes, and then, with eyes wide and other very expressive facial gestures, she would punctuate audience laughter with, "Ooooh. I didn't say that. . . . I never said that!"

In April 1972, Midler was Johnny Carson's opening act at the Sahara Hotel in Las Vegas. She had a successful Carnegie Hall concert and later that summer was performing at the Schaefer Music Festival in Central Park. She had a new manager, Aaron Russo, developing with him a battling relationship that also dominated her private life, although he was then married. Her first album—*The Divine Miss M*—was released by Atlantic Records in November 1972, and it rose to number nine on the charts. The disc contained her campy "Leader of the Pack" and the rhythmic "Chapel of Love." Two singles from the LP became major hits: "Do You Want to Dance?" and the even more popular "Boogie Woogie Bugle Boy." The latter was her tribute to the Andrews Sisters, and the song did much to revive interest in that vintage singing group. Meanwhile, she made a coast-to-coast U.S. tour. In Los Angeles she played at the Troubadour, and on New Year's Eve, 1972, in New York she appeared at Philharmonic Hall, part of the prestigious Lincoln Center complex.

In 1973, Bette continued to tour, including a sold-out engagement at the Dorothy Chandler Pavilion in Los Angeles. She was on a Burt Bacharach TV special in February 1973 (ABC-TV) with Peter Ustinov and Stevie Wonder. Her new backup Harlettes were Charlotte Crossley, Sharon Redd, and Robin Grean, and the extended tour included both Honolulu and Los Angeles's Universal Amphitheater. At the latter engagement, Maxene and Patty Andrews (the surviving members of the three Andrews Sisters) came up onstage to join Bette for "Boogie Woogie Bugle Boy."

In December 1973, Midler began a three-week engagement at New York's Palace Theater, a near one-woman show where she sang Kurt Weill's "Surabaya Johnny," "Hello in There," and all her standards, including a production number of "Lullaby of Broadway." She told vulgar jokes, wittily trashed the rich element in the audience, and was a sold-out hit. (A few weeks later at the nearby Winter Garden Theater, Liza Minnelli had an equally packed engagement, making the two diverse personalities rivals for being the *new* Miss Show Business.) In early 1974, Bette won a Grammy Award as Best New Artist for her debut LP, and she was given a special Tony Award (like Liza Minnelli) for her Broadway concert engagement. Midler was also named one of the ten worst-dressed women of the year by California designer, Mr. Blackwell. He described her as "potluck in a laundromat." It all added to her allure, as did the success of her second album *Bette Midler* (1973).

In 1974, Bette spent several months in Europe recovering from emotional overstress. It was also the year that a low-class religious satire, *The Divine Mr. J,* opened. Bette had played the screen role of a hip Virgin Mary in this production for $250 in 1971, a 16mm amateurish production that wasn't released until the spring of 1974. By then its marketing campaign was altered to exploit Midler as its "star" in her film debut. The singer asked fans not to attend the movie, which had a short run in New York City, with Midler's followers picketing the theater. Later in the year, Bette interviewed with director Mike Nichols about costarring with Warren Beatty and Jack Nicholson in *The Fortune* (1975). However, it was Stockard Channing who won the role in this unsuccessful movie comedy.

Along with Elton John and Flip Wilson, Bette guested on the Cher special on CBS-TV (February 12, 1975). Barry Manilow had already left her entourage by the time Midler opened in the spring of 1975 at New York City's Minskoff Theater in Bette Midler's *Clams on the Half Shell Revue*. The expensively mounted production featured such outré items as Bette emerging from a huge clamshell as a mermaid, singing in the arms of King Kong, and zipping across the stage in a wheelchair. Her ten-week stand, which included characterization skits, grossed nearly $2 million. In 1976 she went on *The Depression Show* tour, a condensed version of her *Clams on the Half Shell* production, adding a Statue of Liberty tribute for the bicentennial. When her third album, *Songs for the New Depression,* was released she called it a "whimsical, reactionary album." Most critics disliked it. It reached only twenty-seventh place on the charts.

Her next tour included Caesars Palace in Las Vegas where, as had become a tradition, audience reaction was not especially positive. While in Cleveland, her show was taped live for presentation on the HBO Cable channel on June 19, 1976. This airing of *The Fabulous Bette Midler Show* allowed home audiences to witness the unexpurgated Bette Midler as network TV censors would never have permitted her to appear. It was far more engaging than her conventional appearance on a Neil Sedaka television special that September.

Plans for Bette to appear in 1977 with the New York City Ballet in Kurt Weill's light opera *The Seven Deadly Sins* did not materialize. By now actor Peter Riegert had replaced Aaron Russo as her steady boyfriend, and she appeared, along with Rosemary Clooney, Debbie Reynolds, Bob Hope, Donald O'Connor, and others on Bing Crosby's *A 50th Anniversary Gala* (CBS-TV, March 28, 1977). Her two-record *Live at Last* (live) album contained the song "You're Moving Out Today," written by Carole Bayer Sager, Bruce Roberts, and Bette. As a change of venue and format in late 1977, Bette went on a tour of small clubs throughout the United States. Nevertheless, she remained her usual self-deprecating self. (Among her typical quips was "They were going to star me in a movie called *Close Encounters of the Worst Kind*, but I declined.") She traded insults with the Harlettes and sang her assortment of songs, including heartfelt ballads. Then she starred in her first network special, *Ol' Red Hair Is Back* (NBC-TV, December 8, 1977), and although she toned down her act, she was sufficiently unique to gain audience response. However, her fifth album, *Broken Blossom*, released in December 1977, sold poorly.

In 1978, Midler embarked on an extensive world tour with the New Harlettes (Linda Hart, Katie Sagal, and Frannie Eisenberg), which included stopovers in England, Denmark, Sweden, Germany, France, and Australia. By early 1979, Bette had severed her working relationship with Aaron Russo, at about the same time as her mother's death from cancer (January 1979). That spring, Bette's new album, *Thighs & Whispers,* was released. Years later she would admit, "By that point, I was just grabbing at straws." She came to consider the disco novelty number "Nights in Black Leather" as the low point of her recording career. However, another single from the album, "Married Men," reached number forty on the charts, her first single hit in nearly six years. After more play dates (the abbreviated tour was called *Bette! Divine Madness*), Bette Midler made her real feature film debut.

In the 1970s there had been talk of Midler starring in screen biographies of Sophie Tucker and Texas Guinan, and her manager had turned down roles for her in *Nashville* (1975), *King Kong* (1976), and *Foul Play* (1978). For Midler, her role as the tragic Janis Joplin–like singer in *The Rose* (1979) was a tour de force. It was an intense dissection of a rock singer on a self-propelled joyride to self-destruction. *Variety* reported, "It's a tribute to the talent of Midler herself that she makes a basically unsympathetic and unlikable character attractive at all." For her exhaustive and exhausting performance, she was Oscar nominated but lost the Best Actress Award to Sally Field of *Norma Rae*. The soundtrack album to *The Rose* reached number twelve on the charts, and two Midler singles from the movie, "When a Man Loves a Woman" and "The Rose," were on the top-forty charts. She won a Grammy Award for Best Contemporary/Pop Female Solo Vocal for the song "The Rose."

The Rose grosssed over $19 million in domestic film rentals, but Bette could not find an appropriate follow-up property. (Concerning this bleak period, she observed later, "Once I saw myself on the big screen and had my dream, I was simply lost. There was no new goal.") She took her *Divine Madness* show to Broadway for six weeks in 1980 and for a $850,000 fee re-created it on film (1980) in concert at the Pasadena Civic Auditorium. However, neither proved to be box-office bonanzas. The soundtrack album for *Divine Madness* reached number thirty-four on the charts, and the single "My Mother's Eyes" reached the number thirty-nine spot. Her saucy memoirs of her recent European tour, *A View From a Broad*, was published in the spring of 1980. Despite the fact that it contained a lot of imagined happenings to enliven the tome, it was a best-seller.

Much has been written about Bette Midler's *The Jinx* (1982), a trouble-plagued movie that was ridiculed as entertainment and did extremely poor business commercially. It costarred Ken Wahl in a black comedy set in and around Lake Tahoe with Midler as the country singer anxious for the demise of her obnoxious blackjack dealer lover (Rip Torn). The experience left Midler with a nervous breakdown and with no further screen offers. (She recalled, "That was the first time I realized that I was not as divine as I thought I was.") She went on the road with *De Tour*, which reflected a strong New Wave music influence. But her show still had such rowdy numbers as "Pretty Legs and Great Big Knockers." For her December 31, 1982, appearance at the Universal Amphitheater, Barry Manilow reunited with her onstage. Her album *No Frills* fared badly, but her children's book, *The Saga of Baby Divine* (1983), was number three on the *New York Times* fiction best-seller list. To continue reaching her audience, Bette made the "Beat of Burden" video and single record in January 1984.

In December 1984 in Las Vegas, Midler married Martin von Haselberg, a Los Angeles commodities trader. (He was also a "performance" artist under the name Harry Kipper.) After nearly three years of no film activity, she returned to picture making. She was to have starred in *My Girdle Is Killing Me*, about a Hollywood star down on her luck. Instead, she was hired for the Paul Mazursky comedy *Down and Out in Beverly Hills* (1986), a wacky entry based on a French film. She played an intense Beverly Hills housewife who sets a chain of amusing reverberations into play when she allows a skid-row bum (Nick Nolte) to stay in the guest bedroom of her mansion. The picture grossed $28.277 million in domestic film rentals and did much to revive the film careers of Richard Dreyfuss (as her on-camera husband) and Midler.

Also for Touchstone Films and Buena Vista Releasing (all part of the Walt Disney Organization), Bette starred in the caper comedy *Ruthless People* (1986). She was the obnoxiously loud but still good-hearted wife that philandering spouse Danny DeVito refuses to ransom from kidnappers. It successfully exploited Bette's raucous comedy style, and the movie grossed $31.443 in domestic film rentals. Her debut comedy album *Mud Will Be Flung Tonight* was released in 1986. In November that year, she gave birth to her first child, Sophie Frederica Alohani von Haselberg. ("She is not named after Sophie Tucker, contrary to what people might think," insisted Midler.) Shortly before her father died in 1986, Bette and he were reconciled after years of strained relations.

The R-rated *Outrageous Fortune* (1987) paired Midler with Shelley Long as two diverse personalities both in love with a seemingly nice school teacher (Peter Coyote). Its popularity led Touchstone Pictures to sign Midler to a long-term, multiple-picture deal in which she was to headline three films as well as to develop/produce/star in additional properties. For *Big Business* (1988), both she and Lily Tomlin played twins, leading to a madcap cascade of slapstick errors. In the full-length animated feature *Oliver & Company*, loosely inspired by Charles Dickens's *Oliver Twist*, Bette provided the voice for the poodle Georgette and sang "Perfect Isn't Easy." Her March 1988 HBO Cable special, *Bette Midler's Mondo Beyondo*, featured her husband Martin von Haselberg in one of its more infantile skits. By July of 1988, Midler had extended her pact with Touchstone Pictures for four additional motion pictures, making her one of the most successful film stars in contemporary Hollywood.

Midler's reputation was capped by her bravura performance in *Beaches* (1988), which offered her as C. C. Bloom, a pop singer whose friendship over the decades with Barbara Hershey forms the film's texture. This mishmash of a movie received very mixed responses, but the reviews for Midler were extremely positive. (*People* magazine stated, "It's hard to think of a more enticing invitation to a movie than these two words: Bette Midler.") The project was packaged by All Girl Productions, a production company that Midler formed with Margaret Jennings South and Bonnie Bruckheimer-Martell. The picture grossed a strong $55 million in its first twenty-five weeks of national distribution. The soundtrack album rose to number two in the charts, and her hit single from it, "Wind Beneath My Wings," reached to number one, displacing Madonna's "Like a Prayer" from the top spot. (Thereafter the song became a trademark number for the songstress in her club acts or TV appearances.) In early 1989, Midler filmed *Stella*, the latest remake of that archetypical tearjerker *Stella Dallas*. The movie proved to be an uncomfortable vehicle for the leading lady, who struggled between comedy and pathos in this lumbering update of the classic drama of mother love.

As Bette entered the 1990s, she was in her mid-forties, a difficult transition time for most actresses. Her new album was *Some People's Lives* on the Atlantic label. Brian Buss (www.allmusic .com) judged it "one of the singer's strongest collections." The disc's hit single, "From a Distance," won a Grammy Award.

It was nearly two years before the star's next film, *For the Boys*, reached the screen. The scenario traced her life as a World War II USO singer and her struggling relationship with a chauvinistic, self-absorbed comedian (James Caan). The expensively produced vehicle grossed a mild $17.86 million at the domestic box office, and the soundtrack album did not fare well, either. After the movie's release, entertainer Martha Raye sued Midler and Twentieth Century-Fox, alleging that the story line had been stolen from Martha's own life. (Raye, then in declining health, lost the court action.) Also that year Bette joined Woody Allen in *Scenes From a Mall*. With Paul Mazursky directing, it proved to be a misfire in which neither Bette (playing second fiddle to Woody) nor Allen (who had rarely been directed by anyone other than himself) proved able to overcome the predictable tale of a Los Angeles couple celebrating their anniversary and finding their marriage falling apart.

The highlight of 1992 for Bette was her appearance on May 21, 1992, on the next-to-last episode of Johnny Carson's nearly thirty-year reign as king of *The Tonight Show*. Midler sang a comic, touching song to Carson, causing the usually unemotional talk show host to become misty-eyed.

Hocus Pocus (1993) was envisioned by the Walt Disney Studio as family entertainment, but the resultant story of three ancient witches (Midler, Sarah Jessica Parker, and Kathy Najimy) who are brought back to contemporary America was an awkward blend of comedy and horror. It grossed an unremarkable $39.514 million in domestic distribution. Bette fared much better with her next project, a TV adaptation of the stage musical *Gypsy*.

Many years had passed since Ethel Merman struck Broadway gold with the musical *Gypsy* (1959), and Rosalind Russell and Natalie Wood had starred with less effect in the movie adaptation (1962). However, both productions—especially Merman's—had become benchmarks of musical comedy. Nevertheless, fearless as always, on December 12, 1993, Midler played the demanding role of Mama Rose in CBS-TV's three-hour telefeature production of the Arthur Laurents story line with music by Jule Styne and lyrics by Stephen Sondheim. She sang such numbers as "Some People," "Everything's Coming Up Roses," and "Rose's Turn." An approving *Daily Variety* enthused, "Midler's Rose is explosive, riveting and impossible, yet impossible not to love. Younger and feistier than Merman's Rose, with much of the insanity that marked Tyne Daly's 1989 stage revival Midler presents a stage mother who loves and tortures her two daughters with equal vigor." For her performance, Bette won a Golden Globe, and the soundtrack album did well with music buyers. Also in 1993, her compilation album, *Experience the Divine* (Atlantic), sold over one million copies. Finally, that year, Bette, having trimmed down her figure, was on tour, after a decade away from the concert stage. On the road, accompanied by her tacky jokes, sentimental ballads, and outrageous backup group, she played a thirty-five date engagement at New York's Radio City Music Hall, and by that mid-December was doing her thing at the Universal Amphitheater in Los Angeles.

In the mid-1990s, when not involved in promoting her environmental causes, Bette was touted to star/produce such screen vehicles as *My Fair Larry* (a comedic update of *Pygmalion*), a remake of the 1966 Walter Matthau–Jack Lemmon classic dark comedy *The Fortune Cookie* with Candice Bergen as her costar, the comedy *Scrambled Eggs*, a big-screen version of the old TV series *Green Acres* (1965–71), a musical biography of 1920s club hostess Texas Guinan, and a screen adaptation of Iris Rainer Dart's novel *Show Business Kills*. None of these projects came to be. Instead, the Divine Miss M released another Atlantic album (1995's *Bed of Roses*), a ballad-heavy release, which went gold in sales. The next year, she joined with Goldie Hawn and Diane Keaton for *The First Wives Club*, a raucous comedy of three women getting even with their past mates. Made on a $28 million budget, the surprise hit grossed over $105.444 million in domestic distribution. With the feature such a success, there was talk of a sequel (which has yet to come to be), and new projects for each of the leading ladies who had proved they were still box-office worthy.

However, Midler's follow-up movie was a disappointment. It was the trite domestic comedy *That Old Feeling* (1997). She was far more effective in her on-camera observations on unorthodox comedy writer/comedian Bruce Vilanch in the documentary *Get Bruce* (1999). Bette had a fleeting cameo in the telefeature *Jackie's Back* (Lifetime Cable, June 14, 1999), a mockumentary starring Jenifer Lewis. Meanwhile, Midler had success with her album *Bathhouse Betty* (1998), released on Warner Bros. Records. The disc, which reflected the raucous Bette of her continental Bathhouse days of decades ago, went gold. In October 1999, she began a thirty-two city *Divine Miss Millennium* tour.

The black comedy *Drowning Mona* (2000) cost $16 million to make and included in its cast Danny DeVito, Jamie Lee Curtis, and Neve Campbell. Midler played the meanest woman in her small town. The repercussions from her death formed the plotline. With its mixture of acting styles and meandering plot, it failed to capture moviegoers' attention. Earlier, in 1998, Michelle Lee had starred in a modestly well-received telefeature about flamboyant novelist Jacqueline Susann (1926–1974), the famous author of *The Valley of the Dolls* (1968) and other trashy best-sellers. In what could have been effective casting, Bette was hired to essay the distinctive writer in a big-screen biography. However, *Isn't She Great* (2000), in which Nathan Lane was badly miscast as her husband/manager, was artistically and financially a bust. Ironically, only in her uncredited cameo in Mel Gibson's *What Women Want* (2000) did Midler get to be in a screen hit that year.

Finding leading assignments in movies harder to obtain now that she was in her mid-fifties, Midler succumbed to starring in a TV series. At one point she was to headline *The Harlettes*, playing the leader of a singing group. That did not come to be, nor did a projected series that would have been a mix of *Topper* (1937) and *The Ghost and Mrs. Muir* (1947), each of which had been TV series themselves; Bette would have played a kvetchy ghost. Instead on October 11, 2000, she debuted on CBS-TV in *Bette* (which her All-Girls Production helped to produce). In this half-hour comedy she played—of all things—herself, a Beverly Hills Jewish matron/celebrity who must balance the often conflicting needs of her career and family. The unoriginal sitcom only came to life when the half-hour show allowed Bette to break into song. Soon after it went on the air, there was no doubt that the show was a flop in the making. Changing cast members did not help, nor did Midler's rather unprecedented badmouthing the series in any public forum she could. By March 7, 2001, after seventeen aired episodes, the show was cancelled. During this troubled point in her career, Midler released her second Warner Bros. album, *Bette*. For the 2002 film, *Divine Secrets of the Ya-Ya Sisterhood*, Midler served as co-executive producer but was not part of the on-screen cast.

Having survived several fallow periods and come back with a vengeance, it was likely that Bette Midler would hit her artistic stride yet again. Some years before she told the *Washington Post*: "You can get trampled on every step of the way. I find it amazing that I keep picking myself up and dusting myself off and keep plowing on."

Filmography

Hawaii (UA, 1966)
Scarecrow in a Garden of Cucumbers (New Line, 1971) (voice only)
The Divine Mr. J (National Entertainment, 1974)
The Rose (20th-Fox, 1979)
Divine Madness! (WB, 1980) (also script)
Jinxed (MGM/UA, 1982)
Down and Out in Beverly Hills (BV, 1986)
Ruthless People (BV, 1986)
Outrageous Fortune (Touchstone, 1987)
Big Business (Touchstone, 1988)
Oliver & Co. (BV, 1988) (voice only)
Beaches (Touchstone, 1988) (also producer)
Stella (Touchstone, 1989)
For the Boys (20th-Fox, 1991) (also producer)

Scenes From a Mall (Touchstone, 1991)
Hocus Pocus (BV, 1993)
Gypsy (CBS-TV, 12/12/93)
Get Shorty (MGM, 1995)
The First Wives Club (Par, 1996)
That Old Feeling (Univ, 1997)
Get Bruce (Miramax, 1999) (documentary)
Jackie's Back! (Lifetime Cable, 6/14/99)
Fantasia 2000 (BV, 1999) (cohost)
Drowning Mona (Destination Films, 2000)
Isn't She Great (Univ, 2000)
What Women Want (Par, 2000)
Crossover (Independent Film Channel Cable, 9/24/2001) (documentary)
Divine Secrets of the Ya-Ya Sisterhood (WB, 2002) (executive producer only)

Broadway Plays

Fiddler on the Roof (1966) (replacement)

TV Series

Bette (CBS-TV, 2000–2001) (also executive producer, music, song)

Some of My Best Friends (2001) (executive producer only)

Album Discography

LPs

Beaches (Atlantic SD-81933) [ST]
Broken Blossom (Atlantic SD-19151)
Bette Midler (Atlantic SD-7270)
Clams on the Half Shell (Atlantic SD2-9000) [OC]
Divine Madness (Atlantic SD-16022) [ST]
The Divine Miss M (Atlantic QD/SD-7238)
Live at Last (Atlantic SD-9000)

Mud Will Be Flung Tonight (Atlantic 81291)
No Frills (Atlantic 80070)
Oliver & Co. (Walt Disney Records 012) [ST]
The Rose (Atlantic SD-16010) [ST]
Songs for the New Depression (Atlantic SD-18155)
Thighs & Whispers (Atlantic SD-16004)

CDs

Bath House Bette (WB 47078, WB WDCR-2170)
Beaches (Atlantic 81973-2) [ST]
Beaches/Some People's Lives/Divine Madness (Musicrama)
Bette (WB 47873)
Bette Midler (Atlantic 82779-2)
Bette of Roses (Atlantic 82823-2)
Broken Blossoms (Atlantic 82780-2)
The Divine Collection (Atlantic 82497-2)
Divine Madness (Atlantic 82781-2) [ST]
The Divine Miss M (Atlantic 82785-2)
Experience the Divine: Greatest Hits (Atlantic 80667-2, WEA WTVD-80667)
For the Boys (Atlantic 82329-2) [ST]

Gypsy (Atlantic 82551-2) (ST/TV)
Live at Last (Atlantic 81461-2)
Mud Will Be Flung Tonight (Atlantic 81291-2)
No Frills (Atlantic 82783-2)
Random Acts (WB)
The Rose (Atlantic 82778-2) [ST]
Sing-A-Long, Vol. 1 (Priddis Music 1024)
Sing-A-Long, Vol. 2 (Priddis Music 1052)
Sing-A-Long, Vol. 3 (Priddis Music 1078)
Some People's Lives (Atlantic 82129-2)
Songs for the New Depression (Atlantic 82784-2)
That Old Feeling (MCA MCAD-11589) [ST]
Thighs & Whispers (Atlantic 87286-2)

Ann Miller

(b. Lucille Ann Collier, Houston, Texas, April 12, 1923)

Brassy, lacquered, robust, perpetually girlish: These descriptions clung to Ann Miller—she of the golden gams—who tap-danced vigorously across stage and screen for many decades, outlasting most of her performing contemporaries. Despite the insistence by some that she was high camp, Miller always remained as professionally enthusiastic as when she began in the business in the early 1930s. She was a club performer and a contractee at two lesser studios (RKO and Columbia) before, midway in her screen career, coming to MGM. She was ready, willing, and able to shine. However, by 1948, Metro was in decline and there were few musicals being produced on the lot. She, as always, made the best of the situation.

Ann Miller's signatures were her fabulous legs (syndicated columnist Walter Winchell tagged her "Legs Miller"), a distinctive terpsichorean strut, a vibrant song style, an extra-wide smile, and that gushy belief in herself. She was renowned for being charmingly lightheaded. When learning they were casting *Ari*, the stage version of *Exodus*, she called her agent and said, "If they're going to do a musical about Ari, I want to play Jackie Onassis." She admitted that once when she injured her foot and went to the doctor for an X ray, she was given a form to complete. "It said 'occupation' and I didn't know whether I should write, singer, dancer, or actress. So I just wrote STAR."

She was born April 12, 1923 (*not*, she insists, 1919 as her studio biography once listed) in Houston, Texas. Her father (John Alfred Collier) was a criminal lawyer. Her mother (Clara), from whom she inherited her enthusiasm and naiveté, sent the girl to dancing school at the age of three to cure a case of childhood rickets. She soon was proficient at "quick-style" dance numbers and was performing at local functions. At age ten, she placed first in a Big Brothers' personality contest. When Lucille (as she was christened) was eleven, her parents divorced. Clara, who was nearly totally deaf and could not hold a job, dreamed of making her child a dancing star, and the two moved to Hollywood. Once in Los Angeles all they seemed to find was an occasional dancing engagement at the Rotary or Lions Club. Piano accompanist Harry Fields suggested that underaged Lucille change her name to Anne (with an "e") Miller. Billed as a "tap-dancer with a new style," she won a talent contest, giving her a two-week engagement at $50 weekly. With strategic padding to fill out her figure, thirteen-year-old Anne was hired for a brief chorus job in *Devil on Horseback* (1936), a minor contemporary Western at Grand National Pictures.

Later, in 1936, Anne accepted a dancing job at the Bal Tabarin Club in San Francisco. During her three-week stand there, Lucille Ball (then a blonde actress at RKO) happened to be in the audience, accompanied by Benny Rubin (at the time a studio talent scout). Ball thought Miller should be screen-tested. She was, and RKO hired her at $150 weekly. Her new screen name was Ann Miller. She made her debut in *New Faces of 1937*. She had no dialogue, just tap-danced a bit in her inimitable fast style. (There were inevitable comparisons to MGM's reigning tap-dancing star, Eleanor Powell, whose style was more athletic and less theatrical.)

Gene Autry, Ann Miller, and Jimmy Durante in *Melody Ranch* (1940).
[Courtesy of JC Archives]

In the glamour-packed *Stage Door* (1937), Ann had lines but no dancing, while in *Radio City Revels* (1938), which featured Milton Berle, she began to shine. *Variety* enthused of the new dancing personality, "She carries the romantic interest well, is a cute charming personality and has a lot of poise. . . . Miss Miller is a right smart tapster. . . ." She was loaned to Columbia Pictures for the classic *You Can't Take It With You* (1938). Director Frank Capra recalled, "She played Alice's [Jean Arthur] sister, Essie, the awkward Pavlova, played her with the legs of Marlene [Dietrich], the innocence of Pippa, and the brain of a butterfly that flitted on its toes."

Ann and Lucille Ball were merely window dressing in the Marx Brothers's less-than-hilarious *Room Service* (1938), Miller's seventh and final RKO picture, where she was earning $250 weekly. She was caught in a career rut, and her agents convinced her that she needed a Broadway success to reestablish her movie worth. She left RKO and went to New York to join Willie and Eugene Howard, Ella Logan, and the Three Stooges in *George White's Scandals of 1939*. It opened on August 28, 1939, and closed less than four months later. However, the revue served its attention-gathering purpose well. (Robert Coleman of the *New York Daily Mirror* stated that "Ann is terrific.

She's an eye tonic, has loads of style and a personality that whirls with hurricane force across the footlights.") Now, there was renewed studio interest in her. She chose to return to RKO for third-featured billing in *Too Many Girls* (1940), starring Lucille Ball, Frances Langford, and introducing Desi Arnaz. The musical proved unremarkable and did little for Miller's career. She moved over to a lesser studio (Republic Pictures) to make an ambitious (by that film company's standards) Gene Autry Western, *Melody Ranch* (1940). On-screen, Ann had to compete for audience attention with Champion the horse and the comedy antics of Jimmy Durante.

In 1941, Ann signed a one-picture contract at Columbia. *Time Out for Rhythm* teamed her with Rudy Vallee. She was given three dance routines, choreographed by LeRoy Prinz, including a prime solo dance number, "A-Twiddlin' My Thumbs." With a favorable response to this "nervous A" (her words), movie studio head Harry Cohn signed Ann to a long-term contract. Rita Hayworth may have been the queen of the studio's lavish musicals, but Ann was around to highlight the minor musical quickies for which the lot was famous. After playing in a Western with Glenn Ford, *Go West, Young Lady* (1941), she was loaned to Paramount for two pictures. In the wacky service comedy *True to the Army* (1942), she took attention away from costars Judy Canova and Allan Jones with her amazingly fast tap-dancing. ("Wait until you hear her answer a machine gun with taps," the *Hollywood Reporter* alerted.) When her next picture, *Priorities on Parade* (1942)—about working women in war plants—debuted on Broadway, Ann starred in the stage show at the flagship Paramount Theater.

Years later, Ann's *Reveille With Beverly* (1943), about a female radio disc jockey, would be best remembered for a brief appearance on-screen by the young Frank Sinatra. Nonetheless, she was very proficient in her obligatory tap-dancing routine, "Thumbs Up and V for Victory." In *Hey, Rookie* (1944), she did her version of a harem dance ("Streamlined Sheik"), while in *Jam Session* (1944) she was outnumbered by six dance bands (including Louis Armstrong's) but tapped her way through the "No Name Jive" number. Costing around $400,000 each, all of Ann Miller's Columbia features made money. They gave her ample opportunity to dance and highlighted her gorgeous figure (usually in black abbreviated tights). Her more-than-competent singing, such as "You Came Along, Baby" in *Eadie Was A Lady* (1945), was often overlooked because of her flashy toe-tapping. In *Eve Knew Her Apples* (1945), a poor remake of *It Happened One Night*, she did not dance at all, but had four pleasing song numbers, including "I'll Remember April."

Columbia was planning finally to star Ann in a major screen musical, the Technicolor *The Petty Girl*, when she and the studio clashed. She had married millionaire industrialist Reese Llewellyn Milner on February 16, 1946, and he insisted she abandon her movie career. Columbia's Harry Cohn sued her and won a $150,000 judgment. She settled the dispute by starring in *The Thrill of Brazil* (1946). She was now pregnant, but, according to Ann, her husband in a drunken rage beat her and threw her down the stairs. She lost her baby and broke her back. She and Milner divorced and her studio contract lapsed.

MGM's Louis B. Mayer had long been an admirer of Ann Miller. The two had been on the social scene together before her marriage. He had been particularly impressed by her vivacious performance in *Eadie Was a Lady*, playing a Boston coed who works as a burlesque dancer at night. When a leg injury forced Cyd Charisse out of MGM's *Easter Parade* (1948), Mayer arranged for Ann to test for the role of dancing star Nadine Hale, who loses Fred Astaire to Judy Garland. It was one of her flashiest and most substantial roles as the "other woman." Ann was riveting in her

"Shaking the Blues Away" tap number. Her performance was all the more amazing because she still wore a back brace from her recent fall.

MGM signed Ann to a contract to join the ranks of their screen musicals stock company. She insisted later, "I never played politics, I never was a party girl, and I never slept with any of the producers," which may be why the studio never promoted her as a major star. Along with Cyd Charisse and Ricardo Montalban, she performed the "Dance of Fury," a much-needed diversion in Frank Sinatra's *The Kissing Bandit* (1948). Then she was among those with the crooner and Gene Kelly in *On the Town* (1948), where Ann was peppery in her "Prehistoric Joe" dance routine. Because MGM was bent on survival, it gave little thought to Ann's career progress. She was wasted in the Red Skelton comedy *Watch the Birdie* (1950), but did much better in *Texas Carnival* (1951), with Skelton and Esther Williams—dancing, smiling, and singing. On loan to Howard Hughes's RKO, Miller danced "Let the Worry Bird Worry for You" in *Two Tickets to Broadway*. A scheduled production number, "It Began in Yucatan," was cut when she injured her back during filming. Once more she was in tandem with Red Skelton in Metro's *Lovely to Look At* as showgirl Bubbles Cassidy. In this remake of Jerome Kern's *Roberta,* Ann danced zestfully through "I'll Be Hard to Handle" supported by a male chorus all wearing wolf masks.

Her two best MGM assignments were both in 1953. In the overlooked *Small Town Girl,* with Jane Powell and Farley Granger, Miller portrayed a Broadway star. In this movie, she had a fascinating Busby Berkeley–choreographed interlude, "I Gotta Hear the Beat," in which she tapped merrily in the midst of a stage full of protruding musical instruments (and the disembodied hands playing them). It was in sharp contrast to her flamenco routine in the picture. By far the greatest musical she ever appeared in was the movie version of Cole Porter's *Kiss Me, Kate* (1953). It was shot in 3-D, and Miller had several showstopping numbers: "Why Can't You Behave?" "Always True to You Darling, In My Fashion," "Tom, Dick or Harry," and the highly erotic "Too Darn Hot." (*Variety* judged the latter "a spectacular sizzler.")

As MGM wound down in the 1950s, so did Ann's movie assignments. She was in two 1956 comedies, the second being a poor remake of *The Women* called *The Opposite Sex.* Ann inherited the role of the avaricious fortune hunter, played in the 1938 screen original by Paulette Goddard. When Janis Paige was given the role Ann had been promised in *Silk Stockings* (1957), Ann and MGM ended their partnership.

Now that Ann's screen career was over, she adapted: "I could sing and dance. And I had a very strong mother. That helped a lot. . . . She was there if anything went wrong. She was like my manager, really." In 1958, Miller married Texas oilman William Moss, previously wed to former child star Jane Withers. According to Miller, it was "a disaster that lasted three years." Thirteen days after her divorce in May 1961, she wed Texas oil millionaire Arthur Cameron on the rebound. That was annulled in 1962, and once again she returned to the Beverly Hills mansion she had purchased for her mother.

Ann had made her television debut on NBC-TV on October 6, 1957, on a Bob Hope comedy special. Later there would be guest visits to *The Perry Como Show* (1959), *The Ed Sullivan Show* (1960), and *The Hollywood Palace* (1964). Because of her gushy gusto she was a favorite TV talk show guest. There was occasional club work, and she served as "unofficial ambassadress" at Hilton Hotel openings worldwide. She explained about her relationship with hotel tycoon Hilton, "Conrad and I are just good friends. He likes to dance."

When she starred in a Houston, Texas, production of *Can-Can* in early 1969, her career had a great resurgence. It brought her to the attention of the producers of *Mame*, who needed a fresh replacement for the hit Broadway musical now entering its third year. She was a far different Mame Dennis than had been Angela Lansbury or her successors, and for the newcomer, Onna White choreographed a special tap sequence interpolated into the "That's How Young I Feel" number. She opened in New York City on May 26, 1969, to solid reviews and remained with the show till it closed in January 1970.

For many couch potatoes, Ann Miller was best known for starring in the extravagant Heinz soup commercial in 1971. She appeared on a rising, eight-foot-high soup can and tap-danced violently to "Let's Face the Gumbo and Dance." Hermes Pan choreographed this unforgettable number. She led a summer tour of *Hello, Dolly!* and later that year (November 15, 1971) she was with Ann-Margret and Fred Gwynne in the NBC-TV adaptation of *Dames at Sea*. As temperamental Broadway luminary Mona Kent, Miller executed a spectacular tap number, "Wall Street." The next summer she toured in *Anything Goes* with Tab Hunter, and during the run at the St. Louis Municipal Opera, she was injured onstage (by a steel curtain). It was feared she would never perform again, but eventually she did (appearing in a tour of *Panama Hattie*). She also authored her autobiography, *Miller's High Life* (1972). "Norma Lee Browning researched the dates and tacked things together, but I wrote most of it in longhand on legal pads," Ann said.

As a girlfriend of the movie-studio president (portrayed by Art Carney), Ann Miller was one of many former movie stars appearing in the nostalgia fiasco *Won Ton Ton, The Dog Who Saved Hollywood* (1976). She made news as the featured attraction of the million-dollar Milliken industrial show in 1978 and 1979 produced at the Waldorf-Astoria's Grand Ballroom. Said one reviewer of her show routine, "Between her extraordinary hair, her gold sequin tights, the 'Ridin' High' music and her tap shoes, there was little more to ask of her." Her *Cactus Flower* tour (1978–79), in which a tap routine was inserted for her, was followed by the greatest success of her moviemaking years and thereafter. It was the starring role in *Sugar Babies*. Originally she wanted Red Skelton or Milton Berle as her colead, but she "settled" for Mickey Rooney (who in turn thought she was too tall for him). The bawdy burlesque revue had a five-city pre-Broadway tour before opening at the Mark Hellinger Theater on October 8, 1979. Filled with hoary routines, decorative chorines, and the very broad mugging of Rooney, it was a surprise hit. The show was given a sharp uplift by Ann's enthusiastic dancing and singing, including a military number she had first done in *Reveille With Beverly* and later at MGM in *Hit the Deck*. At age fifty-six, Ann could still wow an audience with her tapping, her fine figure, and t-h-a-t hair! Rex Reed (*New York Daily News*) noted, "I loved the fact that Mickey Rooney and Ann Miller have proved, once again, there's nothing like the old pros."

Sugar Babies lasted for 1,208 Broadway performances, closing in the late summer of 1982 and then embarking on a lengthy road tour. During this Broadway period, Miller's mother was dying in Los Angeles, and Ann commuted every weekend to visit her. (On one of these red-eye flights, she lost an uninsured million-dollar, thirty-carat diamond ring in the rest room.) Ann also joined with Ethel Merman, Carol Channing, Van Johnson, Della Reese, and Cab Calloway in a two-hour *Love Boat* excursion on ABC-TV (February 27, 1982). When *Sugar Babies* reached Los Angeles—again—in early 1984, Ann explained about her marathon run in the show, "As you get older you get stronger, it seems. I know that I can dance most of the kids in our show into the ground." (By this point Miller had earned an estimated $2 million from the show.) By September 1985, Ann had played the *Sugar Babies* lead 1,406 times. Once a strap on her shoe popped during an intricate dance number. She took off both shoes and danced barefoot. Also in 1985 she donated a pair of her tap shoes (she called them "Moe and Joe") to the Smithsonian Institute. They were displayed next to Ginger Rogers's movie gowns and Irving Berlin's piano.

The *Sugar Babies* saga continued when she and Rooney starred in the London edition (Savoy Theater, September 20, 1988). The British were more impressed by the leads than by the ragamuffin show itself. "Miss Miller clicketty clicks across the stage with those famous legs in better shape than the Eiffel Tower" (*Daily Express*). "Ann Miller, whose tap-dancing is as innocently delightful, and as energetic, as it was in those MGM musicals of 40 years ago." (*Daily Telegraph*). Because Rooney decided he was homesick, the show closed in early January 1989. Back in California, Miller admitted, "I love Hollywood and honestly, I'm tired of being away from home." In February 1989, she and Mickey Rooney were among the MGM alumnae appearing on the televised opening of the Disney–MGM Studios theme park in Florida.

In the 1990s, Ann was one of the several cohosts of *That's Entertainment! III* (1994) and frequently turned up on documentaries devoted to Hollywood's golden age and its array of stars, especially those at MGM. She appeared in an episode of the sitcom *Home Improvement* in 1993 and was the subject of an A&E Cable network biography in 2000. In 1995 she was the recipient of the fifth annual Diversity Award in Los Angeles. In October 1997 Miller received the Lifetime Achievement Award at the Multicultural Moton Picture Assocation's fifth annual Diversity Awards held at the Beverly Hilton Hotel. That November, the Friars Club in Beverly Hills saluted Ann, who was given their Spotlight Award. The year 1998 saw her featured in a revival of the musical *Follies* at the Paper Mill Playhouse in Millburn, New Jersey. Playing Carlotta Campion (the role original on Broadway by Yvonne De Carlo), Miller got to sing "I'm Still Here." She performed that anthem and other numbers at a Hollywood Bowl concert in September 1999. After many years away from feature films, Ann had a role in David Lynch's dark movie *Mulholland Drive* (2001) playing a ditzy Los Angeles landlady. In describing his legendary cast member, filmmaker Lynch assessed, "She's a no-baloney gal, a fantastic Hollywood gal."

Looking back on her long-lasting career, Ann Miller once reflected, "I worked so hard all my life dancing, that my idea of happiness is to dress up in beads and go out. So I married three playboys who loved to go to parties, but the minute they owned you, they lost interest and the fights started. . . . I'm a survivor. You have to be in this business." Regarding her bigger-than-life public image, Miller has noted "I was weaned on caviar and champagne, and all my life I have tried to be an 8-by-10 glossy. I try to give the impression that everything's perfect, that the eyelashes and hair are always in place and that stars never go to the bathroom . . . but sometimes I do get tired of it all. It was particularly hard on my marriages when I never wanted my husbands to see me with rollers and face cream."

Filmography

The Devil on Horseback (GN, 1936)
New Faces of 1937 (RKO, 1937)
The Life of the Party (RKO, 1937)
Stage Door (RKO, 1937)
Radio City Revels (RKO, 1938)
Having Wonderful Time (RKO, 1938)

Tarnished Angel (RKO, 1938)
You Can't Take It With You (Col, 1938)
Room Service (RKO, 1938)
Hit Parade of 1941 (Rep, 1940)
Too Many Girls (RKO, 1940)
Melody Ranch (Rep, 1940)

Time Out for Rhythm (Col, 1941)
Variety Reel (Unk, 1941) (s)
Stars Past and Present (Unk, 1941) (s)
Screen Stars Snapshots Series 21, No. 21 (Col, 1941) (s)
Go West, Young Lady (Col, 1941)
True to the Army (Par, 1942)
Priorities on Parade (Par, 1942)
Reveille With Beverly (Col, 1943)
What's Buzzin' Cousin? (Col, 1943)
Hey, Rookie (Col, 1944)
Carolina Blues (Col, 1944)
Jam Session (Col, 1944)
Eadie Was a Lady (Col, (l945)
Eve Knew Her Apples (Col, 1945)
The Thrill of Brazil (Col, 1946)
Easter Parade (MGM, 1948)

The Kissing Bandit (MGM, 1948)
On the Town (MGM, 1949)
Watch the Birdie (MGM, 1950)
Two Tickets to Broadway (RKO, 1951)
Texas Carnival (MGM, 1951)
Lovely to Look At (MGM, 1952)
Small Town Girl (MGM, 1953)
Kiss Me, Kate (MGM, 1953)
Deep in My Heart (MGM, 1954)
Hit the Deck (MGM, 1955)
The Opposite Sex (MGM, 1956)
The Great American Pastime (MGM, 1956)
Won Ton Ton, The Dog Who Saved Hollywood (Par, 1976)
The Freshman (Tri-Star, 1990)
That's Entertainment! III (MGM, 1994) (cohost)
Mulholland Drive (Univ, 2001)

Broadway Plays

George White's Scandals of 1939 (1939)
Mame (1969) (replacement)

Sugar Babies (1979)

Album Discography

LPs

Dames at Sea (Bell System K-4900) [ST/TV]
Deep in My Heart (MGM E-3153, MGM SES-54ST) [ST]
Deep in My Heart/Words and Music (MCA 5959) [ST]
Easter Parade (10″ MGM E-502, MGM E-3227, MGM SES-40ST) [ST]
Hit the Deck (MGM E-3163, MGM SES-43ST) [ST]
Kiss Me, Kate (MGM E-3077, Metro M/MS-525, MGM SES-44ST, MCA 25003 [ST]
Lovely to Look At (10″ MGM E-150, MGM E-3230, MGM SES-50ST) [ST]

Lovely to Look At/Show Boat (MGM E-3230) [ST]
Lovely to Look At/Summer Stock (MCA 39084) [ST]
On the Town (Show Biz 5603, Caliban 6023) [ST]
Pagan Love Song/Hit the Deck/The Pirate (MGM 2SES-43ST) [ST]
Small Town Girl (Scarce Rarities 5503) [ST]
That's Dancing! (EMI America SJ-17149) [ST]
That's Entertainment! (MCA MCA2-11002) [ST]
Two Tickets to Broadway (RCA LPM-39) [ST]

CDs

Deep In My Heart (MCA MCAD-5949, Sony Music Special Products AK-47703) [ST]
Easter Parade (Sony Music Special Products AK-45392, Turner Classic Movies/Rhino R2-71960-2) [ST]
Follies (TVT Soundtrax 1030) [OC]
Hit the Deck (Turner Classic Movies/Rhino R2-76668-2, EMI 794123) [ST]
Hit the Deck/Royal Wedding (MGM/EMI MGM-15) [ST]

Kiss Me, Kate (Sony Music Special Products AK-46196, EMI 854538, CBS UK 70728) [ST]
Lovely To Look At (MCA MCAD-39084, Sony Music Special Products AK-47027) [ST]
Reveille With Beverly/Jam Session (Hollywood Soundstage 4407) [ST]
Sugar Babies (Varese Sarabande VSD-5453, Varese Sarabande IRB-9012) [OC]
That's Entertainment! III (Angel CDQ-55215) [ST]

Michael York and Liza Minnelli in *Cabaret* (1972).
[Courtesy of Michael R. Pitts]

Liza Minnelli

(b. Liza May Minnelli, Hollywood, California, March 12, 1946)

It is not just that most people mispronounced and misspelled Liza Minnelli's name. More than that, for much of her early life, Liza had to live in the shadows cast by her illustrious, high-voltage mother, Judy Garland. Then Liza suddenly blossomed forth as a major young performer in the mid-1960s, surprising everyone, including herself and her (at times envious) mother. At that point, Liza endured the blunted praise of critics and fans alike who insisted they could see the legendary Judy in Minnelli's every mannerism and vocal gesture. In reaction, Liza insisted dramatically that she was her very own person and never, never would she be or become an imitation of her famous (and soon to be late) mother.

But the Liza Minnelli who won an Academy Award, an Emmy, and several Tonys in the early-to-mid 1970s, soon proved herself wrong. Like her much-documented mother, Liza became intertwined in a series of romances and marriages that seemed to dissipate the thrust of her career. Like Judy, Liza became dependent upon drink and drugs over the years. (But unlike Garland, she went very public in the mid-1980s when she sought treatment for these addictions.) Like mama, Minnelli had great careers highs and lows. Also like Judy, she even made a cinematic trip over the Rainbow into the splendid Land of Oz, albeit in a cartoon feature.

Onstage, in cabarets and on the concert circuit, Liza was for a long time a consistent major attraction. Her verve, pizzazz, and savvy was displayed wonderfully. However, Liza never enjoyed a high-level recording career. Especially after the mid-1970s, her albums had a limited, specialized appeal, brought about more by their subject matter than her chic song styling. On television, she was at her best as a supercharged guest performer rather than as a sustaining star of her own specials. And on-screen, the quite talented Liza never recovered from the career setbacks of three consecutive flops: *Lucky Lady* (1976), *A Matter of Time* (1976), and *New York, New York* (1977).

Liza May Minnelli was born in Hollywood, California, on March 12, 1946. She was the only child of her MGM movie star mother and Garland's second husband, Metro-Goldwyn-Mayer movie director Vincente Minnelli. When Liza was less than three years old, she made her screen debut playing the daughter of Garland and Van Johnson in the closing moments of the MGM musical, *In the Good Old Summertime* (1949).

Years later, Liza admitted, "The kind of childhood I had can make you or break you." She was referring to the fact that her mother was living on an emotional roller coaster heading for an eventual crash. Before Liza was five, her mother had been hospitalized recurrently for emotional breakdowns. Judy had been suspended, rehired, suspended, and then fired from her home away from home, MGM. Garland had attempted suicide and in 1951 had divorced Vincente Minnelli. The next year, Garland had married promoter Sid Luft and then embarked on a series of comebacks onstage (at the Palace Theater) and in films (*A Star Is Born*, 1954). With Luft, Garland would have two additional children (Lorna and Joey), and suffer a long string of separations and reconciliations as her career went through several more highs and lows.

Meanwhile, Liza had to cope. "I've had knocks, but I'm not sure it's not better to have them when you're young. At least it teaches you how to handle them when they come later." Because her mother was frequently on concert tours, in debt, in and out of love, or in emotional retreat, much of Liza's youth was spent growing up fast. She was pushed into being her mother's confidante, arbiter, and sidekick, all the while moving from place to place and school to school. Her schooling was haphazard and encompassed educational stays on the West Coast, East Coast, and later in England and Switzerland.

When Garland had been headlining her successful Palace Theater comeback in 1952, Liza had come onstage one evening and danced for the audience while mama sang "Swanee." But thereafter Liza insisted that she was not interested in show business. However, like Judy, she could and did change her mind. In 1954 Vincente Minnelli used Liza as an extra in his new MGM comedy, *The Long, Long Trailer*. She was cast in the wedding scene where Lucille Ball and Desi Arnaz marry. However, before the picture was released, Liza's few screen moments were cut. In 1955, Art Linkletter interviewed her on his TV show. In December 1956, she was on CBS-TV to introduce the network's then annual showing of the Garland classic, *The Wizard of Oz* (1939). Her equally awkward cohost was her mother's costar from that fantasy picture, Bert Lahr. Liza made an appearance on Jack Paar's TV talk show in 1958 and on April 24, 1959, she was on Gene Kelly's CBS-TV special, dancing with him to "For Me and My Gal" (the title tune of one of the several pictures Kelly made with Garland). By the time Liza was among those on *Hedda Hopper's Showcase* in January 1960, she was nearly five-feet five-inches and a plump 165 pounds.

Throughout 1960, Liza was enrolled at the High School for the Performing Arts in New York City. Her crush on a fellow student—who was moonlighting in the chorus of the Broadway musical *Bye Bye Birdie*—led her to become really enthused about the theater. One of her other friends at school was Marvin Hamlisch, in his pre–Academy Award days as a music/song composer. It was with Hamlisch that Liza made a demonstration record, but no record label showed any interest in their talent.

By the spring of 1961, Liza had transferred to public high school in Scarsdale, New York, living with one of her father's relatives. Garland would flit in and out of town as the mood hit her. That summer, while Garland was vacationing on Cape Cod (among those wanting to be in proximity to President John F. Kennedy's summer White House at Hyannis Port), Liza worked as an unpaid apprentice at the Cape Cod Melody Tent in Hyannis. That next year at Scarsdale High, Liza starred in a school production of *The Diary of Anne Frank*, a show that was sent on a goodwill tour to Israel, Greece, and Italy during the summer of 1962. Meanwhile, both attracted to and repelled by the idea of following in her mother's footsteps, Liza was hired to record the voice of Dorothy in a feature-length cartoon version of *Journey Back to Oz* (aka: *Return to Oz*) that would not be theatrically released until 1974.

After her *Anne Frank* tour on the Continent, Liza remained in London for schooling and then transferred briefly to the Sorbonne in Paris. But she had decided she wished to be in New York City and that she wanted to be in show business. Her mother, busy performing in Las Vegas and coping with an unhappy marriage, reluctantly agreed. At age sixteen, Liza embarked on her New York phase, taking acting and speech classes, doing magazine modeling, and surviving. Being Judy Garland's daughter helped Liza get cast in an off-Broadway revival of *Best Foot Forward* that opened April 2, 1963. She was paid $34 weekly. Shortly before that debut, Garland (who could be a mentor or a monster) arranged with her good friend Jack Paar for Liza to appear again on his TV talk show. Introduced as Dyju Langard, a new Armenian discovery, Liza sang for the television audience. Only later in the program did Paar revealed her identity. Of her *Best Foot Forward* appearance, New York drama critic Walter Kerr wrote, "Liza Minnelli is certainly appealing, and would be even if she wasn't Judy Garland's daughter." More encouraging was Liza being selected as a Promising Newcomer by Daniel Blum's *Theater World* annual.

Still trailing in her mother's powerful wake, Liza appeared on Garland's CBS-TV weekly variety series. In November 1963, Liza and Judy did several duets together on air, and the teenager was again on the television program in December, this time joined by halfsister Lorna and half-brother Joey. Early the next year Liza was "starred" at the Paper Mill Playhouse in Milburn, New Jersey, in the musical *Carnival!* There was much publicity when a near-hysterical Judy, claiming to be upset by Liza's recent bout of flu, threatened legal action if her daughter endangered her health by performing in the show. Even with all this attendant hoopla, Liza went on with the proceedings, and the engagement was a success. Later in 1964, Liza played in the comedy *Time Out for Ginger* at the Bucks County Playhouse in New Hope, Pennsylvania, and that summer teamed with Elliott Gould for a tour of *The Fantasticks*. She made her dramatic acting debut on the "Nightingale for Sale" segment (CBS-TV, October 24, 1964) of *Mr. Broadway*.

One of the major turning points of Liza's career occurred on November 8, 1964. Her mother, having failed with her own TV series, was making another return to the London Palladium. In a moment of being friend not foe, she asked Liza to costar with her for the engagement. Liza was determined to succeed, but was unprepared for her mother's competitiveness onstage. She recalled, "Working with her was something else. I'll never be afraid to perform with anyone ever again after that terrifying experience." The onstage duel between two generations of performers was a draw to some and an unqualified success for Liza to others. From this English engagement, Liza Minnelli emerged as a full-fledged performing talent that would become more refined as the years passed.

Liza had already been featured on the cast album from *Best Foot Forward* and, in December 1964, Capitol Records (for whom her mother had made several albums in the 1950s) released *Liza! Liza!* The latter album featured the song "Maybe This Time," written by the team of Fred Ebb and John Kander. Ebb, in particular, had already became Liza's mentor, and he did a great deal to groom her professional image. He also favored her trying out for a new musical he and Kander had composed, *Flora, the Red Menace.* Produced by Hal Prince and directed by George Abbott, the show opened on Broadway on May 11, 1965. The musical received mixed reviews, but Liza was praised. The show folded after 89 performances, but Liza won a Tony Award as Best Musical Actress of the Year.

In 1965, Liza starred with Vic Damone on TV in a whimsical musical *The Dangerous Christmas of Red Riding Hood* and was a guest on one of Frank Sinatra's TV specials. She debuted at the Plaza Hotel's Persian Room in February 1966, part of a cabaret tour that encompassed London and Los Angeles. More importantly to her, she auditioned for the role of Sally Bowles in the Broadway musical *Cabaret.* However, a Britisher (Jill Haworth) played the part when the show opened in November 1966 for a 1,166-performance run.

It was Judy Garland who used industry connections to pave the way for Liza gaining a cameo assignment in the British-filmed *Charlie Bubbles* (1968). Liza played an American who becomes the secretary and mistress of a quirky writer (Albert Finney). *Variety* was unenthusiastic about her smallish role: "Miss Minnelli gets a trifle cloying, but is okay." It was also Garland who introduced her daughter to Liza's future husband. In 1965, Judy had hired Australian Peter Allen and his partner Chris Bell to be part of her club act. She thought the talented Allen would make a fine husband for Liza, although the latter had mixed feelings during their courtship over the next two years. Nevertheless, on March 3, 1967, they were married in New York City.

Just as Liza had campaigned hard for the stage role in *Cabaret*, she became enamored of the role of the sensitive Pookie Adams in *The Sterile Cuckoo* (1969), a film project that Alan J. Pakula had in mind. When he finally received financial backing from Paramount Pictures and agreed to hiring her, she turned down the lead in the pending Broadway musical *Promises, Promises* (1969). In retrospect it is hard to imagine anyone else as the kookie Pookie Adams who finds love with a shy college freshman (Wendell Burton) only to see him outgrow her. So telling was her performance that she was nominated for an Academy Award, but she lost the Best Actress Oscar to Maggie Smith (of *The Prime of Miss Jean Brodie*).

Liza was already in rehearsal for her next film, Otto Preminger's *Tell Me That You Love Me, Junie Moon* (1970), when her mother—now in her fifth marriage—died of an "accidental" overdose of barbiturates in London on June 22, 1969. Liza maturely rose to the occasion, handling all the details of the funeral that took place in New York City in the midst of much hysteria on the part of Judy's fans. For playing the screen role of Junie Moon, the rape victim whose face and arms are scarred by battery acid, Liza was paid $50,000. The oddball film was a box-office flop. Meanwhile, Liza was a hit on the club circuit, especially in Las Vegas. On June 29, 1970, she headlined her own special on NBC-TV. She earned $500,000 that year.

A lot happened to Liza in 1972. She and Peter Allen divorced, and she was engaged in a highly publicized and media-covered cross-global romance with Desi Arnaz Jr. (She was twenty-six; he was nineteen.) She also finally got to play in *Cabaret*, starring in the film version, which was shot in Munich. Within the story line that focused on the loves and tribulations of an American singer in a decadent club in 1930s' Berlin, Liza gave much dimension to the role of Sally Bowles. She turned the hit musical's theme song "Cabaret" into her trademark number, and added the poignant "Maybe This Time" to the roster of songs within this film musical. For her performance she won the Best Actress Oscar. On September 10, 1972, she starred in the TV Special *Liza With a 'Z'* and the hour-long show won an Emmy Award. The Columbia LP of that TV special rose to number nineteen on the album charts. (Her 1973 LP, *Liza Minnelli the Singer*, reached number thirty-eight on the charts; the last time one of her albums made the top forty.)

In the next year, Liza earned as much attention for her international romances as for her performances. She was linked, among others, with Peter Sellers, Edward Albert, Assaf Dayan, and Ben Vereen. Then, in January 1974, she appeared for three sold-out weeks at Manhattan's Winter Garden Theater in concert, receiving as much attention for lip-synching some of her song numbers as for her Bob Fosse–style dance strutting. (She received a special Tony Award for this stage turn.) Her April 30, 1974, special on NBC-TV, *Love From A to Z*, teamed her with Charles Aznavour, who had introduced her when she had appeared a few years before in concert at the Olympia Theater in Paris.

Liza was also one of the cohosts of the MGM salute, *That's Entertainment!* (1974), in which she narrated the section focusing on Judy Garland's studio musicals. The producer of that documentary was Jack Haley Jr., whose father had costarred with Judy in *The Wizard of Oz* and *Pigskin*

Parade. On September 15, 1974, Liza and Jack Haley Jr. were married. The huge wedding reception was hosted by Vincente Minnelli and Sammy Davis Jr. at Ciro's on the Sunset Strip in Hollywood. The couple would divorce in 1978. (She remained friendly with Haley, and when he died on April 21, 2001, Liza was one of those who spoke at his memorial tribute.)

Somehow Liza could not follow up the screen success of *Cabaret.* She starred in a big-budgeted musical *Lucky Lady* (1976), dealing with rum-running in the 1930s. It also focused on a bizarre ménage à trois that included Liza, Burt Reynolds, and Gene Hackman. The gaudy production was a financial bust. Vincente Minnelli had been suffering from poor health and an inability to get backing for any new movie projects. As a gesture to her ailing father, Liza agreed to star in *A Matter of Time* (1976), a frequently incoherent quaint fantasy romance that teamed her with Ingrid Bergman and Charles Boyer. It proved to be an arty flop.

In contrast, there was much interest in her next picture, another big musical, this time set in the 1940s big band era. *New York, New York* (1977) costarred Minnelli with Robert De Niro and was directed in a too-meticulous manner by Martin Scorsese. John Kander and Fred Ebb provided the memorable title song for Liza (another of her signature numbers). However, before general release the splashy "Happy Endings" production number was deleted, and many viewers said this cut (later restored for reissues) was one of the causes for the picture's failure. (The situation was reminiscent of Judy Garland and the editing turmoil surrounding *A Star Is Born.*) Its failure, in tandem with her two past flops, left Liza without a film career.

For six weeks in the summer of 1975, Liza took over the lead role in the Broadway musical *Chicago* (which for years thereafter would be touted as a potential joint film project for her and Goldie Hawn). On October 29, 1977, *The Act*, starring Liza, opened on Broadway. With songs by Kander and Ebb and directed by Martin Scorsese, the musical offered a Las Vegas club star (Liza) performing her act while flashbacks recount her rocky life and marriage (to Barry Nelson). Said the *New York Times*, "It displays the breathtaking presence of Liza Minnelli, and her command of a force that is the emotional equivalent of what a good coloratura achieves in top form. . . ." The show lasted 233 performances, and Liza won another Tony Award. In 1979 she was seen briefly as a temporary replacement—playing Lillian Hellman—in the off-Broadway drama *Are You Now Or Have You Ever Been.* In December 1979 Liza wed Mark Gero, a one-time stage manager turned sculptor. He was seven years her junior. Over the next several years, Liza suffered numerous miscarriages, and her marriage was a very much on-and-off-again situation. (It eventually ended in divorce in the early 1990s.)

With club performances and occasional TV outings as her chief venues, Liza had to wait four years before gaining another movie role. *Arthur* (1981) was a starring vehicle for British comedian Dudley Moore, who excelled as the drunken, spoiled multimillionaire who finds true love and redemption with a shoplifting waitress (Liza). The popular movie grossed $42 million in domestic film rentals. While Liza was effective in her performance, the industry did not regard the picture as a Liza Minnelli picture. (Dudley Moore was *the* star, and the comedy netted John Gielgud a Best Supporting Actor Oscar as Arthur's stuffy butler.) Liza was again in a movie career slump.

On Broadway, Liza was listed as the top-billed draw of *The Rink* (1984), another Kander and Ebb musical, but it was colead Chita Rivera (as her mother) who stole the limelight. By the time the unexceptional show closed after 204 performances, Liza had left the cast (replaced by Stockard Channing). In July 1984, Minnelli entered the Betty Ford Center in Rancho Mirage,

California, for treatment of "Valium and alcohol abuse." Accompanied to her destination by Lorna Luft and bolstered by another Ford Center alumnus (Elizabeth Taylor), Liza admitted publicly, "I've got a problem and I'm going to deal with it." She was much interviewed then and later, and confessed that thereafter she suffered several dependency setbacks.

When not performing in clubs, Liza was back to guest-starring on-camera in such passable fare as *The Muppets Take Manhattan* (1984). She cohosted *That's Dancing!* (1985), a big-screen documentary coproduced by her ex-husband (Jack Haley Jr.) and featuring clips of a multitude of screen song-and-dance talent, including Judy Garland. Then Minnelli made her telefeature debut in *A Time To Live* (NBC-TV, October 28, 1985) playing a real-life mother/author whose son (Corey Haim) is combating muscular dystrophy. The effective drama won a Christopher Award.

Her father, Vincente Minnelli, died in July 1986, leaving $1 million of his estate to Liza, and the next year she participated in a PBS-TV tribute entitled *Minnelli on Minnelli*. As her mother had done twenty-six years prior, Liza played a sold-out (three-week) engagement at Carnegie Hall in May 1987, which brought her rave reviews and led to a new double-LP album set recorded live at the concert. That winter she underwent a five-week European concert tour joined by pianist/ singer Michael Feinstein, a good friend.

One of the more interesting concepts for a TV special was the ABC-TV offering (June 7, 1988), *Sam Found Out: A Triple Play*. In a trio of playlets (costarring with Ryan O'Neal, Lou Gossett Jr., and John Rubinstein) Liza acted out three different scenarios about what happened "after Sam found out." As a showcase for Liza, it was only fitfully successful. Nevertheless, it was far better than her two 1988 pictures. In *Rent-a-Cop*, she reteamed with Burt Reynolds, whose cinema track record had floundered as badly as hers. She played a Chicago prostitute enmeshed in homicide and police corruption. The tacky movie quickly disappeared from distribution. More promising was *Arthur 2: On the Rocks*. But, like most sequels, it could not live up to its predecessor. Liza was as winning as before (her screen character had undergone positive changes), but the plot ploy had worn thin, and only the brief reappearance of John Gielgud as the deceased butler/ confidant gave the tiresome movie any resonance. Made for $15 million, it grossed only $7.5 million in domestic film rentals.

Decades before Judy Garland had been a charter member of Frank Sinatra's Rat Pack. In turn, Liza and Sinatra had become pals over the years. When Dean Martin dropped out of *The Ultimate Event* tour headlining Sinatra, Martin, and Sammy Davis Jr. in 1988, Liza substituted. She joined her new teammates for a heavy schedule of play dates at home and abroad, climaxed by a taping of their sold-out concert tour for a Showtime Cable TV special that played in May 1989. The trio made additional appearances, and Liza returned to solo performing on the club circuit.

When not performing her cabaret act, Minnelli was a participant in charity events, such as *Dance for Life*, a December 8, 1990, event held at the Santa Monica Civic Auditorium on behalf of the charity, Vital Options. After the embarrassing *Arthur 2: On the Rocks* and *Rent-A-Cop* in 1988, there was much anticipation when Liza made a new feature, *Stepping Out*. Joined by Shelley Winters, Julie Waters, and an ensemble cast, Minnelli played a middle-aged former Broadway chorus dancer who finds herself teaching tap-dance lessons in upstate New York. Paramount was unsure how to handle this intimate story and its assemblage of superior actors (none of whom, however, were hot at the box office). Thrown into delayed release, the quasi-musical quickly disappeared from distribution.

In October 1991, the European media touted that Liza was engaged to Billy Stritch, the twenty-something pianist who had been part of the cabaret trio of Montgomery, Plant and Stritch. He and Minnelli became "inseparable" and while traveling together in Germany were cornered by a reporter at a Frankfurt jewelry shop where they were buying fun rings. Misassumptions and joking around led to the news scoop. Besides, Liza had not officially been divorced from husband Mark Gero. In 1992, Minnelli had a highly successful engagement at Radio City Music Hall, working into her show anecdotes about her father Vincente Minnelli, who had been a designer at the showplace back in the 1930s. The high-energy evening was aired as a PBS-TV special on December 6, 1992. In June 1993, the songstress performed at Carnegie Hall, joined in the week-long concertizing by her longtime friend, French singer Charles Aznavour. Also that month, Liza joined with her half-sister Lorna Luft in performing a medley on the June 6 Tony Awards ceremony that Minnelli was hosting. Said the bubbling star about her sibling: "We're just women who admire and really know each other. We allow each other to have the weaknesses the public doesn't allow us to have." That year Minnelli was the subject of a new biography, this one by Wendy Leigh and entitled *Liza: Born a Star*.

Liza was among the several performers (including James Belushi, Gena Rowlands, Dudley Moore, and Robert Wagner) who performed in the Linda Yellen–directed *Parallel Lives* (1994). The made-for-cable feature revolved around men and women of assorted ages melding together during a fraternity/sorority reunion. The gimmick of the project was that much of the dialogue was improvised on the set. When not doing her club act, Liza was active in AIDS charities, including making a video for a new song, "The Day After That," that was a hopeful anthem for those suffering from the disease.

By the mid-1990s, Minnelli was often more in the news for her hip and knee replacement surgeries than for her performing. In June 1995, she appeared at the Cerritos Center for the Performing Arts in Southern California. The *Los Angeles Times* reported, "Instead of filling the stage with high-voltage, rapid-fire dance steps, she brought the focus in much closer via more subtle strutting, her classic, mime-like arm and hand movements, and richly multilayered lyrical interpretations. The result was a far more intimate show than she has offered in past appearances." On November 23, 1995, Liza could be seen on the CBS-TV movie *West Side Waltz*, which featured Shirley MacLaine, Liza, and Jennifer Grey in an intimate drama of three "misfits" living on New York City's West Side who have interlocking associations. Regarding this play of aging and renewal, the *Hollywood Reporter* judged, "Minnelli, playing a spinsterish [sweet but glum] middle-aged woman, gives a beautiful performance that wouldn't be overkill to call of Emmy caliber." Then it was back to the club circuit, with Minnelli headlining at Bally's in Las Vegas in May 1996. As always the supermarket tabloids were full of stories and pictures suggesting that the veteran talent was still a party animal involved in substance abuse, impetuous relationships with boy toys, and so on. In January 1997, Liza took over for Julie Andrews in the Broadway musical *Victor/Victoria* so Andrews could have a month's vacation from her Herculean stage work. Reporting on her performance in the show, the *New York Times* described (January 14, 1997): "So what if her dancing seems a tad uncertain? So what if her voice wanders strangely. . . . So what if she looks like a cute toy penguin when she wears a tuxedo. . . . As always, Ms. Minnelli's voice, of a limited range, tends to circle notes before finally landing on them. But it remains a big, heartfelt voice . . . that does more than justice to the bland melodies of Henry Mancini and the appallingly strained lyrics of Leslie Briscusse. And when she stands onstage, alone in the spotlight, her hair slicked back, her hands clenched and her voice at full throttle, she inevitably evokes her mother in her fabled late concert appearances."

By 1999, the supermarket papers were full of news that Liza had finally conquered her substance abuse and was attending twelve-step program meetings. She had also slimmed down from her recent ballooning weight cycle. In July 1999, she told syndicated columnist Liz Smith: "I want the people who care about me to know I'm taking care of myself. I'm looking forward to performing again and giving back to my fans and friends the love they have shown me by being healthy. I feel there is no shame in taking positive action."

Back in 1997, when Liza was recovering from throat surgery, she took to watching many of her father's movies again. It led to conceive the idea for *Minnelli on Minnelli*, which opened at the Palace Theater on Broadway on December 8, 1999. A tribute to the films of Vincente Minnelli, the production encompassed slides of family photographs as well as clips and songs from his pictures (as performed by Liza and her six-member male chorus). The *New York Times* detailed, "Though she still sports the black helmet of hair that has been her trademark for decades, Ms. Minnelli is at first almost unrecognizable. It's not just that she is substantially heavier; it's that the famously dynamic Ms. Minnelli, who has had hip replacement surgery several [years] ago, seems so sedentary." The reviewer concluded, "This strange, awkward evening will be remembered less as one of song than as a conscious manipulation of a fragile, needy persona." *Daily Variety*'s reporter observed, "Minnelli is one of the last practitioners of a particular strain of showbiz that draws on this mutual, personal give and take: We sustain our favorites with our love and loyalty as they have sustained us with their artistry." The limited-run show led to a cast album release. On January 31, 2000, Liza was the subject of a tribute by the Drama League head at the Pierre Hotel ballroom in Manhattan.

Minnelli on Minnelli was scheduled to tour across America. However, the Chicago engagement in May 2000 had to be cancelled when Liza was hospitalized in New York City for treatment of a severe hip condition. It proved that the star had double pneumonia as well and had to cancel her planned tour. She was in Fort Lauderdale, Florida, in September 2000 planning to find a new home in South Florida. In mid-October she was admitted to a local hospital there where she was treated for viral encephalitis, from which she almost died. In spring 2001, Minnelli underwent further hip and back surgery. Later, on the set of the TV special *Michael Jackson: 30th Anniversary Special* (2001), the diva met TV producer David Gest, seven years her junior. They soon became engaged and planned to wed (her fourth, his first) in March 2002. Said the jubilant bride to be: "Everything I've been through was worth it to find David." The ceremony was held in New York City and proved to be a celebrity-filled circus. It garnered tremendous media coverage.

Having reached the age where many superstars had already faded and/or retired, Liza Minnelli proved that, like her legendary mother, she was a survivor. While the talented Liza showed great verve and promise in her early adult years in show business, she became in later life—like movie star Elizabeth Taylor—an enduring icon, revered for having overcome so many professional and personal missteps. It did not seem to matter to the public that Minnelli's glory days as an entertainer were in the past.

Filmography

In the Good Old Summertime (MGM, 1949)
Charlie Bubbles (Univ, 1968)
The Sterile Cuckoo (Par, 1969)
Tell Me That You Love Me, Junie Moon (Par, 1970)
Cabaret (AA, 1972)
That's Entertainment! (MGM, 1974) (cohost)
Journey Back to Oz [Return to Oz] (Filmation, 1974) (voice only)
Lucky Lady (20th-Fox, 1976)
A Matter of Time (AIP, 1976)
Silent Movie (20th-Fox, 1976)

New York, New York (UA, 1977)
Arthur (Orion/WB, 1981)
The King of Comedy (20th-Fox, 1983)
The Muppets Take Manhattan (Tri-Star, 1984)
That's Dancing! (MGM, 1985) (cohost)
A Time to Live (NBC-TV, October 28, 1985)
Rent-A-Cop (Kings Road Entertainment, 1988)
Arthur 2: On the Rocks (WB, 1988)
Stepping Out (Par, 1991)
Parallel Lives (Showtime Cable, 8/14/94)
West Side Waltz (CBS-TV, 11/23/95)
Jackie's Back (Lifetime Cable, 6/14/99)

Broadway Plays

Flora, The Red Menace (1964)
Chicago (1975) (replacement)
The Act (1978)

The Rink (1984)
Victor/Victoria (1997) (replacement)

Album Discography

LPs

The Act (DRG 6101)
Best Foot Forward (Cadence 4012/24102; Stet DS-15003) [OC]
Cabaret (ABC ABCD-752; MCA AB-752) [ST]
Christmas With Judy (Minerva MIN LP 6JG-XST) w. Judy Garland, Lorna Luft, Jack Jones
Come Saturday Morning (A&M 4164)
The Dangerous Christmas of Red Riding Hood (ABC ABC/ABCS-536) [ST/TV]
Flora, the Red Menace (RCA LOC/LSO-1111) [OC]
Foursider (A&M 3524)
It Amazes Me (Cap T/ST-2271)
Liza at Carnegie Hall (Telarc DG-15502)
Live at the London Palladium (Cap WBO/SWBO-2295, Cap ST-11191) w. Judy Garland
Live at the Olympia Hall (A&M 4345)

Liza at the Winter Garden (Col TC-32854)
Liza Live at Carnegie Hall (Altel Sound Systems—no number)
Liza! Liza! (Cap T/ST-2174)
Liza Minnelli (A&M 4141)
Liza Minnelli (CBS/Sony Japan FCPA-534)
Liza With a "Z" (Col KC-31762) [ST/TV]
Lucky Lady (Arista 4069) [ST]
Maybe This Time (Cap SM-11080)
New Feelin' (A&M 4272)
New York, New York (UA UA-LA750) [ST]
Nina (Oceania SO-69301) [ST]
Portrait of Liza (Reader's Digest RD1-7099)
Return to Oz [Journey Back to Oz] (Filmation RFO101) [ST/TV]
The Singer (Col KC-32149)
There Is a Time (Cap T/ST-2448)
Tropical Nights (Col PC-34887)

CDs

The Act (DRG CDRG-6101) [OC]
All That Jazz (Sony Music Special Products CK-31053)
A&M Gold Series (A&M 397080-2)
Aznavour/Minnelli: Paris—Plais de Congres (EMI Holland 8324262) w. Charles Aznavour
Back to Back Hits (CEMA Special Markets S21-18250) w. Judy Garland
Best Foot Forward (DRG 15003) [OC]
The Best of Liza Minnelli: The Millennium (A&M 490877)

Cabaret (Col/Sony COL-466117-2)
Cabaret (MCA MCAC-37125, MCA MCAD-250428) [ST]
City Lights (Promo Sound CD-3572) [OC]
The Collection (Polygram 551-815-2, PID 475332, Spectrum/Karussell/A&M 551-815-2)
Flora, the Red Menace (RCA 09026-60821-2) [OC]
Foursider (A&M 75021-6013-2)
Frank Sinatra in Italy (Drive 534) w. Frank Sinatra, Sammy Davis Jr.

Gently (Angel 35430)

Hot Enough (Music Options MO-3025)

It Was a Good Time—The Best of Judy Garland & Liza Minnelli (Curb D2-77777) w. Judy Garland

Judy and Liza Together (Curb D2-77587) w. Judy Garland

The Life (RCA 09026-68001-2) [OC]

Liza! (SMSP A23804)

Liza Minnelli (A&M D3243595)

Liza Minnelli at Carnegie Hall: The Complete Concert (Telarc 2CD-85502)

Liza Minnelli at Carnegie Hall: The Highlights (Telarc CD-85502)

Liza Minnelli Live From Radio City Music Hall (Col CK-53169)

Liza Minnelli Max 20 (A&M Japan MAX-214)

Liza With a "Z" (Col CK-31762) (ST/TV)

The Magic Collection—Liza Minnelli (ARC MEC-949051)

Master Series—Liza Minnelli (Polygram International Music/A&M 540-781-2)

Maybe This Time (Cap C21K-48443)

Millennium Edition (Polymedia 490-590-2)

Minnelli on Minnelli (Angel 7243-5-2405-2-3)

Music Reflexion (Selected Sound Carrier LL-4912)

My Own Space (MCPS/Roman Music 290091)

New York, New York (EMI E21Y-46090) [ST]

Results (Epic EK-45098)

The Rink (TER 1091) [OC]

The Singer (Col CK-32149, Geffen 24195)

16 Biggest Hits (Legacy CK-53778)

Stepping Out (Milan 73138-35606-2) [ST]

Together (Curb D21K-77587) w. Judy Garland

A Touch of Class (Disky TC-883682)

Tropical Nights (CBS/Sony Japan 25DP-5375)

Ultimate Collection (Hip-O Records 556504)

The Wonderful Music of Liza Minnelli (WMO 90329)

Carmen Miranda

(b. Maria do Carmo Miranda da Cunha in Marco de Canavezes, near Lisbon, Portugal, February 9, 1909; d. Los Angeles, California, August 4, 1955)

South-of-the-border countries have long had show-business personalities who translated well into the North American entertainment scene, including Dolores Del Rio, Lupe Velez, Maria Montez, Katy Jurado, and, more recently, Sonia Braga and Salma Hayek. But no one took the North American continent more by storm than Carmen Miranda. After her whirlwind arrival on Broadway in 1939, and soon thereafter in the movies, the United States was never the same.

Pre–Carmen Miranda, a banana was a banana and a grape was a grape and they were meant for eating. But Miranda used fruits interlaced with flowers to assemble wild, colorful cornucopia hats. They adorned her exotic face, setting off her flashing eyes and wide mouth as she sang exotically, danced the samba, and enchanted the public with her exotic outfits and affected scatter-brained persona. She spoke in a wild flurry of broken English and often vocalized in Portuguese. Her darting, expressive fingers (bedecked with massive costume jewelry, with those l-o-n-g, painted nails) were always flying everywhere, punctuating her volatile rhythm and directing attention to her multihued costumes. She was tagged, appropriately, the "Brazilian Bombshell," and in the World War II era when the U.S.-South American "Good Neighbor Policy" was a political expediency, she was the best good will ambassador the southern continent could have with its northern neighbor.

Later, after her death, Carmen Miranda was regarded as a delicious show-business oddity, a high queen of camp viewed as more a joke (in the United States) than as an institution (as viewed by some in her adopted homeland of Brazil). That assessment was shameful, because Carmen was extremely talented. Moreover, she was a shrewd merchandiser of her flamboyant, oversized persona: a foreigner who coped effectively in an era when patronizing Americans believed anyone not homegrown was to be somewhat pitied.

Carmen Miranda was born Maria do Carmo Miranda da Cunha in Marco de Canavezes, near Lisbon, Portugal, on February 9, 1909. Her parents, José Pinto Cunha and Maria Emilia (Miranda), moved to Rio de Janeiro three months later, where Maria's father was a barber. Carmen had three sisters, one older (Olinda) and two younger (Cecilia and Aurora, the latter of whom also went into show business) and two younger brothers, Gabriel and Mario.

Even while being schooled at the Convent of Saint Teresenha, Carmen was already thinking of a show-business career. She recalled, "When the sisters asked me to play a role in the school plays, I always inserted my own lines in the parts I was interpreting and the sisters didn't like that." Through a childhood acquaintance, Carmen obtained a department store job, but devoted more energy to entertaining her coworkers with songs than to working. One person who witnessed one of these impromptu performances helped her obtain a weekly singing spot on a local radio

Carmen Miranda in *That Night in Rio* (1941).
[Courtesy of JC Archives]

station. She kept her show-business activities secret because her conservative parents thought such a career unsuitable for their daughter. In 1928, Carmen appeared at the National Institute of Music festival and made a strong impression with both the critics and the public. An executive from the South American division of RCA Records heard Carmen on the radio, and she was signed to a recording contract in late 1929. (She later would record in Rio de Janeiro for Brunswick and Odeon.) By 1931, her chief rival in the singing field was the popular Raquel Meller. By this time, Carmen's family had decided to accede to her theatrical career, and her father had become her business manager, although Carmen made all her own decisions. She termed her song style *con moviemento*, a quick way of describing her enthusiastic format, with its gyrating hips, rolling eyes, and facile hand gestures used to punctuate her rapid-fire words.

Carmen appeared in local Rio nightclubs and in 1930 performed in the revue *Vai Dar o Que Falar* at the Joao Caetano Theater in Rio. In 1933, she made her film debut in *A Voz do Carnaval*, a semidocumentary of the famed Rio Carnival. She can be spotted in a few sequences, shown singing in front of a microphone. In the variety musical feature *Alo, Alo Brasil* (1935), her sister Aurora (already a vocalist) also appeared, as the two sisters had done previously in *Estudantes* (1935). The two songsters were together once again in *Alo, Alo Carnaval* (1936), and Carmen made her final South American–made film, *Banana da Terra*, for producer Wallace Downey. It was released by MGM of Brazil in 1939.

By this point, Carmen was an extraordinarily well-established recording artist—by 1939 she had made more than three hundred singles—and her cabaret appearances were always very well attended. She had toured South America's leading cities nine times with her act and was already considered a national institution. While playing the Caino Urca in Rio, she was noticed by Claiborne Foster, a former actress and now wife of Maxwell J. Rice, a Pan American Airlines official based in Brazil. Foster wrote Claude Greneker, press agent to theatrical producer Lee Shubert, that Carmen was a performer worthy of the showman's consideration. On his next trip to Brazil, Shubert saw Carmen perform.

The Broadway impresario offered Carmen a contract to come north to the United States, *if* she would learn English. She retorted that "the public likes my songs in Portuguese, and if you want me, it will be on those terms." After more negotiation, Carmen signed a three-year contract with Shubert and headed north by ship, arriving in New York on May 17, 1939. The novelty of this exotic entertainer had preceded her, and the press was on hand to greet the five-feet two-inches celebrity (she wore thick platform shoes and high hats to disguise her shortness). Although she spoke Portuguese, Spanish, and French, she insisted that her (very accented) English vocabulary was limited to saying "money, money, money . . . hot dog. I say yes, no, and I say, money, money, money, and I say turkey sandwich and I say grape juice." Aloysio Oliveria, the lead performer in her Banda da Lua (which she brought north to accompany her numbers in Shubert's shows) served as her interpreter.

Carmen was rushed into rehearsals for *Streets of Paris*, a musical revue that opened in New York on June 19, 1939. She had three solo numbers in the show, including "South American Way." Said one Broadway critic, "Her face is too heavy to be beautiful, her figure is nothing to write home about and she sings in a foreign language. Yet she is the biggest theatrical sensation of the season." Carmen and *Streets of Paris* were a major hit. When not performing onstage at the Broadhurst Theater, Carmen could be heard on such radio variety shows as Rudy Vallee's. She also appeared on the roster of the late show at the Waldorf-Astoria's club and played vaudeville engagements.

In 1940, Twentieth Century-Fox was making many musicals, with a particular emphasis on Technicolor productions. The studio's head, Darryl F. Zanuck, was wise enough to know that fostering Latin American–U.S. friendship would be favorably viewed by the U.S. government. Thus it was a natural for Carmen and the studio to come together. She signed to make a specialty appearance in *Down Argentine Way* (1940), a lusciously filmed but frivolous Don Ameche–Betty Grable production. Because Miranda was bound contractually to remain in New York, the studio shot her scenes at the Movietone Studios in Manhattan, while the greater part of the movie, set in Buenos Aires, was lensed in Hollywood. For her contributions, Carmen was paid $20,000 (minus the contractual commissions owed to the Shuberts). The *New York Times* noted when the film was released that "Miss Miranda sings 'South American Way' and a few Spanish trifles scorchily, but we don't see enough of her. . . ." Twentieth Century-Fox was already remedying that situation. They signed Carmen to a long-term contract and intended to provide the public with many opportunities on the big screen to witness her enticing " 'Souse' American Way."

When Carmen returned to Rio in July 1940, Brazilian President Vargas declared it a national holiday, but Carmen learned quickly that the Brazilians were unappreciative of her having "gone Hollywood" and for internationalizing a caricature of their native ways. This perception greatly saddened Carmen, who now felt alienated from her beloved homeland. She returned to the States to find the Shuberts uncertain of how next to showcase her. They considered presenting her in a modern version of *Carmen* or of teaming her in a revue with Maurice Chevalier. Neither came to be.

After conferring with her sister Aurora (now playing nightclub engagements in America) and advising her to turn down a minor MGM contract as well as a bid from the Shuberts, Carmen went to California to appear in *That Night in Rio* (1941) in support of Alice Faye and Don Ameche. It became evident that Fox, having provided her with an English instructor (named Zacharias Yaconellei), had helped her language problem, because her dialogue in this musical was far more intelligible. She had two big numbers: "Chica, Chica, Boom, Chic" and "I Yi Yi, Yi," both of which became permanent parts of her repertoire. She was backed by her Bando da Lua and did the samba. However, some critics insisted Hollywood was Americanizing her too much. She was now earning $4,000 weekly, which she had to share fifty-fifty with the Shuberts. She was then teamed on-camera with Alice Faye, John Payne, and Cesar Romero in the lush *Weekend in Havana* (1941). As fiery club performer Rosita Rivas, she sang "The Nango" and assorted other tunes and wore an array of attention-grabbing costumes (most of which she designed herself). "Where else," asked the *New York Times*, "can you meet Carmen Miranda wriggling devilishly with harvest baskets on her head, except in whatever capital a Fox musical is set? How Miss Miranda gets around—and all the time standing in one spot!" By now she was grossing $5,000 weekly. On March 23, 1941, she imprinted her shoe and handprints at Grauman's Chinese Theater. She was officially part of Hollywood movie lore.

The Shuberts brought Carmen back to Broadway, teaming her with Olsen and Johnson, Ella Logan, the Blackburn Twins, and others in the musical revue *Sons o' Fun* (December 1, 1941). The show was a hodgepodge of slapstick, songs, and skits. Richard Watts Jr. (*New York Herald Tribune*) concluded, "In her eccentric and highly personalized fashion, Miss Miranda is by way of being an artist and her numbers give the show its one touch of distinction." Her rousing showstopper was "Thank You, North America." On June 1, 1942, she left the production; her Shubert contract had expired. Meanwhile she made recordings for Decca Records, including "Chica, Chica, Boom Chic," "The Tic-Tac of My Heart," "Manuelo," and "Chatanooga Choo Choo."

Carmen was now a full-time Hollywood star. However, off-camera, as on-screen, she remained an industry enigma. She liked nightlife, but never drank or smoked, nor was she linked romantically with anyone (there were rumors of a Brazilian lawyer she had left behind in 1939). Her mother and brother Gabriel had moved to California to be with her, her father having died in 1938. If her next feature, *Springtime in the Rockies* (1942), lacked much-needed creative verve with its predictable backstage tale featuring Betty Grable and John Payne, it boasted Harry James's band and the zesty presence of Carmen, who was developing into a seasoned comedienne. Although Carmen was already mastering English, she wisely retained the illusion of her original accent. On a different note, there had been a ruckus at Fox when press photographers, taking candids on a set where Carmen was twirling away, revealed in their glossies that she wore (that day) no undergarments beneath her long skirts. The studio had frowned on the "adverse" publicity. This incident would crop up for years thereafter, often cited as the reason Fox finally lost interest in her.

Of all Carmen Miranda's feature films—and often it was hard to differentiate any one of her pictures from another—her most memorable was *The Gang's All Here* (1943), which boasted the "new" Carmen who had had plastic surgery to reshape her nose. The film starred Alice Faye, featured Benny Goodman and His Band, and was directed with abandon by Busby Berkeley. Never was the choreographer more expansive, fluid, or erotic than in Carmen's lavish set piece "The Lady in the Tutti-Frutti Hat." It showcased Miranda at her most dazzling, despite her top-heavy, fruit-laden chapeau. Miranda competed for the filmgoer's attention with dancing bananas (phallic imagery much written about in later decades). But the film, which cast her as Dorita the Broadway performer who adores but does not win James Ellison (Faye does), illustrated the major impediment in the furtherance of Carmen's career momentum. Hollywood believed moviegoers would not accept her in the status of a leading lady who wins the heart of an American leading man; so she remained a high-energy diversion, always cast as the star's peppery friend or jealous rival. Caught in such a narrow mold, Carmen was bound to wear out her welcome.

She had three 1944 features. In *Four Jills in a Jeep*, a tribute to show-business entertainment of troops at the war front, Miranda appeared in a radio broadcast setting to present "Ay Ay Ay." It was her first black-and-white Hollywood feature. She was top-starred in *Greenwich Village*, supported by Don Ameche, William Bendix, and Vivian Blaine. She murdered the English, sang a few numbers, and moved on to *Something for the Boys*, a distillation of Cole Porter's stage musical. It costarred Vivian Blaine and Perry Como, and Miranda offered "Samba Boogie." The silly plot had her portraying Chiquita Hart, whose tooth fillings act as a radio transmitter. Plans for her to star in an original musical *Brazilian Bombshell* did not materialize.

Carmen now was earning more than $200,000 yearly, but her star at Twentieth Century-Fox was dimming. She was to have starred in *Riocabana* but instead was in the black-and-white *Doll Face* (1945), based on a bad Gypsy Rose Lee play, in which Vivian Blaine had the lead. The *New York Herald-Tribune* alerted, "Carmen Miranda does what she always does, only not as well." She was in support of Miss Blaine for the fourth time in *If I'm Lucky* (1946), and the *New York Times* complained that here she was just "an animated noise."

Once World War II was over, public tastes changed, and Carmen and Twentieth Century-Fox parted company in January 1946. Her specialized brand of entertainment was no longer required. She signed a long-term contract with Universal, but when that studio merged into Universal-International, the new regime had no concrete plans for her. Her one picture in 1947 was United Artists' *Copacabana*, which featured Groucho Marx (without his brothers). She had two roles: as a Latin songstress and as a French harem-veiled thrush wearing a blonde wig. The picture did mild business. She did club work in Florida, and then—on March 17, 1947, at the Good Shepherd Church in Beverly Hills—the Catholic Carmen married the Jewish David Sebastian, whose brother-in-law had invested in *Copacabana*. Sebastian would become her business manager. In May 1947, Carmen played the actual Copacabana Club in New York and the next year did cabaret work in Las Vegas and was at the London Palladium that April.

Meanwhile, MGM, which had a far-ranging roster of specialty performers to decorate its musical entries, hired Carmen for two features, both starring Jane Powell and produced by Joe Pasternak. In *A Date With Judy* (1948), Miranda was Rosita Conchellas, a dance instructress who accidentally gets Wallace Beery into marital strife. In this vehicle, she worked in tandem with Xavier Cugat and His Orchestra. Her big number was a delightful rendition of "Cuanto La Gusta." For *Nancy Goes to Rio* (1950), Carmen supplied the local color, wore a blonde hairdo, and performed "Ca-Room Pa Pa."

Amidst rumors she was having a baby in 1948 (she later suffered a miscarriage) and continuing marital problems with her husband, Carmen continued to ply the nightclub circuit, earning $7,500 weekly. Later, Paramount used Carmen to enhance their Dean Martin–Jerry Lewis vehicle *Scared Stiff* (1953) set in Cuba, but the comedy was weak and Miranda's routines/songs were all too familiar. Also in 1953 she went on a four-month tour to Europe that concluded with performances in Sweden and Finland.

While performing in Cincinnati in October 1953, Miranda collapsed (from exhaustion), and plans for her to tour several of the Shubert theaters in the United States were dropped. She began suffering from despondency over her diminished career and her longtime rift with her homeland. She underwent electroshock therapy, and when that failed to cure her, her physician suggested a return visit to Brazil. Accompanied by her sister Aurora, she arrived in Rio de Janeiro on December 3, 1954, her first visit home in fourteen years. Her widespread acceptance by her fellow country people did much to restore her confidence. She recuperated there until April 4, 1955, when she returned north to rejoin her husband.

In April 1955, Carmen performed at the New Frontier Hotel in Las Vegas and in July enjoyed a highly popular club tour of Cuba. Thereafter, she returned to Los Angeles to recuperate from a recurring bronchial ailment. She was next scheduled to guest on Jimmy Durante's TV show. On August 4, 1955, while taping a vigorous mambo number with Durante and Eddie Jackson, she almost fell during the final sequence and murmured, "I'm all out of breath." That night, after attending a party, she returned home, where she collapsed and died of a heart attack. After Catholic services in Hollywood, her husband and Carmen's mother accompanied the body to Rio for burial. An estimated one million people lined the streets to bid her farewell. She was buried on August 13, wearing a simple red suit and the red beads of a rosary. Miranda's family directed that the Jimmy Durante show be aired. It was shown on October 15, 1955, with the producer substituting a long shot of Carmen's dance finale and omitting her telltale final words.

In 1957, David Sebastian shipped many of Carmen's effects to Rio, where it was hoped a museum would be started, devoted to Miranda's career. Such a shrine did open in 1976. Tourists still visit Miranda's gravesite located at the Cemiterio Sao Joao Batista in Rio.

Hollywood was not through with Carmen. In Twentieth Century-Fox's *Beloved Infidel* (1959), there is a scene with Deborah Kerr and Gregory Peck leaving a movie theater that is showing *That Night in Rio*. In the same studio's *Myra Breckinridge* (1970), there is a clip of Carmen singing "Chica, Chica, Boom Chic" from *That Night in Rio*. In MGM's *That's Entertainment!* (1974), there is a bit of Miranda in the ensemble song number from *A Date With Judy*. Over the decades, there have been several compilation record albums released both in the United States and in South America of Carmen's many recordings. In 1989 *Brazilian Bombshell*, a biography of Carmen by Martha Gil-Montero, was published. Five years later, the colorful celebrity was the subject of an offbeat documentary. Entitled *Carmen Miranda: Bananas Is My Business*, it was written, directed, and coproduced by Helena Solberg. In this dramatic biography/documentary of the unique Portuguese star, Leticia Monte portrayed Carmen as a teenager, while Eric Barreto impersonated (for exotic effect) Miranda in the fantasy sequences. Later came the 1997 Brazilian-made documentary, directed by Rogério Sganzerla, an eighty-two-minute study of the one-of-a-kind performer. In 2001, Soraya Ravenle starred in Rio De Janeiro as the late entertainer in *South American Way: The Carmen Miranda Musical*. The hit show, with its revisionist point of view, focused on Carmen's controversial status in Brazil during the 1940s. Carmen was criticized for not being a "real" Brazilian, and because the Caucasian made her mark in Hollywood as a caricatured Pan-American singing in a musical style conceived in the black slums of her adopted homeland. Also, as part of the resurgence in interest in Miranda in the new millennium, Ney Matogrosso issued an album of songs long associated with Carmen.

For the record, Carmen Miranda's distinctive personality and headgear were responsible for United Fruit's Chiquita Banana advertisements. Imogene Coca imitated Carmen onstage in *The Straw Hat Revue* (1939). On the big screen, Hilda Navarez did a Miranda imitation in *Angels With Broken Wings* (1941), and Cass Daley did an improvisation of the Miranda mystique in the movie *Ladies' Man* (1947). However, the two best impersonations of the legendary Miranda were executed by Mickey Rooney in the film *Babes on Broadway* (1941) and by Milton Berle on his early 1950s teleseries. Nevertheless, despite their zest, none of these parodies caught the vibrant and unique flavor that was the witty and daring Carmen Miranda.

Filmography

A Voz do Carnaval (Braz, 1933)
Estudiantes (Braz, 1934)
Alo, Alo, Brazil (Braz, 1935)
Alo, Alo Carnaval (Braz, 1936)
Banana da Terra (Braz, 1938)
Down Argentine Way (20th-Fox, 1940)
That Night in Rio (20th-Fox, 1941)
Weekend in Havana (20th-Fox, 1941)
Springtime in the Rockies (20th-Fox, 1942)
The Gang's All Here [The Girls He Left Behind]
    (20th-Fox, 1943)

Four Jills in a Jeep (20th-Fox, 1944)
Greenwich Village (20th-Fox, 1944)
Something for the Boys (20th-Fox, 1944)
Hollywood on Parade (Col, 1945) (s)
All Star Bond Rally (20th-Fox, 1945) (s)
Doll Face [Come Back to Me] (20th-Fox, 1946)
If I'm Lucky (20th-Fox, 1946)
Copacabana (UA, 1947)
A Date With Judy (MGM, 1948)
Nancy Goes to Rio (MGM, 1950)
Scared Stiff (Par, 1953)

Broadway Plays

The Streets of Paris (1939)

Sons o' Fun (1941)

Album Discography

LPs

The Brazilian Bombshell (Ace of Hearts 99, MCA Coral CP-99, MCA Coral COP-6821, EMI CRLM-1060)

The Brazilian Fireball (World Record Club SH-114)

Carmen Miranda: A Pequna Notavel (RCA Camden CALB-5173)

Carmen Miranda Live—Rare Broadcast Performances (Amalgamated 149)

Carmen Miranda—Radio Broadcasts (Records Macumbeiros Churrasco M-809) w. Jimmy Durante

The Compleat Carmen Miranda (AEI 2101)

Cuanto la Gusta (Rio Brasil LP-1901)

Down Argentine Way (Hollywood Soundstage 5012) [ST]

Down Argentine Way/Springtime in the Rockies (Caliban 6003, Hollywood Soundstage 5013) [ST]

Four Jills In a Jeep (Hollywood Soundstage HS-407) [ST]

The Gang's All Here (CIF 3003) [ST]

Greenwich Village (Caliban 6026) [ST]

Nancy Goes to Rio (10″ MGM E-508, MGM SES-53ST) [ST]

Quanto La Gusta (Rio 1900)

Something for the Boys (Caliban 5030) [ST]

South American Way (MCA Coral MCL-1703, EMI/MCA Coral CDL-8029)

Springtime in the Rockies (Pelican 128) [ST/R]

20 Anos de Saudade (RCA Camden Brazil 107.0214)

Weekend in Havana/That Night in Rio (Curtain Calls 100/14) [ST]

CDs

Absolute Best Sambas (Recording Arts ABCD-111)

Acero Especial (BMG Brasil V-10026)

Anthology (One Way MCAD-22124) w. The Andrews Sisters

Balance (EMI Brasil 076.422531)

Bananas Is My Business (Fox Lorber 1211)

The Best of Carmen Miranda (ABCD Japan AB-115)

The Brazilian Bombshell (Harlequin HQ-CD33)

The Brazilian Bombshell (Legend LGCD-6005)

Brazilian Bombshell—25 Hits (ASV CD-AJA-5242)

Carmen Miranda (EMI Japan TOCP-8571)

Carmen Miranda (Miran Sur CH-524)

Carmen Miranda (RCA Brasil 74321-52777-2)

Carmen Miranda (RCA Japan BVCP-2078)

Carmen Miranda and Aurora Miranda (Motodiscos 054-7947221)

Carmen Miranda and Aurora Miranda, Vol. 2 (Motodiscos 054-795323)

Carmen Miranda 1930-45, Vol. 2 (Harlequin HQ-CD94)

Carmen Miranda 1939-50 (Decca MVCE-241863)

Cocktail Hour (Columbia River Entertainment Group CRG-218026)

The Gang's All Here (Sandy Hook CDSH-2009) [ST]

Holiday in Mexico/Weekend in Havana (Great Movie Themes 60036) [ST]

Junto de Voces (Revivendo Musicas RCD-020)

Lady Be Good/Four Jills In a Jeep (Great Movie Themes 60029) [ST]

The Lady in the Tutti Frutti Hat (Harlequin HQ-CD133)

A Melhos de Carmen Miranda (BMG Brasil 7321-49645-2)

Nancy Goes to Rio (MCA MCAD-5952) [ST]

A Pequeña Notavel (Revivendo RVCD-037)

Raizes Do Samba (EMI Brasil 522167-2)

Revivendo: Carmen Miranda (Revivendo Musicas RVCD-003)

Samba (Absolutely Free 111)

Sambas (Musica Latina MIN-55035)

Siempre Notavel (BMG 74321-152774-2)

South American Way (Jasmine JASCD-317)

South American Way (Saludas 62063)

Grace Moore

(b. Mary Willie Grace Moore, Nough, Tennessee, December 5, 1898; d. near
Copenhagen, Denmark, January 26, 1947)

During the mid-1930s, opera diva Grace Moore, after a few unremarkable features at MGM in
the early part of the decade, returned to moviemaking. In a series of surprisingly successful films
that the dramatic soprano made for Columbia Pictures, she almost single-handedly brought opera
to the masses. Such was her impact on the Hollywood movie industry that she was Oscar-nominated
for her performance in 1934's *One Night of Love*. Like Lawrence Tibbett and Nelson Eddy, Moore
had a varied career that not only encompassed the operatic stage, but also Broadway revues, recordings, radio, and movies. Although her singing career was past its prime when she was killed in an
air crash in 1947, this lyrical soprano was still a potent force in opera. Her popularity abroad
equaled or even exceeded that in her homeland; she was given France's Chevalier du Legion
d'Honneur in addition to accolades from a dozen other countries.

Mary Willie Grace Moore was born on December 5, 1898, in Nough, Tennessee, the daughter
of a clerk/traveling salesman (Richard Lawson Moore) and his wife Tessie Jane Stokely. (Other
children in the family were Herbert, Martin, the twins Estel and Emily, Richard, James, and Anna.)
She was five when the family moved to Knoxville, and they later relocated to the mining town of
Jellico. After finishing high school in Jellico, Grace attended a Baptist seminary in Louisville,
Kentucky (with the thought of doing missionary work), but decided, instead, to focus on singing,
musical theory, Freud, and English at the Ward-Belmont College in Nashville, Tennessee. Then,
against her father's wishes, she continued her vocal studies at the Wilson-Greene Music School in
Washington, DC.

In 1919, Moore went to New York City (again much against her father's wishes) to pursue
a theatrical career. For a six-month period, she lost her voice, which required a long rest to cure.
Returning to voice lessons, she studied under the guidance of the Metropolitan Opera's resident
throat specialist and vocal pedagogue Dr. P. Mario Marafioti, a friend of the great Italian tenor
Enrico Caruso. After traveling with a road production, Grace was spotted in a Greenwich Village
club (the Black Cat Café) by George M. Cohan, who suggested she try her luck in musical comedy.
In 1920 the young singer was signed for a featured spot (singing "Oh Moon of Love") in the revue
of *Hitchy-Koo of 1920* with Raymond Hitchcock and Julia Sanderson; she was also Sanderson's
understudy. The show debuted in Boston at the Colonial Theater on September 7, 1920, and then
moved to Broadway at the New Amsterdam Theater on December 19, 1920, for a seventy-one-
performance run. *Town Gossip*, with Grace in the singing lead, closed in Baltimore in September
1921. The revue *Up in the Clouds* (also called *Above the Clouds*) with Skeets Gallagher toured and
then came to New York City, where it played on the subway circuit.

Intent on gaining admission to the world of opera, Grace realized she needed to travel to
France to further her studies. For the next two years, she underwent intensive voice training and

Grace Moore and André Luguet in *Jenny Lind*, the French-language version of *A Lady's Morals* (1930). [Courtesy of JC Archives]

worked with the German-American Opera Company in Paris. In France she met Irving Berlin, who suggested she return to Broadway to join in his new *Music Box Revue of 1923*. Thus, in the fall of 1923, she joined with Frank Tinney, the Brox Sisters, and Robert Benchley for 273 performances in this Irving Berlin production. The next year she starred in Berlin's *Music Box Revue of 1924* with Clark and McCullough, Fanny Brice, Oscar Shaw, the Brox Sisters, and Claire Luce. Among her songs in this production was "What'll I Do?" Despite her growing success onstage, Grace Moore still wanted to sing grand opera, and she continued her opera studies. However, she failed two auditions at New York's Metropolitan Opera.

An invitation from opera diva Mary Garden led Grace to the diva's apartment in Monte Carlo, where she studied with opera coach Richard Barthélemy. She remained in Europe for the next two years studying opera under the patronage of Otto Kahn. Returning to the United States once again, she did concert work, and then, on February 7, 1928, she made her Metropolitan debut in the soprano role of Mimi in Giacomo Puccini's *La Bohème*. Because of her Broadway background, Moore's opera bow attracted much attention, including that of the focal figures of the famed Algonquin circle. Among the audience that night were one hundred friends from Tennessee, including its two U.S. senators. She was to remain at the Metropolitan Opera for nearly two decades (except for three seasons in the mid-1930s), and from 1928 to 1931 she sang the roles of Juliette in Charles Gounod's *Romeo et Juliette*, Micaela in Georges Bizet's *Carmen*, Marguerite in Gounod's *Faust*, and the title role in Jules Massenet's *Manon* before going to Paris in 1929 to appear at the L'Opera Comique. Her debut role there was again Mimi of *La Bohème*, but she also sang the title role in Gustave Charpentier's *Louise*. (The latter role was generally considered by critics to be her best characterization.)

By now Hollywood was interested in the acclaimed opera singer. MGM, who had already signed Lawrence Tibbett, contracted Grace for pictures, assuming that the public would enjoy seeing an opera singer (who was not overweight—once she lost a required fifteen pounds) and listening to more highbrow music. It was stipulated that her pictures would be made during the summers, so she could continue developing her opera career. She made her screen debut in 1930 in *A Lady's Morals* (reviewed as *The Soul Kiss*) as the famous Swedish singer Jenny Lind in a contrived plot that had her working for P. T. Barnum (Wallace Beery) and in love with a young composer (Reginald Denny). In the feature, she offered "Casta Diva" from Vincenzo Bellini's *Norma* and "Rataplan" from Gaetano Donizetti's *The Daughter of the Regiment* in addition to such popular numbers as "Is It Destiny?" "I Heard Your Voice," and "Lovely Hour." *Variety* rhapsodized that Moore was "an actress of an indescribable charm, with the added appeal of a voice that registers magically on the mechanical, with a human quality that gives it remarkable appeal." The general moviegoing public was less impressed, preferring more down-to-earth entertainment and heroines who did not display such an apparent air of superiority. (Moore also starred in a French-language version of *A Lady's Morals* called *Jenny Lind*).

In 1931 Grace costarred with Lawrence Tibbett in Sigmund Romberg's *The New Moon* (called *Parisian Belle* on TV). MGM changed the setting from the original stage operetta, with Moore now as a Slavic princess who is the subject of rivalry between a Russian lieutenant (Tibbett) and his commander (Adolphe Menjou). She sang "Softly as in a Morning Sunrise," "One Kiss," and dueted with Tibbett on "Wanting You" and "Lover Come Back to Me." *Variety* opined, "There's a doubt as to whether it will be easily digested by the average picturegoer." There were rumors of Grace being temperamental on the set, problems with the front office about her dieting, and worst of all, poor box-office returns on both pictures. MGM cancelled her contract. Moore returned to Broadway in *The DuBarry* (1932), which had an eighty-seven performance run. The previous year (on July 15, 1931 in Cannes) she had wed Valentin Parera, a Spanish movie actor.

Undaunted by her Hollywood failure, Moore hoped to returned to filmmaking in general and MGM in particular. When that studio began preparation for Franz Lehar's classic operetta *The Merry Widow*, she was very receptive to their bid to headline the feature. However, problems arose as to whether she or colead Maurice Chevalier would have top billing, and when the studio favored Chevalier she left the project (to be replaced by Jeanette MacDonald).

Harry Cohn's Columbia Pictures thought he could merchandize the temperamental Ms. Moore for public consumption and hired her at $25,000 per picture. When the mogul began to have misgivings and indicated that he wanted to end their agreement, she threatened to sue. Instead, he allowed production on *One Night of Love* to proceed, although when he decided to cut the operatic sequences to save costs she paid for them in exchange for a percentage of the film's profits.

Now much glamorized and made more human, she was cast as a promising music student who falls in love with her teacher (Tullio Carminati). He deserts her, but returns in time to make her Metropolitan debut a rousing success. In the film, she introduced her most popular number, "Ciribiribin," and also sang the title song, plus several opera arias. She recorded the two pop numbers for Brunswick Records. (She had been recording for nearly a decade, having made her first discs in 1925 for Victor Records with songs from the *Music Box Revue of 1924*. In 1927, she had recorded selections from *La Bohème, Carmen*, and Puccini's *Madame Butterfly* for Brunswick, and in 1932 she had performed a trio of songs from *The DuBarry* for Victor, including a duet with Richard Crooks on "Without Your Love.")

The modestly budgeted *One Night of Love* proved to be one of the surprise film successes of 1934, earning Moore an Academy Award nomination as Best Actress (she lost to Claudette Colbert of Columbia's *It Happened One Night*), as well as garnering Oscars for Best Sound Recording and Best Scoring. It was named one of the ten best films of the year by the trade publication *Film Daily*. Thanks to *One Night of Love* and *It Happened One Night*, Columbia Pictures became a major Hollywood studio and not just a step up from poverty row.

Irving Thalberg at MGM was now intent on having her back at the studio for the announced *Rose-Marie* and *Maytime*. However, scheduling problems intervened, and Jeanette MacDonald inherited both movie roles, released respectively in 1936 and 1937. By then Thalberg had died and Metro was no longer eager for Grace's services. Meanwhile, she made her second Columbia picture. In *Love Me Forever* (1935), she portrayed an heiress who loses all her money and becomes a café singer, eventually making a successful debut in grand opera. She sang the title song (also recorded for Decca) and "Whoa!" plus several operatic excerpts. Next came *The King Steps Out* (1936), directed by Josef Von Sternberg, with Grace as a princess posing as a commoner. She attracts the attention of a handsome young king (Franchot Tone) who requires a bride. She sang "Shall We Remain?" "Stars in My Eyes," "Learn to Lose," and "The End Begins," all of which she recorded for Decca Records. Again there were more rumors of conflicts on the sound-stage sets.

Continuing in its attempt to make Moore a more empathetic heroine on-screen, Columbia teamed her with dapper Cary Grant in *When You're in Love* (1937). She was the Australian opera star who takes part in a marriage of convenience with an artist (Grant) so she can gain entrance into the United States to sing at a musical festival produced by her uncle (Thomas Mitchell). In this popular musical, Moore sang a variety of songs like "Siboney," "Minnie the Moocher" (to show how down-to-earth she could be), "In the Gloaming," and Franz Schubert's "Serenade," as well as abbreviated arias from Puccini's operas *Madame Butterfly* and *Tosca*.

In what proved to be Grace's final Columbia outing, *I'll Take Romance* (1937), she played a Metropolitan opera singer who reneges on her promise to sing in Buenos Aires because of a more lucrative professional offer from Paris. She is kidnapped by an American producer (Melvyn Douglas) who brings her to Rio to fulfill her obligations. Besides arias from Giuseppe Verdi's *La Traviata*, Fredrich Von Flotow's *Martha*, and Puccini's *Madame Butterfly* (the latter actually a duet with Frank Forest), she also performed the folk song, "She'll Be Comin' 'Round the Mountain."

By now the popularity of opera in films, which Moore had started with *One Night of Love*, had severely waned, aided by other studios diluting the formula: RKO with Lily Pons features, Paramount's use of contralto Gladys Swarthout, and even Republic's attempt to make a movie star of Grace Talley. (MGM, in contrast, had found a successful formula with light operettas starring Jeanette MacDonald and Nelson Eddy.) Columbia and Grace Moore ended their partnership.

While making films for Columbia, Moore had made her London operatic debut as Mimi in *La Bohème* on June 6, 1935 at the Covent Garden Opera House. In the United States she became a popular performer on radio. In early 1935, she starred in the radio series *Open House* for a season, and from 1936 to 1937 she headlined *General Motors Concert* on NBC on Sundays. From May 1 to June 16, 1937, she was on the Saturday-night CBS program *The Nash Show*, and in April 1938 she appeared with Andre Kostelanetz (who was married to her screen rival Lily Pons) on the CBS network's *The Chesterfield Show* on Wednesday nights for three months. Grace continued to give concerts, perform at the Metropolitan, and make records for Decca and RCA Victor. She was renowned for her high lifestyle: villas in Italy and Cannes and a mansion in Hollywood, lavish party giving, and traveling with an extensive entourage. As she explained about her moviemaking years, "I already had some of the fame, but Hollywood gave me the rich lace trimmings, the royal robes, the furs, the jewels, the international celebrity. . . ."

When there were no forthcoming film offers from Hollywood, Moore went to France in the summer of 1938 to star in what proved to be her final film, the opera *Louise*. It was directed by the famed Abel Gance (who had made the landmark silent film *Napoleon*, among others). The picture received scattered, unimpressive release in the United States in 1940. (On January 28, 1939, she sang the title role of *Louise* at the Metropolitan.) Meanwhile, the coming of World War II cut Grace Moore off from her lucrative European popularity. She began nurturing new operatic talent, both in sponsorship and through coaching. Her star protégée was Dorothy Kirsten.

Grace continued at the Met and made concert tours across the country. As a goodwill gesture for the State Department, she made a South American tour in 1941. On December 18, 1941, she debuted in the lead of Puccini's *Tosca* at the Met, later performing the role in Canada and Chicago. During the war, she toured with the USO both at home and abroad. Her autobiography, *You're Only Human Once*, was published in 1944.

Following the war's end in 1945, Grace resumed working in Europe (she celebrated the liberation of Paris with a concert at the Paris Opera on July 24, 1945) and back in the United States. While on a concert tour, she was killed in a plane crash over Copenhagen, Denmark on January 26, 1947. In the ensuing years, her records have continued to be reissued and her (non-MGM) movies retain their appeal to film buffs. In 1953, Kathryn Grayson portrayed Grace Moore in a disappointing feature *So This Is Love* (1953) released by Warner Bros. The pedestrian musical biography gave little indication of what Grace More had done for Hollywood, as recognized when Grace, in May 1934, had received the National Service Fellowship Medal from the Society of Arts and Sciences for "distinctive service in the arts, especially for conspicuous achievement in raising the standard of cinema entertainment."

Filmography

A Lady's Morals [The Jenny Lind Story/The Soul Kiss] (MGM, 1930)*
New Moon [Parisian Belle] (MGM, 1930)
One Night of Love (Col, 1934)
Inside Opera (Col, c. 1935) (s)
A Dream Comes True (Vita, 1935) (s)

Love Me Forever (Col, 1935)
The King Steps Out (Col, 1936)
I'll Take Romance (Col, 1937)
When You're in Love (Col, 1937)
Louise (Fr, 1940)
*Also French-language version.

Broadway Plays

Hitchy-Koo of 1920 (1920)

Music Box Revue of 1923 (1923)

Music Box Revue of 1924 (1924)

The DuBarry (1932)

Radio Series

Open House (NBC, 1935–36)

General Motors Concert (NBC, 1936–37)

The Nash Show (CBS, 1937)

The Chesterfield Show (CBS, 1938)

Album Discography

LPs

The Art of Grace Moore (Camden CAL-519, RCA International 90040)

Grace Moore (Empire 801)

Grace Moore in Opera and Song (Rhapsody 6018)

Grace Moore in Opera and Songs (10″ RCA LCT-7004)

Grace Moore Sings (Decca DL-9593)

Irving Berlin: 1909-1939 (JJA 19744)

The Memorable Radio Years, 1935-45 (Star-Tone 217)

The Music of Broadway (JJA 19779)

One Night of Love (Amalgamated 248) [ST]

Opera and Song (Tap 334)

Parisian Belle [New Moon] (Amalgamated 168, Pelican 2020) [ST]

When You're in Love (Caliban 6044) [ST]

CDs

Charpentier: Louise (Naxos Historical 8.110102-04)

Love Me Forever (PEP 9116)

One Night of Love (Memoir 424)

The Radio Years (Enterprise R458)

So This Is Love (ASV CD-AJA-5257)

Dennis Morgan

(b. Stanley Morner, Prentice, Wisconsin, December 30, 1910; d. Fresno California, September 8, 1994)

Dennis Morgan was a solid utility performer on film. He was handsome (always with a twinkle in his eyes and a dimpled smile), a fine tenor singer, and had a pleasing disposition on-camera (and off-). Thus, he became an unobtrusive leading man in dozens of feature films in the 1940s and 1950s, eventually developing into one of Warner Bros.' highest-paid stars before the inroads of television ended his movie career. In many respects his screen career could be compared to that of George Murphy's, except Morgan was a singer, while Murphy traded on his dancing skills. While not an overly distinctive movie crooner, Dennis Morgan proved to have the staying power lacking in many of his contemporaries, because he could switch from singing roles to dramatics and back again with relative ease.

He was born Stanley Morner on December 30, 1910, in Prentice, Wisconsin. His father was a banker who also owned a number of logging camps. As he was growing up, young Stanley worked as a lumberjack for his father (who later became his manager), eventually maturing to a solid six-feet two-inches. Because of his hard work at the logging camps, he excelled in school sports, including baseball, football, basketball, and track.

After graduating from high school in Marshfield, Wisconsin, Stanley attended Carroll College in Waukesha, Wisconsin. There he continued to participate in sports as well as working as a radio station disc jockey at WTMJ in Milwaukee for $35 weekly. In addition, he took music lessons and became a soloist with the campus glee club. After college graduation, Morner decided on a musical career—one in opera—and obtained a job with a Chautauqua troupe performing Charles Gounod's *Faust*. After a tour with the group, he landed a job singing on radio in Milwaukee as well as performing as a soloist in various church choirs. From there he worked in vaudeville and then went to Chicago, where he studied at the Chicago Musical College and performed at the State Lake Theater. He negotiated a singing engagement at the Empire Room of the Palmer House. This job led to radio work on NBC as the singing star of the *Silken Strings* program, plus the lead in a production of George Frideric Handel's *Xerxes* with a small opera company. It was there that he was heard by opera diva Mary Garden, who recommended him to Metro-Goldwyn-Mayer in Hollywood.

Stanley Morner arrived in Hollywood in 1935 with his wife Lillian. She was his high school and college sweetheart, whom he had married in 1933. (They would have three children: Stanley, James, and Kristin.) Under his own name, he had a lead in the independently produced *I Conquer the Sea* (Academy Pictures, 1936), portraying a Portuguese harpooner who loses his life at sea. *Variety* noted, "Stanley Morner contributes the best all around performance, though a bit mawkish in early scenes." He was at MGM for a year, appearing in small roles in such varied MGM products as *Suzy* (1936), *Song of the City* (1937), and *Navy, Blue and Gold* (1937). His best showcase came

Dennis Morgan in *My Wild Irish Rose* (1947).
[Courtesy of JC Archives]

in *The Great Ziegfeld* (1936), singing the song "A Pretty Girl Is Like a Melody." However, after he filmed the sequence, the studio decided they wanted a different voice for the number and dubbed in Allan Jones singing the song for the release print.

In 1938, the actor-singer left MGM, where he was not progressing, and went to Paramount, where he called himself Richard Stanley. But, the best he could get was small parts in three entries, two of them gangster programmers: *King of Alcatraz* (1938—as a ship's first mate) and *Persons in Hiding* (1939). From there he went to Warner Bros., and changing his name again to Dennis Morgan, he won the unsympathetic lead in a "B" picture called *Waterfront* (1939) as a hot-tempered longshoreman. That same year, he also played a newlywed husband whose father (Fred Stone) comes to live with him and his new bride (Gloria Dickson) in *No Place to Go.* Following this outing, he portrayed an intern who tries to save his girl (Rosemary Lane) from a mad scientist (Humphrey Bogart) in *The Return of Dr. X.*

In 1940, Dennis was cast as a member of the famous World War I battalion in *The Fighting 69th,* portrayed a pilot in *Flight Angels,* a policeman in *Tear Gas Squad,* and a mountie after a murderer in the remake of *River's End.* That year the studio loaned him to RKO Radio for the role of a wealthy playboy who is enchanted by a working girl (Ginger Rogers) in *Kitty Foyle.* The extremely popular movie netted Rogers an Oscar. It also established Morgan as a reliable leading man. After that, Warner Bros. kept him on its lot exclusively, using him in a variety of ways: leading man in light comedy, a purveyor of strong dramatic roles, a singer in musical comedies, and the star of an occasional Western. As a result of this versatility, Morgan became one of filmdom's most popular male stars of the era.

After scoring in *Kitty Foyle,* Dennis was cast as a husband who cannot decide romantically between his wife (Merle Oberon) and a beautiful newspaperwoman (Rita Hayworth) in the comedy *Affectionately Yours* (1941). He was one of the notorious Younger Brothers in *Bad Men of Missouri* (1941), his first feature with Jane Wyman. The year 1942 found him starring in three solid dramas: *In This Our Life,* as a surgeon who leaves his wife (Olivia de Havilland) for her sister (Bette Davis); in the Technicolor *Captains of the Clouds,* as a member of the Royal Canadian Air Force; and as a wartime aircraft plant worker in *Wings for the Eagles,* his first screen pairing with both Ann Sheridan and Jack Carson. The next year, he and Carson were vaudevillians in *The Hard Way,* which had Carson marrying pretty Joan Leslie, with all three of them coming under the tyrannical thumb of her ambitious sister (Ida Lupino) with tragic results. Morgan, as an aspiring singer, and Joan Leslie were also paired as lovers in the all-star musical *Thank Your Lucky Stars* (1943). They sang "Ridin' for a Fall" and "No You, No Me," and Morgan soloed on "Good Night, Good Neighbor."

Dennis was given the lead in the modernized movie version of the operetta *The Desert Song* (1943), in which he played Paul Hudson, the secret leader of the North African Riffs, who vies with sinister Bruce Cabot for the affections of beautiful Margot (Irene Manning). In the film, he sang the title song, "One Flower Grows Alone in Your Garden," "One Alone," and "The Riff Song," all of which he recorded for Columbia Records. Throughout the mid- and late 1940s, Morgan recorded for Columbia, ranging from songs he sang in his Warner Bros. features to traditional numbers like "The Battle Hymn of the Republic" and "The Lost Chord" (which he performed with the Cathedral Choir of the First Presbyterian Church of Hollywood) to making 78 rpm albums of Irish songs and Franz Lehar compositions. After leaving Columbia Records,

Morgan did not pursue his recording career, although in the 1950s he did record a single for Decca, "When the Shadows Fall" / "I'll Give You All My Love."

In 1944, Morgan was cast in another Warner Bros. studio all-star musical, *Hollywood Canteen*, in which he and Joe E. Brown dueted on "You Can Always Tell a Yank." Then he was seen in one of his best-remembered film roles, that of composer Jack Norworth to Ann Sheridan's Nora Bayes in *Shine on Harvest Moon* (1944). It was a spirited, if overlong, period musical that gave him an opportunity to sing a number of vintage songs, including "By the Light of the Silv'ry Moon." *Variety* applauded that Morgan "smacks over his vocal assignments in fine style." For a change of pace, he was cast in the drama *The Very Thought of You* (1944), playing a soldier who returns home from the war to face domestic troubles with his young bride (Eleanor Parker).

Dennis was featured again as a service flier in *God Is My Co-Pilot* (1945) and then switched to a comedy role in *Christmas in Connecticut* (1945). He was the sailor rescued after being marooned on a raft for eighteen days and sent to the home of a writer (Barbara Stanwyck) for the yuletide holidays, where the woman writer was intent on fooling both he and her publisher (Sydney Greenstreet) into believing she has a family. As a seasonal favorite on television, it is one of Morgan's most shown pictures. On October 10, 1945, Morgan portrayed composer Stephen Foster in "Swanee River," a segment of CBS radio's *Lux Radio Theater*. In this adaptation of the 1939 picture (in which Don Ameche had played Foster), Morgan performed several of the composer's songs, although the bulk of them were delivered by Al Jolson, repeating his screen role of E. P. Christy. The following June, Morgan made a guest appearance on Jack Carson's CBS radio show.

During World War II, Morgan's screen career had escalated (along with the studio's Errol Flynn and John Garfield) while many leading men were away in military service. Nevertheless, his status continued to improve after the armistice, despite the competition of demobilized movie stars and the changing tastes of moviegoers. At the height of his stardom in the mid- to late 1940s, Morgan, who never had script approval on his vehicles, was receiving one thousand letters weekly and had a $6,000 weekly salary. He continued to alternate between drama and musical comedies. In 1946, the studio teamed him with another industry workhorse, Jack Carson, in two lightweight but fun pictures: *The Time, the Place and the Girl* (in which Morgan sang "A Gal in Calico" and "Rainy Night in Rio") and *Two Guys From Milwaukee*, where he was a prince who learns about ordinary life from a garrulous cabbie (Carson). *One More Tomorrow* (1946; shot in early 1944) was a remake of *The Animal Kingdom* (1932). Dennis portrayed a rich playboy (one of his frequent screen personae) who became smitten with a radical magazine editor (Ann Sheridan); a few years later the film would be used as an example of leftist propaganda that had "infiltrated" Hollywood products.

Another noteworthy musical role came in 1947, when Dennis played Irish entertainer Chauncey Olcott in the biopic *My Wild Irish Rose*, and again he sang a variety of vintage tunes, like "Hush-a-Bye (Wee Rose of Killarney)." The prettified Western *Cheyenne* (1947) cast Dennis as a gambler in love with the wife (Jane Wyman) of an outlaw (Bruce Bennett). (Later, the feature was retitled *The Wyoming Kid*.) He reteamed with Jack Carson for the comedy *Two Guys From Texas* (1948), a pleasing remake of *The Cowboy From Brooklyn* (1938), in which they portrayed out-of-work vaudevillians stranded on a Texas ranch. In its highlighted scene, the two were caricatured in animated hijinks with Bugs Bunny. Morgan's next feature, *One Sunday Afternoon* (1948), was a retread of *The Strawberry Blonde* (1941), with Morgan in James Cagney's old role as a turn-of-the-century dentist who wonders if he married the right girl. He sang the title number plus "Wait Till the Sun Shines, Nellie" and "One Little, Sweet Little Girl."

Then, it was back to dramatics for the melodrama *To the Victor* (1949), about French wartime collaborators being placed on trial, and following this, he was the object of Jane Wyman's amorous machinations in *The Lady Takes a Sailor* (1949). The last of his popular pairings with Jack Carson was *It's A Great Feeling* (1949), which had them play themselves while attempting unsuccessfully to wangle backing for a film on the Warners' lot—until they discover singing waitress Doris Day. Morgan and Day sang "Blame My Absent-Minded Heart" while the three stars performed "There's Nothing Rougher Than Love."

By 1950, Dennis Morgan was forty (and noticeably stockier). The competition of TV had severely damaged the studio's economics, and Warner Bros. had a new singing star, Gordon MacRae. But Morgan still had his contract to complete. He was reteamed with Ginger Rogers for *Perfect Strangers* (1950), in which they were fellow jurors who fall in love. In *Pretty Baby* (1950), he was involved with a young woman (Betsy Drake) who becomes a success due to a gimmick, while in *Raton Pass* (1951)—a rather unsturdy Western—he was a cattle baron fleeced by his wife (Patricia Neal), who gains revenge by aligning homesteaders against her. In his final studio musical, *Painting the Clouds With Sunshine* (1951), a remake of *The Gold Diggers of Broadway* (1929), Morgan was one of three rich men sought after by a trio of Las Vegas husband hunters. In 1952, he played a rancher forced into a showdown with a gunman (Philip Carey) in the programmer *Cattle Town*, and he completed his Warner Bros. contract with the Joan Crawford melodrama (her final for the studio) *This Woman Is Dangerous* (1952), in which he was a doctor who falls in love with the moll (Crawford) of a gangster (David Brian).

Like many movie stars at this time, Dennis negotiated a termination of his studio pact. Instead of opting for a one-time settlement, he asked that payments be made over a ten-year period, thus giving him a healthy income for the next decade. During the next several years, he turned to television, appearing on such anthology series as *General Electric Theater, Pepsi Cola Playhouse, Fireside Theater, Ford Theater, Stage Seven*, and a *Best of Broadway* adaptation of "Stage Door." In 1955, he starred in the low-budget Columbia Western *The Gun That Won the West* as the leader of a cavalry troop that holds off a Sioux attack with new Springfield rifles. For RKO, he was in an economy adventure opus, *Pearl of the South Pacific* (1955), where he and partner David Farrar have Virginia Mayo masquerade as a missionary in order to steal tropical natives' pearls.

Morgan's final starring picture was a Columbia "B" entry called *Uranium Boom* (1956), where he and William Talman fight over Patricia Medina and a uranium mine. He then returned to TV for guest roles in *Star Stage, Telephone Time*, and *Alfred Hitchcock Presents*, before starring as private investigator Dennis Chase in the 1959 NBC-TV summer replacement series *21 Beacon Street*. Thereafter, Morgan did guest shots on the TV shows *Saints and Sinners* and *Dick Powell Theater* in the early 1960s.

After more than two decades in the limelight (but never part of the Hollywood social scene—he was a happily married family man), Morgan moved from his La Canada home to a Fresno ranch with his wife Lillian and enjoyed his well-invested earnings. In memory of the untimely death of his screen partner and pal Jack Carson in 1963, Dennis became a spokesman throughout the United States for the American Cancer Society, raising funds in his friend's memory. In 1968, Morgan returned to the screen in *Rogue's Gallery* as a suspect in a murder case involving a framed private eye (Roger Smith), and he also did a guest shot on the CBS-TV series *Petticoat Junction*.

Mostly he donated his time as a speaker for the American Cancer Society. In 1974, he guested on the TV special "Grammy Salutes Oscar," but the next year he rejected a $10,000 per week offer to star in a stage revival of *The Vagabond King*. Looking much older, Morgan showed up in a guest cameo in Paramount's *Won Ton Ton, the Dog Who Saved Hollywood* (1976). As a lark, the former movie star acted in stage productions in his home state of Wisconsin, sometimes with the Campus Community Players at the University of Wisconsin Center (in Marshfield-Wood County). His last acting appearance was in a guest role on the ABC-TV series *The Love Boat* in 1980, in which he was teamed with his old Warner Bros. friend, Jane Wyman.

Dennis, who was named singer of the year in 1947 by the Music Trades Association, was politically active and in the 1950s was a major supporter of President Dwight D. Eisenhower. Although Morgan considered running for Congress, the only political office he held was that of honorary mayor of Crescenta-Canada Valley. In later years, the singer-actor, who had been in a serious auto accident, suffered from heart problems. He died in a Fresno hospital of respiratory failure on September 7, 1994. His wife of sixty years was with him when he passed away.

Filmography

As Stanley Morner

I Conquer the Sea (Academy Pictures, 1936)
Suzy (MGM, 1936)
Piccadilly Jim (MGM, 1936)
Down the Stretch (WB, 1936)
The Great Ziegfeld (MGM, 1936)

Old Hutch (MGM, 1936)
Song of the City (MGM, 1937)
Navy Blue and Gold (MGM, 1937)
Mama Steps Out (MGM, 1937)

As Richard Stanley

Men With Wings (Par, 1938)
King of Alcatraz (Par, 1938)

Persons in Hiding (Par, 1938)

As Dennis Morgan

Waterfront (WB, 1939)
Ride, Cowboy Ride (Vita, 1939) (s)
The Return of Dr. X (WB, 1939)
No Place to Go (WB, 1939)
The Singing Dude (Vita, 1940) (s)
Three Cheers for the Irish (WB, 1940)
The Fighting 69th (WB, 1940)
Tear Gas Squad (WB, 1940)
Flight Angels (WB, 1940)
River's End (WB, 1940)
Kitty Foyle (RKO, 1940)
Affectionately Yours (WB, 1941)
Bad Men of Missouri (WB, 1941)
Captains of the Clouds (WB, 1942)
In This Our life (WB, 1942)
Wings for the Eagle (WB, 1942)
The Hard Way (WB, 1942)
Thank Your Lucky Stars (WB, 1943)
Stars on Horseback (Vita, 1943) (s)
The Desert Song (WB, 1943)
The Shining Future (Vita, 1944) (s)

The Very Thought of You (WB, 1944)
Hollywood Canteen (WB, 1944)
Shine on Harvest Moon (WB, 1944)
God Is My Co-Pilot (WB, 1945)
Movieland Magic (Vita, 1945) (s)
Christmas in Connecticut [Indiscretion] (WB, 1945)
One More Tomorrow (WB, 1946)
Two Guys From Milwaukee [Royal Flush] (WB, 1946)
The Time, The Place and the Girl (WB, 1946)
Cheyenne [The Wyoming Kid] (WB, 1947)
My Wild Irish Rose (WB, 1947)
Always Together (WB, 1947)
To the Victor (WB, 1948)
Two Guys From Texas [Two Texas Knights] (WB, 1948)
One Sunday Afternoon (WB, 1948)
It's a Great Feeling (WB, 1949)
The Lady Takes a Sailor (WB, 1949)

Perfect Strangers [Too Dangerous to Love] (WB, 1950)
Pretty Baby (WB, 1950)
Raton Pass [Canyon Pass] (WB, 1951)
Painting the Clouds With Sunshine (WB, 1951)
This Woman Is Dangerous (WB, 1952)
Cattle Town (WB, 1952)

The Nebraskan (Col, 1953)
The Gun That Won the West (Col, 1955)
Pearl of the South Pacific (RKO, 1955)
Uranium Boom (Col, 1956)
Rogue's Gallery (Par, 1968)
Won Ton Ton, the Dog Who Saved Hollywood (Par, 1976)

Radio Series

Silken Strings (NBC Blue, 1933–35)

TV Series

21 Beacon Street (NBC, 1959)

Album Discography

LPs

Hollywood Canteen (Curtain Calls 100/11-12) [ST]
It's a Great Feeling (Caliban 6015) [ST]
The Merry Widow (10″ Cap ML-2064) w. Risë Stevens
My Wild Irish Rose and Other Songs (Col ML-4272)

Painting the Clouds With Sunshine (10″ Cap L-291, Caliban 6012) [ST]
Swanee River (Totem 1028) [ST/R]
Thank Your Lucky Stars (Curtain Calls 100/8) [ST]
The Time, the Place and the Girl (Titania 511) [ST]

CDs

Thank Your Lucky Stars (Sandy Hook CDSH-2012) [ST]

That's Entertainment, Part 2 (Sony Music Special Products A2K-46872) [ST]

Helen Morgan in *Show Boat* (1936).
[Courtesy of JC Archives]

Helen Morgan

(b. Helen Riggins, Danville, Illinois, August 2, 1900; d. Chicago, Illinois,
October 8, 1941)

Helen Morgan's plaintive voice will forever be that of the definitive torch singer of the 1920s. Sitting atop a piano and twisting a chiffon scarf, she sang forlorn songs of unrequited love, loneliness, and endless longings for wayward men. While her career encompassed successes in vaudeville, Broadway, nightclubs, motion pictures, and recordings, she was much like the heroines she sang about. In fact, most of her life she fought a battle against alcohol abuse. Eventually drink caused her untimely death at just over forty years of age.

She was born Helen Riggins in Danville, Illinois, on August 2, 1900, the daughter of French-Canadian parents. While still in her teens, she went to Chicago, where she attended Crane High School. While in school, Helen worked at a variety of manual-labor jobs, like boxing crackers, as a clerk at Marshall Field's department store, and then as a lingerie model—all before starting to sing in honky tonks, such as the Green Mill Club, in 1918. An attractive young woman, she won several beauty contests, and with the prize money she came to New York City. She worked in small cabarets before landing a singing job in Billy Rose's Backstage Club.

In 1920, Helen was hired to sing in the chorus of Florenz Ziegfeld's Broadway show *Sally*, starring Marilyn Miller. She remained with it during its two-year run before going to Chicago, where she had a winning engagement at the Café Montmartre. Late in 1922, she returned to Gotham and, during the next three years, eked out a living singing in small clubs and doing bits in vaudeville and musical revues, including a season of "Grand Guignol" plays in Greenwich Village. She won a small role in *George White's Scandals of 1925*, which led to a featured role in *Americana* (1926), where she sang "Nobody Wants Me." As a result of her popularity in this show, Helen was used as a front for several popular speakeasies, where she appeared as the star attraction, including the House of Morgan, Chez Helen Morgan, Helen Morgan's Summer House, and Helen Morgan's 54th Street Club. It was here she developed her famous style of sitting on a piano clutching a scarf and singing sad love songs. It soon made her one of New York's most popular club attractions.

In 1927, often accompanied by Leslie A. "Hutch" Hutchinson, Helen made her recording debut on Brunswick Records, and that summer and fall she was performing in London, where she also recorded for Brunswick. Returning to the United States, Helen Morgan was cast in her most famous role, that of the beautiful, but tragic, mulatto Julie in Jerome Kern and Oscar Hammerstein II's celebrated stage musical *Show Boat*, which opened at the Ziegfeld Theater on December 27, 1927, for a 572-performance run. In the landmark show, she sang her two most famous songs, "Bill" and "Can't Help Lovin' Dat Man," which she recorded for RCA Victor, a company she would remain with until 1934.

By the time *Show Boat* debuted, the songstress also had become a headliner in vaudeville, and during the musical's run in 1928, she was arrested for Prohibition law violations at one of her speakeasies. Needless to say, the event made headlines. In July 1929, Helen appeared in the cabaret entertainment at the Ziegfeld Roof atop the New Amsterdam Theater. On September 3, 1929, she opened in another Jerome Kern–Oscar Hammerstein musical, *Sweet Adeline,* as the young daughter of a beer garden owner who becomes a famous singing star. In that show, she performed two more of her famous torch songs, "Why Was I Born?" and "Don't Ever Leave Me." The show ran for 234 performances. (When Warner Bros. translated the property to the screen in 1935, Irene Dunne won the lead.)

Universal acquired the screen rights to *Show Boat,* but chose to revamp the musical numbers in its part-talkie film of 1929. Alma Rubens was cast as the trouble-plagued Julie. However, for the New York City showings of the film, an eighteen-minute sound prologue was added, which included Morgan singing "Bill." That fall, the vocalist made her own feature film acting debut to critical acclaim in Rouben Mamoulian's *Applause* for Paramount, shot at their Astoria, Long Island, facility. In this innovative dramatic story, Morgan was superb as aging burlesque queen Kitty Darling, who brings her young daughter (Joan Peers) into her show at the behest of her shady comedian lover (Fuller Mellish Jr.), who has designs on the girl. Helen sang "What Wouldn't I Do for That Man," "Give Your Little Baby Lots of Lovin'," and "I've Got a Feeling I'm Falling." The *New York Times* endorsed that Morgan "does remarkably well," adding that she "speaks her lines with feeling and she plays her part with ability." Late in 1929, she made a guest appearance in the Paramount musical (also filmed at the Astoria Studio) *Glorifying the American Girl.* In the big production number, she reprised "What Wouldn't I Do for That Man" from *Applause.*

In 1930, Helen starred in her third Paramount picture, *Roadhouse Nights,* which cast her as Lola Fagan, a songstress who saves her former boyfriend, a newspaper editor (Charles Ruggles), from her gangster employer (Fred Kohler). Outside of Jimmy Durante's antics, the entry had little to offer. Morgan returned to Broadway in the summer of 1931 for *Ziegfeld Follies of 1931.* The production ran for 165 performances and also starred Harry Richman, Ruth Etting, Hal LeRoy, Jack Pearl, Buck and Bubbles, and Mitzi Mayfair. By this time, Helen's drinking was so severe she had to sit onstage in order to perform. Costar Etting later said Morgan drank to give herself courage because she was petrified of live audiences.

In the early 1930s, Helen continued to star in vaudeville, nightclubs, and in 1932 was again playing Julie in *Show Boat* at the Casino Theater in New York. In 1933, she married Maurice Maschke Jr., but they were divorced two years later. In 1934, she starred on the CBS radio program *Broadway Melodies.* That year, she was starring in *Memories* at the Biltmore Theater in Los Angeles and made her first Hollywood feature films: Fox's *Marie Galante* and Paramount's *You Belong to Me.* In the former she sang "It's Home" and "Song of a Dreamer," and in the latter she warbled "When He Comes Home to Me." Neither of these (melo)dramas were starring vehicles for her.

In 1935, Morgan had three film roles. She made a guest appearance as herself in the Rudy Vallee–Warner Bros. musical *Sweet Music,* where she performed "I See Two Lovers." At Warner Bros.–First National, she appeared with Al Jolson and Ruby Keeler in *Go Into Your Dance* singing "The Little Things You Used to Do." She also starred in the RKO production *Frankie and Johnny,* set in the bowery of the 1890s and concerns a good-time gal (Morgan) who is done wrong by her two-timing boyfriend (Chester Morris). In it she sang the title folk ballad, "Give Me a Heart to Sing To" (both recorded for Victor Records), "Rhythm in Your Feet," and "If You Want My

Heart." Unfortunately the picture was so badly received it gained few showings, and RKO soon sold it to fledgling Republic Pictures, which issued the lackluster picture in 1936.

Helen's final screen appearance was to reprise Julie in Universal's production of *Show Boat* (1936) starring Irene Dunne and Allan Jones. Again she sang "Bill" and "Can't Stop Lovin' Dat Man," and gave a favorable account of herself in the classic musical. Unfortunately, her drinking had grown only worse. It was reported that during filming she would arrive on the set drunk every day and had to be placed under a cold shower and filled with coffee before she could emote before the cameras.

Morgan toured in *George White's Scandals of 1936*, and in 1937 she was the featured vocalist on Ken Murray's CBS radio program. Also that year she returned to England for a tour. Rudy Vallee reported in his autobiography *My Time Is Your Time* (1962) that during a performance in London she became ill due to her excessive drinking and had to be helped offstage. Rudy volunteered to take her place.

Alcohol continued to dominate Helen's life, and after the late 1930s her show-business career was an on-again, off-again affair. She stopped recording entirely after a session with Brunswick early in 1935. Due to her drinking problem, Helen had difficulty obtaining club bookings as the 1930s progressed. In 1941 she married Los Angeles car dealer Lloyd Johnson. By then she had pulled herself together enough to appear in a touring version of the now rather tattered *George White's Scandals* revue. During its Chicago engagement at the State Lake Theater she was hospitalized with cirrhosis of the liver. She died on October 8, 1941, in the same city where she had commenced her career.

In the mid-1950s interest in Helen Morgan was reactivated, thanks to movies being made about famous stars who had become alcoholics: Susan Hayward as Lillian Roth in *I'll Cry Tomorrow* (1955) and Dorothy Malone as Diana Barrymore in *Too Much, Too Soon* (1957). On April 16, 1957, Polly Bergen had the title role in the CBS-TV *Playhouse 90* program "Helen Morgan," which re-created the star's life and songs. Bergen also recorded an LP album, *Bergen Sings Morgan*, for Columbia Records. The same year, Ann Blyth portrayed Helen Morgan (to lesser results than Bergen) in the Warner Bros. fiction *The Helen Morgan Story*. The movie, which suffered from a clichéd scenario, was highlighted by an excellent music track comprised of Helen's famous torch songs and dubbed by Gogi Grant. RCA issued a best-selling soundtrack album from the otherwise mundane movie ("little more than a tuneful soap opera," complained *Variety*).

Later, with cable television and videos/DVDs resurrecting so many of the early 1930s' features and short subjects, viewers had the opportunity to study Helen Morgan. In these offerings, she may not be at her physical or emotional peak, but there are always flashes of dramatic poignancy, and her song numbers consistently reaffirm her unique singing style.

Filmography

Applause (Par, 1929)
Show Boat Prologue (Univ, 1929) (s)
Glorifying the American Girl (Par, 1929)
Roadhouse Nights (Par, 1930)
The Gigolo Racket (Vita, 1931) (s)
Manhattan Lullaby (Educational, 1933) (s)
The Doctor (Educational, 1934) (s)

Marie Galante (Fox, 1934)
You Belong to Me (Par, 1934)
Sweet Music (WB, 1935)
Go Into Your Dance (FN, 1935)
Frankie and Johnny (RKO, 1935)
Show Boat (Univ, 1936)

Broadway Plays

Sally (1920)
George White's Scandals of 1925 (1925)
Americana (1926)

Show Boat (1927)
Sweet Adeline (1929)
Ziegfeld Follies of 1931 (1931)

Radio Series

Broadway Melodies (CBS, 1933–34)
The Ken Murray Show (CBS, 1937)

The Open House (NBC, 1941)

Album Discography

LPs

Fanny Brice/Helen Morgan (RCA LPV-561)
Go Into Your Dance (Golden Legends 2000/2, Hollywood Soundstage 402, Sandy Hook 2030) [ST]
Helen Morgan Sings (Audio Rarities 2330)
The Legacy of a Torch Singer (Take Two TT-220)

Let's Have Fun (Mar-Bren 744, Nostalgia Enterprises 002)
Show Boat (Columbia Special Products 55)
Show Boat (Vertinge 2004, Xeno 251) [ST]
The Torch Singer and the Mountie (Amalgamated 205) w. Nelson Eddy
Torch Songs (X LVA-1006) w. Fanny Brice

CDs

Here Comes the Show Boat (Columbia Music Special Products A55) [ST]
More Than You Know (Box Office ENB-CD-15/95) w. Ruth Etting
Torch Song Trio (Crystal Stream Audio IDCD61) w. Ruth Etting, Libby Holman.

The Ultimate Show Boat (Pavilion GEMS-0060) [ST]
You Can't Have Everything/Go into Your Dance/You'll Never Get Rich (Great Movie Themes 60014) [ST]

George Murphy

(b. George Lloyd Murphy, New Haven, Connecticut, July 4, 1902; d. Palm Beach, Florida, May 3, 1992)

Typed as a congenial and versatile song-and-dance man who appeared in scores of films from the early 1930s to the 1950s, blue-eyed George Murphy was always regarded as a dependable player. While his screen image as a clean-cut Irish-American was not charismatic, he could always be relied on for a workmanlike performance. He was an astute achiever who knew how to keep active in show business while many of his contemporaries faded. In later years he moved out of one limelight into another—as a major politician. As such he was one of the first show-business celebrities to hold a national office, that of U.S. senator. Through him the barrier against actors in politics was broken, thus permitting his fellow Republican Ronald Reagan later to ascend to the presidency.

He was born on July 4, 1902, in New Haven, Connecticut, the son of track coach Michael Charles Murphy (the man who trained the 1912 Olympic team led by Jim Thorpe). When the senior Murphy died in 1913, the family moved to Detroit to be with Mrs. Murphy's family. While a student at the University of Detroit High School, fifteen-year-old George ran away from home to join the navy. However, he was soon discharged when his true age was discovered. A small sports scholarship got the young man into the Peddie School in Highstown, New Jersey, and later he received a full scholarship at New York's Pawling School. There he took up public speaking, and a speech on Theodore Roosevelt earned him the Chauncey Depew Oratory Award.

After graduation in 1921, George went to Yale University to major in engineering. To support himself, he worked in the summers as a bouncer at a club, at loading coal, and at other menial jobs. He dropped out of Yale in 1924, due to bad grades and an injury received at the coal mine. That autumn, he relocated to New York City, where he became a stock-market runner. When he had lived in Detroit, Murphy had met a girl named Juliette Henkel, who was now working in Gotham as dancer Julie Johnson. Murphy had natural dancing rhythm, so the two formed a duo and worked at parties and clubs before landing a stint with George Olsen and His Orchestra performing the dance craze of the day: the Varsity Drag (which was from the hit Broadway musical *Good News*). When not working with Olsen, Murphy and Johnson appeared with Emil Coleman's orchestra. When Herbert Morrison, a London producer, came to New York to cast the London edition of *Good News*, he saw the couple dance and signed them to appear in the show. (Murphy and Julie married on December 28, 1926.)

After the London run of *Good News*, the now-celebrated couple returned to the United States, where they were signed in 1929 to appear in the Bert Lahr musical *Hold Everything*, replacing Jack Whiting and Betty Compton. They stayed with the show on Broadway for the remainder of its eight-month run and then went on tour, returning for the 1931 Broadway revue *Shoot the Works* that also featured a young Imogene Coca. After that stint, George went solo, appearing in a supporting role in the long-running George Gershwin musical *Of Thee I Sing* (1932). This was followed by a featured part in Jerome Kern's *Roberta* (1933), which also included Tamara, Bob

Thelma Todd and George Murphy in *After the Dance* (1935).
[Courtesy of JC Archives]

Hope, and Fred MacMurray. As a result of being in this popular musical, Murphy was signed to a Hollywood contract by producer Samuel Goldwyn. He made his movie debut in the Eddie Cantor musical *Kid Millions* (1934) as Ann Sothern's dancing partner. The two of them performed a duet of "Your Head on My Shoulder."

After his film bow, Murphy signed with Columbia Pictures, but only made a quartet of pictures for that studio, three of them musicals with Nancy Carroll: *Jealousy* (1934), *I'll Love You Always* (1935), and *After the Dance* (1935). Following *The Public Menace* (1935) with Jean Arthur, he made *Woman Trap* (1936) with Gertrude Michael at Paramount and *Top of the Town* (1937) with Doris Nolan at Universal. By now, George had negotiated an MGM contract where his first outing was *Women Men Marry* (1937), a programmer with Claire Dodd, followed by the murder mystery *London by Night* (1937). The latter was the first feature in which he obtained top billing. *Variety* reported, "Murphy handles himself very capably, speaks lines well and acquits himself creditably as a romantic lead. . . ."

Broadway Melody of 1938 (1937) was George's first major musical for Metro, and he had an opportunity to dance, partnered with the studio's Eleanor Powell. Next, he was loaned to Universal to join with Alice Faye (on loanout from Twentieth Century–Fox) for *You're a Sweetheart* (1938), and they worked well together. *Variety* commended, "Murphy has acquired a rather pleasing singing voice on top of his dancing skill." Another loanout—this time to Twentieth Century–Fox—resulted in one of George's best-remembered film assignments, playing opposite Shirley Temple in *Little Miss Broadway* (1938). After this hit, MGM found it profitable to loan Murphy to Universal for a trio of features: *Letter of Introduction* (1938), *Hold That Co-Ed* (1938), and *Risky Business* (1939). He was back on the home lot for *Broadway Melody of 1940* (1940) but now in support of two top dancers: Fred Astaire and Eleanor Powell.

Murphy was Judy Garland's leading man in *Little Nellie Kelly* (1940) and did so well as the husband/father that the studio planned to cast him with Garland in *For Me and My Gal* (1942). However, by the time that musical went into production, younger Gene Kelly had been hired by the studio, and he was given Murphy's role with George recast as the partner who loses Judy to Gene.

Several of George Murphy's loanouts in the early 1940s were to RKO Radio, which did far better by him than did his home lot. In 1941, RKO starred him in the delightful *A Girl, a Guy and a Gob* as the sailor who vies with a rich young man (Edmond O'Brien) for pretty Lucille Ball. Just as good was RKO's comedy *Tom, Dick and Harry* (1941), with Murphy as one of three men pursuing fickle Ginger Rogers. At the same time, all that his home studio, MGM, offered the actor-hoofer was a costarring role with Ann Sothern in *Ringside Maisie* (1941), a popular but low-budget studio series. RKO provided with him starring assignments in two popular budget films, *The Mayor of 44th Street* and *The Navy Comes Through*, both in 1942. Murphy was at United Artists for the musical *The Powers Girl* (1942) and returned home for the grade "A" picture *Bataan* (1943), a grimly effective wartime drama in which he demonstrated credible dramatics. The studio continued to prosper by loaning him out. He was at Warner Bros. for Irving Berlin's *This Is the Army* (1943), playing Ronald Reagan's father; he was the World War I veteran who staged a big show for the new war's servicemen.

This progression between big and small pictures continued, which gave no positive pattern to Murphy's screen career. MGM wasted him as a musical producer feuding with his old-time vaudevillian dad (Charles Winninger) in *Broadway Rhythm* (1944), a project once planned for Mickey Rooney and Judy Garland. George was with Eddie Cantor in RKO's *Show Business* (1944), a modest look at the changes in vaudeville over the decades. The highlight of this picture was a send-up of grand opera by Murphy, Cantor, Constance Moore, and Joan Davis. Murphy was the ambitious stage producer in RKO's *Step Lively* (1944), which showcased the young Frank Sinatra. For the same studio's *Having Wonderful Crime* (1945), a good comedy-mystery, he and Carole Landis were honeymooners mixed up in a series of murders with a detective (Pat O'Brien).

In 1946, MGM again relegated Murphy to a Maisie movie with series' star Ann Sothern, this time *Up Goes Maisie* (1946). For the remainder of his screen career, he would stay at the studio except for a loanout to Columbia for the taut semidocumentary melodrama *Walk East on Beacon* (1952), which cast him as an FBI agent chasing after foreign spies. Murphy had one of the two (Greta Garbo had the other) MGM contracts that paid for fifty-two weeks a year, not the standard industry practice of being on salary for only forty weeks per year.

During the 1940s, several things happened to change George Murphy's life, if not his congenial screen image. In 1940, he campaigned actively for Republican Wendell Wilkie for U.S. president and gained the close friendship of fellow Republican and MGM chief Louis B. Mayer. From 1940 to 1943, George was vice president of the Screen Actors Guild, and he served as its president for two terms beginning in 1944. (He had been one of the guild's first members in the late 1930s.)

In the war years, Murphy helped organize entertainment for servicemen through the Hollywood Victory Committee, and after the war he and Robert Montgomery formed the Hollywood Republican Committee. In 1948, George attended the Republican National Convention as a delegate for California governor and presidential candidate Earl Warren. In 1950, the Academy of Motion Picture Arts and Sciences gave Murphy a special Oscar for his contributions to the film industry, and in 1952 he was placed in charge of entertainment for the Republican National Convention, a post he held again in 1956 and 1960. From 1953 to 1954, Murphy was chairman of the Republican National Convention. Meanwhile, he and his wife (who had retired from show business) continued a quiet home life with their children: Dennis (born in 1939) and Melissa (born in 1943). In addition, Murphy worked on radio during this time on such series as the *Kraft Music Hall* and *Suspense*. On January 29, 1948, he starred in the "History in the Making" segment of the radio show *Proudly We Hail*, sponsored by the U.S. Air Force, and he hosted the 1948 summer NBC radio program *Let's Talk Hollywood* and the next year hosted a big-money game show, *Hollywood Calling*, for the same network.

Murphy continued appearing in MGM products, his most notable role being Pop among the GI ensemble in *Battleground* (1949), a fine World War II drama about the assault on Bastogne. After making *Talk About a Stranger* (1952), which costarred future first lady Nancy Davis (Reagan), his next film role was in *Deep in My Heart* (1954), as the master of ceremonies in an aquacade scene featuring Esther Williams. However, the entire sequence was deleted from the release print. Nevertheless, George remained with MGM in a public-relations capacity, promoting the studio in particular and the movie industry in general. He hosted the MGM syndicated radio show *Good News From Hollywood* (1953) and did the same chore on the ABC-TV *MGM Parade* (1955).

Although Louis B. Mayer had been ousted as MGM chief in 1951 by Dore Schary and his regime, Murphy continued on good terms with Schary until 1957, when Schary accused George of attempting to aid Mayer in a return to power. Murphy quit his MGM job and became the vice president in charge of public relations for Desilu Studios (owned by Lucille Ball and Desi Arnaz) until 1959. The next year, he took over as a director and corporate vice president for the Technicolor Corporation. Also in 1960 (August 1), he was seen in the CBS-TV comedy pilot *You're Only Young Twice*, which failed to sell as an ongoing series.

In 1964 George Murphy became the Republican candidate for the U.S. Senate in California, easily defeating Pierre Salinger, who had briefly held the post following the death of Sen. Clair Engle. In 1966, Murphy underwent surgery for throat cancer, and while it was successful, it lowered his speaking voice to a hoarse whisper, contributing to his defeat for reelection in 1970. As a campaign tool that year he published his memoirs, *Say . . . Didn't You Used to Be George Murphy?*—a title that kidded his screen image. After leaving the senate, he became a partner in the public-relations firm, Washington Consultants, Inc. In 1973 his wife Juliette (an invalid for several years) died, and Murphy sold their Beverly Hills mansion and moved into an apartment. In 1976, he produced the television special *The All-American Bicentennial Minstrels*. One of his rare later public appearances occurred when former costar (and fellow Republican) Shirley Temple was honored at an American Cinema Awards fund-raiser in Irvine, California, in 1989.

In the 1980s, Murphy built a retirement home in North Carolina's Great Smoky Mountains and lived there in the summer, spending winters in Florida. He married former model Bette Blandi in 1982. He died of leukemia at their Palm Beach, Florida, home on May 3, 1992, at the age of eighty-nine. He was survived by his second wife, a son (Dennis), a daughter (Melissa), and four grandchildren.

Filmography

Kid Millions (UA, 1934)
Jealousy (Col, 1934)
After the Dance (Col, 1935)
Public Menace (Col, 1935)
I'll Love You Always (Col, 1935)
Woman Trap (Par, 1936)
Top of the Town (Univ, 1937)
Women Men Marry (MGM, 1937)
London by Night (MGM, 1937)
Broadway Melody of 1938 (MGM, 1937)
You're a Sweetheart (Univ, 1937)
Little Miss Broadway (20th-Fox, 1938)
Letter of Introduction (Univ, 1938)
Hold That Co-Ed [Hold That Girl] (Univ, 1938)
Risky Business (Univ, 1939)
Hollywood Hobbies (MGM, 1939) (s)
Broadway Melody of 1940 (MGM, 1940)
Two Girls on Broadway [Choose Your Partner] (MGM, 1940)
Public Deb No. 1 (20th-Fox, 1940)
Little Nellie Kelly (MGM, 1940)
A Girl, A Guy and a Gob [The Navy Steps Out] (RKO, 1941)
Tom, Dick and Harry (RKO, 1941)
Ringside Maisie [Cash and Carry] (MGM, 1941)
Meet the Stars—Hollywood Visits the Navy (Republic, 1941) (s)
Picture People #10 (RKO, 1941) (s)

Rise and Shine (20th-Fox, 1941)
The Mayor of 44th Street (RKO, 1942)
For Me and My Gal [For Me and My Girl] (MGM, 1942)
The Navy Comes Through (RKO, 1942)
The Powers Girl [Hello! Beautiful] (UA, 1942)
Show Business at War (20th-Fox, 1943) (s)
Bataan (MGM, 1943)
This Is the Army (WB, 1943)
Broadway Rhythm (MGM, 1944)
Show Business (RKO, 1944)
Step Lively (RKO, 1944)
Having Wonderful Crime (RKO, 1945)
Up Goes Maisie [Up She Goes] (MGM, 1946)
The Arnelo Affair (MGM, 1947)
Cynthia [The Rich, Full Life] (MGM, 1947)
Tenth Avenue Angel (MGM, 1948)
The Big City (MGM, 1948)
Border Incident (MGM, 1949)
Battleground (MGM, 1949)
No Questions Asked (MGM, 1951)
It's a Big Country (MGM, 1951)
Walk East on Beacon [The Crime of the Century] (Col, 1952)
Talk About a Stranger (MGM, 1952)
Deep in My Heart (MGM, 1954) (scene deleted from release print)
1955 Motion Picture Theater Celebration (MGM, 1955) (s) (host) (documentary)

Broadway Plays

Hold Everything (1929) (replacement)
Shoot the Works (1931)

Of Thee I Sing (1931)
Roberta (1933)

Radio Series

Let's Talk Hollywood (NBC, 1948)
Hollywood Calling (NBC, 1949–50)
Good News From Hollywood (Synd, c. 1953)

TV Series

MGM Parade (ABC, 1955–56)

Album Discography

LPs

Broadway Melody of 1938 (Motion Picture Tracks MPT 3) [ST]
Broadway Melody of 1940 (CIF 3002) [ST]
For Me and My Gal (Sountrak STK-107) [ST]
George Murphy for U.S. Senator (American United AU2)

Kid Millions (CIF 3007) [ST]
Show Business (Caliban 6034) [ST]
Step Lively (Hollywood Soundstage 412) [ST]
This Is the Army (Hollywood Soundstage 408, Sandy Hook 2035) [ST]
You're a Sweetheart (Scarce Rarities 5502) [ST]

CDs

Broadway Melody 1936-40 (Great Movie Themes 60007) [ST]
For Me and My Gal (Turner Classic Movies/Rhino R2-722204) [ST]

Moon Over Miami/Broadway Melody of 1938 (Great Movie Themes 60030) [ST]
Step Lively (Great Movie Themes 60006) [ST]
This Is the Army (Hollywood Soundstage 4009) [ST]

Willie Nelson

(b. William Hugh Nelson, Abbott, Texas, April 30, 1933)

One of the leaders in the "outlaw" movement in country music in the 1970s, Willie Nelson had long established himself as one of the genre's top songwriters as well as being a popular performer and recording artist. His change from the clean-cut singer of the 1960s to the long-haired, bearded troubadour of the next decade led to a surprising widening of Willie Nelson's popularity. Not only did his hard-core country fans not desert him, but he also found himself a whole new audience with rock fans, as well as urban popular-music lovers. By expanding his song repertoire to include pop standards, progressive country, and country rock, Nelson became one of the top record sellers of the 1970s and 1980s. He became noted for his strong, somewhat raspy singing with his trademark clipped phrasing. In addition, his wide television exposure led to a lucrative movie career. During the 1980s, he starred in some half dozen Western movies, making him the premiere cowboy star of the decade and allowing him to assume John Wayne's mantle as the top star of this otherwise rather moribund genre.

William Hugh Nelson was born in Abbott, Texas, on April 30, 1933, the son of Ira and Myrle (Greenhaws) Nelson. He was the younger of two children (his older sister Bobbie has been a member of his touring band for many years). After his parents divorced, Willie and his sister were raised by their paternal grandparents. When he was six, his blacksmith grandfather gave him a guitar. Willie learned to play by ear, mostly from listening to such shows as *Louisiana Hayride* and *Grand Ole Opry* on radio. While in high school, he worked as a cotton picker.

After graduating in 1949, Nelson worked for a time as a disc jockey and began his career as a professional singer. In 1950, he joined the air force, but a back injury resulted in his discharge. He attended Baylor University in Waco, Texas, for a semester and then left, opting, instead, to sing in local honky-tonks. There he met sixteen-year-old Martha Mathews, a full-blooded Cherokee Indian who was working as a carhop, and they married. (They would have three children: Lana, Susie, and Billy.) During the day, Nelson had jobs selling Bibles, rug sweepers, and encyclopedias. He became a disc jockey in San Antonio, which began his period of working for radio stations in Texas, California, and Oregon until the late 1950s, when he began performing again on a regular basis. He also started composing songs, and in the early 1960s, he moved to Nashville. By now he was drinking heavily, and he made a suicide attempt.

Willie met and befriended performer-songwriter Hank Cochran, who arranged for Nelson's contract as a staff writer for Pamper Music. Ray Price was part owner of the firm, and he hired Nelson as bass guitarist for his band, the Cherokee Cowboys. Nelson's songs also began selling. (He had sold his first major composition "Night Life" for $150 in order to buy a car to get to Nashville.) Soon other performers were having hit records with his songs, such as Patsy Cline with "Crazy," Ray Price with "Night Life," Billy Walker with "Funny How Time Slips Away," and Faron Young with the top-selling "Hello Walls." Nelson himself earned a recording contract with

Willie Nelson performing on TV for a charity fundraiser in the 1990s.
[Courtesy of Echo Book Shop]

Liberty, and in 1962 he was on the charts with "Mr. Record Man," "Touch Me," and "There's Gonna Be Love in My House," along with a duet with Shirley Collie on "Willingly" (the two were married in 1963 following Nelson's divorce from his first wife), followed, in turn, by "You Took My Happy Away" in 1964.

The mid-1960s were successful ones for Willie Nelson with income from his song compositions, nightclub performing, and personal-appearance work due to his record success; and in 1964 he was made a member of the Grand Ole Opry. He also signed a contract with RCA Victor and had a string of modest sellers like "Johnny One Time" and "San Antonio." During the 1966–67 television season, he was a regular on the syndicated *The Ernest Tubb Show*, often singing the program's weekly spiritual.

Financial setbacks, the loss of his home in a fire, and the breakup of his second marriage—plus his growing alienation with the slick type of music being produced in Nashville—caused Nelson to leave Music City in the early 1970s. He settled in Austin, Texas, where he became a popular celebrity. It was at this time he began his annual July 4 picnics in Running Springs, which drew a conglomerate of music lovers from hard rockers to hard-core country lovers. Nelson also left RCA in 1971 and began singing with Columbia in 1974 as his own producer under his Lone Star

Records label. In 1975, his Columbia single of the old Roy Acuff standard, "Blue Eyes Crying in the Rain," climbed to number one on the country charts, and his album *Red Headed Stranger* also reached first place as well as breaking into the top-forty pop album charts. Nelson then embarked on a grueling schedule of tours.

In 1973, Nelson had been inducted into the Nashville Songwriters' Hall of Fame. In 1975, he had his first involvement with movies when he was heard singing "Stay All Night, Stay a Little Longer" on the soundtrack of the Roy Rogers feature *MacKintosh & T. J.* After that, Nelson had a string of hit records like "I Love You a Thousand Ways," "Help Me Through the Night," "Heartbreak Hotel" (with Leon Russell), plus successful releases on RCA, United Artists, and other labels, such as "Crazy Arms," "Sweet Memories" and "There'll Be No Teardrops Tonight." Meanwhile, there were his best-selling albums for Columbia, as well as reissue material, plus a series of duet albums with some of his favorite country performers (Webb Pierce, Faron Young, Roger Miller, Hank Snow). He did a group of LPs with Waylon Jennings, and their 1976 RCA LP, *Wanted! The Outlaws* with Jessi Colter (Jennings's wife) and Tompall Glaser is credited with galvanizing the integration of music rebels with traditional country music.

Willie Nelson made his first appearance in a feature film in the Austin-lensed *Outlaw Blues* (1977) about a songwriting ex-con (Peter Fonda) who sets out to regain his filched songs with the aid of a pretty backup singer (Susan Saint James). Nelson's annual July 4 party was documented in 1979 in a theatrical film, and he also sang on the soundtrack of *Voices* (1979) for United Artists. That year also found him as Robert Redford's pal in *The Electric Horseman*, and his easy, laid-back performance, plus his several songs in this picture, were about the only good things the critics enjoyed in this glossy reworking of *Lonely Are the Brave* (1962) now set in Las Vegas.

As a result of his solid work on *The Electric Horseman*, Willie landed his first starring film role in *Honeysuckle Rose* (1980)—retitled *On the Road Again* for TV—as veteran country singer Buck Bonham. After years of toiling on the road, he is on the threshold of stardom, but forgets his loyal wife (Dyan Cannon) for a fling with his sideman's (Slim Pickens) nubile daughter (Amy Irving). While the film was essentially a remake of *Intermezzo* (1939) but set in the country, the movie found a ready audience, and it made Willie Nelson a commercial film entity. For the singer's fans (many of whom thought the project was semibiographical), the picture was a treasure trove of Nelson songs, with the star performing his favorites like "Whiskey River" and "Uncloudy Day." It also had him doing newer items like the title tune and "Angel Flying Too Close to the Ground," both of which became chart hits for him on Columbia Records.

In 1981, Nelson and Hank Cochran, who had appeared in *Honeysuckle Rose*, wrote the songs for the film *Ruckus* (1981), and Nelson costarred in the underrated *Thief* (1981) as Jailbird Okla, a scruffy convict who is involved with the title character (James Caan). During this period, Nelson was also involved in a heavy performance schedule, traveling by bus to over 250 road dates a year plus television appearances (from PBS-TV's *Austin City Limits* to guest spots on variety shows and his own cable TV specials). The early 1980s found him with single hits such as "Heartaches of a Fool," "In the Jailhouse Now" (with Webb Pierce), "Midnight Rider," and "Faded Love" and "Don't You Ever Get Tired of Hurting Me," the latter being duets with Ray Price.

During a 1981 tour of Hawaii, Nelson was hospitalized with exhaustion but was soon back starring in his first Western movie, the highly regarded but poorly distributed *Barbarosa* (1982). In this outing, he had a straight dramatic role as a famous bandit who befriends a young criminal (Gary Busey) while trying to thwart his rich father-in-law's (Gilbert Roland) attempts to have him killed. Then Willie portrayed an actual person, Red Loon, in the 1982 TV movie *Coming Out of the Ice* about Victor Herman (John Savage), a young American unjustly sent to a Soviet prison camp in Stalinist Russia. In 1983, Willie was featured along with Johnny Paycheck, Bo Diddley, and Jerry Garcia in the documentary *Hells Angels Forever*. He and Kris Kristofferson (who toured with Nelson in the late 1970s and who was the subject of the album *Willie Nelson Sings Kristofferson* in 1979) costarred in the story of a popular singer (Nelson) who enlists the aid of his ex-partner (Kristofferson) to get even with one of his crooked backers (Richard C. Sarafin) in TriStar's *Songwriter* (1984). During this period, Nelson organized a series of annual Farm Aid concerts, televised over the Nashville Network, to raise money for financially troubled farmers. (He had lost money farming while living on a two-hundred-acre farm near Nashville in the late 1960s).

In 1986, Willie Nelson was back on the big screen in *Red Headed Stranger*, based on the concept of his 1975 record album of the same name. He was seen as a minister in the old West saddled with an unfaithful wife (Morgan Fairchild) and dealing with the affections of the woman (Katharine Ross) that he learns to love. The movie was his first theatrical release not to make a profit. After that, he was featured in a quartet of Westerns, all made-for-television productions. Nelson made a guest appearance as an army general in *The Last Days of Frank and Jesse James* (NBC-TV, 1986), and he was in the third film version of *Stagecoach* (CBS-TV, 1986). In this poorly received entry, he played Doc Holliday, a strong Native American rights proponent. *Once Upon a Texas Train* (CBS-TV, 1987) presented him as an old-time outlaw hunted by his long time adversary (Richard Widmark), a former Texas Ranger. Burt Kennedy produced, directed, and wrote this ingratiating tale, as he did with Nelson's *Where the Hell's That Gold* (CBS-TV, 1988). The latter focused on outlaws Nelson and Jack Elam being hunted by both U.S. and Mexican authorities because of their border-smuggling activities. Willie also appeared briefly singing the title song he wrote for the Home Box Office Cable TV feature *Baja Oklahoma* (1988). On May 20, 1989, he appeared in an NBC-TV special with Dolly Parton and Kenny Rogers, an open-air concert taped at Houston's Johnson Space Center.

Willie Nelson was named the winner of the American Music Awards special Award of Merit in 1989, just one of many prizes and citations he has garnered since the 1970s. Among his accolades are several Grammys, the Country Music Association's Entertainer of the Year (1979), and many laurels for his many songs. His autobiography, *Willie*, with Bud Shrake, was published in 1988, but that year also found him involved in a complicated personal scenario when his live-in companion Anne-Marie D'Angelo gave birth to his son on Christmas Day. Early the next year Nelson's third wife, Connie (Koepke) Nelson, whom he had married in 1972 (and who was the mother of his daughters Paula and Amy), announced she was suing him for divorce. Nelson and D'Angelo were married the next year.

Despite all his successes—and many failures—Willie Nelson continued to do what he did best: travel and sing. At a gig at the Caesars Palace Circus Maximus Show Room in Las Vegas in 1988 he said, "I haven't changed. I'm doing basically the same thing I've been doing all along. Our music is good, and I think it just took a long time for anyone to hear it. And the people who hear it like it and want to be a part of it."

In the mid-1980s, Nelson teamed with Johnny Cash, Waylon Jennings, and Kris Kristofferson for the highly successful Columbia album *Highwayman*, and they followed it with *Highwayman 2* in 1990. The quartet of country stars toured together, resulting in the feature-length video *Highwaymen Live* in 1990, followed by *The Highwaymen: On the Road Again*, a 1993 documentary on their European tour.

The decade of the 1990s saw some erosion in Willie Nelson's career, although he retained much of his in-person popularity with fans in his never-ending road tours and annual Farm Aid music festivals. In 1990, the Internal Revenue Service announced the star owed over $16 million in back taxes and proceeded to collect by stripping him of most of his assets. To raise money, he recorded a two-cassette tape album *The IRS Tapes: Who'll Buy My Memories*, and with the help of friends and fans he negotiated a settlement with the IRS in 1993. The same year, he was named to the Country Music Hall of Fame, designated "Native American of the Year" and his home state dubbed him a "Living Texas Legend." Also in 1993 he was given a tribute in the CBS-TV special *The Big Six-O*, which celebrated his sixtieth birthday. Seventy-five name performers worked with him on the album *Across the Borderline* that year. Leaving Columbia Records in the mid-1990s, Nelson recorded for a variety of labels like Justice, Liberty, and Island. In 1998, Nelson was an honoree at the annual Kennedy Center Honors and that year he was also inducted into the Texas Music Hall of Fame.

Willie Nelson's acting career continued in the 1990s. He opened the decade by teaming with Kris Kristofferson in the TV western *Pair of Aces* in which he was a safecracker awaiting trial and in the custody of a Texas Ranger (Kristofferson) who is after a serial killer. A sequel, *Another Pair of Aces: Three of a Kind*, followed the next year. Willie was the now-reformed outlaw who joins up with his Texas Ranger pal (Kristofferson) to clear another lawman accused of murder. In 1991, Nelson also played himself in the Dolly Parton starrer, *Wild Texas Wind*, but was offscreen for three years before returning as a lawyer in *Dust to Dust* in 1994. That year, he also appeared as himself in the musical Western *Big Country*, and in 1995 he was again himself in *Big Dreams & Broken Hearts: The Dottie West Story*, a TV biopic starring Michele Lee as Dottie West.

In 1996, Willie starred as Grandpa Lium in the sci-fi feature *Starlight*. The next year he did a trio of pictures: He was Billy (Catcher) Poole in the dud comedy *Gone Fishin'*; he was himself in the documentary *Anthem*; and he was Johnny Dean in *Wag the Dog*, a contemporary comedy about a White House staffer (Robert De Niro) who enlists the aid of a Hollywood producer (Dustin Hoffman) to engineer a fake war with Albania to take the heat off the chief executive's involvement in a sex scandal. Willie was very amusing as the singer-composer who writes a song to support the venture. He was just as good in the marijuana-themed comedy *Half Baked* (1998), and he appeared as himself in *The Hi-Lo Country* (1998). In 1999 Willie and Kris Kristofferson reteamed in the TV movie *Outlaw Justice* as two aged gunmen who get their old gang members back together to take revenge for the murder of a friend. Nelson also played himself in three other 1999 features: two comedies, *Dill Scallion* and *Austin Powers: The Spy Who Shagged Me*, and the direct-to-video documentary about the University of Texas football coach, *The Story of Darrell Royal*. In 2000, Nelson was in the outer-space western adventure *Stardust*, and the next year he was seen in *The Journeyman*.

The veteran singer also guest-starred on various TV series, mostly in the 1990s. Besides appearing on musical shows like *Austin City Limits* and a variety of cable and network specials (including the August 14, 2000, two-hour concert *Live by Request* on A&E Cable), he also did dramatic work, beginning with a segment of the police action show *Miami Vice* in 1984. Among the other series on which he guested after 1990 included *Hot Country Nights, Nash Bridges, The Awful Truth, Space Ghost: Coast to Coast*, and *Dr. Quinn, Medicine Woman*. Nelson also provided voice-overs on the TV animated series *King of the Hill* and *The Simpsons*. In 1992, he was the subject of the home-video documentary *Willie Nelson—My Life*, issued by Music Video Distributors.

As the new century loomed, Willie Nelson remained as active as ever. While he did movies and TV appearances, he mainly continued to tour, promote his annual Farm Aid and Fourth of July picnic festivals, and work at his Pedernales recording studio and golf course near Austin, Texas. He was author of 2002's *The Facts of Life: And Other Dirty Jokes* which he labeled, "one-part song lyrics, one-part photographs, and ten parts bulls***." In the midst of the reminiscences, photos, and song words, there was an occasional philosophical gem: "Ninety-nine percent of the world's lovers are not with their first choice. That's what makes the jukebox play."

Once when the multitalented Nelson was asked if he ever considered retirement, the indefatigable Willie replied, "All I do is play music and golf—which one do you want me to give up?"

Filmography

Puzzle (Garbanzo Studios, 1974) (voice only)

MacKintosh & T.J. (Univ, 1975) (voice only)

Outlaw Blues (WB, 1977)

Country Cookin' (Dallas County Community College District, 1977) (s)

Renaldo and Clara (Circuit Films, 1978) (song only)

Willie Nelson's 4th of July Celebration (Alston/Zanitsch International, 1979)

Voices (UA, 1979) (voice only)

The Electric Horseman (Col/Univ, 1979)

Honeysuckle Rose [On the Road Again] (WB, 1980) (also songs)

Ruckus [The Loner] (New World, 1981) (co-songs only)

Thief (UA, 1981)

Barbarosa (Univ, 1982)

Coming Out of the Ice (CBS-TV, 5/23/82)

Hells Angels Forever (Marvin Films, 1983)

Welcome Home (Col, 1984) (song vocal only)

Songwriter (TriStar, 1984) (also co-songs)

Porky's Revenge (20th-Fox, 1985) (song only)

Red Headed Stranger (Alive Films, 1986)

Amazons (New Horizon, 1986)

Stagecoach (CBS-TV, 5/18/86)

The Last Days of Frank and Jesse James (NBC-TV, 2/16/86)

Once Upon a Texas Train (CBS-TV, 1/3/88) (video title: Texas Guns)

Baja Oklahoma (Home Box Office Cable, 2/20/88) (also song)

Walking After Midnight (Kay Film, 1988)

Where the Hell's That Gold? (CBS-TV, 11/13/88) (video title: Dynamite and Gold)

Welcome Home (Col, 1989) (voice only)

Pair of Aces (CBS-TV, 1/14/90)

Another Pair of Aces: Three of a Kind (CBS-TV, 4/9/91)

Wild Texas Wind (NBC-TV, 9/23/91)

Dust to Dust (Movie Reps International, 1994)

Big Country (Iwerks Entertainment, 1994)

Big Dreams & Broken Hearts: The Dottie West Story (TNN Cable, 1/22/95)

Starlight (Astral, 1996)

Anthem (Zeitgeist Films, 1997) (documentary)

Wag the Dog (New Line Cinema, 1997)

Gone Fishin' (BV, 1997)

Half Baked (Univ, 1998)

The Hi-Lo Country (Gramercy Pictures, 1998)

Dill Scallion (The Asylum, 1999)

Outlaw Justice (CBS-TV, 1/24/99)

Austin Powers: The Spy Who Shagged Me (BV, 1999)

The Story of Darrell Royal (Hall of Legends Sports, 1999) (documentary)

Stardust (Cyber Sci-Fi, 2000)

The Journeyman (Unk, 2001)

Crossover (Independent Film Channel Cable, 9/24/2001) (documentary)

TV Series

The Ernest Tubb Show (Synd, 1966–67)

Album Discography

LPs

Alabama (Quicksilver 1013) w. Jerry Lee Lewis

Always on My Mind (Col FC-37951)

And Then I Wrote (Liberty LST-7239) w. Leon Russell

Angel Eyes (Col FC-39363) w. Ray Charles, Jackie King

Bandana Land (Heritage RSRD-181920)

Best of 2 Super Artists Sing Gospel (Arrival BU-1654) w. George Jones

The Best of Willie Nelson (Capitol/CEMA 4XLL-9391)

The Best of Willie Nelson (EMI 1C-064-82878)

The Best of Willie Nelson (Liberty LN-10118)

The Best of Willie Nelson (Liberty Special Products SLL-8296)

The Best of Willie Nelson (RCA AH1-4420, RCA AYK1-5143)

The Best of Willie Nelson (UA UA-LA086-F)

Blue Skies (CBS 10025)

Both Sides Now (RCA LSP-4294)

Brand on My Heart (Col PC-39977) w. Hank Snow

Broken Promises (Quicksilver 5048)

Charlie's Shoes (Quicksilver DECP-02) w. Billy Walker

City of New Orleans (Col FC-39145)

Classic Willie Nelson (Music for Pleasure MFP-5602)

Collector's Series (RCA AHL1-5470)

Columbus Stockade Blues and Other Country Favorites (Camden CAS-2444, Camden 7018, Pickwick ACL-7018)

Country and Western Classics (Time-Life P3-16946)

Country Classics (Astra 102)

Country Classics (Columbia Special Products P16911)

Country Club: The Hits of Willie Nelson (RCA KEL1-8015)

Country Favorites, Willie Nelson Style (RCA LPM/LSP-3528)

Country Willie (EMI TC-EMS-1252)

Country Willie (Liberty LN-10013)

Country Willie (UA UA-LA410-E)

Country Willie—His Own Songs (RCA LPM/LSP-3418)

Country Winners (Camden ACL1-0326)

Danny Davis, Willie Nelson and the Nashville Brass (RCA AHL1-3549)

Diamonds in the Rough (Delta DLP-1557)

Don't You Ever Get Tired of Hurting Me (RCA CLP1-5174)

Double Barrel (LT 1961)

Early Willie (Potomac P7-1000)

Early Willie: Collector's Edition (Potomac P7-1000)

18 Golden Hits (Masters MA-11141183)

18 Great Songs (Design DELP-308) w. Waylon Jennings

The Electric Horseman (Col JS-36327) [ST]

Even Then (Country Fidelity CFX-213)

Faces of a Fighter (Lone Star L-4602)

The Family Bible (MCA 3258)

The Family Bible (Songbird 37167)

Funny How Time Slips Away (Col FC-39484) w. Faron Young

The Ghost of the Ghost (Hot Schaltz HS-0052-1)

Good Hearted Woman (Pair PDK2-1114)

Good Ol' Country Singin' (Camden CAL-2703)

Good Times (RCA LSP-4057)

Greatest Hits (Camden CL-8514)

Greatest Hits (ERA/RCA Special Products DPK1-0675) w. Waylon Jennings

Greatest Hits and Some That Will Be (Col KC2-37542)

Half Nelson (Columbia FCT-39990)

HBO Presents Willie Nelson & Family (HBO—no number) [ST/TV]

Hello Walls (Pickwick 3584)

Hello Walls (Sunset SUM-1138/SUS-5138, Liberty LRP-33081)

Help Me Make It Through the Night (RCA NL-89475)

Here's Willie Nelson (Liberty LST-7308)

The Highwayman (Col 40056) w. Waylon Jennings, Johnny Cash, Kris Kristofferson

Historic Reissue (Bridge 100.027-2)

Home Is Where You're Happy (82 Music Co. LSM-906)

Home Is Where You're Happy (Showcase SHLP-111, ONN 39)

Honeysuckle Rose (Col S2-36752) [ST]

The Hungry Years (Plantation PLC-53)

I Just Don't Understand (Classic Sound CLASSIC-7560)

I'd Rather Have Jesus (Arrival NU-719-4) w. Bobbie Nelson

In the Jailhouse Now (Col PC-38095) w. Webb Pierce

Island in the Sea (Col CK-40487)

Just Plain Willie—The Unreleased Tapes, Vols. 1-3 (Col P17726-8)

Just Willie (Casino CASINO-151)

Laying My Burdens Down (RCA LSP-4404)

The Legend Begins (Takoma 7104)

Let's Pretend (Blue Ribbon BR-47541)

Live Country Music Concert (RCA LPM/LSP-3659)

The Longhorn Jamboree Presents Willie Nelson and Friends (Plantation PLP-24, Charly CR-30120) w. Jerry Lee Lewis, Carl Perkins, David Allan Coe

Love and Pain (Aura 1003, Out of Town Distributors OTD-8641)

MacKintosh & T. J. (RCA APL-1520 [ST]

The Magic of Willie Nelson (Banner BTR-2542)

Make Way for Willie Nelson (RCA LPM/LSP-3748)

Me and Paul (Col 40008)

Mellow Moods of the Vintage Years: Written and Sung by Willie Nelson (82 Music Co. LSM-609)

Minstrel Man (RCA AHL1-4045)

Monte Alban Mezcal Proudly Presents Willie Nelson, Country Superstar (RCA/Candlelite DVL1-0446)

My Own Peculiar Way (RCA LSP-4111)

My Own Way (RCA AHL1-4819)

Night Life (Plantation PLC-207)

Old Friends (Col PC-38013) w. Roger Miller

Once More With Feeling (RCA DPL1-0496)

One for the Road (Col KC2-36064) w. Leon Russell

The Original Willie Nelson (Classic Collection KC-10101)

Outlaw Reunion, Vol. 1 (Aura A-1010, Out of Town Distributors OTD-8647, Sundown SDLP-1005) w. Waylon Jennings

Outlaw Reunion, Vol. 2 (Aura A-1011, Out of Town Distributors OTD-8648, Sundown SDLP-1007) w. Waylon Jennings

Outlaws (Topline 133) w. David Allan Coe

Pancho and Lefty (Epic FE-37958) w. Merle Haggard

Partners (Columbia PCT-39394)

The Party's Over (RCA LPM/LSP-3858)

Phases and Stages (Atlantic 7291)

The Poet (Accord 7236)

Porky's Revenge (Col JS-39983) [ST]

A Portrait in Music (Premier KCBR-1016)

Pretty Paper (Col JC-36189)

Pride Wins Again (Maverick 1004)

The Promiseland (Col JC-36189)

Rainy Day Blues (Plantation PLC-224)

Red Headed Stranger (Col KC-33482)

Reply (Sierra FEDB-5507)

San Antonio Rose (Col JC-36476) w. Ray Price

Seashores of Old Mexico (Col 40293) w. Merle Haggard

Seasons of the Heart (Pickwick CAK-2444)

Second Fiddle (Axis AX-701238)

Shotgun Willie (Atlantic 7762)

Slow Down Old World (Aura 1002, /Out of Town Distributors OTD-8692, Sundown SDLP-1006)

Somewhere Over the Rainbow (Col FC-36883)

A Song for You (Hallmark SHM-3127, Pickwick PWKS-578)

Songwriter (Col FC-39531) [ST]

The Sound in Your Mind (Col KC-34092)

Spotlight on Willie Nelson (Camden ACL1-0705)

Stardust (Col JC-35305)

Super Hits (Classic Sound Classic-40022)

Super Hits (Evergreen 2690252, Point 261114, Black Tulip 2690254)

Sweet Memories (RCA AHL1-3243, RCA AYL1-4300)

Take It to the Limit (Col FC-38562) w. Waylon Jennings

Take Me As I Am (Cap 4XLL-8312)

Texas in My Soul (RCA LSP-3937)

Texas Tornados (Plantation PLP-54) w. Mickey Gilley, Johnny Lee

There'll Be No Teardrops Tonight (UA UA-LA930-H)

Things to Remember (Creative Sounds S11-3548, Media Music MM-37184)

To Lefty, From Willie (Col KC-34695)

Together Again (Delta 1139) w. Johnny Bush

Touch Me (EMI ED-2606831)

Tougher Than Leather (Col QC-338248)

The Troublemaker (Col KC-34112)

Tudor Record Vintage Series, Vol. 1 (Tudor TR-1444-04) w. David Houston

Tudor Record Vintage Series, Vol. 2 (Tudor TR-1143-04) w. Mickey Gilley

20 Early Memories (Plantation PLC-2000)

20 Golden Classics (Astan 20021)

20 Golden Classics (Big Country 2430513)

20 of the Best (RCA International 89137)

20 Outlaw Reunion Hits (Astan 20020) w. Waylon Jennings

Vintage Willie Nelson (Delta CTA-7014, Delta DLP-1151)

Voices (Planet P-9002) [ST]

Walking the Line (Epic FE-40821) w. Merle Haggard, George Jones

Wanted! The Outlaws (RCA APL1-1321) w. Waylon Jennings, Jessi Colter, Tompall Glaser

Waylon and Willie (RCA AFL1-2686, AYK1-5134) w. Waylon Jennings

What Can You Do to Me Now (RCA APL1-1234, RCA AYL1-3958)

Wild and Willie (Allegiance 5010)

Willie (RCA CPL1-7158)

Willie and David (Plantation PLP-411) w. David Allan Coe

Willie and Family Live (Col KC2-35642) w. Johnny Paycheck, Emmylou Harris

Willie Before His Time (RCA APL1-2210)

Willie Nelson (Audio Fidelity ZCCGAS-757)

Willie Nelson (Exact 249)

Willie Nelson and Bob Wills (Merit MC-105)

Willie Nelson and David Allan Coe (Plantation 41)

Willie Nelson and Family (RCA LSP-4489)

Willie Nelson and Faron Young (Romulus A-6056, Mid South T-6056)

Willie Nelson and His Texas Friends (Merit MC-101)

Willie Nelson and Johnny Lee (Quicksilver 5005, Astan 20022)

Willie Nelson: Collector's Edition Promo (Premore PL-66)

Willie Nelson Live (RCA APL1-1487)

Willie Nelson: Nashville (82 Records 122982)

Willie Nelson, 1961 (Shotgun 1961)

Willie Nelson Sings Kris Kristofferson (Col JC-36188)

Willie Nelson, Vol. 1 (Golden Circle GC-47503)

Willie Or Won't He (Allegiance 5005)

The Willie Way (RCA LSP-4760)

Winning Hand (Monument 38389-1) w. Kris Kristofferson, Dolly Parton, Brenda Lee

Without a Song (Col FC-39110)

The Words Don't Fit the Picture (RCA LSP-4653)

The World of Willie Nelson (Warwick WW-2204)

WWII (RCA AHL1-4455) w. Waylon Jennings

Yesterday's Wine (RCA LSP-4568, RCA AHL1-1102, RCA AYL1-3800)

CDs

A & E Biography . . . Anthology (Cap Nashville 20015)

Across the Borderline (Col CK-52752)

Across the Tracks (Telstar TCD-2317)

Allegiance Extra (Delta CDP-72922)

All of Me (Sony 4878732)

All-Time Greatest Hits, Vol. 1 (RCA 8556-2-R)

All-Time Greatest Hits, Vol. 2 (RCA 2695-2-R)

Always on My Mind (Col CK-37951, GSS GSS-5280)

Always on My Mind (Delta 6096)

Always on My Mind/Best of Willie Nelson (Prism PLATCD-578)

Always on My Mind & Other Big Hits Live (BCD CT-55445)

Always: 20 Superb Songs (Prism PLATCD-116)

And Then I Wrote (Liberty C214-32464, Liberty CDP-7243)

Augusta (Coast to Coast Records CTC-0305, Sundown/Magnum 80) w. Don Cherry

Back to Back (EMI-Cap Special Markets 23739) w. George Jones

Backtracks (Renaissance 603)

Best of Gospel (MCA MCAD-20560) w. Merle Haggard

The Best of Johnny Cash & Willie Nelson—37 Outlaw Country Classics (Master Song 550312)

The Best of Willie Nelson (EMI Manhattan E214-48398-2)

The Best of Willie Nelson (Liberty C214-48398)

The Best of Willie Nelson (RCA 07863-56335-2)

The Best of Willie Nelson (Starlight CDS-51023)

The Best of Willie Nelson: The Early Years (EMI-Cap Special Markets 98876)

Blame It on the Times (ABM ABMMCD1215)

Blame It on the Times (Javelin HADCD-132)

Born for Trouble (Col CK-45492)

Broken Promises (Century/PNEC PLCD-1010)

Building Heartaches (Laserlight 12-938)

Burning Memories (Kingfisher 20) w. Waylon Jennings

Christmas With Willie Nelson (Regency V20037)

City of New Orleans (Col CK-39145)

A Classic, Unreleased Collection (Rhino R2-71462)

Classic Collection: 23 of His Best (AIM AIM-30003CD)

Classic Willie (BMG Special Products 44525-2, KRB Music Companies KRB1104-2)

Classics (Sony Music Special Products A-52062/ KRB Music Companies KRB7026-2)

Clean Shirt (Epic EK-47462) w. Waylon Jennings

Col Stockade Blues (Delta 6090) w. Dolly Parton, Ronnie Milsap

Col Stockade Blues (Delta 6092)

Country Legends (Object FPF05A)

Country Legends Reunion (Legacy Entertainment ATP034) w. Waylon Jennings

Country Outlaw (Soundsational CDMA-4011)

The Country Store Collection (Masterpiece CD-CST-42) w. Waylon Jennings

Country Willie (EMI-Manhattan E21K-48399)

Country Willie: His Own Songs (Buddha 99676)

Country Winners (Pair PDC2-1007)

Crying (Excelsior EXL-20072, St. Clair 2377) w. Waylon Jennings

December Days (Laserlight 12-937)

Early Times (Plane COCY-90038)

Early Tracks (Sun R4-70345)

Early Years (Master 503202)

The Early Years (Scotti Bros. 72392-75437-2, Scotti Bros. 32057)

The Early Years: The Complete Liberty Recordings Plus More (2-Liberty C22U-28077)

The Electric Horseman (Col CK-36327) [ST]

The Essential Willie Nelson (Cedar GFS-048)

The Essential Willie Nelson (RCA 07863-66590-2)

Face of a Fighter (MK 30042)

Flesh & Blood (Varese Sarabande VSD-5460) [ST]

Forever Gold (St. Clair FGD-58162)

Forrest Gump (Epic Soundtrax E2K-66329) [ST]

Funny How Times Slips Away: Best of Willie Nelson (Camden 74321487272)

Georgia on My Mind (Columbia River Entertainment Group CRG-110020)

Golden Hits (Masters MACD-61020)

Gone Fishin'(Hollywood HR-62119-2) [ST]

Good Ol' Country Singin' (RCA Camden Classics 6120)

Good Old Country (St. Clair 7815)

Gospel Favorites (MCA MCAD-20784)

Gospel's Best (MCA MCAD-20478) w. Merle Haggard

Great Willie Nelson (Ronco CDSR-016)

Greatest Hits (Excelsior 1332/EXL-10732)

Greatest Hits (MSHRM 4780392)

Greatest Hits (St. Clair 1332)

Greatest Hits (& Some That Will Be) (Col CGK-37542)

Greatest Hits—Live in Concert (BCI BCCD-295)

Greatest Songs (Curb/CMEA D21K-77366)

The Gypsy (Pedernales/Free Falls FFE-7014-2) w. Jackie King

Half Nelson (Col CK-39990)

Healing Hands of Time (Liberty 7243-8-30420-2-9, EMI K21X-30420)

Heartaches (Prestige CDSGP-052)

Heroes (BMG 4321202732) w. Waylon Jennings

Highwayman (BCD GLD-2580) w. Johnny Cash, Waylon Jennings, Kris Kristofferson

Highwayman (Col CK-40056) w. Johnny Cash, Waylon Jennings, Kris Kristofferson

Highwayman 2 (Col CK-45240) w. Johnny Cash, Waylon Jennings, Kris Kristofferson

Hill Country Christmas (Finer Arts FAR-9705-2) w. Bobbie Nelson

His Greatest Hits and Finest Performances: Collectors' Edition of Original Recordings (Reader's Digest RBA-133/A)

Home Is Where You're Happy (Success 16182CD)

Home Is Where You're Happy (Time Music TT-1225)

Honeymoon in Vegas (Epic Soundtrax EK-52845) [ST]

Honeysuckle Rose (Col CGK-36762) [ST]

Honky Tonk Heroes (Free Falls Entertainment 7008)

A Horse Called Music (Col CK-45046)

How Great Thou Art (Finer Arts FA-9605-2) w. Bobbie Nelson

The Hungry Years (Sony Music Special Products A22354)

I Let My Mind Wander (Kingfisher KF60019-2)

I'd Rather Have Jesus (Bald Eagle Productions NU-719-1) w. Bobbie Nelson

In the Jailhouse Now (CBS PCT-38095) w. Webb Pierce

In the Jailhouse Now/Brand on My Heart (DCC Compact Classics 198) w. Webb Pierce, Hank Snow

Is There Something on Your Mind (Tring International GRF032)

Island in the Sea (Col CK-40487)

Just One Love (Justice JR-1602-2, Buddha 99718)

King of the Outlaws (Charly CDCD-1088)

The Legend Begins (Pair PCD2-1333) w. Shirley Collie

The Legendary Willie Nelson (Sony Music Special Products BT-23335)

The Legends of Country Music (Madacy 5337)

Love and Pain (Forever Music Group 0403)

Love Songs (Legacy CK-62183)

The Many Sides of Willie Nelson (Sony Music Special Products A322736)

Me & Paul (DCC Compact Classics DZS-191)

Milk Cow Blues (Island 542-517)

Moonlight Becomes You (Justice JR-1601-2, Buddha 99717)

My Heroes Have Always Been Cowboys (RCA 2338-2-R) [ST]

Nashville Was the Roughest (Bear Family BCD-15831)

Night and Day (Pedernales/Free Falls FF-7002-2)

Night Life (Laserlight 15-485)

Nite Life: His Greatest Hits & Rare Tracks 1959-71 (Rhino R2-70987)

Oh Boy Classics Presents Willie Nelson (Oh Boy 401)

Old Friends (Pickwick PWKS-4041) w. Waylon Jennings

Old Friends/Funny How Time Slips Away (Koch 8039) w. Roger Miller, Faron Young, Ray Price

Old Time Religion (Laserlight 12-114) w. Bobbie Nelson

On the Road Again (BCD GLD-25346O)

On the Road Again (Col A/BT-21281)

On the Road Again (Col CK-21100)

One for the Road (Col CGK-36064) w. Leon Russell

One Step Beyond (Prestige CDSGP-096, Starburst SM-11)

The Original Outlaws: The Encore Collection (BMG Special Products 44662) w. Waylon Jennings

Outlaw Reunion (Tring International GRF058) w. Waylon Jennings

Outlaws (BCD CTS-55407) w. Waylon Jennings

Pancho & Lefty (Epic 37958) w. Merle Haggard

Pancho & Lefty & Rudolph: Country Christmas Super Hits (Col/Nashville CK-67296) w. Merle Haggard

Peace in the Valley: The Gospel Truth Collection (Promised Land Music PLMCD-052158) w. Willie Nelson Jr.

Phases & Stages (Atlantic Nashville 82192-2)

Phases & Stages/Shotgun Willie (Mobile Fidelity UDCD-581)

Partners (Col CK-39894)

Pretty Paper (Col CK-36189)

Profile of Willie Nelson (Profile PRO-33112)

The Promiseland (Col CK-40327)

Pure Willie (Jerden 7010)

Rainbow Connection (Island 314-548-810-2)

Red Headed Stranger (Col CK-33482, Col CK-63589)

Revolutions of Time . . . The Journey 1975-1993 (Col/Legacy C3K-64796)

The Road Goes on Forever (Liberty C21Z-28091) w. Johnny Cash, Waylon Jennings, Kris Kristofferson

San Antonio Rose (Col CK-36476) w. Ray Price

Seashores of Old Mexico (Epic PET-40293) w. Merle Haggard

Shotgun Willie (Atlantic 7262-2, Rhino 7262)

Singer, Songwriter (Platinum Disc Corp. 14512)

Singer, Songwriters (Sony Music Special Products A21130) w. Eddie Rabbitt

Six Hours at Pedernales with Special Guest: Curtis Potter (Step One SOR-0084)

16 Biggest Hits (Legacy CK-69322)

16 Great Songs (16 Tons CD-11006)

16 Great Songs (16 Tons CD-11009) w. Waylon Jennings

Slow Down Old World (Forever Music Group 04111)

Somewhere Over the Rainbow (Col CK-36883)

The Sound in Your Mind (Col CK-34092)

Spirit (Island 314-524-242-2)

Spotlight on Willie Nelson (Javelin HADCD-132)

Standard Time (Sony Music Special Products A26915)

Stardust (Col CK-35305, Legacy CK-65946)

A Step Beyond (Direct Source CY-60052)

Suffering in Silence (That's Country TC-007)

Super Hits (Black Tulip 2690254, Point 2661114)

Super Hits (Col 4989502)

Super Hits (Col CK-64184)

Super Hits (CSI Classics-40022)

Super Hits, Vol. 2 (Col CK-67295)

Sweet Memories (GSC Music/BMG Special Products 15331)

Sweet Memories (RCA 07863-55975-2)

Switchback (RCA 07863-66993-2) [ST]

Teatro (Island 524-548)

3 For 3 (St. Clair 3815) w. Kenny Rogers

Things to Remember (BCD CTS-55401)

Things to Remember (That's Country TC-006)

To Lefty From Willie (Col CK-34695)

To Lefty From Willie/Always on My Mind (Legacy CK-61391)

Touch Me (Golgram GG045)

Tougher Than Leather (Col CK-38248)

20 Golden Greats (Cleopatra 843)

20 Golden Hits (Masters MA/MC-911121183)

20 of the Best (Amiga 8-56-363)

Ultimate Legends (Ultimate Music Collection ULT-40662)

The Very Best of Willie Nelson (Legacy CK-65825)

VH1 Storytellers (American Recording CK-69416) w. Johnny Cash

Walking the Line (Epic FET-40821) w. Merle Haggard, George Jones

Wanted! The Outlaws (RCA CD-66841-2, RCA 5976-2-RRE, BMG Entertainment 66841-2) w. Waylon Jennings, Jessi Colter, Tompall Glaser

Waylon & Willie (RCA 58401-2, Buddha 99773) w. Waylon Jennings

Waylon & Willie: WWII (Buddha 99668) w. Waylon Jennings

What a Wonderful World (Col CK-44331)

White Lightning (Delta 6130) w. Waylon Jennings

Who'll Buy My Memories, Vol. 1 & Vol. 2 (Col A2K-52981/2/3)

Willie (RCA 5988-2-R)

Willie & Conway (King Special KSCD-473) w. Conway Twitty

Willie & Family Live (CBS 2-G2K-35642)

Willie Nelson (Bridge 100.277-2)

Willie Nelson (CD Sounds CDFX-6741)

Willie Nelson (Delta 64017)

Willie Nelson (Newsound NST-112)

Willie Nelson (Quality QED-068)

Willie Nelson (Time Life Music 3661-2)

Willie Nelson & Eddie Rabbitt (Madacy 848)

Willie Nelson & Friends (Sony Music Special Products PCD-4601)

Willie Nelson & Waylon Jennings (Goldies GLD-63125)

Willie Nelson Christmas (KRB Music Companies KRB3506-2)

Willie Nelson Double CD (Classic World Productions 9905)

Willie Nelson: Original Artist (Fat Boy FATCD-125)

Willie Nelson Sings Kristofferson (Col CK-36188)

Willie Nelson Sings 28 Great Songs (Hollywood HT/HCD-405)

Willie Nelson, Vol. 1 (BCI Eclipse 64705)

Willie Nelson, Vol. 2 (BCI Eclipse 64708)

Willie Standard Time (Sony Music Special Products A26915)

Willie, Waylon & Friends: 36 All-time Favorites! (GSC Music 15447) w. Jessie Colter, Hank Williams Jr.

Without a Song (Col CK-39110)

Yours Always (Madacy 3134)

Yours Always (Sony Music Special Products A21562)

Olivia Newton-John in *Grease* (1978).
[Courtesy of JC Archives]

Olivia Newton-John

(b. September 26, 1948, Cambridge, England)

In the mid–1970s, one of the most popular country singers in the United States was *not* from Nashville, but was a petite young British woman who had grown up in Australia. To many critics she was bland in her vocal interpretations ("if white bread could sing"), but to her devotees, she was sweet in spirit and pure in sound. Within a few years, blonde, blue-eyed Olivia Newton-John crossed over into pop music, emerging with a new, tougher image and a more mainstream sound. *Grease* (1978) costarred her with John Travolta, and she demonstrated she could be more than cotton-candy sweet. From that movie musical megahit to the embarrassing failure of *Xanadu* (1980)—with Gene Kelly—was a long but quick movie career drop. (Ironically the *Xanadu* soundtrack album and several of its singles proved that Newton-John still had clout with record buyers.) When another fantasy film (*Two of a Kind,* 1983, also with John Travolta) was a total box-office dud, Olivia abandoned moviemaking (or vice versa). Meanwhile, she continued experimenting as a songwriter, an ecologist, and a businessperson. Musically, she moved from the satirical teasing image of "Let's Get Physical" to the more middle-of-the-road "The Rumour," an Elton John tune. Despite playing with her innocent image throughout the 1980s, Olivia's pure, dulcet voice, with its childlike overtones, remained intact. Later in life, she became a pert, safe icon for her middle-aged fans, several restrained leaps from the more current Madonna.

She was born on September 26, 1948, in Cambridge, England, the daughter of Bryn and Irene (Born) Newton-John. There was an older brother (who became a doctor) and an older sister (who became an actress). Her Welsh father had planned to have a career in opera, but instead taught German at King's College, Cambridge University. Her mother was the daughter of Max Born, a Nobel Prize–winning German physicist. When Olivia was five, Mr. Newton-John was appointed headmaster of Ormond College in Melbourne and the family migrated to Australia. When she was eleven, her parents divorced and Olivia moved with her mother to an apartment in Melbourne. The teenager was already expressing a strong interest in music, particularly in the singing styles of Tennessee Ernie Ford, Joan Baez, Nina Simone, and Ray Charles. Her mother gave her an acoustic guitar when she thirteen, and this led to her performing in a coffeehouse (owned by her sister and her sister's then-husband) on weekends. Thereafter, with three female friends, she formed a singing group, the Sol Four, and they sang traditional jazz material. At fourteen, Olivia (known as "Livvey") won a Hayley Mills look-alike contest, and two years later, having appeared on several local television shows (such as *The Go Show*), she won a talent contest. The prize was a free trip to England.

Olivia debated for nearly two years before accepting the trip. When she did fly to London, she abandoned further schooling and dropped plans (fostered by her mother) to attend the Royal Academy of Dramatic Arts. She decided to make England her home and became involved with several musical groups. Eventually she came to the attention of American music producer Don

Kirschner (who had prefabricated the Monkees singing group). He was in the process of creating a new synthetic rock combo. He recalled, "when I heard her sing, I knew we could get a great, sweet sound out of her." The group (three males and one female) was dubbed Toomorrow (deliberately misspelled) and in 1970 they appeared on film in the science-fiction musical *Toomorrow*. With songs by Ritchie Adams and Mark Barkan, the movie failed to arouse much enthusiasm and quickly disappeared. *Variety* noted that the Toomorrows, cast here as students paying for their education by performing, were "fresh and cleancut, with girl warbler Olivia Newton-John being particularly promising as a screen potential."

Next, artistic Olivia teamed with fellow Australian Pat Carroll, and together, the two female singers began playing pub dates and appearing on television. When Carroll's visa expired and she returned to Australia temporarily, Olivia continued on her own as a single performer, which led to her association with the group the Shadows and with singer Cliff Richard. She began appearing on *The Cliff Richard Show* on British television. For a time she dated Bruce Welch, a member of the Shadows who spun off with other group members into the act Marvin, Welch, and Farrar.

Olivia first rose to prominence in the British music industry in 1971 with her middle-of-the-road version of Bob Dylan's "If Not for You" (which that summer rose to number twenty-five on the United States singles chart). In 1971, Olivia was created an Officer of the Order of the British Empire, being named Best British Girl Singer. She continued with such British hits as "Banks of the Ohio," "What Is Life," and "Take Me Home, Country Roads," all the time veering farther away from folk and closer to country music. Meanwhile, she continued to appear on television and to tour (Britain, Australia, and Japan) with Cliff Richard. Her producer on many of her recordings was guitarist John Farrar (who later married Olivia's old performing partner, singer Pat Carroll). Newton-John's song "Let Me Be There" was unique on the United States record charts by starting on the country charts and then reaching sixth position on the pop charts in early 1974.

Olivia toured the United States for several months in 1974, including playing at the Hilton in Las Vegas (as an opening act) and Harrah's Club in Lake Tahoe. She also was named Female Vocalist of the Year by the Country Music Association (as well as by their British counterpart) and won a Grammy for Best Country and Western Female Vocal ("Let Me Be There"). Her victory upset many American-bred country singers, including Dolly Parton (who later became a friend), Tammy Wynette, and Johnny Paycheck. (The latter said when forming the splinter organization the Association of Country Entertainers, "We don't want somebody out of another field coming in and taking away what we've worked so hard for.") Newton-John did not help matters when, while accepting the CMA Award, she remarked ingenuously, "It's probably the first time an English person won an award over Nashville people." Country-music purists were even more incensed the next year (1975), when Olivia won two Grammys (Record of the Year and Best Contemporary/Pop Female Solo Vocal) for "I Honestly Love You."

By now, Olivia, who had been recording in England with the Pye label, was contracted with MCA Records. "I Honestly Love You" rose to number one on the charts, as did "Have You Never Been Mellow" (written and produced by John Farrar) in 1975. For "Please, Mr. Please" (1975) she received the ASCAP Country Music Award. For the movie drama *The Other Side of the Mountain* (1975) she sang the soundtrack vocal "Richard's Window."

In October 1975, Olivia became a Las Vegas headline act at the Riviera Hotel. The *Los Angeles Times* described, "Her gentle, whispery vocal tone and sweet, delicate appearance/manner are . . . more important in establishing her appeal onstage than range, dynamics, phrasing and the other technical measure of a singer's talent." Her fifth gold album in a row was *Don't Stop Believin'* (1976), which was deliberately recorded in Nashville (and did a great deal to end the controversy over a foreign pop singer having invaded country turf). She had already appeared on several TV specials—including those of Bob Hope (1974), Perry Como (1975), John Denver (1975), and Glen Campbell (1976)—when she hostessed her own hour-long variety special. Produced by Lee Kramer, *The Olivia Newton-John Show* (ABC-TV, November 17, 1976), featured such guests as Rock Hudson, Ron Howard, Lee Majors, and Nancy Walker. It received sharp raps from reviewers doubting the capability of her charisma to carry a full show, but the ratings were high, and she was back on ABC-TV with another special, *Olivia* (May 17, 1978), with guests ABBA and Andy Gibb.

Such Newton-John songs as "Don't Stop Believin' " (1976) and "Sam" (1977) rose to the top forty (but not on top) on the charts. However, increasingly, critics insisted that her cloyingly virtuous image and overly sweet song delivery were self-defeating. In May 1977, she appeared successfully in concert at the Metropolitan Opera House in New York City, winning over some of her prior detractors. Said the *New York Times,* "Miss Newton-John's soprano isn't as negligible as some think. . . ." She then went on a tour of Great Britain, which included a TV special and an appearance before the queen of England.

By late 1977, Olivia announced that she was to costar in the screen version of the long-running Broadway hit *Grease.* John Travolta had already been signed to play the lead male role of Danny. She claimed she screen-tested for the part of Sandy (who converts from an overly wholesome coed into a leather-clad motorcycle-ette to win the love of her beau) because, "I didn't want to go into something I couldn't handle or have something to say about. I was playing a naive girl but I didn't want her to be sickly." *Grease* was released by Paramount Pictures in the summer of 1978, grossing eventually over $96 million in domestic film rentals. *Variety* agreed that "Newton-John registers very impressively—far better than the usual personality casting one has come to expect. . . ." Within this slick satire on the rock 'n' roll era, she soloed "Hopelessly Devoted to You" (which rose to number three on the charts as a single disc) and dueted with John Travolta on "Summer Nights" (which became a number-five hit single) and "You're the One That I Want" (written especially for the film by John Farrar, it reached number one on the charts). All three songs became number-one hits on the British singles chart. Previous to the summer 1978 phenomenon of the *Grease* film and album, Olivia had a well-publicized tiff with MCA Records. She claimed they were not promoting her sufficiently, and she sought to end their five-year contract. Post *Grease,* matters were resolved and she continued recording with the label.

With her revamped image courtesy of *Grease,* Olivia pulled farther away from her girl-next-door mold with her album *Totally Hot.* It contained the hit song "A Little More Love." She turned down *Grease* producer Allan Carr's offer to have her star in the movie musical *Can't Stop the Music* (1980) but did agree to appear in *Xanadu* (1980), a film musical of high intention but little entertainment value. She was the muse who comes to earth and finds herself being courted by a wealthy man (Gene Kelly) and a punk rocker (Michael Beck). The expensive but dreadful production was a financial fiasco. However, interestingly enough, the soundtrack music was a big success. "Magic" (written by John Farrar) became a number-one hit for her. The title tune peaked in eighth position, and her duet ("Suddenly") with Cliff Richard reached number twenty on the charts. The *Xanadu* soundtrack album went platinum, selling over one million copies. On April 14, 1980,

ABC-TV telecast her latest special, *Olivia Newton-John's Hollywood Nights.* Her duet single "I Can't Help It" with Andy Gibb was in the top ten songs in the spring of 1980.

"I wanted peppy stuff because that's how I'm feeling," insisted Newton-John when she recorded the hit album *Physical* (1980), which had two top ten songs: "Physical" and "Make a Move on Me." Listeners to the song "Physical" could clearly discern its suggestive lyrics. However, seeing the music video of "Physical" (which won a Grammy as Best Video of the Year) or watching Olivia perform the rousing, provocative song on her TV special (*Olivia Newton-John: Let's Be Physical,* ABC-TV, February 8, 1982) was a far more exciting matter. It proved that the singing star had now become the happy queen of sassy pop tunes. *Billboard* magazine named "Physical" the top single of 1982. Because she could now reach her audiences through TV specials and music videos, Olivia cut down on her touring (especially after her controversial concert in Sun City, South Africa, in August 1982), with which she had never been completely comfortable. She concentrated more on her private life, including her love and care of stray animals. With her longtime friend Pat Carroll, she opened the first of the Koala Blue boutiques (selling Australian wares) in Los Angeles. She ended her several year's romantic relationship with her American businessman manager Lee Kramer and began dating Matt Lattanzi, the twenty-two-year-old dancer/extra she had met on the set of *Xanadu.*

Olivia starred in a cable TV special (*Olivia Newton-John in Concert*) on HBO on January 23, 1983, mixing her past and present images, but getting more intriguing response for her punk persona in such songs as "Heart Attack." Plans for her to costar with Bryan Brown in D. H. Lawrence's *Kangaroo* fell apart. (Judy Davis starred in the movie project with Colin Friels in 1986.) Instead, Newton-John returned to moviemaking in the disastrous $14 million *Two of a Kind* (1983). It cast her as a would-be actress from Australia who becomes involved with an inventor-turned-robber (John Travolta). Both characters were greedy and not particularly likeable, which made it all the more difficult for four angels from above to use the duo as an example of potential human goodness so the Supreme Being would not flood the Earth. The trite, whimsical production failed badly at the box office. Nevertheless, the *Two of a Kind* album (for which she cowrote some of the songs) was popular, and "Twist of Fate" from the film rose to number five on the charts.

On December 12, 1984, Olivia wed Matt Lattanzi at her Malibu home. It was not until the next fall that she returned to the recording limelight with her album *Soul Kiss,* which carried her even farther away from her former "Miss Apple Blossom" image. The album (with such songs as "Toughen Up," "Culture Shock," and "The Right Moment") only reached number twenty-nine on the charts, and the twenty-minute music video of the album was considered more gross and artificial than playfully shocking. On January 17, 1986, Olivia gave birth to a girl named Chloë. Having become a mother, she spent most of her time as a homemaker, although in midyear she made the video and recorded "The Best of Me" with David Foster. She also opened more branches of the Koala Blue stores. When asked in the summer of 1988 how she kept in shape at age thirty-nine she replied, "It's called motherhood."

HBO promoted *Olivia Newton-John in Australia* (July 30, 1988) as a "picture-postcard concept special." In this bicentennial salute to her adopted homeland, she sang several selections from her new album, *The Rumour* (her first since 1985). She was rated cute, but the concept was branded "dorky." As for *The Rumour, People* magazine judged it "Lively, funny, thoughtful, varied." The title tune was cowritten by Elton John, who sang backup for her; she collaborated on several of the other tunes. However, the disc was not a hit. (The next year she signed with David Geffen's record label and made the children's album *Warm and Tender*.)

In January 1989, Olivia was named celebrity businesswoman of the year by the National Association of Women Business Owners. She and her partners (Pat Carroll Farrar and David Sidell) were operating nine Koala Blue stores with twenty licensed franchisees around the country. Her new business-executive status reflected what she had admitted a few years earlier: "I don't have the desire I think a lot of performers feel, to get the applause. It's not life and death to me. I like to sing, and I love doing what I'm doing, but it's not a dire need." However, two years later, the Los Angeles–based Koala Blue company filed for bankruptcy protection. To recoup the losses from her failed business venture, Newton-John chose to return to the concert stage with her *Back to Basics* tour that was to premiere in Las Vegas in August 1992. But that summer her father died of cancer, and Olivia learned that she had a malignant tumor in her right breast. It required she undergo a modified radical mastectomy at Los Angeles' Cedars-Sinai Medical Center in mid-July. Her tour was cancelled. Two years later, after continued cancer treatment, the songstress returned to acting, appearing in the holiday telefeature *A Christmas Romance* (CBS-TV, December 18, 1994) opposite Gregory Harrison and with her daughter Chloë in the cast. Explaining what appealed to her about the project, Olivia said, "There's no sex. It's a family movie."

In April 1995, Newton-John announced that her marriage to Matt Lattanzi—long believed to be in trouble but a situation put on hold during her lengthy cancer treatment—was in the process of ending. (In late 1999, Lattanzi, forty, wed twenty-eight-year-old Cindy Jessup, who had formerly been his daughter Chloë's babysitter when he and Olivia were married.) By 1996, Newton-John was visible on several media fronts. She had a cameo role in the AIDS drama *It's My Party* starring Eric Roberts and hosted the cable network special *Lifetime Applauds the Fight Against Breast Cancer* (October 21, 1996).

In 1994, the revival of *Grease!* had become a Broadway hit, and four years later the 1978 hit movie version was reissued for a special twentieth anniversary edition. The hoopla renewed public interest in both Olivia and her long-ago film musical costar John Travolta. Newton-John continued to make guest appearances on TV specials, recorded a new Nashville-flavored, self-produced album (*Back With a Heart* on the MCA label), and was a strong and visible advocate in the fight against cancer. In 1998, *People* magazine chose Olivia as one of their fifty Most Beautiful People in the World. Late the next year, the songster joined Delta Burke and Beau Bridges for filmmaker Del Shores's *Sordid Lives,* an independent picture about a small-town Texas family dealing with the funeral of the mother. (The darkly comic movie—in which Olivia played a gum-chewing, guitar-twanging local—was eventually released to little public response in 2001.) In September 2000, Olivia was on hand in Sydney, Australia, along with Italian tenor Andrea Bocelli to carry the torches in front of the Sydney Opera House before the Olympic Games began. Onstage she shared "Dare to Dream" with Australian superstar John Farnham to kick off the competition.

Continuing with occasional albums (*Country Girl, One Woman's Live Journey*), Newton-John in fall 2000 was dating forty-four-year-old cameraman Patrick McDermott, her escort for the past four years. She made occasional concert engagements, including performing at the Las Vegas Hilton Theater in August 2001. In late 2001, Olivia starred in the made-for-cable feature *The Wilde Girls,* in which she was seen as a former rock star not wanting the same lifestyle for her teenaged daughter (played by her real-life offspring Chloë).

Planning to write her autobiography, Olivia said of her life-changing cancer battle: "Now I wake up and I'm grateful for each and every morning. I'm thrilled to get older . . . It's funny, but now I am known more for being a breast cancer survivor than for being a performer. It makes me proud to be someone who can inspire and help people. Maybe that was supposed to be my job all along."

Filmography

Toomorrow (Br, 1970)
The Other Side of the Mountain [A Window to the Sky] (Univ, 1975) (voice only)
Grease (Par, 1978)
Xanadu (Univ, 1980)
Two of a Kind (20th-Fox, 1983) (also songs)
She's Having a Baby (Par, 1988) (uncredited)
A Mom for Christmas (Disney Channel Cable, 12/17/90)

The Global Forum (WB., 1990)
Madonna: Truth or Dare (Miramax, 1991) (documentary)
A Christmas Romance (CBS-TV, 12/18/94)
It's My Party (UA, 1996)
Sordid Lives (Regent Entertainment, 2001)
The Wilde Girls (Showtime Cable, 11/4/2001)
Not Under My Roof (Children's Health Environmental Coalition, 2001) (s) (documentary)

Album Discography

LPs

Angel of the Morning (TLA 50137)
Back to Basics: The Essential Collection 1971–92 (Mer 512641-1)
Banks of the Ohio (Interfusion L-34320)
Clearly (MCA 3015)
Clearly Love (MCA 2148)
Come on Over (MCA 2186, MCA 3016)
Crystal Lady—Golden Double 32 (EMI EMS-65001/2)
Don't Stop Believin' (MCA 2223, MCA 3107)
Early Olivia (EMI EMS-1322)
First Impressions (EMI EMC-3055, EMI-Electrola 1C062-95957)
Grease (RSO RS-2-40012) [ST]
Greatest Hits (MCA 3028)
Greatest Hits, Vol. 2 (MCA 5347)
Have You Never Been Mellow (MCA 2133)
I Love You, Honestly I Love You (Music for Pleasure SRSJ-8060)
If Not for You (Uni 73117)
If You Love Me, Let Me Know (MCA 411, MCA 3013)
It's My Party (Varese Sarabande VSD-5701) [ST]
Let Me Be There (MCA 389, MCA 3012)

Long Live Love (EMI 3028)
Love Performance (EMI EMS-91010)
Love Songs (Music for Pleasure)
Making a Good Thing Better (MCA 2280, MCA 3018)
Music Makes My Day (Pye 28185)
Never Been Mellow (MCA 3014)
Olivia (Pye 28168)
Olivia & Tom—Super Stars (TLA 50138) w. Tom Jones
Olivia Newton-John (Pye 28155)
Olivia Newton-John (Supraphon 113-226920)
Olivia Newton-John, Best (Jasrac R-950102)
The Other Side of the Mountain (MCA 2086) [ST]
Physical (MCA 5229)
Retrato (EMI 6331)
The Rumour (MCA 53294)
Soul Kiss (MCA 6151)
Special Collection (EMI EMCJ-7949301)
Toomorrow (RCA CSA-3008) [ST]
Totally Hot (MCA 3067, Mobile 040)
20 Greatest Hits (EMI EMTV-36)
Two of a Kind (MCA 6127) [ST]
Xanadu (MCA 6100) [ST]

CDs

Back to Basics: The Essential Collection 1971–92 (Geffen GEFD-24470, Mer 512641-2, RMD 53361)
Back With a Heart (MCA Nashville 70030, Festival D1735, DTS Entertainment 1019, MVCZ 10009, UMD 80487)
Banks of the Ohio (Success 22533CD, Tring International JHD039)

The Best of Olivia Newton-John (EMI 9243-52101-2-4, EMI CDMFPE-6430, PID 537522)
Clearly Love (MCA MCAD-3111, Festival D21037, Festival D35704)
Collector's Guide Box Set (Griffin GCD-373-0)
Come On Over (MCA MCAD-31082, Festival D35847)

Come On Over/Clearly Love (MCA MCAD-5882)

Country Girl (EMI 7243-494970-2-3)

Don't Stop Believin' (MCA MCAD-1610, Festival D2103, Festival D36023)

Don't Stop Believin'/Totally Hot (MCA MCAD-5878)

Early Olivia (EMI EMS-1322, EMI CDP-792-019-2)

EMV Easy: The Olivia Newton-John Collection (EMI 7243-52269-2-4)

48 Original Tracks (EMI CDEM-1503, EMI CDP-82711-2, MSI/EMD 27110)

Gaia (Griffin DSHCD-7017, Festival D21045, CMC 44002-2, CA 851-50566)

Get Physical (S.I.A.E. ON-1006)

Grease (Polydor 825-095-2) [ST]

Grease: 20th Anniversary (Polydor 044041-2) [ST]

Great Hits (Festival D35375)

The Great Olivia Newton-John (Redx RXBOX-31053)

The Greatest (EMI TOP-51065)

Greatest Hits (MCA MCAD-522, Festival D21048)

The Greatest Hits Collection (Mer 518942-2)

Greatest Hits—Double Gold (Bellaphon 993-07-033)

Greatest Hits 2 (MCA MCAD-5347, EMI CDP7-460192)

Greatest Hits, Vol. 2 (MCA MCAD-5347, Festival D36449)

Greatest Hits, Vol. 3 (Festival D21050, EMI 72434979321, EMI 7243-8-56820-2-5)

Have You Never Been Mellow (MCA MCAD-1676, Griffin GCD-373-2, Festival D21046, Festival D35465, EMI EMC-3069, EMI EMS-63027, MSI 3455, Toshi D21046)

Her Greatest Hits (MSI 86033)

Highlights From "The Main Event" (BMG 74321-638832) w. John Farnha, Anthony Warlow

I Honestly Love You (EMI SE-865722, Musicrama 66016)

I Honestly Love You—Her Greatest Hits (EMI WM-860332)

If Not for You (Festival D19809)

If You Love Me, Let Me Know (MCA MCAD-31018)

Legend (EMI 7243-497648-2-8)

Let Me Be There (MCA MCAD-31017, Festival D21035)

Long Live Love (Festival D21036, Festival D35230)

Love Songs (Festival D26449)

Love Songs—A Collection (MSI 138239)

Magic: The Very Best of Olivia Newton-John (MCA 585233)

Making a Good Thing Better (MCA MCAD-1682, Festival D36277)

Mis Momentos (EMI 7243-855608-28)

Music Makes My Day (Festival D21035, Festival D25026)

Olivia (EMI CP21-6073, Festival D21034, Festival D34658)

Olivia Newton-John (Festival D453771B)

One Woman's Live Journey (Festival D32259, PID 63582)

Physical (MCA MACD-31110)

Rumour (MCA MCAD-6245, MCA MCAD-31083, Festival D21044, Phonogram 834-957.2, Universal Special Markets 6245)

Simply the Best (Disky E-865722)

Simply the Best: I Honestly Love You—Her Greatest Hits (Disky SE-865722)

Singles + 10 (PID 439432)

The Singles: Australian Tour Souvenir (Festival TVD-93361)

Songs From Heathcliff (EMI 7243-835762-2-7) w. Cliff Richard

Soul Kiss (MCA MCAD-6245, MCA MCAD-31083)

'Tis the Season (Hallmark Cards) w. Vince Gill, Bradford Singers, the London Symphony Orchestra

Totally Hot (Festival D21041, PID 44852)

Two of a Kind (MCA MCAD-11738) [ST]

The Very Best of Olivia Newton-John (EMI 7243-494563-2-7)

Warm and Tender (Geffen 24257-2)

Xanadu (MCA MCAD-11857, Sony Music Europe 486600-2) [ST]

Donald O'Connor and Martha Stewart in *Are You With It?* (1948).
[Courtesy of JC Archives]

Donald O'Connor

(b. Donald David Dixon Ronald O'Connor, Chicago, Illinois, August 28, 1925)

During the World War II era, Donald O'Connor was so popular that Universal Pictures kept him on the studio payroll for two years while he was in the armed services. O'Connor grew up in show business and went from a youth to a young man before the movie camera. A multitalented performer, O'Connor was equally at home with drama, comedy, or music, and he was one of filmdom's more energetic and pliable dancers, probably due to his early circus training. O'Connor was mainly associated with motion pictures, where he passed through four career phases: as a child player at Paramount; as the boisterous teenager of many inept Universal musicals of the 1940s; as the human companion to Francis the Talking Mule in that popular, if inane, picture series; and as the costar of the classic *Singin' in the Rain* (1952), made during his brief stay at MGM in the early 1950s. He was also a performer in vaudeville, nightclubs, television, and the stage. His well-rounded career demonstrated that he was a performer of considerable depth, although his image was primarily that of a song-and-dance man.

Donald David Dixon Ronald O'Connor was born August 28, 1925, in Chicago, the son of John " Chuck" O'Connor and Effie Irene Crane, who were vaudeville performers. With their three older children (John, William, and Arlene) the parents formed the O'Connor Family that did an acrobatic act, at times commanding a big salary. When Donald was an infant, his sister was killed by a hit-and-run driver, and his father died a few months later. Other family members, including baby Donald, were added to the act, and by the time he was four years old the boy had his own singing-and-dancing act. In 1936, he and brothers Jack and Billy appeared in a novelty number in the Warner Bros. film *Melody for Three* (1937). This led to local work in Hollywood where Donald was signed by Paramount for the role of the little brother in *Sing You Sinners* (1938). One of the highlights of this screen musical was his duet with Bing Crosby on the song "Small Fry."

Thanks to his success in *Sing You Sinners*, Donald was given a Paramount studio contract, and he next starred in *Sons of the Legion* (1938) as a juvenile delinquent who is helped by the sons of American Legionnaires. He was the impish Huckleberry Finn in *Tom Sawyer, Detective* (1938) helping to solve a murder. Then he was typecast as an orphan in three studio releases: *Unmarried* (1939), *Night Work* (1939), and *Death of a Champion*. He closed out his uneventful, bread-and-butter Paramount tenure (at $900 weekly) with the role of the youth who becomes Gary Cooper in the remake of *Beau Geste* (1939). Donald had literally outgrown his studio contract by shooting up ten inches in height, and he could no longer be cast in young boy roles. As the studio informed him, "You've come into that awkward age. It's tough on kid stars. Some can hold on but not many, and there just aren't any parts around here for you." As a result he rejoined his family's vaudeville act and they toured for two years, including an engagement in Australia.

When the family act disbanded in 1941 (Effie retired and Jack became a dance director at Warner Bros.), Donald joined Universal Pictures, where he would remain for nearly fifteen years.

His first trio of studio entries starred the Andrews Sisters, but more importantly they teamed him with Peggy Ryan. Eventually she and Donald would become Universal's (budget) answer to MGM's successful duo, Judy Garland (whom Donald had known as Frances Gumm on the vaudeville circuit) and Mickey Rooney. The first film, *What's Cookin'?* (1941), had O'Connor and Ryan as part of a group of entertainers hoping for a radio booking. *Variety* printed, "Young Donald O'Connor. . . . catches attention with a standout juvenile performance and displays a clicko screen personality."

After doing yeoman duty in *Give Out, Sisters* and *Private Buckaroo* (both 1942, with Ryan and the Andrews Sisters), things got better for Donald in *Get Hep to Love* (1942). He had second billing as the teenager sought after by star Gloria Jean and her rival Peggy Ryan (with whom he did a lively jitterbug). He and Ryan were in support of Allan Jones and Gloria Jean in *When Johnny Comes Marching Home* (1942), but in *It Comes Up Love* (1943) he became Gloria Jean's leading man in a light romance. He and winsome Gloria costarred again in *Mr. Big* (1943) as teenagers who turn their school's pageant into a musical. As always O'Connor made the most of his screen time, demonstrating a breezy, carefree personality and the ability to break into effortless song, dance, or comedy at the slightest provocation. In *Top Man* (1943), he had top billing for the first time in his pictures, playing a young collegiate who becomes the head of the family when his father (Richard Dix) is recalled to active duty. That year Donald was voted a Star of Tomorrow.

The year 1944 proved to be O'Connor's busiest at Universal. He and Peggy Ryan executed a jitterbug number in the all-star *Follow the Boys,* and in *This Is the Life* he vied with Patric Knowles for Susanna Foster's affections. *The Merry Monohans* presented O'Connor and Ryan as siblings whose vaudevillian father (Jack Oakie) is reunited with his ex-love (Rosemary DeCamp), who has a singing daughter (Ann Blyth). Ryan and Blyth were rivals for O'Connor in the musical comedy *Chip Off the Old Block,* while he and Peggy were back for a specialty routine, "He Took Her Out for a Sleigh Ride in the Good Old Summertime," in the big-budget musical *Bowery to Broadway.*

Donald and Peggy Ryan next costarred in *Patrick the Great* (1945), which found O'Connor and his father (Donald Cook) vying for the same Broadway role. By the time the picture was released in the spring of 1945, O'Connor was in the Army Air Force. For the next two years, he did more than three thousand shows across America entertaining soldiers for the Special Services. Just prior to enlisting, on February 6, 1944, he had eloped with Gwendolyn Carter (whom he had known while at Paramount) to Tijuana, Mexico, where they were married. Their daughter Donna was born in the summer of 1945.

When Donald returned to films in the summer of 1947, Universal was undergoing extensive corporate changes, but the new regime had great use for such a strong utility performer as O'Connor. He was now an adult and was matched with Deanna Durbin in *Something in the Wind* (1947), in which he used his acrobatic training for a strenuous rendition of "I Love a Mystery." He got mixed up with eccentric Marjorie Main and a town of hillbillies in *Feudin', Fussin' and A-Fightin'* (1948) while performing "Me and My Shadow," and he was a math wizard who joins a carnival in *Are You With It?* (1948). A bit sturdier was the college comedy *Yes Sir, That's My Baby* (1949), with O'Connor vocalizing "They've Never Figured Out a Woman" and dueting with Gloria DeHaven on the title song and "Look at Me." During this period O'Connor made several appearances on Bing Crosby's radio variety show.

In 1949, Donald starred in *Francis,* the movie that was to have a major impact on his career. He played Peter Stirling, an army lieutenant who becomes involved with the garrulous title character, a talking mule (voice of Chill Wills). The silly programmer proved so popular that during the 1950s the Francis series rivaled Universal's Ma and Pa Kettle entries, and Donald starred in a half dozen of these steady moneymakers. The property revived his sagging career, but he regarded the entries as a mixed blessing and referred to the period as "my-mule-and-me era."

In 1950, the star headlined the amusing Western satire *Curtain Call at Cactus Creek* as well as the not-so-funny sendup of buccaneer movies, *Double Crossbones,* in which he was a falsely accused criminal who becomes a part of Captain Kidd's (Alan Napier) crew. In the fall of 1951, Donald starred on the *Colgate Comedy Hour* on NBC-TV in a monthly segment (*The Donald O'Connor Show*). The variety show ran for three seasons, and in 1953 O'Connor earned an Emmy Award for the program.

Despite the inroads TV was making into movie attendance, O'Connor continued to churn out a large quantity of pictures like *The Milkman* (1950), which teamed him with Jimmy Durante in shenanigans involving murder. In 1952, he went to MGM for two musicals. The first, *Singin' in the Rain,* was the best film of his career. It focused on the early days of sound musicals, with comedic Donald stealing the show (from costars Gene Kelly and Debbie Reynolds) with his songs "Make 'Em Laugh" and the energetic "Moses Supposes." (Later he would say, "You know the secret of why Gene Kelly and I looked good together? While most performers turn to the right when dancing, Gene and I both turn to the left.")

The second MGM musical top-billed him in *I Love Melvin* (1953) as a magazine photographer after a pretty starlet (Debbie Reynolds). Although made on a limited budget, the feature grossed $4.5 million at the box office. At Twentieth Century-Fox, Donald costarred with Ethel Merman in *Call Me Madam* (1953), with he and Ethel dueting on "You're Just in Love." In addition, he soloed on Irving Berlin's "What Chance Have I With Love," and he and Vera-Ellen performed "It's a Lovely Day Today."

Thanks to the success of this trio of loanouts, Universal assigned O'Connor to their own musical *Walking My Baby Back Home* (1953) as a GI who uses an inheritance to start his own band. He performed the title song and "Rampart Street Parade." Illness caused Danny Kaye to replace O'Connor in Paramount's *White Christmas* (1954) starring Bing Crosby, but Donald went back to Twentieth Century-Fox for *There's No Business Like Show Business* (1954). He was one of the members of a show-business clan who sings "A Boy Chases a Girl" and who romances Marilyn Monroe. In 1954, he also starred in the biweekly half-hour NBC-TV series *The Donald O'Connor Show,* which ran for one season. He concluded his Universal contract with *Francis Joins the Navy* (1955). (When O'Connor refused to do yet another Francis installment, Mickey Rooney was hired for *Francis in the Haunted House* [1956], which wiped out the movie series.)

O'Connor and his wife had divorced in 1953, and on October 11, 1956, he wed Gloria Noble. They eventually had three children: Alicia, Donald, and Kevin. The year before his second marriage, O'Connor conducted the Los Angeles Philharmonic's world premiere of his symphony "Reflections d'un Comique," and for the next several seasons he did occasional symphony conducting.

In 1956 O'Connor costarred with Bing Crosby as a television star who does a Broadway show with a has-been (Crosby) in the Paramount musical *Anything Goes.* (It was O'Connor's last screen musical because, he admitted, he was earning too much money in other mediums to pursue a dying genre any further.) For the same studio he starred in the title role of *The Buster Keaton*

Story (1957), a disservice to both the star and its subject. O'Connor then appeared on TV on CBS's *Playhouse 90* and the *DuPont Show of the Month*'s production of "The Red Mill" before starring in his own special on NBC-TV in the fall of 1960. He also worked in nightclubs, and that year became a partner in the Riverside Hotel in Reno, Nevada.

Donald returned to motion pictures in the title role of the misguided fantasy *The Wonders of Aladdin* (1961). In the derivative *Cry for Happy* (1961), he and two sailor buddies (Glenn Ford and James Shigeta) made an orphanage out of a geisha house. When O'Connor headlined at the Hotel Americana in New York City in 1963, he received a salary of $12,000 per week. The next year, he toured in the stage musical *Little Me*, which Embassy Pictures planned to make (but never did) as a movie starring O'Connor. Universal had much changed by the time O'Connor returned there in 1965 to support Sandra Dee and Bobby Darin in the thin comedy *That Certain Feeling*. In 1966, he made a teleseries pilot, *The Hoofer*, which did not sell. On *ABC Stage 67*, he starred in the original TV musical "Olympus 7–0000" in the fall of 1966. In addition, he hosted *The Hollywood Palace* (ABC-TV) a few times and did TV commercials. In 1968, he had a good stint in Las Vegas in a truncated version of *Little Me*, and that fall he headed the syndicated ninety-minute weekday talk program *The Donald O'Connor Show*, which aired for a season.

During the 1970's period, when he looked much bloated and overweight, O'Connor remained active, although he was sidelined for a time by a heart attack and bypass surgery. During the decade, he appeared on TV in the 1971 NBC-TV special *Li'l Abner* and had guest roles in series like *The Girl With Something Extra*, *Ellery Queen*, *The Bionic Woman*, *Police Story*, and *Hunter*. Early in the decade, he toured in *Promises, Promises*, and in 1976 he was on the road in *Where's Charley?* He also headlined *Weekend With Feathers*, which never reached Broadway. That year his daughter Donna made her film bow in *All the President's Men*, whose cast also included Kerry Sherman, Peggy Ryan's daughter. On film, O'Connor was one of the cohosts of the MGM musical compilation *That's Entertainment!* (1974), but only movie clips of him were used in its sequel, *That's Entertainment, Part 2* (1976).

In the 1980s, O'Connor appeared on such TV fare as *The Music Mart* (a 1980 pilot that did not sell), *The Love Boat*, *Alice*, *Fantasy Island*, *Simon and Simon*, and *Hotel*. He returned to films in 1981 at Paramount for the featured role of Evelyn Nesbitt's (Elizabeth McGovern) dance teacher in *Ragtime*, and the next year he did a guest bit in the feature *Pandemonium*. In March 1981, Donald had a four-performance run on Broadway in *Bring Back Birdie*, the abortive sequel to the past stage hit *Bye Bye Birdie*. It was during this period that O'Connor admitted publicly that he was dealing with his drinking habit, which had plagued him for decades. (In 1978, his wife Gloria and the children had left Donald, hoping the tough love would shock him into dealing with his alcoholism. A few weeks later, he spent three months in substance-abuse treatment at an Amityville, New York, facility. Thereafter he was reunited with his family.)

O'Connor's next movie appearance was as the Lory Bird on the CBS-TV movie *Alice in Wonderland*, late in 1985. Onstage he did a concert/club tour in tandem with Jane Powell and, later, with Debbie Reynolds. In early 1989, he became a stage producer when he opened the Donald O'Connor Theater in Studio City, California, and later that year he toured the country in a cabaret act with Mickey Rooney.

By the early 1990s, O'Connor had reshaped his life in more ways than one. In 1990 he had quadruple-bypass surgery, which required him to change his diet, exercise habits, and lifestyle. By 1992, Donald was back to performing forty weeks a year around the United States, with return engagements in Las Vegas. Said O'Connor, who accepted a featured role in Robin Williams's *The Toys* (1992), "I'm no longer a superstar. Now I'm working on being a quasar, because stars wear out. Quasars go on forever."

In October 1995, O'Connor, a past president of the Thalians, received the charity group's Mr. Wonderful Award. The next years, he was a guest on episodes of the sitcoms *Frasier* and *The Nanny* and was in the fantasy feature *Father Frost.* In 1997, he appeared to advantage as a dance host aboard a luxury cruise ship in the Walter Matthau–Jack Lemmon big-screen comedy *Out to Sea* (1997). On May 21, 1997, Donald was the subject of a evening of film clips and commentary at the Film Society of Lincoln Center. That year, O'Connor who had relocated to Sedona, Arizona, began a weekly talk show on the Senior Citizen Network. Entitled *Senior Lifestyle,* he was teamed with another ex–child star, Jane Withers. In February 1999, while performing in *The Fabulous Palm Springs Follies,* a musical revue being presented in the California desert community, O'Connor suffered heart and lung failure brought on by double pneumonia. Three months later he returned to the show, insisting, "Rumors of my death were highly exaggerated." He vowed at the time, "As long as there's a stage waiting for me, I'm not going to die!"

Thanks to his big-budget musicals of the 1950s, Donald O'Connor's reputation endured as the personification of the agile, comic song-and-dance man. Ironically these movies represented only a small part of his musical-film output, but his genre outings for Universal in the 1940s paled in comparison to them. Unlike MGM, which lavished substantial production values and music scores on its Judy Garland–Mickey Rooney offerings, Universal hacked out the Donald O'Connor–Peggy Ryan efforts in quick fashion. Their assembly-line look always showed, but despite everything talented Donald O'Connor always sparkled.

Filmography

Melody for Two (WB, 1937)
Men With Wings (Par, 1938)
Sing You Sinners (Par, 1938)
Sons of the Legion (Par, 1938)
Tom Sawyer, Detective (Par, 1938)
Million Dollar Legs (Par, 1939)
Unmarried [Night Club Hostess] (Par, 1939)
Death of a Champion (Par, 1939)
Night Work (Par, 1939)
On Your Toes (WB, 1939)
Beau Geste (Par, 1939)
What's Cookin'? [Wake Up and Dream] (Univ, 1942)
Get Hep to Love [She's My Lovely!] (Univ, 1942)
Give Out, Sisters (Univ, 1942)
It Comes Up Love [A Date With an Angel] (Univ, 1942)
When Johnny Comes Marching Home (Univ, 1942)
Private Buckaroo (Univ, 1942)
Mister Big (Univ, 1943)
Top Man (Univ, 1943)
Follow the Boys (Univ, 1944)
This Is the Life (Univ, 1944)
The Merry Monahans (Univ, 1944)

Chip off the Old Block (Univ, 1944)
Bowery to Broadway (Univ, 1944)
Patrick the Great (Univ, 1945)
Something in the Wind (Univ, 1947)
Feudin', Fussin' and A-Fightin' (Univ, 1948)
Are You With It? (Univ, 1948)
Yes Sir, That's My Baby (Univ, 1949)
Francis (Univ, 1949)
Curtain Call at Cactus Creek [Take the Stage] (Univ, 1949)
The Milkman (Univ, 1950)
Double Crossbones (Univ, 1950)
Francis Goes to the Races (Univ, 1951)
Singin' in the Rain (MGM, 1952)
Francis Goes to West Point (Univ, 1952)
I Love Melvin (MGM, 1952)
Call Me Madam (20th-Fox, 1953)
Walking My Baby Back Home (Univ, 1953)
Francis Covers the Big Town (Univ, 1953)
There's No Business Like Show Business (20th-Fox, 1954)
Francis Joins the WACS (Univ, 1954)
Francis in the Navy (Univ, 1955)
Anything Goes (Par, 1956)
The Buster Keaton Story (Par, 1957)

The Wonders of Aladdin (MGM, 1961)
Cry for Happy (Col, 1961)
That Funny Feeling (Univ, 1965)
That's Entertainment! (MGM, 1974) (co–host)
Ragtime (Univ, 1981)
Pandemonium (MGM/UA, 1982)
Alice in Wonderland (CBS-TV 12/9–10/85)

A Time to Remember [Miracle in a Manager]
    (Film World, 1987) (made in 1984)
Toys (20th-Fox, 1992)
Bandit: Bandit's Silver Angel (NBC-TV, 10/10/94)
Father Frost (Plaza Entertainment, 1996)
Out to Sea (20th-Fox, 1997)

Broadway Plays

Bring Back Birdie (1981)

TV Series

The Colgate Comedy Hour (NBC, 1951–54)
The Donald O'Connor Texaco Show (NBC,
    1954–55)

The Donald O'Connor Show (Synd, 1968)
Senior Lifestyle (Synd, 1997–98)

Album Discography

LPs

Anything Goes (Decca DL-8318) [ST]
Call Me Madam (10″ Decca DL-5465, Stet 15024)
    [ST]
Donald O'Connor Music (Palette 1021) w. Brussels
    Symphony
Follow the Boys (Hollywood Soundstage 50120)
    [ST]
Give Out, Sisters (Vertinge 2004) [ST]
I Love Melvin (10″ MGM E-140, MGM SES-
    52ST) [ST]
Olympus 7-0000 (Command O7) [ST/TV]
A Rose on Broadway (Cozy PL-9206) [ST/TV]

Singin' in the Rain (10″ MGM E-113, MGM E-
    3236, Metro M/S-599) [ST]
That Old Song and Dance (Minerva MIN 6JG-
    FSS) w. Judy Garland
That's Dancing! (EMI America SJ-17149) [ST]
That's Entertainment! (MCA MCA2-11002) [ST]
That's Entertainment, Part 2 (MGM MG-1-5301,
    MCA 6155) [ST]
There's No Business Like Show Business (Decca
    DL-8091, MCA 1727) [ST]
Yes Sir, That's My Baby (Caliban 6019) [ST]

CDs

Bring Back Birdie (Varese Sarabande VSD-5440)
    [OC]
Singin' in the Rain (Sony Music Special Products
    AK-45394, Turner Classic Movies/Rhino R2-
    71963, Great Movie Themes 60006) [ST]

There's No Business Like Show Business (Varese
    Sarabande VSD-5912) [ST]
Two Weeks—With Love/I Love Melvin (Sony
    Music Special Products AK$-48609) [ST]